Simon, Neil

The collected plays of Neil Simon, volume II

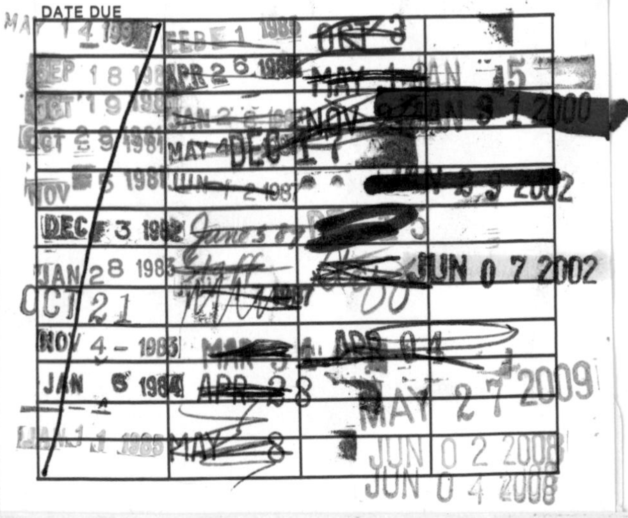

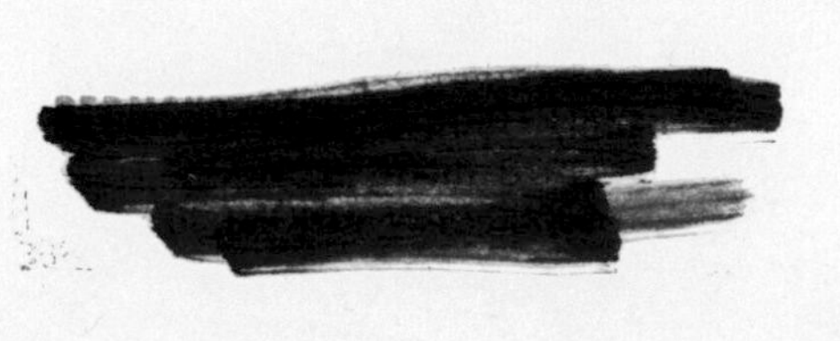

The COLLECTED PLAYS *of* Neil Simon

VOLUME II

The COLLECTED PLAYS *of* Neil Simon

VOLUME II

With an Introduction by Neil Simon

Random House
New York

Grateful acknowledgment is made to the following for permission to reprint previously published material:
Edwin H. Morris & Company: Lyrics from *Little Me* by Carolyn Leigh. Copyright © 1962 by Carolyn Leigh and Cy Coleman. All rights throughout the world controlled by Edwin H. Morris & Company, a division of MPL Communications, Inc. International Copyright Secured. All rights reserved. Used by permission.

Warner Bros. Inc., lyrics from "The Man I Love" by Ira Gershwin. Copyright © 1924 New World Music Corp. Copyright renewed. All rights reserved. Used by permission of Warner Bros. Music.

Tempo Music, Inc. and Edwin H. Morris and Co., lyrics from "Flamingo" by Ted Grouya. Copyright © 1941 by Tempo Music, Inc. Copyright renewed, assigned to Edwin H. Morris & Co., a division of MPL Communications, Inc.

Library of Congress Cataloging in Publication Data

Simon, Neil.
The collected plays of Neil Simon, Vol. II

Vol. 1 has title: The comedy of Neil Simon.
PS3537.1663A6 1979 812'.5'4 79-5081
ISBN 0-394-50770-3

Manufactured in the United States of America

98765432

FIRST EDITION

For
Marsha, Ellen and Nancy

Contents

The COLLECTED PLAYS *of* Neil Simon

VOLUME II

Introduction

"As Time Flies By"

Where were we? Has it been eight years since last we met on those smooth white pages that served as an introduction to the first seven plays created by that schizophrenic half man–half monster? It was March 10, 1971, as I recall. How have you been? . . . Really? . . . Well, I've had my ups and downs. Not that you would notice too much from my outward appearance. The hair thinned just a bit, a little grayer around the temples, some lines around the eyes that seem to suggest character more than decay, no more than three pounds added to a still lithesome frame and an agility around the tennis courts that bring "oohs" and "ahs" from the aging members of the club who usually match up the "Bypasses" against the "Pacemakers" in the semiweekly doubles matches. All in all, life has, in the words of Barney Cashman in *Red Hot Lovers,* "not only been very kind, but has gone out of its way to ignore me."

Alas, like Dorian Gray, the true picture is hidden in the attic of the mind, locked and kept from view to all except wife, family, a few close friends and a plethora of medical men who daily struggle to keep the deadly radiation of neurosis from melting down and destroying this Prolificity Plant and all who live in a radius of its emotional and co-working environs. On a day like all others, I awoke to the first sign of danger. A duodenal ulcer appeared and panic spread through the central nervous system. The plant was immediately shut down and six hundred and twelve spicy foods and alcoholic beverages were laid off. Cottage cheese and Carnation non-fat milk had to show identifying badges before they were allowed to enter the lower digestive tract . . . Meetings were held in the brain, and college-type white cells marched out defiantly carrying placards that proclaimed, "We don't want Neurotic Energy," "No More Neuks," "Right to Live, Not

Live to Write" . . . Paranoia set in. "What if suddenly all the Creative Plants broke down at once? What if ulcers spread across the writing community like the plague? Would there be enough help? Would there suddenly be odd and even days for Antacid Tablets?" The overworked, overwrought, overloaded machinery came to a halt. All ideas were given a six-month paid vacation and were told either to relocate or to wait until the plant was rehauled and inspected and found safe enough to go back into production. Some ideas, already half typed and ready to be born, lay unloved and unnurtured on the yellow bond paper, withered and died. Others huddled together for protection in a top right-hand drawer, hoping against hope they would not be forgotten. Now came the difficult and arduous task of looking for causes, of dismantling an enormously productive piece of creative equipment which suddenly seemed to break down and malfunction at the peak of its thought-to-be-limitless potential.

On a quiet, cool and perfect spring night in New York a few weeks later, the first clue appeared. It was to be a week of quiet relaxation for me. Dinner dates with friends, two plays, a ballet and a drink with Woody Allen at the Russian Tea Room comparing notes where life had taken us since the days we worked on the old Garry Moore Show (*Annie Hall* and *The Goodbye Girl* were easier to write than a funny lead-in to Jo Stafford's next song). The days were spent idly walking up the west side of Madison Avenue to see the galleries, the boutiques, the antique shops, and down the east side to ogle the deep-dark chocolate cakes in Greenberg's window and the girls bouncing out of Yves St. Laurent's, both of whom got equal attention from my salivary glands. The ulcer in my stomach, which demanded to be fed every fifty-three minutes, was assuaged by saltine crackers bulging from every conceivable coat pocket, and seemed incompatible with the pleasantness of my surroundings and that I had two hit shows running on Broadway. In addition to this, the film of *Chapter Two* was about to be shot in New York, a new play, *I Oughta Be in Pictures,* was written and ready to go into rehearsal in December, and another film, *Seems Like Old Times,* set to shoot in California the following February. If ever a man wanted more out of life, he was not only a glutton but a fool.

On the night I speak of, this gluttonous fool decided to look in on his two current attractions. I saw the first act of *Chapter Two,* now in its second year with a superb and dedicated new cast, then jaunted down four blocks to see the second act of *They're Playing Our Song,* which not only was playing to a Standing Room Only audience of the most vociferous, enthusiastic and appreciative group of theatergoers I've encountered in a long time, but had, in addition, just paid off and was now in profit. Even the ulcer decided to skip a meal to see Lucie Arnaz and Robert Klein. After all, how often does an affliction get a free ticket to a Broadway show?

Did I sit back and revel in my good fortune? Did I relax and watch boyhood ambitions being fulfilled before my eyes? Not if you were born in the Bronx, in the Depression and Jewish, you don't. In each case, at each show, I reacted in the same manner. It was like going to simultaneous opening nights with all the accompanying fears and traumas. I found myself annoyed and irritated when latecomers arrived, causing an entire row to rise one after the other like ducks in a shooting gallery and distracting everyone who sat behind them, so that my favorite line in the play was barely audible, let alone laughed at. I gunned down insensitive coughers with the high-powered rifle I carry in the back of my brain for such emergencies; I put body language on every syllable uttered by the actors, wishing they wouldn't turn their heads at that moment or drop their voices at another, and mostly I wished I had rewritten the whole bloody thing while I reached back in my arsenal, got out two hand grenades and blew up the air-conditioning system and six elderly usherettes who were chatting pension-talk near the exit sign.

My inner rage was so intense that my ulcer threatened to attack my teeth if I didn't keep quiet. It hardly mattered to me that these were both successful shows, enjoying long runs and having long since passed the acid test of critics (not without its usual slings and arrows, causing considerable personal pain but no significant damage to life and longevity), or that the present audience, by their vocal approval, were having the time of their lives . . . give three or four rows. What mattered was that I left the theater with my stomach tied not only in knots—it was braided. Instead of the even, relaxed breathing I was taught in meditation, mine was coming in quick, short gasps, not unlike the kind you experience if you are in bed at three o'clock in the morning and suddenly hear your window being opened from the outside.

I got home that night, undressed, brushed my teeth, looked in the mirror and saw a man holding a glass of water in one hand and a Valium, an ulcer pill, two extra-strength Tylenol and an Inderal, which helps lower blood pressure, in the other. I prayed that that man wasn't me. The pajamas and the slippers fit, and the face matched the one in the photograph on my wife's side of the bed. The man in the mirror was definitely me and neither one of us was very happy about it.

The ulcer knocked three times on the duodenum and yelled up, "Let's move it, Buster. We need some milk and cottage cheese down here." The blood pressure yelled back at the ulcer, "Be quiet, will you? We're trying to get some rest. Otherwise we come upstairs and bang on this guy's head." Then someone in the digestive tract got really angry and said, "You guys have been asking for this all night," whereupon he opened Flood Gates 2, 4 and 7, sending cascades of acidity over intestinal walls, wiping out lunch, dinner and what felt like a small town in southern Mississippi.

I know that I personally writhed and anguished in pain, but the face in the mirror smiled tauntingly as if it had a life of its own and smirked, "Well, big shot, how does it feel to be a success?"

I glanced to the side and the cut-glass mirror in the shower reflected my pained expression dozens of times over, straight out of an early Orson Welles movie. And the myriad of images of this suffering soul nodded and said in unison, "Someone's trying to tell you something, fella!" I have never before heard the Mormon Tabernacle Choir in my bathroom offering me sage symphonic advice. ". . . telling you something, fella fella fella fella fella," it echoed and bounced against the tiles until it faded away in silence. The message got through. I had been given a gift. A reprieve. Another chance to re-examine and re-evaluate my life; to redirect my energies so that I would no longer stand in front of a bathroom mirror every night with a glass of water in one hand and a mini-pharmaceutical outlet in the other. My joy was enormous. I wanted to raise my eyes up to heaven and whisper my love and gratitude to the Almighty, but I was already on the thirty-fifth floor, and looking up struck me as being redundant.

Success, I grant you, is relative. From an outsider's point of view, it is measured by the degree of his admiration, respect, envy or disdain. From inside looking out, it is no greater nor less than you perceive yourself. I have dozens upon dozens of awards, nominations and tributes, most of which hang in my bathroom on a wall facing the commode. I am too vain to store them in the basement and humble enough to know they seem to be in the right perspective from the low vantage point I view them from. I rejoice in the flattering letters I receive from my peers and thoughtful admirers who rank my plays anywhere from "a delightful evening" to "worthy of Molière." They do not, however, counterbalance the humiliation endured on the opening night of *God's Favorite,* when a kindly semi-invalided woman in her mid-seventies beckoned to me at the final curtain as I made my way backstage, took me by the arm, looked me straight in the eye and said, "Mr. Simon . . . shame on you!" It's moments like this that take the lustre out of an opening-night party.

I am in a no man's land of self-evaluation. On a Tuesday I see myself as so gifted that I think the cornflakes I left over for breakfast should immediately be wrapped and sent to some Literary Museum for bronzing and held for posterity. (Walter Matthau's mother once said, "Walter, you don't have to act anymore. You're too big a star.") Come around on a Thursday and I will grovel at your feet to take me on as a shipping clerk in a dockside factory that manufactures "I Love New York" ashtrays. My confidence not only blows with the wind but is susceptible to the currents caused by a butterfly at rest.

Espying Woody Allen one night at a corner table in Elaine's shortly after his delightful *Manhattan* had opened to reviews which bestowed upon him such accolades as "genius" and "the most mature comic mind in America," I toyed despondently with my fettucini, rationalizing my own achievements by throwing myself such bitter crumbs as "Oh, well, I'm taller than he is," or, "I'm glad they didn't call *me* a genius. How can you ever top yourself?" But it was merely a cosmetic job that didn't cover up my true feelings for Woody. I was naturally envious of the critical acclaim showered upon him. Showered, hell. It was a downpour. Not only did it bother me that he was being extolled to the pantheon of greats, it bothered me that it bothered me. I am not without my supporters, but I often feel it will go no further than Clive Barnes's succinct evaluation: "Neil Simon is destined to remain rich, successful and underrated." Thank you, Clive. If you're my gift horse, it's not your mouth I'm looking at. I have no wish to be poor, unsuccessful and overrated. My admiration for Woody is enormous. Not just for the body of his work, but for the uncompromising dignity he maintains in striving for excellence. Jealousy fades away under the unadulterated rays of admiration.

However, what struck me about Woody as he sat there with his face all over *Time* magazine's cover was that he was toying with his linguini just as despondently as I was. His face was so long that he didn't need a napkin to cover up the faded army shirt that has been his uniform long before our military forces thought of it. When I walked over to congratulate him and ask how he was feeling about it all, he replied, "Oh, all right." It was such a mournful response that I suspected he had just learned he had contracted a disease so dreadful that it doesn't end in death but causes one to live in pain for three hundred years. When I saw his dour expression, I saw my own reflected agony. I was not exactly along skid row career-wise myself, and yet the acidity in my stomach was as sour as the look on his face. After Woody won the Academy Award for *Annie Hall,* someone remarked to him, "You must be very happy." His reported reply was, "I have no time for happiness." He didn't seem to be dealing with good fortune any better than I was, and if misery loves company, we should have taken out a wedding license that night. But the next afternoon at the Tea Room the common bond was found. "The fun is getting there," we both agreed. "The work is the joy. The results are just something you have to deal with. You resent the catcalls and don't trust the ones who overpraise."

I don't know Woody well enough to accuse him of terminal *misanthropia.* He makes too many people happy to be joyless himself. Nor do I myself wish to appear ungrateful for the rewards that can't find wall space in my john, or unduly bitter for the times I'm dismissed by academia. But these recent observations have crystallized and finally made themselves clear to me. To wit: "I must take my work seriously, but not the results. I can control only what I write and not what others write about my writing. To agree with the ayes and negate the nays is a foolish pastime." To get gastric lesions because four people walked out of your play, or euphoria because someone asks for your autograph, will eventually misdirect your intentions and you will work to please rather than be pleased with your work. If success brings no more happiness than failure, what *does* give me joy? (We are, for the moment, leaving aside the main sources of contentment: wife, family, friends, good health, *The Maltese Falcon* and Chinese food. We are dealing solely with the creative spirit here and that won't take much longer, I promise.)

I am most alive and most fulfilled sitting alone in a room, hoping that those words forming on the paper

Little Me

LITTLE ME, based on *Little Me,* by Patrick Dennis, *opened at the Lunt-Fontanne Theatre on November 17, 1962, starring Sid Caesar; directed by Cy Feuer and Bob Fosse; choreography by Bob Fosse; lyrics by Carolyn Leigh; music by Cy Coleman; presented by Feuer & Martin.*

THE SCENES

THE PRESENT:	Belle's estate in Southampton, Long Island
THE PAST:	Venezuela, Illinois
	Peoria
	Chicago
	Somewhere in France
	On the North Atlantic
	Hollywood
	Monte Carlo
	A Principality in Middle Europe
	The Dakotas

Act One

SCENE I

The curtain rises on an ornate, lavish room. A chaise is downstage right, a table up right, and a grand piano up left. Two suits of armor flank the center French door. A BUTLER, *preceded by a* BARTENDER, *is ushering a young man into the room. It is* PATRICK DENNIS. *He carries a tape recorder.*

BUTLER Right this way, please. If you'll kindly wait here, I'll try to locate Miss Poitrine.

PATRICK She is expecting me. Patrick Dennis, the author? I'm going to work with her on her autobiography.

BUTLER Oh, yes. She asked to be informed just as soon as you arrived. *(He opens the small door which is the breastplate of a suit of armor and picks up the telephone which is hidden there)* Chapel, please.

PATRICK Chapel? She has her own chapel?

BUTLER Oh, good morning, Padre. Would you kindly inform Miss Poitrine that Mr. Dennis is waiting here in the Rumpus Room.

PATRICK The Rumpus Room?

BUTLER Thank you, Padre . . . Oh, and bless you too. *(He hangs up the phone and turns to* PATRICK*)* She'll be here directly.

PATRICK Her own chapel. Incredible. *(The* BARTENDER *opens the piano top, which reveals a hidden bar.* PATRICK *is astonished, then crosses to the table covered with photographs of* BELLE *and various men. He reads the inscription)* "Belle and Fred on honeymoon."

PATRICK Well, she was married again, wasn't she?

BUTLER To the entire table.

PATRICK Extraordinary woman.

(Chimes sound. The BUTLER *motions to the* BARTENDER *to prepare the drink)*

BUTLER Excuse me.

*(*OLDER BELLE *sweeps into the room. She is large and flamboyant)*

OLDER BELLE Mr. Dennis! . . . Mr. Dennis! *(She sweeps past him directly to the* BARTENDER *to her drink. The* BUTLER *exits)* Patrick! . . . My first meeting with my Boswell! *(She takes* PATRICK*'s hand)* I do hope I didn't keep you waiting. But I just couldn't dash out of the chapel.

PATRICK I understand.

OLDER BELLE It's my portrait. I'm sitting for a stained-glass window.

(She drinks and returns the glass to BARTENDER*'s tray. The* BARTENDER *goes to the piano)*

PATRICK How . . . inspiring.

(The BUTLER *reenters, followed by* THREE HAIRDRESSERS*)*

BUTLER Excuse me, madam. The hairdressers are here from New York.

OLDER BELLE Oh, dear. We're terribly busy, darlings. Why don't you do the poodles first?

PATRICK That really isn't necessary. During the next few days you can go about your daily routine as though I weren't here. I'll just follow you around with my tape recorder. *(He opens it up)* Have you ever used one?

OLDER BELLE Indirectly. I once found one under my bed in a hotel room in Atlantic City . . . *(She goes to the chaise and sits)* But we don't need to mention that.

PATRICK Oh, but we do! Today, the reader can spot a phony life story in the table of contents. They want the truth. Names, dates, places, vivid descriptions . . . *(Music starts)* Leave out the "intimate" details, and you can kiss the Book-of-the-Month Club goodbye.

OLDER BELLE The truth! . . . What a challenge!

(BELLE, PATRICK and the SERVANTS sing "The Truth")

DENNIS

The all-revealing truth?

BELLE

The mass-appealing truth!

DENNIS

The blood-congealing truth?

BELLE

The ir-regardless truth—

BOTH

The truth!

MEN *(Spoken)*

The truth!

BELLE

As through a haze
I see a Doubleday's—
And shining in a windowful
Of Arthur Miller plays,
The truth!

MEN

The truth?

BELLE

An odyssey
Entitled "Little Me"
As told to Patrick Dennis in its whole entirety
By me!

DENNIS

The truth!

BELLE

All hail to "Little Me"
The book that's bound to be
Prohibited from passage through the mail—
But nonetheless on sale
Throughout the land!
And printed by demand
In Esperanto,
Japanese
And Braille!

With the areas I'll expose,
I'll annihilate Gypsy Rose;
As for practic'lly Proustian prose:
Mary Astor,
Meet your master!
Stack me up with all three Gabors,

MEN

Oh-oh!

BELLE

I'll reduce 'em to cut-rate stores!

MEN

Oh, no!

BELLE

And Louella dear, you'll get yours
With the end-all
Casey Stendhal
Truth!

MEN

Truth!
Truth!
Truth!

The D. H. Lawrence truth!

BELLE

With an index!

MEN

In floods and torrents, truth!

DENNIS

Illustrations!

BELLE

The plain, plebeian truth,

MEN

Inspirational!

DENNIS

The Brendan Behan truth!

BELLE

Educational!

MEN

In black and white, the truth!

DENNIS

Do you mean it?

BELLE

You're goddamn right, the truth!

DENNIS

In the language of Thoreau,
Rousseau

BELLE

And Harriet Beecher Stowe!

ALL

For God and Home and Underpriv'leged
Youth—
The truth!
The truth!
The truth!
The truth!

(After the number, BELLE *sits on the chaise as two* HAIRDRESSERS *begin to work on her hair. The* BUTLER, BARTENDER *and one* HAIRDRESSER *exit)*

PATRICK All right, Belle. You're a writer now. Tell it all. From the very beginning.

OLDER BELLE Little Me . . . Chapter One . . . "The Belle's First Toll" . . . It was May in the little town of Venezuela, Illinois . . . and a brand-new century got up out of bed, yawned and got dressed. Good morning, 1900 . . . Say Hello to Belle Schlumpfert.

(She smiles at PATRICK, *pleased with her prose. Fade-out)*

Light comes up behind scrim on a tumbledown shack in Drifters' Row. In the distance are all the fine and stately homes of the Bluff.

OLDER BELLE I lived alone with Momma . . . As the years passed glumly by, we were as poor as church mice, living in a tumbledown shack in Drifters' Row . . . (YOUNG BELLE, *aged sixteen, steps out on the ramshackle porch.* BELLE *is lovely, starry-eyed and well-stacked. Dressed raggedly)* By the time I was sixteen, I had bloomed into a lovely and delicate young flower. In fact, there were those who thought I had overbloomed. Girls shunned me and boys were afraid of me. And so, with the exception of a few workmen on the Rock Island Line, no one wanted to play with little me . . .

(Blackout on OLDER BELLE. *She,* PATRICK *and* TWO HAIRDRESSERS *exit. Lights come up on Drifters' Row and the scrim goes up.* MOMMA *steps out on the porch wearing a flaming-red dress)*

MOMMA Well, Belle, honey, I'm off to work.

BELLE All right, Momma. Say hello to Mrs. Louise for me.

MOMMA Not *Mrs.* Louise, baby, *Madam.* She's French . . . How do I look, baby?

BELLE Like a bright-red angel . . . Oh, Momma, when I grow up I wanna be a nurse just like you.

MOMMA I'm not really a nurse, sugar . . . I just like to make people feel good. Well, I gotta go. And, sweetie, don't forget to throw out the garbage.

BELLE All right. Momma, will you be home early?

MOMMA No, hon. We got two new girls today, and I gotta stay late and take inventory.

(She exits. GEORGE MUSGROVE *runs on stage.* GEORGE *is skinny and freckle-faced, the same age as* BELLE*)*

GEORGE Hya, Belle.

BELLE Oh, hello, George . . . What have you got there?

GEORGE Cards. Let's cut the deck. High card for a kiss.

BELLE I can't, George. I've got to throw out the garbage. And, George Musgrove, put away those cards. You should try to lead a clean, decent life like the folks up on the Bluff.

(She exits into the shack)

GEORGE The Bluff! The Bluff! That's all you ever think about. You stick your nose up too high in the air, Belle, and you'll get disappointment up both nostrils.

*(*GEORGE *exits as three young kids from up on the Bluff enter. All are well-dressed and carry picnic baskets)*

BRUCEY Come on, girls, we'll be late for the picnic.

RAMONA You can go on ahead if you want, Brucey, we're waiting here for Noble.

BRUCEY You're always waiting for Noble. You'd think just 'cause he's captain of the football, baseball, boxing, debating and tumbling teams, he was something special.

RAMONA Well, he *is!* There's nothing Noble Eggleston can't do. *(She looks off to the right)* Ooh, there he is! *(She yells and waves)* Noble! . . . Noble, here we are! *(Suddenly a young boy comes in, tumbling across the stage, flipping hand over hand right past the group)* Wait, Noble, you're going too fast.

(The boy flips right off into the wings, then comes quickly back and stands there breathing hard. He has a big smile)

NOBLE Hi, gang! I guess I must have overtumbled. *(*NOBLE EGGLESTON, *sixteen years old, is an Edwardian Jack Armstrong, clean of body, mind and spirit)*

RAMONA Hi, Noble . . .

NOBLE May I carry your basket, Ramona? *(He takes her picnic basket)*

RAMONA Noble, you're so strong . . . *(Points to his neck)* Is that a new muscle?

NOBLE *(Nods and flexes the muscle on his neck)* It came out last night . . . while I was sleeping. Say, gang, where are we?

BRUCEY I took a shortcut. This is Drifters' Row.

RAMONA *(Aghast)* Drifters' Row! I've never been down here before. *(Sniffs)* What's that horrible odor?

NOBLE *(Sniffs)* Smells like Poverty!

RAMONA It gives me the creeps. *(She shivers)* Let's get out of here.

BRUCEY Yes. Let's go. *(They all start to go except* NOBLE*)*

NOBLE Wait, gang! *(They all stop and turn to him)* I just got a swell idea. Where are we all going to now? A picnic, right?

BRUCEY AND OTHERS Right!

NOBLE And where did we just come from? Another picnic, right?

BRUCEY AND OTHERS Right!

NOBLE And where are we all going to after this picnic? To lunch!

BRUCEY AND OTHERS Right!

NOBLE Well, I say . . . Instead of eating seven or eight meals today, we take our baskets chockful of good food and give them to a worthy starving family of our choice?

(They all look at one another, puzzled)

BRUCEY But why?

NOBLE Why? Because that's the democratic way. Eat until you think you're gonna bust, and then give away the leftovers . . .

BRUCEY You're crazy, Noble. Come on, girls.

(He pulls one girl offstage)

RAMONA Are you coming, Noble?

NOBLE I'll be with you in a minute, Ramona. Just a minute. *(She exits. He crosses to the porch of the shack)* Hellooooo, is anyone in that thing? *(He moves upstage of the porch)* Helloo!

(Just as he looks directly into the door YOUNG BELLE *appears with a large pail of garbage. She hauls back to throw it out and they both freeze as the arc picks up* OLDER BELLE *to the right)*

OLDER BELLE It was then, with that pail of garbage in my hands, that I saw Noble for the first time in my life. The moment I saw him, my heart brimmed with passion, and yet, the only words I could find to say were . . .

(Blackout on OLDER BELLE *just as* YOUNG BELLE *heaves the pail of garbage at* NOBLE*)*

YOUNG BELLE Oh! I'm awfully sorry.

NOBLE *(Smiles and wipes the garbage off)* That's all right. You've got to throw your garbage somewhere.

BELLE Oh, what a mess . . . Can I get you anything?

NOBLE *(Examining contents on his shoulders)* No, I don't think you left anything out. It's all here.

BELLE Here, let me help you brush it off.

(She raises her hand to brush NOBLE*'s shoulder)*

NOBLE Oh, no . . . you don't have to.
(He puts his hand up and they touch. At the touch, their "I Love You" theme plays from out of nowhere . . . She removes her hand and the music stops. They both react)

BELLE What was that?

NOBLE I don't know. You touched me . . . And you turned something on. *(*BELLE *touches him again experimentally. The music starts. She removes her hand and again it stops. He looks puzzled)* Well, anyway. My name is Noble Eggleston, and I live up on the Bluff. In the biggest and best house.

BELLE Oh! And I'm Belle Schlumpfert.

NOBLE Gosh, that's a pretty name.

BELLE Thank you.

NOBLE You're welcome. I was just passing by, and I heard you people starving and I thought I'd come and bring you this basket chockful of good food.

BELLE Oh, gee, that's sweet of you. But no, thank you. I couldn't accept a gift.

NOBLE It's not a gift. It's charity! I feel sorry for you.

BELLE Thank you. Gee, that's very nice of you, Noble. Thank you.
*(*RAMONA *comes back onstage)*

RAMONA Noble, come on. We're all waiting.

NOBLE I'll be with you in a minute, Ramona. *(*RAMONA *exits)* Belle, this Saturday night my mother is throwing me a Sweet Sixteen party. If you're through eating by then, would you come?

BELLE Me? Up on the Bluff? Oh, yes, Noble, I'd love to.

NOBLE Good. Then, I'll see you Saturday night . . . *(He extends his hand and they shake. The love theme plays even louder this time. He withdraws his hand and the music stops)* I'd better go before we wake up the whole neighborhood.

BELLE Little me up on the Bluff! Maybe I'm aiming too high . . .

(And she sings "The Other Side of the Tracks")

But my heart says, "Reach for the stars!"
And my heart I cannot deny—
Though it's my hard luck
That I'm sorta stuck
On the farthest one in the sky . . .
So my eyes are destined to wander,
And my brain no more to relax—
For there's nothing farther out yonder
Than the other side of the tracks!

On the other side of the tracks,
It's a long and difficult climb—
But the air up there
On the bill of fare
Is a choice of lemon or lime!
And the muscles keeping your nose up
Are the only muscles you tax—
Oh, I envy someone who grows up
On the other side of the tracks.

(The chorus sings "Rich Kids Rag")

1ST GIRL
We—are the wealthy children from
the right side of the tracks.

1ST BOY
That's right.

2ND BOY
We're rich.

3RD BOY
He's right.

1ST GIRL
We're here to celebrate Noble
Eggleston's sixteenth birthday.

2ND GIRL

He's cute.

3RD GIRL

Oh.

4TH GIRL

Oh.

5TH GIRL

Oh.

6TH GIRL

Oh.

1ST GIRL

Hey.

ALL

What?

1ST GIRL

Let's do our favorite dance.

ALL

Swell.

1ST GIRL

The rich kids rag.

ALL

Oh, boy!
Get set
Ready
Go.

(They dance)

SCENE 3

Interior of the Egglestons' elegant living room. Rich boys and girls are dancing. During the number they all attempt to out-snob each other. After the number NOBLE *and* RAMONA *enter.* NOBLE *keeps looking around the room.* BENTLEY, *the butler, enters)*

RAMONA Noble, you haven't paid any attention to me the whole evening. Who are you looking for?

NOBLE *(Still looking around)* I'm not looking for anyone. Why should I be looking for anyone?

*(*MRS. EGGLESTON, NOBLE*'s mother, comes down the stairs. She is an elegant, overpowering woman. She has a purple velvet case in her hands)*

RAMONA Noble, there's your mother. Good evening, Mrs. Eggleston.

NOBLE *(Turns to his mother)* Oh, good evening, Mother. May I take this opportunity to thank you for this wonderful party. I just realized I'm sixteen years old today. I'm not a child anymore. I'm a full-grown, mature man. Ready to take his place in the world. I suddenly have hopes and desires. Suddenly I'm a man! At last—a man!

MRS. EGGLESTON Blow your nose!

NOBLE Yes, Mother.

(He takes out his handkerchief and blows his nose)

MRS. EGGLESTON I too am aware of the importance of this day, Noble. And on this occasion, I'd like you to have these.

(She gives him the case)

NOBLE *(Opens the case)* Thank you, Mother. Gosh . . . a set of matching trust funds! That's swell! Oh, Bentley, would you kindly put these in my piggy vault.

(The BUTLER *crosses to* NOBLE*)*

BUTLER Yes, sir. And there's a strange young lady at the door . . . from Drifters' Row.

NOBLE *(Happy)* That must be Belle! Show her in.

*(*BUTLER *goes up the stairs and exits)*

MRS. EGGLESTON Drifters' Row? Noble, have you gone mad?

NOBLE I don't understand, Mother.

MRS. EGGLESTON Noble, you can't afford to be seen with that kind. You're an Eggleston. Our family goes back nearly four hundred years, to the earliest *rich* people. Remember your heritage, Noble. Our good name can only be perpetuated if blue blood marries blue blood. No other color will do, Noble. It must be a deep navy blue.

(She turns to go)

NOBLE But, Mother . . . Mother . . . Please . . .

MRS. EGGLESTON I'm sorry, Noble.

(She exits. NOBLE *looks after her glumly as* BELLE *enters wearing* MOMMA*'s red dress. Everyone in the room stops and turns to look at this strange creature from another world.* NOBLE *crosses, looking for her. She is fixing her skirt.* NOBLE *backs into her and the music plays rhapsodically)*

NOBLE Belle!

BELLE Noble!

(The snob RICH KIDS *whisper and point at* BELLE*)*

NOBLE *(Takes* BELLE*'s arm and pulls her aside)* Gosh, Belle—you look so pretty in your dress, I hardly recognize you without your rags.

BELLE You look nice too, Noble.

NOBLE Well, I *always* look nice. I was thinking about you all week. Last night I went by your house, but you were still eating . . .

BELLE I've been thinking about you too, Noble.

NOBLE You know, Belle, my mother says you're not good enough for me, and yet, I have a feeling for you . . . that . . . I could never have for a *nice* girl. *(He grabs her hand and sings "I Love You," with* BELLE *and the chorus)*

NOBLE

I love you
As much as I am able
Considering I'm wealthy
Considering you're poor

BELLE

That's very nice because
I love you!

CHORUS *(Echo effect)*

She loves you, she loves you, she loves you . . .

NOBLE

I know it!

BELLE

As much as I am able

CHORUS

Considering her background

BELLE

Considering your mother
Considers me a boor—
My passion will endure for you

NOBLE

And I will always love you

BELLE

My heart I'll keep secure for you

NOBLE

Though other girls are so far above you—

To show you
I am democratic
Considering you're riffraff—
And I am well-to-do
As Noble

CHORUS
Noble-Noble-Noble-Noble

NOBLE
And worthy of the label

CHORUS
Label-label-label-label

NOBLE
As much as I am able

NOBLE and BELLE
I love you.
(After the song, MRS. EGGLESTON *and* RAMONA *approach)*

MRS. EGGLESTON Noble! Who is this . . . person?

NOBLE Mother, this is Belle Schlumpfert from the wrong side of the tracks. Belle, this is my mother, from the right side.

BELLE How do you do, Mrs. Eggleston.

MRS. EGGLESTON *(Ignores her)* Noble, I want this person out of the house.

NOBLE But, Mother—please . . . Can I . . . Mother . . .

*(*MRS. EGGLESTON *gives him an icy stare and crosses left with* RAMONA*)*

NOBLE *(Reluctantly turns to* BELLE*)* I'm sorry, Belle. It's nothing personal . . . It's just *you*!

BELLE I see. Before your mother would ever accept me, I must have what you have. Wealth and culture.

NOBLE And don't forget social position.

BELLE Very well, then. If that's what I need, I'll go out into the world and get it. Will you wait for me, Noble?

NOBLE I certainly will.

MRS. EGGLESTON *(From across the room)* *Noble!*

NOBLE *(To* BELLE*)* But you'd better hurry.

BELLE *(Starting to exit)* I'll be back someday, Noble. Wait for me . . . Wait for me.

(She stumbles on the stairs. Everyone breaks out into loud laughter. MRS. EGGLESTON *exits.* BELLE *bursts into tears and exits—on the platform)*

NOBLE *(Runs up the steps and stomps his foot)* All right —*stop it! (The laughter stops abruptly)* Well, have we all had our big laugh? Do we realize what we've just done? We've just thrown out the girl with the kindest heart . . . the purest soul . . . and the best build in town!

(Blackout)

SCENE 4

Exterior of the Eggleston home. BELLE *enters crying. Suddenly* GEORGE MUSGROVE, *with a valise, comes running by. He stops.*

GEORGE Belle, Belle, I've been lookin' all over for you. I came to say goodbye.

BELLE Goodbye?

GEORGE A friend of mine just opened up a chain of crap games in the Middle West. Maybe someday I'll be able to send for you.

BELLE Thank you, George, but I'm going to be busy myself for the next few years.

GEORGE Doin' what?

BELLE Looking for wealth, culture and social position.

GEORGE You're making a mistake, Belle. Someday you're gonna get kicked right in the heart. But if you ever need me—remember, all you've got to do is snap your fingers . . . *(He snaps his fingers)* . . . and George Musgrove will be there.

BELLE I'll remember, George.

GEORGE So long, Belle. I'm goin' to Chicago to grow up.

(He exits)

BELLE *(Looks after him, then says with determination)* I *will* get there someday . . . I will! *(She sings "The Other Side of the Tracks"—reprise)*

YOUNG BELLE

On the other side of the tracks
That is where I'm goin' to be—
On the other side
Of the great divide
Between fame and fortune and me!
Gonna put my shadows behind me,
Give my inhibitions the ax—
And tomorrow morning you'll find me
On the other side of the tracks!

On the other side of that line,
Where the life is fancy and free,
Gonna sit and fan
On my fat divan
While the butler buttles the tea!
But for now I'm facin' the fences,
And I can't afford to relax—
'Cause the whole caboodle commences
On the other side of the tracks!

So I'm off and runnin'
Over the rail—
I'm goin' gunnin'
After the quail!
Off and runnin'—
Send me my mail
To the great big world on the other side
The great big world on the farther side
The great big world on the other side
Of the tracks!

On the other side
On the other side
To the great big world on the other side
Of the tracks.

Lights up on OLDER BELLE *seated at a table with a standing mirror, trying on tiaras and much-bejeweled bracelets, being shown to her by a handsome and finely tailored* SALESMAN. *She is also narrating to* PATRICK DENNIS *and the tape recorder.*

OLDER BELLE I was determined to win Noble. But to accomplish my new ambition, I knew I had to seek my fortune in the outside world.

PATRICK *(Into the mike)* Chapter Two . . . "Goodbye Green Pastures, Hello Blue Horizons."

OLDER BELLE To travel took money. I thought perhaps I might borrow it from our friends and neighbors in Drifters' Row—*(Throws the jewels on the table and turns to the* SALESMAN*)* No, Jacques, these are too formal. I just want something to knock around the pool in. *(To* PATRICK*)*—never realizing that at the moment these poor people were facing a dilemma far worse than little mine.

(Blackout)

Interior of a small-town bank. PINCHLEY JUNIOR *and* MISS KEPPLEWHITE *are arranging papers on the desk.*

MISS KEPPLEWHITE Hurry, hurry, Mr. Pinchley will be in any second.

JUNIOR I'm doing it as fast as I can.
(He drops a book)

MISS KEPPLEWHITE And be careful. You heard him yesterday. One more stupid mistake and you're fired.

JUNIOR Do you think he really would? His own son?

MISS KEPPLEWHITE *(Reacts)* Watch it! The Grouch is here!

*(*NURSE *wheels in eighty-eight-year-old* AMOS PINCHLEY *to the left of the desk. He is withered and sour. A cane rests in his hand. His head is down and he seems to be dozing)*

JUNIOR G-good morning, Father.

NURSE One moment, please. An eighty-eight-year-old man needs a little more time than most of us to get started in the morning. *(She leans over and says in the old man's ear)* Good morning, Mr. Pinchley. *(She shakes him gently.* PINCHLEY *stirs. His head rises slowly, then his lips start to quiver. Life is slowly awakening within him)*

PINCHLEY Gemumba . . . Gemumble . . .

NURSE He's coming around.

PINCHLEY Goomorbaw . . .

NURSE That's it, Mr. Pinchley. Come on.

PINCHLEY Goo mormee . . . Goo mormee . . .

NURSE Come on. Get those lips moving.

PINCHLEY Goo mormee . . . morming . . . Goo morming . . .

NURSE That's it. That's it! You're almost up!

PINCHLEY Morning . . . Morning . . . Good morning! Good morning!

(He growls)

NURSE He's all right now. He has another two hours before he goes under again . . . I'll be back at twelve. Goodbye, Mr. Pinchley.

(He mutters and chuckles as she goes, as though he enjoys being nasty)

JUNIOR *(Smiling but fearful)* Good morning, Father.

PINCHLEY Good morning, Nincompoop! Well, let's start making money . . . Money money money money . . . That's the most important thing. What's first?

JUNIOR There's a crowd of dirty people outside. From Drifters' Row.

PINCHLEY Probably come to grovel and beg.

MISS KEPPLEWHITE Shall I call the Fire Department and have them hosed out?

PINCHLEY No. I haven't had a good grovel and beg in weeks . . . Show them in.

*(*MISS KEPPLEWHITE *nods and exits)*

JUNIOR It's about those evictions, Father. Don't you think we're being too harsh? I mean, maybe we should show them a little kindness.

PINCHLEY Kindness? *(He swings his cane savagely.* JUNIOR *ducks just in time)* This is a bank, son, not a mother!

(MISS KEPPLEWHITE *enters, followed by a group of people)*

MISS KEPPLEWHITE Come in, please. And wipe your feet.

(They all pause and wipe their feet. They walk in. At the head of the group are MOMMA *and* MR. KLEEG*)*

PINCHLEY Well? Well?

KLEEG *(Steps forward. He is afraid, as they all are, of the power of men like* PINCHLEY*)* Er . . . Mr. Pinchley.

PINCHLEY Sir.

KLEEG Sir . . . We poor people of Drifters' Row have come to ask—

PINCHLEY *Beg!*

KLEEG —beg you to listen to our plea. We've been given our eviction notice.

PINCHLEY Oh my.

KLEEG The sheriff says if we don't have the money, he's going to throw us out tonight.

PINCHLEY Oh, that's terrible.

KLEEG Can't we have a little time?

PINCHLEY How much time would you need?

KLEEG Next week.

PINCHLEY When next week? Say, Monday?

KLEEG Yes, yes, Monday.

PINCHLEY Would you have all of it by Monday?

KLEEG Yes, yes, all of it. Can we stay, Mr. Pinchley?

PINCHLEY No, but it was fun getting your hopes up. Hee, hee, hee!

JUNIOR But, Father . . .

(PINCHLEY *brandishes his cane)*

KLEEG Come on, folks. It's no use.

(They all nod and start out, when BELLE *enters)*

BELLE Wait! *(They all stop and turn)* Are you going to give up without a fight? Are you going to let yourselves be treated like animals?

MOMMA Belle, be quiet!

BELLE No! It's time someone spoke up to him. *(She turns to* PINCHLEY*)* Mr. Pinchley, you're a mean, miserly, nasty, rotten old man!

(They all gasp)

JUNIOR Nobody ever talked to my father like that.

*(*PINCHLEY *is shaking, cannot get his mouth open)*

MISS KEPPLEWHITE Mr. Pinchley, are you all right?

JUNIOR He's choking on anger! Try to get his mouth open.

*(*MISS KEPPLEWHITE *forces* PINCHLEY*'s mouth open)*

PINCHLEY You! *(He points the cane at* BELLE*)* With the dimples and the big mouth! Come closer.

JUNIOR *(Crosses right, pushing people to the side)* Everyone else out, please . . . This isn't going to be pleasant.

MOMMA Don't say anything foolish, honey. He's a powerful man.

(They all exit, leaving BELLE, JUNIOR *and* PINCHLEY *alone. He stares at her)*

PINCHLEY Come closer, Dimples. *(*BELLE *nervously moves in closer.* PINCHLEY *takes his cane and measures the distance between him and* BELLE*)* A little closer. *(*BELLE *moves within striking distance)* Good! I want to kill you, I don't want to wound you. Now, say it!

BELLE You're a mean, miserly, nasty, rotten old man—

PINCHLEY *(Raises his cane)* And here it comes!

BELLE —and everyone in this town *hates* you!

PINCHLEY *(Stops at the top of his swing)* Hates me?

BELLE Yes, *hates* you, Mr. Pinchley . . . you're a hated man. *(She takes the cane from* PINCHLEY *and puts it on the desk)* I feel sorry for you, because there's no one in this whole wide world who really loves you.

PINCHLEY That's a lie. That's a dastardly lie—and I'll prove it right now. Nincompoop! *(Points to* JUNIOR*)* You love me . . . don't you?

JUNIOR I respect my father. Because he is rich and powerful.

PINCHLEY *(Smiles and nods)* And what else?

JUNIOR *(Puzzled)* And what else is there?

PINCHLEY You know . . . *(Trying to prompt him)* Lo—lo—

JUNIOR Lo—?

PINCHLEY Lo—

JUNIOR Lo—?

PINCHLEY Lo—

JUNIOR Lo—?

PINCHLEY Love!

JUNIOR Love, Father?

PINCHLEY *(Screams)* Yes, love, you idiot! Get out of here and don't come back till you love me.

*(*JUNIOR *runs out)*

BELLE He didn't even know the meaning of the word. The plain truth is . . . no one likes you, do they, Mr. Pinchley? *(*PINCHLEY *bows his head)* It's not a pleasant thing, is it? To be hated?

PINCHLEY I'm not crazy about it, no . . . Nobody seems to like me. Even on Christmas Eve the carolers stand outside my window and sing threatening Christmas songs.

BELLE I'm really not surprised.

PINCHLEY That's just because I'm a rich, rotten old man.

(He is breaking down)

BELLE That's not true, Mr. Pinchley. You're only rotten on the top . . . *(Music starts under the dialogue)* *Everybody* has a little good in them . . . somewhere.

PINCHLEY *(Hopefully)* Even me, Dimples?

BELLE Even you!

(And she sings "Deep Down Inside," joined by PINCHLEY*)*

BELLE

Somewhere, there's a darn' nice fella,
Deep down inside!

PINCHLEY

Deep down inside?

BELLE

Deep down, in the ol' subcellar—
Somewhere, though I think he fell a-
Sleep down inside—
Deep down,
Dig-a, dig-a
Deep down inside!

(Speaks) *You* try it now!

PINCHLEY Gosh, I'm ashamed.

BELLE Go on!

PINCHLEY All right. Here goes.

(Sings)

Sometimes, I am darn' near human
Deep down inside!

BELLE

Deep down inside, Mr. Pinchley?

PINCHLEY

Deep down, where the bass is boomin'

Sometimes, gotta take that broom 'n
Sweep down inside—
Sweep down,
Dig-a, dig-a
Deep down inside!
(Speaks) Hey, *I like it!*

BELLE Keep going!

BELLE and PINCHLEY
No man is a true Pariah, deep down inside—
Deep down inside—

PINCHLEY
Deep down, in the old spare tire!

BOTH
No man is a true Uriah
Heep down inside!
There's a lover that you just can't keep down—
Deep down inside!
Deep down inside!
(After the first chorus, PINCHLEY*'s emotions are soaring)*

BELLE *(Elated)* We found it, Mr. Pinchley. We found that little bit of good in you.

PINCHLEY You think some people would like me?

BELLE Try it and see.

PINCHLEY All right, I will. *(Screams)* Junior!
*(*JUNIOR *rushes in)*

JUNIOR Did you scream, Father?

PINCHLEY How about you and me—going out and having dinner sometime?

JUNIOR *(Overwhelmed with emotion)* Oh, Daddy!

PINCHLEY *(Turns to* BELLE*)* He called me Daddy!

BELLE He likes you.

PINCHLEY And I don't even like him.

(They continue to sing "Deep Down Inside," this time joined by JUNIOR*)*

JUNIOR

In even the worst of varmints
You'll find a good deed

BELLE

Down under the outer garments
Of malice and greed

PINCHLEY

That little gold streak is shining,
Believe it or not!

ALL

That is, if you don't mind mining
'Til
You hit rock bottom!

JUNIOR

Strip down,

BELLE

Rip down,

PINCHLEY

Meet a real pip down

JUNIOR

Deep down

BELLE

Deep down

PINCHLEY

Inside!

JUNIOR

Deep down

BELLE

Deep down

PINCHLEY

Inside!

JUNIOR
Slip down,

BELLE
Zip down,

PINCHLEY
Take a little trip down!

JUNIOR
Go down,

BELLE
Low down,

PINCHLEY
Meet a good Joe down

ALL
Under your hide—
On that shovel get a real good grip
And
Dip down in-
Down down in-
Dip down inside!

PINCHLEY *(To* BELLE*)* Gosh, do you think . . . *other* people would like me too?

BELLE Of course, Mr. Pinchley. If you'll only give them a chance.

PINCHLEY Oh . . . all right, I will. *(Screams) Other people! (All the people from Drifters' Row rush in)* Other people . . . I'm tearing up all the mortgages on Drifters' Row! You can live there for free! *(They all say "Free?")* And Monday . . . the painters are coming! *(They all say "Painters?")* And starting this winter—heat!

(They all say "Heat!" They cheer and join in another chorus)

CHORUS
Three cheers for Pinchley, he's true blue!
We knew evinch'lly he'd come through!
'Cause

TWO MEN

Pinchley is a real nice human
Deep down inside!
Deep down inside!

PINCHLEY

Deep down, there's a vi'let bloomin'!

CHORUS

Pinchley ain't a low, inhuman creep down inside—

ONE MAN

He's a fella with a heart *that* big—

CHORUS

All you've gotta do is dig, dig, dig!

ALL *(As dance starts)*

Stoop down,
Snoop down

BELLE and PINCHLEY

Get the real poop down

ALL

Deep down
Deep down
Down where?
Deep down
Deep down

PINCHLEY

Right there!

ALL

Swoop down
Troop down

BELLE and PINCHLEY

Bring a little group down

ALL

Get down
Set down

BELLE

Meet a good bet down

ALL

Under your hide!

BELLE

(Don't let down)

ALL

Then rise up and give a hip, hip, hip
Hip!
Three cheers for Pinchley, he's okay!
We knew essinch'lly he's grade-a,
'Cause
No man is a mean old geezer
Clear down inside!

BOYS

(No mean geezer)

ALL

Peer down inside!

GIRLS

(He's a pleaser)

PINCHLEY

Here down in the geezer-freezer!

ALL

No man'll deny that he's a
Dear down inside—

PINCHLEY *(Speaks)* Dear Miss Schlumpfert—you've been such a comfort!

ALL

Deep, deep, deep down—
Deep down inside!

In even the worst of varmints
You'll find a good deed—
Down under the outer garments
Of malice and greed
That little gold streak is shining,
Believe it or not!

That is, if you don't mind mining
'Til
You hit rock bottom!

Somewhere there's a darn nice fellow
Deep down
Deep down
Inside!
Slip down,
Zip down,
Take a little trip down!

Go down,
Low down,
Meet a good Joe down
Under your hide—
On that shovel get a real good grip
And
Dip down in-
Dip down in-
Dip down inside—

Somewhere there's a darn nice fella'
Down in the old subcellar
Somewhere there's a darn nice fella'
Deep down inside!
(The people from Drifters' Row exit)

BELLE Look, Mr. Pinchley. Now *everyone* likes you.

PINCHLEY That's all because of you, Dimples. And now that you did something nice for me, it's only right that I do something nice for you.

BELLE *(Gesturing)* No. No.

PINCHLEY What's right is right. What would you want more than anything else in the whole wide world?

BELLE Oh, that's easy. To leave Venezuela. And go to some great center of culture, like Peoria, and learn the really important things in life—diction, manners and French cooking!

PINCHLEY Well, that takes money.

BELLE Yeah.

PINCHLEY *(Takes out bankroll and blows dust from it)* Here it is.

BELLE *(Takes the bankroll)* Oh, thank you, Mr. Pinchley, thank you. *(She kisses him on the cheek)* Look! Even *I* like you! *(She exits happily)* Whee!

PINCHLEY And you know what? *(He beams) So do I! (He sings)*

Three cheers for Pinchley
He's true blue.
He's a fella with a heart that big,
All you gotta do is dig, dig, dig.

(The music swells up—lights fade out as he wheels himself off)

OLDER BELLE *and* PATRICK *are on a golf course A* GOLF PRO *has his arms around her, demonstrating a swing.* PATRICK *carries the tape recorder and pulls a caddy rack.*

OLDER BELLE Thanks to my kind and generous benefactor, I moved to Peoria to begin a new life. *(She swings the club. To the* PRO*)* How'm I doing, Arnold?

PRO Just fine, ma'am. Just fine.

OLDER BELLE *(To* PATRICK*)* But back in Venezuela the local gossipmongers began their evil work. *(She is moving left across the stage)* And oh, how they could twist the truth. The fact that sweet old Mr. Pinchley spent every weekend with me in my hotel in Peoria was grist for their mill. But good banker that he was, he was merely trying to protect his investment. However, my good character was besmirched. And then, on one peaceful Saturday afternoon in June, my character received the worst besmirchment of all.

(Blackout)

SCENE 8

A hotel room in Peoria. BELLE, *in a negligee, is balancing a book on her head, walking up and down and enunciating clearly.*

BELLE How-now-brown-cow. Brown-cow-how-now. *(There is a knock at the door) Entrez*—come in!

(The door opens. There stands PINCHLEY, *without wheelchair)*

PINCHLEY Hi, Dimples.

BELLE Mr. Pinchley!

PINCHLEY Hello there . . . Dimples!

(He walks in, gives a little skip and a hop)

BELLE Mr. Pinchley—you're walking!

PINCHLEY And skipping and hopping and jumping. Thanks to you, I found out my legs weren't lame—they were just nasty!

BELLE Oh, Mr. Pinchley, isn't that wonderful!

PINCHLEY You know what I did yesterday, Dimples?

BELLE What?

PINCHLEY I smiled. I smiled from nine to one, took a half-hour for lunch, and smiled till six.

BELLE Imagine that.

PINCHLEY All because of you, Dimples. You know, Dimples, there's a big difference in our ages—I'm an octogenarian and you're a teen-agenarian—well, I'll give you a business proposition . . . Will you marry me?

BELLE *(Crosses right in astonishment)* Marry you?

PINCHLEY And in return, when I go I'll leave you wealth, culture and social position.

BELLE But . . . I love another boy. You'd never be happy with me.

PINCHLEY Happy? Happy? *(He takes a gun out of his breast pocket)* Do you see that?

BELLE A *gun!*

PINCHLEY Yes, a gun. I bought it as a present. I was going to shoot myself for my birthday.

BELLE Oh no!

PINCHLEY Oh yeah. But I don't have to do that, Dimples, not if you say you'll marry me. What do you say, Dimps?

BELLE *(Reacts)* Wealth, culture and social position . . . I say—yes! *(PINCHLEY puts the gun back in his breast pocket)* And thank you for everything, Mr. Pinchley. Thank you.

(She throws her arms around him and hugs him tightly. We hear a gunshot. PINCHLEY feels his heart. His legs begin to shake. He sits down on the bed)

PINCHLEY I think you thanked me right through the heart.

BELLE *(Sobs)* Oh no!

PINCHLEY Oh yeah.

BELLE Is it bad?

PINCHLEY The bullet's about an eighth of an inch above my heart. I mustn't move . . . or I'll die.

BELLE You mustn't die. *(She shakes him vigorously)* You mustn't die.

PINCHLEY That's it!

(He dies. Blackout)

SCENE 9

Prison bars come up from the floor. An arc picks up BELLE *behind them. A* NEWSBOY *enters shouting headlines.*

NEWSBOY Extra . . . "Millionaire Slain in Love Nest" . . . "Sweet Little Old Man Murdered" . . . "I Didn't Do It Says Well-Built Teen-ager" . . . Read all about it . . .

(Two men enter and buy a paper, and both read the headline)

NEWSBOY . . . "Girl Guns Geezer" . . . Get your paper . . . Extra . . . *(He exits. The two men look at each other. They are the Buchsbaum brothers,* BERNIE *and* BENNY*— two squat, dyspeptic middle-aged men)*

BERNIE Are you thinking what I'm thinking, Benny?

BENNY I'm thinking what you're thinking, Bernie.

(They cross to BELLE*, behind bars)*

BERNIE Miss Schlumpfert?

BENNY *(Going to left of the bars)* How do you do. We're—

BERNIE —the Buchsbaum Brothers.

BENNY I'm Benny!

BERNIE And I'm Bernie!

BENNY Benny and Bernie!

BERNIE The Buchsbaum Brothers!

BELLE Lawyers?

BENNY No!

BERNIE Bookers.

BENNY Yes!

BERNIE In vaudeville.

BENNY Vaudeville bookers.

BERNIE Benny and Bernie Buchsbaum.

BENNY The Vaudeville Bookers.

BELLE How do you do?

BERNIE How do we do?

BENNY Tell her how we do.

BERNIE Sensational—

BENNY —is how we do.

BERNIE But with *you*—

BENNY We'll do better

BERNIE —is how we'll do.

BENNY "Dimples"—

BERNIE How would *you*—

BENNY —like to be—

BERNIE —a star!

BELLE A star?

BENNY A star!

BERNIE For the Buchsbaum Brothers . . .

BENNY Vaudeville circuit.

BERNIE Top billing.

BENNY Fancy salary.

BERNIE Spic-and-span dressing room.

BENNY Like a star.

BELLE But I'm in jail!

BERNIE *(Smiles, happily)* A talented kid.

BENNY For thirty cents' worth of bullets—

BERNIE —you got a million dollars' publicity.

BELLE But I can't sing and I can't dance.

BENNY Singers we got!

BERNIE Dancers we got!

BENNY *Killers* we ain't got.

BELLE But I'm on trial for my life. *(Bernie and Benny sing "Be a Performer")*

BOTH

So resulting from a few illegal capers
You are starring in the papers
Just go over with a jury and in jig-time
Join the Buchsbaums in the big time!
So you'll try a little trill
From *Traviata*
*(*BELLE *tries and fails)*
So it's not your style sonata!
When a girl has got
What you have got a lotta
You know what you've got?
You've got something hot!

BERNIE

So here's a good tiding

BENNY

If men you are killing

BERNIE

A talent you're hiding

BENNY

To be a performer!

BOTH

So be a performer!

BENNY

And soon you'll be riding

BOTH

If God should be willing
The crest of your life!

BENNY

You ain't a Pavlova

BERNIE

An Eleonora Duse

BENNY

But looking you over

BOTH

You'll be a performer
You'll be a performer

BERNIE

A lollapalooza

BENNY

And rolling in clover—

BOTH

Just pass the test of your life!
So up the river
They would send you—
But with Mother Nature helping to defend you
Who could send you
Very far?

BENNY

Sobbing in a dress that clings to
All the things you are!

BERNIE

So listen to Bernie

BENNY

And listen to Benny

BOTH

Forget the attorney
And be a performer
And be a performer
We mean a performer

BENNY

Unless you, God forbid,

BERNIE

Get hung for what you did

BOTH

Ho, ho, you naughty kid—
Just fulfill this small request of your life—

BENNY

So be a performer!

BELLE

I'll be a performer!

BOTH

You'll be thankful all
The rest of your long and healthy—
(knock wood)—life!

ANNOUNCER *(Offstage, over mike)* Hear ye, hear ye. This court is now in session.
The State of Illinois vs. Dimples Schlumpfert.

(Light hits MRS. EGGLESTON *above scrim with her right hand raised)*

MRS. EGGLESTON I do. She was a cheap, vulgar gold digger!

(Blackout, then light up on MISS KEPPLEWHITE *above scrim with her right hand raised)*

MISS KEPPLEWHITE I do. She was a sixteen-year-old vamp!

(Blackout, then light up on another witness above scrim—a WOMAN *who stands with her right hand raised)*

WOMAN I do. I never met her but I'm sure I wouldn't have liked her!

(Blackout, then light up on witness stand below scrim. NOBLE EGGLESTON, *in a college sweater with large letters* H *and* Y *on the front, stands there with the* DEFENSE LAWYER*)*

NOBLE *(Hand raised)* I certainly do!

DEFENSE LAWYER Your name is?

NOBLE Noble Eggleston.

DEFENSE LAWYER You were away at college when the unfortunate incident occurred, were you not?

NOBLE Yes, I were.

DEFENSE LAWYER Tell me, Mr. Eggleston, what university do you attend?

NOBLE Harvard and Yale. I won a double scholarship.

DEFENSE LAWYER And what are you studying at Harvard and Yale?

NOBLE Medicine and law. I hope some day to become a legal doctor.

DEFENSE LAWYER And your records show that in every year in high school you were voted the most brilliant and most popular student in your class.

NOBLE And best-looking three out of four. One year I had a little complexion trouble.

DEFENSE LAWYER Then, do you, the pride and honor of Venezuela, Illinois, after searching down deeply into your heart and conscience, believe that that lovely, fragile young girl is capable of murder?

NOBLE Belle Schlumpfert is the sweetest, kindest thing I've ever known. I love her . . . and a person as good as I am could never love a murderess.

DEFENSE LAWYER Thank you. You may have saved her life.

NOBLE It was my pleasure!

(Blackout)

VOICE OVER P.A. The Buchsbaum Brothers proudly present . . . direct from her triumphant two-week trial . . . Miss Dimples Schlumpfert and her police escort.

(Roller drop comes down. BELLE *and* FOUR POLICEMEN *enter. They sing "Oh! Dem Doggone Dimples")*

BELLE

Oh!
Dem Doggone Dimples!
Oh!
Dey did it again!
Tell me why a little indentation
Should start a criminal investigation!
Oh!
Dem doggone dimples!
If
I ever go to da pen—
Oh!
Oh!
Oh!
Oh!
Dey did it again!

POLICEMEN

At eighty-eight

BELLE

Oh!

POLICEMEN

He seemed the fatherly kind
You wouldn't think

BELLE

Oh!

POLICEMEN

That it would enter his mind
But sure enough

BELLE

Oh!

POLICEMEN

His shining armor corroded—
As she expressed it when the gun exploded
"Boom"—

BELLE

Oh!
Dem doggone dimples!
Oh!
I never know when—
Oh!

POLICEMEN

Oh!

BELLE

Oh!

POLICEMEN

Oh!

BELLE

Dey'll do it again.
Oh!

POLICEMEN

Oh!

BELLE

Uh-oh!
Dey did it again!

*(*BELLE *and the* POLICEMEN *exit. They return for another bow)*

Lights come up on OLDER BELLE, *in white coveralls, sculpting a clay figure.* PATRICK DENNIS, *in a tiger skin, is posing. He is also holding the tape recorder.*

OLDER BELLE In my very first public appearance, I was a smash hit. *(*BELLE *and her* POLICE ESCORT, *who have frozen their bow, now unfreeze and exit)* After seeing my performance, the critic for the Chicago *Daily Tribune* said: "Dimples Schlumpfert is the best singing acquitted killer in town . . ."

PATRICK You were on your way up.

OLDER BELLE Only to come crashing down again. *(She pushes* PATRICK*'s arm down, and the statue's)* I was fired six weeks later when the Buchsbaum Brothers found a new headliner, Peaches Davis, who shot her millionaire husband at the wedding.

PATRICK And you were on your way down.

OLDER BELLE But determined to bounce back up again. *(She pushes* PATRICK*'s arm up again as well as the statue's)* Which I did . . . all the way up to the Skylight Roof on top of the Breakstone Hotel. I was a pioneer in the annals of entertainment. I had the distinction of becoming the very first Camera Girl ever to take a picture in a night club.

(Blackout)

SCENE 13

In the dark a flashlight explodes. The lights come up on the Skylight Roof. BELLE, *dressed as a camera girl, has just snapped a picture of a smiling group. The camera is an old, huge affair mounted on a tall tripod.*

BELLE Thank you. Your picture will be ready in just two weeks.

(She lifts the camera and tripod and moves to another place. NOBLE, MRS. EGGLESTON *and* RAMONA *enter. They follow the* HEADWAITER *to a table.* BRUCEY, *who is seated at a table with friends, rises and comes downstage. The* HEADWAITER *exits)*

BRUCEY Noble! Noble Eggleston!

NOBLE Brucey! You son of a gun! How are things at Princeton?

BRUCEY Rah, rah.

NOBLE Rah, rah.

BRUCEY What are you doing in Chicago?

NOBLE I'm here to announce my engagement.

BRUCEY Well, say . . . congratulations.

NOBLE I'd like you to meet my fiancée, Ramona VanderVeld, the girl my mother picked out.

BRUCEY Well, the best of luck to both of you.

NOBLE Thanks a lot. And Rah. Rah.

*(*BRUCEY *returns to his table.* NOBLE *sits down at the table with his mother and* RAMONA*)*

MRS. EGGLESTON Noble, why don't you have a picture taken with Ramona?

NOBLE Gosh, that's a wonderful idea. Oh, Camera Girl!

BELLE *(Turns and comes down to* NOBLE*)* Yes, sir. Would you—

NOBLE Belle!

BELLE Noble!

NOBLE Belle . . . What are you doing working here as a Camera Girl?

BELLE I'm working here as a Camera Girl.

NOBLE Oh!

BELLE You never answered my letters, Noble.

NOBLE Yes, I did. Every one. I know, because I gave them to my mother to mail . . .

BELLE Hello, Mrs. Eggleston.

*(*MRS. EGGLESTON *turns away)*

NOBLE It's no use. She still can't stand you. But I still think about you. Every minute of every waking day, my thoughts are only of you. *(*RAMONA *coughs. He turns to her)* Oh, this is my fiancée, Ramona Vander-Veld.

BELLE Your fiancée?

NOBLE My mother picked her out.

BELLE But you promised.

NOBLE But my mother—

BELLE You said you'd—

NOBLE But my mother—

BELLE Oh, Noble!

(She bursts into tears and runs off)

NOBLE Belle, wait—

MRS. EGGLESTON Noble!

NOBLE No, Mother. I've tried to fight it—with every ounce of blue blood in my veins—but it's no use. I love her, and there isn't anything you can say or do to change it.

MRS. EGGLESTON We're going home!

NOBLE I'll get the coats.

(They all exit. THREE FRENCH GIRLS *enter. They sing)*

ALL
Messieurs et dames

IST GIRL
Bon soir

2ND GIRL
Bon soir

3RD GIRL
Bon soir

IST GIRL
Enchanté

3RD GIRL
Enchanté

2ND GIRL
Ze Skylight Roof is proud to present

3RD GIRL
Ze toast of *cinq*—five continents

IST GIRL
Direct from Gay Paree—

ALL
Ho Ho

3RD GIRL
Ze one

IST GIRL:
Ze only

2ND GIRL

Ze debonaire

ALL

Ze man-about-town

IST GIRL

He sings

3RD GIRL

He dances

2ND GIRL

He struts
Ze expert on ze affaires of ze heart,

ALL

Monsieur Hot Stuff himself,
Val du Val.

(Musical play-on. Spotlight hits curtain and VAL DU VAL *enters, wearing a straw hat. Thunderous applause from the patrons)*

VAL Sank you, ladies and gentlemen, sank you, sank you, sank you. Or as you say in English—*Th* ank you! But now, I would like you to meet my assistant, Colette—the very beautiful, the very wonderful Colette. *(*COLETTE *appears, a pretty, dark-haired girl carrying a drum)* Colette travels with me and she lives in the same hotel, in separate room . . . *(Kisses her hand)* . . . sometimes. And now I should like to sing at you about love. *(A chair is brought out and placed for* VAL *so he can sit at a piano made by the hands of the girls in his show)* Not the little love that goes plinky-linkly-plink . . . *(As he pretends to play, the real piano in the pit makes the actual sounds)* . . . but the French love that goes BOOM-BOOM. *(His elbow pounds the keys)* My famous "BOOM-BOOM" song.

*(*VAL *and the* GIRLS *sing the* "Boom-Boom" song*)*

VAL

Poor Pierrot, I hear him yet
In pursuit of his Pierrette

With the same old urgent message to impart
What it was she never found out—
For the point was always drowned out
By the vi'lent cannonading of his heart *(*BOOM-BOOM*)*

He'd say, "Pierrette"—
And clear his throat.
"Lest we forget—"
*(*And here I quote:*)*

If ze girl BOOM-BOOM
And ze boy BOOM-BOOM
And zey get togezzer and zey both BOOM-BOOM
C'est Le Grand BOOM-BOOM
Et Le Grand BOOM-BOOM
Zats ze one BOOM-BOOM for me!

Oh, a stray BOOM-BOOM occasionally may
Prove a gay BOOM-BOOM and carry you away;

But ze prime BOOM-BOOM—
Zat's sublime BOOM-BOOM—
Won't be true,
Not if you
All ze time BOOM-BOOM!
What I mean is, my chérie—
Save Le Grand BOOM-BOOM for me!
(They dance)

ALL

Oh a stray BOOM-BOOM occasionally may
Prove a gay BOOM-BOOM and carry you away
For ze dream BOOM-BOOM—
Zat supreme BOOM-BOOM—

VAL

Is for two
People who
Like a team BOOM-BOOM!
What I mean is, my chérie

ALL

Save Le Grand BOOM-BOOM for me!

(After the number there is great applause. VAL *bows, then runs off through the curtains. It is a section of a room with a ledge and window.* BELLE *has climbed up on the ledge and is just about to jump when* VAL *comes in and grabs her)*

VAL Why do you do this crazy thing? Why?

BELLE *(She buries her face in her hands)* Let me go. Let me go. I have nothing left to live for.

VAL What a shameful thing to say. A pretty girl like you.

BELLE But you don't understand. The boy I love . . . is going to marry someone else.

VAL Love! I thought so. Let me tell you a little story. There once was a French boy who was een love wiz a French girl. They were very much in love. They were going to get married een the leetle town where zey lived. One day a man from ze city meets ze girl. He is charming . . . he is clever . . . and soon ze girl runs away wiz him, leaving ze poor French boy in tears. He too wanted to keel himself—but he didn't. After a while he got over it, and today, he is a famous person in France. I suppose you've already guessed I am telling a story about myself . . . But now I have Colette and I am very happy.

BELLE When did you meet Colette?

VAL I just told you. When I took her from that French boy in the village.

BELLE Do you really think I'll get over it too, maybe?

VAL Of course you will. When it comes to love, always leesten to a Frenchy.

(A tall, attractive MAN *in tuxedo enters)*

MAN Second show, Val.

VAL Yes. *(To the* MAN*)* Keep an eye on her. She likes to jump. *(* VAL *goes through the curtain into the night club. The* HEADWAITER *enters, goes to* VAL, *gives him a note and exits)*

MAN Is there anything ya need?

BELLE No, I'm all right now.

MAN Remember what I once told ya, Belle? If ya ever need me, all ya gotta do is—

BELLE —snap your fingers! *(He snaps)* George! George Musgrove! Gosh, you really *did* grow up since Drifters' Row . . . What are you doing here?

GEORGE I own this club, baby.

BELLE *Your* club?

GEORGE That's right. And I got a cozy little apartment right downstairs.

(There is a drum cue as the lights come up on VAL *in the night club)*

VAL Ladies and gentlemen. Ze management has asked me to make two very important announcements. The first one: Zere will be a special New Year's Eve show, six dollairs a couple with noisemakers. And ze second announcement ees: *(He looks at a piece of paper) World War I* ees declared! *(Pandemonium. A* MAN *rushes by)* Where are you going?

MAN War is declared!

VAL War! That's terrible!

(He rushes off)

BELLE War! Oh, George, how terrible.

GEORGE Don't worry about it, baby. The Allies are eight-to-five favorites. How about you and me goin' down to my apartment and playin' a game of two-handed romance?

(He bites her neck)

BELLE But I still love Noble.

GEORGE Forget him. It ain't in the cards for you two.

(He bites her neck again)

BELLE Don't, George . . .

(She walks away from him)

GEORGE Don't fight it, Belle. Our hearts are shuffled. Let's cut the deck!

*(*GEORGE*, in the empty club, sings "I've Got Your Number")*

You've got no time for me—
You've got big things to do!
Well, my sweet chickadee,
I've got hot news for you!

I've got your number—
I know you inside out—
You ain't no Eagle Scout
You're all at sea.

Oh, yes, you'll brag a lot,
Wave your own
Flag a lot;
But you're unsure a lot—
You're a lot
Like me,
Oh—

I've got your number—
And what you're looking for—
And what you're looking for
Just suits me fine:

We'll break those rules a lot
We'll be damned
Fools a lot—
But then, why should we not—
How could we not
Combine?
When I've got your number, and
I've got the glow you've got—
I've got your number
And baby, you know, you've got mine.

What do you say, Belle baby? This is big George talking.

BELLE Well, I . . . *(Music rhythm and beat catch* BELLE. GEORGE *comes up to her and playfully snaps her garter)* Oh, stop it, George.

GEORGE I'd tango on a dime for you, Belle baby.

BELLE You know I'm not that kind of girl, George.

GEORGE I know. I know.

BELLE *(On second garter snap)* Oh, George! *(Again music and beat catch* BELLE*)* Oh, well . . . it's wartime.

(She stretches out her arms to him)

GEORGE *(Sings)*

I've got your number, and, baby, you know
You've got mine!

*(*GEORGE *picks* BELLE *up and carries her offstage)*

OLDER BELLE, PATRICK *and a* BALLET MASTER. *She is taking a ballet lesson and is dressed accordingly.*

OLDER BELLE The next morning, George left to join the Navy, but he left me with renewed faith in myself . . . a will to live—and pregnant. Once again my overgenerous nature had brought me nothing but trouble . . . Those first nine months of the war were very difficult for me *and* America!

PATRICK *(Into the mike)* Chapter Three . . . "Talcum and Gun Powder"!

OLDER BELLE Noble was commissioned a captain in the Army Air Corps because of his brilliant football record . . . and sailed for France before he could marry Ramona. One night, still in a delicate condition, I was invited to a "Farewell, Doughboy" party by some friends from my vaudeville days.

(Blackout)

SCENE 15

A small, gaily decorated apartment. SOLDIERS *and* GIRLS *are dancing to the music of a pianola.* BELLE *enters. She is about six months pregnant.*

1ST GIRL Hey, everyone, look who's here. You remember Belle Schlumpfert . . . Miss Dimples.

BELLE *(Shyly)* Hello.

2ND GIRL Gee, we're glad you could come, Belle. How've you been?

BELLE Oh, just fine. A little sick in the mornings.

3RD GIRL Hey, Belle, there's someone here we want you to meet.

BELLE Gosh, girls, I don't think I'd be very good company.

1ST GIRL He's real sweet.

2ND GIRL A typical American farm boy.

3RD GIRL I think this is his first party. He's in the kitchen. Making fudge.

1ST GIRL I'll call him. *(She shouts)* Oh, Fred! Fred!

*(*FRED POITRINE *enters in an ill-fitting uniform and thick glasses.* FRED *is a happy poor soul. His afflictions do not seem to bother him.* FRED *goes happily through life with a smile, and no catastrophe can dampen his high spirits)*

FRED *(Sings)* "Mademoiselle from Armentières, parlez-vous . . ." *(He shakes hands with one soldier, then crosses to a couple who are kissing passionately.* FRED *taps him on the shoulder)* Bert, snap out of it.

Let's have some fun . . . "Mademoiselle from Armentières . . ."

IST GIRL Fred! Hey, Fred . . .
(She waves)

FRED Hi! Who's talking?

IST GIRL It's me, Fred.

2ND GIRL He has a little trouble with his eyes.

FRED *(Gives* IST GIRL *a piece of paper)* Here's your song sheet. We're gonna sing "Mademoiselle from Armentières . . ."

IST GIRL Later, Fred. We'd like you to meet a wonderful person.

2ND GIRL Fred, this is Belle Schlumpfert.

BELLE Hello.

FRED Hi. I'm Fred Poitrine. U.S. Army . . . 646717. That's my serial number in case you can't remember my name. Gosh, this is a swell party!

IST GIRL Well, we'll leave you two to get acquainted.

2ND GIRL See you later, Fred.
*(*BERT *and his* GIRL *cross left directly in front of* FRED*)*

FRED Hya, Bert, Hey, Bert, hi! Hi, Bert! *(*MAN *ignores him)* That's my best friend, Bert. He's crazy about me. I talk to him after lights out in the barracks. I talk to him about the farm and the cows and the chickens and the eggs. I keep talking all night long. I keep talking and talking and talking and talking. Last night his gun went off right near my head, but it was an accident.

BELLE What do you do in the army, Fred?

FRED I'm a rear guard clerk.

BELLE What's a rear guard clerk?

FRED In case of defeat, I type up the surrender. Say, can I get you a drink or something? *(He crosses in front of* BELLE*)* A glass of beer or some punch?

BELLE *(Looks down)* Oh, no, Fred. I'm only allowed to have milk.

FRED I respect you for that . . . *(He turns and sees* BERT *about to kiss his* GIRL*)* Hya, Bert . . . What are you so moody about? Whyn't you have some fun? *(*BERT *looks disgusted and moves away.* FRED *turns back to* BELLE*)* That's my best friend, Bert.

BELLE It's nice to have a buddy, isn't it?

FRED It sure is. He promised to show me what to do with my bayonet, later.

BELLE Gee, you're a very sweet boy, Fred. And you have such a kind, gentle face . . . Your eyes are brown, aren't they?

FRED No, they're blue. My glasses fell in the fudge . . .

(A SERGEANT *rushes in)*

SERGEANT *(Blows his whistle)* Attention, doughboys, all members of the Twenty-fifth Illinois are shippin' out. Report to barracks immediately.

(He exits. A loud moan goes up from all)

2ND GIRL Well, kids, let's make this the last dance.

FRED Hey, wait a minute. Instead of dancing, why don't we all get married?

2ND GIRL *(Astonished)* Get married?

FRED Yeah.

2ND GIRL Gee, that's a great idea. How about it, everybody?

(They all cheer and rush for a partner. FRED *looks at each girl hopefully as she passes right by him. He is disappointed. Then he turns and sees* BELLE*)*

FRED You remember me, Belle . . . 646717?

BELLE Yes, Fred.

FRED Oh, good. Something tells me we need each other. What I want to ask is . . . would you marry me?

BELLE Me? You mean you want to marry me? But why, Fred? You hardly know me.

FRED I guess it's because I'm kinda lonely, and I guess it's because I want someone to come home to . . . and I guess it's because you kinda remind me of my mother.

BELLE Do I?

FRED Yes. She's fat too.

BELLE Oh, but—Fred, don't you know why? Look at me? Look at my condition.

FRED Well, if it bothers you, don't drink so much milk.

BELLE Oh, Fred, you're so innocent. Don't you understand . . . I'd only want to marry you for your name.

FRED Fred? You like it so much?

(A SOLDIER *rushes in with a* PREACHER*)*

SOLDIER Hey, everyone. I just woke up a preacher. He says because of the war, he'll make a special allowance and marry us all right here and now.

(They all cheer)

FRED What do you say, Belle?

BELLE Oh, Fred, the answer is yes. And do you know what I'm hoping for more than anything else in the whole wide world? A boy!

FRED Well, you don't have to hope anymore—I am a boy!

(The PREACHER *stands on the couch as he begins to*

speak, all the couples group themselves about him in a tight knot)

PREACHER Will you all gather neatly before me, please.

FRED *(He is trying to get everybody together)* Come on, everybody . . . get a girl. We're getting married.

*(*FRED *moves behind the group lined up in front of the* PREACHER. *There is no space for him and finally he elbows his way next to* BELLE *and another* GIRL. *He stares at the other* GIRL*)*

PREACHER Dearly beloved, we are all gathered here on this joyous occasion to join this crowd in holy matrimony. Do you men of the Twenty-fifth Illinois promise to love, honor and cherish these girls?

MEN We do.

PREACHER And do you, lovely flowers of American womanhood, promise in sickness and health, war and peace, to love and obey, this gallant platoon?

GIRLS We do.

PREACHER Then, with the power vested in me, I now pronounce you men and wives. *(They all kiss.* FRED *is still looking at the* PREACHER*)*

BELLE *(Turning to* FRED*)* Fred, aren't you going to kiss me?

FRED I don't think it would be very proper.

BELLE Why not?

FRED I just married this girl.
(Points to the GIRL *next to him)*

BELLE No, Fred, you married me.

FRED No, you married this fellow right here.
(Points to the MAN *on the other side of* BELLE*)*

BELLE No, Fred. He married her.
(Points to the GIRL *standing next to the* MAN*)*

FRED We ought to get it straightened out. Did anyone happen to notice who I married?

3RD GIRL Belle. You married Belle.

FRED I did? Oh, good. *(The* PREACHER *gets down off the couch and exits)*

BELLE *(Takes* FRED *downstage)* Well, Fred, now that we're married, you can kiss me.

FRED Kiss you? Gosh, I never counted on that.
*(*BELLE *closes her eyes and waits.* FRED *reacts shyly)*

BELLE Fred, haven't you ever been kissed before? *(He shakes his head shyly "no")* Oh, come on, Fred, it's easy.

FRED *(Has difficulty making the connection)* What do we do with the noses?

BELLE One on each side.

FRED Oh . . . You go to the right, or else we'll crash.
*(*FRED *again has difficulty)*

BELLE Closer, Fred . . .

FRED What do you do with your teeth?

BELLE Your lips cover your teeth.

FRED The lips cover your teeth? Isn't nature wonderful?

BELLE Don't talk anymore, Fred. We're going to kiss now. *(They kiss . . . then part)* Fred, you're blushing.

FRED I have to blush. It's the only thing that keeps me from fainting.
(Fred sings "Real Live Girl")

FRED

Pardon me, miss,
But I've never done this
With a real, live girl—
Strayed off the farm
With an actual arm-

Ful of real, live girl!
Pardon me if your affectionate squeeze
Fogs up my glasses and buckles my knees
I'm simply drowned
In the sight and the sound
And the scent
And the feel
Of a real,
Live
Girl!

(They kiss. The SERGEANT *reenters)*

SERGEANT Okay, Yanks. Let's go.

(Everyone ad-libs goodbye and leaves)

FRED Gosh. Well, this is it, Mrs. Poitrine.

BELLE Mrs. Poitrine . . . From now on I'm Belle Poitrine.

SERGEANT Let's go, Poitrine.

(He exits)

FRED They're calling you, Belle.

BELLE No, they're calling you, Fred.

FRED Oh, I guess it must be something about the war . . . Goodbye, Belle. Bye.

(He starts to go)

BELLE Fred! *(He stops)* Come back to me. *(He nods . . . then turns and walks back to her)* Not now. After the war.

(He leaves again)

FRED Oh, after the war . . . Hey, Bert, wait for me. Why are you running?

(He runs off)

(Blackout)

The dark stage is suddenly aglow with bursting gunfire, accompanied by cannon roar and bomb whistles. It stops, and light comes up on 2ND GIRL *reading a letter. She is surrounded by girls and* BELLE.

2ND GIRL *(Reading)* "Dear Suzie, we're finally at the front. It's pretty rough on all of us. Miss you terribly."

(Blackout, then light comes up on a SOLDIER *in no man's land behind her. Blackout)*

3RD GIRL *(Lights comes up on her as she reads)* "Dear Kitty, we're in on the big push now. I've got your picture in my pocket and it keeps me going."

(Blackout, then light up on another SOLDIER, *bayonet in hand, in no man's land. Blackout, then light up on* BELLE *seated on the couch amid the other girls)*

BELLE *(Reads)* "Dear Belle, at last I'm in action."

(Blackout. Light up on FRED *downstage left at typewriter.* FRED *starts to type and repeats aloud)*

FRED "Dearest Quartermaster, please send us two dozen of your very finest officer's dinner napkins . . . as we are . . ." *(He catches his pinky in the keys)* Oh, Medic, Medic . . .

(Blackout, then light up on the GIRLS *again,* BELLE *reading a telegram)*

BELLE "The War Department regrets to inform you that your husband, Private Fred Poitrine, died in action from a serious digit wound."

*(*BELLE*'s head lowers)*

3RD GIRL You should be very proud of him, Belle.

BELLE Yes. My only regret is that Fred never saw Baby.

*(*2ND GIRL *is behind the couch and holding* BABY *in a pink blanket)*

2ND GIRL And she wants her momma.

BELLE Sweet angel. Poor Baby. She had two fathers and never saw either one of them.

*(*MOMMA *rushes on, holding a newspaper)*

MOMMA Belle . . . Belle . . .

BELLE Not now, Momma, please!

(She looks down at the telegram)

MOMMA It's about Noble!

BELLE Noble??

(She quickly crumples the telegram and throws it away and stands up holding BABY*)*

MOMMA Listen! *(She opens the newspaper and reads)* "France. November 12th. Allied Flying Ace, Colonel Noble Eggleston, nine-time winner of the Victoria Cross, was shot down today over the front lines."

*(*BELLE *drops onto the couch)*

MOMMA "Colonel Eggleston has to his credit twenty-seven enemy planes destroyed in the air, thirteen on the ground . . . and six in the factory."

BELLE Momma, is he alive?

MOMMA "Colonel Eggleston is believed to be alive but until further confirmation he will be listed as missing in action . . . There will be a two-minute silent prayer today at the Harvard-Yale game. A minute for each side!

BELLE He's alive, I know it. Noble's alive. He *must* be! *(She gets up)* Momma, take Baby.

(She hands her BABY*)*

MOMMA Belle, where are you going?

BELLE To France. To finish the job that men like Fred and Noble started. My personal goals must wait now. Our boys need cheering up. And I'm going to do it with my God-given talent.

MOMMA That's Momma's little girl!

BELLE I won't be back until I've found Noble. Goodbye, Momma. *(She kisses* MOMMA*)* Goodbye, Baby! *(She kisses* BABY*)* Hello, France!

(Blackout)

(Light up on NOBLE *in trench coat, helmet and goggles . . . sitting on a bench. A* GERMAN SOLDIER *in pointed helmet enters carrying a package)*

GERMAN SOLDIER Vell, Herr Prisoner of War Eggleston, how are you feeling today?

NOBLE You'll get no information from me, Jerry.

GERMAN SOLDIER Brave *Schweinehund.* Ah, I have for you a package.

NOBLE A package from Ramona. Ramona sent me a package? *(He opens the box)* Oh, she knitted me some socks—no, they're cookies!

GERMAN SOLDIER We also have for you a newspaper . . . from Illinois.

(He hands it to NOBLE*)*

NOBLE *(Reads)* A newspaper from Illinois . . . Belle! She's in France. I've got to see her. I've got to escape and see her.

GERMAN SOLDIER Escape? From here? Impossible.

NOBLE Oh, yeah. *(Points)* Oh, there's the Kaiser. *(The* SOLDIER *turns his head.* NOBLE *punches him with all his might in the stomach. The* SOLDIER *does not even blanch. He looks at* NOBLE*)* How about a bribe?

GERMAN SOLDIER A bribe, yes!

(Blackout)

SCENE 17

It is the base hospital somewhere in France. The remains of a church are up left. SOLDIERS *are seated on camp stools and an old church pew and talking when one* SOLDIER *runs on.*

1ST SOLDIER Hey, you guys! Good news! Guess who's coming?

2ND SOLDIER Reinforcements?

1ST SOLDIER No. Better yet—Belle Poitrine.
(The SOLDIERS *get up)*

3RD SOLDIER Is she bringing all of her girls?
*(*1ST SOLDIER *nods "yes")*

SOLDIERS "Real, live girls!"

2ND SOLDIER Hey, Sarge, you've seen her before. What does she really look like?
(The SOLDIERS *surround the* SERGEANT*)*

SERGEANT Well, she's got red hair . . .

2ND SOLDIER And?

SERGEANT And . . . blue eyes . . . I tell you, fellows, she's terrific.

ALL SOLDIERS *(Sing)* "Real, live girl!"

4TH SOLDIER Hey, did you boys hear what happened at Belleau Wood? *(They all crowd around him)* C Company got lost with six of them.

3RD SOLDIER Germans?

4TH SOLDIER No. Belle and her girls.

IST SOLDIER Well, what happened?

(The SOLDIERS *huddle around* 4TH SOLDIER, *who whispers)*

2ND SOLDIER No, kidding?

(Again they huddle)

ALL SOLDIERS Chee . . .

ALL *(Sing)* "Real, live girls!"

(They sing "Real, Live Girl")

ALL

Nothing can beat
Getting swept off your feet
By a real, live girl—
Dreams in your bunk
Don't compare with a hunk
Of a real, live girl!
Speaking of miracles, this must be it!

2ND SOLDIER

Just when I started to learn how to knit—

ALL

I'm all in stitches
From finding what riches
A waltz can reveal
With a real,
Live
Girl!
(They dance)
Real, live girl.

Real, live girl.
I've seen photographs
And facsimiles
That have set my head off in a whirl—
But
No work of art
Gets you right in the heart
Like a real, live girl—
Take your statues of Juno
And the Venus de Milo—

2ND SOLDIER
(Mee lo*)*

4TH SOLDIER
When a fellow wants—you know

ALL
We know

Who wants substitutes—
I'll overlook
Everyone in the book
For a real,

3RD SOLDIER
Sexy Sally or Suzabelle—

ALL
Take your Venetian
Or Roman or Grecian
Ideal—

4TH SOLDIER
I'll take something more use-a-belle

2ND SOLDIER
Girls were like fellas.
Was once my belief—

ALL
What a reversal—

2ND SOLDIER
And what a relief!

ALL
I'll take the flowering hat
And the towering heel
And the squeal
Of a real,
Live
Girl!

2ND SOLDIER *(Speaks)* That's charming, absolutely charming.

ALL

Real, live girl.
Real, live girl
Go be a holdout for Helen of Troy—
I am a healthy American boy—

I'd rather gape
At the dear little shape
Of the stern
And the keel
Of a full-time vocational,
All-operational

Girl!

(After the number, BELLE *and the* GIRLS *rush on, shouting greetings. The* GENERAL *enters and crosses to* BELLE*)*

GENERAL Miss Poitrine, we've been looking forward to this for some time. I'm General Milton "Over-the-Top" Schreiber. I'd like to welcome you to our base hospital.

BELLE Thank you, General.

GENERAL *(Taking her right a few steps)* Miss Poitrine, how can the Army ever thank you? You've worked miracles for these boys of ours. With your singing and dancing and writing letters and assisting in major operations.

BELLE America is my nation too, General.

GENERAL I think I'll be able to repay you in some measure. I've some news about your Colonel Eggleston.

BELLE Noble? Is he alive?

GENERAL Very much so. He escaped from an enemy prison camp, stole a plane, captured Field Marshal Werner Schlecter and flew back to France, taking important aerial photographs on the way.

BELLE That's Noble. Never too busy to help his country. Where is he now?

GENERAL He's in his plane most of the time. He only comes down for fuel and mail . . .

(A NURSE *enters from the door in the church ruins)*

NURSE General, we're having trouble with 107 again.

GENERAL The Frenchman, eh? Pity. No one seems to be able to help the poor chap.

BELLE What is it, General?

GENERAL A French officer. Amnesia. Total loss of memory. We found him wandering around in no man's land asking what side he's on. And he has a letter. He keeps reading it and crying.

BELLE Perhaps I might be able to do something. Could I try, General?

GENERAL Can't see what harm it would do. Nurse!

(The NURSE *opens the door and a* FRENCH OFFICER, *with a dazed look, appears. He reads a letter)*

BELLE Val! . . . Val!

GENERAL You know him?

BELLE It's Val du Val, the great French entertainer. He once saved my life.

NURSE *(Taking* VAL*'s arm)* Come along, sir.

VAL *(Indignant)* Take your hands off me. Do you know who I am?

NURSE No.

VAL Neither do I . . . I don't know who I am.

(He sighs and goes back to reading his letter as he goes to the church pew)

BELLE *(Goes to* VAL*)* Val . . . Val, look at me. Look at me, Val. Don't you remember me?

VAL *(Looks at her, shakes his head)* No . . . No, I don't remember.

BELLE *(Turns to* GENERAL*)* What caused it, General?

GENERAL It was an emotional shock. I believed it was caused by that letter. He won't let anyone see it.

BELLE Val, you may not remember me, but I want to help you. Won't you tell *me* what the letter says?

VAL *(Looks at her and nods)* The letter? It says . . .
(He double-talks in French)

BELLE What does that mean?

VAL I don't know. I forgot French.

GENERAL I can translate. It's from his sweetheart, Colette.

BELLE *(Takes the letter from* VAL *and gives it to the* GENERAL*)* Colette. She used to assist him in the act.

GENERAL *(Reads)* It says, "My darling. A year I have waited for you. I love you, I need you, I miss you and I have jilted you. A French girl needs romance, so I married my cousin who is too short to go in the army."

VAL Colette . . . Colette . . .

BELLE Do you remember Colette?

VAL No. But whoever she is, she should drop dead. *(Grabs the letter from the* GENERAL*)* Did you hear that letter?

GENERAL It's no use. He's been jilted by his girl, so he's trying to block out all memory of her.
(A SOLDIER *rushes on stage)*

SOLDIER General Schreiber. Report from headquarters, sir. We have to evacuate the hospital. The enemy big guns have advanced to within two miles.
(In the distance we hear two loud cannon booms)

VAL What was that?

GENERAL The enemy cannons.

VAL Boom-boom?

GENERAL That's right. Cannons go boom-boom.

VAL Boom-Boom.

BELLE Wait, General, I think I have an idea.

GENERAL I'm sorry. We have no time.

BELLE But it could save his whole future.
(Cannons)

VAL Boom-Boom?

GENERAL Very well. But please hurry.

BELLE Thank you, General.

GENERAL *(To a* SOLDIER*)* Prepare the trucks for evacuation. And get a very fast car for me.
*(*SOLDIERS *and* NURSES *start to move out.)*

BELLE *(Goes to* VAL *as cannons are heard again)* Val, listen to me. We haven't got much time. The Germans are coming closer.
(They sing "Boom-Boom")

VAL Boom-Boom?

BELLE Val, listen to the cannons. Val, try to remember.

(She sings)
"If ze girl—

(Cannons)

VAL Boom-Boom . . .

BELLE
"And ze boy . . .
(Cannons)
"And zey get together and zey both . . .
(Cannons)

VAL
Boom-Boom . . .

BELLE *(Speaks)* That's it, Val, that's it . . .
"C'est La Grande . . .
(Cannons)

VAL
Boom-Boom . . .

BELLE
"Et La Grande . . .
(Cannons)

VAL
Boom-Boom . . .

BELLE & VAL *(Sing together)*
"Zat's ze one Boom-Boom for me."

VAL I remember. I'm Val du Val, ze great French entertainer. Oh, yes, I remember.
(He does a tap dance)

BELLE Yes, Val, you remembered . . .
(They embrace)

VAL Oh, Belle, thank you, thank you. You made me remember. Belle, you mustn't leave me now . . . I need you. Promise you'll never leave me.

BELLE Yes, Val, I promise . . . I'll never leave you.

GENERAL Ready to move out, Captain?

VAL *(Snaps to attention)* The name is Du Val, General. Val du Val. Big *V* little *d* big *V.* Wait for me. *(Turns to* BELLE*)* I want to get my gun, my helmet and my orchestrations. *(He throws her a kiss)* Wait for me.
(He exits into the hospital)

GENERAL It's a miracle. With just a little understanding, you've accomplished what our best doctors couldn't do.
(Cannons. A SOLDIER *comes in from the right.* ANOTHER SOLDIER *races across the stage)*

SOLDIER General, we don't have room for all the equipment. What'll we do, sir?

GENERAL Just take the medicine and the beer.

(The SOLDIER *salutes and exits. Suddenly the door flings open and there in a trench coat, aviator's helmet and goggles stands* NOBLE*)*

NOBLE Belle!

BELLE Noble!

(The "I Love You" theme is heard. They rush to each other, stop, and then embrace. The GENERAL *exits)*

NOBLE *(Releasing* BELLE*)* We're still in tune, Belle.

BELLE Oh, Noble, it's so good to see you. Are you all right, darling? Tell me the truth. You look tired.

NOBLE I am a little tired. I was just shot down.

BELLE Oh, Noble, I've missed you so. Do you ever think of me?

NOBLE Think of you? I've named my plane after you. It's called "The Flying Riffraff."

(The GENERAL *enters with* TWO SOLDIERS. *He sends* ONE SOLDIER *off. Cannons are heard again)*

GENERAL We're about to move out, Colonel.

NOBLE I realize that, sir. *(To* BELLE*)* Belle, look. We don't have much time. Tomorrow morning at six o'clock I have a dogfight appointment with Baron von Richthofen and his entire Flying Circus.

BELLE Oh, Noble, no . . .

NOBLE Yes. *Somebody* has to do it, Belle. Eddie Rickenbacker's got the mumps.

BELLE Oh, Noble, I'm so worried.

NOBLE Belle, I want to ask you one question. Will you marry me tonight?

BELLE Marry you? But I haven't got wealth, culture or social position.

NOBLE Belle, in these ravaged days all of us are equal. If we wait until after the war is over, I'll be *better* than you again. What do you say, Belle?

BELLE Oh, darling, yes. Of course, of course.
(They embrace)

NOBLE Good. I'll get an overnight pass.

BELLE But, Noble, what will your mother say?

NOBLE My mother? When you get back home, just tell her we got married. *(Gets to the door and turns)* No, you better tell her I got killed.
(He exits into the hospital)

GENERAL Congratulations, Miss Poitrine.
(Cannons. A SOLDIER *enters)*

SOLDIER General, we're all ready to move out, sir.

GENERAL Good. Start that group out immediately.

SOLDIER Yes, sir.

GENERAL Get all the men into the trucks and put the girls in my car.

SOLDIER Yes, sir.
(He exits. The hospital door flies open and VAL *with helmet and beaming happily appears)*

VAL Ready, Belle?

BELLE *(Runs up to him. Joyously)* Val, I have wonderful news. I'm going to Paris to marry Noble.

VAL Who am I? Where am I?
(He exits through the door)

GENERAL I'm afraid he's slipped back again.

BELLE But why?

GENERAL Du Val thinks you've jilted him. Just as Colette did. He would have been all right if you had stayed with him . . . but of course, that's not your concern.

(The door opens and there is NOBLE *in trench coat and goggles)*

NOBLE *(Turns and yells back inside)* I never saw you before in my life. Crazy Frenchman. *(To* BELLE*)* Ready, Belle? Excuse me, General.

BELLE *(Fighting back tears)* I—I'm sorry, Noble, but I've changed my mind.

NOBLE What do you mean?

BELLE I mean . . . I can't marry you.

NOBLE But you've got to. I just put a deposit down on a hotel room.

BELLE Don't you understand what I'm trying to say, Noble? *(The great lie)* I—I don't love you anymore.

NOBLE I don't believe you, Belle. You just don't stop loving a person like me just like that.

BELLE I'm sorry, Noble. *(Cannons)* Please go away.

NOBLE Very well, goodbye, Belle.

BELLE Goodbye, Noble.

(They shake hands. The "I Love You" theme plays)

NOBLE Well, I guess there was one left over.

(He exits into the hospital)

BELLE *(In tears)* Oh, Noble . . . He doesn't understand. He'll never understand.

(Cannons)

GENERAL All right, let's get these men moving. We've wasted enough time already. Are you coming, Miss Poitrine?

BELLE In a second, General. But first I'm going to repay someone an old favor—I'm going to marry that great French entertainer.

VAL *(Enters from the door)* Val du Val, that's me!

(He does a tap dance)

BELLE Hello, Val!

VAL Boom-Boom, Belle.
(They embrace)

GENERAL All right, let's move out.
(The GENERAL *exits. The troops move up the ramp.* VAL *salutes, throws a kiss and exits. Next we see him carrying a wounded soldier up the ramp. Cannons)*

BELLE *(Sings, with tears in her eyes)*
But wherever you may be, oh Noble,
Save La Grande Boom-Boom for me.
*(*VAL *waves to her)*

Curtain

Act Two

SCENE I

OLDER BELLE in a steam box; just her head can be seen. PATRICK, holding his jacket, and with sleeves rolled up and tie loosened, stands at the left holding a microphone. The BUTLER is standing next to BELLE holding a tray with a martini pitcher and glass.

OLDER BELLE What torture we women endure to shed a few meager pounds. Now . . . where was I?

PATRICK *(Holds the mike to her)* You just got married.

OLDER BELLE To whom?

PATRICK Val du Val.

OLDER BELLE Oh, yes. A dash more martini. *(The BUTLER holds the glass to her lips)* Thank you. The war in France was finally over, and as most of you know, the Allies won. Val taught me the old act and together we toured the continent.

PATRICK *(Into the mike)* Chapter Four . . . "Twenty-eight Thousand Miles of Sheer Entertainment."

(He points the mike back at BELLE)

OLDER BELLE But after five years of "Boom-Boom" and foreign food, I grew homesick and desperate to see Baby. We booked passage on the maiden crossing of the S.S. *Gigantic,* a voyage that few will ever forget . . . More steam, Patrick.

(PATRICK turns steam valve and simultaneously we hear a steamship whistle and we light up behind a scrim-traveler on the deck of the S.S. Gigantic. *Blackout)*

SCENE 2

OLDER BELLE *continues her narration as all activity on deck continues in pantomime.* VAL *and* YOUNG BELLE *stroll on deck arm in arm.*

OLDER BELLE Val and I were as happy as two people could be, considering we were both in love with two other people . . . On the second night out, Val decided to stroll around the deck trying to work out a brand-new number for the act, called "Zoom-Zoom" . . . *(*VAL *pantomimes "Zoom-Zoom," doing it much the way he did "Boom-Boom." He goes off working on the number, leaving* YOUNG BELLE *alone)* . . . when lo and behold, who should appear from the cocktail lounge but the Buchsbaum Brothers, who were now producers of the big Broadway hit *Cheezit, My Husband. (The* BUCHSBAUMS *appear through doorway and nod their greetings to* BELLE, *puffing away on their cigars)* We planned a gala reunion dinner for that night. But unbeknownst to me, there was still another passenger aboard from out of my past—Noble Eggleston.

(Blackout on OLDER BELLE. *The scrim-traveler goes out.* BELLE *walks off. The* CAPTAIN *enters)*

CAPTAIN Excuse me.

BUCHSBAUMS Oh, good evening, Captain.

CAPTAIN We're coming into some very thick fog. All passengers are cautioned not to wander around the ship this evening.

BERNIE Oh! Is there any danger, Captain?

CAPTAIN No, no. None at all . . . unless, of course, we hit something!

(They all exit. Sound of foghorn again. BELLE *comes on, looking around)*

BELLE Val! Val, where are you? *(A man walks on. They walk past each other, smile hesitantly, back up to look at each other, and then walk on a step)* Noble?

NOBLE Belle?

(They recognize each other)

BELLE Noble!

NOBLE Belle! *(They make a move toward each other, then stop awkwardly, remembering they are no longer free)* What a wonderful surprise . . . banging into you like this.

BELLE It's . . . it's been a long time, Noble.

NOBLE Yes, it's been a long time.

BELLE I've been reading about you . . . and following your career. In medicine and law. You're a surgeon now, aren't you?

NOBLE And a judge!

BELLE That's wonderful.

NOBLE And a husband and a father.

BELLE Oh! That's nice! *(She being very brave about all this)* What have you got?

NOBLE A boy and a wife.

BELLE Who did you marry?

NOBLE You remember Ramona. The girl with wealth, culture and social position. They're very happy.

BELLE They?

NOBLE She and my mother.

BELLE Funny how everything turned out, isn't it? I mean, after promising to wait for each other.

NOBLE We were so young.

BELLE Two silly kids.

NOBLE Two childish children.

BELLE A childhood romance. It's really very funny, isn't it?

NOBLE A scream!

(They both throw back their heads and laugh heartily . . . then suddenly they touch and their "I Love You" theme swells about them. They throw their arms about each other)

BELLE Oh, Noble, isn't there *some way* we can go on seeing each other?

NOBLE *(Despairingly)* Belle, what's the matter with you? Do you want to go sneaking around back alleys . . . checking into cheap hotels . . . lying to our family and friends? Is that what you want?

BELLE Of course not.

NOBLE Oh! Well, it was just a suggestion. I think a man up on A deck was listening.

BELLE A man? Val! It was Val! I know it.

NOBLE Who's Val?

BELLE My husband. Oh, Noble, do you think he heard?

(The STEWARD *comes on with a note in his hand)*

STEWARD A note for you, ma'am. From the gentleman on A deck.

BELLE *(Takes the note)* It's Val's handwriting. *(She opens it and reads)* "Dear Lady, who am I? Where are we?" . . . Oh, no. He's lost his memory again. He thinks I've jilted him . . . Noble, you've got to help me.

NOBLE I can't. I've got to get all the women and children in the lifeboats.

BELLE Lifeboats? Why?

NOBLE Because we're going to hit that iceberg.

(We see an iceberg appear, then hear a crash as NOBLE *and* BELLE *are shaken. People start to scramble on deck in confusion and panic)*

PEOPLE Help! Help! . . . We're sinking! We're sinking! . . . Help!

NOBLE Belle, I may be busy for the next hour or so. Whatever happens, I'd like you to know—*(He sings)* "I love you . . . as much as I am able . . ."

*(*TWO SAILORS *and* TWO STEWARDS *rush on)*

1ST SAILOR *(Very excited)* Mr. Eggleston, We can't find the captain anywhere. What'll we do?

NOBLE Don't panic—I'll take over! . . . You—lower the lifeboats!

1ST SAILOR Aye aye, sir.

(He salutes and rushes off to lower the lifeboats)

NOBLE You—get all the women and children!

2ND SAILOR Aye aye, sir.

(He salutes and runs off)

NOBLE You—batten down the hatches!

1ST STEWARD *(On the upper deck)* Aye aye, sir.

(He rushes off)

NOBLE And you—send out an S O S and start yelling for help!

2ND STEWARD *(On the upper deck)* Aye aye, sir. Help! Help!

(He rushes off)

BELLE Oh, Noble, you're wonderful.

NOBLE That's because—*(He sings)* "I love you . . . as much as I am able . . . considering we're sinking . . ." *(He speaks)* Hold it . . . You! In the yellow dress. *(Women are in line waiting to go over the side as* NOBLE *reaches out, grabs the dress of one and rips it off her. A man in a white uniform stands humiliated)* Aren't you ashamed, Captain?

(The CAPTAIN *lowers his head and goes back inside the ship embarrassed)*

1ST SAILOR *(On upper deck)* Mr. Eggleston, there's not enough room in the boats. What'll we do?

NOBLE There's plenty of room in the water. Bring all the non-swimmers to me.

1ST SAILOR Aye aye, sir.

(He runs off)

BELLE Oh, Noble, no matter what happens, I want you to know—*(She sings)* "I love you . . . as much as I am able . . ."

*(*1ST SAILOR *returns with about six or eight people)*

1ST SAILOR Here are the non-swimmers, sir.

NOBLE All right, everyone, listen to me. I've got two minutes to teach you how to swim. You only get one lesson. So pay attention! *(As he speaks he demonstrates action. The non-swimmers try to follow the action)* Push with the left . . . *(He pushes out the left arm)* Pull with the right . . . *(He pulls with the right arm)* Push with the left . . . Pull with the right . . . Breathe in, breathe out . . . breathe in . . . breathe out . . . *(He breathes from the chest)* Frog, kick . . . frog, kick . . . frog, kick . . . *(He is lifted up to demonstrate)* All together now. Push pull breathe frog kick, push pull breathe frog kick. Keep practicing. You'll be in the water in a minute . . . *(The non-swimmers practice. To* BELLE, *he sings)* "What happens I see with you . . ."

BELLE *(Sings)* "Oh, Noble, you're a wonder . . ."

NOBLE *(To the group)* All right—the minute's up. Everybody in the water.

1ST SAILOR Into the water, everyone.

(They all jump in as NOBLE *shouts to them. A woman in a green polka-dot dress and babushka walks daintily up to the edge of the group.* NOBLE *pulls off the babushka)*

NOBLE Captain! I don't want to have to ask you again! *(The* CAPTAIN *snaps his fingers, as if to say "Nuts" and slinks off)* Where were we? Oh yes.

BELLE *(Sings)* "How grand it is to be with you."

NOBLE *(Sings)* "Considering that we're going under." *(The* FOUR SAILORS *and* STEWARDS *carry in the non-swimmers looking half drowned)*

1ST SAILOR It's the non-swimmers, sir. They're all rotten swimmers.

NOBLE Quick—artificial respiration. First class here. Tourist over there. *(The* SAILORS *stack the non-swimmers up in a single-file pile, one on top of the other.* NOBLE *bends over the top one and begins applying first aid)* In with the good air, out with the bad . . .

BELLE *(Sings)* "My darling . . . how nobly you're behaving . . ."

NOBLE All right, everybody in the water again. *(The* SAILORS *half carry them to the rail and push them over. A woman in a green polka-dot dress crosses again past* NOBLE *as he turns and screams)* All right, what do you say, Captain! *(He pulls off the dress. It is a woman, who tries to shield herself)* I'm terribly sorry, madam. The captain wears the same kind of dress.

1ST SAILOR *(Looking over the rail)* They're going down again, sir.

NOBLE Throw them a line. *(The* SAILORS *throw them a line and give one end to* NOBLE. *He starts to pull the rope slowly as he sings)* "I love you . . . as much as I am able . . . Considering I'm saving, the passengers and crew . . ." *(The rope is pulled all the way and on the end hang all the non-swimmers)* All right now, everybody. Push, pull, breathe, frog, kick.

NON-SWIMMERS Push pull breathe frog kick.

NOBLE You're on your own. *(He lets go of the rope and they all fall back into the sea. He sings)* "As Noble . . .

BELLE *(Sings)* "Reliable and stable . . .

BOTH "As much as I am able . . ."
(The ship is tilting. He puts the life preserver around BELLE *as they hang on)*

BOTH "I . . . love . . . you . . . !"
(Blackout)

OLDER BELLE and PATRICK both lying on rubbing tables, wrapped in towels. They face out front while TWO MASSEURS work on them.

OLDER BELLE The ship went down, but thanks to the heroic efforts of Noble Eggleston, every one of the passengers and crew were saved, except one . . .

PATRICK Your husband!

OLDER BELLE Poor Val had lost his memory again, fell into the water, forgot how to swim and drowned.

PATRICK And you?

OLDER BELLE I sued the steamship company and won two million dollars for the loss of my husband and luggage.

PATRICK You had achieved the first of your goals. You now had wealth.

OLDER BELLE All I needed was culture and social position.

PATRICK But Noble wasn't free.

OLDER BELLE A few years later, on October 29th, 1929—Black Thursday—Noble's wife received a letter from her family.

(Blackout. Lights up on RAMONA, holding a letter and sobbing. MRS. EGGLESTON appears)

MRS. EGGLESTON Why, Ramona, child—whatever is the matter, dear?

RAMONA Oh, Mother Eggleston. Father's entire fortune was wiped out in the crash and he's going to take a job as a common laborer. My family no longer has wealth or social position . . .

(She sobs)

MRS. EGGLESTON *(Puts her arm around* RAMONA*)* There, there, child. It isn't the end of the world . . . Come on, sweet, let's see a smile. *(*RAMONA *manages a little smile)* That's better. Now, do you know what we're going to do? You're going to put on your prettiest dress and hat and then we'll all go downtown to the lawyer's office and have the marriage annulled!

(Blackout. Lights up on OLDER BELLE *and* PATRICK*)*

PATRICK Well, there was a chance for you again.

OLDER BELLE But where to find my next goal—culture? Then suddenly came the answer, with one simple little phone call.

PATRICK Who was it?

OLDER BELLE Who else . . . but the Buchsbaum Brothers! Who recently had turned their chubby little talents westward, to the silver screen.

(Blackout)

SCENE 4

OPERATOR'S VOICE *(In the dark)* Hello, Hollywood. One moment on your call to New York.

(Lights up on BERNIE, *seated, with a phone in his hand. To his left stands* BENNY*)*

BERNIE Well, what are you gonna tell her?

BENNY Let me think.

BERNIE Are you gonna tell her we're broke? That the studio's bankrupt?

BENNY Let me think.

BERNIE How are you gonna ask her for two million dollars?

BENNY I got it. We'll make her a partner . . . put her in pictures.

BERNIE Are you crazy? She's got no talent.

BENNY We're in trouble. It's our only chance. *(Into the telephone)* Hello, Belle. This is Benny.

BERNIE And Bernie.

BENNY Benny and Bernie!

BERNIE The Buchsbaum Brothers!

BENNY Belle, how'd you like to be a movie star? . . . *(Disappointed)* Oh, I see!

BERNIE We're in trouble?

BENNY Yeah! *(Nods)* She said yes!

(Blackout)

SCENE 5

Light up on YOUNG BELLE. *She is hanging up the phone.*

BELLE Hollywood!

BELLE My shortcut to culture . . . I'll bring *art* to the world . . . You can't look down your nose at that, Mrs. Eggleston . . . Oh, Noble, I'll make you so proud of me . . . *(Shiver of delight)* Hollywood! But oh, the loneliness of public adulation. *(Sings "Poor Little Hollywood Star")*

Once you were an ordinary av'rage little girl from Illinois—

Once it was an ordinary av'rage little life—and what a joy!

Sudden success

(Sign appears—a variety headline reading "Buchbaums—Poitrine—Form Vita-Belle")

Caught you, I guess
High on its glittering bough—
Blithe and merry, ordinary, av'rage little girl—

(Sign appears—a variety headline reading: "Belle to Popularize Classics. Shooting Starts")

Where are you now?

(She sits on the apron, feet dangling in the pit)

Carefully dressed
Carefully coached
Di-a-mond-braceleted, emerald-brooched—
Just to be loved from afar,
Poor little Hollywood star!
One of the rare,
One of the great
Everyone's idol,

But nobody's mate
Poor little fairy-tale Queen—

(Theatre marquee appears reading: World Premiere . . . Introducing BELLE POITRINE *in "Moby Dick")*

How do you fill the void
Under that celluloid sheen?

Smile for your fans
Live for your art
What if nobody gives *that* for your heart?

(Theatre marquee appears reading: BELLE POITRINE *in "Mata Hari")*

This is the very last stop
Where can you go from the top?

(Sign is held centerstage)

MAN'S VOICE Oh, Mata . . . I don't care if you are a spy . . . I love you, Mata.

BELLE'S VOICE And I love you, Harry.

(Additional marquees appear during the following lyric: BELLE POITRINE *as "Dr. Jekyll and Mrs. Hyde";* BELLE POITRINE *as Joan of Arc in "Flaming Youth";* BELLE POITRINE *in "The Sweetheart of Gunga Din";* BELLE POITRINE *in "Ben Her";* BELLE POITRINE *in "Hello Quo Vadis, Hello, with Free Dishes")*

BELLE

But,
Never relax
Never give in—
Pull in those longings,
And stick out that chin—
Loved and adored as you are,
Your melancholy would seem just a trifle bizarre
In this jolly wood—
Poor little shiny,
Secure
Little Hollywood Star!

(Blackout)

SCENE 6

The office of the BUCHSBAUM BROTHERS. *The two of them are seated side by side behind a large desk. In front of* BENNY *there is a sign that reads "Benny" and in front of* BERNIE *a similar sign that reads "And Bernie." With them is the assistant director standing above the center chair. He holds a movie clapboard. There is a bench downstage, and a table.*

BERNIE You know what we're in, Benny?

BENNY Trouble—

BERNIE —is what we're in, Benny!

BENNY Culture she wanted.

BERNIE We shoulda listened to the Warner Brothers . . .

BENNY For three dollars—

BERNIE —you buy yourself a football—

BENNY —and you got yourself a nice little college picture.

BERNIE Right?

ASSISTANT DIRECTOR Right, Mr. Buchsbaum!

BERNIE Who asked ya?

BENNY Can't you see we're in trouble?

BERNIE Don't you read *Variety*?
(They both pick up Variety, *each holding a page and reading aloud)*

BENNY "Buchsbaum Studio—"

BERNIE —future at stake."

BENNY "Brothers gamble millions—"

BERNIE "—on Belle Poitrine religious epic—"

BENNY "—*Moses Takes a Wife!*"

BERNIE "—filmed in glorious Biblicolor—"

BENNY "—providing they can find a director!"

(They put down the paper)

BERNIE Which we haven't found.

BENNY Which means we're in trouble.

ASSISTANT DIRECTOR It's one o'clock. I ordered your lunch.

BERNIE Lunches we don't need.

BENNY Directors we need.

(The SECRETARY *sticks her head in the left door)*

SECRETARY The boy is here from the luncheonette.

ASSISTANT DIRECTOR Have him bring it in.

SECRETARY *(To the* BOY *outside)* Bring it in.

(A DELIVERY BOY *enters. He carries sandwiches and drinks in a cardboard carton, and goes to the right of the desk. He has a German accent. He is actually old for a delivery boy and there is something very sad, almost tragic about this obvious misfit. The* SECRETARY *crosses to the bench. The* ASSISTANT DIRECTOR *sits)*

BOY Hot stuff. Watch yourself here. All hot.

(He puts down the carton on the desk and starts to take out the food)

BERNIE How about Lipman? He's a good director.

BENNY Lipman turned us down.

BOY Chicken gumbo?

SECRETARY I'm the chicken gumbo.

BOY *(As he brings the soup to her)* You're the chicken gumbo.

BENNY How about Perlman?

BERNIE Perlman?? A *lousy* director.

BENNY You're right. Forget him.

BERNIE I did. He turned us down.

BOY *(Back at the carton on the desk)* Hot lentil?

ASSISTANT DIRECTOR I'm the hot lentil.

BOY *(Brings him the soup)* You're a hot lentil.

BENNY Did you ask Berman?

BERNIE Yes. He's leaving town.

BENNY When is he leaving town?

BERNIE As soon as I asked him.

BOY *(Back again at the carton on the desk)* Tuna fish, hold der mayo?

BENNY I'm hold the mayo.

BOY *(Bringing the sandwich to him)* You're holding the mayo.

BERNIE Is Zeissman working?

BENNY Zeissman? No!

BERNIE Call him.

BENNY I called him. He said he's working.

BOY *(Back at the carton on the desk)* Tomato herring on roll.

ASSISTANT DIRECTOR On roll is for me.

BOY *(Gives him the sandwich)* You're rolling a tomato herring.

BERNIE How about Vogel? Call him.

BENNY I called him. They told me he moved away.

BERNIE Where'd he move to?

BENNY Vogel wouldn't tell me.

BOY *(Back at the carton on the desk)* Hot pastrami, all fat?

BERNIE All fat is mine.

BOY *(Puts the sandwich in his hand)* All fat is yours.

BENNY There must be another director. But who? Who?

BOY Who gets der pickle? I got a dripping pickle here.

(The door opens and BELLE *rushes in. The* BOY *places the pickle in* BERNIE*'s outstretched hand)*

BELLE *(Goes to the left of the desk)* Listen, everyone! I think I've got one.

BENNY A director?

BERNIE For *Moses Takes a Wife?*

SECRETARY Who?

ASSISTANT DIRECTOR Where?

BENNY What's his name?

BOY Lorna Doones?

(The ASSISTANT DIRECTOR *indicates he gets the Lorna Doones)*

BELLE They talk about him on the set. He used to work here years ago on the old lot. His name is . . . Schnitzler.

BERNIE Schnitzler?

BENNY *Otto* Schnitzler??

BOY A package of Vings, cork-tip cigarettes?

BELLE You know about him?

BENNY He was once a big director in Europe.

BERNIE Then he came here and laid a big egg.

BOY A frozen Milky Vay and a box of jujubes.

(The SECRETARY *indicates these are for her, and the* BOY *walks across to give them to her)*

BELLE Where is Schnitzler now?

BERNIE Laughed out of pictures. He's got some crummy little job now.

BENNY I think he's a delivery boy.

BERNIE That's it. For a luncheonette.

BELLE Which luncheonette?

BOY *(As he crosses back to his carton on the desk)* Der vun across der street.

BENNY That's right. The one across the street.

BELLE Then he must deliver lunches to this studio.

BOY *(Reading from an itemized bill)* That'll be a dollar eighty for der lunch.

(They all suddenly stop as they realize who is standing before them. They all rise)

BERNIE It can't be!

BOY (SCHNITZLER) Oh, but it is! I'll prove it to you. Chicken gumbo's a qvarter . . . Hot pastrami is a qvarter . . .

BENNY AND BERNIE Schnitzler!

ASSISTANT DIRECTOR Otto Schnitzler!

BELLE *(Going toward him)* Is it true? Are you *the* Otto Schnitzler?

*(*BENNY *and* BERNIE *follow* BELLE. *The* SECRETARY *moves to the* ASSISTANT*'s right)*

SCHNITZLER *(Nods and hangs his head in shame)* Yeah, it's true . . . I'm Schnitzy.

BELLE Oh, Mr. Schnitzler. A man of your reputation. This is terrible.

SCHNITZLER Vell, I don't make der prices, lady. Chicken gumbo's a qvarter, it's a qvarter.

ASSISTANT DIRECTOR Otto Schnitzler—a delivery boy.

BELLE What caused your downfall, Mr. Schnitzler?

SCHNITZLER What caused my downfall? I'll tell you what caused my downfall. It was prejudice and bigotry. Just because I come here from the old country and I talk different and I dress different . . . They were all prejudiced and bigoted against me.

BELLE Because you were a foreigner?

SCHNITZLER Yeah. And I also happened to make twelve rotten pictures in a row.

BELLE Benny . . . Bernie . . . But he was a great director once. He only made twelve mistakes. Why not give him another chance?

(BENNY and BERNIE go back to the desk and sit down, picking up copies of the Variety and read. BELLE goes to right of the desk)

SCHNITZLER *(Kneels left of the desk)* Please . . . I've never begged before. But for this I'll get down on my knees and beg. I know I was once a tyrant and a dictator. But failure has changed all that. I'm a humble man now. I'm filled with humbility. Please —with my last vestige of human dignity—give me this one chance to redeem myself . . .

(They all look at the BUCHSBAUMS. SCHNITZLER pulls himself up from the floor and goes toward the door)

BELLE Benny . . . Bernie . . . Please!

(BENNY and BERNIE lower their copies of Variety, *look at each other, shrug, then nod "yes")*

BELLE *(To SCHNITZLER)* Wait! *(He stops and turns)* Mr. Schnitzler, you have the job. I'll see you on the set tomorrow morning at eight.

SCHNITZLER *(Pulls out a monocle and places it in his eye)* You'll be there at six and if you're late, you're fired.

(He exits and slams the door)

*(*BELLE *and the* ASSISTANT DIRECTOR *follow him off. The* SECRETARY *exits. The* BUCHSBAUM BROTHERS *come downstage. They sing "Be a Performer"—reprise)*

BENNY
A heartburn you needed

BERNIE
A headache you wanted

BENNY
So now you succeeded

BERNIE
So be a producer

BENNY
So be a producer

BOTH
So be a producer

BERNIE
A million-dollar toy
You give an errand boy
(While they sing the following, the office set is removed, leaving the next scene visible)

BENNY
Oh boy, oh boy, oh boy.

BERNIE *(Speaks)* Go be a producer.

A biblical movie set. A camera is upstage center. A throne is up left. A CAMERAMAN *and* THREE ACTORS *dressed in Egyptian costumes enter.*

ASSISTANT DIRECTOR *(Walks on with a small box containing props)* Quiet on the set, please! Quiet on the set!

BERNIE *(Shaking hands with* BENNY*)* Good luck, Benny.

BENNY Good luck, Bernie.

ASSISTANT DIRECTOR All right, let's settle down. Ready, Mr. Schnitzler?

*(*SCHNITZLER *enters carrying a riding crop. He is a different man)*

SCHNITZLER Ready! And it better be good. Now, where's my star?

*(*BELLE *enters.* SCHNITZLER *gives his riding crop to the* ASSISTANT DIRECTOR*)*

BELLE Here I am, Schnitzie.

SCHNITZLER Good. We got all the props?

ASSISTANT DIRECTOR Props are here, Mr. Schnitzler.

SCHNITZLER I want to run this down chust vunce with the props, den we shoot it. Now, where is my king?

(The man playing the KING *comes downstage.* SCHNITZLER *puts his arms around* BELLE *and the* KING*)*

ASSISTANT DIRECTOR Look, pussycats. This is the big scene of the picture. You got to remember who you are in this scene. You are the Pharaoh—all-powerful. Whatever you see, you take. Whatever you want, you take. You see her . . . you want her . . . you can't have her . . . Why? Because she doesn't love you. *(To* BELLE*)* You are not in love with the Pharaoh. You are in love with a common slave . . . Moses. Remember the name. When you hear about this you are angry. You are infatuated with anger . . . You are a cacophony of angriness. You want to kill her. But how? Your pet snake, which is an asp—filled with venom and poison. You take the snake and throw it right on her.

*(*SCHNITZLER *picks up the snake from a box which the* ASSISTANT DIRECTOR *is holding and throws it at* BELLE. *She screams)*

BELLE Oh, take it away! Take it away!

SCHNITZLER Vot the hell is the matter? It's not a real snake. It's a toy! F.A.O. Schwarz! You don't think we'd use a real snake on a star?

BELLE I'm sorry . . . It looked so real.

SCHNITZLER It's supposed to look real. We're making a picture here. We're spending a couple of bucks, you know.

BELLE Yes!

SCHNITZLER Good! Now! Der miracle takes place. Der snake does not bite you. Why? Because the snake knows that there is too much goodness in you for the venom and poison to overcome. This is his first defeat. You have never been defeated before. Now you are defeated, so you want to show her you are still a man, and you can die like a man. Then you call for your royal dagger. You pick it up, and right in front of her you plunge it into your heart! *(He grabs the knife and demonstrates by plunging it into his heart)* Then you look aghast, and *(Indicating* BELLE*)* you stand with pride. Then when you see—*(He stops . . . He looks down at the knife, then out front, then to the* ASSISTANT DIRECTOR*)* Oh, prop boy . . . you couldn't find a fake knife? *(The* ASSISTANT DIRECTOR *shakes his head "no")* You looked all over Hollywood and you couldn't find a fake knife. *(The* ASSISTANT DIRECTOR *nods)* All der novelty shops . . . sold out? They had a run on them? *(The* ASSISTANT DIRECTOR *nods)* Couldn't find vun? You found a fake snake, but not a fake knife? *(The* ASSISTANT DIRECTOR *shakes his head)* So you got a real one!

(The ASSISTANT DIRECTOR *nods.* SCHNITZLER *falls back into the arms of the* KING*)*

BELLE Oh, Schnitzie! This is terrible. Should I call a doctor?

SCHNIZLER Only if you expect to be sick!

(Blackout)

SCENE 8

PATRICK is sitting at a garden table. OLDER BELLE, carrying a white tennis racket, and the tennis instructor, enter.

PANCHO Very good game, Miss Poitrine.

OLDER BELLE Thank you, Pancho. See you tomorrow. *(He exits)* As a final tribute to the late great Schnitzler, I finished directing the picture myself.

PATRICK And how was it received?

OLDER BELLE Financially? Not well. But we *were* an artistic triumph. From the highest education center in the country, Harvard University, the *Harvard Lampoon* voted *Moses Takes a Wife* "the most unbelievable Picture of the Year" and awarded us . . . the Golden Turkey! *(She pulls the cloth off the statuette)* The highest symbol of culture in our society.

PATRICK You had achieved your goal.

OLDER BELLE I had surpassed it. I became one of the wealthiest women in America.

PATRICK The public had discovered your talent.

OLDER BELLE No. They had discovered oil on the back lot of the studio.

PATRICK You now had wealth *and* culture.

OLDER BELLE Yes, but oh, the price that I had paid. All those dear departed husbands and friends—Mr. Pinchley, Val du Val, Fred and now Schnitzie.

PATRICK And still you pursued Noble?

OLDER BELLE Yes. Although he seemed further out of reach than ever. He had just been awarded the Nobel Prize for Medical Research and had assisted Clarence Darrow on the Leopold and Loeb case.

PATRICK But you didn't give up?

OLDER BELLE No. I needed only social position. But it was difficult to think of that . . . *(*YOUNG BELLE *enters in a black tennis dress carrying a black tennis racket)* . . . while still in mourning.

*(*OLDER BELLE *and* YOUNG BELLE *sing "Little Me")*

OLDER BELLE

There was I—
Schnitzie dead and gone—
All alone and friendless,
What was I to do?

YOUNG BELLE

What to do?
What to do?
Here am I—
How can I go on
Chasing down these endless
Cul-de-sacs and hallways?
Who would see me through?

OLDER BELLE

Well, I ask of you—

BOTH

Who would see me through
As always?

OLDER BELLE

Who to tell my troubles to?

YOUNG BELLE

Lend a sympathetic ear—

OLDER BELLE

Who to cheer me when I'm blue?

YOUNG BELLE
Wipe away each little tear

OLDER BELLE
When there's no one left

YOUNG BELLE
I am not bereft:

BOTH
There is always Little Me!

OLDER BELLE
(Old Reliable!)

YOUNG BELLE
When a year goes down the drain

OLDER BELLE
And I haven't made a cent

YOUNG BELLE
When I fall in love in vain

OLDER BELLE
Or I give it up for Lent

YOUNG BELLE
Friends can fly the coop

OLDER BELLE
Leave me in the soup

BOTH
Who'll come through with lentils—
And to get to fundamentals:
When the chips are really down,
Who would not be out of town?

OLDER BELLE
(Or a blabbermouth?)

YOUNG BELLE
Who do I esteem most?

OLDER BELLE
Who do I adore most?

YOUNG BELLE
Who deserves the cream most?

OLDER BELLE
Who built up the candy store most?

BOTH
Who comes first and foremost,
Obviously
(When you add it all up)
Everlovin' Little Me!

OLDER BELLE
Rise or fall

YOUNG BELLE
Loyal friend

OLDER BELLE
Through it all

YOUNG BELLE
To the end

OLDER BELLE *(Speaks)* . . . And suddenly my spirits began to soar . . . almost miraculously I had shown myself the way.

YOUNG BELLE I know what I'll do.

OLDER BELLE I knew then what I had to do.

YOUNG BELLE I'll go to Europe!

OLDER BELLE Had I known then what I know now.

YOUNG BELLE I'll find social position!

OLDER BELLE What cruel fate awaited me there.

YOUNG BELLE Somehow! Some way!

OLDER BELLE But I was determined.

YOUNG BELLE Nothing can stop me now, Noble.

OLDER BELLE You tell him, honey!

(They go back to singing. PATRICK *is moved out)*

BOTH

When it comes to parlez-vous
Who could parlez-vous a few?

OLDER BELLE

(With the best of 'em)

YOUNG BELLE

Who will earn that bounty?

OLDER BELLE

Who'll pursue that quarry?

YOUNG BELLE

Like a Northwest Mountie

OLDER BELLE

Only built like Mata Hari!

BOTH

Who'll get Lochinvar e-
ventually?

OLDER BELLE

In a little black sheer

YOUNG BELLE

With a little bit here

OLDER BELLE

And a little "*Mon cher*"

YOUNG BELLE

And a little bit there

OLDER BELLE

*(*Just a *little* bit!*)*

YOUNG BELLE

Who will make you sorry?
Wait and see,
Mrs. Eggleston!

BOTH

Yours sincerely, Little
I mean merely Little
Yours sincerely, Little Me!

(The lights fade)

SCENE 9

The Casino in Monte Carlo. The gambling table is center. Above it is a throne chair. GEORGE MUSGROVE *enters and is greeted by* VICTOR, *the director of the Casino. Others, in formal dress, stand around the table.*

VICTOR Ahh, Monsieur Musgrove.

GEORGE Hiya, Victor.

VICTOR Is Miss Poitrine with you tonight?

GEORGE Belle's never *with me,* Victor. I'm just following her around Europe . . . waiting! Maybe I'll have better luck at the tables.

VICTOR Oh, I'm sorry, monsieur. All tables are closed tonight. Because of the "Game."

GEORGE Game? What game?

VICTOR You have not heard? About the biggest game Monte Carlo has ever seen? One spin of the wheel, just one, between the Bank and His Royal Highness . . . Prince Cherny of Rosenzweig.

GEORGE Rosenzweig?

VICTOR The tiny duchy. It's the only country ever to be defeated in war by Luxembourg. They are destitute and now the Prince comes to gamble everything, in hopes of saving Rosenzweig from financial ruin.

GEORGE The poor sucker. Just like me. If it ain't a dame, it's a duchy.

(He disappears as YULNICK *appears at the top of the staircase, and announces . . .)*

YULNICK His Royal Highness, Prince Cherny of Rosenzweig. *(He turns)* Your Majesty. *(The* PRINCE *enters, resplendent in Graustarkian royal uniform. He is followed by a* LACKEY, *who carries a tray)* Your Highness, I beg of you. Forget this madness. To gamble everything, it is too dangerous.

PRINCE Yulnick, my people are starving. They look to me to fill their plates. I *must* gamble.

YULNICK Please, Your Majesty—the danger, I meant, was to yourself. You know your condition better than I do. You read Dr. Zoltan's report. It wouldn't take much . . .

PRINCE Yulnick, I have no choice. I must gamble.

(They cross to the table. The PRINCE *sits)*

VICTOR Ladies and gentlemen, because of the enormous stakes and consequences of this game, we ask your indulgence in maintaining complete and absolutesilence...*Merci beaucoup. (He looks at the* PRINCE*)* The Bank is ready, Your Majesty.

(The PRINCE *nods to* YULNICK*)*

YULNICK His Majesty is ready.

VICTOR *Allons! Nous commençeons* . . . Chips, Your Majesty? *(The* PRINCE *motions to the* LACKEY, *who places the tray on the table)* How—how much is that?

PRINCE My entire treasury—Two million gold plotkees.

(He sways into YULNICK*'s arms. The crowd reacts)*

YULNICK Your Majesty, are you all right? Are you all right?

PRINCE I'm all right . . . I'm all right . . .

VICTOR Your Majesty, it is your bet. What number, please?

PRINCE The number . . . What number? I got an idea. Let it come from the people. Let the people pick the number. *(Turns to a* WOMAN *standing nearby)* Excuse me, madame. Would you kindly tell me your age?

WOMAN I'm twenty-four, Your Majesty.

PRINCE Twenty-four . . . That will be the day.

*(*MOMMA *and* BELLE *enter)*

BELLE I've made up my mind, Momma. If nothing happens tonight, I'm going home.

VICTOR Please, madame, the Prince must have silence.

BELLE Prince? Did he say Prince?

YULNICK *(To the* PRINCE*)* Belle Poitrine, the American film star.

*(*BELLE *turns and goes to the* PRINCE*)*

PRINCE Pardon me, beautiful American film star . . .

BELLE Yes, Your Honor . . .

PRINCE Oh, how charming. There is an old proverb in my country which goes . . . *(Polish double-talk)* . . . which means: Beautiful lady always brings good luck. I was wondering . . . would you kindly make the bet for me?

BELLE Me? But I couldn't possibly do that. I could never take that responsibility. Why, if you lost, I would never forgive myself.

YULNICK Please, madame, to refuse the Prince now would be—

PRINCE Yulnick, please. We must not insist. I make the bet myself.

(Polish double-talks "Eenie, meenie, minie, mo")

YULNICK Thirty-six.

PRINCE Thirty-six Black is the number. Thirty-six Black is the bet.

MOMMA I think you insulted the Prince, honey.

BELLE I did?

MOMMA You shouldna' done it. It may bring him bad luck.

BELLE Do you really think so?

VICTOR The bet is Thirty-six Black . . . and the wheel spins.

(BELLE makes up her mind)

BELLE Make it Nineteen Red.

(She moves the bet)

VICTOR And the winner . . . Thirty-six Black . . .

(The crowd gasps. The PRINCE is stunned. He goes into Polish double-talk. Then he pulls out a gun)

YULNICK Your Majesty—no! Put away the gun.

PRINCE No, Yulnick. It's the only way. *(Suddenly he points the gun at VICTOR)* This is a stickup.

(But before he can proceed, pain takes hold of him and he crumples)

VICTOR Quick, get a doctor.

(VICTOR dashes out and the people are all ushered out by the LACKEY)

YULNICK There is no time for a doctor. The Prince is a very sick man. *(He takes off his coat)* In my pocket there's a hypodermic needle. *(Snaps his fingers)* Hurry, give it to me. Quickly! Quickly!

BELLE I'll get it! *(She reaches into YULNICK's coat pocket, takes out the instrument and gives it to YULNICK)* Here! *(YULNICK is busy rolling up the sleeve of the PRINCE. He takes the instrument from BELLE without looking, and injects the PRINCE with it. BELLE taps him on the shoulder)* Will he be all right?

YULNICK I don't think so.

BELLE Why not?

YULNICK *(Holds up the instrument)* You gave me my fountain pen . . .

OLDER BELLE *and* PATRICK *ride across the stage on a tandem bicycle.*

OLDER BELLE I was overcome with utter remorse and regret. If only somehow I could make it up to the Prince. Finally, a generous guard took pity on me and permitted me to enter the Prince's bedchamber . . . where I stayed for two weeks. Night and day I did my best to comfort the ailing monarch, relying greatly on the few lessons I had learned from my mother about nursing. Was it any wonder that this simple and well-meaning gesture was turned into wild tales of an illicit tryst in the castle? But even the vilest of tongues was silent when it was learned the end was very near . . .

The royal bedchamber. A huge bed is center. The PRINCE *lies dying, surrounded by weeping women and grief-stricken men. A* DOCTOR *has a gauge attached to the* PRINCE*'s arm.*

DOCTOR *(Left of the bed)* Eighty-nine . . . ninety . . . ninety-one . . . ninety-one and a half . . . *(He turns to* YULNICK *and shakes his head somberly)*

YULNICK *(Right of the bed)* How is he?

DOCTOR When it hits a hundred, he dies.

PRINCE *(With great effort)* Yu— Yulnick!

YULNICK Yes, Your Majesty?

PRINCE Yulnick, I—I want—

DOCTOR Ninety-two . . . ninety-two and a half . . .

YULNICK *(To the* PRINCE*)* What did you want, Your Majesty?

PRINCE I want to say goodbye to all my people.

YULNICK Yes, Your Majesty.

PRINCE The big criers first.
(Music starts)

YULNICK Your Prince.
*(*YULNICK *motions to the faithful to approach. They enter. The* PRINCE *sings the "Goodbye" song with the chorus)*

PRINCE
Goodbye!

PEOPLE
Goodbye!

PRINCE
Goodbye!

PEOPLE
Goodbye!

PRINCE
Goodbye

1ST MAN
Ve hate to see you die!

PRINCE
Vell, anyvay
Goodbye!

PEOPLE
Goodbye!

PRINCE
Goodbye!

PEOPLE
Goodbye!

PRINCE
Goodbye!

YULNICK
You couldn't put it off?

PRINCE
I'd luff to put it off
But den,
Ve'd only haff to do dis painful scene again,
So let's
Just say
Goodbye!

So:
Goodbye, Yulnick,
Goodbye, Yishe,
Goodbye, Sam,
I'm sure gonna miss ya—

Goodbye, Melnick,
You, too, Myron,
Pardon my expirin'—
Goodbye country
It's been fun
You know I hate to rule and run,
But I must get some dying done,
So everyvun,
Goodbye!
(The People sob and sniffle)

PRINCE *(Speaks)* Don't cry!
(Sings)
Someday ve'll say Hello!

PEOPLE
Ve hate to see you blow

PRINCE
I'll greet you in der sweetest land I know

PEOPLE
We hope it isn't soon.

PRINCE
It's gonna be so *vun*derbar,
So full of dat
Funiculi, funicula
It almost pays to go.

DOCTOR Ninety-three!

PEOPLE Ohhh . . .

PRINCE
So,
Sing, Natasha!
You too, Bradley!
(Not you, Sal,
You sing very badly!)
Dance, Matilda,
'Til I holler
For der fun'ral poller!
Down vit rotten rhetoric
I'm really feeling very sick

So sing or dance or do a trick
But qvick
I gotta die!
(One of them does a dance)

PRINCE A good jumper.

YULNICK Your Highness, the winemakers of the Province of Pollusk wish to bid you a fond farewell.
(They dance)

PRINCE That's good—now take out the pits.

YULNICK Your Royal Volunteer Army wishes you to know that they will guard you on your trip to the great battlefield beyond.
(The soldiers do a sword dance)

PRINCE AND CHORUS

PRINCE Vatch out you don't cut yourselves.

YULNICK From the Vetchman Province, wishing to bid you a happy dying, are the lovely virgins. *(Virgins dance. As they finish and surround the bed, the* PRINCE *swoons)* Your Highness, speak to us. Say something.

PRINCE I'll take these two—but don't throw away the others.

PEOPLE

So, good night, sweet Prince
Good night, Highness
(They place flowers on the bed)

PRINCE

Me, oh my, will I have sinus.

PEOPLE

We forgive the royal fumbles,

PRINCE

That's the way the kingdom crumbles.
(Music up and an ANGEL *appears over the bed headboard beckoning. The* PRINCE *gestures impatiently)*

PRINCE Wait a minute—will you wait a minute!

PEOPLE

So long . . .

PRINCE

So long

PEOPLE

Ta ta

PRINCE

Ta ta

PEOPLE

Goodbye!

(They dance again. BELLE *enters)*

BELLE How are you, Your Majesty?

(She hands a cup to YULNICK *and sits down on the bed)*

PRINCE *(Smiles)* Belle! My little Florence Nightingale . . .

(He ends up in a bowl of pain)

BELLE Where does it hurt?

PRINCE On my leg—where you're sitting.

BELLE Oh, I'm sorry.

(She gets up)

DOCTOR Ninety-seven . . . ninety-seven and a half . . . ninety-eight . . .

BELLE *(Takes the goblet from* YULNICK*)* Your Majesty, I brought you your wine.

PRINCE *(Takes the goblet)* Thank you, Belle. Ah, wine. How I used to love wine . . . And this will be the last . . . the last wine I will ever drink. Well—here's to a long life!

DOCTOR Ninety-eight and a half . . . ninety-nine!

YULNICK If only he could have saved Rosenzweig before he died.

DOCTOR Ninety-nine and a quarter!

BELLE Rosenzweig *will* be saved, Your Majesty.

DOCTOR Ninety-nine and a *half!*

BELLE There was a boy who once taught me the joy of giving charity. *(She takes a check from her bodice)* Here! Enough to save Rosenzweig . . . Seventy million plotkees.

DOCTOR One hundred!

(He picks up the sheet to cover the PRINCE, *but the* PRINCE *stops him and takes another look at the check)*

PRINCE Hold it! *Seventy million plotkees!*

DOCTOR It's ninety-*nine!* . . . ninety-*eight!* It's going down.

PRINCE *Seventy million plotkees!*

DOCTOR Ninety-six . . . ninety-five . . .

YULNICK It's going down! Down . . . Oh, my Prince!

DOCTOR It's back to normal.

YULNICK He's going to live! He's going to live! *(He rushes to the window and shouts)* Long live the Prince!

(There is a tremendous roar from the crowd outside. The PRINCE *raises his hand for quiet and everybody stops shouting suddenly)*

PRINCE *(Takes* BELLE*'s hand in his and smiles at her)* Belle, because of you, Rosenzweig lives. Because of you, *I* live. Belle, would you kindly kneel. *(*BELLE *kneels)* In gratitude I award you the Royal Star . . . *(He gives her a medallion)* . . . and with it the title the Countess Zoftic.

(Everyone bows to the new countess, who rises in happiness)

BELLE A countess . . . You've given me social position, and I . . . *(She cries)* Oh, Your Highness, can you forgive me?

PRINCE *(Drinks from the goblet)* Forgive you? For what?

BELLE I didn't want you to suffer at the end . . . so I poisoned the wine!

(The PRINCE *continues to drink the wine. Then, resigned to his fate, he puts down the goblet, lies back in bed and sings)*

PRINCE

"Goodbye, Yulnick . . . Goodbye Yisha . . ."

(The DOCTOR *pulls the sheet over his head and places the crown on top. Dimout)*

OLDER BELLE *moves out on the chaise from her Southampton Rumpus Room with* PATRICK *and his tape recorder.*

OLDER BELLE Bravely the Prince died. As he was going, he muttered something to me. We'll never really know what.

PATRICK But we can guess.

OLDER BELLE Yes, we can. Saddened, I sailed for home. But good news awaited me. Noble had won political office, and once again had asked me to be his wife.

(Blackout)

Light up on stage left, where we see NOBLE, *in a dark suit, with one hand raised, and flanked by* TWO JUSTICES *in black robes, each holding a Bible. They stand before a desk.*

1ST JUSTICE . . . and do you, Noble Eggleston—

2ND JUSTICE —swear to uphold and fulfill the laws and duties of office?

NOBLE I do!

1ST JUSTICE Congratulations, sir.

2ND JUSTICE Congratulations, sir.

NOBLE Thank you.
(Both JUSTICES *exit.* BELLE *enters)*

BELLE Oh, Noble, I'm so proud of you. Just think, you're Governor of North Dakota.

NOBLE And South Dakota. Well, Belle, you finally got it—wealth and culture and social position.

BELLE Oh, Noble, we've waited so long for this. And at last our dream is come true. *(Picks up a bottle of whiskey and two glasses)* Let's drink to our future.

NOBLE But, darling, I never drink.

BELLE But this is a special occasion, darling.

NOBLE But drinking is against my extremely high principles.

BELLE Oh, come on, Noble. There's no harm in having one drink to our happiness. Please—just for me?

NOBLE Very well, sweetheart. Just for you. Here's to us. *(He takes a small sip and puts the glass down on the desk)* You know, Belle, I think we ought to build a little house high up on a—

(He stops and returns to the drink on the desk. He freezes into a position of drunken stupor as a huge, oversized newspaper comes down, framing him as if he were the picture on the front page. The headline screams in huge letters: "DRUNKEN GOVERNOR IMPEACHED." Lights up on OLDER BELLE *and* PATRICK, *on the chaise, on the opposite side of the stage)*

OLDER BELLE The wedding never took place. Within three weeks, Noble had guzzled away our future. Disgraced and humiliated, he disappeared. I sought seclusion in Southampton. It was *I* now who lived up on the Bluff. And here I waited for Noble's return . . . as the years passed by. And I waited . . . and waited . . . And then, one Christmas night . . .

OLDER BELLE*'s Rumpus Room in Southampton. A Christmas tree all decorated and lit up is seen outside through the doors. Gathered around a table laden with food are the* BUCHSBAUM BROTHERS *and* MOMMA, *and other guests. The* BUTLER *and the* BARTENDER *are serving drinks.*

OLDER BELLE *(Crossing into set)* Merry Christmas, everyone! *(They greet her)* Benny and Bernie!

BENNY The Buchsbaum Brothers.

OLDER BELLE Oh, it's so good to have you all here tonight. To be surrounded by all the ones you love best . . . almost.

BENNY You know what this occasion calls for?

BERNIE A toast!

BENNY Is what it calls for.

(Music starts)

OLDER BELLE Well, it may not be Emily Post to say it, but . . .

(She sings "Here's to Us" joined by the others)

OLDER BELLE AND CHORUS

Here's to us,
My darling, my dear—
Here's to us tonight;

Not for what might happen next year,
For it might not be nearly
As bright

But, here's to us
For better or worse—

And for thanks to a merciful star;
Skies of blue
And muddling through
And for me and for you
As we are!

ALL

And here's to us
For nothing at all
If there's nothing at all we can praise

OLDER BELLE

Just that we're
Together and here
For the rest of our beautiful days

ALL

Here's to us

ALL

Forever and always!
(The lights dim on the room)

The lights go up on the exterior of the house. A torn and tattered old bum enters and looks longingly through the window at the warm scene inside. It is NOBLE, *or rather, the shell of him.*

NOBLE What a fool—what an utter fool I've been! To throw away all that . . . *(Indicating the house)* . . . just for this! *(Indicating the bottle in his hand) That's* better than this. People only use this when they haven't got *that* . . . I had all that, and I threw it away for this . . . How about that?

*(*GEORGE MUSGROVE *enters, his arms laden with Christmas gifts)*

GEORGE Hey, you! Bum! What are you doing at that window?

NOBLE Nothing. Nothing, sir. *(He shivers)* Say, could . . . could you spare a dime for an ex-governor, sir?

GEORGE Noble! Noble Eggleston!

NOBLE Who are you? George . . . George Musgrove!

GEORGE Noble, what's happened to you? We've looked everywhere. What have you been doing?

NOBLE Oh, I've been very busy . . . I'm a full-time rummy now.

GEORGE Noble, come on in out of the cold. Belle has been waiting for you so long.

NOBLE No! No! She mustn't see me like this. A dirty drunken old bum. These aren't even my clothes. I took them off a snowman.

GEORGE But she loves you. She always has.

NOBLE I know that, George. But I'm paying the price for class distinction.

GEORGE Noble, what are you going to do?

NOBLE I'll go back into medicine. *(He staggers)* There's a tramp steamer leaving for the South Seas that needs a drunken old doctor.

GEORGE Will you ever come back? To Belle?

NOBLE I don't know, George. If I ever lick this thirst. *(He licks his dry lips)* Take care of her, George. She's all we've got now, buddy. *(He pats* GEORGE*'s shoulder, then starts off. He stops and turns)* George, the South Seas is this way, isn't it?

*(*GEORGE *nods,* NOBLE *waves and exits. The exterior piece flies out and the lights come up on the living room)*

OLDER BELLE Who was that you were talking to, George?

GEORGE Oh, er . . . no one, Belle. Just a dirty old bum.

(He goes into the house. Lights dim in the living room. OLDER BELLE *turns again to* PATRICK *to resume her narrative.* GEORGE *and guests exit)*

OLDER BELLE A dirty old bum who, had he not fallen to temptation, might today have been Chief Justice of the Supreme Court, and Personal Physician to the President . . .

PATRICK And you never saw him again?

OLDER BELLE Never . . . The love of my life was gone —although I did see his mother, Mrs. Eggleston, a week later. In front of the Plaza Hotel. She was selling apples.

PATRICK Destiny often leads us on strange roads.

OLDER BELLE And I was still traveling on mine. On New Year's Day, Momma came rushing into the room flushed with excitement.

(Lights up on the living room as MOMMA *rushes in)*

MOMMA Belle! Belle, honey, she's home! Baby's home!

*(*OLDER BELLE *crosses into room)*

OLDER BELLE Baby? Where's my baby?

*(*YOUNG BELLE, *now playing* BABY, *enters, the same sweet, sixteen-year-old girl her mother was at the beginning of the play)*

BABY Momma!

OLDER BELLE Oh, sugar. Let me look at my college girl.

MOMMA It's you all over again, Belle.

BABY Momma, I want you to meet someone. *(She calls off)* All right, darling. *(A young man, about nineteen years old, enters. It is* JUNIOR. *He wears a sweater with large block letters JG)* Momma, I'd like you to meet—

OLDER BELLE *(Astonished)* Noble! Noble Eggleston!

JUNIOR Noble Junior, ma'am. Did you know my father?

OLDER BELLE *(Nods meaningfully)* We met—once.

JUNIOR When he was the governor . . . or the drunk?

OLDER BELLE Both. Where did you two meet?

BABY At my prom. Noble goes to Juilliard.

JUNIOR And Georgia Tech.

OLDER BELLE Juilliard and Georgia Tech?

JUNIOR I'm going to be a musical engineer.

BABY *(Goes to* NOBLE*'s left)* Momma, we want to get married.

OLDER BELLE So soon? . . . so soon. But you hardly know each other . . . *(To* JUNIOR*)* Do you love her? Do you know what love *is?*

JUNIOR I think so. Ever since I met her, I've been sick to my stomach.

OLDER BELLE Come here . . . I want to make sure. *(They sit on a small couch)* Now, give me your hands. *(They each hold out a hand)* Now—touch!

(They touch. The "I Love You" Theme music swells)

Yes . . . You are in love!

(The lights fade on them)

OLDER BELLE *returns to* PATRICK. MOMMA *exits.*

OLDER BELLE Baby and Noble Junior were married and live happily today in Scarsdale. Noble Junior is the chief construction engineer for Lincoln Center . . . and conducts there at night.

(GEORGE MUSGROVE *enters)*

GEORGE Belle, can I see you a minute?

OLDER BELLE Yes, George. Mr. Dennis, this is my very last husband, George Musgrove.

GEORGE Hi.

(He puts his hand in greeting. OLDER BELLE *touches him and listens. No music. She shrugs, "What a pity")*

PATRICK How do you do.

GEORGE I've just received a call from the state police. They say a prowler has been seen lurking around the house.

OLDER BELLE A prowler?

GEORGE Don't worry about it, honey. Not with me around.

(Suddenly the center French doors fly open and there, brandishing a gun, in rags and carrying a basket of apples is MRS. EGGLESTON*)*

MRS. EGGLESTON Don't move—anyone. I've waited a long time for this.

OLDER BELLE Mrs. Eggleston!

MRS. EGGLESTON It's you! *You* ruined everything. You had to climb, higher and higher, until you got to the top. And then you pushed me and Noble off . . . Well, Mrs. Rich and Famous Belle Poitrine—*you're* the one who's going to be pushed now!

OLDER BELLE No. You're wrong. I loved Noble . . .

(She moves left toward MRS. EGGLESTON*)*

MRS. EGGLESTON Stand back!

OLDER BELLE You're making a mistake. Please! For Noble's sake . . . give me the gun.

(She reaches to grab the gun)

MRS. EGGLESTON Stop or I'll shoot.

(But OLDER BELLE *lunges for* MRS. EGGLESTON *and they both struggle for the gun, when suddenly through the French doors* NOBLE, *in black turtleneck sweater, Navy pea jacket and maritime cap, appears)*

NOBLE *(Happily)* I'm back!

(And the gun goes off . . . NOBLE, *stunned, grabs his stomach)*

OLDER BELLE Noble!

MRS. EGGLESTON My boy!

*(*OLDER BELLE *rushes to* NOBLE*'s side. He holds on to his stomach)*

NOBLE I just gave up drinking. I walk into a room . . . a gun goes off . . . and who gets shot? *(He looks at his stomach; then, puzzled, he looks up)* It's not me!

GEORGE *(On the other side of the room, looks down at* his *stomach)* It's me!

OLDER BELLE George! *(She rushes to him as he falls to the floor)* George, are you all right?

NOBLE I'll take care of it, Belle. I'm a doctor.

OLDER BELLE He's dead!

MRS. EGGLESTON *(Sobs)* I killed him!

NOBLE I'll take care of it, Mother. I'm a lawyer.

OLDER BELLE Poor George . . . and yet all along, I think he knew it would end like this.

NOBLE It's not the end, Belle . . . it's just the beginning.

PATRICK *(Into the mike)* Chapter Twelve . . . "Sunset in Southampton."

*(*OLDER BELLE *and* NOBLE *come downstage center. The scenery moves off and now a bright red sunset appears. They turn, touch hands, their "Theme" soars and they walk into the sunset into their future)*

Curtain

The Gingerbread Lady

THE SCENE

The action takes place in a brownstone apartment in New York's West Seventies.

ACT ONE

A late afternoon in mid-November.

ACT TWO

Three weeks later—about 9:00 P.M.

ACT THREE

The following morning.

Act One

The scene is the third-floor apartment in a brownstone in the West Seventies. It consists of a living room, a bedroom and, to the left, a kitchen. The rooms are fairly large, with high ceilings and what were once very nice wood panelings, now painted over. In the mid-thirties and forties this was a great place to live. The furniture is very good and probably very attractive but one could hardly tell any more; it has fallen into disrepair. Against the wall there is a small, battered piano that is covered with photographs, all of a theatrical nature. A stack of mail is on the table.

A man's sheepskin coat is draped over a chair. From the kitchen we hear the faucet running and a man humming. He comes out with a vase he has just filled with fresh flowers. JAMES PERRY *is in his early forties, portly and probably homosexual. Probably but not obviously. He wears slacks with a dark blue turtleneck sweater. He first goes to the window and peers out and down, looking for the arrival of someone; then he turns back and looks for a place to put the vase. He tries the piano, changes his mind, then settles on the coffee table. It doesn't please him much.*

JIMMY I hate it. *(The doorbell rings. He looks at his watch nervously, then crosses to the door and asks without opening)* Who is it?

MANUEL *(Offstage)* Groceries.

(JIMMY *opens the door and glares at the delivery boy,* MANUEL, *who is Spanish and about twenty. He is holding two large grocery bags in his arms)*

JIMMY Where were you? I thought you went out of business. Put them in the kitchen, please.

MANUEL *(At doorway)* Mrs. Meara live here?

JIMMY Yes, Mrs. Meara lives here. Would you please put them in the kitchen.

MANUEL *(Not moving)* Is fourteen dollars twenny-eight cents.

JIMMY Fine. Terrific. That's a charge. Just put them in the kitchen.

(JIMMY *starts to walk away but notices that the boy is not moving*)

MANUEL Mr. D'Allessandro say to me I mus' have fourteen dollars and twenny-eight cents.

JIMMY No, you don't understand. Mrs. Meara has a charge account. *Charge—account!* Do you know what that is?

MANUEL *(Nods)* Tha's a charge account.

JIMMY That's right. It's an account and you charge it. I don't live here. I'm a friend of Mrs. Meara. You charge it to her account.

MANUEL Mr. D'Allessandro say to me eef they say to you, eet's a charge account, you say to them eet's fourteen dollars and twenny-eight cents.

JIMMY Do you want me to get on the phone and call Mr. D'Allessandro? What's the number?

MANUEL The number? The telephone number? Ee's seven-six-six-something, I don't know, I never call them . . . Eef you speak to Mr. D'Allessandro, he's gonna say to you eet's fourteen dollars and twenny-eight cents.

JIMMY *(Irritated)* I don't have to call Food Fair, you know. They have canned goods in Bohack's, too.

MANUEL Bohack's is nice. My cousin works for Bohack's. They all the same, you know.

JIMMY *(Glares at him)* . . . I don't have fourteen dollars and twenty-eight cents. I have no money on me.

MANUEL Oh, well, tha's okay. I'm sorry.

(He turns)

JIMMY Where are you going?

MANUEL Back to Mr. D'Allessandro.

JIMMY Wait a minute. I'll look. *(He takes his wallet from his back pocket. The boy smiles at him.* JIMMY *turns his back so the boy can't see into his wallet. He takes out one bill)* I have ten dollars.

MANUEL *(Shrugs)* I leave you one package.

JIMMY *(Glares more angrily)* Wait here. *(He starts for his sheepskin coat, notices that the boy has edged inside a step or two)* That's far enough.

MANUEL Wha's a matter, Meester, you afraid I come inside, I rob you house? I don' rob no houses.

JIMMY I don't care what you do, just wait there.

MANUEL I got a good job, I don' have to rob houses.

JIMMY *(Half to himself as he goes through his pockets)* Yeah, in the daytime. *(He takes a passbook out of his pocket, along with some loose dollar bills. He holds the book in one hand and counts money as he crosses back)* How much was that again?

MANUEL Same thing, fourteen dollars twenny-eight cents. *(The boy puts down the packages.* JIMMY *takes out four singles and hands them to the boy, but in the process he drops the passbook on the table. The boy picks it up and looks at it)* Oh, I use to have thees. Unemployment book. You unemployed, Meester?

JIMMY *(Grabs it back)* None of your damned business. Who asked you? You've got your fourteen dollars. You can leave now.

MANUEL *(Holds out his hand)* And twenny-eight cents.

JIMMY *(Reaches into his pocket and takes out the change. He hands it to the boy, one coin at a time)* Ten . . . fifteen, twenty-five, twenty-six, twenty-seven, twenty-eight cents. *(The boy looks at it, and nods his head in agreement)* That's all. There's no tip. I don't live here. I don't tip where I don't live.

MANUEL I don' wan' no tip. You ain't even got a job. I don' need your tips.

JIMMY And I don't need your goddamned sympathy. You're very fresh for a delivery boy.

MANUEL Wha's a matter, you don' like Spanish people?

JIMMY Who the hell said anything about Spanish people? *You're* the only one I don't like. Will you please leave now?

MANUEL *(At the door)* I know the kin' of people *you* like, Meester.

(He makes two kissing sounds with his pursed lips)

JIMMY *Get out of here! (The boy smiles and rushes out, the door closing behind him.* JIMMY *bolts the door, then crosses to the grocery bags, still fuming)* I wouldn't live in this neighborhood if you paid me . . . *(He picks up the bags and starts for the kitchen)* Can't say a thing any more, everyone is so goddamned race conscious . . . Lousy spic! *(He goes into the kitchen. We hear the rustle of the paper bags as the phone rings.* JIMMY *comes out with a can of coffee in his hand and crosses to the phone)* Hello? . . . No, she's not, I'm expecting her home any minute. Who's calling, please? . . . Well, in regards to what? . . . Oh! Well, I'm sure Mrs. Meara hasn't paid her phone bill intentionally. She's been away sick for the past ten weeks . . . But you're not going to cut it off, are you? She'll pay it as soon as she gets home . . . Fourth notice already, my goodness . . . But you must realize she's good for it. I mean this is Evelyn Meara, the singer . . . It must be in by Tuesday, yes, I'll tell her that. Thank you very much, I appreciate that. *(He hangs up. To the phone)* Wait three years to get one but you rip 'em out fast enough, don't you? *(He starts opening the can. The front doorbell rings.* JIMMY *turns and looks at the door. He is extremely anxious. He puts the can of coffee down on a chair, wipes his hands on his pants and goes to the door. He calls out without opening)* Who is it?

TOBY *(Offstage)* It's us. We're home.

(JIMMY *starts to open the door, but it doesn't work, since he's forgotten that he bolted it. He tries to unbolt it but has a little difficulty at first)*

JIMMY *(Calls out)* Wait a second, I'm so damned nervous. *(He finally opens it, and* TOBY LANDAU *enters. She is a very pretty woman, in her early forties—but you'd never believe it. That's because she spends most of her waking hours trying to achieve that effect. She is well dressed in a smartly tailored suit. She carries a large, heavy, but not very elegant suitcase)* Look at me, I'm shaking.

TOBY *(Entering)* Don't complain to me. I just spent four hours in a taxi on the Long Island Expressway. Look out the window, you'll see a very rich cab driver.

(She looks around the apartment)

JIMMY Where is she? *(He looks out the doorway)* Evy? Where's Evy?

TOBY She's saying hello to a neighbor . . . I thought you were going to clean the apartment. Didn't you say you would clean the apartment for Evy?

JIMMY I tried rearranging the furniture, but it always came out like a bus terminal in Passaic. Where is she? Is she all right?

TOBY Yes, but you're going to be shocked when you see her. She lost forty-two pounds.

JIMMY Oh, my God.

TOBY I will tell you right here and now that a rest home for drunks is the most depressing place in the world.

JIMMY I never thought she'd last it out. I'm so nervous. What do I say to her? How do I act in front of her?

TOBY You hug her and love her and, above all, you must trust her.

JIMMY I'll kill her if she ever takes another drink . . . Where the hell is she?

(We hear EVY*'s voice just outside the door)*

EVY *(Offstage)* I'm out in the hall. Are you ready?

JIMMY Ready.

(EVY *enters, wearing a mink coat and carrying books*)

EVY All right, say it, I'm gorgeous, right?

JIMMY Oh, my God, I don't believe it. Who is she? Who is this beautiful woman?

EVY It better be me or I'm out twenty-seven hundred bucks.

JIMMY Am I allowed to hug you?

EVY You're allowed.

(JIMMY *rushes into her arms and hugs her. He feels her*)

JIMMY It's true. It's gone. Forty-two pounds are gone. Where did it go to?

EVY You want it? It's in the suitcase.

JIMMY I can't get over it. It's like talking to a stranger. Somebody introduce me.

TOBY Jimmy, this is Evelyn Meara. Remember? She used to sing in clubs?

JIMMY That fat lady? Who used to drink a lot? Use foul language? No. This is a nice skinny woman. You put a dress on her, you can take her anywhere.

EVY I don't want to go anywhere. I want to be right here in my own apartment . . . Oh, it's so good to be home. *(Looks around)* Jesus, it looks different when you're sober. I thought I had twice as much furniture.

TOBY Will you sit down? (*To* JIMMY) She won't sit down. She stood all the way in the taxi coming home.

JIMMY You must be starved. When did you eat last?

EVY I had chicken salad in July. I'm not hungry.

TOBY The doctors told me she worked harder than any patient there. Even the nurses were so proud of her.

EVY It's the truth. I was the best drunk on my floor . . . *(Looking at the sectional)* Christ, now it's coming back to me. I threw the other half of this out the window.

JIMMY I want to make you something. Let me make you a tongue and Swiss on toast and a pot of coffee. Sit down. I'll be five minutes.

EVY I thought my mother lived in Ohio. Leave me alone. I tortured myself to lose forty-two pounds.

TOBY Jimmy, stop it, you'll get Evy nervous.

JIMMY I'm worried about her. If someone doesn't make it for her she doesn't eat.

EVY There's plenty of time to eat next year. I'm all right. I'm home. Let me enjoy myself.

JIMMY Who's stopping you? *(To* TOBY, *softly)* She look all right to you? (TOBY *nods*) Is there anything she has to take? Pills or anything?

TOBY Just some tranquilizers. She has them in her bag.

JIMMY But nothing heavy? No serious stuff?

TOBY Just a mild sedative to help her sleep.

EVY *(At the kitchen door)* If you doctors want to be alone, I can go back to Happy Valley . . . What are you whispering about?

JIMMY We're not whispering. We're talking softly.

EVY You were whispering.

JIMMY We were not whispering. We were talking softly.

EVY Why were you talking softly?

JIMMY Because we don't want you to hear what we're saying . . .

TOBY Jimmy's worried about you, that's all.

EVY If he's worried, let him worry a little louder. I can't stand whispering. Every time a doctor whispers in the hospital, the next day there's a funeral.

JIMMY I'm sorry. I'm sorry.

EVY It took ten weeks to cure me and five minutes for you to drive me crazy.

TOBY Jimmy didn't mean it, darling.

EVY What are you blaming him? You were whispering too.

TOBY I had to. He whispered a question to me.

JIMMY All right, can we drop it?

TOBY I didn't even bring it up.

EVY Jesus, I got along better with the nuts on Long Island.

JIMMY I'm sorry, Evy. All right? I'm nervous I'm gonna say the wrong thing. I don't know how to act in front of somebody who just got home from the cure five minutes ago.

EVY You act natural. The way you always acted with me.

JIMMY This is the way I always acted with you.

EVY Yeah? Well, maybe that's why I started to drink.

TOBY My God, what a homecoming.

EVY *(Wilts a little)* Hey, listen, I'm sorry. Maybe I am nervous . . . Don't pay attention to me. Jimmy, you know what I'd love more than anything else in the world? A tongue and Swiss on toast and a pot of coffee.

JIMMY Do you mean it?

EVY I dreamt of it every night. First I dreamt of sex, then a tongue and Swiss on toast.

JIMMY I'll bring you the sandwich. The rest I can't help you with.

(He exits into the kitchen)

TOBY *(Looking at herself in the mirror)* And what can I do, Evy?

EVY You can stop looking at yourself and give me a cigarette.

TOBY You *are* nervous, aren't you?

EVY I hated that place so much I used to save up matches, planning to burn it down. It was a goddamn prison. And then when it came time to leave I was afraid to go . . . I suddenly felt comfortable there . . . Can I have my cigarette, please?

TOBY That's almost a whole pack since we left the hospital. Are you sure they said it's all right to smoke?

EVY Once you pay your bill and check out, they don't care if you get knocked up by a dwarf. *(Takes the cigarette and smokes)* I thought I'd have a million things to do once I got home. I'm here six minutes, I'm bored to death.

TOBY You've got to give yourself time, Evy. And then you're going to start your life all over again and you're going to grow up to be a beautiful wonderful person like me.

EVY What's that? What's that crap you're putting on your face?

TOBY It's a special crap that protects the skin. Have you noticed you've never seen pores on me? As long as you've known me, have you ever seen a single pore on my face?

EVY I've never even seen your face . . . Who are you, anyway?

TOBY A woman can never be too pretty. It's her feminine obligation. I love my looks, don't you?

EVY You're gorgeous. If you went bald and lost your teeth, you'd still be cute-looking. Leave yourself alone.

TOBY I can't. Isn't it terrible? I'm obsessed.

EVY You remind me of the psycho in the room next to me. She used to shampoo her eyelashes every night. Thought all the doctors were in love with her. An eighty-seven-year-old virgin screwball.

TOBY What a sweet story . . . You just going to sit there forever? Aren't you going to unpack or something?

EVY Unpack what? A pair of pajamas and a bottle of mineral oil? Besides, I'm never going in that bedroom again. I ruined half my life in there. The next half I'm playing it safe.

TOBY I understand perfectly. But how will you get to the bathroom?

EVY Over the roof and down the pipes. Just worry about your face, all right?

TOBY I can worry about both. I wish I could stay with you tonight.

EVY Then why don't you stay with me tonight?

TOBY I have to meet Martin at Pavillon for dinner. It's business—I distract the client.

EVY Some friend you are.

TOBY Don't say it like that. I'm a wonderful friend. I'm sensitive. You want me to be hurt?

EVY Don't pout. You'll crack your make-up and start an avalanche on your face.

TOBY Anyway, Jimmy can stay with you tonight.

JIMMY *(Sticks his head in through the kitchen window)* Jimmy has an audition at five forty-five.

TOBY You said you'd be free tonight.

JIMMY I was until the audition came up. I have to eat, you know.

TOBY Can't you cancel it? For Evy?

JIMMY I wouldn't cancel it for Paul Newman.

TOBY Oh, God, Evy, I'm sorry. What will you do tonight?

EVY I'll turn on television and stand stark naked in front of Merv Griffin. What the hell do you think I'm going to do all alone?

TOBY You could call Polly. She's probably home from school by now.

EVY I'm not ready to see my daughter yet, thank you. What I'd really like to do is move the hell out of this dump.

TOBY Then why don't you move?

EVY Because, dumb-dumb, I still pay a hundred and twenty dollars for three and a half rooms. It's on a sublet from Mary Todd Lincoln.

TOBY You can borrow from Marty and me until you go back to work again.

EVY Work? Singing in clubs? The last job I had was two years ago in Pittsburgh. I broke the house record. Fell off the stool seventeen times in one show.

TOBY That's old news, I don't want to hear about it.

EVY I shared a dressing room with a female impersonator who had the hots for me. I think we made it, but I forget which way.

TOBY You don't have to sing in clubs. There's television—Martin knows people in advertising. You can be a cat in a tuna fish commercial, you'll make a fortune . . . I've got to go.

EVY So soon?

TOBY I'm afraid so, Marty's waiting.

EVY Just gonna dump me here like a basket case, heh? I thought you were going to stay and grow old with me.

TOBY Don't be silly. I'm never growing old . . . I won't go if you're really desperate.

EVY When have you known me when I wasn't desperate?

TOBY Never. If you need me I'll be at Martin's office and then at Pavillon. Can I send you anything?

EVY How about the headwaiter?

TOBY Armand? He doesn't go for women.

JIMMY *(Entering with a tray with cups of coffee)* Send him anyway, we'll find something for him to do.

TOBY Evy, this may be one of the happier days of my life.

EVY Toby, if you didn't come to pick me up today . . .

TOBY I told you. I'm always way the hell out on Long Island early Thursday mornings. Tell me once more how pretty I am.

EVY Helen of Troy couldn't carry your compact.

TOBY I believe you, Evelyn. I really do. I'll call you from the restaurant. *(She goes to the door; stops)* Evy . . . say it just once more.

EVY Say what?

TOBY What you promised me in the taxi.

EVY *(A pause)* I will be a good girl. For ever and ever.

TOBY Oh, Christ, I'm going to cry—there goes my make-up.

(She exits quickly. EVY *turns to* JIMMY*)*

JIMMY You skinny bastard, I'm so proud of you.

EVY Is that why you didn't visit me once in ten weeks?

JIMMY I can't go to hospitals, you know that. I pass out in hospitals. If I ever get hit by a car I tell them, "Take me to a drugstore, never a hospital."

EVY It wasn't a hospital. It's a sanitarium for drunks.

JIMMY They had white shoes and cotton balls, that's enough for me. *(He hands her a cup of coffee)* Didn't I call you almost every day? Didn't I send you popular novels?

EVY Queen Alexandra and her hemophiliac son? Couldn't you send me a sex manual, for chrissakes?

JIMMY I'm sorry I was nice to you. Next time I'll just send you a get-sober telegram.

EVY How much do I owe you for the groceries?

JIMMY We got 'em free. I had an affair with the delivery boy.

EVY Next time *I'll* answer the door. Give me the bill.

JIMMY Don't be ridiculous. Where would I get money?

EVY You were just in a show.

JIMMY That was in October and we ran two nights and were closed by the police. Please don't ask me what I had to do naked with six people on the stage.

EVY Was it something sexual?

JIMMY I couldn't tell, I had my eyes closed . . . That is the goddamned last time I will ever take my clothes off in public. Not only have I not worked since then, I can't even get a lousy date any more. You know what I did to keep alive? God is my judge, I worked in Bonwit's selling snakeskin toilet-seat covers, on my mother's life.

EVY *(At the window, looking out)* I don't see any men on the streets. Little boys, fags, hippies, but no men.

JIMMY What kills me is that I'm so good. I'm such a good actor I can't stand it. But I'm too late. Show business is over this year. There will be no more entertainment in the world after June. Maybe you'll see a person whistling or humming on the street, but that's all. I was born too talented and too late. What are you doing at the window? Who are you looking for?

EVY Nothing.

JIMMY You look tired. Why don't you lie down for a while?

EVY I don't want to lie down.

JIMMY You've got to lie down sometime.

EVY That's an old wives' tale. I've known people to stand for years at a time . . .

JIMMY *(Lost in his own problems)* I won't get this job tonight. They'll turn me down. I'm auditioning for some nineteen-year-old putz producer who has seventy-five thousand dollars and a drama degree from Oklahoma A&M . . . First time he walked into the theater he fell off the stage, broke two ribs . . . Some chance an intelligent actor has today . . . Oh, God, I want to be a star so bad. Not a little star. I want to be a big star with three agents and two lawyers and a business manager and a press agent, and then I'd fire all of them and get new ones because I'm such a big star. And I'd make everyone pay for the twenty-two years I poured into this business. I wouldn't do benefits, I wouldn't give money to charity. I would become one of the great shitheels of all time. Isn't that a wonderful dream, Evy!

EVY *(Looks around)* She didn't leave any cigarettes. Stupid dumb broad.

JIMMY *(Takes a crumpled pack out of his shirt pocket)* Here. Take whatever I have. My money, my blood, whatever you want—only calm down, because I don't trust you when you get nervous.

EVY I just made up my mind: I don't like you.
(She takes one of the cigarettes)

JIMMY You never liked me. For fifteen years it's been a one-sided friendship. I'm the one who always worries about you, picks you up off the floor, puts you to bed, feeds you—and for what? Christmas you gave me the one lousy album you made in 1933 . . . Well, I'm through. I can't take it any more. You're skinny and sober, take care of yourself now.

EVY How'd you like a big wet kiss on the mouth?

JIMMY How'd you like a tongue and Swiss on toast? Sit down, it's ready.
(He starts for the kitchen)

EVY *(Yells)* Jimmy, will you stay here and talk to me!

JIMMY *(Stops)* What do you want to talk about?

EVY Anything, dammit, pick a subject.

JIMMY Why don't you ask me, Evy? Why don't you get it over with and *ask me?* . . . No, I have not seen him or spoken to him, all right?

EVY *(A pause; she nods)* All right.

JIMMY I'm lying. I saw him at the bar in Downey's last week. I don't think he's doing well because he had one beer and ate all the pretzels in the dish . . .

EVY Was he alone?

JIMMY Yes. I know because when he left I watched him through the window hoping he'd get hit by the Eighth Avenue bus . . . What else do you want to know?

EVY Nothing. I was curious, not interested.

JIMMY Oh, really? Is that why you keep staring out the window? Is that why you won't go into the bedroom? What are you afraid of, you'll see his lousy ghost sitting on the john doing the *Times* crossword puzzle? . . . Go on. Go in the bedroom and get it over with, for chrissakes.

(EVY looks at him, then goes into the bedroom. It is quiet a moment. Then we hear EVY from the bedroom)

EVY How'd you get the Bloody Mary stains off the wallpaper?

JIMMY I hung your bathrobe over them.

EVY *(Reenters living room)* You know what I'll do? I'll repaint the room white. The whole bedroom white, top to bottom. Walls, floors, bedspreads, shoes, stockings, everything white. And I'm going to forget everything that ever happened in there and I'm going to become one happy, TV-watching, Protestant, square-assed lady, how about that?

JIMMY Nixon'll be thrilled.

(The doorbell rings. EVY looks startled)

EVY Are you expecting anyone?

JIMMY I don't even live here. Should I answer it? They're just going to ring again. *(It rings again)* See!

(EVY nods. He opens the door. It's the Spanish delivery boy with one package in his arms)

MANUEL I forget the soda. Six cans Coca-Cola, six cans Canada Dry ginger ale. Two dollars, forty cents.

JIMMY I paid you before, didn't I?

(He tries to grab the package)

MANUEL You paid me for las' time, you dint pay me for this time. Two dollars and forty cents, please.

JIMMY *(Angry)* Did you tell D'Allessandro that Mrs. Meara is going to take her business somewhere else?

MANUEL He don' care. He say, "Take the Coca-Cola somewhere else."

EVY *(Steps forward)* What's wrong?

JIMMY There's nothing wrong. *(To the boy)* Wait out there. I'll get your money.

(JIMMY takes the bags and goes into the kitchen)

MANUEL I don' wanna come in your house.

(EVY steps out into the center of the room so that she is in view of the boy for the first time)

EVY Jimmy, don't leave him out in the hall like that. *(To* MANUEL*)* That's all right, you can come in.

(The boy looks at her and smiles)

MANUEL Oh. Okay.

(He steps in)

EVY *(Smiles at him)* I'm Mrs. Meara.

MANUEL Oh, yes? Hello, Mrs. Meara, nice to meet you. *(He nods his head a few times, looks her up and down)* I brought you six cans Coca-Cola, six cans Canada Dry ginger ale. Okay?

EVY I don't see why not. That's a charge. And put fifty cents on for yourself.

MANUEL Oh, thank you very much.

EVY You're welcome.

MANUEL But I need two dollars, forty cents. Mr. D'Allessandro say to me—

EVY I know what Mr. D'Allessandro said to you. It's all right. You tell him Mrs. Meara is home and will take care of everything by check again. Will you do that?

MANUEL Yes. I'm going to tell him that. But he's going to tell me not to tell him that.

EVY What's your name?

MANUEL Mr. D'Allessandro.

EVY No, *your* name.

MANUEL *My* name? You want to know *my* name? Manuel.

EVY Manuel?

MANUEL *(Nods)* Manuel. Yes, that's my name. Manuel. Eet's Spanish.

(JIMMY *comes out of the kitchen*)

EVY I haven't seen you before, Manuel. What happened to the other boy?

MANUEL Pablo? Pablo got married and is now work in a better job. Bloomingdale's.

EVY Really? He seemed so young.

MANUEL They don' care how old you are in Bloomingdale's.

EVY I mean to get married.

MANUEL Oh, Pablo is twenny years old, same as me.

EVY You're twenty?

(JIMMY *has been watching this with consternation*)

MANUEL Tha's me, twenny.

EVY Well, let's hope that you get married and find a better job too, Manuel.

MANUEL Eet's okay eef I find a better job, but I don' wanna get married. I'm okay now, you know what I mean?

EVY *(Smiles)* You mean you have lots of girl friends, is that it?

MANUEL Sure. Why not?

EVY Well, you tell Mr. D'Allessandro I will send him his check the first thing every month. Will you do that?

MANUEL The first thing every month. Tha's what I'm gonna tell him.

EVY And put fifty cents on for yourself. I don't have any change just now.

MANUEL Tha's awright . . . I come again. You take care of me another time—you know what I mean? (*There is a slight suggestiveness in his tone that does not go unnoticed by* EVY *or* JIMMY) Goo'bye, Mrs. Meara. (*To* JIMMY) Okay, Meester, eet's okay now, we're good friends again, all right?

(*He winks at* JIMMY *and exits, closing the door behind him*)

JIMMY (*Yells*) Jesus Christ! Why didn't you invite him in to listen to your Xavier Cugat records? Are you crazy?

EVY Oh, come on, he's a delivery boy.

JIMMY I saw the look he gave you and I know what he wants to deliver.

EVY I'm not in *that* kind of trouble yet . . . maybe in a few weeks, but not yet.

JIMMY I can't trust you. I can't trust you alone for ten minutes.

EVY I can be trusted for ten minutes.

JIMMY I know you, Evy. I wouldn't leave you with the Pope during Holy Week . . . Haven't you had enough trouble this year?

EVY I've had enough for the rest of my life. For Christ's sake, I'm not going to shack up with a delivery boy. I don't even have a quarter to give him a tip.

JIMMY You'll charge it like everything else.

EVY Oh, God, Jimmy, I really love you. You don't know how good it is to have somebody worried about you.

JIMMY Well, I hate it. I have enough trouble worrying about me. I'm forty years old and I can't get a job with or without clothes any more. If you want to carry on with Pancho Gonzales, that's up to you.

EVY (*Puts her arms around* JIMMY) Of all the stinking people in this world, you sure ain't one of them.

JIMMY Well, I'm glad you finally realize all the others are stinking.

EVY Why don't you marry me?

JIMMY Because you're a drunken nymphomaniac and I'm a homosexual. We'd have trouble getting our kids into a good school.

EVY Give me a kiss. *(He kisses her lightly)* Come on. Give me a real kiss. Who the hell's gonna know?

(He kisses her with feeling)

JIMMY God will punish us for the terrible thing we're doing.

EVY Don't get depressed but you get me very excited.

JIMMY I don't have to stay and listen to this kind of talk. *(Breaks away from her)* I've got to go. If you promise to behave yourself, I may be nice to you when I'm a star.

EVY We could live together in Canada. They don't do sex in Canada.

JIMMY *(Putting on his bag)* Stop it, Evy, you're confusing my hormones. I'm late.

EVY Jimmy!

JIMMY *(Stops)* What?

EVY Nothing. I just love you and want to thank you for being here today.

JIMMY Don't thank me, just pray for me. Pray that I get this show because I think it's the last one in the world

EVY Will you call me the minute you hear anything?

JIMMY It's off-Broadway, there are no phones. *(On his way out)* I bought you that Stouffer's macaroni that you love. And some Sara Lee cheesecake. And I made you enough coffee until February. Will you remember to drink it?

EVY Drinking is one thing I remember.

JIMMY And get some sleep.

EVY I promise.

JIMMY And if José Ferrer shows his face again, don't open the door. The only groceries he's bringing next time are his own.

(He exits, closing the door behind him. EVY *turns and looks at the empty apartment with full realization that she is alone, alone again for the first time in months. She picks up her suitcase and literally throws it into the bedroom)*

EVY All right, don't panic, we'll take it one night at a time. *(She looks around, puffs up the pillows on the sofa, then sits down on it)* . . . And that's it for the week! *(She crosses to the piano, plays a few notes of "Close to You," then sings the first line)* . . . Thank you, thank you . . . For my next number, Ed Sullivan and I will make it right here on this stage . . . *(She sighs heavily. She is fighting to keep from losing control of herself. She looks at the phone, goes over to it quickly, sits and dials . . . Into the phone)* Hello? . . . Is Miss Meara there? . . . No, not *Mrs.* Meara, *Miss!* . . . Oh? How long ago? . . . Well, when she gets in, would you please tell her— *(Suddenly a key turns in the lock and the front door opens.* POLLY MEARA *stands there with one large, heavy suitcase.* POLLY *is seventeen, pretty, with long straight hair and no pretensions. She wears blue jeans, a sweater and a jacket. There is a long and emotional pause as the two stare at each other across the room. Then* EVY *speaks into the phone)*—never mind, I just heard from her.

(She hangs up and stares at POLLY*)*

POLLY I don't want to get your hopes up, but I have reason to believe I'm your daughter!

EVY No, you're not. *My* daughter would have called first . . . *(No longer able to contain herself)* . . . You rotten kid, you want to give me a heart attack? *(They rush to each other, arms around each other in a huge, warm embrace.* EVY *squeezes her tightly)* Oh, God, Polly, Polly . . .

POLLY I was hoping I'd get here before you. But I was late getting out of school. Of all damn days . . .

(They break the embrace. EVY *wipes her eyes)*

EVY Okay, I'm crying. You satisfied? You just destroyed a helpless old woman . . . Well, why the hell aren't you crying?

POLLY I'm too happy. I can't believe it. My God, look at you.

EVY What do you think?

POLLY You're gorgeous. Skinniest mother I ever had. I can wear your clothes now.

EVY What size dress do you wear?

POLLY Five.

EVY Tough, kid, I wear a four. *(Wipes teary eyes again)* Damn, I knew this would happen. You weren't supposed to know I was home. I needed three days before I could face you.

POLLY I called the hospital this morning. You didn't think I could wait, did you?

EVY Neither could I. Oh God, give me another hug, I can't stand it. *(They embrace)* All right, if we're going to get physical, let's close the door. There's enough talk about me in this building.

(EVY *closes the door.* POLLY *goes to get the suitcase from in front of the door*)

POLLY I'll get that.

(She picks it up)

EVY Have you had dinner yet?

POLLY I haven't even had lunch. I was too nervous.

EVY I just loaded up for the winter. We'll have a food festival. Come on, take your coat off, let me look at you. Hey, what'd you do with your hair?

POLLY Nothing.

EVY I know. It's been three months. When you gonna do something?

POLLY Don't bug me about the way I look. I'm not that secure yet.

(She heads for the bedroom with the suitcase)

EVY I should have your problems. Where you going with that?

POLLY In the bedroom.

EVY What is it?

POLLY *(Looks at it)* Looks like a suitcase.

EVY Thanks, I was wondering. What's in the suitcase?

POLLY *(Shrugs)* Dresses, shoes, books, things like that.

EVY Why do you have things like that in your suitcase?

POLLY Well, otherwise they fall on the floor.

EVY All right, no one likes a smart-ass for a daughter. What's going on here?

POLLY Nothing's going on. Can't I stay?

EVY Tonight? You know you can.

POLLY Okay. I'm staying tonight.
(She starts for the bedroom again)

EVY With all that? You must be some heavy sleeper.

POLLY Okay, *two* nights. Let's not haggle.

EVY Hey, hey, just a minute. Put the suitcase down. (POLLY *looks at her, then puts it down*) . . . Now look at me.

POLLY I'm looking.

EVY And I know what you're thinking. Oh, no, you don't.

POLLY Why not?

EVY Because I don't need any roommates, thank you . . . If you had a beard, it would be different.

POLLY I don't want to be your roommate, I just want to live with you.

EVY You lonely? I'll send you to camp. You have a home, what are you bothering me for?

POLLY You can't throw me out, I'm your flesh and blood.

EVY I just got rid of my flesh, I'm not sentimental.

POLLY I've already decided I'm moving in. You have nothing to say about it.

EVY In the first place, idiot, you're not allowed to live here. It's not up to you or me.

POLLY And in the second place?

EVY I don't need a second place. The first one wiped us out. You live where your father tells you to live.

POLLY Exactly. Where do I put the suitcase?

EVY Are you telling me *your* father gave you permission to move in here with me?

POLLY Right.

EVY *Your* father?

POLLY That's the one.

EVY A tall man, grayish hair, wears blue suits, spits a little when he talks?

POLLY Would you like to speak to him yourself?

EVY Not sober, I don't. What does your stepmother think about this? What's her name, Lucretia?

POLLY Felicia.

EVY Felicia, some name. He must spit pretty good when he says that. Did she ever get that clicking in her teeth fixed?

POLLY Nope. Still clicking.

EVY That's a nice way to live, with a spitter and a clicker. Thank God he didn't get custody of me too.

POLLY That's why I'm begging you to take me in. I can't do my homework with all that noise.

EVY God's truth, Polly? He really said yes?

POLLY He likes me. He wouldn't kid around with my life.

EVY Why don't I believe it?

POLLY We've been talking about it for months. He knows how hard you've been trying. He spoke to your doctor, he knows you're all right . . . And he thinks you need me now.

EVY *Now* I need you? Where does he think I've been the last seven years, Guatemala?

POLLY He knows where you've been.

EVY And what about you? Is this what you really want?

POLLY I've been packed for three years. Every June I put in bigger sizes.

EVY You wanna hear something? My whole body is shaking. I'm scared stiff. I wouldn't know the first thing about taking care of you.

POLLY I'm seventeen years old. How hard could it be?

EVY I'll level with you—it's not the best thing I do. I was feeling very motherly one time, I bought a couple of turtles, two for eighty-five cents, Irving and Sam. I fed them once—in the morning they were floating on their backs. I don't think I could go through that again.

POLLY I'm a terrific swimmer.

EVY Jesus, the one thing I hoped I wouldn't have is a dumb daughter. What kind of influence would I be on you? I talk filthy. I have always talked filthy. I'm a congenital filthy talker.

POLLY Son of a bitch.

EVY I don't think that's funny.

POLLY Well, I just got here, give me a chance.

EVY What the hell is the big attraction? I thought we were doing fine with visiting days.

POLLY When I was nine years old, do you remember what you gave me for Christmas?

EVY An empty bottle of Dewar's White Label? I don't know, I can't remember yesterday.

POLLY Don't you remember the gingerbread house with the little gingerbread lady in the window?

EVY If you say so.

POLLY I always kept it to remind me of you. Of course, today I have the biggest box of crumbs in the neighborhood. Come on, be a sport. Buy me another one this Christmas.

EVY I don't know if I could afford it.

POLLY What are you afraid of?

EVY Of leaving you with the crumbs again . . . You know what I'm like.

POLLY I've seen you drunk. Mostly I hated it but once or twice you sure were cute.

EVY You only saw dress rehearsals. I was very careful around you. A mother doesn't like to get too pissed around her own daughter. Am I supposed to say things like that in front of you? Pissed?

POLLY If you can do it, you can say it.

EVY There are other things I can't tell you . . . Ah, Christ, I might as well tell you. You knew about Lou Tanner.

POLLY I met him here a few times.

EVY Did you know we lived here together for eight months?

POLLY I didn't think he got off a bus in those pajamas.

EVY Jesus, at least have the decency to be shocked.

POLLY There's a sixteen-year-old girl who just left school because she's pregnant. You're forty-three. If you're not allowed, who is?

EVY How'd I suddenly end up with the Mother of the Year Award?

POLLY I don't want to judge you, Evy. I just want to live with you.

EVY You're seventeen years old, it's time you judged me. I just don't want you to get the idea that a hundred and eighty-three pounds of pure alcohol is something called Happy Fat . . . Many a night I would have thrown myself out that window if I could have squeezed through . . . I'm not what you'd call an emotionally stable person. You know how many times I was *really* in love since your father and I broke up? I met the only man who ever really meant anything to me about seven, maybe eight, times. Mr. Right I meet at least twice a week . . . I sure know true love when I see it. It's wherever I happen to look.

POLLY You don't have to tell me any of this.

EVY *I do,* dammit . . . I want you to know everything, Polly, before you make up your mind. I lived here with that guitar player for eight of the happiest months of my life. Well, why not? He was handsome, funny, ten years younger than me, what more could a woman want? . . .

He sat in that chair all day working and writing and I fed him and clothed him and loved him for eight incredible months . . . And then that dirty bastard—I'm sorry, I'm going to try not to do that any more.

POLLY Good.

EVY No, the hell with it. That dirty bastard. He walked out on me in the middle of the night for an eighteen-year-old Indian hippie. "Princess-Screw-the-Other-Woman" . . . Wait'll she gets old and starts looking like the face on the nickel. And he doesn't have a penny, not a cent. Well, her moccasins'll wear out, we'll see how long that affair lasts . . . But I sat at that window for six weeks, waiting and hoping while I ran through two liquor stores in this neighborhood alone . . . Finally Toby came in one day and found me face-down in the bathtub . . . I woke up in a sanitarium in Long Island, and the rest isn't very interesting unless you like stories about human torture . . . But I went through it and I'm here. And I figure, pussycat, that I have only one more chance at this human-being business . . . and if I blow it this time, they'll probably bury me in some distillery in Kentucky . . . And if this is the kind of person you'd like to live with, God has cursed me with one of the all-time-great schmucks for a daughter.

POLLY *(Smiles)* How'd you like to come and speak at my school?

EVY *(Adores her for this)* I think I would rather have you than a mink coat that fits. (*She hugs* POLLY) You still want to take a shot at it?

POLLY After that story, I'd pay for a seat.

EVY Oh, no. If you move in, it's a whole new ball game. If you're going to live here with me, we turn this place into "Little Women." Clean sheets, doilies on the furniture, TV *Guide*, a regular American family.

POLLY And we can go to church on Sunday. By the way, what religion are we?

EVY I'll look it up. I've got it here somewhere . . . I'm going to get a job. Not in show business—a real job.

(She starts pacing)

POLLY I get home from school at four, I could start dinners.

EVY Can you cook?

POLLY No, but I can get them started.

EVY Is that all you can do?

POLLY I can ride a horse.

EVY That's it. When we're starving to death, you're the one who rides for help.

POLLY Can I unpack now?

EVY Yes, you can unpack now! . . . Holy Christ, Polly, I am suddenly so excited. How did I get so lucky?

POLLY *(Shrugs)* Some people have it all.

(POLLY *starts into the bedroom with the suitcase*)

EVY See what looks good in the kitchen, I'll put your things away.

(EVY *starts for the bedroom as* POLLY *starts for the kitchen. They pass each other on the way*)

POLLY So far we're doing terrific.

(EVY *disappears into the bedroom.* POLLY *is in the kitchen. Both are offstage*)

EVY *(Offstage)* What the hell do you have in here, Yankee Stadium?

POLLY *(Offstage)* It's my record collection.

(The doorbell rings)

EVY *(Offstage)* I see a lot of panties here but I don't see any bras. Don't you wear a bra?

POLLY *(Offstage)* No. Am I missing a big thrill?

(POLLY *comes out of the kitchen. She looks toward the bedroom, but apparently* EVY *hasn't heard it.* POLLY *crosses and opens the door.* LOU TANNER *is standing there. He is in his mid-thirties, with scruffy, unmanageable hair, a full, bushy mustache, a dirty turtleneck sweater and light-tan desert boots, very worn. He is, despite his appearance, attractive.* POLLY *is shaken by his ill-timed arrival)*

POLLY Hello, Lou!

LOU *(Looks at her, then past her into the room)* Hello, Polly.

EVY *(Offstage)* I'm not going to ask you what these pills are for because I don't want to know and I don't want to hear.

LOU She all right?

POLLY *(Still shaken)* What? . . . Yes. She's fine.

LOU Can I come in?

POLLY *(Looks toward the bedroom worriedly)* Yes, sure. *(He steps into the room. She closes the door behind him)* How are you?

LOU I thought she'd be alone . . . Maybe I ought to come back later.

POLLY No. No, I'm sure she'll want to see you. *(Calls out)* Mother! . . . Someone's here.

(LOU *stares at the bedroom door as* POLLY *eyes him nervously.* EVY *appears in the bedroom doorway. She has probably recognized* LOU*'s voice. She comes out of the bedroom and faces* LOU)

LOU Hello, Evy.

EVY *(Trying to be cool)* Hello, Lou . . .

(There is a moment of awkward silence)

LOU You look fabulous.

EVY Thank you.

LOU How'd you lose so much weight?

EVY Sheer happiness.

POLLY *(This is no place for her)* I'll finish unpacking. I'll see you, Lou.

EVY That's all right, you can stay.

POLLY I'd rather not, if you don't mind. (*Nods at* LOU) Lou.

(She exits quickly into the bedroom. EVY *and* LOU *stand there eyeing each other)*

LOU I checked the hospital. They told me you were coming home today. Rough scene, heh?

EVY No, I loved it. They showed movies Saturday nights . . . How's Pocahontas?

LOU We split about a month ago.

EVY Ah, that's too bad. What was the problem, couldn't she make it rain?

LOU She couldn't make it, period. A lot of sexual hangups among the Cherokees. *(Looks around)* You going to offer me a cigarette?

EVY No, but you're welcome to take a bath. You look like the second week of the garbage strike. You living indoors somewhere?

LOU Eddie Valendo's on the road, I'm using his place.

EVY I hope he left you food, you look a little shaky.

LOU Musicians don't eat, Evy, you know that. We live on "soul."

EVY Whose?

LOU I wouldn't turn down a bottle of cold beer.

EVY You asking or begging?

LOU Is that what you want to hear? Okay, I'm begging.

EVY I always knew you'd make it big some day. *(Hands him a cigarette)* Here. There's one left. Smoke it when you're older.

LOU *(Tries to grab her)* That's my Evy.

EVY *(Pulling away)* You are one, priceless, unbelievable bastard. You had to walk in here today, didn't you? You had to time it so you'd get me holding my nerves together with spit and coffee.

LOU What'd you want me to do, phone you from a pay station in Walgreen's? "Hi, Evy, guess who this is?"

EVY The only thing stopping you was the dime.

LOU Come on, Evy, I walked seventeen blocks in borrowed shoes. Talk nice to me.

EVY Like nothing ever happened, right?

LOU No, it happened. We'll talk about it. But it's hard when you don't look at me. I get the feeling I'm suddenly left all alone in this room.

EVY *(Turns and looks at him)* I know the feeling well.

LOU I'll say one thing for the Indians. Generally speaking, they're not a vindictive people.

EVY Really, Lou? What'd she do when you walked out on her? Ride into the sunset? Do a little sun dance? Wriggle and bounce her firm little body? You want to tell me about her tight little eighteen-year-old body, Lou?

LOU Not particularly.

EVY Come on. Lay it on me. Talk that hip, colorful language you dig so much. Tell me your problems, Lou, you'll get a lot of sympathy from me.

LOU No problems, Ev. Nothing that can't be worked out.

EVY Lou, I'm forty-three years old and I'm trying to be a grown-up lady. The doctors told me I'm not allowed to drink any more or have affairs with thirty-three-year-old guitar players . . . I thank you for this visit. Now go home, find someone your own age and light up some Astro-Turf or whatever you're smoking these days.

LOU *(Smiles)* If nothing else, Evy, you have a way with a phrase. I used to quote you. Word for word. Of course, this dumb little Indian chick never saw the humor. We communicated in other ways. But whenever I needed a good honest laugh, I had to quote you, Ev. You weren't in the room, but you were there, you know what I mean?

EVY It's an image I think I'll cherish forever . . . Listen, Polly is here and I think we ought to cut this short.

LOU I want to come back, Ev. *(There is a pause)* Today, tomorrow, next week . . . but I want to come back.

EVY I see! . . . Would that be with or without meals?

LOU Maybe with a little humility. I'll scrape up whatever I can.

EVY I don't want you to steal just for me.

LOU There it is, Ev. That's what I've come back for. A little stimulation.

EVY Try a vibrator.

LOU Try letting up for two minutes. Take an interest, Ev, ask me how my work is coming.

EVY How's your work coming, Lou?

LOU Gee, it's nice of you to take an interest. I'm writing. I'm not selling anything, but I'm writing.

EVY *(Without emotion)* I am *enormously* pleased for you.

LOU You don't give a crap, do you? You never did give a good goddamn.

EVY That's too hysterical to be answered.

LOU Oh, you cared about *me.* I never questioned that. Affection, love, passion, you had it by the tonnage. All I had to do was look at you with anything less than indifference and you were ready to jump in the sack with your shoes on.

EVY Forgive me. Frigidity is not one of my major hangups.

LOU I could have been a counterman at Riker's, it wouldn't have made any difference to you.

EVY *Nothing* made any difference to me except you.

LOU You didn't give a damn if the stuff I wrote was good or not as long as it was finished. "It's terrific, Lou, now come to bed."

EVY You wrote it, you played it, I listened to it. Short of publishing it there wasn't a hell of a lot more I could do.

LOU You never really liked it, did you? You never thought I had any real talent, did you?

EVY I loved it. Everything you wrote I loved.

LOU Bullshit.

EVY That's a better way of putting it.

LOU Then why the hell didn't you say so?

EVY I had enough trouble getting affection from you without giving you bad reviews.

LOU I can't believe it. You hated everything I wrote and you never said a word to me until now.

EVY I'm sorry your ego is hurt posthumously. All right, I think you're very promising. I'll take a page ad in *Variety*, now leave me alone.

LOU You know, Evy, you are the biggest ball-breaking insufferable pain-in-the-ass woman I ever met—and I'm standing here enjoying it . . . I'm cut up and bleeding from abuse and humiliation but at least I know I'm in the room with a living human being . . . *(Softening)* I haven't had a good all-out-fight like that in three months . . . I have also, in that time, not put down a piece of music worth the price of the paper . . . Maybe you're right. At best I'm mediocre. But mediocre is better than wasting good music sheets . . . Come on, Evy. The truth is, while I was here, I functioned. And when I functioned, you functioned.

EVY Evy and Lou functioning: one of the great love stories of all time.

LOU *(With some humor)* Well, maybe not the greatest, just the most original . . . What do you say, Ev? Make a contribution to the world of serious music.

EVY I already gave.

LOU Christ, Evy, you want me to say it, I'll say it. I need you very badly.

EVY For how long, Lou? Until you run off with the Chinese hatcheck girl at Trader Vic's?

LOU Evy, I swear—

EVY Don't make me any promises. I just left a hospital filled with people waiting for promises.

LOU Come on, for chrissakes, you had that problem for twenty years before you ever met me.

EVY No argument. I just don't want it for twenty years after.

LOU What are you going to tell me, you're cured? You had buttermilk for twelve weeks and now you'll live happily ever after? . . . There's still a whole life to get through, Evy . . . I'm not coming in here offering you any phony promises. Sure, in six weeks I may find another cute-assed little chick, and in eight weeks they might find you under the piano with a case of Thunderbird wine. Then again, maybe not. Together, Evy, we don't add up to one strong person. I just think together we have a better chance.

EVY What I need now is a relative, not a relationship. And I have one in there unpacking.

LOU Who are you kidding?

EVY She'll be here in the morning. That's good enough for me.

LOU The mornings have never been your problem.

EVY We were just going to have dinner. I'd ask you to stay but it's just the immediate family.

LOU Well, it was kind of a slow afternoon, I just thought I'd ask . . . I'm really glad to see you in good shape, Ev . . . Take care of yourself.

EVY That's the general idea.

LOU *(At the door)* You still have ten seconds to change your mind. *(He waits. No reply)* My, how time flies.

(He opens the door, about to go)

EVY Lou! *(He stops, turns; there is a pause)* Will you call me sometime? Just to say hello?

LOU *(Looks at her)* Probably not.

(He turns, goes, closing the door behind him. EVY *stands there a moment. The bedroom door opens.* POLLY *comes out)*

POLLY I didn't hear a word . . . But can I say something?

EVY Only if it'll make me laugh . . . Are you unpacked yet?

POLLY It would take me two minutes to put it all back.

EVY If you're unpacked, then wash your hands, set the table and light the stove. It's dinner time.

POLLY *(Brightly)* Okay, Evy.

EVY And none of the Evy crap . . . I'm your mother. I want a little respect, for chrissakes!

(EVY *starts to remove the tablecloth from the table as* POLLY, *beaming, exits into the kitchen*)

Curtain

Act Two

It is three weeks later, about nine o'clock at night. POLLY *is thumbing through a private phone book. She finds a number and dials. She looks at her watch, concerned.*

POLLY *(Into the phone)* . . . Hello? . . . Is this Joe Allen's Bar? . . . Could you tell me if Evelyn Meara is there, please? . . . *Evy* Meara, that's right . . . I see . . . Was she there at all today? . . .

(The front door opens, unseen by POLLY. EVY *enters carrying a Saks Fifth Avenue shopping bag)*

EVY I'm here, I'm here. Just what I need, a trusting daughter.

(She closes the door)

POLLY *(Into the phone)* Never mind. Thank you.

(She hangs up and turns to EVY. EVY *puts down the packages)*

EVY If you knew what a terrific day I had you wouldn't be worrying about me . . . I've got sensational news . . . I was picked up today . . . He was eighty-six years old with a cane and a limp, but he really dug me. I don't think he could see me or hear me too good but we really hit it off . . . If I don't get any better offers this week, I'm going to contact him at the Home. Hello, pussycat, give your mother a kiss. *(She kisses* POLLY *on the cheek;* POLLY *receives it coldly)* What's wrong?

POLLY It's almost nine o'clock.

EVY You're kidding?

POLLY *(Points to the clock on the mantel)* I'm not kidding. It's almost nine o'clock.

EVY All right, don't get excited. What did I miss, the eclipse, what happened?

POLLY You don't call, you don't leave a note, you don't tell me where you're going to be. I'm expecting you home for dinner at six-thirty and you don't show and I'm scared to death. What happened? Where were you?

EVY Hanging around the men's room in the subway . . . I had a good day. You want to hear the details or you want to yell at me?

POLLY I want to yell at you.

EVY You can't yell at me, I'm your mother. I missed your dinner. Oh, God, Polly, I'm sorry. What did you make?

POLLY I don't know. Something out of the cookbook. It was brown and it was hot . . . If you want some, it's in the kitchen now. It's yellow and it's cold.

EVY *(Hugging her)* Don't be mad at me. All I've got in the world is you and that eighty-six-year-old gimp—don't be mad at me. Let me tell you what happened today.

POLLY Did you eat?

EVY Yes, I think so . . . Listen to what happened. I ran into this old girl friend of mine who used to work in the clubs—

POLLY What do you mean, you think so? Don't you know if you ate or not?

EVY I ate, I ate! I had a sandwich for lunch. I'll run up to Lenox Hill and take an x-ray for you . . . Will you listen to my story?

POLLY You mean you haven't had anything to eat except lunch?

EVY It didn't say "lunch" on the sandwich. Maybe it was a "dinner" sandwich, I don't know. What are you taking in school this week, nagging? Let me tell you my story.

POLLY You don't sleep well and I never see you eat, so I'm worried about you.

EVY Who says I don't sleep well?

POLLY I watch you at night.

EVY Then *you're* the one who doesn't sleep well.

POLLY You're in the living room until five, six in the morning, pacing and smoking and coughing. I hear you in there.

EVY It's the television. I listen to cancer commercials.

POLLY Making phone calls in the middle of the night . . . Who were you calling at four o'clock in the morning?

EVY The weather bureau.

POLLY At four o'clock in the morning?

EVY I like to know what it's going to be like at five o'clock . . . Jesus! Two more years of this, you're going to be a professional pain in the ass.

POLLY Okay, fine with me. If you don't give a crap, I don't give a crap.

EVY And watch your goddamned language.

POLLY If you don't watch yours, why should I watch mine?

EVY I talk this way. It's an impediment. You want me to wear braces on my mouth?

POLLY You might as well. You never *eat* anything except a cup of coffee for breakfast.

EVY What the hell difference does it make?

POLLY Because if you don't take care of your body, it's not going to take care of you.

EVY I don't want to take care of my body. I want somebody else to take care of it. Why do you think I'm talking to eighty-year-old men?

POLLY You're infuriating. It's like talking to a child.

EVY *(Turns away)* I don't get any respect. How the hell am I going to be a mother if I don't get any respect?

POLLY How am I going to respect you when you don't respect yourself?

EVY *(Looks up in despair)* Oh, Christ, I'm a flop mother. Three weeks and I blew it. Don't be angry, Polly. Don't be mad at me.

POLLY And stop apologizing. You're my mother. Make *me* apologize to you for talking the way I did.

EVY It won't happen again, sweetheart, I promise.

POLLY *(Vehemently)* Don't promise *me*, promise yourself! I can't live my life *and* yours. *You've* got to take over, *you've* got to be the one in charge around here.

EVY Listen, you're really getting me crazy now. Why don't you write all the rules and regulations nice and neat on a piece of paper and I'll do whatever it says. Put on one page where I yell at you, and one page where you yell at me . . . Now you want to hear what happened to me this afternoon or not?

POLLY *(It's hard not to like* EVY; POLLY *smiles at her)* What happened this afternoon?

EVY I think I have a job.

POLLY You're kidding. Where?

EVY Well . . . *(Pacing)* I was in Gucci's looking for a birthday present for Toby . . . when suddenly I meet this old girl friend of mine who used to be a vocalist in this singing group . . . Four Macks and a Truck or some goddamned thing . . . Anyway, she can't get over my gorgeous new figure and asks what I'm doing lately and I tell her . . . I'm looking for good honest work, preferably around a lot of single men, like an aircraft carrier, Okinawa, something like that . . . You're looking at me funny. If you're thinking of heating up the cold yellow stuff, forget it.

POLLY I'm just listening.

EVY All right . . . Well, she starts to tell me how she's out of the business now and is married to an Italian with four restaurants on Long Island and right away I dig he's in with the mob. I mean, one restaurant, you're in business; four restaurants, it's the Mafia . . . Anyway, he's got a place in Garden City and he's looking for an attractive hostess who says, "Good evening, right this way please," and wriggles her behind and gets a hundred and ninety bucks a week . . . So I played it very cool, and nonchalantly got down on my knees, kissed her shoes, licked her ankles and carried her packages out the store.

POLLY A hostess in a restaurant? Is that what you want to do?

EVY No, what I *want* to do is be a masseur at the New York Athletic Club but there are no openings . . . Can I finish my story?

POLLY Why don't you finish your story?

EVY Thank you, I'll finish my story . . . So we go around the corner to Schrafft's and she buys me a sherry and we sit there chatting like a couple of Scarsdale debutantes—me, the former lush, and her, a chippie married to Joe Bananas . . . And she writes down the address and I have to be—*(Consults a scrap of paper from her pocket)*—at the Blue Cockatoo Restaurant in Garden City at ten o'clock tomorrow morning, where Lucky Luciano's nephew will interview me. All this in one day, *plus* getting my knees rubbed by an eighty-six-year-old degenerate on the crosstown bus . . . And you're going to sit there and tell me there's no God . . . *(She looks at* POLLY *expectantly, hoping* POLLY *will be as exuberant and enthusiastic about her prospects as she is. But* POLLY *just glares at her)* . . . What's the matter?

POLLY You had a glass of sherry?

EVY *(Turns away)* Oh, Christ.

POLLY Why did you have a glass of sherry?

EVY Because the waitress put it down in front of me.

POLLY They don't put it down in front of you unless you order it. I don't understand you.

EVY I don't understand *you!* I rush home happy, excited, bubbling with good news and who do I find when I get here—a seventeen-year-old cop! I am not loaded, I am not smashed, I am thrilled to death because I spent a whole day out of this house and I came home alive and noticed and even wanted.

POLLY Do you need a drink to feel that?

EVY I was tense, I was afraid of blowing the job. So I had one stinking little drink. Did you ever have a cocktail in Schrafft's? Half of it is painted on the glass.

POLLY That isn't the point. You could have had coffee or tea or milk.

EVY Thank you, Miss, when do we land in Chicago? . . . I don't want to talk about it any more. Go inside and study. When you pass French, we'll discuss it in a foreign language. Until then, shape up or ship out or whatever the hell that expression is.

POLLY *(A pause)* No, listen *(Looks at her quietly a moment)* I think it's terrific.

EVY You think what's terrific?

POLLY About today, about getting the job. I really do. When will you start?

EVY Well, in the first place, I didn't get it yet. And in the second place, I'm not so sure I'm going to take it.

POLLY *(Puzzled)* Then what's all the excitement about?

EVY About being asked . . . About being wanted.

POLLY I'm sorry—I don't think I understand.

EVY *(Goes over to* POLLY *and holds her head in her arms)* Please God, I hope you never do . . . *(Smiles at her, trying to be more cheerful)* Listen, how about one more chance at being a mother? If I screw up, you can buy out my contract for a hundred dollars and I'll move out.

POLLY *(Takes* EVY*'s hand)* Who's going to bring me up?

EVY *(Shrugs)* I'll set you on automatic . . . *(Crosses back to her shopping bag)* Hey, come on, get dressed. We have a party that started fifteen minutes ago.

POLLY What party?

EVY Toby's birthday. *(She takes a present from the shopping bag)* She's forty years old today. She's promised to take off her make-up and reveal her true identity.

POLLY I've got to study. I have a science test on Monday.

EVY Flunk it! Men don't like you if you're too smart. *(She takes out a bottle of champagne. She looks at* POLLY*, who stares at her meaningfully)* I'm pouring! That's all I'm doing is pouring.

POLLY Who's coming?

EVY Jimmy, Marty and Toby.

(EVY *starts to cross to the kitchen with the champagne bottle, and* POLLY *starts for the bedroom*)

POLLY What should I wear? How about the blue chiffon?

EVY You can wear black crepe as long as your boobs don't bounce around.

(She moves toward the kitchen)

POLLY *(At the bedroom door)* Mother?

EVY Yes?

POLLY Don't take that job. You're too good for it. Hold out for something better.

EVY I'm so glad you said that. Who the Christ even knows where Garden City is? . . . Hey, let's have a good time tonight. I'm beginning to feel like my old self again.

POLLY Hey, listen, I forgot to tell you. We have a lunch date tomorrow.

EVY *(In kitchen, busy with bottles)* Who has a lunch date?

POLLY We do. You, me and Daddy.

(EVY *stops what she's doing and comes out to the kitchen doorway*)

EVY *(Dismayed)* *What* Daddy?

POLLY *My* Daddy. You remember, Felicia's husband? . . . Twelve o'clock at Rumpelmayer's.

EVY Why didn't you tell me?

POLLY Because I never see you. *Now* I see you. He just wants to have lunch with us, talk, see how we're getting along.

EVY We're getting along fine.

POLLY He knows. He just wants to see.

EVY You mean he's checking to see what shape I'm in? Christ, he's going to look in my ears, under my fingernails—I'll never pass.

POLLY He just wants to talk.

EVY Is he gonna ask questions, like what's the capital of Bulgaria?

POLLY Stop worrying. It'll be all right. I've got to get dressed. Oh, and if he does, the capital is Sofia.

(She goes into the bedroom)

EVY *(Standing there a moment)* Just what I needed. A physical examination in Rumpelmayer's. *(Starts into the kitchen)* I should have had *two* sherrys today.

(There is a moment's pause. The doorbell rings)

POLLY Are you getting it?

EVY *(Comes out of the kitchen)* If I was getting it I wouldn't be looking for jobs all day . . . Get dressed. *(*EVY *crosses to the door and opens it.* JIMMY *stands there, looking glum and expressionless. He walks past her into the room.* EVY *closes the door)* No kiss? . . . No hello? . . . Aren't you going to look up, maybe you're in the wrong apartment? *(*JIMMY *sits without taking off his coat. He chews his thumbnail. His leg begins to shake)* If you're that hungry, have some nuts. *(He doesn't acknowledge)* What's the matter? What happened?

JIMMY *(His leg is still shaking)* I'm okay, I'm not upset any more, I'm all right . . . I know my leg is shaking but I'm all right.

EVY Why? What's wrong?

JIMMY They pushed the opening of the show back one night . . . It's opening Tuesday instead of Monday.

EVY All right, it's Tuesday instead of Monday. What's so terrible?

JIMMY It's also another actor instead of me. They fired me. The little son of a bitch fired me three nights before the opening.

EVY Oh, Christ.

JIMMY Fired by a nineteen-year-old producer from Oklahoma A&M . . . Look at that leg. Do you realize the tension that must be going on in my body right now?

EVY Oh, Jimmy, no, don't tell me.

JIMMY If he didn't like me, why'd he hire me in the first place, heh? . . . The entire cast is shocked. Shocked, Evy. Three nights before the opening.

EVY They must be shocked.

JIMMY He didn't even get somebody else to tell me. He wanted to tell me himself . . . He stood there with a little smile on his goddamned baby face and said, "Sorry, Jimmy, it's just not working out." Nineteen years old, can you imagine, Evy? . . . Ten thousand kids a month getting drafted and they leave *this* one behind to produce my show.

EVY What can I say? What can I do?

JIMMY Three nights before the opening. My name was in the Sunday *Times* ad. I've got eighteen relatives from Paterson, New Jersey, coming to the opening. Six of them already sent me telegrams . . . My Aunt Rosario sent me a Candygram. I already ate the goddamned candy.

EVY Oh, God, I can't bear it. Tell me what to do for you.

JIMMY Everybody in the cast wanted to walk out on the show. I wouldn't let them. Even the director was crazy about me . . . I can't breathe, I can't catch my breath, I'm so upset . . . I gotta calm down, Evy, I'll be all right.

EVY I know how you feel. I swear. I know exactly how you feel.

JIMMY You do? You know how it feels for a grown man to plead and beg to a child, Evy? A *child!* . . . I said to him, "You're not happy, I'll do it any way you want. Faster, slower, louder, I'll wear a dress, I'll shave my head, I'll relieve myself on the stage in front of my own family— I'm an actor, give me a chance to act." . . . He turned his back on me and shoved a Tootsie Roll in his mouth.

EVY Listen, maybe the play won't be a hit. Maybe it'll be a bomb—it'll close in one night. You're lucky you're out of it.

JIMMY What do you mean, maybe? It's got no chance. It's the worst piece of crap ever put on a stage. That's why

I'm so humiliated. To get fired from a piece of garbage like that, who's gonna want me for something good?

EVY *(Puts her arm around him)* Screw him, sweetheart, you don't need them. *(She hugs him)* Something better'll come along.

JIMMY When? Next Christmas at Korvette's? *(He pulls away from her)* Do you know who they gave my part to? The understudy. He's not even a full-time actor, he drives a cab in the day . . . A Puerto Rican cabdriver. Can't speak English. He got me coffee the first two weeks, now he's got my part . . . Look how my neck is throbbing. That's blood pumping into the brain, I'm going to have a hemorrhage.

EVY You're not going to have a hemorrhage.

JIMMY What am I going to tell my family in Jersey? My sister's taking my twelve-year-old niece, her first time in the theater, never saw me on the stage, she's gonna think she's got a Puerto Rican uncle . . . I was thinking maybe I wouldn't tell anyone. Opening night I'll show up in the theater, walk out on the stage. Two of us will play the same part, one in Spanish, one in English—the critics will love it.

EVY Whatever you say. You want the theater blown up, the kid rubbed out—I'm in with the Mafia, they'd be glad to do it. (JIMMY *still has not removed his sheepskin coat*) . . . But I don't want you upset, not tonight. It's Toby's birthday, I'm counting on you for laughs.

JIMMY *(Looks at his hand)* Look at my fingers. There's no color in the nails. That's a hemorrhage. I'm having a goddamned hemorrhage and I can't find it.

EVY *(Crosses to him, tries to take his coat off)* Give me your coat. Come on, give me your coat, for chrissakes, you wanna catch pneumonia?

JIMMY What the hell difference does it make?

(But JIMMY *suddenly buries his face in his hands and begins to sob, deeply and uncontrollably)*

EVY *(Almost withers at the sight)* Oh, God, Jimmy, no, don't. *(She wrings her hands helplessly)* Jimmy, listen, you can't do this to me . . . Stop it, Jimmy, you hear? I won't stand for it.

JIMMY *(Sobbing)* What the hell am I going to do?

EVY You're not going to crack up on me. I'm not going to get stuck with a dud party. Come on, Jimmy . . .

JIMMY *(Still sobbing)* Who am I kidding, Evy? I'm not going to make it, I'm *never* going to make it in this business.

EVY Go ahead. You want to destroy me? You want to tear my guts out? You know I can't handle it.

JIMMY Twenty-two years and I'm still expecting to get discovered. The oldest goddamned newcomer in show business.

EVY *(Near tears)* Listen, you bastard, if *I* start to cry, it's all over. You really want to see crying? I'll make you look foolish.

JIMMY I should have stayed at Bonwit's. I'd have been a floorwalker today.

EVY No you wouldn't, because you're going to become a star. A great big star! You're already a shitheel—there's no point in wasting it.

JIMMY *(Grabs* EVY *and clings to her)* Don't say anything. Don't say anything to Toby.

EVY I won't. I promise. Not a word.

JIMMY Evy, you've seen me on the stage. You know I can be good. Was I good, Evy? Tell me—I really have to know.

EVY You're the best. There's no one better. You ring a doorbell, the house comes down . . . Let me get you a drink. You'll feel much better if you have a drink.

JIMMY I'm not Olivier. I never said I was Olivier, did I?

EVY I don't even like Olivier. I can't understand him half the time.

(She goes into the kitchen)

JIMMY *(Talking into the kitchen)* Remember *Mr. Roberts* at Bucks County? Or *Born Yesterday* in Westport? I never heard laughs like that in my life . . . Did you? The truth! Did you?

EVY *(Offstage)* I have never heard laughs like that in my life.

JIMMY In my life, I never heard laughs like that . . . And I don't have to get laughs all the time. My God, the things I've done . . . *Phaedra, Mother Courage, Rhinoceros, The Balcony, Detective Story* . . . Jesus, remember *Detective Story?* The second hood? I was incredible.

EVY *(Offstage)* You were brilliant.

(We hear a cork pop from a champagne bottle)

JIMMY When did you see me in *Detective Story?* I did that in Columbus, Ohio.

EVY *(Comes out with the champagne bottle and two glasses)* You were so brilliant I didn't have to see it.

(She hands JIMMY *a glass. He takes it without being aware he has it)*

JIMMY I played the Dauphin in *St. Joan* at the Cleveland Auditorium three years before that nineteen-year-old rich Oklahoma idiot schmuck was born.

(EVY *pours champagne into his glass, then hers)*

EVY (*Takes a sip*) Forget it. He's not worth it.

JIMMY I actually pleaded with him. I humiliated myself in front of the entire cast. I had no shame. No shame, Evy. *(He drinks)* Opening night my mother will throw herself in front of a rented limousine.

EVY That's the best thing that could happen to *your* mother.

(She sips a little more)

JIMMY I don't wish anybody in the world harm. I don't curse anybody. I want everybody to live their lives healthy and without pain . . . But I pray that little bastard gets a Baby Ruth stuck in his throat and chokes him on the spot. *(He drinks more champagne.* EVY *pours more into his glass. He suddenly watches her and realizes what's happening)*

Oh, my God, what am I doing? I'm sitting here drinking with you. Are you crazy? Are you out of your mind? Put that glass down.

(He reaches for it, but she pulls it away)

EVY I'm not drinking, I'm sipping.

JIMMY You've already sipped a whole glass. Give it to me.

EVY You think I'm going to stand here and watch you have a breakdown on ginger ale? I need help too.

JIMMY You put your lips to that glass one more time, you're going to need more than help.

EVY *(Holds the glass up)* All right, I'm through, I'm through. *(Then she raises the glass to her lips and finishes it)* There! All right?

JIMMY Why do you do that to me? Didn't I have enough heartache today?

EVY A grown man is crying, you want me to sit down and read *Newsweek?* I'm sorry, I panicked.

JIMMY You didn't panic, you drank. Panicking is when you scream and run around like a lunatic.

EVY I will. I promise. Next time I'll panic. Better still, don't tell me your problems. You got a twelve-year-old niece, tell her your troubles. Kids love to cry.

JIMMY *(Turns away from her)* I'm standing there drinking with her. I see the glass in her hand and I'm drinking with her.

EVY *(Walks around in front of him to get his attention)* Don't be mad at me. Everybody's mad at me today. Show me a little tenderness, I'll show you a terrific person.

JIMMY *(Looks at her; he wilts)* How could I be mad at you? You loved me in *Detective Story* and never even saw it.

(He hugs her. The doorbell rings)

EVY *(In a low voice)* Don't tell Polly. Don't tell her I drank, tell her I panicked.

JIMMY Some mood I'm in for a party. Christ!

EVY *(Calls out)* Hey, Pol, come on, they're here.

POLLY *(Offstage)* I don't know how to work the brassière.

EVY *(At the door; to* JIMMY*)* Try and be happy tonight. You won't have to do it for another year. (JIMMY *nods cheerlessly at her. She opens the door.* TOBY *stands there, looking absolutely ravishing in a new dress. She smiles at* EVY) Oh, God, that's a pretty woman. Look, Jimmy. Look at the pretty woman.

JIMMY *(Smiles)* Oh, yes. That's a pretty woman.

EVY (*To* JIMMY) Go, sweetheart. Go kiss the pretty woman.

(JIMMY *crosses in front of* EVY *and kisses* TOBY *on the cheek*)

JIMMY Happy birthday, darling.

TOBY *(Smiles)* Thank you.

(*She speaks softly.* EVY *crosses to* TOBY)

EVY Happy birthday, pretty woman. (*She hugs* TOBY)

TOBY Thank you, Evelyn.

(She goes to the sofa and sits down, opening her purse)

EVY *(Looks toward the outside hall)* Isn't Marty with you?

TOBY No.

(JIMMY *closes the door*)

EVY Is he coming later?

TOBY *(Busy powdering)* I don't think so.

EVY (*Looks at* JIMMY, *then at* TOBY) You don't *think* so? Don't you know?

TOBY Yes, I know. He's not coming later. *(Looks around)* Isn't Polly here?

EVY He's not coming for your birthday party? . . . Are you going to tell me he's *working* tonight?

TOBY No, he's not working. He just couldn't come. To my birthday party.

(She takes out the powder puff again and begins to powder her already highly powdered face)

EVY Why not?

TOBY Well, I didn't catch everything he said . . . because he was very busy packing . . . but it seems that Martin wants a divorce. *(She smiles at them as though she has told them nothing more startling than "it's raining outside."* JIMMY *and* EVY *stare at her, stunned.* TOBY *suddenly controls the flood of tears that are threatening to come by patting her hand to her eye, but we do hear a faint sigh from her)* Is there anything to eat in the refrigerator?

(She gets up and quickly crosses into the kitchen to release the floodgates)

JIMMY *(Looks up to heaven, clasping his hands)* Oh, sweet Mother of Jesus! You just going to stand there? Say something to her? Do something. *(But* EVY *stands there)* Toby! Toby!

(He runs off to the kitchen after TOBY. EVY *turns, looks around, sees that no one is looking and quickly pours herself a glass of champagne. She drinks it quickly, then puts the glass down.* POLLY *emerges from the bedroom, looking lovely and feminine)*

POLLY *(Arms extended)* Happy birthday! *(Looks around)* Where's the birthday lady?

EVY *(Motions toward the kitchen)* With the great American actor.

POLLY Do I look all right?

EVY *(Despondent)* Don't count on applause.

(JIMMY *comes out of the kitchen*)

JIMMY She's all right. Give her a couple of seconds. (*To* POLLY) Hello, Angel. Don't you look gorgeous.

POLLY *(Beaming)* I was thinking of wearing this for your opening. Okay? (JIMMY *looks at* EVY, *then crosses away.* POLLY *looks at them, then to* EVY) I detect tenseness. Is there tenseness at this party?

EVY And it's only ten after nine.

(TOBY *comes out of the kitchen. She seems composed*)

TOBY I love the cake, Evy. It's a beautiful cake . . . Oh, Polly, how sweet. How sweet and beautiful you are. I was the same way.

POLLY *(Goes to her)* Happy birthday, Toby.

(They kiss)

TOBY Thank you, darling. It's so good to see you. I never see you. I was so anxious to see you tonight and spend some time with you. I never spend enough time with you. Would you excuse us, darling, I have to talk to your mother.

POLLY *(Puzzled)* Now?

EVY Now.

POLLY *(Shrugs)* I'll study French. Call me when the games begin. *(She goes into the bedroom)*

TOBY She's going to be beautiful, Evy. There is nothing so important in a woman's life as being beautiful . . . *(There is a pause. No one says anything)* Anyone want to hear about my divorce?

JIMMY You're not serious. You had a fight. That's all it was, a little fight, right?

TOBY No, there's going to be an actual divorce. He is, at the very moment we're speaking, getting advice from his brother, the lawyer, and sympathy from his understanding sister-in-law who happens to know a great deal about sympathy because of those two huge warts on the side of her nose . . . I'm fine. I'm perfectly fine. Really.

EVY What happened tonight? Don't describe what you were wearing, just the details.

TOBY There are no details. He wants a divorce, it's that simple . . . Do you have any canapés, darling, I think I forgot to eat in all the excitement.

EVY You caught him at the Americana Hotel with a stewardess from Delta Airlines, right?

TOBY It wouldn't bother me if I caught him at his brother's house with his sister-in-law . . . Or his sister's house with his brother-in-law . . . It's not another woman.

JIMMY Then what is it?

TOBY I must have something to drink.

EVY *(To JIMMY)* The ladies need a drink.

JIMMY *(Quickly)* *I'll* get it.

(He moves hurriedly and gets the champagne bottle from where EVY left it, and pours a glass for TOBY)

TOBY *(Takes a deep breath)* Martin—has grown accustomed to my face. *(She is visibly wounded but is trying hard not to show the hurt)* Accustomed to my touch, accustomed to my voice . . . and I think he's a little bored with my hair. *(She looks at them, forces a smile, sips a little wine)* He's devoted to me . . . He is respectful of me . . . He is indebted to me . . . but he's having a lot of trouble sleeping with me. For some inexplicable reason—"inexplicable" is his word—he has had no desire to make sexual advances towards me. He makes them, but there's no desire. It's as though someone were in back of him "pushing" . . . He is not tired . . . He is not overworked . . . He is not distracted . . . He is simply—"turned off." That's *my* word.

JIMMY *(About to say something helpful)* Toby, for God's sakes—

TOBY Did you know . . . that in 1950 I was voted the prettiest girl at the University of Michigan? . . . An All-American halfback was willing to give up a trip to the Rose Bowl for one night of my favors . . . In 1951 I switched schools and was voted the prettiest girl at the University of Southern California . . . I received, on the average, fifteen sexual proposals a week—at least two from the faculty—

EVY All right, Toby—

TOBY When I was sixteen I was offered a seven-year contract by RKO Pictures. They knew I couldn't act; they didn't even care. They said the way I looked, it wasn't important . . . When I was seventeen years old, a married psychiatrist in Los Angeles drove his car into a tree because I wouldn't answer his phone calls. You can read all of this in my diaries, I still have them.

EVY Toby, please stop.

TOBY When I was nineteen I had an affair with a boy who was the son of the largest book publisher in the world . . . When I was twenty, I had an affair *with* the largest book publisher in the world . . . The son threatened to kill the father but by then I was having an affair with the youngest symphony conductor in the world.

EVY Jimmy, for God's sakes, will you say something to her?

TOBY *(Accelerating)* When I was twenty-three, I *slept* with a member of the British Royal Household. I slept with him. In the British Royal House . . . There is a Senator living in Washington, D.C., today who will vote any way I want him to vote by my spending just one morning in Washington, D.C. . . . I have had more men—men in politics, in the arts, in the sciences, more of the most influential men in the world—in love with me, desirous of me, *hungry* for me, than any woman I ever met in my entire life . . . And that son-of-a-bitch four-hundred-dollar-a-week television salesman tells me *he isn't interested? . . . Then let him get out, I don't need him! (And she begins to sob uncontrollably)* Evy . . . Evy!

(EVY, *of course, is distraught with her own inability to help*)

EVY *(Paces)* Jimmy, do something or I'll kill myself.

(JIMMY *quickly crosses to* TOBY *and sits on the arm of her chair, putting his arm around her to comfort her*)

JIMMY It's all right, Toby, it's all right.

TOBY (*Looks up at* JIMMY) I am still beautiful and I am still desirable, I don't care how old I am.

JIMMY Of course you are, my God! . . . Evy, give her some more wine.

TOBY (*To* EVY) Evy, no woman has ever taken care of herself the way I have. (EVY *goes to the champagne bottle*) I am forty years old today, and my skin is as smooth and as creamy white as it was when I was sixteen.

(EVY *hands* JIMMY *a glass of champagne*)

JIMMY (*Giving the glass to* TOBY) Drink this. Come on, Toby, you'll feel better.

TOBY We spent two months on the beach at Westhampton last summer, and the sun never once touched my body . . . I wore more clothes on the beach than I do in New York in January . . . In Acapulco last year the Mexicans thought I was some kind of a White Goddess. They would bow to me on the streets. Jimmy, remember I told you that story?

JIMMY I remember that story.

TOBY *(Addressing* EVY *again)* Last December in Los Angeles, that boy I had an affair with, the book publisher's son, called me at the Beverly Hills Hotel, *dying* to see me. He came over and we had cocktails in the Polo Lounge . . . He looked like my father. My *father*, Evy . . . And then the waiter came over and, I swear—may God strike me dead as I sit here with my dearest friends—the waiter asked for my I.D. card . . . I don't even think it's twenty-one in California, I think you have to be eighteen. I know it's dark in the Polo Lounge, but it's not *that* dark.

JIMMY (*To* EVY, *as though it would help* TOBY) It's not, I've been there, I know.

TOBY *(Sips a little more champagne)* I'm not a stupid woman, I know that. I've traveled a lot, I'm well-read, well-educated, I went to two universities. I have had marvelous intellectual conversations with some of the most brilliant men in the world . . . but the thing that men admire most in a woman is her femininity and her beauty . . . That's the truth, Evy, I know it is. (*To* JIMMY) Isn't that the first thing you men look for in a woman, Jimmy?

JIMMY *(Hesitates)* Yes, I suppose it is.

TOBY (*Back to* EVY) I know I'm vain, Evy. I never pretended I'm not. I devote my whole day to myself, to my face, to my body . . . I sleep all morning so my eyes won't be red. I bathe twice a day in soft water. I buy the world's most expensive creams. I have a Japanese man who lives in White Plains come down twice a week just to do my feet. Did you know that, Evy? (EVY *nods.* TOBY *turns to* JIMMY) Did you?

JIMMY I didn't know he was Japanese.

TOBY I swear. He says I have the feet of an Oriental woman. Can you imagine, Evy. Born in Grand Rapids, Michigan, with the feet of an Oriental woman . . . But I've never done it for *me.* None of it . . . It's what Martin wanted when he came into his house at night, what all men want—femininity and beauty . . . But Evy, if it no longer interests Martin, then I assure you . . . somewhere, soon, someplace, someone else will be very . . . very . . . very . . . interested!

(Her voice has trailed off, becoming almost inaudible at the end. There is a long, desperate silence in the room)

EVY *(Finally)* For purely medicinal purposes, I'm having a drink.

(She starts for the bottle)

JIMMY *(Warning)* Evy!

EVY I'm only a hundred and thirty pounds but if you try and stop me, I'll kill you . . . *One* drink, for chrissakes.

JIMMY You *had* one drink.

EVY For *your* story. Now I need one for hers.

(She pours a drink)

TOBY *(Looks up as if in the room for the first time)* What's the matter? What's going on?

EVY *Nothing's* going on, but it's going to start right now . . . We've *all* had a few minor setbacks, but it's a birthday party—and I don't give a crap if the room is on fire, we're going to start having some fun. *(She drinks quickly from her wine glass, then looks at the bottle and holds it up)* We need a new bottle. *(Calls out)* Polly! Fun and games.

TOBY *(Pulling her things together)* I'm not staying, I just wanted to talk to someone.

EVY Nobody's leaving this room until we're all happy. Now sit down, dammit. Drink your booze. *(She drinks a little more from her glass. The wine is now beginning to take effect on* EVY*; since she is an alcoholic, it doesn't take much wine or time)* Jesus, what a bunch of depressing people.

(POLLY *comes out)*

POLLY *(With a big smile)* Okay, who do I dance with?

EVY (*Points to* POLLY) Now *that's* the kind of person you invite to a party. (*To* POLLY) So far it's just you and me, kid, but we're gonna goose things up. Put on one of your records. I'll get some more wine. *(Starts for the kitchen)* And none of that folk-singing crap where they throw babies in the Talahachee River. I want some real music, pussycat.

(She goes off into the kitchen)

POLLY *(Looks after her)* Is she all right? What's going on?

JIMMY Nothing. Everything's fine.

TOBY I think I must have upset her. Did I upset her, Jimmy?

JIMMY It's not you, it's everybody. We're all upsetting each other. Some friends . . .

POLLY She had a drink at Schrafft's this afternoon, did she tell you?

JIMMY At Schrafft's? Who the hell goes off the wagon at Schrafft's?

TOBY I shouldn't have said all that to her. I could see she was very upset.

(They both look worriedly toward EVY *in the kitchen . . . A cork explodes.* EVY *comes out with an opened bottle of champagne)*

EVY Goddamned cheap champagne—I had to make the noise with my tongue. Glasses up, everyone. (*She looks at the silent phonograph, then at* POLLY) You're not going to play that louder, right?

POLLY *(Going for the bottle)* Let me pour it, Mother.

EVY Ooh, you hear that? Mother, she calls me. If it's one thing I know how to get, it's respect.

TOBY Evy, don't pay attention to what I said before. Everything's going to be all right, honestly.

EVY (*To* TOBY) No, listen, you have a major problem. You and Marty are only making it two times a day, if I were you, I'd kill myself.

(She pours wine into TOBY's *glass)*

TOBY *(Embarrassed)* Evy, please. Can we discuss this later?

EVY What's the matter? You're worried about Polly? *My* Polly? You don't know about kids today, do you? (*She puts her arm around* POLLY) She could give you a sex lecture right now, your eyebrows would fall out. (*To* POLLY) Am I right? Is that the truth, Polly?

(POLLY *forces a smile and shrugs*)

JIMMY May I have the wine, please?

EVY What do you think, kids learn about sex today the way you and I did? In rumble seats? They have closed-circuit television—(*To* POLLY) Am I right? Actual demonstrations. Two substitute teachers go at it in the gymnasium and the kids take notes. Is that the truth?

POLLY *(Smiles, embarrassed)* That's the truth.

EVY It's the truth. Polly has a sixteen-year-old girl friend in school who got knocked up for homework. Am I lying? Heh?

POLLY *(Weakly)* Nope.

EVY (EVY *pours some wine into her own glass and drinks it. She laughs)* Oh, Christ, that's funny. *(No one else laughs)* Look how funny you all think it is . . . Gee, what a terrific party. Later on we'll get some fluid and embalm each other. Polly, get a glass. You have to drink to Toby's birthday.

POLLY *(Reaches for the bottle)* Can I pour it myself?

EVY *(Holding back the bottle)* What's the matter, you don't trust me? One glass, that's all I'm going to have . . . My daughter is worried about me. *(She puts her arm around* POLLY *again)* Do you know what it is to have a daughter worried about you? It is the *single greatest* pleasure in the world . . . In the *world* . . . (*To* TOBY) You can have your toes tickled by a Jap—I'll take a daughter worrying about me any time. *(She sips from her glass. She is beginning to lose coordination and control)* I don't even deserve it. The truth, Polly, I don't deserve it. You grew up, you saw the bus driver more than you saw me, am I right?

JIMMY Polly, why don't you get the cake?

EVY No, it's all right, Polly and I understand each other. We have an agreement. She doesn't bug me about the past and I don't bug her about not wearing underwear.

TOBY Evy, stop, you're embarrassing her.

EVY I am not. Am I embarrassing you, sweetheart? I'm not embarrassing you, am I?

POLLY *(Good-naturedly)* I'll let you embarrass me if you let me take your glass.

EVY *(Holds the glass away from* POLLY *but ignores her remark)* I told you I'm not embarrassing her. I mean the girl is *beautiful.* Toby, if you saw her sleeping in the raw you'd kill yourself. It's all firm. Remember "firm"? . . . You don't remember firm.

POLLY *(Forcing a smile)* Okay, *now* I'm getting embarrassed.

EVY *(Going right on)* The body of a young woman is God's greatest achievement . . . Of course, He could have built it to last longer, but you can't have everything.

TOBY Evy, it's my birthday and you're not making me very happy. Let's not have any more wine.

EVY Why doesn't everybody relax? It's like a goddamn telethon for palsy. Come on, a toast. A toast for my friend Toby. Jimmy, you do it. You're the toastmaster . . . A toast, everyone.

JIMMY Evy, I don't think anyone's in the mood.

EVY Well, *put* 'em in the mood. What else you got to do? You're not working!

(She pulls the reluctant JIMMY *to the middle of the floor)*

JIMMY I'm never good at these things. I never know what to say.

EVY Glasses up, everyone.

(She stands next to POLLY. EVY *seems to be unaware of the tension she is causing in the room. Once on alcohol, she enters a world of her own)*

JIMMY *(Holds up his glass)* To Toby . . . whom we all love and cherish. Happy birthday.

POLLY Happy birthday, Toby.

(They all drink)

TOBY Thank you.

EVY That's the toast? Sounds like she died of leukemia. "Fifty dollars donation in memory of Toby Landau, who we loved and cherished . . ." She's alive, for chrissakes—tell her what a great broad she is.

TOBY It was a lovely toast, Evy . . . and I'm very touched.

EVY You're a great broad, Toby. I want you to know it. Only one who came to see me in the hospital. I'll never forget you for that—

TOBY Evy, stop, I'm going to cry again.

EVY I don't care if you whistle Dixie through your ass, I'm telling you I love you . . . (TOBY *looks at* POLLY) Whoops, sorry, Polly. Mother's being naughty.

(She pours some more wine into her glass)

JIMMY Evy, will you give me that bottle?

EVY When it's empty, pussycat.

POLLY Mother, should I get the cake now?

EVY I'll *tell* you when to get the cake. I'm not ready for the cake yet. What the hell's the big rush with the cake? I didn't rent it, I bought it outright . . . I'm still telling Toby how much I love her. *(She points to* TOBY *with the hand holding the glass. The wine spills on* TOBY*'s dress)* Oh, Christ, Jesus, I'm sorry . . . *(Tries wiping it with her hand)* On your birthday, got you right in the crotch . . . Polly, get me a Kleenex or something.

TOBY It's all right, it'll dry.

EVY It's ruined. Your two-hundred-and-fifty-dollar dress is ruined . . . Listen, I want you to take my mink coat. I paid thirty-two hundred bucks for it in 1941. You can get about four dollars for it now and I'll pay you a little bit each week.

(She's still rubbing TOBY*'s dress)*

TOBY Evy, it's all right, it's an old dress.

EVY No kidding? I'll buy it from you. What do you want, about twenty dollars? I mean, it's not worth more, it's got a goddamned wine stain right in the front.

JIMMY Polly, why don't you get the cake?

EVY *(Screams)* Don't you touch that cake! I'm emceeing this party—

TOBY Evy, please don't drink any more.

JIMMY Evy, I'm asking you nicely for the last time. Put down the wine.

EVY I am. I'm putting it down as fast as I can. (*She crosses to* TOBY) Listen, I got a first-class idea. Why don't you two move in with us? We don't need anybody else . . . Just us four girls. What do you say?

TOBY *(About to fall apart)* Evy, I've got to go. *(Crossing the room)* Thank you for the party.

EVY What party? Two salted peanuts, everyone took turns crying, and you fink out on me.

TOBY Evy, I can't sit here and watch what's happening. *(At the door)* Polly, take care of her. I'll call you in the morning . . . (*To* EVY) Evy—I'm sorry if I did this to you.

(She can't say any more; she turns and runs out)

EVY *(Calls out)* Wait a minute. Your present. I didn't give you your present. Polly, get her back.

POLLY She's gone, Mother.

EVY (*Playfully goes to* JIMMY) I believe this is your dance, Colonel Sanders, and by the way, I love your finger-lickin' chicken.

JIMMY Evy, Evy, you stupid bitch.

EVY Hey, hey, watch that kind of talk. I have a daughter here someplace.

JIMMY Then why do you act this way in front of her?

POLLY Jimmy, it's all right.

JIMMY It's *not* all right. She's drunk and disgusting and she doesn't give a damn about herself or anyone else. Well, then damn it, neither do I. Go on. Finish the bottle. Finish the whole goddamn case, for all I care.

EVY Okay, buster, you just talked yourself out of an opening-night party.

JIMMY And you just drank yourself out of a couple of friends. I don't want to see you any more, Evy. I swear to God. I am through. Finished forever, I've *had* it . . . Goodbye, Polly, I'm sorry.

(He goes quickly to the door)

EVY How about a little kiss goodbye? *(She grabs his arm)* Come on, one little kiss on the lips. It'll make all the New York papers.

JIMMY Let go of me, damn it!

(He wrenches from EVY *and runs out, leaving the door open.* EVY *rushes to the door and yells out)*

EVY *(Pleading)* Jimmy! Jimmy, come back, I'm sorry . . . Jimmy, don't leave me, you're the only man in my life. *(But he's gone. She comes back into the apartment.* EVY *tries to compose herself in front of* POLLY*)* I guess this would be a good time to get the cake.

POLLY I'm not hungry. I've got homework to do. I'll clean up later.

EVY Oh, you're mad at me. I don't know what I did, but you're mad at me, right?

POLLY I'm not mad at you, Mother.

EVY What then? You're ashamed? Ashamed of your sweet little old mother because she had two tiny glasses of domestic wine?

POLLY I'm not ashamed.

EVY *Then what are you?*

POLLY I'm sorry . . . I'm just plain sorry.

(She looks at EVY*, then slowly goes into the bedroom and closes the door behind her.* EVY *stands there)*

EVY *(Loudly)* Sorry for what? For me? Well, don't be sorry for me because I don't need your goddamned teen-age pity . . . I'm terrific, baby, haven't you noticed? Cost me twenty-seven hundred bucks and I'm skinny and terrific and I can have any dirty old man in the neighborhood . . . *(Suddenly softening)* Oh, Jesus, Polly, I'm sorry *(Crosses to the bedroom door)* Polly, don't be mad . . . Come on out. We'll have our own private party . . . Look! Look, I'm gonna put on some music. *(Goes to the record player)* I've just had a request to play one of my old numbers. *(Takes out her album)* Come listen to mother sing when she was a big star, darling. *(Puts the record on the machine)* Well, not exactly a big star . . . But I once had a sandwich named after me at the Stage Delicatessen . . . *(The music starts. We hear* EVY *singing. She stands there listening, drinking from the wine glass)* That's not bad, is it? It's not bad . . . It's not *thrilling* but it's not bad. *(She sings along, looking around the room)* This is about the same size audiences I used to get.

(She crosses to the bedroom door) Polly, please come out . . . I don't want to listen to me all by myself . . . Polly? *(No answer. She looks at the phone)* I am *not* going to listen all by myself . . . *(She crosses to phone, takes a deep breath and dials. Into the phone)* . . . Hello? Lou? . . . You alone? . . . Guess who wants to come over to your place?

Curtain

Act Three

It is the following morning, Saturday, about eleven o'clock. POLLY *is seated on the piano bench, staring aimlessly and worriedly.* TOBY, *in a polo coat over pajamas, sits on a chair, nervously smoking.*

TOBY I'm not worried.

POLLY You've told me that since eight o'clock this morning, Toby.

TOBY *(Puffs again)* She's all right. She's done this before. I am not worried.

POLLY Is that why you've had nine cigarettes since you got here?

TOBY I have other problems on my mind besides your mother's disappearance. *(Puffs)* If I get nicotine stains on my teeth, I'll never forgive her.

POLLY She just walks out and disappears all night without saying a word. Where the hell could she be?

TOBY Don't swear, darling, your mother wouldn't like it . . . You really should get some sleep, angel. You're going to get little ugly puffy rings under your eyes.

POLLY I'm sorry, Toby. I've never gone through this before.

TOBY She's put me through it for twelve years. That's why I wear such heavy make-up. Underneath this is my mother.

POLLY *(Determined)* I'm not going to forgive her, Toby, I swear . . . The minute I hear she's all right, I'm not going to forgive her.

(She starts to cry, rushes into the bedroom and closes the door behind her. TOBY *picks up her coffee cup and starts to go into the kitchen, when the door opens. It's* EVY, *hiding her face)*

TOBY Well, good morning.

EVY That's entirely possible.

TOBY Do you know what time it is?

EVY 'November?

TOBY Evy!

EVY Later, Toby. I have to go to the john.

TOBY I refuse to talk to your unbrushed hair all morning. Turn around and look at me. (EVY *turns around, revealing a black-and-blue eye*) Oh, God—your eye! Evy, what have you done?

EVY You want to be my friend, Toby? No questions and no sympathy. I'm all right.

TOBY I don't think I *want* to hear about it.

EVY Where's Polly?

TOBY She's been up all night calling everyone. I made her go in and lie down.

EVY Well, if she sleeps for three weeks I may get away with it.

TOBY You don't seem to be acting much like a woman who just got beaten up.

EVY I didn't get beaten, Toby, just punched. One clean little punch, I never even felt it.

TOBY Really? Have you seen what you look like?

EVY Compared to you, what difference does it make? . . . I'm all right, I promise you.

TOBY Sit down. Let me put some ice on it.

EVY I've already had medical attention. A dog licked my face while I was down.

TOBY Who did it?

EVY What difference does it make?

TOBY Because I feel responsible.

EVY Come on, Toby. I got what I asked for last night because I wasn't getting anything else. *(She sits)* All right, I'm sitting. Are you happy now?

TOBY How can I be happy when your face is half smashed in? How many places did you have to go before you found what you were looking for?

EVY Just one. If there's one thing I know how to do, it's shop.

TOBY *(Turns away)* Oh, Christ, Evy, sometimes you disgust me.

EVY That seems to be the general feeling around town.

TOBY It was Lou Tanner, wasn't it?

EVY That's him. The man I love.

TOBY Jesus, I knew it. There was always something about him that frightened me. You could see it in his eyes.

EVY Never mind the eyes, it's the big fist you gotta watch . . . I wouldn't hate you if you left me alone now, Toby.

TOBY Why did you go there, Evy?

EVY He plays requests—I was lonesome.

TOBY Why did you start drinking yesterday? Everything was going so good for you. Why, Evy?

EVY What do you want, a nice simple answer? When I was six years old my father didn't take me to the circus . . . How the hell do I know why I do anything?

TOBY Didn't you learn anything in ten weeks at the hospital?

EVY The doctor tried to explain, but I was too busy making a pass at him . . . If I knew, Toby, would it make any difference?

TOBY It would help.

EVY If you haven't eaten in three months you don't want a description of food, you want a little hot something in the plate.

TOBY And did you get your fill last night, Evy? Did you get your little hot something in the plate?

EVY No, but we negotiated for a while . . .

TOBY With someone like that? A deadbeat musician who doesn't give a damn about hitting some drunken woman.

EVY You just don't get hit like that, you gotta ask for it . . . I happened to make a bad choice. I broke his guitar. I smashed it against the refrigerator, handed him the pieces and said, "Now you can look for work you're equipped to do." I thought it was cute. The man has no sense of humor.

TOBY The truth, Evy. When he was beating you, did you enjoy it?

EVY Well, for a second there I said to myself, it hurts like hell—but it sure beats indifference. *(She gets up)* Is there anything in the kitchen? I'm always hungry after a fight.

TOBY *(Angrily)* What fight? There was no fight. You just stood there and let him beat the crap out of you.

EVY That's right, pussycat.

TOBY The way you let *everybody* beat the crap out of you.

EVY Same as you. Only Marty doesn't punch, he just walks out on you. In your own adorable way, you're no better off than I am.

TOBY *(Still angry)* At least my face isn't beaten to a pulp.

EVY Terrific. You spent forty years being gorgeous and all you've got to show for it is a turned-up little nose . . . We cried for you yesterday; today is my turn.

TOBY At least I've *tried* to make things work. I've at least made the *effort.*

EVY The only effort you make is opening your compact. If you powdered Marty once in a while instead of your face, you'd be wearing *his* pajamas now instead of yours.

TOBY I powdered my goddamned face because I was afraid every time Marty looked at me too closely. Afraid he'd see what I was becoming.

EVY Terrific. Why don't you spend the rest of your life in the Beverly Hills Polo Lounge? You can put on a Shirley Temple dress and suck a lollipop . . . And next year you'll have an affair with the book publisher's grandson . . .

TOBY Go to hell.

EVY Toby, you know I love you. We're the same kind of broads. We both manage to screw up everything . . . The only difference is, you dress better doing it.

TOBY Damn you, Evy. Damn you for being so goddamned honest all the time. Who needs the truth if this is what it gets you?

EVY Listen, I'm willing to live a lie. As far as I'm concerned, I'm twenty-two with a cute little behind. Now find me a fellow who believes it.

TOBY You're not twenty-two, you're forty-three. And you're an alcoholic with no sense of morality or responsibility. You've never had a lasting relationship with anyone who wasn't as weak or as helpless as yourself. So you have friends like Jimmy and me. Misfits who can't do any more than pick up your discarded clothes and empty glasses. We all hold each other up because none of us has the strength to do it alone. And lovers like Lou Tanner whose only talent is to beat your bloody face in and leave you when something better comes along. I know what I am, Evy. I don't like it and I never have. So I cover the outside with Helena Rubenstein. I use little make-up jars, you use quart bottles—and poor Jimmy uses a little of both . . . Some terrific people . . . But by some strange miracle, in there—*(Indicates bedroom)*—is a girl who is crazy in love with you because she's too young to know any better . . . But keep it up, Evy, and she'll get to know better before you can say Jack Daniels . . . The way I see it, you've got two choices. Either get a book on how to be a mature, responsible person . . . or get her out of here before you destroy her chance to become one. There's your honesty and truth, Evy. It's a perfect fit. How do you like it?

EVY Actually, I was looking for something in a blue.

TOBY That's the first time in my entire life I ever told anyone off. I think I'm going to be sick.

EVY Look who's getting to be a real person. (*She goes over and puts her arms around* TOBY) Next week, with a little luck, you'll throw away the eyelashes.

TOBY Don't hate me, Evy. I still need a little help from my friends. Tell me you don't hate me.

EVY *Hate* you? I'm having trouble seeing you.

TOBY So am I. But the picture's getting clearer . . . Come on, let me put something on your disgusting eye.

EVY I got a big scene to play with Polly. I don't need an audience. Go on home.

TOBY I can't. Marty's still there collecting some papers and things.

EVY You want to take some advice from a drunk? Go home, wash the crap off your face, put on a sloppy house-dress and bring him a T-V dinner. What the hell could you lose?

TOBY Nothing . . . Wouldn't it be funny if you were right?

EVY Of course I'm right. I'm always right. That's how I got where I am today.

TOBY Jesus, I suddenly hate my face . . . What I'd love to do is get rid of the goddamned thing.

EVY No, you don't. You're going to send it to me by messenger. *This* lady is still in trouble.

TOBY I'm going. *(Goes to the door)* I'm scared to death, but I'm going . . . I suddenly feel ten years older . . . Look, Evy. Look at the pretty old lady.

EVY You'll love it. Little boys'll help you across the street.

TOBY *(Opens the door)* Evy, don't tell Polly the truth about what happened. Lie a little. Protect her. That's what mothers are for.

EVY I'll say I was walking along West End Avenue and was hit by the Eastern Airlines shuttle to Boston.

TOBY It needs work. I'll call you from home later. I have to stop off first and blow up my beauty parlor.

(She exits, closing the door behind her. EVY *sits there a moment.* POLLY *comes out)*

POLLY Good morning.

EVY *(Her back to her)* You're up. Did you get any sleep?

POLLY No. There was terrible news on the radio. Someone was hit by an Eastern Airlines shuttle to Boston.

(EVY turns around and reveals herself to POLLY)

EVY It was me . . . How do you like it?

POLLY Wow. It's terrific. Goes very nice with this neighborhood. Listen, I don't have any steak to put on that. Will bacon and eggs do?

EVY You're not going to yell at me, is that it?

POLLY I thought you were going to yell at me. I didn't go to sleep last night either. *(Suddenly POLLY rushes into EVY's arms)* Oh, Evy, Evy, I'm so glad to see you.

EVY *(Winces)* The jaw, the jaw, watch the jaw.

POLLY Listen, don't tell Toby. I promised her I wouldn't forgive you.

EVY She's not even my friend any more. She's too old for me.

POLLY Starting tomorrow I'm not speaking to you. But I'm so glad to see you today.

EVY *(Pulls her to the sofa)* You got to admit, it's not a dull place to live.

POLLY Listen, we're not going to discuss it. It never even happened. Can I get you anything?

EVY If you move from me, you'll get worse than I got.

(She hugs her. There's a moment's pause)

POLLY I had a drink.

EVY What?

POLLY I made myself a Scotch at two o'clock in the morning. The Excedrin P.M. wasn't working, and I had to do something to stop the throbbing in my head.

EVY Did it stop?

POLLY No, but it made it bearable . . . Is that what it's like, Evy? Is that what it does? Make things bearable?

EVY *(Nods)* Mm-hmm. And if you take enough, it even stops the throbbing . . . Jesus, three weeks and I turned my daughter into a lush.

POLLY I hated it. I'll never take another drop in my life. From now on I'm sticking with marijuana.

EVY That's mama's good girl.

POLLY *(Pulls back)* Hey, listen, we better get moving. We have a lunch date in a half an hour, remember?

EVY What lunch date?

POLLY I told you last night. With Daddy, at Rumpelmayer's.

EVY Are you serious? With me looking like Rocky Graziano? He'll send you to a convent.

POLLY We could put something on it. Some powder or something. Or you could wear a hat. With a little veil.

EVY I could sit behind a big screen and talk through a microphone. I can't go to Rumpelmayer's looking like this.

POLLY We'll think of something . . . How about, you just did a Tareyton commercial?

EVY How about just forgetting it?

POLLY We can't. He's expecting you. What about a pair of dark sunglasses?

EVY It's not just the eye, baby. I have a hangover and the shakes. When I start spilling water on his lap, he's gonna notice something.

POLLY But if you don't show up, he'll think something is wrong.

EVY How right could things be if you show up with a punchy mother? . . . Is Melissa coming too?

POLLY Felicia.

EVY Felicia . . . Can you picture that scene? I walk into Rumpelmayer's looking like a dead fish, and she clicks in her coffee and he spits in his sherbet.

POLLY She's not coming. It's just the three of us. He wants to talk to us together. I promised him that when I came here.

EVY Well, unpromise him. I'm not going.

POLLY *(Giving up)* Okay . . . I'll tell him you're not feeling well. I'll figure out something. We'll do it again next week. (POLLY *goes for her coat*) In the meantime, will you see a doctor?

EVY Yes, angel.

POLLY When?

EVY As soon as I look better.

POLLY I'll bring you back a coffee malted and a toy. Get some sleep. I'll be home in an hour.

(She opens the door, about to go)

EVY Polly!

POLLY *(Stops; turns)* Yes?

EVY Maybe you'd better not make another date for next week . . . Not yet, anyway.

POLLY You'll be all right by next Saturday. It's not that bad, really.

EVY It's not the eye I'm worried about . . . It's the rest of the person.

POLLY *(Closes the door)* What are you saying, Mother?

EVY Nothing, baby . . . It's just that I don't know if I'm pulled together yet . . . You saw how suddenly everything unraveled yesterday . . . They warned me in the hospital that after a while I might expect some sort of setback.

POLLY Okay, you had a little setback . . . Onwards and upwards.

EVY Didn't you ever hear of downwards?

POLLY I've heard of it. You wouldn't like it there. It's worse than Garden City.

EVY Polly, I don't think I'm ready for you yet. I don't think I can handle it.

POLLY Handle what? I put on three pounds since I'm here.

EVY Mostly Sara Lee's cheesecake.

POLLY I'm alive, I'm healthy, I'm not floating on my back. What's wrong, Mother?

EVY Mother, heh? Some mother . . . When am I here? I'm out all day doing absolutely nothing and I still manage to come home late. I saw you more when you didn't live with me.

POLLY I'm not complaining.

EVY Well, complain, damn it! What are you so forgiving for? I was a slob last night. A pig and a slob.

POLLY It only happened once.

EVY Wait, it's early, the new schedule didn't come out yet. Besides, it didn't happen once . . . Before last night there was an occasional beer on a wet, lonely afternoon, a couple of glasses of wine on a sunny, lonely afternoon—and once, after a really rotten Swedish movie, a double vodka.

POLLY Okay, so forget downwards and upwards. We'll try sideways for a while.

EVY What we'll try is that you'll go home for a couple of weeks until I pull myself together. That's all, baby, just a couple of weeks. And when you get back, I'll be a regular Doris Day type mother, okay? Freckles and everything.

POLLY If I leave now, you know where you'll be in two weeks. You still have another eye left.

EVY Polly, please—

POLLY And in two weeks you'll find a reason to add another two weeks. And before you know it, Evy, I'll be all grown up and won't even need you any more.

EVY Listen, you weren't in such bad shape when you got here.

POLLY *(Angrily)* Is it such a goddamned big deal to need somebody? If you can need a bottle of Scotch or a Lou Tanner, why can't you need me?

EVY I do need you, baby. I just don't want to use you. Like the rest of the company around here . . . In a few weeks you'll know the regular routine. You'll get a two-hour storm warning, then wait in your bedroom until all the bottles are empty and all the glasses are smashed, and in the mornings there'll be a lot of Alka-Seltzers and black coffee and crying and forgiving and promises, and we'll live happily ever after for two more weeks. And in a year or so you won't even mind it. Like Jimmy and Toby . . . But they have nothing better to do with their lives. You're only seventeen.

POLLY They're just friends. I'm your daughter.

EVY You get my point?

POLLY No! . . . What *is* it, Evy? Am I getting kicked out because you're afraid I'm going to grow up to be a crutch instead of a person? Or do you just want to be left alone so there's no one here to lock up the liquor cabinet?

EVY You're going to be late for Rumpelmayer's.

POLLY *Screw* Rumpelmayer's!

EVY *(Looks at* POLLY *and smiles)* My, my . . . Look how quickly you can learn if you pay attention.

POLLY I'm sorry.

EVY Go on. Please, Polly. Go now.

POLLY Don't I get to argue my side?

EVY Not today. Mother is hung over.

POLLY I see . . . Okay . . . If the room's not for rent, it's not for rent . . . When do you want me out?

EVY All right, let's not get maudlin. You're not moving to the Philippines, just 86th and Madison.

POLLY *(Nods)* I'll be back for my stuff later.

EVY I'll get everything ready. If nothing else, I'm a terrific packer.

POLLY I'm glad you finally found something to keep you busy.

(She glares at EVY, *then crosses to the door. She turns and looks at* EVY*)*

EVY *(A pause)* What?

POLLY I was just wondering if you were going to say good-bye.

EVY Not unless you want to see a major breakdown.

POLLY Never mind. It's the thought that counts.

(The phone rings. POLLY *exits, closing the door behind her.* EVY *is at her low ebb. She crosses to her mink coat and takes out a pint bottle of liquor. She pours it into a glass and sits down on a chair, her legs up on a stool. The phone stops ringing. She drinks. After a moment the doorbell rings. She pays no attention. We hear* JIMMY*'s voice)*

JIMMY Evy? . . . Evy, it's Jimmy . . . Evy, I know you're there. I just saw Polly on the stairs. *(She drinks)* Damn it, Evy, answer me.

EVY Evy's not here. She moved. This is a recording.

JIMMY *(Pounds on the door)* Evy, I'll break this door down, I swear . . . I know what you're doing in there. *(A pause)* Three seconds, Evy. If it's not open in three seconds, I'm breaking it down.

(She drinks. Suddenly the door breaks down and JIMMY*'s body hurtles into the room and onto the floor.* EVY *looks at him)*

EVY Jesus, I didn't think you could do it.

JIMMY *(Gets up, moves to her)* I knew it. I knew you'd be here with a glass in your hand drinking yourself—*(He notices her eye)* Oh, my God. Look at you. Look at your face.

EVY If you're going to throw up, use the bathroom.

JIMMY He beat you. The son of a bitch beat you.

EVY And if you try to take this away from me, I'll show you how it was done.

JIMMY It was Lou Tanner, wasn't it? Toby just called me. I'll find him. If it takes me the rest of my life, I'll track that son of a bitch down and kill him.

EVY Once he hears, he'll never sleep another night . . . Will you close the drapes, Jimmy? And then leave me alone like a good boy.

JIMMY *(He closes the drapes)* Sure. I'll leave you alone. I turn my back for two seconds, they have to call the emergency squad. What happened? How did he beat you?

EVY How many ways are there? You get hit and you fall down.

JIMMY Look at your eye. What did he hit you with, his guitar?

EVY No, the guitar was the preliminaries.

JIMMY I want to know the details, Evy. How did he beat you?

EVY Since when are you interested in sports?
(In a fit of anger, he pushes her)

JIMMY You think it's so goddamned funny—go look at yourself.

EVY How come everybody's so physical lately? Where were you all when I needed you?

JIMMY Have you called the police? Have you seen a doctor? What have you done?

EVY Outside of bleeding, not very much. You want the goddamned case, I give it to you. If you're interested in my welfare, get me another glass, then turn out the light and get out of here. Leave me alone, Jimmy, please . . .

JIMMY I'll never forgive myself for running out last night. Never. *(He turns off the alcove light. He goes back to* EVY *on the sofa, and puts his arm on her)* It's all right, baby . . . We got through it before, we'll get through it again.

EVY And again . . . and again . . .

JIMMY Feel better?

EVY Much . . . There was this movie with Jean Simmons.

JIMMY English or American?

EVY English. And she was in love with this boy.

JIMMY Stewart Granger? David Niven? Michael Wilding?

EVY He was very short with blond hair.

JIMMY Short English actor. Blond hair. Alec Guinness? Michael Caine?

EVY Miles? Mills?

JIMMY Mills. John Mills. *Great Expectations*, directed by David Lean, with Valerie Hobson, John Mills, Francis Sullivan, and introducing Jean Simmons. What about it?

EVY She had this crazy old aunt who spent forty years in a wedding dress. The boy she loved never showed up for the wedding. Never saw him again but she never changed a thing for forty years. Cobwebs on the goddamned wedding cake. And she never went out into the city and she closed all the shutters and never let the sun into the house. She was covered with dust, this crazy old broad. Sat there in the dark, rotting and falling apart . . . Mice nibbling away at the wedding gifts . . . And as I watched her I remembered saying to myself, "She doesn't seem so crazy to me."

JIMMY Martita Hunt played the aunt. Her dress caught fire and she burned to death, screaming on the floor. Try not to think of it.

EVY I'm okay. There ain't no cobwebs on me.

JIMMY What can I get you? Let me get you something. Coffee? A sandwich? Something to drink? I'll even let you have a real drink, how about that?

EVY It's no fun that way. I have to sneak it.

JIMMY If I go away, if I leave you alone, will you take a nap?

EVY For you? Anything.

JIMMY Not for me. For yourself.

EVY Well, we'll split it. I'll sleep a little for you and a little for me . . . Will you turn the rest of the lights out? (JIMMY *crosses and turns out another light*) I can still see you, Charley. *(He turns out the remaining light. The room is almost in total darkness, except for the light in the kitchen)* That's better.

(JIMMY *moves in the dark and stumbles against a stool*)

JIMMY Christ, now I can't find the door.

EVY Don't worry about it, darling. Come to bed.

JIMMY Bitch, go to sleep. *(He has found the door and opens it)* I'll take a walk in Central Park. If I'm not back in an hour, I found true happiness.

(He goes, closing the door behind him)

EVY And get something for me, you bastard.

(She is alone. She gets up, crosses to the record player and switches on the record again. Her voice is heard, singing the song from last night. She pours herself another drink and goes back to the piano, drinking and listening. Suddenly the front door opens and POLLY *stands there in the doorway, looking worriedly into the dark room)*

POLLY *(Concerned)* Mother? Are you all right?

EVY *(In the shadows)* What are you doing here?

(She gets up quickly)

POLLY I forgot my wallet. I don't have carfare . . . What's the matter with the lights?

EVY Nothing. I have a headache.

POLLY Well, no wonder. It's so depressing in here. Like some ghost movie on the late show.

EVY *(Turns off the record player)* *Great Expectations*, directed by David Lean. (POLLY *switches on a light.* EVY *winces from the glare)* Christ, do you have to do that?

POLLY I have to find my wallet. I'll be out in a minute.

(POLLY *starts to look around and then finds the half-empty liquor bottle on the table where* EVY *was sitting. She holds up the bottle, turns and looks at* EVY)

EVY Well, if that's your wallet, take it and go.

POLLY It's not my wallet. It looks like yours.

EVY All right, what do you want, a reward? Put it down and go. Can't you see I'm trying to take a nap?

POLLY Some nap.

(She turns on another light and then another lamp)

EVY What are you doing? I don't want those lights on. Leave those lights alone.

POLLY So you can sit here in the dark, drinking?

EVY It's not hard, I know where my lips are. (POLLY *goes to the windows*) Get away from those curtains.

POLLY *(Opening one curtain)* Sitting here in the dark like some crazy spook. I have a crazy spook for a mother.

EVY And I have a disrespectful pain in the ass for a daughter. That's what I get for sending you to a private school.

POLLY *(Opening the other curtains)* Why don't you get some bats and owls in here? Fly around the room on a broomstick. Crazy old spook mother.

EVY Where's my pocketbook? Take a taxi, buy a car—only get out of here.

POLLY And you can sit here and finish the rest of the bottle, right?

EVY I wasn't drinking, I was meditating.

POLLY Ten more minutes and you'd have meditated right out on the floor. That's why you want to be alone.

EVY I'm not alone. Jimmy was here. And he's coming back in an hour.

POLLY And he'll do whatever you ask him, right? Turn out the lights, seal up the windows, refill your bottles? Anything as long as Evy's happy.

EVY Yes! Yes, dammit! Now get out of here and leave me alone!

POLLY That's why you kicked me out. Because you're afraid of me. Aren't you, Mother? Admit you're afraid of me.

EVY Don't test me. One more word, you'll walk into Rumpelmayer's looking like me.

POLLY Go ahead, hit me. I don't mind a little pain, Mother. It sure beats indifference!

EVY Jesus, you can't say a word around here without you listening at the door.

POLLY I don't have to listen through the door. When you're drunk, they can hear you in Brazil.

EVY I won't stand for this kind of talk.

POLLY Yes, you will. You'll stand for anything!

EVY Stop it! Stop it, Polly!

POLLY Then *make* me! Do something about it!

EVY I won't be talked to this way. I swear, you're going to get it, Polly.

POLLY I'm waiting. Please! Give it to me. Evy!

EVY Not from me. From your father. I swear to God, I'm going to tell your father.

POLLY *(Yells)* *Then tell him!* Tell him what I've become after three weeks. You want things to tell him about, Evy? *(Picks up a glass)* Here! *(She hurls it against the bookcase, smashing it to pieces)* All right? Now come to Rumpelmayer's and tell him . . . Only please don't sit in the dark for the rest of your life.

(POLLY *has burst into tears. She kneels, crying.* EVY *finds it difficult to go to her. It is quiet for a moment*)

EVY Couldn't he have picked a nice out-of-the-way restaurant in Nebraska?

POLLY *(Turns around hopefully)* You mean you've changed your mind?

EVY I didn't change anything.

POLLY All right, don't change your mind. Just change your dress. You can change your mind on the way over.

EVY *(Looks to heaven)* She's *his* daughter. I have too much class for a daughter like this.

POLLY Listen, how about if I don't come back as a daughter? I could be a house guest. I'll just stay till I'm thirty-five, then get out. I promise.

EVY Didn't we just settle all that?

POLLY You and your daughter settled all that. I'm a stranger. Why don't you show me the rest of the apartment?

EVY *(Again, up to heaven)* Who is she? Who sent this monster to torment me?

POLLY Felicia. She can't stand any of us.

(POLLY *has clearly won.* EVY *wilts and opens her arms.* POLLY *runs in*)

EVY Oh, God, I'm not strong enough to resist you . . . I suppose I'll be speaking at your school next week.

POLLY We've got fifteen minutes. What can we do with your face in fifteen minutes?

EVY Christ, I don't know. There's a one-hour cleaners around the corner.

POLLY You've known Toby Landau for twelve years and you never heard of make-up? Come on, sit down.

EVY We'll never get away with it.

POLLY Yes, you will.

(She takes out a compact from her purse)

EVY I'll get twenty years for impersonating a mother.

POLLY Good. We'll share a cell together.

EVY The hell we will. I'm forty-three years old. Someday I'm getting my own place.

(POLLY *starts to apply make-up under the eye*)

POLLY Now remember. Once we get there, don't be nervous. Just be cool and nonchalant.

EVY What if I do something stupid like eat the ice cream with a fork?

POLLY Then I'll eat mine with a fork. He'll look at us, think *he's* wrong, and eat *his* with a fork . . . Try not to move.

EVY Who would believe this? A middle-aged drunk with a black eye is worried about impressing a forty-seven-year-old spitter.

POLLY All right, I'm through.

EVY How does it look?

POLLY Much better.

EVY *(Picks up the compact and looks at herself)* It's *not* better. It looks like I was punched in the eye and someone put make-up on it.

POLLY If we don't get away with it, we'll tell him the truth. He's a terrific person, Evy. He'll understand the truth.

EVY About Lou Tanner?

POLLY No. The Eastern Airlines shuttle to Boston. Come on. Let's get a decent dress on you. You look like you're collecting for UNICEF.

EVY Polly.

POLLY What?

EVY When I grow up, I want to be just like you.

Curtain

The Prisoner of Second Avenue

The Scene

The entire action takes place in a Manhattan apartment, on Second Avenue in the upper eighties.

Act One

Scene One: Two-thirty in the morning on a midsummer's day.
Scene Two: Late afternoon, a few days later.

Act Two

Scene One: Mid-September; about one in the afternoon.
Scene Two: Midafternoon, two weeks later.
Scene Three: A late afternoon in mid-December.

Act One

SCENE I

The scene is a fourteenth-floor apartment in one of those prosaic new apartment houses that grow like mushrooms all over New York's overpriced East Side. This one is on Second Avenue in the upper eighties. The management calls this a five-and-a-half-room apartment. What is visible to us is the living room–dining room combination, a small, airless and windowless kitchen off the dining room, a French door that leads to a tiny balcony or terrace off the living room, and a small hallway that leads to two bedrooms and bathrooms.

This particular dwelling has been the home of MEL *and* EDNA EDISON *for the past six years. What they thought they were getting was all the modern luxuries and comforts of the smart, chic East Side. What they got is paper-thin walls and a view of five taller buildings from their terrace.*

The stage is dark. It is two-thirty in the morning and a hot midsummer's day has just begun.

It is silent . . .

In pajamas, robe and slippers, MEL EDISON *sits alone on the tiny sofa, smoking a cigarette. He rubs his face anxiously, then coughs . . .*

MEL Ohhh, Christ Almighty.

(A light goes on in the bedroom. EDNA, *his wife, appears in her nightgown)*

EDNA What's wrong?

MEL Nothing's wrong.

EDNA Huh?

MEL Nothing's wrong. Go back to bed.

EDNA Are you sure?

MEL I'm sure. Go back to bed. *(*EDNA *turns and goes back into the bedroom)* Oh, God, God, God.

*(*EDNA *returns, putting on her robe. She flips the switch on the wall, lighting the room)*

EDNA What is it? Can't you sleep?

MEL If I could sleep, would I be sitting here calling God at two-thirty in the morning?

EDNA What's the matter?

MEL Do you know it's twelve degrees in there? July twenty-third, the middle of a heat wave, it's twelve degrees in there.

EDNA I told you, turn the air conditioner off.

MEL And how do we breathe? *(Points to the window)* It's eighty-nine degrees out there . . . eighty-nine degrees outside, twelve degrees inside. Either way they're going to get me.

EDNA We could leave the air conditioner on and open the window.

(She goes into the kitchen)

MEL They don't work that way. Once the hot air sees an open window, it goes in.

EDNA We could leave the air conditioner off for an hour. Then when it starts to get hot, we can turn it back on.

(She comes out, eating from a jar of applesauce)

MEL Every hour? Seven times a night? That's a good idea. I can get eight minutes sleep in between working the air conditioner.

EDNA *I'll* do it. *I'll* get up.

MEL I asked you a million times to call that office. That air conditioner hasn't worked properly in two years.

EDNA . I called them. A man came. He couldn't find anything wrong.

MEL What do you mean, nothing wrong? I got it on Low, it's twelve goddamned degrees.

EDNA *(Sits down, sighing)* It's not twelve degrees, Mel. It's cold, but it's not twelve degrees.

MEL All right, seventeen degrees. Twenty-nine degrees. Thirty-six degrees. It's not sixty-eight, sixty-nine. A temperature for a normal person.

EDNA *(Sits on the sofa)* I'll call them again tomorrow.

MEL Why do they bother printing on it High, Medium and Low? It's all High. Low is High. Medium is High. Some night I'm gonna put it on High, they'll have to get a flamethrower to get us out in the morning.

EDNA What do you want me to do, Mel? You want me to turn it off? You want me to leave it on? Just tell me what to do.

MEL Go back to sleep.

EDNA I can't sleep when you're tense like this.

MEL I'm not tense. I'm frozen stiff. July twenty-third.

(He sits down on the sofa)

EDNA You're tense. You were tense when you walked in the house tonight. You've been tense for a week. Would you rather sleep in here? I could make up the cot.

MEL You can't even sit in here. *(Picks up the small puff pillows from behind him)* Why do you keep these ugly little pillows on here? You spend eight hundred dollars for chairs and then you can't sit on it because you got ugly little pillows shoved up your back.

(He throws one of the pillows on the floor)

EDNA I'll take the pillows off.

MEL Edna, please go inside, I'll be in later.

EDNA It's not the air conditioner. It's not the pillows. It's something else. Something's bothering you. I've seen you when you get like this. What is it, Mel?

MEL *(Rubs his face with his hands)* It's nothing. I'm tired.

(He gets up and goes over to the terrace door)

EDNA I'm up, Mel, you might as well tell me.

MEL It's nothing, I'm telling you . . . I don't know. It's everything. It's this apartment, it's this building, it's this city. Listen. Listen to this. *(He opens the terrace door. We hear the sounds of traffic, horns, motors, etc.)* Two-thirty in the morning, there's one car driving around in Jackson Heights and we can hear it . . . Fourteen stories up, I thought it would be quiet. I hear the subway up here better than I hear it in the subway . . . We're like some kind of goddamned antenna. All the sound goes up through this apartment and then out to the city.

EDNA We've lived here six years, it never bothered you before.

MEL It's worse now, I don't know why. I'm getting older, more sensitive to sounds, to noise. Everything. *(He closes the door, then looks at himself)* You see this? I had that door opened ten seconds, you gotta wash these pajamas now.

EDNA *(Anything to please)* Give them to me, I'll get you clean pajamas.

MEL *(Pacing)* Two-thirty in the morning, can you believe that's still going on next door?

(He points to the wall)

EDNA What's going on?

MEL What are you, trying to be funny? You mean to tell me you don't hear that?

EDNA *(Puzzled)* Hear what?

MEL *(Closer to the wall, still pointing)* That! That! What are you, deaf? You don't hear that?

EDNA Maybe I'm deaf. I don't hear anything.

MEL *Listen*, for God's sakes . . . You don't hear "Raindrops Falling on His Head"? *(He sings)* Da dum de dum da dum de da . . . "too big for his feet" . . . You don't hear that?

EDNA Not when you're singing, I don't hear it.

MEL *(Stares at the wall)* It's those two goddamned German airline hostesses. Every night they got someone else in there. Two basketball players, two hockey players, whatever team is in town, win or lose, they wind up in there . . . Every goddamned night! . . . Somewhere there's a 747 flying around with people serving themselves because those two broads never leave that apartment. *(He grabs* EDNA, *pulls her over to the wall)* Come here. You mean to tell me you don't hear that?

EDNA *(Puts her ear against the wall)* Yes, now I hear it.

MEL You see! Is it any wonder I don't sleep at night?

EDNA *(Moving away from the wall)* Don't sleep with your head next to the wall. Sleep in the bedroom.

MEL Hey, knock it off in there. It's two damn thirty in the lousy morning. *(He bangs on the wall, then stops and looks at it. He points to the wall)* Look at that, I cracked the wall. I barely touched it, the damned thing is cracked.

EDNA It was starting to crack before. There's a leak somewhere; one of the pipes upstairs is broken.

MEL A two-million-dollar building, you can't touch the walls? It's a good thing I didn't try to hang a picture; we all could have been killed.

EDNA They know about it. They're starting to fix it on Monday.

MEL *(He sits down)* Not Monday. Tomorrow. I want that wall fixed tomorrow, it's a health hazard. And they're going to repaint the whole wall, and if it doesn't match, they'll paint the rest of the room, and if that doesn't match, they'll do the rest of the apartment. And I'm not paying for it, you understand?

EDNA I'll tell them.

MEL And tell them about the air conditioner . . . and the window in the bedroom that doesn't open except when it rains and then you can't shut it until there's a flood and then tell them about our toilet that never stops flushing.

EDNA It stops flushing if you jiggle it.

MEL Why should I have to jiggle it? For the money I'm paying here do I have to stand over a toilet in the middle of the night and have to jiggle every time I go to the bathroom?

EDNA When you're through, get back into bed, tell me and *I'll* jiggle it.

MEL *(Turns, glares at her)* Go to bed, Edna. I don't want to talk to you now. Will you please go to sleep.

EDNA I can't sleep if I know you're up here walking around having an anxiety attack.

MEL I'm not having an anxiety attack. I'm a little tense.

EDNA Why don't you take a Valium?

MEL I took one.

EDNA Then take another one.

MEL I took another one. They don't work any more.
(He sits down in a chair)

EDNA *Two* Valiums? They *have* to work.

MEL They don't work any more, I'm telling you. They're supposed to calm you down, aren't they? All right, am I calm? They don't work. Probably don't put anything in them. Charge you fourteen dollars for the word "Valium." *(He bangs on the wall)* Don't you ever fly anywhere? Keep somebody in Europe awake!
(He bangs on the wall again with his fist)

EDNA Stop it, Mel. You're really getting me nervous now. What's wrong? Has something happened? Is something bothering you?

MEL Why do we live like this? Why do we pay somebody hundreds of dollars a month to live in an egg box that leaks?

EDNA You don't look well to me, Mel. You look pale. You look haggard.

MEL I wasn't planning to be up.
(He rubs his stomach)

EDNA Why are you rubbing your stomach?

MEL I'm not rubbing it, I'm holding it.

EDNA Why are you holding your stomach?

MEL It's nothing. A little indigestion. It's that crap I had for lunch.

EDNA Where did you eat?

MEL In a health-food restaurant. If you can't eat health food, what the hell can you eat any more?

EDNA You're probably just hungry. Do you want me to make you something?

MEL Nothing is safe any more. I read in the paper today two white mice at Columbia University got cancer from eating graham crackers. It was in *The New York Times.*

EDNA Is that what's bothering you? Did you eat graham crackers today?

MEL Food used to be so good. I used to love food. I haven't eaten food since I was thirteen years old.

EDNA Do you want some food? I'll make you food. I remember how they made it.

MEL I haven't had a real piece of bread in thirty years. If I knew what was going to happen, I would have saved some rolls when I was a kid. You can't breathe in here. *(He goes out onto the terrace)* Christ, what a stink. Fourteen stories up, you can smell the garbage from here. Why do they put garbage out in eighty-nine-degree heat? Edna, come here, I want you to smell the garbage.

EDNA *(Comes to the door of the terrace)* I smell it, I smell it.

MEL You can't smell it from there. Come here where you can smell it.

EDNA *(Walks to the edge of the terrace and inhales)* You're right. If you really want to smell it, you have to stand right here.

MEL This country is being buried by its own garbage. It keeps piling up higher and higher. In three years this apartment is going to be the second floor.

EDNA What can they do, Mel? Save it up and put it out in the winter? They have to throw it out sometime. That's why they call it garbage.

MEL I can't talk to you. I can't talk to you any more.

EDNA Mel, I'm a human being the same as you. I get hot, I get cold, I smell garbage, I hear noise. You either live with it or you get out.

(Suddenly a dog howls and barks)

MEL If you're a human being you reserve the right to complain, to protest. When you give up that right, you don't exist any more. I protest to stinking garbage and jiggling toilets . . . and barking dogs. *(Yells out)* Shut up, goddamnit.

EDNA Are you going to stay here and yell at the dog? Because I'm going to sleep.

(The dog howls again)

MEL How can you sleep with a dog screaming like that? *(The dog howls again. MEL goes to the edge of the terrace and yells down)* Keep that dog quiet. There are human beings sleeping up here. Christ Almighty!!!!

VOICE *(From above)* Will you be quiet. There are children up here.

MEL *(Yelling up)* What the hell are you yelling at me for? You looking for trouble, go down and keep the dog company.

EDNA Mel, will you stop it! Stop it, for God's sakes!

MEL *(Comes back in; screams at EDNA)* Don't tell *me* to stop it! DON'T TELL ME TO STOP IT!

EDNA I don't know what's gotten into you. But I'm not going to stand here and let you take it out on me . . . If it's too much for you, take a room in the public library, *but don't take it out on me.* I'm going to sleep, *good night!!*

(She turns angrily and heads for the bedroom. She gets almost to the bedroom door before MEL calls to her)

MEL Edna! *(She stops and turns around)* Don't go! . . . Talk to me for a few minutes, because I think I'm going out of my mind.

(She stops, looks at him, and comes back into the living room)

EDNA What is it?

MEL I'm unraveling . . . I'm losing touch!

EDNA You haven't been sleeping well lately.

MEL I don't know where I am half the time. I walk down Madison Avenue, I think I'm in a foreign country.

EDNA I know that feeling, Mel.

MEL It's not just a feeling, something is happening to me . . . I'm losing control. I can't handle things any more.

The telephone on my desk rings seven, eight times before I answer it . . . I forgot how to work the water cooler today. I stood there with an empty cup in my hand and water running all over my shoes.

EDNA It's not just you, Mel, it's everybody. Everybody's feeling the tension these days.

MEL Tension? If I could just feel tension, I'd give a thousand dollars to charity . . . When you're tense, you're tight, you're holding on to something. I don't know where to grab. Edna, I'm slipping, and I'm scared.

EDNA Don't talk like that. What about seeing the analyst again?

MEL Who? Doctor Pike? He's dead. Six years of my life, twenty-three thousand dollars. He got my money, what does he care if he gets a heart attack?

EDNA There are other good doctors. You can see someone else.

MEL And start all over from the beginning? "Hello. Sit down. What seems to be the trouble?" . . . It'll cost me another twenty-three thousand just to fill *this* doctor in with information I already gave the dead one.

EDNA What about a little therapy? Maybe you just need someone to talk to for a while.

MEL I don't know where or who I am any more. I'm disappearing, Edna. I don't need analysts, I need Lost and Found.

EDNA Listen . . . Listen . . . What about if we get away for a couple of weeks? A two-week vacation? Someplace in the sun, away from the city. You can get two weeks' sick leave, can't you, Mel?

(He is silent. He walks to the window and glances over at the plant)

MEL Even the cactus is dying. Strongest plant in the world, only has to be watered twice a year. Can't make a go of it on Eighty-eighth and Second.

EDNA Mel, answer me. What about getting away? Can't you ask them for two weeks off?

MEL *(Makes himself a scotch)* Yes, I can ask them for two weeks off. What worries me is that they'll ask me to take the other fifty weeks as well.

(He drinks)

EDNA You? What are you talking about? You've been there twenty-two years . . . Mel, is that it? Is that what's been bothering you? You're worried about losing your job?

MEL I'm not worried about losing it. I'm worried about keeping it. Losing it is easy.

EDNA Has something happened? Have they said anything?

MEL They don't have to say anything. The company lost three million dollars this year. Suddenly they're looking to save pennies. The vice-president of my department has been using the same paper clip for three weeks now. A sixty-two-year-old man with a duplex on Park Avenue and a house in Southampton running around the office, screaming, "Where's my paper clip?"

EDNA But they haven't actually said anything to you.

MEL They closed the executive dining room. Nobody goes out to lunch any more. They bring sandwiches from home. Top executives, making eighty thousand dollars a year, eating egg-salad sandwiches over the wastepaper basket.

EDNA Nothing has happened yet, Mel. There's no point in worrying about it now.

MEL No one comes to work late any more. Everyone's afraid if you're not there on time, they'll sell your desk.

EDNA And what if they did? We'd live, we'd get by. You'd get another job somewhere.

MEL Where? I'm gonna be forty-seven years old in January. Forty-seven! They could get two twenty-three-and-a-half-year-old kids for half my money.

EDNA All right, suppose something *did* happen? Suppose you *did* lose your job? It's not the end of the world. We don't have to live in the city. We could move somewhere in the country, or even out west.

MEL And what do I do for a living? Become a middle-aged cowboy? Maybe they'll put me in charge of rounding up the elderly cattle . . . What's the matter with you?

EDNA The girls are in college now, we have enough to see them through. We don't need much for the two of us.

MEL You need a place to live, you need clothing, you need food. A can of polluted tuna fish is still eighty-five cents.

EDNA We could move to Europe. To Spain. Two people could live for fifteen hundred dollars a year in Spain.

MEL *(Nods)* *Spanish* people. I'm forty-seven years old, with arthritis in my shoulder and high blood pressure—you expect me to raise goats and live in a cave?

EDNA You could work there, get some kind of a job.

MEL An advertising account executive? In Barcelona? They've probably been standing at the dock waiting for years for someone like that.

EDNA *(Angrily)* What is it they have here that's so damned hard to give up? *What is it you'll miss so badly, for God's sakes?*

MEL I'm not through with my life yet . . . I still have value, I still have worth.

EDNA What kind of a life is this? You live like some kind of a caged animal in a Second Avenue zoo that's too hot in one room, too cold in another, overcharged for a growth on the side of the building they call a terrace that can't support a cactus plant, let alone two human beings. Is this what you call a worthwhile life? Banging on walls and jiggling toilets?

MEL *(Shouts)* You think it's any better in Sunny Spain? Go swimming on the beach, it'll take you the rest of the summer to scrape the oil off.

EDNA Forget Spain. There are other places to live.

MEL Maine? Vermont maybe? You think it's all rolling hills and maple syrup? They have more people on welfare up there than they have pancakes. Washington? Oregon? Unemployed lumberjacks are sitting around sawing legs off chairs; they have nothing else to do.

EDNA I will go anywhere in the world you want to go, Mel. I will live in a cave, a hut or a tree. I will live on a raft in the Amazon jungle if that's what you want to do.

MEL All right, call a travel agency. Get two economy seats to Bolivia. We'll go to Abercrombie's tomorrow, get a couple of pith helmets and a spear gun.

EDNA Don't talk to me like I'm insane.

MEL I'm halfway there, you might as well catch up.

EDNA I am trying to offer reasonable suggestions. I am not responsible. I am not the one who's doing this to you.

MEL I didn't say you were, Edna.

EDNA Then what do you want from me? *What do you want from anyone?*

MEL *(Buries his face in his hands)* Just a little breathing space . . . just for a little while. *(The phone rings.* MEL *looks up at* EDNA*)* Who could that be? *(*EDNA *shakes her head, not knowing)* It couldn't be the office, could it?

EDNA At a quarter to three in the morning?

MEL Maybe they got the night watchman to fire me, they'll save a day's salary.

(It keeps ringing)

EDNA Answer it, Mel, I'm nervous.

*(*MEL *picks up the phone)*

MEL *(Into the phone)* Hello? . . . Yes? . . . Yes, Apartment 14A, what about it? . . . *What??? I'm keeping YOU up???* Who the hell do you think got *me* up to get *you* up in the first place? . . . Don't tell me you got a plane leaving for Stuttgart in the morning . . . I'll talk as loud as I damn well please. This isn't a sublet apartment, I'm a regular American tenant . . . Go ahead and bang on the wall. You'll get a bang right back on yours. *(He covers the phone, then says to* EDNA*)* If she bangs, I want you to bang back.

EDNA Mel, what are you starting in for?

(From the other side of the wall, we hear a loud banging)

MEL Okay, bang back.

EDNA Mel, it's a quarter to three. Leave them alone, they'll go to sleep.

MEL Will you bang back?!

EDNA If I bang back, she's just going to bang back at me.

MEL Will you bang back!!!?

EDNA I'll bang, I'll bang!

(She bangs twice on the wall)

MEL *(Into the phone)* All right? *(From the other side of the wall, they bang again.* MEL *says to* EDNA*)* Bang back! *(She bangs again. They bang from the other side again. He repeats his instructions to* EDNA*)* Bang back! *(She bangs again. They bang again)* Bang back!

(She bangs. The stage goes black, then the curtain falls. The house remains in darkness. A screen drops and the News Logo appears. We hear Roger Keating with the Six O'-Clock Report*)*

VOICE OF ROGER KEATING *(In the darkness)* This is Roger Keating and the *Six O'Clock Report* . . . New York was hit with its third strike of the week. This time the city employees of thirty-seven New York hospitals walked out at 3 P.M. this afternoon. The Mayor's office has been flooded with calls, as hundreds of patients and elderly sick people have complained of lack of food, clean sheets and medicines. One seventy-nine-year-old patient in Lenox Hill Hospital fell in the corridor, broke his leg and was treated by a seventy-three-year-old patient who had just recovered from a gall-bladder operation . . . Two of the most cold-blooded robbers in the city's history today made off with four thousand dollars, stolen from the New York City Home for the Blind. Police believe it may have been the same men who got away with thirty-six hundred dollars on Tuesday from the New York Cat and Dog Hospital . . . Water may be shut off tomorrow, says the New York Commissioner of Health, because of an anonymous phone call made to the bureau this morning, threatening to dump fifty pounds of chemical pollutants in the city's reservoirs. The unidentified caller, after making his threat, concluded with, "It's gonna be dry tomorrow, baby." . . . And from the office of Police Commissioner Murphy, a report that the number of apartment house burglaries has risen seven point two percent in August.

*

SCENE 2

It is late afternoon, a few days later.

At the curtain's rise, the room is in a shambles. Chairs are overturned; drawers are pulled open, their contents scattered all over the floor; the bookcase has been cleared of half of its shelves and articles of clothing are strewn about the room. It is obvious what has happened.

EDNA *is on the phone. She is shaking.*

EDNA *(Sobbing)* Edison, Mrs. Edna Edison . . . I've just been robbed . . . I just walked in, they took everything . . . Edison . . . I just walked in, I found the door open, they must have just left . . . 385 East 88th Street . . . Two minutes sooner, I could have been killed . . . Apartment 14A . . . I don't know yet. Television, the record player, books, clothing . . . They took lots of clothing. My dresses, my coats, all my husband's suits—there's not a thing left in his closet . . . I haven't checked the drawers yet . . . Would you, please? Send somebody right away . . . I'm all alone. My husband isn't home from work yet . . . *Mrs. Edna Edison.* I could have been killed. Thank you. *(She hangs up, then turns and looks at the room. She crosses the room, lifts a chair up and sets it right. Then she goes over to the bureau and starts to look through the drawers. As she discovers new things are missing, she sobs louder)* All right . . . Calm down . . . A drink, I have to have a drink *(She rushes into the kitchen, gets a glass and a few cubes of ice from the refrigerator, then rushes back out into the living room. She rushes to the bar and looks. There are no bottles)* The liquor's gone. They took the liquor. *(She puts the glass down, slumps into a chair, and sobs.)* Valium . . . I want a Valium. *(She gets up and rushes down the small corridor, disappearing into the bedroom. We hear noises as she must be looking through ransacked medicine chests. There are a few moments of silence.* EDNA *has probably fallen onto the bed, sobbing, for all we know. The front door is unlocked and* MEL *enters. He carries his suit jacket and the New York* Post. *His shirt sleeves are rolled up and he looks hot. He closes the door and hangs his jacket in the closet. Consumed with his own thoughts, he doesn't seem to even notice the room. He moves over to the chair, falls into it exhausted, puts his head back and sighs . . . His eyes open, then he looks at the room for almost the first time. He looks around the room, bewildered. From the bedroom we hear* EDNA*'s voice)* Mel? . . . Is that you, Mel?

*(*MEL *is still looking at the room, puzzled.* EDNA *appears cautiously from the bedroom. She comes in, holding a vase by the thin end, and looks at* MEL*)*

MEL Didn't Mildred come in to clean today?

EDNA *(Puts the vase down)* Not today . . . Mondays and Thursdays.

MEL What happened here? . . . Why is this place such a mess?

EDNA We've been robbed.

*(*MEL *looks at her in a state of shock . . . He slowly rises and then looks at the room in a new perspective)*

MEL What do you mean, robbed?

EDNA *(Starts to cry) Robbed! Robbed!* What does robbed mean? They come in, they take things out! *They robbed us!!!*

MEL *(He keeps turning, looking at the room in disbelief—not knowing where to look first)* I don't understand . . . What do you mean, someone just walked in and robbed us?

EDNA What do you think? . . . They called up and made an appointment? *We've been robbed!*

MEL All right, calm down. Take it easy, Edna. I'm just asking a simple question. What happened? What did they get?

EDNA I don't know yet. I was out shopping. I was gone five minutes. I came back, I found it like this.

MEL You couldn't have been gone five minutes. Look at this place.

EDNA *Five minutes,* that's all I was gone.

MEL Five minutes, heh? Then we'd better call the FBI, because every crook in New York must have been in here.

EDNA Then that's who was here, because I was only gone five minutes.

MEL When you came back into the building did you notice anyone suspicious-looking?

EDNA *Everyone* in this building is suspicious-looking.

MEL You didn't see anybody carrying any bundles or packages?

EDNA I didn't notice.

MEL What do you mean, you didn't notice?

EDNA I didn't notice. You think I look for people leaving the building with my television set?

MEL They took the television? *(He starts for the bedroom, then stops)* A *brand new* color television?

EDNA They're not looking for 1948 Philcos. It was here. They took it. I can't get a breath out.

MEL All right, sit there. I'll get a drink.

EDNA *(Sitting down)* I don't want a drink.

MEL A little scotch. It'll calm you down.

EDNA It won't calm me down, because there's no scotch. They took the scotch too.

MEL *All* the scotch?

EDNA All the scotch.

MEL The Chivas Regal too?

EDNA No, they're going to take the cheap scotch and leave the Chivas Regal. They took it all, they cleaned us out.

MEL *(Gnashing his teeth)* Sons of bitches. *(He runs to the terrace door, opens it, steps out on the terrace and yells out) Sons of bitches! (He closes the door and comes back in)* All in five minutes, eh? They must have been gorillas to lift all that in five minutes.

EDNA Leave me alone.

MEL *(Gnashing his teeth again)* Sons of bitches.

EDNA Stop swearing, the police will be here any minute. I just called them.

MEL You called the police?

EDNA Didn't I just say that?

MEL Did you tell them we were robbed?

EDNA Why else would I call them? I'm not friendly with the police. What kind of questions are you asking me? What's wrong with you?

MEL All right, calm down, because you're hysterical.

EDNA I am not hysterical.

MEL You're hysterical.

EDNA You're *making* me hysterical. Don't you understand? My house has just been robbed.

MEL What am I, a boarder? My house has been robbed too. My color television and my Chivas Regal is missing the same as yours.

EDNA You didn't walk in and find it. *I* did.

MEL What's the difference who found it? There's still nothing to drink and nothing to watch.

EDNA Don't yell at me. I'm just as upset as you are.

MEL I'm sorry. I'm excited, too. I don't mean to yell at you. *(Starts for the bedroom)* Let me get you a Valium, it'll calm you down.

EDNA I don't want a Valium.

MEL Take one. You'll feel better.

EDNA I'm not taking a Valium.

MEL Why are you so stubborn?

EDNA I'm not stubborn. We don't have any. They took the Valiums.

MEL *(Stops)* They took the Valiums?

EDNA The whole medicine chest. Valiums, Seconals, aspirin, shaving cream, toothpaste, razor blades. They left your toothbrush. You want to go in and brush your teeth, you can still do it.

MEL *(Smiles, disbelieving)* I don't believe you. *I don't believe you!*

(MEL *looks at her, then storms off and disappears into the bedroom.* EDNA *gets up and picks up a book from the floor. From the far recesses of the bathroom we hear* MEL *scream:)*

MEL *(Offstage)* *DIRTY BASTARDS!!!* *(*EDNA *is holding the book upside down and shaking it, hoping some concealed item will fall out. It doesn't.* MEL *storms back into living room)* I hope they die. I hope the car they stole to get away in hits a tree and turns over and burns up and they all die!

EDNA You read about it every day. And when it happens to you, you can't believe it.

MEL A television I can understand. Liquor I can understand. But shaving cream? Hair spray? How much are they going to get for a roll of dental floss?

EDNA They must have been desperate. They took everything they could carry. *(Shakes the book one last time)* They even found my kitchen money.

MEL What kitchen money?

EDNA I kept my kitchen money in here. Eighty-five dollars.

MEL In cash? Why do you keep cash in a book?

EDNA So no one will find it! Where else am I gonna keep it?

MEL In a jar. In the sugar. Some place they're not going to look.

EDNA They looked in the medicine chest, you think they're not going to look in the sugar?

MEL *Nobody looks in sugar!*

EDNA Nobody steals dental floss and mouthwash. Only sick people. Only that's who live in the world today. *Sick, sick, sick people!*

(She sits, emotionally wrung out. MEL *comes over to her and puts his arm on her shoulder, comforting her)*

MEL It's all right . . . It's all right, Edna . . . As long as you weren't hurt, that's the important thing.

(He looks through the papers on the table)

EDNA Can you imagine if I had walked in and found them here? What would I have done, Mel?

MEL You were very lucky, Edna. Very lucky.

EDNA But what would I have done?

MEL What's the difference? You didn't walk in and find them.

EDNA But supposing I did? What would I have done?

MEL You'd say, "Excuse me," close the door and come back later. What would you do, sit and watch? Why do you ask me such questions? It didn't happen, did it?

EDNA It *almost* happened. If I walked in here five minutes sooner.

MEL *(Walking away from her)* You couldn't have been gone only five minutes . . . It took the Seven Santini Brothers two days to move everything in, three junkies aren't gonna move it all out in five minutes.

EDNA Seven minutes, eight minutes, what's the difference?

MEL *(Opens the door, looks at the lock)* The lock isn't broken, it's not jimmied. I don't even know how they got in here.

EDNA Maybe they found my key in the street.

MEL *(Closes the door. Looks at her)* What do you mean, "found your key"? Don't you have your key?

EDNA No, I lost it. I thought it was somewhere in the house, but maybe I lost it in the street.

MEL If you didn't have your key, how were you going to get back in the house when you went shopping?

EDNA I left the door open.

MEL You–left–the–door–open???

EDNA I didn't have a key, how was I going to get back in the house?

MEL *So you left the door open?* In a city with the highest crime rate in the history of the world, *you left the door open?*

EDNA What was I going to do? Take the furniture with me? I was only gone five minutes. How did they know I was going to leave the door open?

MEL They know! They know! A door opens, it doesn't lock, the whole junkie world lights up. "Door open, fourteenth floor, Eighty-eighth Street and Second Avenue." They know!

EDNA They don't know anything. They have to go around trying doors.

MEL And what did you think? They were going to try every door in this house except yours? "Let's leave 14A alone, fellas, it looks like a nice door."

EDNA If they're going to go around trying doors, they have twenty-three hours and fifty-five minutes a day to try them. I didn't think they would try ours the five minutes I was out of the house. I gambled! I lost!

MEL What kind of gamble is that to take? If you lose, they get everything. If you win, they rob somebody else.

EDNA I *had* to shop. There was nothing in the house to eat tonight.

MEL All right, now you have something to eat and nothing to eat it with . . . Why didn't you call up and have them send it?

EDNA Because I shop in a cheap store that doesn't deliver. I am trying to save us money because you got me so worried the other night. I was just trying to save us money . . . Look how much money I saved us.

(EDNA *starts to pick up things)*

MEL What are you doing?

EDNA We can't leave everything like this. I want to clean up.

MEL Now?

EDNA The place is a mess. We have people coming over in a few minutes.

MEL The *police?* You want the place to look nice for the police? . . . You're worried they're going to put it down in their books, "bad housekeeper"? . . . Leave it alone. Maybe they'll find some clues.

EDNA I can't find out what's missing until I put everything back in its place.

MEL What do you mean? You know what's missing. The television, the liquor, the kitchen money, the medicine chest and the hi-fi . . . That's it, isn't it? *(Pause)* Isn't it? *(EDNA looks away)* Okay, what else did they get?

EDNA Am I a detective? Look, you'll find out.

(He glares at her and looks around the room, not knowing where to begin. He decides to check the bedroom. He storms down the hall and disappears. EDNA, knowing what to soon expect, sits on a chair in the dining area and stares out the window. She takes out a hanky and wipes some dirt from the window sill. MEL returns calmly—at least outwardly calm. He takes a deep breath)

MEL Where are my suits?

EDNA They were there this morning. They're not there now. They must have taken your suits.

MEL *(Still trying to be calm)* Seven suits? Three sports jackets? Eight pairs of slacks?

EDNA If that's what you had, that's what they got.

MEL I'm lucky my tuxedo is in the cleaners.

EDNA *(Still staring out the window)* They sent it back this morning.

MEL Well, they did a good job of it . . . Cleaned me out . . . Left a pair of khaki pants and my golf hat . . . Anybody asks us out to dinner this week, ask them if it's all right if I wear khaki pants and a golf hat. DIRTY BASTARDS!!!!

(In what can only be described as an insane tantrum, he picks up some ashtrays from the sideboard and throws them to the floor of the kitchen, continuing uncontrollably until all his energy and his vitriol have been exhausted . . . He stands there panting)

EDNA It's just things, Mel. Just some old suits and coats. We can replace them. We'll buy new ones. Can't we, Mel?

MEL With what? . . . *With what?* They *fired* me.

(He sits, his back to the wall)

EDNA Oh, my God. Don't tell me.

MEL Well, I'm telling you. *They fired me!* . . . Me, Hal Chesterman, Mike Ambrozi, Dave Polichek, Arnold Strauss . . . Two others, I can't even remember their names . . . Seven of us, in one fell swoop. *Fired!*

EDNA *(She is so distraught that she can't even stir in her chair)* Oh, Mel, I'm so sorry . . .

MEL They called us into the office one at a time. They didn't even have to say it, we knew. We saw it coming. Even the secretaries knew. They couldn't look at you when you said good morning . . . Eighty-five-dollar-a-week girls were bringing me coffee and Danish and not charging me for it. I knew right away.

EDNA Oh, Mel, Mel, Mel . . .

MEL They said they had no choice. They had to make cuts right down the line . . . Seven executives, twelve salesmen, twenty-four in office help—forty-three people in one afternoon . . . It took three elevators two trips to get rid of all the losers . . . Wait'll the coffee and Danish man comes in tomorrow, he'll throw himself out the window.

EDNA And then you come home to this. To get fired and then to come home and find your house has been robbed.

MEL It didn't happen today. It happened Monday.

EDNA Monday? You mean you've known for four days and you haven't said a word to me?

MEL I didn't know how to tell you, I couldn't work up the courage. I thought maybe another job would turn up, a miracle would happen . . . Miracles don't happen when you're forty-seven . . . When Moses saw the burning bush, he must have been twenty-three, twenty-four, the most. Never forty-seven.

(He goes into the kitchen, gets a can of beer)

EDNA What have you done since Monday? Where have you been? What did you do all day?

MEL *(Comes out of the kitchen, sits down, and drinks)* In the mornings I made phone calls, tried to see a few people.

When you're looking for help, you'd be surprised how many people are out to lunch at ten-thirty in the morning . . . In the afternoons? *(He shrugs)* I went to museums, an auction, the office-furniture show at the Coliseum . . . I saw an Italian movie, I saw a Polish movie . . . I saw two dirty movies . . . I met Dave Polichek at the dirty movie. We both lied. Said we were killing time until our next appointment. Some important appointments. I went to Central Park and he went to the Ripley Wax Museum.

EDNA You should have come home, Mel.

MEL Why? I had a very nice bench in the park near the Wollman Skating Rink. For lunch I had my jelly apple and my Fanta orange drink.

EDNA Oh, Mel, I can't bear it.

MEL I came very close to having an affair with a seventy-three-year-old English nanny. We hit it off very well but the baby didn't like me. *(At this point* EDNA *gets up and quickly rushes to* MEL, *who is still sitting. He reaches up and grabs her around the waist, holding on for dear life)* I'll be all right, Edna. I don't want you to worry about me. I'll be all right.

EDNA I know you will, Mel. I know it.

MEL I'll find another job, you'll see.

EDNA Of course you will.

MEL You'll take down the living room drapes, make me a suit, and I'll look for another job.

EDNA *(Hugs him)* Oh Mel, we'll be all right. We will.

(They break)

MEL I played two innings of softball yesterday.

EDNA You didn't.

(He sits on the sofa; she resumes picking up items)

MEL *(Nods)* Mm-hmm. With a day camp for fourteen-year-olds . . . Harvey, the right fielder, had to go for a violin lesson, so I played the last two innings.

EDNA And you hit a home run?

MEL I struck out, dropped two fly balls and lost the game . . . They wanted to kill me.

EDNA I wish I'd been there.

MEL I know I can make the team, I just have to get my timing back. If I don't find a job maybe I'll go back to camp this summer.

EDNA It would take me two minutes to sew in your name tapes. You want to think about it while I make you a cup of coffee?

(She starts for the kitchen)

MEL They didn't get the coffee? They left us the coffee? How come?

EDNA Robbers never go into the kitchen.

MEL Then why didn't you leave the money in the sugar jar?

EDNA Mel, we're insured. We'll get all the money back.

MEL We're lucky if we get half. You think you get two hundred dollars for a two-hundred-dollar coat? They depreciate. You put it on once, button it, it's worth forty dollars.

EDNA Then we'll get half the money back.

MEL Then the premiums go up. You get robbed once and it costs you twice as much to protect half of what you used to have.

EDNA *(Comes out of the kitchen)* Mel, please don't worry about the money. We have something put aside. We're not extravagant. We can live comfortably for a while.

MEL With two girls in college? With our rent, with our food bills, with nothing coming in? . . . We have to get out, Edna. We have to get out of everything.

(He paces around the room)

EDNA I'll go wherever you want, Mel.

MEL I don't mean out of here. Out of obligations. Out of things we don't need that are choking us. I'm gonna quit the gym. I don't need a gym for two hundred and fifty dollars a year. I'll run around the bedroom, it's the only way to keep warm in there anyway . . . And we don't need the Museum of Modern Art. We can watch *Duck Soup* on television. *(Picks up some magazines)* And these goddamn magazines. I don't want *Time, Life* or *Newsweek* any more, you understand. I'm not going to spend my last few dollars to find out that unemployment went up this year.

(He throws them into the wastebasket)

EDNA We don't need *any* of them. We never did, Mel.

MEL *(Looking around, throwing some more junk into the basket)* The garbage! The garbage that we buy every year. Useless, meaningless garbage that fills up the house until you throw it out there and it becomes garbage again and *stinks* up the house. For what? For *what,* Edna?

EDNA I don't know, Mel.

MEL Two dollars' worth of food that comes in three dollars' worth of wrapping. Telephone calls to find out what time it is because you're too lazy to look at a clock . . . The food we never ate, the books we never read, the records we never played. *(He picks up a little thing off the bar)* Look at this! Eight and a half dollars for a musical whiskey pourer. *Eight and a half dollars!* God forbid we should get a little bored while we're pouring our whiskey! Toys! Toys, novelties, gimmicks, trivia, garbage, crap, HORSESHIT!!!

(He hurls the basket to the floor)

EDNA No more. We'll never buy another thing, Mel. I promise. I promise.

MEL *(He is seething with anger)* Twenty-two years I gave them. What did I give them twenty-two years of my life for? A musical whiskey pourer? It's my *life* that's been poured down the drain. Where's the music? Where's a cute little tune? They kick you out after twenty-two years, they ought to have a goddamned brass band.

EDNA All right, don't get upset. You're going to get yourself sick.

MEL You know where my music is? *(He goes over to the wall and points)* There! There it is! It's playing on the other side of that wall. *(Screaming) There's my music after twenty-two years. (He grabs his chest, grimacing)* Ohh!

EDNA What is it, Mel? What's the matter?

MEL I got pains in my chest. It's nothing, don't worry. It's not a heart attack.

EDNA *(Nervously)* What do you mean? Why do you say it's not a heart attack?

MEL Because it's not a heart attack. It's pains in my chest.

EDNA Why are you having pains in your chest?

MEL BECAUSE I DON'T HAVE A JOB. BECAUSE I DON'T HAVE A SUIT TO WEAR! BECAUSE I'M HAVING A GODDAMNED BREAKDOWN AND THEY DIDN'T EVEN LEAVE ME WITH A PILL TO TAKE! *(He rushes out onto the terrace again and screams)* BASTARDS! . . . YOU DIRTY BASTARDS!

(Suddenly a VOICE, *probably from the terrace above, yells down)*

VOICE Shut up, down there! There are children up here!

MEL *(Leans over the terrace wall and yells up)* Don't you yell at me! They took everything! EVERYTHING! They left me with a goddamned pair of pants *and a golf hat!*

VOICE There are children up here! Are you drunk or something?

MEL Drunk? Drunk on what? They got my liquor . . . You wanna keep your children, lock 'em up. Don't you tell me you got children up there.

EDNA Mel, please. You're going to get yourself sick.

VOICE Don't you have any respect for anyone else?

MEL *(Screaming up)* Respect? I got respect for my ass, that's what I got respect for! That's all anybody respects . . .

(And suddenly MEL *gets hit with a torrent of water, obviously from a large bucket. He is drenched, soaked through—completely, devastatingly and humiliatingly . . . He comes back into the room. He is too stunned and shocked to be able to say a word)*

EDNA Oh, God. Oh, God, Mel.

MEL *(Very calmly and quietly, almost like a child who has been hurt)* That's a terrible thing to do . . . That's a mean, terrible thing to do.

(And he sits down on a chair and begins to sob. He just quietly sits there and sobs . . . EDNA *runs out to the terrace and yells up)*

EDNA God will punish you for that . . . I apologize for my husband's language, but God will punish you for that. *(She is crying too. She runs back to* MEL, *picks up some linens from the floor, and begins to dry his face and his head)* It's all right, Mel. It's all right, baby . . .

MEL That's a terrible thing to do to a person . . . I would never do that to anyone.

EDNA *(Wiping him)* Never. You're too good, Mel, too decent. You would never do that . . . It's going to be all right, Mel, I promise. You'll get another job, you'll see . . . And we'll move away from here. Someplace far away . . . You know what we could do? You're so good with kids, you love being with them, we could start a summer camp . . . You would be the head of the camp and I would do the cooking and the girls can be the riding instructors and the swimming instructors. You would like that, wouldn't you, Mel? We'll just have to save some money, that's all. And if you don't get another job right away, I can always be a secretary again. I can work, I'm strong, Mel . . . But you mustn't get sick. You mustn't get sick and die because I don't want to live in this world without you . . . I don't like it here! . . . I don't want you to leave me alone here . . . We'll show them, Mel. We'll show them all.

(She continues to wipe his ears as the curtain slowly falls)

Act Two

SCENE I

It is about six weeks later. It is mid-September, about one in the afternoon.

A radio is on, playing music.

From the bedroom we hear dull, rhythmic thumping sounds. The thump is repeated every few seconds. MEL *emerges from the bedroom. He is wearing khaki slacks, a pajama top, a bathrobe with the belt half open, and a pair of slippers. He has a baseball glove on his left hand and a baseball in his right. He keeps throwing the ball into the glove . . . thump . . . thump . . . thump . . .*

Six weeks of unemployment have turned MEL *into a different man. His eyes seem to be sunken into his sockets; he has rings under his eyes and seems to shave only sporadically. There is also a grimness about him, an anger, an hostility, the look of a man who is suffering from a deep depression coupled with a tendency to paranoia.*

He comes into the living room aimlessly. He has no place to go and no desire to go there. He wanders around the room not seeming to see anything. He walks in all the available walking spaces in the living room and dining room, like a prisoner taking his daily exercise. He keeps banging the ball into his glove with increasing intensity . . . thump . . . thump . . . thump . . .

He throws the ball up against the wall where the banging came from, then he crosses into the kitchen looking for something to eat.

Someone puts a key in the door; it opens. EDNA *rushes in, dressed smartly in a suit and carrying a small bundle of food in a brown paper bag. She throws down a magazine, calls out:*

EDNA Mel? . . . Mel, I'm home. *(She closes the door and enters the living room, turns off the radio, and then goes into the kitchen)* You must be starved. I'll have your lunch in a second. *(She takes things out of the package)* I couldn't get out of the office until a quarter to one and then I had to wait fifteen minutes for a bus . . . God, the traffic on Third Avenue during lunch hour . . . I got a cheese soufflé in Schrafft's, is that all right? I just don't have time to fix anything today, Mr. Cooperman wants me back before two o'clock, we're suddenly swamped with work this week . . . He asked if I would come in on Saturdays from now until Christmas but I told him I didn't think I could. *(She goes into the kitchen and gets out some pots)* I mean we could use the extra money but I don't think I want to spend Saturdays in that office too. We see each other little enough now as it is . . . Come in and talk to me while I'm cooking, Mel, I've only got about thirty-five minutes today. *(*EDNA *has put the casserole on the table and is now going into the kitchen, setting up two places with dishes and silverware)* My feet are absolutely killing me. I don't know why they gave me a desk because I haven't had a chance to sit at it in a month . . . Hi, love. I bought you *Sports Illustrated* . . . Mr. Cooperman told me there's a terrific story in there about the Knicks, he thought you might be interested in it. *(*MEL *tosses the magazine aside with some contempt)* You just can't move up Third Avenue because there's one of those protest parades up Fifth Avenue, or down Fifth Avenue, whichever way they protest . . . Fifteen thousand women screaming, "Save the environment," and they're all wearing leopard coats . . . God, the hypocrisy . . . Come on, sit down, I've got some tomato juice first. *(She pours tomato juice into two glasses.* MEL *listlessly moves over to the table and sits down)* Isn't that terrible about the Commissioner of Police? I mean *kidnapping* the New York Commissioner of Police? Isn't that insane? I mean if the cops can't find him, they can't find anybody. *(She sits down, picks up her glass of juice and takes a sip)* Oh, God, that's good. That's the first food I've had since eight o'clock this morning. We're so busy there we don't even have time for a coffee break . . . He's going to ask me to work nights, I know it, and I just don't know what to say to him . . . I mean he's been so nice to me, he buys me sandwiches two or three times a week, not that I don't deserve it, the way I've been working this past month, but I just don't want to spend any nights down there because I don't even have the strength to talk when I get home any more . . . I don't know where I'm getting the energy, I must have been saving it up for the past twenty-two years. *(She sips again)* I've got to stop talking because I'm all wound up and I'll never stop . . . How are you, darling? You feeling all right? *(*MEL *sits, staring into his tomato juice)* Mel? You all right?

MEL *(Mumbles something affirmative)* Mmm.

EDNA *(Looks at him)* Don't feel like talking much?

MEL Mmm.

EDNA Oh, come on, Mel. I've got to leave in about thirty minutes and I probably won't get home until seven o'-clock. Talk to me . . . What did you do today?

MEL *(He looks at her. He waits a long time before he answers)* I took a walk.

EDNA Oh, that's nice. Where?

MEL From the bedroom to the living room . . .

EDNA *(Nervous about his frame of mind, but restrains herself to keep from putting him on edge)* Is that all?

MEL No. I walked back into the bedroom . . . Once I went into the kitchen for a glass of water. What else you want to know?

EDNA Nothing. You don't feel like talking, that's all right.

MEL I feel like talking. You want to hear about the rest of my morning?

EDNA *(Sensing his anxiety)* I said it's all right, Mel.

MEL I looked out the window three times, listened to Martha Deane and went to the toilet, which is still flushing. I didn't jiggle it, I know you like to do it when you get home.

EDNA *(Sighs, puts down her glass)* All right, what's the matter, Mel?

MEL Nothing. I'm telling you about my terrific morning. You ready for some really exciting news? Martha Deane's guest tomorrow is the Galloping Gourmet. Isn't that exciting? He's going to give the secret recipes of five famous celebrities and we're going to have to guess whose casserole is whose . . . Too bad you're going to miss it.

EDNA You didn't sleep well again last night, did you?

MEL Last night? Was last night the night before this morning? I get them mixed up. I'm so busy with my life.

EDNA I thought you were going to take a walk in the park this morning.

MEL There is no place left for me to walk. I have walked on every path, every bridge and every stone. I know every squirrel in the park and I know where they all hide their nuts.

EDNA I know how cooped up you feel when you stay in the house all day. Maybe we can have lunch in the zoo tomorrow?

MEL I am *not* going to the zoo. I've been there every day for a month. When I walk by, the monkeys nudge each other and say, "He's here again."

EDNA I just thought you might get some exercise. Get into a softball game or something.

MEL There are no softball games. It's September, my whole team is in school.

EDNA They get out at three o'clock. You could wait for them.

MEL *(His voice rising)* I'm seven years older than the father of the pitcher. I am not going to wait for kids to get out of school so I can have someone to play with.

EDNA *(Controlling herself)* There is no reason to scream at me, Mel.

MEL I'm sorry. I'm alone a lot, I forgot what the normal voice range is. Is this any better?

EDNA Never mind, Mel . . . Did anybody call?

MEL Your mother. We exchanged recipes.

EDNA *(She drums her fingers on the table, trying to control herself)* Anyone else?

MEL I am not an answering service. You want me to answer phones, hire me. I need the work.

EDNA I take it then there was nothing in the paper today.

MEL About what?

EDNA You know about what, Mel. About a job.

MEL Yes. Mount Sinai Hospital is looking for surgical

technicians. The problem is my slacks are khaki and they require white.

EDNA I was just asking, Mel.

MEL And I'm just answering. There's a Puerto Rican luncheonette in East Harlem that's looking for a bilingual counterman. And Delta Airlines is looking for hostesses, but I don't want to be away from home that much. Don't you agree?

EDNA Mel, please stop it.

MEL You know what I think my best bet is? Maurice Le Peu in Queens is looking for a hair stylist. I thought I'd practice on you tonight, and if you didn't go bald, I'd give him a call tomorrow.

EDNA *(Throws her napkin down angrily)* What's wrong with you? *What's wrong with you today?*

MEL *(Slams his napkin down violently)* *Today? Today?* . . . How about seven weeks? How about almost two months walking around this apartment like a goddamned prisoner? I used to walk from room to room. Now I walk along the edges of the room so I can have longer walks . . . I have read every page of every book in this apartment. I have read every label of every can of food in the kitchen. Tomorrow I'm going to read underwear sizes. After that, I'm through. I have nothing left to live for.

EDNA *(Gets up)* I'm sorry, Mel. I know you're bored, I know you're unhappy. Tell me what I can do to help you.

MEL I'm forty-seven years old. Do you have to come home to make me lunches?

EDNA I *want* to make you lunches. I'm working, I have a job, I never see you. At least this way we get to spend an hour every day together.

MEL Don't you see how humiliating it is? Everyone in the building knows you come home to make me lunches. The only ones here who get lunches cooked for them every day are me and the six-year-old girl on the fourth floor.

EDNA I don't care what people in this building think.

MEL *I* care! *I CARE!!* . . . They probably think you make me take a nap too . . . I can make my own lunches. I can go out to eat.

EDNA I was just trying to save us money.

MEL What are you going to do in the winter when it snows, come home to put on my galoshes?

EDNA Is this what you do all morning? Walk around the edges of the apartment thinking of things like that? Torturing yourself?

MEL I don't have to torture *myself.* I got dogs, flushing toilets and the Red Baron's two sisters in there.

EDNA All right, what did they do today, Mel? Tell me.

MEL No, listen, I don't want to bother you. I know you've got your own problems at the office. You've got a living to make, don't worry about the house. That's my concern.

EDNA I thought we agreed about my working. I thought we agreed it was all right for me to take this job until something came through for you.

MEL I'm not complaining. You've been very nice to me. You pay the rent, buy the food, bought me a nice new sport jacket . . . Maybe next year you'll take me to Hawaii on United Airlines.

EDNA Do you want me to quit, Mel? Do you want me to leave the job? I'll leave the minute you say so, you know I will.

MEL Not this week. Margaret Truman has Bess Myerson on this Friday, I don't want to miss it. *(*EDNA *gets up and storms into the kitchen. She stands there over the stove and bangs her fist on it in desperation. Finally, after a long silence)* You think I haven't been looking? You think I haven't tried? That's what you think, isn't it?

EDNA *(From the kitchen)* I don't, Mel. I swear I don't. I know how hard you've tried.

MEL There are *no jobs* for forty-seven-years-old men . . . *Nothing! (Picks up* The New York Times*)* Here! Read it! It's all in *The New York Times.* I went out in the hall and stole it from the people next door . . . *I steal newspapers, Edna!*

EDNA *(Bringing in a pot of hot food from the kitchen)* Please, let's not talk about it any more.

MEL You want milk? I can get two quarts of milk every morning. If I wear my slippers they don't hear a thing.

EDNA Stop it, Mel, I don't think that's funny.

MEL I'm just trying to contribute, Edna . . . Just trying to do my share.

EDNA *(Puts some food onto the plate)* Please eat your lunch. It's the last time. I promise I won't make it any more.

MEL Why should you? When you can be in some nice Japanese restaurant eating sukiyaki with Mr. Cooperman sitting around with your shoes off.

EDNA I have never had sukiyaki with Mr. Cooperman.

MEL How about Fettucini with Mr. Feidelson? Look, I know what goes on in offices. I used to be one of the boys too.

EDNA Well, I am not "one of the girls."

MEL How come you get home at seven o'clock when everyone knows nobody works past five o'clock any more.

EDNA *I* work past five o'clock.

MEL Where? At Charley O's? Listen, I understand. A little drink to unwind before you go home to face the little man.

EDNA I don't believe what I'm hearing.

MEL You used to believe it when *I* came home at seven o'clock . . . You think it's a picnic sitting home all day wondering what's going on in that office? Try it sometime.

EDNA I feel like I'm watching my whole life running backwards on a movie screen.

MEL Maybe that's why I can't get a job. Maybe if I put on a wig, some high heels and a pair of hot pants, they'd hire me in a second.

EDNA *(Puts down the dish)* I'll leave the soufflé here. Eat it or not, do whatever you want. I'm leaving. I can't talk to you when you're like this.

MEL *(Mocking)* Have a good day, darling. Don't work too hard. Leave me some quarters for the laundromat.

EDNA *(Starts for the door, then stops)* You know what I would suggest, Mel?

MEL What? What would you suggest, Edna?

EDNA I suggest you either get a very tight grip on yourself . . . or you look for someone to help you.

MEL I don't need any help . . . I'm retired. I got it made.

EDNA You know what I'm talking about. Medical help. A doctor. Some doctor who can talk to you and straighten you out because I am *running out of energy and patience!*

MEL *(Looks at her and smiles)* You think it's all in my mind, don't you? . . . My God, you don't have the slightest inkling of what's been going on. You are so naïve, it's ridiculous.

EDNA What are you talking about, Mel? What's been going on?

MEL *(Smirking, as though he has some secret)* You think it's just by accident I can't find any work? You think it's just the breaks? I'm having a bad streak of luck, is that what you think?

EDNA I think it's the times, Mel. We are going through bad times.

MEL You have no suspicion of the truth, do you? None at all?

EDNA What truth? What truth are you talking about, Mel?

MEL I'm talking about the *plot*, Edna. The *plot.*

(She looks at him for a long time)

EDNA What plot, Mel?

MEL *(He stares at her incredulously, then laughs)* "What plot, Mel?" . . . I'm telling you about the plot and all you can say is, "What plot, Mel?"

EDNA I don't know what plot you're talking about. You mentioned there's a plot and all I can think of to say is, "What plot, Mel?"

MEL What plot? Jeez!
(He turns away from her)

EDNA *(Exasperated)* What plot? WHAT PLOT??

MEL *(He turns back toward her)* The–social–economical–and–political–plot–to–undermine–the–working–classes–in–this–country.

EDNA Oh, that plot.

MEL Yes, *that* plot! Instead of rushing downtown every morning, stay home and listen to the radio once in a while. Listen to the talk shows. Find out what's going on in this country. Ten minutes of WQXR and you'll want to move to Switzerland.

EDNA If it depresses you, Mel, don't listen to the talk shows. Listen to some nice music.

MEL Nice music . . . *(laughs)* Incredible. You're a child. You're an uninformed, ignorant little child . . . They've taken it over, Edna. Our music, our culture, it's not ours any more, it's *theirs.*

EDNA They have our music?

MEL All of it. The arts, the media, every form of mass communication. *They got it, baby!*

EDNA Don't get mad, Mel . . . Who?

MEL *Who? . . . WHO?? . . .* Jesus God in heaven! *Who???*

EDNA Mel, I've got to be in the office in twenty minutes. Please tell me who's taking over so I won't be late.

MEL All right, sit down.

EDNA I may not get a cab, Mel. Can't you tell me who's taking over standing up?

MEL Are you going to sit down?

EDNA Do I have to, Mel? Is it a long name?

MEL *Sit down, for Christ sakes! (*EDNA *sits down, while* MEL *paces)* Now . . . Once you do away with the middle class —what have you got left?

EDNA *(She looks at him. It can't be that easy)* What's left? After you take away the middle class? *(*MEL *nods)* The lower class and the upper class?

*(*MEL *stares at her incredulously)*

MEL I can't talk to you. You have no understanding at all. Go on. Go to work.

EDNA You mean there's another class besides the lower, the middle and the upper?

MEL *(He walks to the center of the room and looks around suspiciously)* Come here.

*(*EDNA *looks at him)*

EDNA I thought you wanted me to sit down.

MEL Will you come here. Away from the walls.

*(*EDNA *gets up and goes over to him in the middle of the room)*

EDNA If it's that secret, Mel, I don't think I want to know.

(He grabs her by the wrist and pulls her to him)

MEL *(In a soft voice)* There *is* a plot, Edna. It's very complicated, very sophisticated, almost invisible . . . Maybe only a half a dozen people in this country really know about it.

EDNA And they told it on the radio?

MEL Yes.

EDNA Then everyone heard it.

MEL Did you hear it?

EDNA No.

MEL Then everyone didn't hear it. How many people you think listen to the radio at ten o'clock in the morning? Everybody is working. But I heard it . . . And as sure as we're standing here in the middle of the room, there is a plot going on in this country today.

EDNA Against whom?

MEL Against me.

EDNA The whole country?

MEL Not me personally. Although I'm a victim of it. A plot to change the system. To destroy the status quo. It's not just me they're after, Edna. They're after you. They're after our kids, my sisters, every one of our friends. They're after the cops, they're after the hippies, they're after the government, they're after the anarchists, they're after Women's Lib, the fags, the blacks, the whole military complex. That's who they're after, Edna.

EDNA Who? You mentioned everyone. There's no one left.

MEL There's someone left. Oh, baby, there's someone left all right.

EDNA Well, I'm sure there is . . . if you say so, Mel.

MEL *(Yells)* Don't patronize me. I know what I'm talking about. I am open to channels of information twenty-four hours a day.

*(*EDNA *is becoming increasingly alarmed at* MEL*'s obvious paranoiac behavior, but doesn't quite know how to handle it yet)*

EDNA Mel, Mel . . . Would you come here for a minute. Just sit with me for a minute. *(He sits down)* Mel . . . You know I love you and believe in you completely. I always have . . . But I just want to say something, I hope you don't misunderstand this—

MEL You think I'm paranoiac? You think I'm having some sort of mental, nervous breakdown because I'm out of work? Because of the pressure, the strain I've been under, because I sound like a deranged person because of the personal hell I have gone through these past seven weeks. Is that it?

EDNA *(Nods)* That's it. That's exactly it, Mel . . . I wouldn't have put it that strongly, but that's more or less it. Exactly.

MEL Do you want proof, Edna? Do you want me to give you actual, indisputable proof?

EDNA *(Trying to be kinder now)* Of what, Mel?

MEL That me, that Dave Polichek, that Mike Ambrozi, Hal Chesterman, twenty-three secretaries, six point seven of the working force in this country today is unemployed not because of a recession, not because of wages and high prices, but because of a well-organized, calculated, brilliantly executed *plot!* Do you want me to give you proof right here and now in this room?

EDNA *(Hesitates)* Well—all right . . . If you want, Mel.

MEL I CAN'T GIVE YOU ANY PROOF!!! . . . *What kind of proof do I have?* I'm out of work, that's my proof . . . They won't let me work!

EDNA Who is it, Mel? Tell me who's behind the plot? Is it the kids? The addicts? The Army? The Navy? The Book-of-the-Month Club? WHO THE HELL IS IT, MEL?

MEL It is the human race! . . . It is the sudden, irrevocable deterioration of the spirit of man. It is man undermining himself, causing a self-willed, self-imposed, self-evident *self-destruction* . . . That's who it is.

EDNA *(Looks at him)* The human race? . . . The human race is responsible for the unemployment?

MEL *(A little smirk)* Surprised, aren't you?

EDNA *(Nods, quite shaken)* I never would have guessed. I kept thinking it was somebody else.

MEL *(Glares at her)* Don't mock me. Don't patronize me and don't mock me.

EDNA I'm not mocking you, Mel.

MEL *You're mocking me!* . . . I know when I'm being mocked. I know what I'm talking about. You're working, you've got a job, you're not affected by any of this.

EDNA I am so affected by it, Mel, you wouldn't believe it was possible . . .

MEL You don't know the first thing I'm talking about . . . You don't know what it is to be in my place . . . You've never stood on line for two hours waiting for an unemployment check with a shirt and tie, trying to look like you don't need the money. And some fat old dame behind the counter screaming out so everyone can hear, "*Did you look for a job this week?*" "Yes, I looked for a job." "*Did you turn down any work this week?*" "What the hell am I doing here if I turned down work this week?" . . . You never walked into your own building and had a ninety-one-year-old doorman with no teeth, asthma and beer on his breath giggle at you because *he's* working . . . You've never been on your own terrace and gotten hit with a bucket of ice-cold ice water . . . I haven't forgotten that son of a bitch! *(He goes to the terrace door, but not out on it, and yells up)* I haven't forgotten you, you son of a bitch!

EDNA Mel, don't start in again. Please don't start in again.

MEL I'm waiting for him. I'm just waiting for him. He's up there now, but one day he's gonna be down there and I'm gonna be up here and then we'll see. One cold, snowy day some son of a bitch in this building is gonna be buried under three feet of snow. They won't find him until the spring. *(Yells up again)* They won't find you until the spring, you son of a bitch!

EDNA Mel, listen to me. Listen to me very carefully. I want you to see a doctor . . . I don't want to put it off any more, Mel, I want you to see a doctor as soon as possible. Today, Mel. Now.

MEL *(Disregarding her, he keeps talking through her speeches)* He thinks I don't know what he looks like . . . I know what he looks like, all right . . . I know what they *all* look like. I've got their faces engraved in my brain.

EDNA *(Going through her pocketbook)* Mel, someone gave me the name of a doctor. They say he's very good and knows about people who've gone through what you're going through . . . I'm going to call him now, Mel. I'm going to call him and make an appointment now.

MEL *(He hasn't heard her)* They can get your clothes, Edna. They can get your clothes, your Valium, your television, your Red Label whiskey, your job, they can get everything. But they can't get your brains . . . That's my secret weapon . . . That and the snow . . . I pray to God it snows tomorrow, I'll wait for him. I bought a shovel today. Oh, yeah.

EDNA *(Finds the number)* I'm calling him, Mel . . . I'm calling him now.

(She goes over to the phone. He goes over to the closet)

MEL Not a little shovel, a big one. The kind they use in airports . . . I'll go without shoes this winter, but I won't go without my shovel. I'll bury him so deep, they'll have to salt him out.

(He takes out a shovel, the bottom part of which is in a box)

EDNA *(At the phone)* I won't go to work this afternoon, Mel. If he's free, I'm going to take you myself . . . Don't stand near the window, Mel.

(She begins to dial. He opens the box and takes out a shiny new shovel)

MEL *(A wild, joyous look on his face)* I live for it. I live for the first snow of the winter . . . He gets home at five fifteen, I checked with the doorman . . . I gave him a five-dollar tip, it was worth it. *(Yells up)* I know what time you get home, you bastard. Try using the service entrance, I got that blocked off too.

EDNA *(Into the phone)* Hello? . . . Is Doctor Frankel there, please? . . . Mrs. Edna Edison . . .

MEL *(To* EDNA, *oblivious of her on the phone)* Do you have any idea, any conception of the impact of two pounds of snow falling from a height of fourteen floors . . . They'll find him in the garage. *(Yells up)* They'll find you in the garage, you bastard . . . I know what you look like.

EDNA Hello? . . . Doctor Frankel? . . . I'm sorry to disturb you, but it's an emergency . . . No, for my husband . . . We've got to see you as soon as possible, Doctor Frankel, as soon as possible . . .

MEL *(He goes out onto the terrace)* And if it doesn't snow this winter, I'll wait till next winter . . . I'm in no hurry, smart ass. *(Yelling up)* I've got nothing but time . . . Nothing but time, baby . . .

(He laughs. The room goes black as the curtain falls. In the darkness, the News Logo appears. We hear the voice of Roger Keating again)

VOICE This is Roger Keating and the *Six O'Clock Report*

. . . No word yet on the unsolved mugging and robbing late last night of New York State Governor Nelson Rockefeller on Sixth Avenue and Forty-eighth Street. The governor will be heard in a special interview on the *Eleven O'Clock News* from his room in Beth Israel Hospital where he is resting, which, incidentally, is entering its fifty-seventh day of the hospital strike . . . "We will not go back to work" was the cry of forty-seven municipal, state and federal judges today, defying the court order of Federal Judge Myron Ackerman. Speaking for the striking judges, Judge Mario Pecona told this to CBS reporter Bethesda Wayne.

JUDGE'S VOICE We will not go back to woik.

GIRL'S VOICE Judge Pecona, isn't this strike unconstitutional?

JUDGE'S VOICE Yes, but we will not go back to woik.

GIRL'S VOICE How do you feel about the two hundred and seventy-three people in prisons now awaiting trial?

JUDGE'S VOICE We are underpaid. We will not go back to woik.

GIRL'S VOICE Do you still feel this way despite the fact that President Nixon has threatened to bring in the National Guard to run the courts?

JUDGE'S VOICE He can do what he wants, we will not go back to woik.

VOICE The *Six O'Clock Report* will follow with a filmed story of how twenty million rats survive under the city . . . But first this message from Ultra-Brite toothpaste.

(The News Logo fades as the curtain rises)

SCENE 2

It is midafternoon, two weeks later.

As the curtain rises, we see three women, all in their late fifties and dressed quite well. Two are on a sofa, one sits in armchair. These are MEL*'s sisters:* PAULINE, PEARL *and* JESSIE. PAULINE *is doing needlepoint. Standing is* MEL*'s older brother,* HARRY. *He wears an expensive business suit. He is looking out the window. A pot of coffee and cups are on the table in front of the women. They sit there silently.*

JESSIE He was always nervous.

PEARL Always.

JESSIE As far back as I can remember, he was nervous. Never sat still for a minute, always jumping up and down. Am I lying, Pearl?

PEARL We're his own sisters, who should know better? Up and down, up and down . . . You want some coffee, Harry? Take some coffee.

HARRY I don't drink coffee.

JESSIE He always used to fidget. Talked a mile a minute . . . He even chewed fast—remember how fast he used to chew?

PEARL Wasn't I there? Didn't I see him chew? I remember . . . Harry, why don't you take some coffee?

HARRY When did you ever see me drink coffee? You're my sister fifty-three years, you never saw me drink coffee. Why would I drink coffee now?

PEARL What do I see you, two times a year? I thought maybe you took up coffee.

PAULINE He wasn't nervous, he was high-strung. Melvin was high-strung.

PEARL I call it nervous. As a baby he was nervous, as a boy he was nervous, in the Army he was nervous. How long did he last in the Army, anyway?

JESSIE Two weeks.

PEARL There you are. He was nervous.

PAULINE Where do you think nerves come from? From being high-strung.

PEARL Then why weren't any of us high-strung? We all had the same parents. He was nervous, he was fidgety, he chewed fast . . . I never saw him swallow.

JESSIE No one could talk to him. Poppa could never talk to him, I remember.

PAULINE How could Poppa talk to him? Mel was three years old when Poppa died.

PEARL If he wasn't so nervous, Poppa could have talked to him.

HARRY I never drank coffee in my life. It's poison. Goes right through the system. *(Looks toward the bedroom)* Who's she on the phone with in there anyway?

PEARL He had the same thing in high school. A nervous breakdown. Remember when he had the nervous breakdown in high school?

HARRY *(Turning to her)* Who you talking about?

PEARL Mel! He had a nervous breakdown in high school. You don't remember?

HARRY What are you talking about? He didn't have a nervous breakdown, he had a broken arm. He fell in the gym and broke his arm.

PEARL I'm not talking about that time.

HARRY And once on his bicycle he broke his tooth.

PEARL I'm not talking about that time.

HARRY Then when are you talking about?

PEARL I'm talking about the time he had a nervous breakdown in high school. I remember it like it was yesterday, don't tell me. Pauline, tell him.

PAULINE Mel never had a nervous breakdown.

PEARL Isn't that funny, I thought he had a nervous breakdown. Maybe I'm thinking of somebody else.

HARRY You can't even remember that I don't drink coffee.

PAULINE He must have had some terrible experiences in the Army.

HARRY In two weeks? He wasn't there long enough to get a uniform. None of you know what you're talking about. There was never anything wrong with Mel. Never. His trouble was you babied him too much. All of you.

JESSIE Why shouldn't we baby him? He was the baby, wasn't he?

HARRY You babied him, that's his trouble. He never had the responsibilities as a child like I did. That's why he can't handle problems. That's why he flares up. He's a child, an infant.

PEARL What if I put some milk in the coffee?

HARRY I DON'T WANT ANY COFFEE!!

JESSIE He doesn't want any coffee, leave him alone.

PAULINE Correct me if I'm wrong, but when Mel was a tiny baby, didn't you think his head was too large for his body?

PEARL Mel? Mel had a beautiful head.

PAULINE I didn't say his head wasn't beautiful. I said it was too large for his body. It always kept falling over to one side.

(She demonstrates)

PEARL *All* babies' heads fall to one side.

(She demonstrates)

PAULINE I know that, but he had trouble getting his up again.

(She demonstrates)

HARRY I was never babied. Poppa wouldn't allow it . . . I was never kissed from the time I was seven years old.

JESSIE Certainly you were kissed.

HARRY Never kissed . . . I didn't need kissing. The whole world kissed Mel, look where he is today. Who's she talking to in there all this time?

PEARL Remember the summer he ran away?

PAULINE He didn't run away for the whole summer. He ran away for one night.

PEARL Who said he ran away for the whole summer?

PAULINE Who said it? You said it. You just said, "Remember the summer he ran away?"

PEARL So? He ran away for *one* night *one* summer.

PAULINE But you should say it that way. Say, "Remember the summer he ran away for one night?" . . . Don't make it sound like he ran away for a whole summer. That crazy he never was.

PEARL Did I say Mel was crazy? Who heard me mention the word crazy? Jessie, did you hear "crazy" from me?

JESSIE I heard "crazy" but I wasn't looking where it came.

PEARL *(To* PAULINE*)* If that's what you believe, *you're* the one that's crazy.

PAULINE All right, if it makes you happy, I'm crazy. Let me be the crazy one.

PEARL Fine. Then it's settled. You're the crazy one.

HARRY Listen, I've got to get back to the office, Jessie's going back to Lakewood tonight, let's try to settle things now. What are we going to do?

PAULINE About what?

HARRY *(Looks at her as though she's deranged)* About *what?* About the Suez Canal. What do you mean, about what? What are we here for? What did Jessie come all the way from Lakewood for? What are we doing in that woman's house, *(Points to the bedroom)* where none of us have been invited for nine years? Our brother. Our sick brother who's had a nervous breakdown, for God's sakes.

JESSIE *(Sniffles, wipes her eyes with a handkerchief)* Every time I hear it—

HARRY What are you crying *now* for? You didn't just hear. You've known for a week.

JESSIE You think I haven't been crying the whole week? He's my brother, it hurts me.

HARRY It hurts all of us. That's why we're here. To try to do something.

PAULINE Harry, let her cry if she wants. She came all the way from Lakewood . . . Go on, Harry.

HARRY Fact number one, Mel has had a nervous breakdown. Fact number two, besides a nervous breakdown, Mel doesn't have a job. The man is totally unemployed.

JESSIE *(Sniffles again)* You think that doesn't hurt me too?

PAULINE Jessie, let him finish, you can cry on the way home.

HARRY Fact—

PAULINE Go on with the facts, Harry.

HARRY Fact number three, besides a nervous breakdown and not having a job, the man is practically penniless . . . I don't want to pass any comments on how a man and a woman mishandled their money for twenty-seven years. It's none of my business how a man squandered a life's savings on bad investments for which he never asked my advice once, the kind of advice which has given me solvency, security and a beautiful summer place in the country. Thank God, *I'll* never have a nervous breakdown . . . None of that is my business. My business is what are we going to do for Mel? How much are we going to give? Somebody make a suggestion. *(The silence is deafening. No one speaks. No one looks at each other. There is a lot of coffee drinking, but no offers as to how much they're going to give . . . After what seems like an hour of silence,* HARRY *speaks again)* Well?

PEARL You're a businessman, Harry. You make a suggestion. You tell us how much we should all give.

HARRY *(Thinks a moment)* Let me have some coffee. *(*PEARL *pours him a cup of coffee)* So let's face the facts . . . The man needs help. Who else can he turn to but us? This is my suggestion. We make Mel a loan. We all chip in X number of dollars a week, and then when he gets back on his feet, when he gets straightened out, gets a job again, then he can pay us all back. That's my suggestion. What do you all think?

(There is a moment's silence. PAULINE *whispers to* PEARL. PEARL *nods)*

PEARL Pauline has a question.

HARRY What's the question?

PAULINE How much is X number of dollars?

HARRY X is X. We have to figure out what X is. We'll talk and we'll decide.

PAULINE I mean is it a big X or a little x?

HARRY It's not even an X. It's a blank until we fill X in with a figure.

PAULINE I'm not complaining. We have to do the right thing. But when you say it like that, "X number of dollars," it sounds like a lot of money . . . I have limited capital, you know.

JESSIE Everybody has limited capital. Nobody has *un*limited capital. Pearl, do you have unlimited capital?

PEARL I wish I did. I'd give Mel X number of dollars in a minute.

PAULINE All I'm asking is, how much is X. I can't figure with letters, I have to know numbers.

JESSIE Harry, don't say X any more. We're not businesswomen, we don't know about X. Say a number that we can understand.

HARRY I can't say a number until I figure out A, how much does Mel need a week, and B, how much are we willing to give. I can't even guess what X is until we figure out how much A and B come to.

PEARL All right, suppose we figure out what A is and what B is. And if we know that, then we'll figure what X is, right?

HARRY Right.

PEARL And now suppose everyone here agrees except one

person. She thinks it's too much. She doesn't want to give X. She wants to give M or W, whatever. What do we do then?

HARRY Forget X. Forget I ever said X. *(He rubs his head and drinks some more coffee)* Let's figure what Mel needs to get over his nervous breakdown . . . His biggest expense is the doctor, right? Edna says he's the best and he has to go five times a week.

PAULINE Five times a week to the best doctor? I'm beginning to see what X is going to come to.

JESSIE Maybe it's not even a nervous breakdown. Doctors can be wrong, too. Remember your pains last year, Pearl?

PEARL It's true. They took out all my top teeth, then found out it was kidney stones.

HARRY I can't believe what I'm listening to . . . You're a hundred and sixty years old between the three of you and not one of you makes any sense . . . If you'll all be quiet for a minute, I'll settle this thing.

PEARL All right, we're quiet. Settle it, Harry.

HARRY The most important thing is that Mel gets well, agreed?

ALL THREE Agreed!

HARRY And that the only way he's going to get well is to see a doctor. Agreed?

ALL THREE Agreed.

HARRY And it is our obligation, as his only living relatives —not counting his wife, no disrespect intended—to bear the financial responsibility of that burden. Agreed?

ALL THREE Agreed.

HARRY And we'll all see this thing through to the end whether it takes a week or a month or a year or even five years. Agreed? *(There is stony silence)* Okay. Our first disagreement.

PAULINE No one's disagreeing. We're all in agreement. Except when you mention things like five years. I don't see any sense in curing Mel and ending up in the poorhouse. If, God forbid, that happened, would he be in any position to help us? He's not too able to begin with.

JESSIE So what should we do, Harry? You know how to figure these things. What should we do?

HARRY Well, obviously we can't afford to let Mel be sick forever. We've got to put a time limit on it. Agreed?

ALL THREE Agreed.

HARRY What do we give him to get better? Six months?

PAULINE It shouldn't take six months. If that doctor's as good as Edna says, it shouldn't take six months.

(The door to the bedroom is heard closing)

PEARL Shhh . . . She's coming.

PAULINE We'll let Harry do the talking.

PEARL And then we'll settle everything. Thank God, it's almost over.

(They all assume a pose of innocence and calm. EDNA *comes out of the bedroom)*

EDNA I'm sorry I was so long. I was just talking to Doctor Frankel. Mel's on his way home, he'll be here in a minute.

HARRY How is Mel? What does the doctor say?

EDNA Well, it's hard to tell. Mel is having a very rough time. He's in a very depressed state, he's not himself. He's completely withdrawn. He sits in that chair sometimes for hours without saying a word. You'll see when he comes in, he's a different person.

JESSIE *(Wipes her eyes with a hanky, sniffs)* It hurts me every time I hear it . . .

PAULINE So what is it, a nervous breakdown? Is it a nervous breakdown? You can tell us. We're his family. It's a nervous breakdown, isn't it?

EDNA Yes, in a way I guess you can say it's a nervous breakdown.

PEARL I knew it, I knew it. He had the same thing in high school.

HARRY So what's the diagnosis? What does the doctor say?

EDNA *(Shrugs)* Mel needs care and treatment. He's a very good doctor, he thinks Mel's going to be all right, but it's just going to take time.

PAULINE How much time? A month? Two months? More than two months?

EDNA He can't tell yet.

PAULINE He can guess, can't he? Three months? Four months? More than four months?

EDNA There's no way of telling yet, Pauline. It could be a month, it could be two months, it could be two *years.*

PAULINE No, two years is out of the question. I refuse to go along with two years.

EDNA I'm not saying it will be. I'm just saying we don't know yet.

HARRY Can I say something? Can I get a word in?

PAULINE *(Turning away from* EDNA*)* I wish you would say something, Harry. I wish you would do the talking.

HARRY Thank you very much.

PAULINE Because two years is ridiculous.

PEARL Go on, Harry.

HARRY We're all very concerned, Edna. Very concerned. After all, he's our brother.

JESSIE Since he was a baby.

HARRY Can I please do the talking?

PEARL Will you let him do the talking, Jessie? . . . Go on, Harry.

HARRY We're very concerned. We appreciate that you're his wife, you're going to do all you can, but we know it's not going to be enough. We want to help. We've talked it out among ourselves and . . . we're prepared to take over the financial burden of the doctor. You take care of the apartment, the food, the miscellaneous, we'll pay the doctor bills. Whatever they come to.

EDNA I'm . . . I'm overwhelmed . . . I'll be very truthful with you, I never expected that . . . I am deeply touched and overwhelmed. I don't know what to say . . .

HARRY You don't have to say anything.

PAULINE Just tell us what you think the bills will come to.

EDNA That's very generous of you all, but I couldn't let you do that. Mel wouldn't let me do it.

HARRY Don't be ridiculous. Where you going to get the money from, a bank? You can't put up a nervous breakdown as collateral.

EDNA I have no idea how long Mel will be in treatment. It could run into a fortune.

HARRY Let us worry about that. The money, we'll take care of.

EDNA But it could run as high as twenty, twenty-five thousand dollars.

(There is a long pause. The sisters all look at HARRY*)*

PAULINE Harry, can I say something to you in private?

HARRY We don't need any private discussions.

PAULINE We just found out what X is . . . Don't you think we ought to discuss X a little further?

HARRY It's not necessary. I don't care what it's going to cost. The three of you can contribute whatever you think you can afford, *I'll* make up the deficit . . . If it's fifteen, if it's twenty, if it's twenty-five thousand, I'll see that it's taken care of, as long as Mel has the best medical treatment . . . That's all I have to say.

(He nods his head as though taking a little bow)

EDNA *(Moved)* I'm—I'm speechless . . . What do I say?

HARRY You don't say nothing.

PEARL We just want to do the right thing.

EDNA I know none of us have been very close the last few years.

PAULINE Nine. Nine years was the last time we were invited.

EDNA Has it been that long? I suppose it's been my fault. Maybe I haven't tried to understand you. Maybe you haven't tried to understand me. Anyway, I appreciate it more than you can imagine, but we really don't need it.

HARRY What are you talking about? Certainly you need it.

EDNA Over the years, we've managed to save something. I have some jewelry I can sell . . .

HARRY You're not going to sell your jewelry.

PAULINE Maybe she doesn't wear it any more. Let the woman talk.

EDNA Mel can cash in his insurance policy and I have my job. I can manage whatever the medical expenses come to, but if you really want to help . . . What I'm worried about is Mel's future.

JESSIE We all are, darling.

EDNA It's not easy for a man of Mel's age to get a job today, to start all over again . . .

HARRY If he knew lighting fixtures, I would take him in a minute.

PEARL Certainly, my God.

EDNA If he could just get out of New York and move to the country somewhere, he would be a hundred per cent better off.

HARRY I agree a thousand per cent.

EDNA I was thinking of a summer camp. Mel is wonderful with children and sports, I could do the cooking, the girls will help out, we can hire a small staff . . . There's a lovely place in Vermont that's for sale. We could have it for next summer. Don't you think Mel would be better off there?

HARRY Again, a thousand per cent.

EDNA They want twenty-five thousand dollars down in cash . . . So instead of giving it to us for the doctor, would you lend it to us for the camp?

(There is a hush, a definite hush. HARRY *looks at* EDNA *in disbelief)*

HARRY A summer camp? . . . Twenty-five thousand dollars for a summer camp?

EDNA The price is a hundred thousand. But they want twenty-five thousand down.

HARRY *A hundred thousand dollars* for a *summer camp??* . . . Run by a man with a nervous breakdown?

EDNA He'll be all right by next summer.

HARRY Do you know what it is for a *normal* person to be responsible for that many boys and girls? The lawsuits you're open for?

EDNA I don't understand. You were willing to give Mel the money for a doctor. Why won't you lend it to him for a camp?

HARRY Because with a camp you can go broke. With a doctor you can go broke too, but you get better.

EDNA All right. *You* pay for the doctor. *I'll* invest in the camp.

HARRY You mean we should pay to get Mel healthy so you can lose your money in a camp and get him sick again? . . . Then you'll come to us for more money for another doctor?

EDNA I thought you wanted to do something. I thought you wanted to help him.

HARRY We *do* want to help him.

EDNA *Then help him!*

HARRY Not when he's sick. When he's better, we'll help him.

EDNA *(Turns to the sisters)* Is that how the rest of you feel? Do you all agree with Harry?

(They all look at one another uncomfortably)

PAULINE *(Looking in her coffee cup)* I am not familiar with Vermont.

JESSIE I'd say yes in a minute, but Harry's the spokesman.

PEARL I'd have to go up and see it first, but I can't travel with my leg.

EDNA All right . . . Forget it. Forget the money, we don't need it. We'll get along without it very nicely, thank you . . . I'm surprised you even offered it . . . It's good to know that the minute Mel is completely recovered and back on his own two strong feet again, I can count on you for help. That's just when we'll need it. *(She starts toward the bedroom)* Will you please excuse me? I've got to make some calls before I go back to the office . . . Just in case I don't see any of you for another nine years, *(Points to the tray)* have some cookies . . .

(She storms into the bedroom, slamming the door behind her. They all look at one another, stunned)

HARRY What did I say that was wrong? You're my witnesses, what did I say that was wrong?

PEARL You said nothing wrong. I'm a witness.

PAULINE The truth is, she doesn't *want* us to help him. She's jealous. And I was willing to give him *anything.*

JESSIE *(To* PEARL*)* Does that mean we're not giving for the doctor either?

PEARL *(To* JESSIE*)* Why don't you pay attention? You never pay attention.

HARRY A man in his condition running a summer camp. I spoke to him on the phone Thursday, he could hardly say hello.

PAULINE Why does she hate us? What did we ever do to her? It's jealousy, that's what it is.

PEARL That's all it is.

PAULINE Jealousy . . . I'd like to get him out of here. He could move in with me, I'd love to take care of him.

HARRY A man in his condition running a summer camp. It would take him until August to figure out how to blow up the volleyball.

JESSIE If nothing is settled yet, can I give my vote to Pauline? I've got shopping to do.

HARRY *Sit down! Nothing has been settled!* . . . We'll have to settle it with Mel.

PEARL With Mel? How can Mel make a decision in his condition?

HARRY Him I can reason with. He's only had a nervous breakdown. *That* woman is crazy! Let me have some more coffee.

(PEARL *starts to pour* HARRY *some more coffee when suddenly we hear a key in the latch and the door opens.* MEL *enters. He looks aged. Perhaps aged isn't the right word. Distant might describe it better. His eyes are ringed and his hair is slightly unkempt; he has a glazed expression on his face. He opens the door and closes it, puts his key in his pocket, and goes across the room and into the kitchen without looking up and without noticing the others sitting there. They all look at him, puzzled and slightly horrified at his behavior. In the kitchen* MEL *pours himself a glass of water and then takes out a small vial of pills. He takes a pill, places it in his mouth and drinks the water. He comes back into the living room. He doesn't seem startled or surprised; it is as though he were sixteen again and coming into a familiar setting. When he speaks, his voice lacks emotion)*

MEL I just had a nice walk.

HARRY *(Goes to him)* Hello, Mel.

MEL *(Looks at him)* From Eighty-second and Park. *(He whispers)* Don't tell Edna. She doesn't like me to walk too far.

HARRY Mel? *(Points to himself)* Do you know who this is?

MEL What do you mean, Harry?

HARRY Nothing. Nothing. *(Points to the girls)* Look who's here to see you, Mel.

(MEL *turns and looks at the sisters)*

MEL *(Smiles)* Why shouldn't they come to see me? They're my own sisters, aren't they? Who has better sisters than I have? *(He opens up his arms to greet them and goes to* PAULINE*)* Pauline! How are you?

(He kisses her. She hugs him)

PAULINE Mel, darling.

MEL *(Turns to* JESSIE*)* And Jessie. Sweet Jessica Jessie . . .

(He kisses her)

JESSIE You look—wonderful, Mel.

(She sniffles and fights back the tears. His back is to PEARL*)*

MEL Everyone's here but Pearl.

PEARL *(How could he miss her?)* Here I am, Mel.

MEL *(Turns around)* There she is, hiding . . . Always hiding from your baby brother.

PEARL I wasn't hiding, Mel. I was just sitting.

HARRY *(Takes* MEL *by the arm)* Mel, sit down. We want to talk to you.

MEL *(Looks at him suspiciously)* Something is wrong. Someone in the family is sick.

HARRY No. No one is sick, Mel . . . Everybody is fine. Sit down.

(He urges MEL *into a chair.* MEL *sits down)*

MEL I had such a nice walk.

JESSIE Isn't that wonderful, Mel. You always used to like to walk.

*(*PEARL *gets up and goes over to the window behind* MEL*. She takes out a hanky and wipes her eyes)*

MEL Remember how I used to like to walk, Jessie?

JESSIE I do, Mel, I was just saying that.

PAULINE You're looking very well, darling.

MEL Thank you, Pauline.

PAULINE Are you feeling all right?

(She swallows the last word)

MEL What's that, darling?

PAULINE I said, are you feeling all right?

MEL Am I feeling all right? . . . Yes . . . Yes, I just had a very nice walk.

PAULINE Oh, that's nice, dear.

MEL *(Looks around)* Where's Pearl? Did Pearl go home?

PEARL *(At the window, behind him)* Here I am, Mel. I didn't go home.

MEL *(Turns around)* There she is. Hiding again . . . She always used to hide from me.

HARRY *(Pacing)* Mel . . .

MEL Yes, Harry?

HARRY *(Stops)* Mel . . .

PEARL Harry wants to say something to you, Mel.

MEL What is it, Harry?

HARRY Nothing, Mel . . . Nothing.

MEL You don't look well to me, Harry. You're working too hard . . . Don't work so hard, Harry.

HARRY I won't, Mel.

MEL You have to relax more. Three things I learned at the doctor's, Harry. You have to relax, you mustn't take the world too seriously . . . and you have to be very careful of what you say when you go out on the terrace.

*(Curtain. News Logo in—*Six O'Clock Report*)*

VOICE OVER This is the *Six O'Clock Report* with Stan Jennings sitting in for Roger Keating, who was beaten and mugged last night outside our studio following the *Six O'Clock Report* . . . A Polish freighter, the six-thousand-ton *Majorska,* sailed into New York harbor in dense fog at 7:00 A.M. this morning and crashed into the Statue of Liberty. Two seamen were injured and electrical damage caused flickering in Miss Liberty's torch. It was the first recorded maritime accident involving the famed statue, although the Polish freighter had been in six previous sea collisions . . . And today, in a midtown hotel following a convention of the National Psychiatric Society, seventeen of the leading psychiatrists in the United States were trapped between floors in an elevator for over forty-five minutes. Panic broke out and twelve of the doctors were treated for hysteria.

SCENE 3

It is mid-December, six weeks later. It is late afternoon.

As the curtain rises, EDNA *is on the phone. She is wearing a winter coat over her suit. A grocery package is in her arms. She has obviously just come in and seems rather distraught.*

EDNA *(Into the phone)* Hello? . . . Is the superintendent there, please? . . . Mrs. Edison. 14A. I have no water. There is no water in the house . . . What do you mean he's out? Out where? I have no water. I just walked in the house . . . Well, if they're fixing the pipes, shouldn't he be in the building? He's getting paid for that, isn't he? . . . I didn't see any sign in the elevator. I have other things on my mind besides reading signs in elevators . . . I have no electricity in the kitchen . . . No, just the kitchen . . . Just–the–kitchen! I don't know why, I'm not an electrician . . . I can't wait until seven o'clock . . . My food is spoiling and you're telling me your husband is out? . . . I don't blame him. I wouldn't hang around this building either if I didn't have to. *(*MEL *has entered from the front door during the phone conversation. She hangs up and stands there)* There's no water. The water is shut off . . . They're fixing the pipes, we won't have any until five, six, seven, they're not sure when . . . And there's no electricity in the kitchen. The refrigerator's off . . . I called the super, he's out.

(She sits down. He goes to the table and puts his paints back in their box. His easel and canvas are left standing)

MEL I'm not going back. I'm not going back to that doctor. He's a quack. He sits there cleaning his pipe, playing with his watch fob, and doesn't know what the hell he's talking about. The man is a quack. If I'm getting better, I'm doing it myself . . . I'm working my *own* problems out. That man sits there playing with a pipe scooper watching *me* get better for forty dollars an hour . . . I got mirrors in the house, I can watch myself get better. I could lay there for fifty minutes, if I don't say a word, he won't say a word. What would kill him *(During this, he has been going to the closet, putting his paint box, easel and canvas away)* to ask me a question? "What's wrong, Mr. Edison? What are you thinking about?" . . . Not him. If I don't bring it up, he don't ask. I'm curing myself, I'm telling you. I see how you look when you come home every night. Killing yourself, breaking your back and for what? To give forty dollars an hour to a pipe cleaner? I can't take it any more, Edna. I can't see you turning yourself into an old woman just for me. What's the point in it? As soon as I'm all right again, I'll be too young for you.

EDNA *(Holding back tears)* Well, I don't think you have to worry about that any more, Mel . . . We went out of business today.

MEL Who did?

EDNA We did. The business that I'm in is out of business. There is no business in that place any more.

MEL They let you go?

EDNA If *they're* not staying, what do they need me for?

MEL You mean completely out of business?

EDNA They went bankrupt. They overextended themselves. One of the partners may go to jail.

(She starts to cry)

MEL You don't go bankrupt overnight. You must have had some inkling.

EDNA *(Crying)* I had *no* inkling . . . I did, but I was afraid to think about it . . . What's happening, Mel? Is the whole world going out of business?

MEL *(Goes over to her)* Okay. It's all right, Edna, it's all right.

EDNA *(Sobbing)* I thought we were such a strong country, Mel. If you can't depend on America, who can you depend on?

MEL Ourselves, Edna. We have to depend on each other.

EDNA I don't understand how a big place like that can just go out of business. It's not a little candy store. It's a big building. It's got stone and marble with gargoyles on the roof. Beautifully hand-chiseled gargoyles, Mel. A hundred years old. They'll come tomorrow with a sledgehammer and kill the gargoyles.

MEL It's just a job, Edna. It's not your whole life.

EDNA You know what I thought about on the way home? One thing. I only had one thing on my mind . . . A bath. A nice, hot bath. *(Sobs again)* And now the water went out of business.

MEL It'll come back on. Everything is going to come back on, Edna. They're not going to shut us off forever.

EDNA *(She yells)* I want my bath! I want my water! Tell them I want my bath, Mel!

MEL It's off, Edna. What can I do? There's nothing I can do.

EDNA *(Yells)* Bang on the pipes. Tell them there's a woman upstairs who needs an emergency bath. If I don't sit in some water, Mel, I'm going to go crazy. Bang on the pipes.

MEL Edna, be reasonable . . .

EDNA *(Screams)* *I banged for you, why won't you bang for me?*

MEL Shh, it's all right, baby. It's all right.

EDNA *(Still sobbing)* It's *not.* It's *not* all right. Why are you saying it's all right? Are you out of your mind? Oh, God, Mel, I'm sorry. I didn't mean that. Please forgive me, Mel.

MEL It's all right, Edna . . . Please calm down.

EDNA I don't know what I'm saying any more. It's too much for me, Mel. I have no strength left, Mel. Nothing. I couldn't open my pocketbook on the bus; a little boy had to help me.

MEL Of course you have strength.

EDNA I have anger, no strength . . . If something happens to me, Mel, who's going to take care of us?

MEL I am. I always took care of you, didn't I?

EDNA But who's going to take care of us now, Mel?

MEL Me, Edna. Me!

EDNA You, Mel?

MEL Don't you trust me, Edna? Don't you believe in me any more?

EDNA Let's leave, Mel. Let's give up and leave . . . Let them have it. Let them have their city . . . Let them keep their garbage and their crooks and their jobs and their broken gargoyles . . . I just want to live out the rest of my life with you and see my girls grow up healthy and happy and once in a while I would like to have some water and take a bath . . . Please, Mel . . . Please.

MEL All right, Edna . . . We'll go . . . We'll go.

(The doorbell chimes)

EDNA *(Yells)* That's the super!

MEL I'll take care of it! Edna, you're very upset. Why don't you relax, and wait in the tub for the water to come on . . .

EDNA All right, Mel . . . I'm sorry if I upset you.

(She turns and goes off into the bedroom. He turns, goes over to the door and opens it. HARRY *stands there; he is carrying an attaché case)*

HARRY Hello, Mel . . . All right if I come in?

MEL *(Surprised)* Sure, Harry, sure. I didn't know you were in New York.

HARRY *(Speaks softly)* I had some business, and besides, I wanted to talk to you. How you feeling? All right?

MEL Don't be so solemn, Harry. It's not a hospital room. I'm all right.

*(*HARRY *enters;* MEL *closes the door)*

HARRY I brought you some apples from the country. *(He opens his attaché case)* Wait'll you taste these. *(He takes some apples from the case)* You always loved apples, I remember . . . Are you allowed to eat them now?

MEL Apples don't affect the mind, Harry. They're not going to drive me crazy. Thank you. That's very nice of you.

HARRY Is Edna here?

MEL Yeah, she's in the tub. She's not feeling very well.

HARRY It's all right. She doesn't want to see me. I understand.

MEL It's not that, Harry. She's very tired.

HARRY The woman doesn't like me. It's all right. The whole world can't love you . . . I feel badly that it's my brother's wife, but that's what makes horse racing. I'm only staying two minutes. I wanted to deliver this in person and then I'll go.

MEL You came eight miles to bring me six apples? Harry, that's very sweet but it wasn't necessary.

HARRY Not the apples, Mel. I have something a little more substantial than apples. *(Reaches in his pocket and takes out a check)* Here. This is for you and Edna . . . The apples are separate.

(MEL takes the check and looks at it)

MEL What's this?

HARRY It's a check. It's the money. Go buy yourself a summer camp. *(Good-naturedly)* Go. July and August, take care of six hundred running noses. Have a good time.

(He gets up to go)

MEL Harry, this is twenty-five thousand dollars.

HARRY Your sisters and I contributed equally, fifty-fifty. I'm telling them about it tomorrow.

MEL I don't understand.

HARRY I don't understand myself. Why would anyone want to run a summer camp? But if that gives you pleasure, then this gives me pleasure . . .

MEL When did Edna ask you for this?

HARRY What's the difference? It's over. Everybody got a little excited. Everyone was trying to do the right thing. Take the money, buy your crazy camp.

MEL Harry!

HARRY Yes?

MEL In the first place . . . thank you. In the second place, I can't take it.

HARRY Don't start in with me. It took me six weeks to decide to give it to you.

MEL I can't explain it to you, Harry. But I just can't take the money.

HARRY Why don't you let me do this for you? Why won't you let me have the satisfaction of making you happy?

MEL You already have, by offering it. Now make me happier by tearing it up. They see this much money in this neighborhood, you'll never make it to your car.

HARRY You let everyone else do things for you. You let everyone else take care of you. Edna, Pearl. Pauline, Jessie. Everybody but me, your brother. Why am I always excluded from the family?

MEL They're three middle-aged widows, they're looking for someone to take care of. I made them a present, I got sick. What do you want from me, Harry?

HARRY I had to work when I was thirteen years old. I didn't have time to be the favorite.

MEL Harry, let's not go into that again. You want to be the favorite, I give it to you. I'll call the girls up tonight and tell them from now on, you're the favorite.

HARRY I'm not blaming you! I'm not blaming you. It's only natural. If there are two brothers in the family and one is out working all day, the one who stays home is the favorite.

MEL Harry, I don't want to seem impolite. But Edna's not feeling well, we have no water, and all our food is defrosting. I'm really not in the mood to discuss why you're not the favorite.

HARRY I lived in that house for thirty-one years, not once did anyone ever sing me "Happy Birthday."

MEL *(Exasperated)* Not true, Harry. You always had a birthday party. You always had a big cake.

HARRY I had parties, I had cakes, no one ever sang "Happy Birthday."

MEL All right, this year I'm going to hire a big chorus, Harry, and we're going to sing you "Happy Birthday."

HARRY Eleven years old I was wearing long pants. Fourteen I had a little mustache . . . At the movies I had to bring my birth certificate, they wanted to charge me adult prices.

MEL I know, Harry. You grew up very fast.

HARRY Did you ever see Pearl's family album? There are no pictures of me as a boy. I skipped right over it. Thousands of pictures of you on bicycles, on ponies, in barber chairs . . . one picture of me in a 1938 Buick. I looked like Herbert Hoover.

MEL I'm sorry, Harry.

HARRY I'm going to tell you something now, Mel. I never told this to anybody. I don't think you've got a brain for business. I don't think you know how to handle money. I don't think you can handle emotional problems. I think you're a child. A baby. A spoiled infant . . . And as God is my judge, many's the night I lay in bed envying you . . . Isn't that something? For a man in my position to envy a man in your position? . . . Isn't that something? What I have, you'll never have . . . But what you've got, I'd like to have just once—just for an hour to see what it feels like to be the favorite.

MEL What if I gave you a big kiss right on the mouth?

HARRY You kiss me, I'll break every bone in your body . . . I'll call you. Listen, forget what I said. I changed my mind. I don't want to be the favorite. Not if I have to be kissed by Jessie and Pauline.

MEL Try it, you might like it.

HARRY I tried it, I didn't like it . . . What if I lent you twelve thousand? You start a small camp. Five boys, two girls.

MEL How about a little kiss on the cheek?

HARRY You're not better yet. I don't care what your doctor says, you've not better yet.

(He leaves, closing the door behind him)

MEL Edna! . . . *EDNA!*

(She comes out, wearing a bathrobe)

EDNA What is it, Mel? What is it?

MEL *(He paces angrily, trying to find the right words, as she stands there waiting)* You asked Harry? You asked my family for twenty-five thousand dollars for a summer camp?

EDNA I didn't ask . . . They offered the money for a doctor . . . I told them I didn't need it for a doctor, I needed it for a camp.

MEL Don't you see how humiliating it is for me to ask my family for money? Don't you see that?

EDNA You didn't ask them. You weren't the one who was humiliated. *I was!* I was the one who sat here in front of the Spanish Inquisition. You were out taking a nice *tranquilized walk in the park.*

MEL Tranquilized? Tranquilized? . . . I was sedated, Edna, not tranquilized. SEDATED!

EDNA I don't care if you were petrified! I was the one who was humiliated . . . Next time *you* be humiliated and *I'll* be sedated!

MEL *(Really loud)* You realize you're talking to a man who just had a nervous breakdown? Don't you have any regard for a man's illness?

EDNA *(Yelling back)* You don't sound sick to me now. You sound like you *always* sound!

MEL I'm not talking about *now,* I'm talking about *then!* I was sedated, Edna, not tranquilized. SEDATED!

EDNA *(Yells)* Well, I wish to God you'd get sedated again so you'd stop yelling at me.

WOMAN'S VOICE *(From above)* Will you shut up down there, you hoodlums!

EDNA *(Rushes out onto the terrace, yells up)* Who are you calling hoodlums?

WOMAN'S VOICE You and your loud-mouthed husband.

EDNA *(Yells up)* Don't you call us names. Your husband isn't half the man my husband is. We haven't forgotten the water. We remember the water.

*(*MEL *goes out onto the terrace)*

WOMAN'S VOICE My husband'll be home in an hour. If you don't shut up down there, you're gonna get more of the same.

EDNA Ha! With what! Where are you gonna get the water? Where's your water, big mouth!?

MEL *(Pulling her away)* Edna, get away from there. *(He is out on the terrace now and calls up)* I'm sorry. My wife didn't mean to yell. We were just discus—*(He gets hit with the pail of water. He reenters the room—drenched)* They did it again . . .

(He sits down)

EDNA *(Sitting, bewildered)* Where did they get the water? . . . Where did they get the water?

MEL People like that always have water . . . They save it so that people like us can always get it.

(They are both seated . . . There is silence for a few moments)

EDNA *(Looks at him)* I think you've behaving very well, Mel. I think you're taking it beautifully this time . . . That shows real progress, Mel. I think you've *grown* through this experience, Mel, I really do. *(And suddenly, behind them on the terrace, we see it begin to snow)* Maybe you're right. Maybe you really *don't* have to go back to the doctor any more . . . I'm so proud of you, Mel, so proud . . . Because you're better than them . . . Better than all of them, Mel . . .

(Snow falls—slowly at first, but steadily increasing. MEL, *sensing something, turns and looks behind him.* EDNA *looks at* MEL, *then turns to look at the terrace to see what* MEL *is looking at. She sees the snow. They look at each other, then turn back and look at the snow again.* MEL *looks at his watch. He looks at the snow once more, then turns and slowly gets up and goes over to the closet.* EDNA *watches him. He opens the closet door and gets out his shovel. He looks at the snow once more, looks at his watch, then goes back and sits in his chair, one hand holding his shovel, the other around* EDNA*'s shoulder, a contemporary* American Gothic. *Then we hear the voice of* ROGER KEATING*)*

ROGER KEATING This is Roger Keating and the *Six O'Clock Report* . . . Heavy snow warnings have been posted along the eastern seaboard tonight, and here in New York a record forty-three inches have been forecast . . . Snow plows were ordered out on the streets and city residents were asked to get out their shovels in a joint effort to show how New Yorkers can live together and work together in a common cause.

Curtain

The Sunshine Boys

The Scene

The action takes place in New York City.

Act One

SCENE ONE: A small apartment in an old hotel on upper Broadway, in the mid-Eighties. It is an early afternoon in midwinter.

SCENE TWO: The following Monday, late morning.

Act Two

SCENE ONE: A Manhattan television studio.

SCENE TWO: The same as Act One. It is two weeks later, late afternoon.

Act One

SCENE I

The scene is a two-room apartment in an old hotel on upper Broadway, in the mid-Eighties. It's rather a depressing place. There is a bed, a bureau, a small dining table with two chairs, an old leather chair that faces a TV set on a cheap, metal stand. There is a small kitchen to one side—partitioned off from the living room by a curtain—a small bathroom on the other. A window looks out over Broadway. It is early afternoon, midwinter.

At rise, the TV is on, and the banal dialogue of a soap opera drones on. In the leather chair sits WILLIE CLARK, *in slippers, pajamas and an old bathrobe.* WILLIE *is in his seventies. He watches the program but is constantly dozing off, then catching himself and watching for a few more minutes at a time. The set drones on and* WILLIE *dozes off. The tea kettle on the stove in the kitchen comes to a boil and whistles.* WILLIE*'s head perks up at the sound; he reaches over nd picks up the telephone.*

WILLIE *(Into the phone)* Hello? . . . Who's this?

(The whistle continues from the kettle, and WILLIE *looks over in that direction. He hangs up the phone and does not seem embarrassed or even aware of his own absent-mindedness. He simply crosses into the kitchen and turns off the flame under the kettle)*

VOICE FROM TV We'll be back with *Storm Warning* after this brief message from Lipton Tea.

WILLIE Don't worry, I'm not going anywhere.

(He puts a tea ball into a mug and pours the boiling water in. Then he goes over to the dining table in the living room, takes a spoon, dips into a jar of honey, and pours it into his tea. He glances over at the TV set, which has just played the Lipton Tea commercial)

VOICE FROM TV And now for Part Three of today's *Storm Warning . . .*

WILLIE What happened to Part Two? I missed Part Two? *(He drinks his tea as Part Three continues and the banal dialogue drones on.* WILLIE *listens as he shuffles toward his chair. The TV set, which is away from the wall, has an electric plug running from it, along the ground and into the wall.* WILLIE, *who never seems to look where he's going, comes up against the cord with his foot, inadvertently pulling the cord out of its socket in the wall. The TV set immediately dies.* WILLIE *sits, then looks at the set. Obviously, no picture. He gets up and fiddles with the dials. How could his best friend desert him at a time like this? He hits the set on the top with his hand)* What's the matter with you? *(He hits the set again and twists the knobs futilely, never thinking for a moment it might be something as simple as the plug. He slaps the picture tube)* Come on, for Pete's sakes, what are you doing there? *(He stares at it in disbelief. He kicks the stand on which it rests. Then he crosses to the phone, and picks it up)* Hello? . . . Sandy? . . . Let me have Sandy . . . Sandy? . . . My television's dead . . . My television . . . Is this Sandy? . . . My television died . . . No, not Willie. Mr. Clark to you, please . . . Never mind the jokes, wise guy, it's not funny . . . Send up somebody to fix my dead television . . . I didn't touch nothing . . . Nothing, I'm telling you . . . It's a crappy set . . . You live in a crappy hotel, you get a crappy television . . . The what? . . . The plug? . . . What plug? . . . Wait a minute. *(He lays the phone down, crosses to behind the set, bends down, picks up the plug and looks at it. He goes back to the telephone. Into the phone)* Hello? . . . It's not the plug. It's something else. I'll fix it myself. *(He hangs up, goes over to the wall plug and plugs it in. The set goes back on)* He tells me the plug . . . When he calls me Mr. Clark then I'll tell him it was the plug. *(He sits and picks up his cup of tea)* The hell with all of 'em. *(There is a knock on the door.* WILLIE *looks at the wall on the opposite side of the room.* Bang all you want, I'm not turning it off. I'm lucky it works.

(There is a pause; then a knock on the front door again, this time accompanied by a male voice)

BEN'S VOICE Uncle Willie? It's me. Ben.

*(*WILLIE *turns and looks at the front door, not acknowledging that he was mistaken about the knocking on the other wall)*

WILLIE Who's that?

BEN'S VOICE Ben.

WILLIE Ben? Is that you?

BEN'S VOICE Yes, Uncle Willie, it's Ben. Open the door.

WILLIE Wait a minute. *(He rises, crosses to the door, tripping over the TV cord again, disconnecting the set. He starts to unlatch the door, but has trouble manipulating it. His fingers are not too manipulative)* Wait a minute . . . *(He is having great difficulty with it)* . . . Wait a minute.

BEN'S VOICE Is anything wrong?

WILLIE *(Still trying)* Wait a minute.

(He tries forcing it)

BEN'S VOICE What's the matter?

WILLIE I'm locked in. The lock is broken, I'm locked in. Go down and tell the boy. Sandy. Tell Sandy that Mr. Clark is locked in.

BEN'S VOICE What is it, the latch?

WILLIE It's the latch. It's broken, I'm locked in. Go tell the boy Sandy, they'll get somebody.

BEN'S VOICE That happened last week. Don't try to force it. Just slide it out. *(*WILLIE *stares at the latch)* Uncle Willie, do you hear me? Don't force it. Slide it out.

WILLIE *(Fiddling with the latch)* Wait a minute. *(Carefully, he slides it open)* It's open. Never mind, I did it myself.

(He opens the door. BEN SILVERMAN, *a well dressed man in his early thirties, enters. He is wearing a topcoat and carrying a shopping bag from Bloomingdale's, filled to*

the brim with assorted foodstuffs and a copy of the weekly Variety*)*

BEN You probably have to oil it.

WILLIE I don't have to oil nothing. The hell with 'em.

*(*BEN *hangs up his coat in the closet)*

BEN *(Crosses to the table with the shopping bag)* You feeling all right?

WILLIE What is this, Wednesday?

BEN *(Puzzled)* Certainly. Don't I always come on Wednesdays?

WILLIE But this is Wednesday today?

BEN *(Puts his bag down)* Yes, of course. Haven't you been out?

WILLIE When?

BEN Today. Yesterday. This week. You haven't been out all week?

WILLIE *(Crossing to him)* Sunday. I was out Sunday. I went to the park Sunday.

*(*BEN *hands* WILLIE *the* Variety. WILLIE *tucks it under his arm and starts to look through the shopping bag)*

BEN What are you looking for?

WILLIE *(Going through the bag)* My *Variety.*

BEN I just gave it to you. It's under your arm.

WILLIE *(Looks under his arm)* Why do you put it there? He puts it under my arm.

BEN *(Starts taking items out of the bag)* Have you been eating properly? No corned beef sandwiches, I hope.

WILLIE *(Opens to the back section)* Is this today's?

BEN Certainly it's today's. *Variety* comes out on Wednesday, doesn't it? And today is Wednesday.

WILLIE I'm just asking, don't get so excited. *(*BEN *shakes his head in consternation)* . . . Because I already read last Wednesday's.

BEN *(Takes more items out)* I got you six different kinds of soups. All low-sodium, salt-free. All very good for you . . . Are you listening?

WILLIE *(His head in the paper)* I'm listening. You got six lousy-tasting soups . . . Did you see this?

BEN What?

WILLIE What I'm looking at. Did you see this?

BEN How do I know what you're looking at?

WILLIE Two new musicals went into rehearsals today and I didn't even get an audition. Why didn't I get an audition?

BEN Because there were no parts for you. One of them is a young rock musical and the other show is all black.

WILLIE What's the matter, I can't do black? I did black in 1928. And when I did black, you understood the words, not like today.

BEN I'm sorry, you're not the kind of black they're looking for. *(He shivers)* Geez, it's cold in here. You know it's freezing in here? Don't they ever send up any heat?

WILLIE *(Has turned a page)* How do you like that? Sol Burton died.

BEN Who?

WILLIE Sol Burton. The songwriter. Eighty-nine years old, went like that, from nothing.

BEN Why didn't you put on a sweater?

WILLIE I knew him very well . . . A terrible person. Mean, mean. He should rest in peace, but he was a mean person. His best friends didn't like him.

BEN *(Goes to the bureau for a sweater)* Why is it so cold in here?

WILLIE You know what kind of songs he wrote? . . . The worst. The worst songs ever written were written by Sol Burton. *(He sings)* "Lady, Lady, be my baby . . ." Did you ever hear anything so rotten? Baby he rhymes with lady . . . No wonder he's dead.

(He turns the page)

BEN This radiator is ice-cold. Look, Uncle Willie, I'm not going to let you live here any more. You've got to let me find you another place . . . I've been asking you for seven years now. You're going to get sick.

WILLIE *(Still looking at* Variety*)* Tom Jones is gonna get a hundred thousand dollars a week in Las Vegas. When Lewis and I were headlining at the Palace, the *Palace* didn't cost a hundred thousand dollars.

BEN That was forty years ago. And forty years ago this hotel was twenty years old. They should tear it down. They take advantage of all you people in here because they know you don't want to move.

*(*WILLIE *crosses to the table and looks into the shopping bag)*

WILLIE No cigars?

BEN *(Making notes on his memo pad)* You're not supposed to have cigars.

WILLIE Where's the cigars?

BEN You know the doctor told you you're not supposed to smoke cigars any more. I didn't bring any.

WILLIE Gimme the cigars.

BEN What cigars? I just said I don't have them. Will you forget the cigars?

WILLIE Where are they, in the bag?

BEN On the bottom. I just brought three. It's the last time I'm doing it.

WILLIE *(Takes out a bag with three cigars)* How's your family? The children all right?

(He removes one cigar)

BEN Suddenly you're interested in my family? It's not going to work, Uncle Willie. I'm not bringing you any more cigars.

WILLIE I just want to know how the children are.

BEN The children are fine. They're wonderful, thank you.

WILLIE Good. Next time bring the big cigars.

(He puts two cigars in the breast pocket of his bathrobe and the other one in his mouth. He crosses into the kitchen looking for a light)

BEN You don't even know their names. What are the names of my children?

WILLIE Millie and Sidney.

BEN Amanda and Michael.

WILLIE What's the matter, you didn't like Millie and Sidney?

BEN I was *never* going to name them Millie and Sidney. You forgot, so you made something up. You forget everything. I'll bet you didn't drink the milk from last week. I'll bet it's still in the refrigerator. *(Crosses quickly, and opens the refrigerator and looks in)* There's the milk from last week.

WILLIE *(Comes out of the kitchen, still looking for a light)* Do they know who I am?

BEN *(Looking through the refrigerator)* Who?

WILLIE Amanda and Sidney.

BEN Amanda and Michael. That you were a big star in

vaudeville? They're three years old, Uncle Willie, you think they remember vaudeville? *I* never saw vaudeville . . . This refrigerator won't last another two days.

WILLIE Did you tell them six times on *The Ed Sullivan Show?*

(He sits, tries a cigarette lighter. It's broken)

BEN They never heard of Ed Sullivan. Uncle Willie, they're three years old. They don't follow show business. *(Comes back into the living room and sees* WILLIE *with the cigar in his mouth)* What are you doing? You're not going to smoke that now. You promised me you'd only smoke one after dinner.

WILLIE Am I smoking it? Do you see smoke coming from the cigar?

BEN But you've got it in your mouth.

WILLIE I'm rehearsing . . . After dinner I'll do the show.

BEN *(Crossing back into the kitchen)* I'm in the most aggravating business in the whole world and I never get aggravated until I come here.

(He opens the cupboards and looks in)

WILLIE *(Looking around)* So don't come. I got Social Security.

BEN You think that's funny? I don't think that's funny, Uncle Willie.

WILLIE *(Thumbing through* Variety*)* If you had a sense of humor, you'd think it was funny.

BEN *(Angrily, through gritted teeth)* I have a *terrific* sense of humor.

WILLIE Like your father—he laughed once in 1932.

BEN I can't talk to you.

WILLIE Why, they're funny today? Tell me who you think is funny today, and I'll show you where he's not funny.

BEN Let's not get into that, huh? I've got to get back to the office. Just promise me you'll have a decent lunch today.

WILLIE If I were to tell a joke and got a laugh from you, I'd throw it out.

BEN How can I laugh when I see you like this, Uncle Willie? You sit in your pajamas all day in a freezing apartment watching soap operas on a thirty-five-dollar television set that doesn't have a horizontal hold. The picture just keeps rolling from top to bottom—pretty soon your eyes are gonna roll around your head . . . You never eat anything. You never go out because you don't know how to work the lock on the door. Remember when you locked yourself in the bathroom overnight? It's a lucky thing you keep bread in there, you would have starved . . . And you wonder why I worry.

WILLIE Calvin Coolidge, that's your kind of humor.

BEN Look, Uncle Willie, promise me you'll eat decently.

WILLIE I'll eat decently. I'll wear a blue suit, a white shirt and black shoes.

BEN And if you're waiting for a laugh, you're not going to get one from me.

WILLIE Who could live that long? Get me a job instead of a laugh.

BEN *(Sighs, exasperatedly)* You know I've been trying, Uncle Willie. It's not easy. There's not much in town. Most of the work is commercials and . . . well, you know, we've had a little trouble in that area.

WILLIE The potato chips? The potato chips wasn't my fault.

BEN Forget the potato chips.

WILLIE What about the Shick Injector? Didn't I audition funny on the Shick Injector?

BEN You were very funny but your hand was shaking. And you can't show a man shaving with a shaky hand.

WILLIE Why couldn't you get me on the Alka-Seltzer? That's my kind of comedy. I got a terrific face for an upset stomach.

BEN I've submitted you twenty times.

WILLIE What's the matter with twenty-one?

BEN Because the word is out in the business that you can't remember the lines, and they're simply not interested.

WILLIE *(That hurt)* I couldn't remember the lines? I COULDN'T REMEMBER THE LINES? I don't remember that.

BEN For the Frito-Lays potato chips. I sent you over to the studio, you couldn't even remember the address.

WILLIE Don't tell me I didn't remember the lines. The lines I remembered beautifully. The name of the potato chip I couldn't remember . . . What was it?

BEN Frito-Lays.

WILLIE Say it again.

BEN Frito-Lays.

WILLIE I still can't remember it—because it's not funny. If it's funny, I remember it. Alka-Seltzer is funny. You say "Alka-Seltzer," you get a laugh. The other word is not funny. What is it?

BEN Frito-Lays.

WILLIE Maybe in *Mexico* that's funny, not here. Fifty-seven years I'm in this business, you learn a few things. You know what makes an audience laugh. Do you know which words are funny and which words are *not* funny?

BEN You told me a hundred times, Uncle Willie. Words with a "K" in it are funny.

WILLIE Words with a "K" in it are funny. You didn't know that, did you? If it doesn't have a "K," it's not funny. I'll tell you which words always get a laugh. *(He is about to count on his fingers)*

BEN Chicken.

WILLIE Chicken is funny.

BEN Pickle.

WILLIE Pickle is funny.

BEN Cupcake.

WILLIE Cupcake is funny . . . Tomato is *not* funny. Roast beef is *not* funny.

BEN But cookie is funny.

WILLIE But cookie is funny.

BEN Uncle Willie, you've explained that to me ever since I was a little boy.

WILLIE Cucumber is funny.

BEN *(Falling in again)* Car keys.

WILLIE Car keys is funny.

BEN Cleveland.

WILLIE Cleveland is funny . . . Maryland is *not* funny.

BEN Listen, I have to get back to the office, Uncle Willie, but there's something I'd like to talk to you about first. I got a call yesterday from C.B.S.

WILLIE Casey Stengel, that's a funny name; Robert Taylor is not funny.

BEN *(Sighs exasperatedly)* Why don't you listen to me?

WILLIE I heard. You got a call from N.B.C.

BEN C.B.S.

WILLIE Whatever.

BEN C.B.S. is doing a big special next month. An hour and a half variety show. They're going to have some of the biggest names in the history of show business. They're trying to get Flip Wilson to host the show.

WILLIE Him I like. He gives me a laugh. With the dress and the little giggle and the red wig. That's a funny boy . . . What's the boy's name again?

BEN Flip Wilson. And it doesn't have a K.

WILLIE But he's *black*, with a "K." You see what I mean?

BEN *(Looks to heaven for help. It doesn't come)* I do, I do. The theme of this variety show—

WILLIE What's the theme of the show?

BEN *The theme of the show* is the history of comedy dating from the early Greek times, through the days of vaudeville, right up to today's stars.

WILLIE Why couldn't you get me on this show?

BEN I *got* you on the show.

WILLIE Alone?

BEN With Lewis.

WILLIE *(Turns away)* You ain't got me on the show.

BEN Let me finish.

WILLIE You're finished. It's no.

BEN Can't you wait until I'm through before you say "no"? Can't we discuss it for a minute?

WILLIE I'm busy.

BEN Doing what?

WILLIE Saying "no."

BEN You can have the courtesy of hearing me out. They begged me at C.B.S. *Begged* me.

WILLIE Talk faster, because you're coming up to another "no."

BEN They said to me the history of comedy in the United States would not be complete unless they included one of the greatest teams ever to come out of vaudeville, Lewis and Clark, The Sunshine Boys. The vice-president of C.B.S. said this to me on the phone.

WILLIE The vice-president said this?

BEN Yes. He is the greatest Lewis and Clark fan in this country. He knows by heart every one of your old routines.

WILLIE Then let *him* go on with that bastard.

BEN It's one shot. You would just have to do it one night, one of the old sketches. They'll pay ten thousand dollars for the team. That's top money for these shows, I promise you. Five thousand dollars apiece. And that's more money than you've earned in two years.

WILLIE I don't need money. I live alone. I got two nice suits, I don't have a pussycat, I'm very happy.

BEN You're *not* happy. You're miserable.

WILLIE *I'm happy!* I just *look* miserable!

BEN You're dying to go to work again. You call me six times a day in the office. I can't see over my desk for all your messages.

WILLIE Call me back sometime, you won't get so many messages.

BEN I call you every day of the week. I'm up here every Wednesday, rain or shine, winter or summer, flu or diphtheria.

WILLIE What are you, a mailman? You're a nephew. I don't ask you to come. You're my brother's son, you've been very nice to me. I appreciate it, but I've never asked you for anything . . . except for a job. You're a good boy but a stinking agent.

BEN I'M A GOOD AGENT? Damn it, don't say that to me, Uncle Willie, I'm a *goddamn good agent!*

WILLIE What are you screaming for? What is it, such a wonderful thing to be a good agent?

BEN *(Holds his chest)* I'm getting chest pains. You give me chest pains, Uncle Willie.

WILLIE It's *my* fault you get excited?

BEN Yes, it's *your* fault! I only get chest pains on Wednesdays.

WILLIE So come on Tuesdays.

BEN *(Starts for the door)* I'm going. I don't even want to discuss this with you any more. You're impossible to talk to. FORGET THE VARIETY SHOW!

(He starts for the door)

WILLIE I forgot it.

BEN *(Stops)* I'm not coming back any more. I'm not bringing you your *Variety* or your cigars or your low-sodium soups—do you understand, Uncle Willie? I'm not bringing you anything any more.

WILLIE Good. Take care of yourself. Say hello to Millie and Phyllis.

BEN *(Breathing heavily)* Why won't you do this for me? I'm not asking you to be partners again. If you two don't get along, all right. But this is just for one night.

One last show. Once you get an exposure like that, Alka-Seltzer will come begging to *me* to sign you up. Jesus, how is it going to look if I go back to the office and tell them I couldn't make a deal with my own uncle?

WILLIE My personal opinion? Lousy!

BEN *(Falls into a chair, exhausted)* Do you really hate Al Lewis that much?

WILLIE *(Looks away)* I don't discuss Al Lewis any more.

BEN *(Gets up)* We *have* to discuss him, because C.B.S. is waiting for an answer today, and if we turn them down, I want to have a pretty good reason why. You haven't seen him in—what? ten years now.

WILLIE *(Takes a long time before answering)* Eleven years!

BEN *(Amazed)* You mean to tell me you haven't spoken to him in eleven years?

WILLIE I haven't *seen* him in eleven years. I haven't *spoken* to him in twelve years.

BEN You mean you saw him for a whole year that you didn't speak to him?

WILLIE It wasn't easy. I had to sneak around backstage a lot.

BEN But you spoke to him onstage.

WILLIE Not to *him*. If he played a gypsy, I spoke to the gypsy. If he played a lunatic, I spoke to the lunatic. But that bastard I didn't speak to.

BEN I can't believe that.

WILLIE You don't believe it? I can show you witnesses who *saw* me never speaking to him.

BEN It's been eleven years, Uncle Willie. Hasn't time changed anything for you?

WILLIE Yes. I hate him eleven years more.

BEN Why?

WILLIE Why? . . . You never met him?

BEN Sure I met him. I was fifteen years old. I met him once at that benefit at Madison Square Garden and once backstage at some television show. He seemed nice enough to me.

WILLIE That's only twice. You had to meet him three times to hate him.

BEN Uncle Willie, could I make a suggestion?

WILLIE He used to give me the finger.

BEN The what?

WILLIE The finger! The finger! He would poke me in the chest with the finger. *(He crosses to* BEN *and demonstrates on him by poking a finger in* BEN*'s chest every time he makes a point)* He would say, "*Listen,* Doctor." *(Pokes finger)* "I'm *telling* you, Doctor." *(Pokes finger)* "You know what I *mean,* Doctor." *(Pokes finger.* BEN *rubs his chest in pain)* Hurts, doesn't it? How'd you like it for forty-three years? I got a black and blue hole in my chest. My wife to her dying day thought it was a tattoo. I haven't worked with him in eleven years, it's just beginning to fade away . . . The man had the sharpest finger in show business.

BEN If you work with him again, I promise you I'll buy you a thick padded undershirt.

WILLIE You think I never did that? One night I put a steel plate under my shirt. He gave me the finger, he had it in a splint for a month.

BEN Something else must have happened you're not telling me about. You don't work with a person for forty-three years without some bond of affection remaining.

WILLIE You wanna hear other things? He used to spit in my face. Onstage *the man would spit in my face!*

BEN Not on purpose.

WILLIE *(Turns away)* He tells me "not on purpose" . . . If there was some way I could have saved the spit, I would show it to you.

BEN You mean he would just stand there and spit in your face?

WILLIE What do you think, he's stupid? He worked it into the act. He would stand with his nose on top of my nose and purposely only say words that began with a "T." *(As he demonstrates, he spits)* "*T*ootsie Roll." *(Spit)* "*T*inker *T*oy." *(Spit)* "*T*yping on the *t*ypewriter." *(Spits.* BEN *wipes his face)* Some nights I thought I would drown! I don't know where he got it all from . . . I think he would drink all day and save it up for the night.

BEN I'll put it in the contract. If he spits at you, he won't get paid.

WILLIE If he can get another chance to spit at me, he wouldn't *want* to get paid.

BEN Then will you answer me one question? If it was all that bad, why did you stick together for forty-three years?

WILLIE *(Turns; looks at him)* Because he was terrific. There'll never be another one like him . . . Nobody could time a joke the way he could time a joke. Nobody could say a line the way he said it. I knew what he was thinking, he knew what I was thinking. One person, that's what we were . . . No, no. Al Lewis was the best. The *best!* You understand?

BEN I understand.

WILLIE As an actor, no one could touch him. As a human being, no one *wanted* to touch him.

BEN *(Sighs)* So what do I tell C.B.S.? No deal because Al Lewis spits?

WILLIE You know when the last time was we worked together?

BEN Eleven years ago on *The Ed Sullivan Show.*

WILLIE Eleven years ago on *The Ed Sullivan Show.* July twenty-seventh. He wouldn't put us on in the winter when people were watching, but never mind. We did The Doctor and the Tax Examination. You never saw that, did you?

BEN No, but I heard it's wonderful.

WILLIE What about a "classic"? A *classic!* A *dead* person watching that sketch would laugh. We did it maybe eight thousand times, it never missed . . . *That* night it missed. Something was wrong with him, he was rushing, his timing was off, his mind was someplace else. I thought he was sick. Still, we got terrific applause. Five times Ed Sullivan said, "How about that?" We got back into the dressing room, he took off his make-up, put on his clothes, and said to me, "Willie, if it's all the same to you, I'm retiring." I said, "What do you mean, retiring? It's not even nine o'clock. Let's have something to eat. He said, "I'm not retiring for the night. I'm retiring for what's left of my life." And he puts on his hat, walks out of the theater, becomes a stockbroker and I'm left with an act where I ask questions and there's no one there to answer. Never saw the man again to this day. Oh, he called me, I wouldn't answer. He wrote me, I tore it up. He sent me telegrams, they're probably still under the door.

BEN Well, Uncle Willie, with all due respect, you really weren't getting that much work any more. Maybe he was getting tired of doing the same thing for forty-three years. I mean a man has a right to retire when he wants, doesn't he?

WILLIE Not him. Don't forget, when he retired himself, he retired me too. And goddamn it, I wasn't ready yet. Now suddenly maybe he needs five thousand dollars, and he wants to come crawling back, the hell with him. I'm a single now . . .

BEN I spoke to Al Lewis on the phone last night. He doesn't even care about the money. He just wants to do the show for old times' sake. For his grandchildren who never saw him.

WILLIE Sure. He probably retired broke from the stock market. I guarantee you *those* high-class people never got a spit in the face once.

BEN Did you know his wife died two years ago? He's living with his daughter now, somewhere in New Jersey. He doesn't do anything any more. He's got very bad arthritis, he's got asthma, he's got poor blood circulation—

WILLIE I'll send him a pump. He'll outlive *you*, believe me.

BEN He wants very much to do this show, Willie.

WILLIE With arthritis? Forget it. Instead of a finger, he'll poke me with a cane.

BEN C.B.S. wants you to do the doctor sketch. Lewis told me he could get on a stage tonight and do that sketch letter perfect. He doesn't even have to rehearse it.

WILLIE I don't even want to discuss it . . . And in the second place, I would definitely not do it without a rehearsal.

BEN All right, then will you agree to this? Just rehearse with him one day. If it doesn't work out, we'll call it off.

WILLIE I don't trust him. I think he's been planning this for eleven years. We rehearse all week and then he walks out on me just before the show.

BEN Let me call him on the phone. *(Going over to the phone)* Let me set up a rehearsal time for Monday.

WILLIE WAIT A MINUTE! I got to think about this.

BEN We don't have that much time. C.B.S. is waiting to hear.

WILLIE What's their rush? What are they, going out of business?

BEN *(Picks up the phone)* I'm dialing. I'm dialing him, Uncle Willie, okay?

WILLIE Sixty-forty—I get six thousand, he gets four thousand . . . What the hell can he buy in New Jersey anyway?

BEN *(Holding the phone)* I can't do that, Uncle Willie . . . God, I hope this works out.

WILLIE Tell him I'm against it. I want him to know. I'll do it with an "against it."

BEN It's ringing.

WILLIE And he's got to come here. I'm not going there, you understand?

BEN He's got to be home. I told him I would call about one.

WILLIE Sure. You know what he's doing? He practicing spitting.

BEN *(Into the phone)* Hello? . . . Mr. Lewis? . . . Ben Silverman . . . Yes, fine, thanks . . . I'm here with him now.

WILLIE Willie Clark. The one he left on *The Ed Sullivan Show.* Ask him if he remembers.

BEN It's okay, Mr. Lewis . . . Uncle Willie said yes.

WILLIE With an "against it." Don't forget the "against it."

BEN No, he's very anxious to do it.

WILLIE *(Jumping up in anger)* WHO'S ANXIOUS? I'M AGAINST IT! TELL HIM, you lousy nephew.

BEN Can you come here for rehearsal on Monday?. . . Oh, that'll be swell . . . In the morning. *(To* WILLIE*)* About eleven o'clock? How long is the drive. About two hours?

WILLIE Make it nine o'clock.

BEN Be reasonable, Willie. *(Into the phone)* Eleven o'-clock is fine, Mr. Lewis . . . Can you give me your address, please, so I can send you the contracts? *(He takes a pen out of his pocket and writes in his notebook)* One-one-nine, South Pleasant Drive . . .

WILLIE Tell him if he starts with the spitting or poking, I'm taking him to court. I'll have a man on the show watching. Tell him.

BEN West Davenport, New Jersey . . . Oh-nine-seven-seven-oh-four . . .

WILLIE I don't want any—*(Spitting)*—"*T*oy *t*elephones *t*apping on *t*in *t*urtles." Tell him. Tell him.

Curtain

SCENE 2

It is the following Monday, a few minutes before eleven in the morning.

The stage is empty. Suddenly the bathroom door opens and WILLIE *emerges. He is still wearing his slippers and the same pajamas, but instead of his bathrobe, he has made a concession to the occasion. He is wearing a double-breasted blue suit-jacket, buttoned, and he is putting a handerchief in his pocket. He looks in the mirror, and brushes back his hair. He shuffles over to the window and looks out.*

There is a knock on the door. WILLIE *turns and stares at it. He doesn't move. There is another knock, and then we hear* BEN*'s voice.*

BEN'S VOICE Uncle Willie. It's Ben.

WILLIE Ben? Is that you?

BEN'S VOICE Yes. Open up. *(*WILLIE *starts toward the door, then stops)*

WILLIE You're alone or he's with you?

BEN'S VOICE I'm alone.

WILLIE *(Nods)* Wait a minute. *(The latch is locked again, and again he has trouble getting it open)* Wait a minute.

BEN'S VOICE Slide it, don't push it.

WILLIE Wait a minute. I'll push it.

BEN'S VOICE *DON'T* PUSH IT! SLIDE IT!

WILLIE Wait a minute. *(He gets the lock open and opens the door.* BEN *walks in)* You're supposed to slide it.

BEN I rushed like crazy. I didn't want him getting here before me. Did he call or anything?

WILLIE Where's the *Variety?*

BEN *(Taking off his coat)* It's Monday, not Wednesday. Didn't you know it was Monday?

WILLIE I remembered, but I forgot.

BEN What are you wearing? What is that? You look half-dressed.

WILLIE Why, for him I should get *all* dressed?

BEN Are you all right? Are you nervous or anything?

WILLIE Why should *I* be nervous? *He* should be nervous. I don't get nervous.

BEN Good.

WILLIE Listen, I changed my mind. I'm not doing it.

BEN *What?*

WILLIE Don't get so upset. Everything is the same as before, except I'm not doing it.

BEN When did you decide this?

WILLIE I decided it when you asked me.

BEN No, you didn't. You told me you *would* do it.

WILLIE Well, it was a bad decision. This time I made a good one.

BEN Well, I'm sorry, you have to do it. I've already told C.B.S that you would be rehearsing this week and, more important, that man is on his way over here now and I'm not going to tell him that you called it off.

WILLIE We'll leave him a note outside the door.

BEN We're not leaving any notes. That's why I came here this morning, I was afraid you would try something like this. I'm going to stay until I think you're both acting like civilized human beings, and then when you're ready to rehearse, I'm going to leave you alone. Is that understood?

WILLIE I'm sick. I woke up sick today.

BEN No, you're not.

WILLIE What are you, a doctor? You're an agent. I'm telling you I'm sick.

BEN What's wrong?

WILLIE I think I got hepatitis.

BEN You don't even know what hepatitis is.

WILLIE If you got it, what's the difference?

BEN There's nothing wrong with you except a good case of the nerves. You're not backing out, Willie. I don't care what kind of excuse you make, you're going to go through with this. You promised me you would give it at least one day.

WILLIE I'll pick another day.

BEN TODAY! You're going to meet with him and rehearse with him TODAY. Now *stop* and just behave yourself.

WILLIE What do you mean, "behave yourself"? Who do you think you're talking to, Susan and Jackie?

BEN *Amanda* and Jackie!—Michael! I wish I were. I can reason with them. And now I'm getting chest pains on Monday.

WILLIE Anyway, he's late. He's purposely coming late to aggravate me.

BEN *(Looking out the window)* He's not late. It's two minutes after eleven.

WILLIE So what is he, early? He's *late!*

BEN You're *looking* to start trouble, I can tell.

WILLIE I was up and dressed at eight o'clock, don't tell me.

BEN Why didn't you shave?

WILLIE Get me the Shick commercial, I'll shave. *(He looks in the mirror)* I really think I got hepatitis. Look how green I look.

BEN You don't get green from hepatitis. You get yellow.

WILLIE Maybe I got a very bad case.

BEN *(Looks at his watch)* Now you got me nervous. I wonder if I should call him? Maybe he's sick.

WILLIE *(Glares at him)* You believe *he's* sick, but me you won't believe . . . Why don't you become *his* nephew?

(Suddenly there is a knock on the door. WILLIE *freezes and stares at it)*

BEN That's him. You want me to get it—

WILLIE Get what? I didn't hear anything.

BEN *(Starts toward the door)* All right, now take it easy. Please just behave yourself and give this a chance. Promise me you'll give it a chance.

WILLIE *(Starts for the kitchen)* I'll give it every possible chance in the world . . . But it's not gonna work.

BEN Where are you going?

WILLIE To make tea. I feel like some hot tea.

(He crosses into the kitchen and closes the curtain. Starts to fill up the kettle with water)

BEN *(Panicky)* *NOW? NOW?* *(*BEN *looks at him, exasperated; a knock on the door again and* BEN *crosses to it and opens it.* AL LEWIS *stands there. He is also about seventy years old and is dressed in his best blue suit, hat, scarf, and carries a walking stick. He was probably quite a gay blade in his day, but time* *has slowed him down somewhat. Our first impression is that He is soft-spoken and pleasant—and a little nervous)* Mr. Lewis, how do you do? I'm Ben Silverman.

(BEN, nervous, extends his hand)

AL How are you? Hello. It's nice to see you. *(His eyes dart around looking for* WILLIE. *He doesn't see him yet)* How do you do?. . . Hello . . . Hello . . . How are you?

BEN We met before, a long time ago. My father took me backstage, I forget the theater. It must have been fifteen, twenty years ago.

AL I remember . . . Certainly . . . It was backstage . . . Maybe fifteen, twenty years ago . . . I forget the theater.

BEN That's right.

AL Sure, I remember.

(He has walked into the room and shoots a glance toward the kitchen. WILLIE *doesn't look up from his tea-making)*

BEN Please sit down. Uncle Willie's making some tea.

AL Thank you very much.

(He sits on the edge of the table)

BEN *(Trying hard to make conversation)* Er. . . Did you have any trouble getting in from Jersey?

AL My daughter drove me in. She has a car.

BEN Oh. That's nice.

AL A 1972 Chrysler . . . black . . .

BEN Yes, the Chrysler's a wonderful car.

AL The big one . . . the Imperial.

BEN I know. I drove it.

AL My daughter's car?

BEN No, the big Chrysler Imperial. I rented one in California.

AL *(Nods)* No, she owns.

BEN I understand . . . Do you come into New York often?

AL Today's the first time in two years.

BEN Really? Well, how did you find it?

AL My daughter drove.

BEN No, I mean, do you find the city different in the two years since you've been here?

AL It's not my New York.

BEN No, I suppose it's not. *(He shoots a glance toward the kitchen.* WILLIE *still hasn't looked in)* Hey, listen, I'm really very excited about all this. Well, for that matter, everyone in the industry is.

AL *(Nods, noncommittally)* Well, we'll see.

(He looks around the room, scrutinizing it)

BEN *(He calls out toward the kitchen)* Uncle Willie, how we doing? *(No answer. Embarrassed, to* AL*)* I guess it's not boiling yet . . . Oh, listen, I'd like to arrange to have a car pick you up and take you home after you're through rehearsing.

AL My daughter's going to pick me up.

BEN Oh, I see. What time did you say? Four? Five?

AL She's going to call me every hour.

BEN Right . . .

(Suddenly WILLIE *sticks his head out of the kitchen, but looks at* BEN *and not at* AL*)*

WILLIE One tea or two teas?

BEN Oh, here he is. Well, Uncle Willie, I guess it's been a long time since you two—

WILLIE One tea or two teas?

BEN Oh. Er, nothing for me, thanks. I'm just about leaving. Mr. Lewis? Some tea?

AL *(Doesn't look toward* WILLIE *)* Tea would be nice, thank you.

BEN *(To* WILLIE*)* Just the one, Uncle Willie.

WILLIE You're sure? I got two tea balls. I could dunk again.

BEN *(Looks at his watch)* No, I've got to get back to the office. Honestly.

WILLIE *(Nods)* Mm-hmm. One tea.

(On his way back in, he darts a look at LEWIS, *then goes back into the kitchen. He pulls the curtain shut)*

BEN *(To* LEWIS*)* Well, er . . . Do you have any questions you want to ask about the show? About the studio or rehearsals or the air date? Is there anything on your mind that I could help you with?

AL Like what?

BEN Like, er, the studio? Or the rehearsals? Or air date? Things like that?

AL You got the props?

BEN Which props are those?

AL The props. For the doctor sketch. You gotta have props.

BEN Oh, props. Certainly. What do you need? I'll tell them.

(Takes out a pad; writes)

AL You need a desk. A telephone. A pointer. A blackboard. A piece of white chalk, a piece of red chalk. A skeleton, not too tall, a stethoscope, a thermometer, an "ahh" stick—

BEN What's an "ahh" stick?

AL To put in your mouth to say "ahh."

BEN Oh, right, an "ahh" stick.

AL A look stick, a bottle of pills—

BEN A look stick? What's a look stick?

AL A stick to look in the ears. With cotton on the end.

BEN Right. A look stick.

AL A bottle of pills. Big ones, like for a horse.

BEN *(Makes a circle with his two fingers)* About this big?

AL That's for a pony. *(Makes a circle using the fingers of both hands)* For a horse is like this. Some bandages, cotton, and eye chart—

BEN Wait a minute, you're going too fast.

AL *(Slowly)* *A*-desk . . . *a*-telephone . . . *a*-pointer . . .

BEN No, I got all that—after the cotton and eye chart.

AL A man's suit. Size forty. Like the one I'm wearing.

BEN Also in blue?

AL What do I need two blue suits— Get me a brown.

BEN A brown suit. Is that all?

AL That's all.

WILLIE *(From the kitchen, without looking in)* A piece of liver.

AL That's all, plus a piece of liver.

BEN What kind of liver?

AL Regular calves' liver. From the butcher.

BEN Like how much? A pound?

AL A little laugh is a pound. A big laugh is two pounds. Three pounds with a lot of blood'll bring the house down.

BEN Is that it?

AL That's it. And a blonde.

BEN You mean a woman—

AL You know a blond nurse that's a man?. . . Big! As big as you can find. With a big chest—a forty-five, a fifty—and a nice bottom.

BEN You mean a sexy girl with a full, round, rear end?

AL *(Spreads hands apart)* About like this. *(Makes a smaller behind with his hands)* This is too small. *(Makes a bigger one)* And this is too big. *(Goes back to the original one)* Like this is perfect.

BEN I know what you mean.

AL If you can bring me pictures, I'll pick out one.

BEN There's a million girls like that around.

AL The one we had was the best. I would call her, but she's maybe fifty-five, sixty.

BEN No, no. I'll get a girl. Anything else?

AL Not for me.

BEN Uncle Willie?

WILLIE *(From the kitchen)* I wasn't listening.

BEN Well, if either of you thinks of anything, just call me. *(Looks at his watch again)* Eleven-fifteen—I've got to go. *(He gets up)* Uncle Willie, I'm going. *(He crosses to* LEWIS *and extends his hand)* Mr. Lewis, I can't express to you enough how happy I am, and speaking for the millions of young people in this country who never had the opportunity of seeing Lewis and Clark work, I just want to say "thank you." To both of you. *(Calls out)* To *both of you,* Uncle Willie.

AL *(Nods)* I hope they won't be disappointed.

BEN Oh, they won't.

AL I know they won't. I'm just saying it.

BEN *(Crosses to the kitchen)* *Goodbye,* Uncle Willie. I'm going.

WILLIE I'll show you the elevator.

BEN I *know* where it is. I'll call you tonight. I just want to say that this is a very happy moment for me. To see you both together again, reunited . . . The two kings of comedy. *(Big smile)* I'm sure it must be *very exciting* for the both of you, isn't it? *(No answer. They both just stare at him)* Well, it looks like we're off to a great start. I'll call you later . . . Goodbye.

(He leaves and closes the door. They are alone. WILLIE *carries the two teas to the dining table, where the sugar bowl is. He pours himself a teaspoonful of sugar)*

WILLIE *(Without looking in* AL*'s direction)* Sugar?

AL *(Doesn't turn)* If you got.

WILLIE *(Nods)* I got sugar. *(He bangs the sugar bowl down in front of* AL, *crosses with his own tea to his leather chair and sits. And then the two drink tea . . . silently and interminably. They blow, they sip, they blow, they sip and they sit. Finally)* You like a cracker?

AL *(Sips)* What kind of cracker?

WILLIE Graham, chocolate, coconut, whatever you want.

AL Maybe just a plain cracker.

WILLIE I don't have plain crackers. I got graham, chocolate and coconut.

AL All right, a graham cracker.

WILLIE *(Without turning, points into the kitchen)* They're in the kitchen, in the closet.

*(*AL *looks over at him, a little surprised at his uncordiality. He nods in acknowledgment)*

AL Maybe later.

(They both sip their tea)

WILLIE *(Long pause)* I was sorry to hear about Lillian.

AL Thank you.

WILLIE She was a nice woman. I always liked Lillian.

AL Thank you.

WILLIE And how about you?

AL Thank God, knock wood—*(Raps knuckles on his cane)* —perfect.

WILLIE I heard different. I heard your blood didn't circulate.

AL Not true. My blood circulates . . . I'm not saying *everywhere*, but it circulates.

WILLIE Is that why you use the cane?

AL It's not a cane. It's a walking stick . . . Maybe once in a great while it's a cane.

WILLIE I've been lucky, thank God. I'm in the pink.

AL I was looking. For a minute I thought you were having a flush.

WILLIE *(Sips his tea)* You know Sol Burton died?

AL Go on . . . Who's Sol Burton?

WILLIE You don't remember Sol Burton?

AL *(Thinks)* Oh, yes. The manager from the Belasco.

WILLIE That was Sol Bernstein.

AL Not Sol Bernstein. Sol *Burton* was the manager from the Belasco.

WILLIE Sol *Bernstein* was the manager from the Belasco, and it wasn't the Belasco, it was the Morosco.

AL Sid *Weinstein* was the manager from the Morosco. Sol *Burton* was the manager from the Belasco. Sol *Bernstein* I don't know *who* the hell was.

WILLIE How can you remember anything if your blood doesn't circulate?

AL It circulates in my *head.* It doesn't circulate in my *feet.*

(He stomps his foot on the floor a few times)

WILLIE Is anything coming down?

AL Wait a minute. Wasn't Sid Weinstein the songwriter?

WILLIE No for chrissakes! That's SOL BURTON!

AL Who wrote "Lady, lady, be my baby"?

WILLIE That's what I'm telling you! Sol Burton, the lousy songwriter.

AL Oh, *that* Sol Burton . . . He died?

WILLIE Last week.

AL Where?

WILLIE *(Points)* In *Variety.*

AL Sure, now I remember . . . And how is Sol Bernstein?

WILLIE I didn't read anything.

AL Good. I always liked Sol Bernstein. *(They quietly sip*

their tea. AL *looks around the room)* So-o-o . . . this is where you live now?

WILLIE Didn't I always live here?

AL *(Looks again)* Not in here. You lived in the big suite.

WILLIE This *is* the big suite . . . Now it's five small suites.

(AL *nods, understanding)*

AL *(Looks around)* That's what they do today. Anything to squeeze a dollar. What do they charge now for a small suite?

WILLIE The same as they used to charge for the big suite.

(AL *nods, understanding)*

AL I have a very nice room with my daughter in New Jersey. I have my own bathroom. They don't bother me, I don't bother them.

WILLIE What is it, in the country?

AL Certainly it's in the country. Where do you think New Jersey is, in the city?

WILLIE *(Shrugs)* New Jersey is what I see from the bench on Riverside Drive. What have they got, a private house?

AL Certainly it's a private house. It's some big place. Three quarters of an acre. They got their own trees, their own bushes, a nice little swimming pool for the kids they blow up in the summertime, a big swing in the back, a little dog house, a rock garden—

WILLIE A what?

AL A rock garden.

WILLIE What do you mean, a rock garden? You mean for rocks?

AL You never saw a rock garden?

WILLIE And I'm not that anxious.

AL It's beautiful. A Chinaman made it. Someday you'll take a bus and you'll come out and I'll show you.

WILLIE I should drive all the way out to New Jersey on a bus to see a rock garden?

AL You don't even know what I'm talking about. You have to live in the country to appreciate it. I never thought it was possible I could be so happy in the country.

WILLIE You don't mind it's so quiet?

AL *(Looks at him)* They got noise in New Jersey. But it's a quiet noise. Birds . . . drizzling . . . Not like here with the buses and trucks and screaming and yelling.

WILLIE Well, it's different for you. You like the country better because you're retired. You can sit on a porch, look at a tree, watch a bush growing. You're still not active like me. You got a different temperament, you're a slow person.

AL I'm a slow person?

WILLIE You're here fifteen minutes, you still got a whole cup of tea. I'm finished already.

AL That's right. You're finished, and I'm still enjoying it. That was always the difference with us.

WILLIE You're wrong. I can get up and make a *second* cup of tea and enjoy it twice as much as you. I like a busy life. That's why I love the city. I gotta be near a phone. I never know when a picture's gonna come up, a musical, a commercial . . .

AL When did you do a picture?

WILLIE They're negotiating.

AL When did you do a musical?

WILLIE They're talking.

AL When did you do a commercial?

WILLIE All the time. I did one last week.

AL For what?

WILLIE For, er, for the . . . what's it, the potato chips.

AL What potato chips?

WILLIE The big one. The crispy potato chips . . . er . . . you know.

AL What do I know? I don't eat potato chips.

WILLIE Well, what's the difference what the name is?

AL They hire you to sell potato chips and you can't remember the name?

WILLIE Did you remember Sol Burton?

AL *(Shrugs)* I'm not selling Sol Burton.

WILLIE Listen, I don't want to argue with you.

AL I didn't come from New Jersey to argue.

(They sit quietly for a few seconds. AL *sips his tea;* WILLIE *looks at his empty cup*

WILLIE *(Finally)* So-o-o . . . What do you think? . . . You want to do the doctor sketch?

AL *(Thinks)* Well, listen, it's very good money. It's only a few days' work, I can be back in New Jersey. If you feel you'd like to do it, then my feeling is I'm agreeable.

WILLIE And my feeling they told you.

AL What?

WILLIE They didn't tell you? My feeling is I'm against it.

AL You're against it?

WILLIE Right. But I'll do it if you want to.

AL I don't want to do it if you're against it. If you're against it, don't do it.

WILLIE What do you care if I'm against it as long as we're doing it? I just want you to know *why* I'm doing it.

AL Don't do me any favors.

WILLIE Who's doing you a favor? I'm doing my nephew a favor. It'll be good for him in the business if we do it.

AL You're sure?

WILLIE Certainly I'm sure. It's a big break for a kid like that to get big stars like us.

AL That's different. In that case, I'm against it too but I'll do it.

WILLIE *(Nods)* As long as we understand each other.

AL And I want to be sure you know I'm not doing it for the money. The money goes to my grandchildren.

WILLIE The whole thing?

AL The whole thing. But not now. Only if I die. If I don't die, it'll be for my old age.

WILLIE The same with me.

AL You don't have grandchildren.

WILLIE My *nephew's* children. Sidney and Marvin.

AL *(Nods)* Very good.

WILLIE Okay . . . So-o-o, you wanna rehearse?

AL You're not against rehearsing?

WILLIE Why should I be against rehearsing? I'm only against doing the show. Rehearsing is important.

AL All right, let's rehearse. Why don't we move the furniture, and we'll make the set.

(They both get up and start to move the furniture around. First each one takes a single chair and moves it into a certain position. Then they both take a table and jointly move it away. Then they each take the chair the other one had moved before, and move it into a different place. Every time one moves something somewhere, the other moves it into a different spot. Finally WILLIE *becomes aware that they are getting nowhere)*

WILLIE Wait a minute, wait a minute. What the hell are we doing here?

AL I'm fixing up the set, I don't know what you're doing.

WILLIE You're fixing up the set?

AL That's right.

WILLIE You're fixing up the set for the doctor sketch?

*(*AL *looks at him for a long time without saying a word. It suddenly becomes clear to him)*

AL Oh, the *doctor* sketch?

(He then starts to pick up a chair and move it into another position. WILLIE *does the same with another chair. They both move the table . . . and then they repeat what they did before. Every time one moves a chair, the other one moves the same chair to a different position.* WILLIE *stops and looks again)*

WILLIE Wait a minute! Wait a minute! We're doing the same goddamn thing. Are you fixing up for the doctor sketch or are you redecorating my apartment?

AL I'm fixing up for the doctor sketch. If you'd leave what I'm doing alone, we'd be finished.

WILLIE We'd be finished, but we'd be wrong.

AL Not for the doctor sketch. I know what I'm doing. I did this sketch for forty-three years.

WILLIE And where was I all that time, taking a smoke? Who did you think did it with you for forty-three years? That was *me*, mister.

AL Don't call me mister, you know my name. I never liked it when you called me mister.

WILLIE It's not a dirty word.

AL It is when you say it.

WILLIE Forgive me, *sir.*

AL Let's please, for Pete's sakes, fix up for the doctor sketch.

WILLIE You think *you* know how to do it? You fix it up.

AL It'll be my pleasure. *(*WILLIE *stands aside and watches with arms folded as* AL *proceeds to move table and chairs and stools until he arranges them exactly the way he wants them. Then he stands back and folds his arms the same way)* There! *That's* the doctor sketch!

WILLIE *(Smiles arrogantly)* For how much money?

AL I don't want to bet you.

WILLIE You're afraid to lose?

AL I'm afraid to *win.* You don't even have enough to buy a box of plain crackers.

WILLIE —Don't be so afraid you're gonna win—because you're gonna lose! That's not the doctor sketch. That's the gypsy chiropractor sketch.

AL You're positive?

WILLIE I'm *more* than positive. I'm *sure.*

AL All right. Show me the doctor sketch.

WILLIE *(Looks at him confidently, then goes to a chair, picks it up and moves it to the left about four inches, if that much. Then he folds his arms over his chest)* There, *that's* the doctor sketch!

AL *(Looks at him)* You know what you are, Willie? You're a lapalooza.

WILLIE *(Nods)* If I'm a lapalooza, you're a mister.

AL Let's please rehearse the sketch.

WILLIE All right, go outside. I'm in the office.

AL You gonna do the part with the nurse first?

WILLIE You see a nurse here? How can I rehearse with a nurse that's not here?

AL I'm just asking a question. I'm not allowed to ask questions?

WILLIE Ask whatever you want. But try to make them intelligent questions.

AL I beg your pardon. I usually ask the kind of question to the kind of person I'm talking to . . . You get my drift?

WILLIE I get it, mister.

AL All right. Let's skip over the nurse. We'll start from where I come in.

WILLIE All right, from where you come in. First go out.

AL *(Takes a few steps toward the door, stops and turns)* All right, I'm outside. *(Pantomimes with his fist, knocking on a door)* Knock, knock, knock! I was looking for the doctor.

WILLIE Wait a minute. You're not outside.

AL Certainly I'm outside.

WILLIE If you were outside, you couldn't see me, could you?

AL No.

WILLIE Can you see me?

AL Yes.

WILLIE So you're not outside. Go *all* the way outside. What the hell kind of a rehearsal is this?

AL It's a rehearsing rehearsal. Can't you make believe I'm all the way out in the hall?

WILLIE I could also make believe you were still in New Jersey, but you're not. You're here. Let's have a professional rehearsal, for chrissakes. We ain't got a nurse, but we got a door. Let's use what we got.

AL *(Sighs deeply)* Listen, we're not gonna stop for every little thing, are we? I don't know how many years I got left, I don't wanna spend it rehearsing.

WILLIE We're not gonna stop for the little things. We're gonna stop for the big things . . . The door is a big thing.

AL All right, I'll go through the door, I'll come in, and then we'll run through the sketch once or twice, and that'll be it for today. All right?

WILLIE Right . . . Unless another big thing comes up.

AL *(Glares at him)* All right, I'm going out. I'll be right back in. *(He crosses to the door, opens it, stops and turns)* If I'm outside and my daughter calls, tell her to pick me up in an hour.

(He goes out and closes the door behind him)

WILLIE *(Mumbles, half to himself)* She can pick you up *now* for all I care. *(He puts his hands behind his back, clasps them, and paces back and forth. He calls out)* All right! Knock, knock, knock!

AL *(From outside)* Knock, knock, knock!

WILLIE *(Screams)* *Don't say it,* for God's sakes, *do it! (To himself)* He probably went *crazy* in the country.

AL *(From outside)* You ready?

WILLIE *(Yells)* I'm ready. Knock, knock, knock! *(*AL *knocks three times on the door)* Come in. *(We see and hear the doorknob jiggle, but it doesn't open. This is repeated)* All right, come in already.

AL *(From outside)* It doesn't open—it's stuck.

WILLIE *(Wearily)* All right, wait a minute. *(He shuffles over to the door and puts his hand on the knob and pulls. It doesn't open)* Wait a minute.

(He tries again, to no avail)

AL *(From outside)* What's the matter?

WILLIE Wait a minute.

(He pulls harder, to no avail)

AL Is it locked?

WILLIE It's not locked. Wait a minute. *(He tries again; it doesn't open)* It's locked. You better get somebody. Call the boy downstairs. Sandy. Tell him it's locked.

AL *(From outside)* Let me try it again.

WILLIE What are you wasting time? Call the boy. Tell him it's locked.

*(*AL *tries it again, turning it in the other direction, and the door opens. They stand there face-to-face)*

AL I fixed it.

WILLIE *(Glares at him)* You didn't fix it. You just don't know how to open a door.

AL Did my daughter call?

WILLIE You know, I think you went crazy in the country.

AL You want to stand here and insult me, or do you want to rehearse the sketch?

WILLIE I would like to do *both*, but we ain't got the time . . . Let's forget the door. Stand in here and say "Knock, knock, knock."

AL (AL *comes in and closes the door. Sarcastically)* I hope I can get *out* again.

WILLIE I hope so too. *(He places his hands behind his back and paces)* All right. "Knock, knock, knock."

AL *(Pantomimes with his fist)* Knock, knock, knock.

WILLIE *(Singsong)* Enter!

AL *(Stops and looks at him)* What do you mean "Enter"? *(He does it in the same singsong way)* What happened to "Come in"?

WILLIE It's the same thing, isn't it? "Enter" or "come in." What's the difference, as long as you're in?

AL The difference is we've done this sketch twelve thousand times, and you've always said "Come in," and suddenly today it's "Enter." Why today, after all these years, do you suddenly change it to "Enter"?

WILLIE *(Shrugs)* I'm trying to freshen up the act.

AL Who asked you to freshen up the act? They asked for the doctor sketch, didn't they? The doctor sketch starts with "Come in," not "Enter." You wanna freshen up something, put some flowers in here.

WILLIE It's a new generation today. This is not 1934, you know.

AL No kidding? I didn't get today's paper.

WILLIE What's bad about "Enter" instead of "Come in"?

AL Because it's different. You know why we've been doing it the same way for forty-three years? Because it's good.

WILLIE And you know why we don't do it any more? Because we've been doing it the same way for forty-three years.

AL So, if we're not doing it any more, why are we changing it?

WILLIE Can I make a comment, nothing personal? I think you've been sitting on a New Jersey porch too long.

AL What does that mean?

WILLIE That means I think you've been sitting on a New Jersey porch too long. From my window, I see everything that goes on in the world. I see old people, I see young people, nice people, bad people, I see hold-ups, drug addicts, ambulances, car crashes, jumpers from buildings—I see everything. You see a lawn mower and a milkman.

AL *(Looks at him for a long moment)* And that's why you want to say "Enter" instead of "Come in"?

WILLIE Are you listening to me?

AL *(Looks around)* Why, there's someone else in the room?

WILLIE You don't know the first thing that's going on today?

AL All right, what's going on today?

WILLIE Did you ever hear the expression "That's where it is"? Well, this is where it is, and that's where I am.

AL I see . . . Did you ever hear the expression "You don't know what the hell you're talking about"? It comes right in front of the *other* expression "You *never* knew what the hell you were talking about."

WILLIE *I* wasn't the one who retired. You know why you retired? Because you were tired. You were getting old-fashioned. I was still new-fashioned, and I'll *always* be.

AL I see. That's why you're in such demand. That's why you're such a "hot" property today. That's why you do movies you don't do, that's why you're in musicals you're not in, and that's why you make commercials you don't make—because you can't even remember them to *make* them.

WILLIE You know what I *do* remember? I remember what a pain in the ass you are to work with, that's what I remember.

AL That's right. And when you worked with this pain in the ass, you lived in a *five*-room suite. Now you live in a *one*-room suite . . . And you're still wearing the same goddamn pajamas you wore in the five-room suite.

WILLIE I don't have to take this crap from you.

AL You're lucky you're getting it. No one else wants to give it to you.

WILLIE I don't want to argue with you. After you say "Knock, knock, knock," I'm saying "Enter," and if you don't like it you don't have to come in.

AL You can't say nothing without my permission. I own fifty percent of this act.

WILLIE Then say *your* fifty percent. I'm saying "Enter" in my fifty percent.

AL If you say "Enter" after "Knock, knock, knock" . . . I'm coming in all right. But not alone. I'm bringing a lawyer with me.

WILLIE Where? From New Jersey? You're lucky if a *cow* comes with you.

AL Against *you* in court, I could *win* with a cow.

(He enunciates each point by poking WILLIE *in the chest)*

WILLIE *(Slaps his hand away)* The *finger?* You're starting with the finger again?

(He runs into the kitchen and comes out brandishing a knife.)

AL I'll tell you the truth now. I didn't retire. I *escaped.*

WILLIE *(Wielding the knife)* The next time you give me the finger, say goodbye to the finger.

AL *(Hiding behind a chair)* Listen, I got a terrific idea. Instead of working together again, let's never work together again. You're crazy.

WILLIE I'm crazy, heh? I'M CRAZY!

AL Keep saying it until you believe it.

WILLIE I may be crazy, but you're *senile!* You know what that is?

AL I'm not giving you any straight lines.

WILLIE Crazy is when you got a couple of parts that go wrong. Senile is when you went the hell out of business. That's you, mister. *(The phone rings.* AL *moves toward the phone)* Get away from that phone. *(He drives the knife into the table.* AL *backs away in shock.* WILLIE *picks up the phone)* Hello?

AL Is that my daughter?

WILLIE Hello . . . How are you?

AL Is that my daughter? Is that her?

WILLIE *(To* AL*)* Will you shut up? Will you be quiet? Can't you see I'm talking? Don't you see me on the phone with a person? For God's sakes, behave like a human being for five seconds, will you? WILL YOU BEHAVE FOR FIVE SECONDS LIKE A HUMAN BEING? *(Into the phone)* Hello? . . . Yes . . . Just a minute. *(To* AL*)* It's your daughter.

(He sits, opens up Variety*)*

AL *(Takes the phone, turns his back to* WILLIE, *speaks low)* Hello . . . Hello, sweetheart . . . No . . . No . . . I can't talk now . . . I said I can't talk now . . . Because he's a crazy bedbug, that's why.

WILLIE *(Jumps up)* Mister is no good but bedbug is all right?? *(Yells into the phone)* Your father is sick! Come and get your sick father!

AL *(Turns to him)* Don't you see me on the phone with a person? Will you please be quiet, for God's sakes! *(Back into the phone)* Listen, I want you to pick me up now . . . I don't want to discuss it. Pick me up now. In front of the hotel. Don't park too close, it's filthy here . . . I *know* what I promised. Don't argue with me. I'm putting on my coat. I'll wait in the street—I'll probably get mugged . . . All right, just a minute. *(He hands the phone to* WILLIE*)* She'd like to talk to you for a second.

WILLIE Who is it?

AL *(Glares at him)* Mrs. Eleanor Roosevelt . . . What do you mean, who is it? Didn't you just say it's my daughter?

WILLIE I know it's your daughter. I forgot her name.

AL Doris.

WILLIE What does she want?

AL *(Yells)* Am I Doris? She'll tell you.

WILLIE *(Takes the phone)* Hello? . . . Hello, dear, this is Willie Clark . . . Unpleasantness? There was no unpleasantness . . . There was stupidity maybe but no unpleasantness . . .

AL Tell her I'm getting into my coat. *(He is putting his coat on)* Tell her I got one sleeve on.

WILLIE *(Into the phone)* I was hoping it would work out too . . . I bent over backwards and forwards. He didn't even bend sideways . . .

AL I got the other sleeve on . . . Tell her I'm up to my hat and then I'm out the door.

WILLIE It's a question of one word, darling. "Enter"! . . ."Enter"—that's all it comes down to.

AL *(Puts his hat on)* The hat is on. I'm bundled up, tell her.

WILLIE *(Into the phone)* Yes . . . Yes, I will . . . I'll tell him myself. I promise . . . Goodbye, Dorothy. *(He hangs up)* I told her we'll give it one more chance.

AL Not if you say "Enter." "Come in," I'll stay. "Enter," I go.

WILLIE Ask me "Knock, knock, knock."

AL Don't fool around with me. I got enough pains in my neck. Are you going to say "Come in"?

WILLIE Ask me "Knock, knock, knock"!

AL I know you, you bastard!

WILLIE ASK ME "KNOCK, KNOCK, KNOCK"!

AL KNOCK, KNOCK, KNOCK!

WILLIE *(Grinding it in)* EN-TERRR!

AL BEDBUG! CRAZY BEDBUG!
(He starts to run out)

WILLIE *(Big smile)* ENNN-TERRRRR!
(The curtain starts down)

AL *(Heading for the door)* LUNATIC BASTARD!

WILLIE ENNN-TERRRR!
Curtain

Act Two

SCENE I

The scene is a doctor's office or, rather, an obvious stage "flat" representation of a doctor's office. It has an old desk and chair, a telephone, a cabinet filled with medicine bottles, a human skeleton hanging on a stand, a blackboard with chalk and pointer, an eye chart on the wall.

Overhead television lights surround the top of the set. Two boom microphones extend from either end of the set over the office.

At rise, the set is not fully lit. A thin, frail man in a hat and business suit sits in the chair next to the doctor's desk, patiently waiting.

VOICE OF TV DIRECTOR *(Over the loudspeaker)* Eddie! *EDDIE!*

(EDDIE, *a young assistant TV director with headset and speaker, trailing wires and carrying a clipboard, steps out on the set. He speaks through his mike)*

EDDIE Yeah, Phil?

VOICE OF TV DIRECTOR Any chance of doing this today?

EDDIE *(Shrugs)* We're all set here, Phil. We're just waiting on the actors.

VOICE OF TV DIRECTOR What the hell is happening?

EDDIE I don't know. There's a problem with the make-up. Mr. Clark wants a Number Seven amber or something.

VOICE OF TV DIRECTOR Well, get it for him.

EDDIE Where? They stopped making it thirty-four years ago.

VOICE OF TV DIRECTOR Christ!

EDDIE And Mr. Lewis says the "ahh sticks are too short.

VOICE OF TV DIRECTOR The what?

EDDIE The "ahh" sticks. Don't ask me. I'm still trying to figure out what a "look" stick is.

VOICE OF TV DIRECTOR What the hell are we making, *Nicholas and Alexandra*? Tell them it's just a dress rehearsal. We'll worry about the props later. Let's get moving, Eddie. Christ Almighty.

*(*WILLIE*'s nephew* BEN *appears onstage. He talks up into the overhead mike)*

BEN Mr. Schaefer . . . Mr. Schaefer, I'm awfully sorry about the delay. Mr. Lewis and Mr. Clark have had a few technical problems backstage.

VOICE OF TV DIRECTOR Yeah, well, we've had it all week . . . I'm afraid we're running out of time here. I've got twelve goddamned other numbers to get through today.

BEN I'll get them right out. There's no problem.

VOICE OF TV DIRECTOR Tell them I want to run straight through, no stopping. They can clean up whatever they want afterwards.

BEN Absolutely.

VOICE OF TV DIRECTOR I haven't seen past "Knock, knock, knock"—"Come in" since Tuesday.

BEN *(Looks offstage)* Right. There they are. *(Into the mike)* We're ready, Mr. Schaefer. I'll tell them we're going to go straight through, no stopping. Thank you very much.

*(*BEN *exits very quickly)*

VOICE OF TV DIRECTOR All right, Eddie, bring in the curtains.

EDDIE What?

VOICE OF TV DIRECTOR Bring in the curtains. Let's run it from the top with the voice over.

EDDIE *(calls up)* Let's have the curtains.
(The curtains come in)

VOICE OF TV DIRECTOR Voice over!

ANNOUNCER The golden age of comedy reached its zenith during a fabulous and glorious era known as Vaudeville—Fanny Brice, W. C. Fields, Eddie Cantor, Ed Wynn, Will Rogers and a host of other greats fill its Hall of Fame. There are two other names that belong on this list, but they can never be listed separately. They are more than a team. They are two comic shining lights that beam as one. For, Lewis without Clark is like laughter without joy. We are privileged to present tonight, in their first public performance in over eleven years, for half a century known as "The Sunshine Boys"—Mr. Al Lewis and Mr. Willie Clark, in their beloved scene, "The Doctor Will See You Now."

(The curtain rises, and the set is fully lit. The frail man in the hat is sitting on the chair as WILLIE, *the doctor, dressed in a floor-length white doctor's jacket, a mirror attached to his head and a stethoscope around his neck is looking into the* PATIENT*'s mouth, holding his tongue down with an "ahh" stick)*

WILLIE Open wider and say "Ahh."

PATIENT Ahh.

WILLIE Wider.

PATIENT *Ahhh!*

WILLIE *(Moves with his back to the audience)* A little wider.

PATIENT Ahhh!

WILLIE *(Steps away)* Your throat is all right, but you're gonna have some trouble with your stomach.

PATIENT How come?

WILLIE You just swallowed the stick.

(The PATIENT *feels his stomach)*

PATIENT Is that bad?

WILLIE It's terrible. I only got two left.

PATIENT What about getting the stick out?

WILLIE What am I, a tree surgeon? . . . All right, for another ten dollars, I'll take it out.

PATIENT That's robbery.

WILLIE Then forget it. Keep the stick.

PATIENT No, no. I'll pay. Take the stick out.

WILLIE Come back tomorrow. On Thursdays I do woodwork. *(The* PATIENT *gets up and crosses to the door, then exits.* WILLIE *calls out)* Oh, Nurse! Nursey!

(The NURSE *enters. She is a tall, voluptuous and overstacked blonde in a tight dress)*

NURSE Did you want me, Doctor?

WILLIE *(He looks at her, knowingly)* Why do you think I hired you? . . . What's your name again?

NURSE Miss MacKintosh. You know, like the apples.

WILLIE *(Nods)* The name I forgot, the apples I remembered . . . Look in my appointment book, see who's next.

NURSE It's a Mr. Kornheiser.

WILLIE Maybe you're wrong. Look in the book. It's better that way.

(She crosses to the desk and bends way over as she looks through the appointment book. Her firm, round rear end faces us and WILLIE. WILLIE *shakes his head from side to side in wonderful contemplation)*

NURSE *(Still down)* No, I was right.

WILLIE So was I.

NURSE *(Straightens up and turns around)* It's Mr. Kornheiser.

WILLIE Are you sure? Spell it.

NURSE *(Turns, bends and gives us the same wonderful view again)* K-o-r-n-h-e-i-s-e-r!

(She turns and straightens up)

WILLIE *(Nods)* What's the first name?

NURSE *(Turns, bends)* Walter.

WILLIE Stay down for the middle name.

NURSE *(Remains down)* Benjamin.

WILLIE Don't move and give me the whole thing.

NURSE *(Still rear end up, reading)* Walter Benjamin Kornheiser.

(She turns and straightens up)

WILLIE Oh, boy. From now on I only want to see patients with long names.

NURSE Is there anything else you want?

WILLIE Yeah. Call a carpenter and have him make my desk lower.

(The NURSE *walks sexily right up to* WILLIE *and stands with her chest practically on his, breathing and heaving)*

Nurse *(Pouting)* Yes, Doctor.

WILLIE *(Wipes his brow)* Whew, it's hot in here. Did you turn the steam on?

NURSE *(Sexily)* No, Doctor.

WILLIE In that case, take a five-dollar raise. Send in the next patient before *I'm* the next patient.

NURSE Yes, Doctor. *(She coughs)* Excuse me, I think I have a chest cold.

WILLIE Looks more like an epidemic to me.

NURSE Yes, Doctor. *(She wriggles her way to the door)* Is there anything else you can think of?

WILLIE I can *think* of it, but I'm not so sure I can *do* it.

NURSE Well, If I *can* help you, Doctor, that's what the nurse is for.

(She exits and closes the door with an enticing look)

WILLIE I'm glad I didn't go to law school. *(Then we hear three knocks on the door. "Knock, knock, knock")* Aha. That must be my next patient. *(Calls out)* Come in! *(The door starts to open)*—and *enter!*

*(*AL *steps in and glares angrily at* WILLIE. *He is in a business suit, wears a wig, and carries a cheap attaché case)*

AL I'm looking for the doctor.

WILLIE Are you sick?

AL Are *you* the doctor?

WILLIE Yes.

AL I'm not *that* sick.

WILLIE What's your name, please?

AL Kornheiser. Walter Benjamin Kornheiser. You want me to spell it?

WILLIE Never mind. I got a better speller than you . . . *(Takes a tongue depressor from his pocket)* Sit down and open your mouth, please.

AL There's nothing wrong with my mouth.

WILLIE Then just sit down.

AL There's nothing wrong with that either.

WILLIE Then what are you doing here?

AL I came to examine you.

WILLIE I think you got everything backwards.

AL It's possible. I dressed in a hurry this morning.

WILLIE You mean you came here for me to examine *you.*

AL No, I came here for me to examine *you.* I'm a tax collector.

WILLIE *(Nods)* That's nice. I'm a stamp collector. What do you do for a living.

AL I find out how much money people make.

WILLIE Oh, a busybody. Make an appointment with the nurse.

AL I did. I'm seeing her Friday night . . .

WILLIE *(Jumps up and down angrily)* Don't fool around with my nurse. DON'T FOOL AROUND WITH MY NURSE! She's a nice girl. She's a *Virginian!*

AL A what?

WILLIE A *Virginian.* That's where she's from.

AL Well, she ain't going *back*, I can tell you that. *(He sits, opens the attaché case)* I got some questions to ask you.

WILLIE I'm too busy to answer questions. I'm a doctor. If you wanna see me, you gotta be a patient.

AL But I'm not sick.

WILLIE Don't worry. We'll find something.

AL All right, you examine me and I'll examine you . . . *(Takes out a tax form as* WILLIE *wields the tongue depressor)* The first question is, How much money did you make last year?

WILLIE Last year I made—

(He moves his lips mouthing a sum, but it's not audible.)

AL I didn't hear that.

WILLIE Oh. Hard of hearing. I knew we'd find something. Did you ever have any childhood diseases?

AL Not lately.

WILLIE Father living or deceased?

AL Both.

WILLIE What do you mean, both?

AL First he was living, now he's deceased.

WILLIE What did your father die from?

AL My mother . . . Now it's my turn. Are you married?

WILLIE I'm looking.

AL Looking to get married?

WILLIE No, looking to get out.
(He looks in AL*'s ear with a flashlight)*

AL What are you doing?

WILLIE I'm examining your lower intestines.

AL So why do you look in the ear?

WILLIE If I got a choice of two places to look, I'll take this one.

AL *(Consulting his form)* Never mind. Do you own a car?

WILLIE Certainly I own a car. Why?

AL If you use it for medical purposes, you can deduct it from your taxes. What kind of car do you own?

WILLIE An ambulance.

AL Do you own a house?

WILLIE Can I deduct it?

AL Only if you use it for medical purposes. Where do you live?

WILLIE In Mount Sinai Hospital . . . Open your shirt, I want to listen to your heartbeat.

AL *(Unbuttons two buttons on his shirt)* Will this take long?

WILLIE Not if I hear something. *(He puts his ear to* AL*'s chest and listens)* Uh-huh. I hear something . . . You're all right.

AL Aren't you going to listen with the stethoscope?

WILLIE Oh, sure. I didn't know you wanted a thorough examination. *(Puts the stethoscope to his ears and listens to* AL*'s chest)* Oh, boy. Ohhh, boyyyy! You know what you got?

AL What?

WILLIE A filthy undershirt.

AL Never mind that. Am I in good health?

WILLIE Not unless you change your undershirt.

AL What is this, a doctor's office or a laundry? I bet you never went to medical school.

WILLIE *(Jumping up and down again)* What are you talkin'? . . . WHAT ARE YOU TALKIN'? . . . I went to Columbia Medical School.

AL Did you pass?

WILLIE Certainly.

AL Well, you should have gone *in!*

WILLIE Never mind . . . I'm gonna examine your eyes now.

AL They're perfect. I got twenty-twenty eyes.

WILLIE That's too much. All you need is one and one.

Look at that chart on the wall. Now put your left hand over your left eye and your right hand over your right eye. *(*AL *does so)* Now tell me what you see.

AL I don't see nothing.

WILLIE Don't panic, I can cure you . . . Take your hands away. *(*AL *does)* Can you see now?

AL Certainly I can see now.

WILLIE You know, I fixed over two thousand people like that.

AL It's a miracle.

WILLIE Thank you.

AL A miracle you're not in jail . . . What do you charge for a visit?

WILLIE A dollar.

AL A dollar? That's very cheap for an examination.

WILLIE It's not an examination. It's just a visit. "Hello and Goodbye" . . . "Hello and How Are You?" is ten dollars.

AL If you ask me, you're a quack.

WILLIE If I was a duck I would ask you . . . Now roll up your sleeve, I wanna take some blood.

AL I can't do it.

WILLIE Why not?

AL If I see blood, I get sick.

WILLIE Do what I do. Don't look.

AL I'm sorry. I'm not giving blood. I'm anemic.

WILLIE What's anemic?

AL You're a doctor and you don't know what anemic means?

WILLIE That's because I'm a specialist.

AL What do you specialize in?

WILLIE Everything but anemic.

AL Listen, can I continue my examination?

WILLIE You continue yours, and I'll continue mine. All right, cross your legs. *(He hits* AL*'s knee with a small hammer)* Does it hurt if I hit you with the hammer?

AL Yes.

WILLIE Good. From now on, try not to get hit with a hammer. *(He throws the hammer over his shoulder. He takes a specimen bottle from the cabinet and returns)* You see this bottle?

AL Yes.

WILLIE You know what you're supposed to do with this bottle?

AL I think so.

WILLIE You *think* so or you *know* so? If you're not sure, let me know. The girl doesn't come in to clean today.

AL What do you want me to do?

WILLIE I want you to go in this bottle.

AL I haven't got time. I have to go over your books.

WILLIE *The hell you will!*

AL If I don't go over your books, the *government* will come in here and go over your books.

WILLIE Don't they have a place in Washington?

AL Certainly, but they have to go where the books are.

WILLIE The whole government?

AL No, just the Treasury Department.

WILLIE That's a relief.

AL I'm glad you're relieved.

WILLIE I wish *you* were before you came in here.
(The door opens and the big-chested NURSE *steps in)*

NURSE Oh, Doctor. Doctor Klockenmeyer.

WILLIE Yes.

NURSE Mrs. Kolodny is on the phone. She wants you to rush right over and deliver her baby.

WILLIE I'm busy now. Tell her I'll mail it to her in the morning.

NURSE Yes, Doctor.
(She exits and closes the door)

AL Where did you find a couple of nurses like that?

WILLIE She was standing on Forty-third and Forty-fourth Street . . . Let me see your tongue, please.

AL I don't want to.
*(*WILLIE *squeezes* AL*'s throat, and his tongue comes out)*

WILLIE Open the mouth . . . How long have you had that white coat on your tongue?

AL Since January. In the spring I put on a gray sports jacket.

WILLIE Now hold your tongue with your fingers and say "shish kabob."

AL *(Holds his tongue with his fingers)* Thickabob.

WILLIE Again.

AL Thickabob.

WILLIE I have bad news for you.

AL What is it?

WILLIE If you do that in a restaurant, you'll never get shish kabob.

AL *(Stands with his face close to* WILLIE*'s)* Never mind that. What about your *t*axes?

(On the "T," he spits a little)

WILLIE *(Wipes his face)* The what?

AL The *t*axes. It's *t*ime *t*o pay your *t*axes to the *T*reasury.

(All the "T's" are quite fluid. WILLIE *wipes his face and glares angrily at* AL*)*

WILLIE I'm warning you, don't start in with me.

AL What are you talking about?

WILLIE You know what I'm talking about. *(Illustrates)* "It's *t*ime *t*o pay the *t*axes." You're speaking with spitting again.

AL I said the right line, didn't I? If it comes out juicy, I can't help that.

WILLIE *(Quite angry)* It doesn't come out juicy unless you squeeze the "T's." I'm warning you, don't squeeze them on me.

*(*VOICE OF TV DIRECTOR *is heard over the loudspeaker)*

VOICE OF TV DIRECTOR Okay, let's hold it a second. Mr. Clark, I'm having trouble with the dialogue. I don't find those last few lines in the script.

WILLIE *(Shouts up)* It's not in the script, it's in *his mouth.*

AL *(Talking up into the mike)* I said the right line. Look in the script, you'll find it there.

WILLIE *(Shouting)* You'll find the words, you won't find

the spit. The spit's his own idea. He's doing it on *purpose!*

AL I don't spit on purpose. I spit on accident. I've *always* spitted on accident. It's not possible to say that line without spitting a little.

WILLIE *(Addressing all his remarks to the unseen director)* *I* can say it. *(He says the line with great delicacy, especially on the "T's")* "It's time to pay your taxes to the Treasury." *(Back to his normal inflection)* There wasn't a spit in my entire mouth. Why doesn't he say it like *that?*

AL What am I, an Englishman? I'm talking the same as I've talked for forty-three years.

VOICE OF TV DIRECTOR Gentlemen, can we argue this point after the dress rehearsal and go on with the sketch?

WILLIE I'm not going to stand here and get a shower in the face. If you want me to go on, either take out the line or get me an umbrella.

VOICE OF TV DIRECTOR Can we *please* go on? With all due respect, gentlemen, we have twelve other scenes to rehearse and we cannot spend all day on personal squabbles . . .

WILLIE I'll go on, but I'm moving to a safer spot.

VOICE OF TV DIRECTOR Don't worry about the moves, we'll pick you up on camera. Now, let's skip over this spot and pick it up on "I hope you don't have what Mr. Melnick had." *(*WILLIE *moves away from* AL*)* All right, Mr. Clark, whenever you're ready.

WILLIE *(Waits a minute, then goes back into the doctor character)* I hope you don't have what Mr. Melnick had.

AL What did Mr. Melnick have?

WILLIE *(Points to standing skeleton)* Ask him yourself, he's standing right there.

AL That's Mr. Melnick?

WILLIE It could be *Mrs.* Melnick. Without high heels, I can't tell.

AL If he's dead, why do you leave him standing in the office?

WILLIE He's still got one more appointment with me.

AL *(Crosses to him)* You know what you are? You're a charlatan! *(As* AL *says that line, he punctuates each word by poking* WILLIE *in the chest with his finger. It does not go unnoticed by* WILLIE*)* Do you know what a charlatan is?

(More pokes)

WILLIE It's a city in North Carolina. And if you're gonna poke me again like that, you're gonna end up in Poughkeepsie.

VOICE OF TV DIRECTOR *(Over the loudspeaker)* Hold it, hold it. Where does it say, "You're going to end up in Poughkeepsie"?

WILLIE *(Furious)* Where does it say he can poke me in the chest? He's doing it on purpose. He *always* did it on purpose, just to get my goat.

AL *(Looking up to the mike)* I didn't poke him, I tapped him. A light little tap, it wouldn't hurt a baby.

WILLIE Maybe a baby elephant. I *knew* I was going to get poked. First comes the spitting, then comes the poking. I know his routine already.

AL *(To the mike)* Excuse me. I'm sorry we're holding up the rehearsal, but we have a serious problem on our hands. The man I'm working with is a lunatic.

WILLIE *(Almost in a rage)* *I'm* a lunatic, heh? He breaks my chest and spits in my face and calls *me* a lunatic!

I'm gonna tell you something now I never told you in my entire life. I hate your guts.

AL You told it to me on Monday.

WILLIE Then I'm telling it to you again.

VOICE OF TV DIRECTOR Listen, gentlemen, I really don't see any point in going on with this rehearsal.

AL I don't see any point in going on with this *show.* This man is persecuting me. For eleven years he's been waiting to get back at me, only I'm not gonna give him the chance.

(The assistant director, EDDIE, *walks out in an attempt to make peace)*

WILLIE *(Half-hysterical)* I knew it! I knew it! He planned it! He's been setting me up for eleven years just to walk out on me again.

EDDIE *(Trying to be gentle)* All right, Mr. Clark, let's settle down. Why don't we all go into the dressing room and talk this out?

AL I didn't want to do it in the first place.

WILLIE *(Apoplectic) Liar! Liar!* His daughter *begged* me on the phone. She *begged* me!

*(*BEN *rushes out to restrain* WILLIE*)*

BEN Uncle Willie, please, that's enough. Come back to the dressing room.

EDDIE Gentlemen, we need the stage. Can we please do this over on the side?

AL *(To the assistant director)* The man is hysterical, you can see for yourself. He's been doing this to me all week long.

(He starts taking off the wig and suit jacket)

WILLIE Begged me. She begged me. His own daughter begged me.

BEN Uncle Willie, stop it, please.

AL *(To the others)* I'm sorry we caused everyone so much trouble. I should have stayed in New Jersey in the first place. *(On his way out. To the assistant director)* He pulled a knife on me last week. In his own apartment he pulled a knife on me. A crazy man.

(He is gone)

WILLIE I don't need you. I *never* needed you. You were nothing when I found you, and that's what you are today.

BEN Come on, Willie. *(Out front)* I'm sorry about this, Mr. Schaefer.

WILLIE He thinks I can't get work without him. Maybe *his* career is over, but not mine. Maybe he's finished, but not me. You hear? not me! NOT M—

(He clutches his chest)

BEN *(Turns and sees him stagger)* Grab him, quick! *(*EDDIE *rushes to* WILLIE, *but it's too late—*WILLIE *falls to the floor.* BEN *rushes to his side)* All right, take it easy, Uncle Willie, just lie there. *(To* EDDIE*)* Get a doctor, please hurry.

(A bit actor and the NURSE *rush onstage behind* BEN*)*

WILLIE *(Breathing hard)* I don't need a doctor. Don't get a doctor, I don't trust them.

BEN Don't talk, Willie, you're all right. *(To the* NURSE*)* Somebody get a blanket, please.

WILLIE *(Breathing fast)* Don't tell him. Don't tell him I fell down. I don't want to give him the satisfaction.

BEN Of course, I won't tell him, Willie. There's nothing to tell. You're going to be all right.

WILLIE Frito-Lays . . . That's the name of the potato chip . . . You see? I remembered . . . I remembered the name! Frito-Lays.

*(*BEN *is holding* WILLIE*'s hand as the lights dim. The curtain falls on the scene. In the dark, we hear the voice of the* ANNOUNCER*)*

ANNOUNCER The golden age of comedy reached its

zenith during a fabulous and glorious era known as Vaudeville—Fanny Brice, W. C. Fields, Eddie Cantor, Ed Wynn, Will Rogers and a host of other greats fill its Hall of Fame. There are two other names that belong on this list, but they can never be listed separately. They are more than a team. They are two comic shining lights that beam as one. For, Lewis without Clark is like laughter without joy. When these two greats retired, a comic style disappeared from the American scene that will never see its likes again . . . Here, then, in a sketch taped nearly eleven years ago on *The Ed Sullivan Show*, are Lewis and Clark in their classic scene, "The Doctor Will See You Now."

(We hear WILLIE*'s voice and that of the first* PATIENT*)*

WILLIE Open wider and say "Ahh."

PATIENT Ahh.

WILLIE Wider.

PATIENT Ahh.

WILLIE A little wider.

PATIENT Ahhh!

WILLIE Your throat is all right, but you're gonna have some trouble with your stomach.

PATIENT How come?

WILLIE You just swallowed the stick.

Curtain

SCENE 2

The curtain rises. The scene is WILLIE*'s hotel room, two weeks later. It is late afternoon.* WILLIE *is in his favorite pajamas in bed, propped up on the pillows, his head hanging down, asleep.*

The television is droning away—another daytime serial. A black REGISTERED NURSE *in uniform, a sweater draped over her shoulders, and her glasses on a chain around her neck, is sitting in a chair watching the television. She is eating from a big box of chocolates. Two very large vases of flowers are on the bureau.* WILLIE*'s head bobs a few times; then he opens his eyes.*

WILLIE What time is it?

NURSE *(Turns off the TV and glances at her watch)* Ten to one.

WILLIE Ten to one? . . . Who are you?

NURSE Don't give me that. You know who I am.

WILLIE You're the same nurse from yesterday?

NURSE I'm the same nurse from every day for two weeks now. Don't play your games with me.

WILLIE I can't even chew a piece of bread, who's gonna play games? . . . Why'd you turn off the television?

NURSE It's either watching that or watching you sleep—either one ain't too interesting.

WILLIE I'm sorry. I'll try to sleep more entertaining . . . What's today, Tuesday?

NURSE Wednesday.
(She bites into a piece of chocolate)

WILLIE How could this be Wednesday? I went to sleep on Monday.

NURSE Haven't we already seen Mike Douglas twice this week?

WILLIE Once.

NURSE Twice.

WILLIE *(Reluctantly)* All right, twice . . . I don't even remember. I was all right yesterday?

NURSE We are doing very well.

WILLIE We are? When did *you* get sick?

NURSE *(Deadly serious, no smile)* That's funny. That is really funny, Mr. Clark. Soon as I get home tonight I'm gonna bust out laughing.

WILLIE You keep eating my candy like that, you're gonna bust out a lot sooner.

NURSE Well, *you* can't eat it and there's no sense throwing it out. I'm just storing up energy for the winter.

WILLIE Maybe you'll find time in between the nougat and the peppermint to take my pulse.

NURSE I took it. It's a little better today.

WILLIE When did you take my pulse?

NURSE When you were sleeping.

WILLIE *Everybody's* pulse is good when they're sleeping. You take a pulse when a person is up. Thirty dollars a day, she takes a sleeping pulse. I'll tell you the truth, I don't think you know what you're doing . . . and I'm not a prejudiced person.

NURSE Well, *I* am: I don't like sick people who tell registered nurses how to do their job. You want your tea now?

WILLIE I don't want to interrupt your candy.

NURSE And don't get fresh with me. You can get fresh with your nephew, but you can't get fresh with me. Maybe *he* has to take it, but I'm not a blood relative.

WILLIE That's for sure.

NURSE That's even funnier than the other one. My *whole* evening's gonna be taken up tonight with nothing but laughing.

WILLIE I don't even eat candy. Finish the whole box. When you're through, I hope you eat the flowers too.

NURSE You know why I don't get angry at anything you say to me?

WILLIE I give up. Why?

NURSE Because I have a good sense of humor. I am *known* for my good sense of humor. That's why I can take anything you say to me.

WILLIE If you nurse as good as your sense of humor, I won't make it to Thursday . . . Who called?

NURSE No one.

WILLIE I thought I heard the phone.

NURSE *(Gets up)* No one called. *(She crosses and puffs up his pillow)* Did you have a nice nap?

WILLIE It was a nap, nothing special . . . Don't puff up the pillows, please. *(He swats her hands away)* It takes me a day and a night to get them the way I like them, and then you puff them up.

NURSE Oh, woke up a little grouchy, didn't we?

WILLIE Stop making yourself a partner all the time. I woke up grouchy. Don't make the bed, please. I'm still sleeping in it. Don't make a bed with a person in it.

NURSE Can't stand to have people do things for you, can you? If you just want someone to sit here and watch you, you're better off getting a dog, Mr. Clark. I'll suggest that to your nephew.

WILLIE Am I complaining? I'm only asking for two things. Don't take my pulse when I'm sleeping and don't make my bed when I'm in it. Do it the other way around and then we're in business.

NURSE It doesn't bother me to do nothing as long as I'm getting paid for it.

(She sits)

WILLIE *(A pause)* I'm hungry.

NURSE You want your junket?

WILLIE Forget it. I'm not hungry. *(She reads)* Tell me something, how old is a woman like you?

NURSE That is none of your business.

WILLIE I'm not asking for business.

NURSE I am fifty-four years young.

WILLIE Is that so? . . . You're married?

NURSE My husband passed away four years ago.

WILLIE Oh . . . You were the nurse?

NURSE No, I was not the nurse . . . You could use some sleep and I could use some quiet.

(She gets up)

WILLIE You know something? For a fifty-four-year-old registered widow, you're an attractive woman.

(He tries to pat her. She swings at him)

NURSE And don't try that with me!

WILLIE Who's trying anything?

NURSE You are. You're getting fresh in a way I don't like.

WILLIE What are you worried about? I can't even put on my slippers by myself.

NURSE I'm not worried about your slippers. And don't play on my sympathy. I don't have any, and I ain't expecting any coming in, in the near future.

WILLIE Listen, how about a nice alcohol rub?

NURSE I just gave you one.

WILLIE No, I'll give *you* one.

NURSE I know you just say things like that to agitate me. You like to agitate people, don't you? Well, I am not an agitatable person.

WILLIE You're right. I think I'd be better off with the dog.

NURSE How did your poor wife stand a man like you?

WILLIE Who told you about my poor wife?

NURSE Your poor nephew . . . Did you ever think of getting married again?
(She takes his pulse)

WILLIE What is this, a proposal?

NURSE *(Laughs)* Not from me . . . I am *not* thinking of getting married again . . . Besides, you're just not my type.

WILLIE Why? It's a question of religion?

NURSE It's a question of age. You'd wear me out in no time.

WILLIE You think I can't support you? I've got Medicare.

NURSE You never stop, do you?

WILLIE When I stop, I won't be here.

NURSE Well, that's where you're gonna be unless you learn to slow up a little.

WILLIE Slow up? I moved two inches in three weeks, she tells me slow up.

NURSE I mean, if you're considering getting well again, you have to stop worrying about telephone calls and messages, and especially about when you're going back to work.

WILLIE I'm an actor—I have to act. It's my profession.

NURSE Your profession right now is being a sick person. And if you're gonna act anywhere, it's gonna be from a sick bed.

WILLIE Maybe I can get a job on Marcus Welby.

NURSE You can turn everything I say into a vaudeville routine if you want, but I'm gonna give you a piece of advice, Mr. Clark . . .

WILLIE What?

NURSE The world is full of sick people. And there just ain't enough doctors or nurses to go around to take care of all these sick people. And all the doctors and all the nurses can do just so much, Mr. Clark. But God, in His Infinite Wisdom, has said He will help those who help themselves.

WILLIE *(Looks at her)* So? What's the advice?

NURSE *Stop bugging me!*

WILLIE All right, I'll stop bugging you . . . I don't even know what the hell it means.

NURSE That's better. Now you're my type again.

(The doorbell rings. The NURSE *crosses to the door)*

WILLIE Here comes today's candy.

(She opens the door. BEN *enters with packages)*

BEN Hello. How is he?

NURSE Fine. I think we're gonna get married.

BEN Hey, Uncle Willie, you look terrific.

WILLIE You got my *Variety?*

BEN *(Goes over to him, and hands him* Variety*)* I also got about two hundred get-well telegrams from just about every star in show business—Lucille Ball, Milton Berle, Bob Hope, the mayor. It'll take you nine months just to answer them.

WILLIE What about a commercial? Did you hear from Alka-Seltzer?

BEN We have plenty of time to talk about that . . . Miss O'Neill, did you have your lunch yet?

NURSE Not yet.

WILLIE She just finished two pounds of appetizers.

BEN Why don't you go out, take an hour or so? I'll be here for a while.

NURSE Thank you. I could use some fresh air. *(Gets her coat. To* WILLIE*)* Now, when I'm gone, I don't want you getting all agitated again, you hear?

WILLIE I hear, I hear. Stop bugging me.

NURSE And don't get up to go to the bathroom. Use the you-know-what.

WILLIE *(Without looking up from his* Variety*)* And if not, I'll do it you-know-where.

(The NURSE *exits)*

BEN *(Pulling up a chair next to the bed)* Never mind, she's a very good nurse.

WILLIE *(Looks in the paper)* Oh, boy, Bernie Eisenstein died.

BEN Who?

WILLIE Bernie Eisenstein. Remember the dance team "Ramona and Rodriguez"? Bernie Eisenstein was Rodriguez . . . He would have been seventy-eight in August.

BEN *(Sighs)* Uncle Willie, could you put down *Variety* for a second?

WILLIE *(Still reading)* Did you bring a cigar?

BEN Uncle Willie, you realize you've had a heart attack, don't you? . . . You've been getting away with it for years—the cigars, the corned beef sandwiches, the tension, the temper tantrums. You can't do it any more, Willie. Your heart's just not going to take it.

WILLIE This is the good news you rushed up with? For this we could have skipped a Wednesday.

BEN *(A pause)* I talked to the doctor this morning . . . and I'm going to have to be very frank and honest with you, Willie . . . You've got to retire. I mean give it up. Show business is out.

WILLIE Until when?

BEN Until *ever!* Your blood pressure is abnormally high, your heart is weak—if you tried to work again you would kill yourself.

WILLIE All right, let me think it over.

BEN *Think what over?* There's nothing to think over. You can't work any more, there's no decision to be made. Can't you understand that?

WILLIE You decide for Ben Silverman, I'll decide for Willie Clark.

BEN No, *I'll* decide for Willie Clark. I am your closest and *only* living relative, and I am responsible for your welfare . . . You can't live here any more, Willie. Not alone . . . And I can't afford to keep this nurse on permanently. Right now she's making more than I am. Anyway she already gave me her notice. She's leaving Monday. She's going to Buffalo to work for a very wealthy family.

WILLIE Maybe she'll take me. I always did well in Buffalo.

BEN Come on, Willie, face the facts. We have to do something, and we have to do it quickly.

WILLIE I can't think about it today. I'm tired, I'm going to take a nap.

(He closes his eyes and drops his head to the side on the pillow)

BEN You want to hear my suggestion?

WILLIE I'm napping. Don't you see my eyes closed?

BEN I'd like you to move in with me and Helen and the kids. We have the small spare room in the back, I think you would be very comfortable . . . Uncle Willie, did you hear what I said?

WILLIE What's the second suggestion?

BEN What's the matter with the first?

WILLIE It's not as good as the second.

BEN I haven't made any yet.

WILLIE It's still better than the first. Forget it.

BEN Why?

WILLIE I don't like your kids. They're noisy. The little one hit me in the head with a baseball bat.

BEN And I've also seen you talk to them for hours on end about vaudeville and had the time of your life. Right?

WILLIE If I stopped talking, they would hit me with the bat. No offense, but I'm not living with your children. If you get rid of them, then we'll talk . . .

BEN I know the reason you won't come. Because Al Lewis lives with his family, and you're just trying to prove some stupid point about being independent.

WILLIE What's the second suggestion?

BEN *(A long sigh)* All right . . . Now, don't jump when I say this, because it's not as bad as it sounds.

WILLIE Say it.

BEN There's the Actors' Home in New Brunswick—

WILLIE It's as bad as it sounds.

BEN You're wrong. I drove out there last Sunday and they showed me around the whole place. I couldn't believe how beautiful it was.

WILLIE You went out there? You didn't have the decency to wait until I turned down living with you first?

BEN I just went out to investigate, that's all. No commitments.

WILLIE The Old Actors' Home: the first booking you got me in ten years.

BEN It's on a lake, it's got twenty-five acres of beautiful grounds, it's an old converted mansion with a big porch . . .

WILLIE I knew it. You got me on a porch in New Jersey. He put you up to this, didn't he?

BEN You don't have to sit on the porch. There's a million activities there. They put on shows every Friday and Saturday night. I mean, it's all old actors—what could be better for you?

WILLIE Why New Jersey? I hate New Jersey . . . I'm sorry they ever finished the George Washington Bridge.

BEN I couldn't get over how many old actors were there that I knew and remembered. I thought they were all dead.

WILLIE Some recommendation. A house in the swamps with forgotten people.

BEN They're not forgotten. They're well taken care of . . . Uncle Willie, I promise you, if you spend one day there that you're not happy, you can come back and move in with me.

WILLIE That's my choice—New Jersey or the baseball bat.

BEN All right, I feel a lot better about everything.

WILLIE And what about you?

BEN What do you mean what about me?

WILLIE *(A pause; looks away)* I won't see you no more?

BEN Certainly you'll see me. As often as I can . . . Did you think I wouldn't come to visit you, Uncle Willie?

WILLIE Well, you know . . . People don't go out to New Jersey unless they have to.

BEN Uncle Willie, I'll be there every week. *With* the *Variety*. I'll even bring Helen and the kids.

WILLIE *Don't bring the kids!* Why do you think I'm going to the home for?

BEN You know, this is the first moment since I've known you, that you've treated me like a nephew and not an agent. It's like a whole new relationship.

WILLIE I hope this one works out better than the other one.

BEN I've been waiting for this for fifteen years. You just wouldn't ever let me get close, Uncle Willie.

WILLIE If you kiss me, I call off the whole thing.

BEN No kiss, I promise . . . Now there's just one other thing I'd like you to do for me.

WILLIE With my luck it's a benefit.

BEN In a way it is a benefit. But not for any organization. It's for another human being.

WILLIE What are you talking about?

BEN Al Lewis wants to come and see you.

WILLIE If you wanted to kill me, why didn't you bring the cigars?

BEN He's been heartsick ever since this happened.

WILLIE What do you think I've been? What is this, the mumps?

BEN You know what I mean . . . He calls me twice a day to see how you are. He's worried to death.

WILLIE Tonight tell him I'm worse.

BEN He's not well himself, Willie. He's got diabetes, hardening of the arteries, his eyes are getting very bad . . .

WILLIE He sees good enough to spit in my face.

BEN He's lost seven pounds since you were in the hospital. Who do you think's been sending all the candy and flowers every day? He keeps signing other people's names because he knows otherwise you'd throw them out.

WILLIE They're *his* flowers? Throw 'em out!

BEN Uncle Willie, I've never asked you to do a personal favor for me as long as I've known you. But this is important—for me, and for you, for Al Lewis. He won't even stay. He just wants to come up and say hello . . .

WILLIE Hello, heh?

BEN That's all.

WILLIE And if he pokes me in the chest with the finger, I'm a dead man. That's murder, you know.

BEN Come on, Willie. Give us all a break.

WILLIE Well, if he wants to come up, I won't stop him. But I can't promise a "hello." I may be taking a nap.

BEN *(Starts toward the phone)* I knew I could count on you, Willie. He's going to be very happy.

(He picks up the phone)

WILLIE You don't have to call him from here. Why should I pay sixty cents for him to come say hello?

BEN *(He dials "O")* It's not going to cost you sixty cents. *(To the operator)* Hello. Would you tell the boy at the desk to send Mr. Lewis up to Mr. Clark's room, please? Thank you.

(He hangs up)

WILLIE *(As near to shouting as he can get)* You mean he's here now in the hotel?

BEN He's been with me all morning. I knew it would be all right.

WILLIE First you commit me to the Old Man's Home, bring that bastard here and *then* you ask me?

BEN *(All smiles)* I'm sorry. I apologize. Never speak to me again . . . But just promise you'll be decent to Al Lewis.

WILLIE I'll be wonderful to him. In my will, I'll leave him *you!*

(He starts to get out of bed)

BEN What are you doing? You're not supposed to be out of bed.

WILLIE You think I'm going to give him the satisfaction of seeing me laying in bed like a sick person? I'm gonna sit in my chair and I'm gonna look healthier than he does.

(He tries weakly to get on his slippers)

BEN The doctor said you're not to get out of bed for *anything.*

WILLIE Lewis coming to apologize to Clark is not anything. To me, this is worth another heart attack. Get my coat from the closet.

BEN *(Starting for the closet)* All right, but just walk slowly, will you, please?

(He opens the closet)

WILLIE And then I want you to move my chair all the way back. I want that son-of-a-bitch to have a long walk.

BEN *(Takes out a bathrobe from the closet)* Here, put this on.

WILLIE Not the bathrobe, the jacket. The blue sports jacket. This is gonna be a *formal* apology.

BEN *(Puts back the bathrobe and takes out the blue sports jacket)* He's not coming to apologize. He's just coming to say hello.

WILLIE If he doesn't apologize, I'll drop dead in the chair for spite. And you can tell him that.

(BEN helps him into the blue sports jacket over the pajamas)

BEN Now I'm sorry I started in with this.

WILLIE That's funny. Because now I'm starting to feel good. *(Buttons the jacket)* Push the chair back. All the way.

(BEN picks up the chair and carries it to the far side of the room)

BEN I thought I was bringing you two together.

WILLIE *(He shuffles over to the chair. BEN helps him to sit)* Put a pillow underneath. Make it two pillows. When I sit, I wanna look down on him.

(BEN puts a pillow under WILLIE)

BEN This is the last time. I'm never going to butt into your lives again.

WILLIE The only thing that could have made today better is if it was raining. I would love to see him apologize dripping wet. *(And then come three knocks on the door: "Knock, knock, knock")* Aha! This is it! . . . *This* was worth getting sick for! Come on, knock again. *(Points his finger in the air, his crowning moment. AL knocks again) En-terrr !*

*(*BEN *crosses to the door and opens it.* AL LEWIS *timidly steps in, with his hat in his hand.* WILLIE *immediately drops his head to his side, closes his eyes and snores, feigning a nap)*

AL *(Whispers)* Oh, he's sleeping. I could come back later.

BEN *(Also whispers)* No, that's all right. He must be dozing. Come on in. *(*AL *steps in and* BEN *closes the door)* Can I take your hat?

AL No, I'd like to hold on to something, if you don't mind.

*(*BEN *crosses over to* WILLIE, *who is still dozing. He bends over and speaks softly in* WILLIE*'s ear)*

BEN Uncle Willie. There's someone here to see you.

WILLIE *(Opens his eyes, stirs)* Heh? What?

BEN Look who's here to see you, Uncle Willie.

WILLIE *(Squints)* I don't have my glasses. Who's that?

AL It's me, Willie. Al . . . Al Lewis.

WILLIE *(Squints harder)* Al Lewis? You're so far away . . . Walk all the way over here. *(*AL *sheepishly makes the trek across the room with hat in hand. He squints again)* Oh, *that* Al Lewis.

AL I don't want to disturb you, Willie. I know you're resting.

WILLIE That's all right. I was just reading my telegrams from Lucille Ball and Bob Hope.

AL Oh, that's nice . . . *(Turns, looks at the vase)* Oh, look at the beautiful flowers.

WILLIE I'm throwing them out. I don't like the smell. People send them to me every day with boxes of cheap candy. They mean well.

AL *(Nods)* They certainly do . . . Well, I just came up to see how you're doing. I don't want to take up your time. I just wanted to say hello . . . So "hello"—and goodbye.

(He starts to put on his hat to go)

WILLIE Wait a minute. You got a few minutes before my next nap. Sit down and talk for a while.

AL You're sure it's okay?

WILLIE I'm sure you got a lot more to say than just "hello" . . . Would you like some tea?

AL I would love some.

WILLIE Go in the kitchen and make it.

BEN I've got a better idea. I'll go down and have the kitchen send up a tray. If I call room service it'll take forever.

(He starts for the door)

WILLIE *(To* BEN*)* You're going? You don't want to hear what Al has to say?

BEN I don't think it's necessary. I'll be back in ten minutes. *(At the door)* It's good to see you, Mr. Lewis . . . It's good to see the *both* of you.

(He nods, then exits, closing the door. There is an awkward silence between the two men for a moment)

AL *(Finally)* He's a nice boy.

WILLIE He's the best . . . Not too bright, but a good boy.

AL *(Nods)* You've got everything you need here?

WILLIE What could I need here?

AL Some books? Some magazines?

WILLIE No, I got plenty to do. I got all my fan mail to answer.

AL You get fan mail?

WILLIE Don't you?

AL I don't even get jury duty.

WILLIE Sure, plenty of people still remember . . . *(He coughs)* Excuse me.

AL You're sure it's all right for you to talk like this?

WILLIE I'm not talking. I'm just answering. *You're* talking. *(There is a long pause)* Why? Is there something special you wanted to talk about?

AL Like what?

WILLIE What do I know like what? How should I know what's on your mind? Do I know why you can't sleep at night?

AL Who said I don't sleep at night! I sleep beautifully.

WILLIE Funny, to me you look tired. A little troubled. Like a person who had something on his conscience, what do I know?

AL I have nothing on my conscience.

WILLIE *(A pause)* Are you sure you looked good?

AL I have *nothing* on my conscience. The only thing I feel badly about is that you got sick.

WILLIE Thank you. *I accept your apology!*

AL What apology? Who apologized? I just said I'm sorry you got sick.

WILLIE Who do you think *made* me sick?

AL Who? *You* did, that's who! Not me. You yelled and screamed and carried on like a lunatic until you made yourself sick . . . and for that I'm sorry.

WILLIE All right, as long as you're sorry for something.

AL I'm also sorry that people are starving in India, but I'm not going to apologize. I didn't do it.

WILLIE I didn't accuse you of India. I'm just saying you're responsible for making me sick, and since you've come up here to apologize, I am gentleman enough to accept it.

AL Don't be such a gentleman, because there's nothing to accept.

WILLIE You're the one who came up here with your hat in your hand not me.

AL It's a twenty-five dollar hat, what was I gonna do, fold it up in my pocket?

WILLIE If you didn't come to apologize, why did you send me the candy and flowers?

AL I sent you candy and flowers?

WILLIE Yes. Because it was on your conscience and *that's* why you couldn't sleep at night and *that's* why you came up here with you hat in your hand to apologize, only *this* time I'm not a gentleman any more and I *don't accept the apology!* How do you like that ?

*(*AL *stares at* WILLIE*)*

AL I knew there was gonna be trouble when you said "Enter" instead of "Come in."

WILLIE There's no trouble. The trouble is over. I got what I want and now I'm happy.

AL What did you get? You got "no apology" from me, which you didn't accept.

WILLIE I don't want to discuss it any more, I just had a heart attack.

*(*AL *stares at* WILLIE *silently)*

AL *(Calmly)* You know something, Willie. I don't think we get along too good.

WILLIE Well, listen, everybody has their ups and downs.

AL In forty-three years, we had maybe one "up" . . . To tell you the truth, I can't take the "downs" any more.

WILLIE To be honest with you, for the first time I feel a little tired myself. In a way this heart attack was good for me. I needed the rest.

AL So what are you going to do now?

WILLIE Well, my nephew made me two very good offers today.

AL Is that right?

WILLIE I think I'm gonna take the second one.

AL Are you in any condition to work again?

WILLIE Well, it wouldn't be too strenuous . . . Mostly take it easy, maybe do a show on Saturday night, something like that.

AL Is that so? Where, in New York?

WILLIE No, no. Out of town . . .

AL Isn't that wonderful.

WILLIE Well, you know me, I gotta keep busy . . . What's with you?

AL Oh, I'm very happy. My daughter's having another baby. They're gonna need my room, and I don't want to be a burden on them. . . . So we talked it over, and I decided I'm gonna move to the Actors' Home in New Brunswick.

WILLIE *(He sinks back onto his pillow, his head falls over to one side, and he sighs deeply)* Ohh, God. I got the finger again.

AL What's the matter? You all right? Why are you holding your chest? You got pains?

WILLIE Not yet. But I'm expecting.

AL *(Nervously)* Can I get you anything? Should I call the doctor?

WILLIE It wouldn't help.

AL It wouldn't hurt.

(The realization that they slipped accidentally into an old vaudeville joke causes WILLIE *to smile)*

WILLIE "It wouldn't hurt" . . . How many times have we done that joke?

AL It always worked . . . Even from you I just got a laugh.

WILLIE You're a funny man, Al . . . You're a pain in the ass, but you're a funny man.

AL You know what you're trouble was, Willie? You always took the jokes too seriously. They were just jokes. We did comedy on the stage for forty-three years, I don't think you enjoyed it once.

WILLIE If I was there to enjoy it, I would buy a ticket.

AL Well, maybe now you can start enjoying it . . . If you're not too busy, maybe you'll come over one day to the Actors' Home and visit me.

WILLIE You can count on it.

AL I feel a lot better now that I've talked to you . . . Maybe you'd like to rest now, take a nap.

WILLIE I think so . . . Keep talking to me, I'll fall asleep.

AL *(Looks around)* What's new in *Variety?*

WILLIE Bernie Eisenstein died.

AL Go on. Bernie Eisenstein? The house doctor at the Palace?

WILLIE That was Sam Hesseltine. Bernie Eisenstein was "Ramona and Rodriguez."

AL Jackie Aaronson was Ramona and Rodriguez. Bernie Eisenstein was the house doctor at the Palace. Sam Hesseltine was Sophie Tucker's agent.

WILLIE Don't argue with me, I'm sick.

AL I know. But why should I get sick too? *(The curtain starts to fall.* WILLIE *moans)* Bernie Eisenstein was the house doctor when we played for the first time with Sophie Tucker, and that's when we met Sam Hesseltine . . . Jackie Aaronson wasn't Rodriguez yet . . . He was "DeMarco and Lopez" . . . Lopez died, and DeMarco went into real estate, so Jackie became Rodriguez . . .

Curtain

Curtain Call

AL Don't you remember Big John McCafferey? The Irishman? He owned the Biltmore Theater in Pittsburgh? And the Adams Theater in Syracuse? Always wore a two-pound diamond ring on his finger? He was the one who used to take out Mary Donatto, the cute little Italian girl from the Follies. Well, she used to go with Abe Berkowitz who was then the booker for the Orpheum circuit and Big John hated his guts because of the time when Harry Richman . . .

The Good Doctor

Synopsis of Scenes

The action takes place in Russia at the turn of the century.

The Concert

Oop Tymbali
Good Doctor Opus #1
Trans-Siberian Railroad
Father and Son
Good Doctor Opus #2
Morning Dance
Dance for the Gathering I
Dance for the Gathering II

Act One

SCENE ONE "The Writer"
SCENE TWO "The Sneeze"
SCENE THREE "The Governess"
SCENE FOUR "Surgery"
SCENE FIVE "Too Late for Happiness"
SCENE SIX "The Seduction"

Act Two

SCENE ONE "The Drowned Man"
SCENE TWO "The Audition"
SCENE THREE "A Defenseless Creature"
SCENE FOUR "The Arrangement"
SCENE FIVE "The Writer"

Act One

SCENE ONE

"The Writer"

WRITER *(In his study)* It's quite all right, you're not disturbing me . . . I would much rather talk than work. Yet here I am, day after day, haunted by one thought: I must write, I must write, I must write . . . This is my study, the room in which I write my stories. I built it myself, actually —cut the timber and fitted the logs. Made an awful mess of it. I do my writing here at the side of the room because the roof leaks directly over my desk. I'd move the desk, but it covers a hole I left in the floor. And the floor was built on the side of the hill, so in heavy rains, the room tends to slide downhill. Many's the day I've stood in this cabin and passed my neighbors standing in the road . . . Still, I'm happy here. Although I don't get enough visitors to suit me. People tend to shy away from writers. They assume we're always busy thinking—not true. Even my dear sweet mother doesn't like to disturb me, so she always tiptoes up here and leaves my food outside the door . . . I haven't had a hot meal in years. But I've done a good deal of writing in here . . . Perhaps too much . . . I look out the window and think that life is passing me at a furious rate. So, I ask myself the question, What force is it that compels me to write so incessantly, day after day, page after page, story after story? And the answer is quite simple: I have no choice. I am a writer . . . Sometimes I think I may be mad . . . Oh, I'm quite harmless. But I do admit to fits of wandering. I'm engaged in conversations where I hear nothing and see only the silent movement of lips and answer a meaningless, "Yes, yes, of course." And all the time I'm thinking, "He'll make a wonderful character for a story, this one." Still, while I'm writing I enjoy it. And I like reading the proofs, but . . . as soon as it appears in print, I can't bear it. I see that it's all wrong, a mistake, that it ought never to have been written, and I am miserable. Then the public reads it:

"Yes, charming, clever." "Charming, but a far cry from Tolstoy." Or "A fine thing, but Turgenev's *Fathers and Sons* is better." And so it will be to my dying day . . . Charming and clever, charming and clever, nothing more. And when I die my friends will walk by my grave and say, "Here lies so and so, a good writer, but Turgenev was better" . . . It's funny, but before you came in, I was thinking to myself, perhaps I should give it up one day. What would I do instead? . . . Well, I've never freely admitted this before, but to you here in the theater tonight, I would like to tell you what I would most like to do with my life. Ever since I was a small child, I always . . . I always . . . Excuse me a moment. Just making a note . . . An idea just occurred to me. A subject for a short story . . . Hmm, yes, yes. It was my mentioning the theater that sparked me. What were we talking about a moment ago? . . . No matter. My thoughts are consumed with this new story. See if this appeals to you . . . It starts in a theater. It starts on the opening night of the new season. It starts with the arrival of all those dear and devoted patrons of the arts who wave and greet each other in the Grand Salon, commenting on how this one looks and how that one is dressed—scarcely knowing what play they are about to see that evening . . . With the exception of one man . . . Ivan Ilyitch Cherdyakov!

(The theater set appears, showing two rows of the audience, facing out toward us)

SCENE TWO
"The Sneeze"

WRITER If Ivan Ilyitch Cherdyakov, a civil servant, a clerk in the Ministry of Public Parks, had any passion in life at all, it was the theater. *(Enter* IVAN CHERDYAKOV *and his* WIFE. *He is in his mid-thirties, mild-mannered and unassuming. He and his wife are dressed in their best, but are certainly no match for the grandeur around them. They are clearly out of their element here. They move into their seats. As his* WIFE *peruses her program,* CHERDYAKOV *is beaming with happiness as he looks around and in back at the theater and its esteemed audience. He is a happy man tonight)* He certainly had hopes and ambitions for higher office and had dedicated his life to hard work, zeal and patience. Still, he would not deny himself his one great pleasure. So he purchased two tickets in the very best section of the theater for the opening night performance of Rostov's *The Bearded Countess. (A splendidly uniformed* GENERAL *and his wife enter, looking for their seats.)* As fortune would have it, into the theater that night came His Respected Superior, General Mikhail Brassilhov, the Minister of Public Parks himself.

(The GENERAL *and his wife take their seats in the first row, the* GENERAL *directly in front of* CHERDYAKOV*)*

CHERDYAKOV *(Leans over to the* GENERAL*)* Good evening, General.

GENERAL *(Turns, looks at* CHERDYAKOV *coldly)* Hmm? . . . What? Oh, yes. Yes. Good evening.

(The GENERAL *turns front again, looks at his program)*

CHERDYAKOV Permit me, sir. I am Cherdyakov . . . Ivan Ilyitch. This is a great honor for me, sir.

GENERAL *(Turns; coldly)* Yes.

CHERDYAKOV Like yourself, dear General, I too serve the Ministry of Public Parks . . . That is to say, I serve *you,* who is indeed *himself* the Minister of Public Parks. I am the Assistant Chief Clerk in the Department of Trees and Bushes.

GENERAL Ahh, yes. Keep up the good work . . . Lovely trees and bushes this year. Very nice.

(The GENERAL *turns back.* CHERDYAKOV *sits back, happy, grinning like a cat. The* GENERAL*'s wife whispers to him and he shrugs back. Suddenly the unseen curtain rises on the play and they all applaud.* CHERDYAKOV *leans forward again)*

CHERDYAKOV My wife would like very much to say hello, General. This is she. My wife, Madame Cherdyakov.

WIFE *(Smiles)* How do you do?

GENERAL My pleasure.

WIFE *My* pleasure, General.

GENERAL How do you do?

(He turns front, flustered. CHERDYAKOV *beams at his* WIFE*; then)*

CHERDYAKOV *(To the* GENERAL*'s wife)* Madame Brassilhov —my wife, Madame Cherdyakov.

WIFE How do you do, Madame Brassilhov?

MADAME BRASSILHOV *(Coldly)* How do you do?

WIFE I just had the pleasure of meeting your husband.

CHERDYAKOV *(To* MADAME BRASSILHOV*)* And I am my wife's husband. How do you do, Madame Brassilhov?

(The WRITER *"shushes" them)*

GENERAL *(To the* WRITER*)* Sorry. Terribly sorry.

(The GENERAL *tries to control his anger as they all go back to watching the play)*

CHERDYAKOV I hope you enjoy the play, sir.

GENERAL I will if I can watch it.

(He is getting hot under the collar. They all go back to watching the performance)

WRITER Feeling quite pleased with himself for having made the most of this golden opportunity, Ivan Ilyitch Cherdyakov sat back to enjoy *The Bearded Countess.* He was no longer a stranger to the Minister of Public Parks. They had become, if one wanted to be generous about the matter, familiar with each other . . . And then, quite suddenly, without any warning, like a bolt from a gray thundering sky, Ivan Ilyitch Cherdyakov reared his head back, and—

CHERDYAKOV AHHHHHHHH—CHOOOOOOOO!!! *(*CHERDYAKOV *unleashes a monstrous sneeze, his head snapping forward. The main blow of the sneeze discharges on the back of the* GENERAL*'s completely bald head. The* GENERAL *winces and his hand immediately goes to his now-dampened head)* Ohhh, my goodness, I'm *sorry,* your Excellency! I'm so terribly sorry!

(The GENERAL *takes out his handkerchief and wipes his head)*

GENERAL Never mind. It's all right.

CHERDYAKOV *All right?* . . . It certainly is *not* all right! It's unpardonable. It was monstrous of me—

GENERAL You make too much of the matter. Let it rest.

(He puts away his handkerchief)

CHERDYAKOV *(Quickly takes out his own handkerchief)* How can I let it rest? It was inexcusable. Permit me to wipe your neck, General. It's the least I can do.

(He starts to wipe the GENERAL*'s head. The* GENERAL *pushes his hand away)*

GENERAL Leave it be! It's all right, I say.

CHERDYAKOV But I splattered you, sir. Your complete head is splattered. It was an accident, I assure you—but it's *disgusting!*

WRITER Shhhh!

GENERAL I'm sorry. My apologies.

CHERDYAKOV The thing is, your Excellency, it came completely without warning. It was out of my nose before I could stifle it.

MADAME BRASSILHOV Shhh!

CHERDYAKOV Shhh, yes, certainly. I'm sorry . . . *(He sits back, nervously. He blows his nose with his handkerchief. Then* CHERDYAKOV *leans forward)* It's not a cold, if that's what you were worrying about, sir. Probably a particle of dust in the nostril—

GENERAL Shhh!

(They watch the play in silence, and CHERDYAKOV *sits back, unhappy with himself)*

WRITER But try as he might, Cherdyakov could not put the incident out of his mind. The sneeze, no more than an innocent anatomical accident, grew out of all proportion in his mind, until it resembled the angry roar of a cannon aimed squarely at the enemy camp. He played the incident back in his mind, slowing the procedure down so he could view again in horror the infamous deed.

*(*CHERDYAKOV, *in slow motion, repeats the sneeze again, but slowed down so that it appears to us as one frame at a time. It also seems to be three times as great in intensity as the original sneeze. The* GENERAL, *also in slow motion, reacts as though he has just taken a fifty-pound hammer blow at the base of his skull. They all go with the slow motion of the "sneeze" until it is completed, when the unseen curtain falls and they applaud. They all rise and begin to file out of the theater, chattering about the lovely evening they have just spent)*

GENERAL Charming . . . Charming.

MADAME BRASSILHOV Yes, charming.

GENERAL Charming . . . Simply charming. Wasn't it charming, my dear?

MADAME BRASSILHOV I found it utterly charming. *(*CHERDYAKOV *stands behind them tapping the* GENERAL*)*

WRITER I was completely charmed by it.

CHERDYAKOV *(still tapping away at the* GENERAL*)* Excuse me, Excellency—

GENERAL Who's tapping? Somebody's tapping me. Who's that tapping?

CHERDYAKOV I'm tapping, sir. I'm the tapper . . . Cherdyakov.

MADAME BRASSILHOV *(Quickly pulls the* GENERAL *back)* Stand back, dear, it's the sneezer.

CHERDYAKOV No, no, it's all right. I'm all sneezed out . . . I was just concerned about your going out into the night air with a damp head.

GENERAL Oh, that. It was a trifle. A mere faux pas. Forget it, young man. Amusing play, don't you think? Did you find it amusing?

CHERDYAKOV Amusing? Oh, my goodness, yes. Ha, ha. So true. Ha, ha. I haven't laughed as much in years. Ha, ha, ha . . .

GENERAL Which part interested you the most?

CHERDYAKOV The sneeze. When I sneezed on you. It was unforgivable, sir.

GENERAL Forget it, young man. Come, my dear. It looks like rain. I don't want to get my head wet again.

MADAME BRASSILHOV You shouldn't let people sneeze on you, dear. You're not to be sneezed at.

(They are gone)

CHERDYAKOV I'm ruined! Ruined! He'll have me fired from Trees and Bushes. They'll send me down to Branches and Twigs.

WIFE Come, Ivan.

CHERDYAKOV What?

WIFE You mustn't let it concern you. It was just a harmless little sneeze. The General's probably forgotten it already.

CHERDYAKOV Do you really think so?

WIFE No! I'm scared, Ivan.

WRITER And so they walked home in despair.

CHERDYAKOV Perhaps I should send him a nice gift. Maybe some Turkish towels.

WRITER Cherdyakov's once-promising career had literally been blown away.

CHERDYAKOV *(As they arrive home)* Why did this happen to me? Why did I go to the theater at all? Why didn't I sit in the balcony with people of our own class? They love sneezing on each other.

WIFE Come to bed, Ivan.

CHERDYAKOV Perhaps if I were to call on the General and explain matters again, but in such a charming, honest and self-effacing manner, he would have no choice but to forgive me . . .

WIFE Maybe it's best not to remind him, Ivan.

CHERDYAKOV No, no. If I ever expect to become a gentleman, I must behave like one.

WRITER And so the morning came. It so happened this was the day the General listened to petitions, and since there were fifty or sixty petitions ahead of Cherdyakov, he waited from morning till late, late afternoon . . .

(CHERDYAKOV moves into the office set)

GENERAL Next! . . . NEXT!

CHERDYAKOV I'm not next, your Excellency . . . I'm last.

GENERAL Very well, then . . . Last!

CHERDYAKOV That's me, sir.

GENERAL Well, what is your petition?

CHERDYAKOV I have no petition, sir. I'm not a petitioner.

GENERAL Then you waste my time.

CHERDYAKOV Do you not recognize me, sir? We met last night under rather "explosive" circumstances . . . I am the splatterer.

GENERAL The what?

CHERDYAKOV The sneezer. The one who sneezed. The sneezing splatterer.

GENERAL Indeed? And what is it you want now? A *Gesundheit?*

CHERDYAKOV No, Excellency . . . Your forgiveness. I just wanted to point out there was no political or antisocial motivation behind my sneeze. It was a nonpartisan, nonviolent act of God. I curse the day the protuberance formed itself on my face. It's a hateful nose, sir, and I am not responsible for its indiscretions . . . *(Grabbing his own nose)* Punish that which committed the crime, but absolve the innocent body behind it. Exile my nose, but forgive me, your kindship. Forgive me.

GENERAL My dear young man, I'm not angry with your

nose. I'm too busy to have time for your nasal problems. I suggest you go home and take a hot bath—or a cold one—take *something,* but don't bother me with this silly business again . . . Gibber, gibber, gibber, that's all I've heard all day. *(Going offstage)* Gibber, gibber, gibber, gibber . . .

*(*CHERDYAKOV *stands alone in the office sobbing)*

CHERDYAKOV Thank you, sir. God bless you and your wife and your household. May your days be sweet and may your nights be better than your days.

WRITER The feeling of relief that came over Cherdyakov was enormous . . .

CHERDYAKOV May the birds sing in the morning at your window and may the coffee in your cup be strong and hot . . .

WRITER The weight of the burden that was lifted was inestimable . . .

CHERDYAKOV I worship the chair you sit on and the uniform you wear that sits on the chair that I worship . . .

WRITER He walked home, singing and whistling like a lark. Life was surely a marvel, a joy, a heavenly paradise . . .

CHERDYAKOV Oh, God, I am happy!

WRITER And yet—

CHERDYAKOV And yet—

WRITER When he arrived home, he began to think . . .

CHERDYAKOV Have I been the butt of a cruel and thoughtless joke?

WRITER Had the Minister toyed with him?

CHERDYAKOV If he had no intention of punishing me, why did he torment me so unmercifully?

WRITER If the sneeze meant so little to the Minister, why did he deliberately cause Cherdyakov to writhe in his bed?

CHERDYAKOV . . . to twist in agony the entire night?

WRITER Cherdyakov was furious!

CHERDYAKOV I AM FURIOUS!

WRITER He foamed and fumed and paced the night through, and in the morning he called out to his wife, "SONYA!"

CHERDYAKOV SONYA! *(She rushes in)* I have been humiliated.

WIFE *You,* Ivan? Who would humiliate *you?* You're such a kind and generous person.

CHERDYAKOV Who? I'll tell you who! General Brassilhov, the Minister of Public Parks.

WIFE What did he do?

CHERDYAKOV The swine! I was humiliated in such subtle fashion, it was almost indiscernible. The man's cunning is equal only to his cruelty. He practically forced me to come to his office to grovel and beg on my knees. I was reduced to a gibbering idiot.

WIFE You were that reduced?

CHERDYAKOV I must go back and tell him what I think of him. The lower classes must speak up . . . *(He is at the door)* The world must be made safe so that men of all nations and creeds, regardless of color or religion, will be free to sneeze on their superiors! It is *he* who will be humiliated by *I!*

WRITER And so, the next morning, Cherdyakov came to humiliate *he.*

(Lights up on the GENERAL *at his desk)*

GENERAL Last! *(*CHERDYAKOV *goes to the* GENERAL*'s desk. He stands there glaring down at the* GENERAL *with a faint trace of a smile on his lips. The* GENERAL *looks up)* Well?

CHERDYAKOV *(Smiles)* Well? Well, you say? . . . Do you not recognize me, your Excellency? Look at my face . . . Yes. You're quite correct. It is I once again.

GENERAL *(Looks at him, puzzled)* It is you once again who?

CHERDYAKOV *(Confidentially)* Cherdyakov, Excellency. I have returned, having taken neither a hot bath nor a cold one.

GENERAL Who let this filthy man in? What is it?

CHERDYAKOV *(On top of the situation now)* What is it? . . . What is it, you ask? You sit there behind your desk and ask, What is it? You sit there in your lofty position as General and Minister of Public Parks, a member in high standing among the upper class and ask me, a lowly civil servant, What is it? You sit there with full knowledge that there is no equality in this life, that there are those of us who serve and those that are served, those of us that obey and those that are obeyed, those of us who bow and those that are bowed to, that in this life certain events take place that cause some of us to be humiliated and those that are the cause of that humiliation . . . and still you ask, "WHAT IS IT?"!

GENERAL *(Angrily) What is it?* Don't stand there gibbering like an idiot! What is it you want?

CHERDYAKOV *I'll tell you what I want!* . . . I wanted to apologize again for sneezing on you . . . I wasn't sure I made it clear. It was an accident, an accident, I assure you . . .

GENERAL *(Stands and screams out) Out! Out, you idiot!* Fool! Imbecile! Get out of my sight! I never want to see you again. If you ever cross my line of vision I'll have you exiled forever . . . WHAT'S YOUR NAME?

CHERDYAKOV Ch—Cherdyakov!

(It comes out as a sneeze—in the GENERAL*'s face)*

GENERAL *(Wiping himself)* You germ spreader! You maggot! You insect! You are lower than an insect. You are the second cousin to a cockroach! The son-in-law of a bed bug! You are the nephew of *a ringworm!* You are nothing, nothing, do you hear me? . . . *NOTHING!*

(CHERDYAKOV *backs away, and returns home)*

WRITER At that moment, something broke loose inside of Cherdyakov . . . Something so deep and vital, so organic, that the damage that was done seemed irreparable . . . Something drained from him that can only be described as the very life force itself . . . (CHERDYAKOV *takes off his coat. He sits on the sofa, head in hands*) The matter was over, for once, for all, forever. What happened next was quite simple . . . (CHERDYAKOV *lies back on the sofa*) Ivan Ilyitch Cherdyakov arrived at home . . . removed his coat . . . lay down on the sofa—and died!

*(*CHERDYAKOV*'s head drops and his hand falls to the floor)*

Blackout

SCENE THREE
"The Governess"

WRITER *(Appears in a spot and addresses the audience)* Wait! For those who are offended by life's cruelty, there is an alternate ending . . . "Ivan Ilyitch Cherdyakov went home, took off his coat, lay down on the sofa . . . and inherited five million rubles." There's not much point to it, but it *is* uplifting. I assure you it is not my intention to paint life any harsher than it is. But some of us are, indeed, trapped. Witness the predicament of a young governess who cares for and educates the children of a well-to-do family.

(Lights up on the MISTRESS *of the house at her desk. She has an account book in front of her)*

MISTRESS Julia!

WRITER Trapped, indeed . . .

MISTRESS *(Calls again)* Julia!

(A young governess, JULIA, *comes rushing in. She stops before the desk and curtsies)*

JULIA *(Head down)* Yes, madame?

MISTRESS Look at me, child. Pick your head up. I like to see your eyes when I speak to you.

JULIA *(Lifts her head up)* Yes, madame.

(But her head has a habit of slowly drifting down again)

MISTRESS And how are the children coming along with their French lessons?

JULIA They're very bright children, madame.

MISTRESS Eyes up . . . They're bright, you say. Well, why not? And mathematics? They're doing well in mathematics, I assume?

JULIA Yes, madame. Especially Vanya.

MISTRESS Certainly. I knew it. I excelled in mathematics. He gets that from his mother, wouldn't you say?

JULIA Yes, madame.

MISTRESS Head up . . . *(She lifts head up)* That's it. Don't be afraid to look people in the eyes, my dear. If you think of yourself as inferior, that's exactly how people will treat you.

JULIA Yes, ma'am.

MISTRESS A quiet girl, aren't you? . . . Now then, let's settle our accounts. I imagine you must need money, although you never ask me for it yourself. Let's see now, we agreed on thirty rubles a month, did we not?

JULIA *(Surprised)* Forty, ma'am.

MISTRESS No, no, thirty. I made a note of it. *(Points to the book)* I always pay my governesses thirty . . . Who told you forty?

JULIA You did, ma'am. I spoke to no one else concerning money . . .

MISTRESS Impossible. Maybe you *thought* you heard forty when I said thirty. If you kept your head up, that would never happen. Look at me again and I'll say it clearly. *Thirty rubles a month.*

JULIA If you say so, ma'am.

MISTRESS Settled. Thirty a month it is . . . Now then, you've been here two months exactly.

JULIA Two months and five days.

MISTRESS No, no. Exactly two months. I made a note of it. You should keep books the way I do so there wouldn't be these discrepancies. So—we have two months at thirty rubles a month . . . comes to sixty rubles. Correct?

JULIA *(Curtsies)* Yes, ma'am. Thank you, ma'am.

MISTRESS Subtract nine Sundays . . . We did agree to subtract Sundays, didn't we?

JULIA No, ma'am.

MISTRESS Eyes! Eyes! . . . Certainly we did. I've always subtracted Sundays. I didn't bother making a note of it because I always do it. Don't you recall when I said we will subtract Sundays?

JULIS No, ma'am.

MISTRESS Think.

JULIA *(Thinks)* No, ma'am.

MISTRESS You weren't thinking. Your eyes were wandering. Look straight at my face and look hard . . . Do you remember now?

JULIA *(Softly)* Yes, ma'am.

MISTRESS I didn't hear you, Julia.

JULIA *(Louder)* Yes, ma'am.

MISTRESS Good. I was sure you'd remember . . . Plus three holidays. Correct?

JULIA Two, ma'am. Christmas and New Year's.

MISTRESS And your birthday. That's three.

JULIA I worked on my birthday, ma'am.

MISTRESS You did? There was no need to. My governesses never worked on their birthdays . . .

JULIA But I did work, ma'am.

MISTRESS But that's not the question, Julia. We're discussing financial matters now. I will, however, only count two holidays if you insist . . . Do you insist?

JULIA I did work, ma'am.

MISTRESS Then you *do* insist.

JULIA No, ma'am.

MISTRESS Very well. That's three holidays, therefore we take off twelve rubles. Now then, four days little Kolya was sick, and there were no lessons.

JULIA But I gave lessons to Vanya.

MISTRESS True. But I engaged you to teach two children, not one. Shall I pay you in full for doing only half the work?

JULIA No, ma'am.

MISTRESS So we'll deduct it . . . Now, three days you had a toothache and my husband gave you permission not to work after lunch. Correct?

JULIA After four. I worked until four.

MISTRESS *(Looks in the book)* I have here: "Did not work after lunch." We have lunch at one and are finished at two, not at four, correct?

JULIA Yes, ma'am. But I—

MISTRESS That's another seven rubles . . . Seven and twelve is nineteen . . . Subtract . . . that leaves . . . forty-one rubles . . . Correct?

JULIA Yes, ma'am. Thank you, ma'am.

MISTRESS Now then, on January fourth you broke a teacup and saucer, is that true?

JULIA Just the saucer, ma'am.

MISTRESS What good is a teacup without a saucer, eh? . . . That's two rubles. The saucer was an heirloom. It cost much more, but let it go. I'm used to taking losses.

JULIA Thank you, ma'am.

MISTRESS Now then, January ninth, Kolya climbed a tree and tore his jacket.

JULIA I forbid him to do so, ma'am.

MISTRESS But he didn't listen, did he? . . . Ten rubles . . . January fourteenth, Vanya's shoes were stolen . . .

JULIA By the maid, ma'am. You discharged her yourself.

MISTRESS But you get paid good money to watch everything. I explained that in our first meeting. Perhaps you weren't listening. Were you listening that day, Julia, or was your head in the clouds?

JULIA Yes, ma'am.

MISTRESS Yes, your head was in the clouds?

JULIA No, ma'am. I was listening.

MISTRESS Good girl. So that means another five rubles off. *(Looks in the book)* . . . Ah, yes . . . The sixteenth of January I gave you ten rubles.

JULIA You didn't.

MISTRESS But I made a note of it. Why would I make a note of it if I didn't give it to you?

JULIA I don't know, ma'am.

MISTRESS That's not a satisfactory answer, Julia . . . Why would I make a note of giving you ten rubles if I did not in fact give it to you, eh? . . . No answer? . . . Then I must have given it to you, mustn't I?

JULIA Yes, ma'am. If you say so, ma'am.

MISTRESS Well, certainly I say so. That's the point of this little talk. To clear these matters up . . . Take twenty-seven from forty-one, that leaves . . . fourteen, correct?

JULIA Yes, ma'am.
(She turns away, softly crying)

MISTRESS What's this? Tears? Are you crying? Has something made you unhappy, Julia? Please tell me. It pains me to see you like this. I'm so sensitive to tears. What is it?

JULIA Only once since I've been here have I ever been given any money and that was by your husband. On my birthday he gave me three rubles.

MISTRESS Really? There's no note of it in my book. I'll put it down now. *(She writes in the book)* Three rubles. Thank you for telling me. Sometimes I'm a little lax with my accounts . . . Always shortchanging myself. So then, we take three more from fourteen . . . leaves eleven . . . Do you wish to check my figures?

JULIA There's no need to, ma'am.

MISTRESS Then we're all settled. Here's your salary for two months, dear. Eleven rubles. *(She puts the pile of coins on the desk)* Count it.

JULIA It's not necessary, ma'am.

MISTRESS Come, come. Let's keep the records straight. Count it.

JULIA *(Reluctantly counts it)* One, two, three, four, five, six, seven, eight, nine, ten . . . ? There's only ten, ma'am.

MISTRESS Are you sure? Possibly you dropped one . . . Look on the floor, see if there's a coin there.

JULIA I didn't drop any, ma'am. I'm quite sure.

MISTRESS Well, it's not here on my desk, and I *know* I gave you eleven rubles. Look on the floor.

JULIA It's all right, ma'am. Ten rubles will be fine.

MISTRESS Well, keep the ten for now. And if we don't find it on the floor later, we'll discuss it again next month.

JULIA Yes, ma'am. Thank you, ma'am. You're very kind, ma'am.

(She curtsies and then starts to leave)

MISTRESS Julia! *(JULIA stops, turns)* Come back here. *(She goes back to the desk and curtsies again)* Why did you thank me?

JULIA For the money, ma'am.

MISTRESS For the money? . . . But don't you realize what I've done? I've cheated you . . . *Robbed* you! I have no such notes in my book. I made up whatever came into my mind. Instead of the eighty rubles which I owe you, I gave you only ten. I have actually stolen from you and still you thank me . . . Why?

JULIA In the other places that I've worked, they didn't give me anything at all.

MISTRESS Then they cheated you even worse than I did . . . I was playing a little joke on you. A cruel lesson just to teach you. You're much too trusting, and in this world that's very dangerous . . . I'm going to give you the entire eighty rubles. *(Hands her an envelope)* It's all ready for you. The rest is in this envelope. Here, take it.

JULIA As you wish, ma'am.

(She curtsies and starts to go again)

MISTRESS Julia! *(JULIA stops)* Is it possible to be so spineless? Why don't you protest? Why don't you speak up? Why don't you cry out against this cruel and unjust treatment? Is it really possible to be so guileless, so innocent, such a—pardon me for being so blunt—such a simpleton?

JULIA *(The faintest trace of a smile on her lips)* Yes, ma'am . . . it's possible.

(She curtsies again and runs off. The MISTRESS *looks after her a moment, a look of complete bafflement on her face. The lights fade)*

SCENE FOUR
"Surgery"

The lights come up on the WRITER, *at the side of the stage.*

WRITER Wait! For those, again, who are offended by life's cruelty, there is an alternate ending . . . Julia was so enraged by such cruel and unjust treatment that she quit her job on the spot and went back to her poor parents—where she inherited five million rubles. It is my intention someday to write a book of thirty-seven short stories—all with that same ending, I do love it so. You know that it has been said that Man is the only living creature that is capable of laughter, and it is that faculty that separates us from the lower forms of life . . . Yet, one must wonder about this theory when we examine some of the objects of our laughter. For example, Pain. Pain, needless to say, is no laughing matter. Unless of course, it's someone else who is doing the suffering. Why the sight of a man in the throes of excruciating agony from an abcessed tooth that has enlarged his jaw to the size of an orange is funny, I couldn't say. It is *not* funny. Not in the least. But in the village of Astemko, where they have very little access to entertainment, a man with a toothache can tickle their ribs for weeks. Certainly, Sergei Vonmiglasov, the sexton, saw nothing humorous about it . . . *(The lights come up on the Surgery Room. There is a chair on one side and on the other is a table with various medical instruments. Enter the* SEXTON, *Vonmiglasov. He is a large, heavyset man wearing a cassock and a wide belt. He is a priest in the Russian Church. A scarf is wrapped around his face and his jaw is enlarged. He crosses the stage and moans in pain)* Yet, as he passed through the village on his way to the hospital, his moans and groans won him more chuckles than sympathetic remarks. Wouldn't they find it even more amusing to know that the good doctor who normally performed the extractions of angry teeth was away at the wedding of his daughter, and the duty fell to his new assistant, Kuryatin, an eager medical student, if—alas, poor sexton—an inexperienced one.

(The WRITER *during this speech "becomes"* KURYATIN, *the assistant. He changes into a not-too-clean doctor's coat and lights a cigar stub. As the* SEXTON *enters the door* KURYATIN *picks up a large, one-word-titled book:* TEETH*)*

SEXTON Ohhh! Ohhh!

KURYATIN Ahh, greetings, Father. What brings you here?

SEXTON The pain is unbearable . . . It is beyond unbearable . . . It is unendurable!

KURYATIN Where exactly is the pain?

SEXTON Where *isn't* it? Everywhere! It's not just the tooth. It's the whole side of my mouth.

KURYATIN How long have you had this agony?

SEXTON Ten years.

KURYATIN *Ten years?*

SEXTON Since yesterday morning it seems like ten years. I must have sinned terribly to deserve this. God must have dropped *all* other business to punish me this way. Where is the doctor?

KURYATIN The doctor is away on personal business. He left the care of his patients in my young, capable hands.

SEXTON But are you a doctor?

KURYATIN In every way except a degree . . . I am a doctor-to-be.

SEXTON Then I'm a patient-to-be. Goodbye.

(He turns, then moans)

KURYATIN *(Trying to stop him from leaving)* I can assure you, the only thing that prevents me from being called "Doctor" is the formality of an examination. I'm skilled. I'm just not "titled." Please, I beg you for this opportunity. Please, sit in the chair, Father.

SEXTON *(Goes over to the chair)* Heaven help me today. *(He sits)* Oghhh . . . even sitting hurts.

KURYATIN No doubt the nerves are inflamed. Once removed, the pain will cease to be.

SEXTON You're going to remove the nerves?

KURYATIN The *tooth* that's connected to the nerve. It's a simple matter of surgery . . .

(Smoke is blown in the SEXTON*'s face)*

SEXTON The cigar!

KURYATIN What?

SEXTON Your cigar is burning my eyes.

KURYATIN I'm sorry. Would you rather I put it out? I only smoke it to steady my nerves.

SEXTON Smoke it. Smoke the cigar.

KURYATIN Thank you. *(Starts to untie the scarf. He can't loosen it, so he takes a large pair of scissors from his coat pocket, yanks the scarf and cuts it quickly. The* SEXTON *screams "Aggghhhhhh!")* There! . . . Now, let's see what we have here.

SEXTON *(Puts his hands up)* I pray for you. I pray to the Saints and to our dear Lord in Heaven . . . Be gentle with me. Spare me pain.

KURYATIN My dear Sexton, we are living in an age of advanced science. In skilled hands, there is no longer need for pain. If it's gentleness you want, it's gentleness you'll have . . . Now, are you ready? *(The* SEXTON *nods)* Good.

Now please open your mouth so I can examine you. *(The* SEXTON *stiffens)* Come, come, open your mouth, please. *(The* SEXTON *grips the chair, but won't open his mouth)* My dear Sexton, inexperienced as I am, I *know* it's essential you open your mouth. It's mandatory to all work concerning the mouth to have it open first. It would be highly impractical for me to pull your tooth from the *outside.* Now, please open up. *(The* SEXTON *opens his lips, but his teeth remain clenched)* Not the lips, the entire mouth. I don't want to brush your teeth, I want to examine them.

SEXTON Will you be gentle?

KURYATIN Didn't I promise you I would?

SEXTON As a child I was promised many things I never got.

KURYATIN There is no pain connected to this part. This part is merely an examination to find out what must be done, where and how. NOW OPEN UP! *(The* SEXTON *opens his mouth)* Good. Now, let's have a look. *(*KURYATIN *peers in. The* SEXTON *groans in pain)* Ahh, yes. There it is. There's the ugly little fellow . . . You're a nasty one, aren't you?

SEXTON Stop talking to it! Don't make friends with it, pull it out!

KURYATIN Don't rush me, I'm evaluating . . . Your tooth has a hole in it big enough to drive a horse and carriage through.

(He gags at what he sees)

SEXTON What is it?

KURYATIN It's even disgusting to look at . . . But if this is going to be my profession, I have to get used to these things. Now then, I'm going to try something.

SEXTON Be gentle.

KURYATIN As though I were your own mother.

SEXTON My mother didn't like me. Gentler.

KURYATIN I want to see how exposed the nerve is . . . All I'm going to do is—*gently*—blow on your tooth. That's all. All right? . . . Excuse me. *(He steps to one side and tests his breath on his hand)* Here goes. *(*KURYATIN *puckers his lips and gently blows into the* SEXTON*'s mouth . . . The scream we hear is bloodcurdling)* I have some information for you . . . The nerve is exposed.

SEXTON Is that how far science has advanced? Blowing on teeth?

KURYATIN *(Going to the instrument table)* It's still inconclusive. More work must be done in this field. So much depends on the temperature of the doctor's breath . . . Ahhh, here we are.

(He picks up a forceps)

SEXTON What are you going to do with that?

KURYATIN The tooth *has* to be pulled. It'll be out quicker than you can spit.

(He goes back to the chair)

SEXTON *(He crosses himself)* Oh, Merciful God . . .

KURYATIN Surgery is nothing. It's all a matter of a firm hand. *Open up!*

SEXTON *(Chants religioso)* I pray for you. May the Lord enlighten your soul. May He give you health and quickness . . . mostly quickness.

KURYATIN *(Sings)* Aaahhh-men.

SEXTON *(Sings along)* Aaahhh-men.

KURYATIN *(Having gotten the* SEXTON *to open his mouth in song, he holds it firmly open)* This will come out easily. Some teeth give you trouble, I admit, but that's only when the roots are deep . . . I hope you prayed for shallow roots. All right, here we go. *(He is just about to enter the*

SEXTON*'s mouth when the* SEXTON *grabs his wrist)* Don't do that. Don't grab my hand. Let go. Let go, I say! *(The* SEXTON *lets go. Then* KURYATIN *starts to enter his mouth again, when the* SEXTON *grabs his wrist once more)* You've got my hand again. If I'm going to pull your tooth I need my hand. Now, let go. *(The* SEXTON *won't let go)* Are you going to let go of my hand? If you don't let go of my hand, I'm going to take these forceps and pull your fingers out . . . *(The* SEXTON *still won't let go, so* KURYATIN *raps him on the knuckles with the forceps. He pulls his hand away in pain)* There! Now, let's try once more. *(The* SEXTON *opens his mouth and* KURYATIN *places the forceps inside)* Good, good. Don't twitch, sit still. You're *twitching* again! . . . Now, the important thing is to get a deep enough hold so we don't break the crown . . .

SEXTON Ohhh . . . Ohhhhhhhhh!
(He clamps his mouth shut)

KURYATIN *(He forces the* SEXTON*'s mouth open and inserts the forceps again)* All right, this time I got a firm grip on the little monster. Now, whatever I do, don't grab my hands. I'm going to have enough trouble with your tooth without *you* interfering. Steady now. When I say three . . . One . . . Two . . . THREE!
(And KURYATIN *pulls . . . and pulls . . . and pulls. The tooth will not give, and the* SEXTON *begins to slide down in his chair.* KURYATIN *keeps pulling, but succeeds only in pulling the* SEXTON *with him—not only down in his seat . . . but clear out of it . . . onto the floor . . . across the floor . . . to the other side of the room . . . and then he finally* yanks *the tooth out as the* SEXTON *screams and moans)*

SEXTON AAAAAAGGGGGHHHHHHHHHHH!!!

KURYATIN *(Falling to one side, victorious)* Got it! Got it! I pulled it out! My first tooth!

SEXTON You pulled it all right! I hope they pull you into the next world like that!
(He feels his face)

KURYATIN *(Looks at the forceps)* Oh, oh, I knew it. The crown broke. You've still got the roots in your mouth. What a mess this is going to be. *I told you not to twitch!*

SEXTON *(Still lying on the floor)* *You butcher! You carpenter!* You're God's vengeance for my sins. Compared to *you,* the toothache was a joy!

KURYATIN *You ignorant peasant!* The only thing harder than the roots in your tooth are the brains in your head. *(He gets up and starts for the* SEXTON*)* Now, get back in the chair. We have unfinished business.

SEXTON *(Having gotten up, he starts to back away from him)* Keep away from me, Sorcerer! If you put your fingers in my mouth, it'll be the first solid food I eat this week.

(The SEXTON *bolts for the door, only to find* KURYATIN *has beaten him there and is blocking his exit)*

KURYATIN You're not leaving here until those roots come out. It's a question of professional pride.

(The SEXTON *dashes away from him. Having gotten* KURYATIN *away from the door, the* SEXTON *runs back toward the door . . . Near exhaustion, they both finally collapse close to each other, too tired to move)*

SEXTON I give up . . .

KURYATIN I failed in my duty.

SEXTON Come, my son. Let us pray for a miracle. *(The* SEXTON, *on his knees, crawls over to* KURYATIN *and helps him up to his knees. Then they both clasp their hands, look heavenward and pray)* Dear Lord in Heaven . . .

KURYATIN Dear God above . . .

SEXTON I plead for this good doctor . . .

KURYATIN I pray for this poor creature . . .

(The lights begin to fade)

SEXTON Keep his hand steady . . .

KURYATIN Keep his mouth open . . .

(The lights continue to fade out slowly)

SEXTON Don't let him falter . . .

KURYATIN Don't let him bite me . . .

SEXTON Hail Mary!

KURYATIN Hail Mary!

SEXTON Hail Mary!

KURYATIN Hail Mary!

SEXTON Hail Mary!

KURYATIN Hail Mary! . . .

Blackout

SCENE FIVE

"Too Late for Happiness"

The scene is a park. A WOMAN, *in her early sixties, sits alone on a bench. She is reading a book. A* MAN, *in his early seventies, enters, carrying a walking stick and wearing a hat and a large scarf around his neck. He tips his hat to her.*

MAN Good afternoon, madame.

WOMAN Good afternoon.

(She goes back to her book. He takes a deep breath of the crisp fall air)

MAN Ahhh . . . Fine weather . . . Fine weather indeed, wouldn't you say, madame?

WOMAN *(Looks up)* I hadn't noticed really . . . Yes, I suppose it is a lovely day.

(She goes back to her book)

MAN Not many more of these left . . . Winter's just beyond that tree there.

WOMAN *(Closes her book, looks at the sky)* Mmm . . . The winters seem to be getting longer lately, have you noticed that? . . . They come sooner and stay longer.

MAN I've noticed it, madame . . . Only in these last few years have I noticed it.

(Music is heard in the background)

WOMAN *(Sings)*

A kind, gentle-looking person
Who's seen his share of life,
A kind, gentle-looking person,
And he's never with a wife.

If this kind, gentle-looking gentleman
Speaks once again to me,
Should this shy, nervous widowed lady
Go out with him for tea?

MAN *(Sings)*
A fine figure of a lady,
With quality and tone,
A fine figure of a lady,
And she always sits alone.

Should this fine figure of a gentleman,
Who's older than the sea,
Ask a fine figure of a lady
If she'd like to share some tea?
(Speaks)
I was wondering, madame . . .

WOMAN Yes?

MAN I, er, I was wondering . . . Do you have the time of day?

WOMAN I don't carry a timepiece.

MAN Ahhh . . . No matter. It wasn't urgent. My business can wait . . . Yes . . . It can wait.
(Sings)
Should this old weather-beaten gentleman
Take one more chance at life?
She reminds me of that sweet lady
Whom I lovingly called wife.

WOMAN *(Sings)*
I had my tender-hearted gentleman.
Can I go through again
All the pain, joy, and all the sorrow
That you get from loving men?

BOTH
Is it too late for happiness?
Too late for flings?
Too late to ask for love?

There aren't many springs
Left for
People who spend their nights
Waiting for the day,
For someone to share delights
Long since passed away.

Too late for happiness,
Too soon for fall,
Too late for anything,
Anything at all . . .

MAN *(Looking up at the sky, speaks)* Seems to be clouding up a bit.

WOMAN Yes. I'm beginning to feel a chill in the air.

MAN Oh? . . . Would you like my scarf for your neck?

WOMAN Thank you, no . . . I should be getting home. It's getting late.

MAN Yes, yes, of course. I was thinking the same thing . . . the same thing. Unless—

WOMAN Yes?

MAN Unless you would care to join me for tea? A cup of hot tea? Might be just the right thing . . . a cup of tea . . .

WOMAN Tea? . . . Tea, you say . . . Well, that's very nice of you. I—I would love to . . .

MAN You would?

WOMAN Yes . . . but not today. It's getting late . . . Perhaps tomorrow.

MAN Yes, yes, of course. Perhaps tomorrow. Good . . . There's always tomorrow . . .

WOMAN Good day, sir.

MAN Good day, madame . . .

BOTH *(Sing)*

Yes, there's still time for happiness,
Time to be gay,
Still time to answer yes—
(Pause)
—but just not today . . .
(They turn and walk off slowly in different directions as the music and lights fade)

SCENE SIX

"The Seduction"

The lights come up on the WRITER. *He is in suit and hat, wears a pince-nez, and is carrying a walking stick. He is seated on a bench in a small public garden.*

WRITER Peter Semyonych was the greatest seducer of other men's wives that I've ever met. He was successful with *all* women, for that matter, but there was a special challenge to beautiful women married to prominent, rich, successful men . . . I could never do him justice; let him tell you in his own words . . .

(He removes his glasses, puts them in his pocket, clears his throat, assumes a more debonair posture—and becomes PETER SEMYONYCH*)*

PETER If I may say so myself, I am the greatest seducer of other men's wives that I've ever met. I say this not boastfully, but as a matter of record. The staggering figures speak for themselves. For those men interested in playing this highly satisfying but often dangerous game, I urge you to take out pen and paper and take notes. I am going to explain my methods. In defense, married women may do likewise, but it will do them little good if they happen to be the chosen victim. My method has never failed . . . Now then, there are three vital characteristics needed. They are: patience, more patience and still more patience. Those who do not have the strength to wait and persist, I urge you to take up bicycling—rowing, perhaps. Seducing isn't for you. Now then, in order to seduce a man's wife, you must, I repeat *must,* keep as far away from her as possible. Pay her practically no attention at all. Ignore her if you must. We will get to her—through the *husband* . . . *(He looks at his watch, then off into the wings)* You are about to witness a practical demonstration, for as it happens I am madly and deeply in love this week. My heart pounds with excitement knowing that she will pass through this garden in a few moments with her husband. Every fiber of my being tells me to throw my arms around her and embrace her with all the passion in my heart. But observe how a master works: I shall be cool almost to the point of freezing. My heart of hearts—and spouse—approaches.

(He turns the other way as the HUSBAND *and his lovely, younger bride approach, taking an afternoon stroll in the park. She carries an umbrella to shade her from the afternoon sun)*

HUSBAND Ahh, Peter Semyonych, fancy meeting you here.

PETER *(Doesn't look at the* WIFE*)* My dear Nikolaich, how good to see you. You're looking well. *(To the audience)* Notice how I'm not looking at her.

HUSBAND Thank you. And you, you gay devil, you're always looking well . . . Excuse me, have you met my wife, Irena? . . . Of course, you have. You sat next to her at dinner at the Veshnovs. Irena, I don't know what this charmer said to you at dinner, but I must warn you that he is a scoundrel, a notorious bachelor and an exceptional swordsman. That's the best I can say for you, Peter.

PETER You exaggerate, Nicky. *(Glances at the* WIFE*)* Madame. Good to see you again.

(He doffs his hat but barely looks at her. She nods back, then turns and looks at the flowers)

HUSBAND We were just taking a stroll. If you're not busy, why don't you walk with us?

PETER That's very kind of you, Nikolaich, but as a matter of fact, I am riveted to this spot. A new romance has just entered my life, and my legs are like pillars of granite . . . Until she is out of my sight, I will be incapable of movement. *(To the audience)* Too much, do you think? As I said, be patient.

HUSBAND Fantastic! You never cease to amaze me. Pretty, I suppose?

PETER Suppose *magnificent*. Suppose *glorious*, and you will suppose correctly.

HUSBAND Any . . . "complications"?

PETER As usual, a husband. I'm afraid my cause looks hopeless.

HUSBAND Nonsense. I'm placing my money on you, Peter. And you know I never bet unless I'm sure of winning. Well, we're off. Good hunting, my boy. Good hunting.

(They start off)

PETER *(Doffs his hat)* Madame! *(Turns to the audience)* Beautifully done, don't you think? I'm sometimes awed by the work of a true professional . . . Did you notice our eyes barely met, we exchanged hardly a word, and yet how much she knows of me already: A) I am a popular bachelor; B) a man in love (always titillating to romantic women); C) a gifted sportsman (a nice contrast to her sedentary husband); and D), and this is most important, a dangerous man with the ladies. Quite frankly, at this point she is disgusted by me: A) because I'm a braggart and a scoundrel; B) because I am shamelessly frank as to my intentions; and C) because she thinks she's not the one I'm interested in. Forgive me if I'm slightly overcome by my own deviousness . . . By the way, are you getting all this down? It gets tricky from here on in. Now then, next step, hypnosis. Not hypnosis with your eyes, but with the poison of your tongue, much like a venomous snake moving in for the kill. And what's more, the best channel is the husband himself. Witness, as I "accidentally" run into him one day at the Club . . .

(He crosses to the "Club." The HUSBAND *is sitting reading a newspaper.* PETER *takes up a newspaper and sits next to him. The* HUSBAND *looks up and notices him)*

HUSBAND Peter. You're looking glum . . . I take it your pursuit isn't going well.

(He laughs)

PETER Is it that obvious? I'm doomed, Nicky. I haven't

seen her since last I met you and your dear wife. I sleep little and eat less. I've had all my shirt collars taken in a half-inch. Ah, Nicky, Nicky, why do I waste my valuable youth chasing women I can never truly call my own? . . . How I envy you.

HUSBAND Me? What's there about me that you envy?

PETER Why, your marriage, of course. A charming woman, your wife, let me tell you.

HUSBAND Really? What is there about her that fascinates you so?

PETER Her grace, her quiet charm, everything. But mostly it's the way she looks at you, Nicky. Oh, if only someone would look at me like that—with such adoring, loving eyes. It must send quivers through your body.

HUSBAND Quivers? No, not really.

PETER A tingle, perhaps? Don't tell me you don't tingle when she looks at you.

HUSBAND Of, of course. By all means. I tingle all the time.

PETER She's an ideal woman, Nicky, believe that from a lonely bachelor and be glad fate gave you a wife like that.

HUSBAND Perhaps fate will be as kind to *you.*

PETER That's what I'm counting on . . . Good heavens, I'm late for my doctor's appointment.

(He rises)

HUSBAND What's he treating you for?

PETER Melancholia . . . Please say hello to your extraordinary wife, but I urge you not to repeat our conversation. It might embarrass her fragile sensitivities . . . *(Sighs, as he walks away)* Ahh, where oh where is the woman for me? *(Out of earshot of the* HUSBAND, *he stops and turns to the audience. A wicked smile)* I *know* where! The question is: "How soon will she be mine?" There is still work to be done—but not by me. That task falls to my aide and accomplice. "Oh, by the way, I saw Peter Semyonych today . . ."

(The lights go down on PETER *and come up on the* HUSBAND *and the* WIFE. *They are at home in their bedroom, preparing for bed)*

HUSBAND Oh, by the way, I saw Peter Semyonych today . . .

WIFE *(Putting up her hair)* Who?

HUSBAND Peter Semyonych. The bachelor . . . We met him in the gardens last week. That attractive fellow . . . you remember.

WIFE I remember what a loathsome man he is.

HUSBAND You may not think so when you hear what he had to say about you.

WIFE Nothing that braggart had to say would interest me.

HUSBAND He spoke most enthusiastically about you . . . He was enraptured by your grace, your quiet charm . . . and he seemed to feel that you were capable of loving a man in some extraordinary way. It was something about your eyes and the way you looked so adoringly. He certainly had a lot to say about you. He went on and on . . . Well, good night, my dear.

(She gets into bed)

WIFE Good night. *(A long pause)* What else?

HUSBAND Hmm?

WIFE What else did he have to say about me?

HUSBAND Peter?

WIFE Whatever that loathsome man's name is . . . What else did Peter Semyonych say about me?

HUSBAND Well, that's more or less it . . . what I told you.

WIFE But you said he went on and on.

HUSBAND He did.

WIFE But you stopped. If he went on and on, don't stop. Either go on and on or let's go to bed.

HUSBAND Well, he said how much he envied me. How much he wanted someone to look at him the way you look at me.

WIFE How does he know how I look at you?

HUSBAND Well, that day in the gardens. He must have been looking at you when you were looking at me. It sent a tingle through my whole body.

WIFE The way I looked at you?

HUSBAND Exactly, my precious.

WIFE But you were looking at him. So you couldn't have seen how I was looking at you. As a matter of fact, I was looking at the flowers because he made me nervous the way he kept avoiding looking at me . . . You must have tingled for some other reason.

HUSBAND It's getting rather confusing . . . The point is, he found you fascinating. I thought it would please you.

WIFE Well, it doesn't. I would rather you didn't tell me such stories . . . Are you planning to see him again soon?

HUSBAND Tomorrow for lunch.

WIFE Well, I would rather not be discussed over lunch.

Tell him that . . . And at dinner you can tell me what he said. Good night, Nicky.

HUSBAND Good night, my angel.

(The lights go down on them and come up on PETER*)*

PETER Good night, my love! *(To the audience)* I'm spellbound by my own powers. I succeeded not only in piquing her interest, but in causing her heart to flutter at the mention of my name—the same man she called loathsome not two minutes ago. All this was accomplished, mind you, while I was home taking a pine-scented bath . . . Luncheon the next day was not only nourishing, but productive. *(He goes over and sits with the* HUSBAND*)* By the way, old man, I ran into Nekrasov yesterday. The artist? It seems he's been commissioned by some wealthy prince to paint the head of a typical Russian beauty. He asked me to look out for a model for him . . . I said I knew just the woman, but I didn't dare ask her myself . . . What do you think of asking your wife?

HUSBAND Asking my wife what?

PETER To be the model, of course. That lovely head of hers. It would be a damn shame if that exquisite face missed the chance to become immortalized for all the world.

HUSBAND For all the world . . . Really? Hmm . . . I see what you mean . . .

PETER Why don't you discuss it with her?

HUSBAND Good idea. I'll discuss it with her. *(He gets up and crosses to the bedroom area. They have been talking as they prepare for bed. To* WIFE*)* . . . So I said I would discuss it with you. What do you think?

WIFE *(Brushing her hair)* I think it's nonsense . . . How did he put it to you? I mean, did he actually say, "a typical Russian beauty"?

HUSBAND Precisely. And that it would be a damn shame if

that exquisite face missed the chance to become immortalized for all the world . . . That's exactly what he said.

WIFE He gets carried away by his own voice . . . Those *exact* words? You didn't leave anything out?

HUSBAND Oh, yes . . . "that lovely face." I left out "that lovely face." He said that a number of times, I think.

WIFE He *does* go on, doesn't he? . . . How many times did he say it? Once? Twice? What?

HUSBAND Let me think. It's hard to remember.

WIFE It's not important . . . but in the future I wish you would write these things down.

(Blackout on them; lights up on PETER*)*

PETER *(To the audience)* Have you seen me near her? Have you heard me speak to her? Has any correspondence passed between us? No, my dear pupils. And yet she *hangs* on my every word uttered by her husband. Awesome, isn't it? . . . We apply this treatment from two to three weeks. Her resistance is weakening, weakening, weakening . . .

(The lights go up on the bedroom again)

HUSBAND *(As usual, preparing for bed)* I think his mind is elsewhere, if you ask me. On some woman, from the looks of him.

WIFE What woman? Has he mentioned any woman in particular?

HUSBAND Oh, no. He's too discreet for that. He'll protect her good name at any cost. Instead, he talks of you all day. Poor fool, I'm beginning to feel sorry for him.

WIFE It's really none of our concern, Nicky, did you ask him to dinner tomorrow?

(There was no break in that last speech)

HUSBAND He's busy.

WIFE The day after, then.

HUSBAND Busy.

WIFE Next week. Next month. When? Doesn't the man eat?

HUSBAND He says he's involved on a very important project, and it will be months before he can see us . . . He did say that with patience and persistence, good things will come to him . . . By the way, he thinks you should go on the stage.

WIFE The stage? Me, on the stage? Why, in heaven's name?

HUSBAND Well, he said—just a moment. I don't want to misquote him.

(He goes to his jacket and takes out a small notebook)

WIFE No, no. Take your time. Try to get it as accurately as possible.

HUSBAND *(Reading)* Ah, yes. He said, "With such an attractive appearance, such intelligence, sensitiveness, it's a sin for her to be just a housewife."

WIFE *(Her hand to her heart)* Oh, dear, he said that?

HUSBAND And that "ordinary demands don't exist for such women."

WIFE Nicky, I don't think I want to hear any more.

HUSBAND "Natures like that should not be bound by time and space."

WIFE Nicky, I implore you, please stop.

HUSBAND And then he says, "If I weren't so busy, I'd take her away from you."

WIFE He said that?

HUSBAND Yes, right there.

(He points to the notation)

WIFE What did you say, Nicky? It's important I know what you said to him then.

HUSBAND *(Laughs)* Well, I said, "Take her, then. I'm not going to fight a duel over her."

(He laughs again)

WIFE Nicky, you mustn't discuss me with him any more. I beg you not to mention my name to him ever again.

HUSBAND But I don't, my love. *He's* the one who always brings up the subject . . . He actually accused me of not understanding you. He shouted at me, "She's an exceptional creature—strong, seeking a way out. If I were Turgenev, I would put her in a novel—*The Passionate Angel,* I would call it" . . . The man is weird. Definitely weird.

(The WIFE *hangs her head disconsolately as the lights black out on them and come up on* PETER*)*

PETER *(To the audience)* He's delivering my love letters, sealing them with kisses, and calls *me* weird—I ask you! . . . So, let's see what we've got so far . . . The poor woman is definitely consumed with a passion to meet me. She is sure I am the only man who truly understands her. Her yawning, disinterested husband transmits my remarks, but it is my voice she hears, my words that sing in her heart . . . The sweet poison is doing its work. I am relentless. There is no room for mercy in the seducing business. Observe how deftly the final stroke is administered. For the faint-hearted, I urge you, look away!

(Lights up on the bedroom again. They are eternally preparing for bed)

WIFE *No,* Nicky! I don't want to hear. Not another word from him. Nothing.

HUSBAND *(Getting undressed)* But exactly. That's what he said. He begged me to tell you *nothing.* He said he knew because of your sweet, sympathetic nature, you would worry to hear of someone else's distress.

WIFE He's in distress?

HUSBAND Worse . . . He's gloomy, morose, morbid, in the depths of despair.

WIFE Oh, no . . . But why? What's the matter with him?

HUSBAND Loneliness . . . He says he has no relatives, no true friends, not a soul who understands him.

WIFE But doesn't he know I . . . *we* understand him perfectly? Doesn't he know how much I . . . *we* appreciate him and commune with him daily? Doesn't he know how much I . . . *we* yearn to be with him? . . . You and I.

HUSBAND I tried to make that clear. I again urged him to come home to dinner with me. But he said he can't face people. He is so depressed he can't stay home . . . He paces in the public garden where we met him, every night.

WIFE What time?

HUSBAND Between eight and nine. *(Gets into bed)* By the way, we're invited to the Voskovecs tomorrow. Is eight o'clock all right for you?

WIFE No, I'm visiting Aunt Sophia tomorrow. She's ill. I'll be there at nine . . . or a little after.

(The lights go down on the bedroom and come up on the gardens where PETER *is strolling, waiting for his prey)*

PETER *(To the audience)* Please, no applause. I couldn't have done it alone. I share that honor with my good friend and collaborator, her husband. He wooed her so successfully that there is no carriage fast enough for her to be in my arms. She ran all the way . . . Observe! *(The* WIFE, *wearing a cloak, rushes into the garden and then stops, breathless)* Now for the conclusion . . . You *will* understand if I ask you to busy yourselves with your programs or such. These next few moments are private and I *am*, after all, a gentleman. *(He turns to the* WIFE*)* My dear

. . . My sweet, dear angel. At last I can speak the words that I've longed—

WIFE *No!* Not a word! Not a sound! Please . . . I couldn't bear it . . . Not until you've heard what's in my heart. *(She takes a moment to compose herself)* For weeks now I've been in torment . . . You've used my husband as a clever and devious device to arouse my passions, which I freely admit have been lying dormant these past seven years. Whether you are sincere or not, you have awakened in me desires and longings I never dreamt were possible. You appeal to my vanity and I succumb. You bestir my thoughts of untold pleasures and I weaken. You attack my every vulnerability and I surrender. I am here, Peter Semyonych, if you want me. *(He starts to reach for her, but she holds up her hand for him to stop)* But let me add this. I love my husband dearly. He is not a passionate man, nor even remotely romantic. Our life together reaches neither the heights of ecstasy nor the depths of anguish. We have an *even* marriage. Moderate and comfortable, and in accepting this condition and the full measure of his devoted love, I have been happy . . . I come to you now knowing that once you take me in your arms, my marriage and my life with Nicky will be destroyed for all time. I am too weak and too selfish to make the choice. I rely on your strength of character. The option is yours, my dear Peter. Whichever one you choose will make me both miserable and eternally grateful . . . I beg of you not to use me as an amusement—although even with that knowledge, I would not refuse you. I am yours to do with as you will, Peter Semyonych . . . If you want me, open your arms now and I will come to you. If you love me, turn your back and I will leave, and never see or speak to you again . . . The choice, my dearest, sweetest love of my life, is yours . . . I await your decision. *(*PETER *looks at her, then turns his head and looks full face at the audience. He wants some advice but none is forthcoming. He turns back to the* WIFE. *He starts to raise his arms for her, but they will not budge. It is as though they weighed ten tons each. He struggles again with no results. He makes one final effort and then quickly changes his mind and turns his back on her)* God bless you, Peter Semyonych . . . I wish that life brings you the happiness you have just brought to me.

(She turns and runs off. PETER *slowly turns out to the audience. Then he reaches into his pocket, puts on his glasses and becomes the* WRITER *again—seeming a little older, and with none of the dash and charm of* PETER*)*

WRITER Peter Semyonych, the *former* seducer of other men's wives, from that day on turned his attentions to single, unmarried women only. . . . Until one day, the perfect girl came along, and the confirmed bachelor married at last. *(He starts to walk off)* He is today a completely happy man . . . except possibly on those occasions when some dashing young officer tells him how attractive he finds his lovely young wife . . .

(Dim-out)

Curtain

Act Two

SCENE ONE
"The Drowned Man"

As the lights come up, we are on a pier at the edge of a dock. It is dusk, a little foggy. In the harbor we can see some lights of distant ships. A foghorn bellows out at sea. The WRITER *enters with his walking stick. He is wearing a great-coat to keep out the evening chill.*

WRITER *(Stops, looks out at the sea, then turns to the audience)* Just getting a little night air to clear my mind. *(He takes a deep breath, then exhales)* Ahhh, that's good. That's wonderful. The sea air is so refreshing, it revitalizes my entire body. *(Another deep breath; exhales)* But my mind is blocked . . . I have no thoughts, no ideas. Most unusual for me. Most times they fill up my brain and overflow it like a cascading fountain. And tonight, nothing . . . And still I have the urge to write. Something will come, never fear, always does. These things happen to all men in my profession at one time or another. Writer's block, we call it. No need to panic, it'll pass soon . . . Wait! Wait! Hold on, an idea is coming. Yes . . . Yes, aha. Aha! . . . Terrible . . . Bad idea. False alarm. Sorry I disturbed you. Not only was it a bad idea, I've already written it. It turned out awful. This won't last long. It's just temporary. However, it's getting to be a very long "temporary." Nothing is coming. My nerves are tightening. Oh, God help me—no, no, I take that back. I mustn't rely on a collaboration with the Almighty. What selfishness . . . to ask God to take time out to help me come up with an idea for a story. Forgive me, dear Lord. I'll go home and try to sleep. Tomorrow is another day. If, however, anything *does* occur to you during the night, I would appreciate it if you would make it known to me. Even if it's just the germ of an idea. It doesn't have to be original. I'm very clever at twisting things around . . . Look how desperate I've become! Asking the Lord to resort to plagiarism for my petty needs. Home . . . I must get home and to bed before this thing becomes serious . . .

(He turns and starts to walk off when a figure appears in the shadows and calls to him)

TRAMP Psst! You, sir. Can I have a word with you, sir?

WRITER *(Turns and looks)* Who's there? . . . I can't see you in the dark.

(The figure steps into the light. His clothes are shoddy and he looks down on his luck. He needs a shave, his gloves have only half fingers, and he smokes a cigarette butt)

TRAMP 'Evening, sir . . . I was wondering, sir, if you might be in the mood for a little, er, "entertainment" this evening?

WRITER *(Suspiciously)* "Entertainment"? I'm sure I don't know what you're talking about.

(He turns away)

TRAMP Sure you do, sir. Entertainment . . . Amusement, so to speak. A little "diversion," if you know what I mean.

WRITER I think I *do* know what you mean and I'm not interested. Go on, off with you. You should know better than to make such a proposal to a gentleman.

TRAMP You've never witnessed anything like *this* before, that I promise you. This is a once-in-a-lifetime offer . . . Not even a *little* bit curious?

WRITER Curiosity is the nature of my profession. But I try to keep it morally elevated . . . Excuse me.

TRAMP Perhaps you're right, sir. On second thought, this might be too much for a gentleman of your "sensitivities."

WRITER *(Turns quickly)* Wait!

TRAMP *(Turns quickly)* Got you with that last one, didn't I?

WRITER I'm just asking, mind you, but, er . . . just exactly what is this "entertainment" you speak of?

TRAMP *(Moves closer, almost confidential)* Well, sir, how would you like to see—a drowned man?

WRITER *(Stares at him)* I beg your pardon?

TRAMP A drowned man! A man with his lungs filled up with salt water and stone dead from drowning. How much would you pay to see that?

WRITER *Pay? Pay* to see a drowned man? Are you insane? I wouldn't look at a drowned man if they paid *me*. Why would I want to see a drowned man? What's the point in looking at a man who drowned? You're mad! Get out of here!

(He prods him away with his stick and starts to walk on, but the TRAMP *runs around in front of him)*

TRAMP Three rubles, sir. That's all it'll cost you. Three rubles to see him first, before he's in the water, then in the agonizing act of drowning and then the grand finale, the man already drowned, rest his soul.

WRITER What are you saying? That the man isn't drowned yet? That he's still alive and well?

TRAMP Not only alive and well, but dry as a bone and standing before you. I'm the drowned man, sir.

WRITER *You?* You're going to drown yourself for three rubles? You expect to charge me for your own suicide? . . . I must get away from this lunatic.

TRAMP No, no, no, you've got it all wrong, sir. I don't actually drown. I *impersonate* a drowned man. I jump into the icy cold water, splash around a bit, flail my arms, yell for help a few times, go under—bubble, bubble, bubble—and then come up floating head down, all puffy like. It sends a chill up your spine . . . Three rubles for individual performances, special rates for groups. Show starts in two minutes.

WRITER I can't believe I'm actually discussing the price of admission to a drowning.

TRAMP You miss the whole point, sir. This is not some sort of cheap thrill. It's a rich tableau filled with social implications. A drama, not tragic, but ironical, in view of its comic features.

WRITER Comic? What's comic about it?

TRAMP I blow up my cheeks and bulge my eyes out. Yell for help in a high squeaky voice. Sounds like a pig squealing. I'm the only one on the waterfront who can do it.

WRITER Do you actually expect me to pay to hear an underwater pig squealer?

TRAMP I've just had a very successful season, sir. Sold out in August. What do you say, sir? Would you like me to book you now for the dinner show?

WRITER What do you mean, dinner show?

TRAMP I jump in, flail around and throw you a nice fish. I think the halibuts are running now, sir.

WRITER Why do I stand here listening to this?

TRAMP I wish you'd make up your mind soon, sir. In five minutes that restaurant throws its garbage in the water. Then it's messy. I have my pride.

WRITER To hell with your pride. It doesn't prevent you from making a living imitating a deceased swimmer.

TRAMP You sure know how to strike at a man's vulnerable points. That was cruel, sir.

WRITER I'm sorry. I didn't mean to be cruel.

TRAMP You completely overlook the finer points to my profession . . . Look here, did you ever see a coal miner at the end of a day? Filth and grime all over his body. Soot up his nostrils and in his ears, black grit in his teeth. Disgusting . . . Or a barber who goes home at night with the cuttings of other people's hair sticking to his hands. It gets in his bread, in his soup, it's nauseating . . . Do you know where a surgeon puts his fingers—

WRITER Oh, please.

TRAMP —or a farmer his feet? Every man who works eventually touches something filthy. On the other hand, I deal with water. Water is wet, it's clean, it's purifying. I don't have to take a bath when I come home at night. I've done it. Can you say the same, sir?

WRITER Do you think I'm going to discuss my toilet habits with you? My God, you're infuriating. There must be a carriage around here. *(Calls out)* Cabbie! Cabbie!

TRAMP You'll regret it. You'll be back one night, bored to death, *dying* to see a good drowning and I'll be gone. This is my last week here. I close on Sunday . . . Next week I'm in Yalta.

(A POLICEMAN *strolls by in the background)*

WRITER There's a police officer. Now if you don't leave me alone, I'll have you arrested for soliciting.

TRAMP I'm not soliciting. I'm in the Maritime Entertainment business.

WRITER Drowning is not *maritime entertainment!* You're a waterfront lunatic. *Officer! Officer!*

TRAMP *(Starting away)* I'm going, I'm going. I'll tell you one thing, the drowning business isn't what it used to be.

(He runs off behind the pier. The POLICEMAN *walks quickly to the* WRITER*)*

POLICEMAN Can I help you, sir?

WRITER There's a man there behind the docks. There. He's been pestering me all evening. I shouldn't be surprised if he were deranged.

POLICEMAN A lot of bad characters around these docks at night, sir. A gentleman like you shouldn't be wandering around here. What was he pestering you about?

WRITER Well, I'm warning you, you're going to find this strange. He wanted to charge me three rubles to watch him drown. Can you imagine?

(The POLICEMAN *looks at him strangely)*

POLICEMAN Strange? . . . It's outright thievery. It's not worth more than sixty kopecks. You can get as fine a drowning as you'd want to see and not pay a penny more. Three rubles. What nerve!

WRITER Officer, you seem to miss the point—

POLICEMAN There's two brothers on the next pier, for one ruble each they'll give you a double drowning. You have to know how to bargain with these men, sir. Get your money's worth.

WRITER It's not a question of price.

POLICEMAN Three rubles . . . Why, the other day, right over there, fourteen men acted out an entire *shipwreck* for three rubles. On a good day, for ten rubles you can get a *whole navy* going down. Yes, sir. Sixty kopecks, that's all *I'd* pay for a good drowning. Stick to your price, sir, and have a nice evening.

(The POLICEMAN *tips his hat and walks off in the opposite direction. The* WRITER *stands there flabbergasted, not knowing what to do)*

WRITER It's come . . . It's finally come . . . The day the world has gone mad has arrived at last.

(The TRAMP *emerges from his hiding place)*

TRAMP Psst! . . . Pssst! I see the officer is gone. What did you tell him, sir?

WRITER Tell him? I told him the truth. That you were mentally unbalanced . . . Unfortunately he was a little more mentally unbalanced than you.

TRAMP Still I appreciate your not causing me any trouble, and in gratitude, I am reducing my price to an all-time low. Eighty kopecks.

WRITER *(Furious)* *Eighty? Eighty, you thief!* You conniving, wretched, deceiving little thief, I won't pay you more than *sixty!*

TRAMP *Sixty?* Sixty kopecks for a drowning? But where's my profit? My *towels* cost me forty kopecks. And another forty for the fella who fishes me out. I'd be losing money on it. What's the point? I might as well stay under.

WRITER You can't cheat me, sir. Sixty kopecks for the drowning, take it or leave it.

TRAMP *(Grumbly)* You're a hard man, sir. A hard man . . . Sixty kopecks it is. *(He sticks out his open hand for his money)* I pray to God my son doesn't want to be a drowner.

WRITER *(Counting out money)* —thirty—forty—fifty—sixty. There's your money. Now where shall I stand?

TRAMP *(Pocketing the money in a handkerchief)* Right on the edge of the dock, sir. Right up close, that's where you'll see all the action.

(He walks to the edge of the dock)

WRITER It's a bit dark down there. You're sure I'll be able to see well?

TRAMP That's what makes it so eerie. The eerier, the more entertaining. All the action's in the last ten seconds anyway . . . Well, here I go. Oh, I almost forgot. When I come up for the third time, yell at the top of your lungs, *Popnichefsky! Popnichefsky!*

WRITER Who's Popnichefsky?

TRAMP He's the fellow who jumps in after me. I can't swim, sir.

WRITER *You can't swim!* Are you trying to tell me you're going to drown without knowing how to swim?

TRAMP That's what makes it so exciting. Popnichefsky always waits till the very last second before jumping in and pulling me out. He's in that restaurant, sir, having a drink. Popnichefsky. Don't forget the name, sir . . . Well, I hope you enjoy the show. If you like it, tell your friends . . . In the soup, as we say. *(He jumps in, yells for help)* Help! Help, I'm drowning! I can't swim, help!

WRITER Over here. A little toward me . . . I can't see you too well there . . .

TRAMP Oh, God! Help! Help, somebody, I'm drowning!

WRITER Good, very good. Yes, well, that's enough of that. I don't want to see that part any more. I don't have all night . . . Can you drown now?

TRAMP Aggglllll . . .

WRITER Do you hear me? I would like to have you drown now . . . Where the devil is he? Ahh, there you are . . . That's the third time, isn't it? *(About to call out for Popnichefsky)* Good heavens, what was that fellow's name?

(Blackout)

SCENE TWO

"The Audition"

VOICE (The WRITER) Next actress, please! Next actress, please!

(A young GIRL *enters and walks to the center of the stage. She is quite nervous and clutches her purse for security. She doesn't know where to look or how to behave. This is obviously her first audition. She tries valiantly to smile and give a good impression. She has a handkerchief in her hand and constantly wipes her warm brow)*

VOICE Name.

GIRL *(Doesn't understand the question)* What?

VOICE Your name.

GIRL Oh . . . Nina.

VOICE Nina? Is that it? Just Nina?

GIRL Yes, sir . . . No, sir . . . Nina Mikhailovna Zarechnaya.

VOICE Age.

GIRL My age?

VOICE Yes, please . . . That means "How old are you?"

GIRL *(Thinks)* How old are you looking for?

VOICE Couldn't you answer the question simply, please?

GIRL Yes, but I just wanted you to know, I can be any age you want—sixteen, thirty . . . In school I played a seventy-eight-year-old woman with rheumatism, and everyone said it was very believable. A seventy-nine-year-old rheumatic woman told me so herself.

VOICE Yes, but I'm not looking for a seventy-eight-year-old rheumatic woman. I'm looking for a twenty-two-year-old girl . . . Now, how old are you?

GIRL Twenty-two, sir.

VOICE Really? I would have guessed twenty-seven or twenty-eight.

GIRL I have a bad head cold, sir. It makes me look older. Last year when I had influenza, the doctor thought I was thirty-nine. I promise I can look twenty-two when you need it, sir.

(She wipes her forehead)

VOICE Do you have a temperature?

GIRL Yes, sir . . . a hundred and three.

VOICE Good God, what are you doing walking around in the dead of winter with a hundred and three temperature? Go home, child. Go to bed. You can come back some other time.

GIRL Oh, no please, sir. I've waited six months to get this audition. I waited three months just to get on the six-month waiting list. If they put me on the end of that list again, I'll have to wait another six months and by then I'll be twenty-three and it'll be too late to be twenty-two. Please let me read, sir. I'm really feeling much better. *(Feels her forehead)* I think I'm down to a hundred and one now.

VOICE I can see you have your heart set on being an actress.

GIRL My heart, my soul, my very breath, the bones in my body, the blood in my veins—

VOICE Yes, yes, we've had enough of your medical history . . . But what practical experience have you had?

GIRL As what?

VOICE Well, for example, the thing we're discussing. Acting. How much acting experience have you had?

GIRL You mean on a stage?

VOICE That's as good a place as any.

GIRL Well, I studied acting for three years under Madame Zoblienska.

VOICE She teaches here in Moscow?

GIRL No. In my high school . . . In Odessa . . . But she was a very great actress herself.

VOICE Here in Moscow?

GIRL No. In Odessa . . .

VOICE You are then, strictly speaking, an amateur.

GIRL Yes, sir . . . In Moscow. In Odessa, I'm a professional.

VOICE Yes, that's all very well, but you see, we need a twenty-two-year-old professional actress in Moscow. Odessa—although, I grant you, a lovely city—theatrically speaking, is not Moscow. I would advise you to get more experience and take some aspirin . . .

GIRL *(Starts off; stops)* I've traveled four days to get here, sir. Won't you just hear me read?

VOICE My dear child, I find this very embarrassing . . .

GIRL Even if you did not employ me, just to read for you would be a memory I would cherish for all of my life . . . If I may be so bold, sir, I think you are one of the greatest living authors in all of Russia.

VOICE Really? That's very kind of you . . . Perhaps we do have a *few* minutes—

GIRL I've read almost everything you've written . . . The articles, the stories. *(She laughs)* I loved the one about—*(She laughs harder)*—the one about—*(She is hysterical)*—oh, dear God, every time I think of it, I can't control myself . . .

VOICE *(Laughs too)* Really? Really? Which story is that?

GIRL *(Still laughing)* The "Death of a Government Clerk." Oh, God, I laughed for days.

VOICE "Death of a Govern—" I don't remember that . . . What was that about?

GIRL Cherdyakov? The sneeze . . . The sneezing splatterer?

VOICE Oh, yes. You found that funny, did you? . . . Strange, I meant it to be sad.

GIRL Oh, it *was* sad. I cried for days . . . It was tragically funny . . .

VOICE Was it, really? . . . And of everything you've read, what was your favorite?

GIRL My *very* favorite?

VOICE Yes, what was it?

GIRL Tolstoy's *War and Peace.*

VOICE I didn't write that.

GIRL I know, sir. But you asked me what my favorite was.

VOICE Well, you're an honest little thing, aren't you? It's refreshing . . . Irritating, but refreshing. Very well, what are you going to read for me?

GIRL I should like to read from *The Three Sisters.*

VOICE Indeed? Which sister?

GIRL All of them . . . if you have the time.

VOICE *All* of them? Good heavens, why don't you read the entire play while you're at it.

GIRL Oh, thank you, sir. I know it all. Act One . . . *(She looks up)* "A drawing room in the Prozorovs' house. It is midday; a bright sun is shining through the large French doors—"

VOICE *That's not necessary!* An excerpt will do nicely, thank you.

GIRL Yes, sir. I would like to do the last moment of the play.

VOICE Good. Good. That shouldn't take too long. Whenever you're ready.

GIRL I've been ready for six months . . . Not counting the three months I waited to get on the six-month waiting list.

VOICE PLEASE, begin!

GIRL Yes, sir. Thank you, sir. *(She clears her throat; then just as she's about to begin)* Oh, sir, could you please say, "Ta-ra-ra boom-de-ay, sit on the curb I may"?

VOICE Certainly not. Why would I say such an idiotic thing?

GIRL I don't know, sir. You wrote it. Chebutykin says it at the end of the play. It would help me greatly if you could read just that one line. I've waited six months, sir. I walked all the way from Odessa . . .

VOICE All right, all right. Very well, then. Ready?

GIRL Yes, sir.

VOICE "Ta-ra-ra boom-de-ay, sit on the curb I may—"

GIRL And Masha says, "Oh, listen to that music! They are leaving us, one has gone for good, forever; we are left alone to begin our life over again. We must live . . . We must live . . ." And Irina says, "A time will come when everyone will know what all this is for . . . *(She is reading with more feeling and compassion than we expected)* . . . why there is all this suffering, and there will be no mysteries; but meanwhile, we must live . . . we must work, only work! Tomorrow I shall go alone, and I shall teach in the school, and give my whole life to those who need it. Now it is autumn, soon winter will come and cover everything with snow, and I shall go on working, working . . ." Shall I finish?

VOICE *(Softly)* Please.

GIRL And Olga says, "The music plays so gaily, so valiantly, one wants to live! Oh, my God! Time will pass, and we shall be gone forever, we'll be forgotten, our faces will be forgotten, our voices, and how many there were of us, but our sufferings will turn into joy for those who live after us, happiness and peace will come to this earth, and then they will remember kindly and bless those who are living now. Oh, my dear sisters . . . it seems as if just a little more and we shall know why we live, why we suffer . . . If only we knew, if only we knew . . ." *(It is still)* Thank you, sir. That's all I wanted . . . You've made me very happy . . . God bless you, sir.

(She walks off the stage . . . The stage is empty)

VOICE *(Softly)* Will someone go get her before she walks all the way back to Odessa . . . ?

(Dim-out)

SCENE THREE

"A Defenseless Creature"

The lights come up on the office of a bank official, KISTUNOV. *He enters on a crutch; his right foot is heavily encased in bandages, swelling it to three times its normal size. He suffers from the gout and is very careful of any mishap which would only intensify his pain. He makes it to his desk and sits. An* ASSISTANT, *rather harried, enters.*

ASSISTANT *(With volume)* Good morning, Mr. Kistunov!

KISTUNOV Shhh! Please . . . Please lower your voice.

ASSISTANT *(Whispers)* I'm sorry, sir.

KISTUNOV It's just that my gout is acting up again and my nerves are like little firecrackers. The least little friction can set them off.

ASSISTANT It must be *very* painful, sir.

KISTUNOV Combing my hair this morning was agony.

ASSISTANT Mr. Kistunov . . .

KISTUNOV What is it, Pochatkin?

ASSISTANT There's a woman who insists on seeing you. We can't make head or tail out of her story, but she insists on seeing the directing manager. Perhaps if you're not well—

KISTUNOV No, no. The business of the bank comes before my minor physical ailments. Show her in, please . . . quietly. *(The* ASSISTANT *tiptoes out. A* WOMAN *enters. She is in her late forties, poorly dressed. She is of the working class. She crosses to the desk, a forlorn look on her face.*

She twists her bag nervously) Good morning, madame. Forgive me for not standing, but I am somewhat incapacitated. Please sit down.

WOMAN Thank you.
(She sits)

KISTUNOV Now, what can I do for you?

WOMAN You can help me, sir. I pray to God you can help. No one else in this world seems to care . . .
(And she begins to cry, which in turn becomes a wail —the kind of wail that melts the spine of strong men. KISTUNOV *winces and grits his teeth in pain as he grips the arms of his chair)*

KISTUNOV Calm yourself, madame. I *beg* of you. Please calm yourself.

WOMAN I'm sorry.
(She tries to calm down)

KISTUNOV I'm sure we can sort it all out if we approach the problem sensibly and quietly . . . Now, what exactly is the trouble?

WOMAN Well, sir . . . It's my husband. Collegiate Assessor Schukin. He's been sick for five months . . . Five agonizing months.

KISTUNOV I know the horrors of illness and can sympathize with you, madame. What's the nature of his illness?

WOMAN It's a nervous disorder. Everything grates on his nerves. If you so much as touch him he'll scream out— *(And without warning, she* screams *a loud bloodcurdling scream that sends* KISTUNOV *almost out of his seat)* How or why he got it, nobody knows.

KISTUNOV *(Trying to regain his composure)* I have an inkling . . . Please go on, a little less descriptively, if possible.

WOMAN Well, while the poor man was lying in bed—

KISTUNOV *(Braces himself)* You're not going to scream again, are you?

WOMAN Not that I don't have cause . . . While he was lying in bed these five months, recuperating, he was dismissed from his job—for no reason at all.

KISTUNOV That's a pity, certainly, but I don't quite see the connection with our bank, madame.

WOMAN You don't know how I suffered during his illness. I nursed him from morning till night. Doctored him from night till morning. Besides cleaning my house, taking care of my children, feeding our dog, our cat, our goat, my sister's bird, who was sick . . .

KISTUNOV The bird was sick?

WOMAN My *sister!* She gets dizzy spells. She's been dizzy a month now. And she's getting dizzier every day . . .

KISTUNOV Extraordinary. However—

WOMAN I had to take care of *her* children and *her* house and *her* cat and *her* goat, and then her bird bit one of my children, and so our cat bit her bird, so my oldest daughter, the one with the broken arm, drowned my sister's cat, and now my sister wants my goat in exchange, or else she says she'll either drown my cat or break my oldest daughter's other arm—

KISTUNOV Yes, well, you've certainly had your pack of troubles, haven't you? But I don't quite see—

WOMAN And then, when I went to get my husband's pay, they deducted twenty-four rubles and thirty-six kopecks. For what? I asked. Because, they said, he borrowed it from the employees' fund. But that's impossible. He could never borrow without my approval. I'd break his arm . . . Not while he was sick, of course . . . I don't have the strength. I'm not well myself, sir. I have this racking cough that's a terrible thing to hear—

(She coughs rackingly—so rackingly that KISTUNOV *is about to crack)*

KISTUNOV I can well understand why your husband took five months to recuperate . . . But what is it you want from me, madame?

WOMAN What rightfully belongs to my husband—his twenty-four rubles and thirty-six kopecks. They won't give it to me because I'm a woman, weak and defenseless. Some of them have laughed in my face, sir . . . *Laughed! (She laughs loud and painfully.* KISTUNOV *clenches everything)* Where's the humor, I wonder, in a poor, defenseless creature like myself?

(She sobs)

KISTUNOV None . . . I see none at all. However, madame, I don't wish to be unkind, but I'm afraid you've come to the wrong place. Your petition, no matter how justified, has nothing to do with us. You'll have to go to the agency where your husband was employed.

WOMAN *What do you mean?* I've been to *five* agencies already and none of them will even *listen* to my petition. I'm about to lose my mind. The hair is coming out of my head. *(She pulls out a handful)* Look at my hair. By the fistful. *(She throws a fistful on his desk) Don't tell me to go to another agency!*

KISTUNOV *(Delicately and disgustedly, he picks up her fistful of hair and hands it back to her. She sticks it back in her hair)* Please, madame, keep your hair in its proper place. Now listen to me carefully. This-is-a-bank. A bank! We're in the banking business. We bank money. Funds that are brought here are banked by us. Do you understand what I'm saying?

WOMAN What are you saying?

KISTUNOV I'm saying that I can't help you.

WOMAN Are you saying you can't help me?

KISTUNOV *(Sighs deeply)* I'm trying. I don't think I'm making headway.

WOMAN Are you saying you won't believe my husband is sick? Here! Here is a doctor's certificate. *(She puts it on the desk and pounds it)* There's the proof. Do you still doubt that my husband is suffering from a nervous disorder?

KISTUNOV Not only do I not doubt it, I would *swear* to it.

WOMAN *Look at it!* You didn't look at it!

KISTUNOV It's really not necessary. I know *full well* how your husband must be suffering.

WOMAN *What's the point in a doctor's certificate if you don't look at it?!* LOOK AT IT!

KISTUNOV *(Frightened, quickly looks at it)* Oh, yes . . . I see your husband is sick. It's right here on the doctor's certificate. Well, you certainly have a good case, madame, but I'm afraid *you've still come to the wrong place. (Getting perplexed)* I'm getting excited.

WOMAN *(Stares at him)* You lied to me. I took you as a man of your word and you lied to me.

KISTUNOV I? LIE? WHEN?

WOMAN *(Snatches the certificate)* When you said you read the doctor's certificate. You couldn't have. You couldn't have read the description of my husband's illness without seeing he was fired unjustly. *(She puts the certificate back on the desk)* Don't take advantage of me just because I'm a weak, defenseless woman. Do me the simple courtesy of reading the doctor's certificate. That's all I ask. Read it, and then I'll go.

KISTUNOV ·But I *read it!* What's the point in reading something twice when I've already *read it once?*

WOMAN You didn't read it carefully.

KISTUNOV I read it *in detail!*

WOMAN Then you read it too fast. Read it slower.

KISTUNOV *I don't have to read it slower. I'm a fast reader.*

WOMAN Maybe you didn't absorb it. Let it sink in this time.

KISTUNOV *(Almost apoplectic)* I *absorbed* it! It *sank* in! I could pass a *test* on what's written here, *but it doesn't make any difference because it has nothing to do with our bank!*

WOMAN *(She throws herself on him from behind)* Did you read the part where it says he has a nervous disorder? Read that part again and see if I'm wrong.

KISTUNOV THAT PART? OH, YES! I SEE YOUR HUSBAND HAS A NERVOUS DISORDER. MY, MY, HOW TERRIBLE! *ONLY I CAN'T HELP YOU! NOW PLEASE GO!*

(He falls back into his chair, exhausted)

WOMAN *(Crosses to where his foot is resting)* I'm sorry, Excellency. I hope I haven't caused you any pain.

KISTUNOV *(Trying to stop her)* Please, don't kiss my foot. *(He is too late—she has given his foot a most ardent embrace. He screams in pain)* Aggghhh! Can't you get this into your balding head? If you would just realize that to come to us with this kind of claim is as strange as your trving to get a haircut in a butcher shop.

WOMAN You can't get a haircut in a butcher shop. Why would anyone go to a butcher shop for a haircut? Are you laughing at me?

KISTUNOV *Laughing!* I'm lucky I'm breathing . . . Pochatkin!

WOMAN Did I tell you I'm fasting? I haven't eaten in three days. I want to eat, but nothing stays down. I had the same cup of coffee three times today.

KISTUNOV *(With his last burst of energy, screams)* *POCHATKIN!*

WOMAN I'm skin and bones. I faint at the least provocation . . . Watch. *(She swoons to the floor)* Did you see? You saw how I just fainted? Eight times a day that happens.

(The ASSISTANT *finally rushes in)*

ASSISTANT What is it, Mr. Kistunov? What's wrong?

KISTUNOV *(Screams)* GET HER OUT OF HERE! Who let her in my office?

ASSISTANT You did, sir. I asked you and you said, "Show her in."

KISTUNOV I thought you meant a human being, not a lunatic with a doctor's certificate.

WOMAN *(To Pochatkin)* He wouldn't even read it. I gave it to him, he threw it back in my face . . . You look like a kind person. Have pity on me. *You* read it and see if my husband is sick or not.

(She forces the certificate on Pochatkin)

ASSISTANT I *read* it, madame. Twice!

KISTUNOV Me too. I had to read it twice too.

ASSISTANT You just showed it to me outside. You showed it to *everyone*. We *all* read it. Even the doorman.

WOMAN You just looked at it. You didn't read it.

KISTUNOV Don't argue. Read it, Pochatkin. For God's sakes, read it so we can get her out of here.

ASSISTANT *(Quickly scans it)* Oh, yes. It says your husband is sick. *(He looks up; gives it back to her)* Now will you please leave, madame, or I will have to get someone to remove you.

KISTUNOV Yes! Yes! Good! Remove her! Get the doorman and two of the guards. Be careful, she's strong as an ox.

WOMAN *(To* KISTUNOV*)* If you touch me, I'll scream so loud they'll hear it all over the city. You'll lose all your depositors. No one will come to a bank where they beat weak, defenseless women . . . I think I'm going to faint again . . .

KISTUNOV *(Rising)* WEAK? DEFENSELESS? You are as defenseless as a charging rhinoceros! You are as weak as the King of the Jungle! You are a plague, madame! A plague that wipes out all that crosses your path! You are a raging river that washes out bridges and stately homes! You are a wind that blows villages over mountains! It is women like you who drive men like me to the condition of husbands like yours!

WOMAN Are you saying you're not going to help me?

KISTUNOV Hit her, Pochatkin! Strike her! I give you permission to knock her down. Beat some sense into her!

WOMAN *(To Pochatkin)* You hear? You hear how I'm abused? He would have you hit an orphaned mother. Did you hear me cough? Listen to this cough.

(She "racks" up another coughing spell)

ASSISTANT Madame, if we can discuss this in my office—

(He takes her arm)

WOMAN Get your hands off me . . . Help! Help! I'm being beaten! Oh, merciful God, they're beating me!

ASSISTANT I am not beating you. I am just holding your arm.

KISTUNOV Beat her, you fool. Kick her while you've got the chance. We'll never get her out of here. Knock her senseless!

(He tries to kick her, misses and falls to the floor)

WOMAN *(Pointing an evil finger at* KISTUNOV, *she jumps on the desk and punctuates each sentence by stepping on his desk bell)* A curse! A curse on your bank! I put on a curse on you and your depositors! May the money in your vaults turn to potatoes! May the gold in your cellars turn to onions! May your rubles turn to radishes, and your kopecks to pickles . . .

KISTUNOV STOP! Stop it, I beg of you! . . . Pochatkin, give her the money. Give her what she wants. Give her anything—only get her out of here!

WOMAN *(To Pochatkin)* Twenty-four rubles and thirty-six kopecks . . . Not a penny more. That's all that's due me and that's all I want.

ASSISTANT Come with me, I'll get you your money.

WOMAN And another ruble to get me home. I'd walk but I have very weak ankles.

KISTUNOV Give her enough for a taxi, anything, only get her out.

WOMAN God bless you, sir. You're a kind man. I remove the curse. *(With a gesture)* Curse be gone! Onions to money, potatoes to gold—

KISTUNOV *(Pulls on his hair)* REMOVE HERRRR! Oh, God, my hair is falling out!

(He pulls some hair out)

WOMAN Oh, there's one other thing, sir. I'll need a letter of recommendation so my husband can get another job. Don't bother yourself about it today. I'll be back in the morning. God bless you, sir . . .

(She leaves)

KISTUNOV She's coming back . . . She's coming back . . . *(He slowly begins to go mad and takes his cane and begins to beat his bandaged leg)* She's coming back . . . She's coming back . . .

(Dim-out)

SCENE FOUR
"The Arrangement"

As the lights come up, we are on a wharf. The WRITER *enters and addresses the audience.*

WRITER This one goes back a good many years ago to my youth . . . I was nineteen years old, to be exact . . . And in the ways of love, I was not only unschooled—I hadn't even been in the classroom. I was so innocent and shy that I actually thought that, since the beginning of time, no woman had *ever* been completely unclothed. As for connubial bliss, I dared not think of it. And as for impregnation, I chose to believe it was caused by the husband giving the wife a most ardent handshake before retiring . . . and let it go at that. But my father was a wonderful man—quite liberal in his thinking. And on the occasion of my nineteenth birthday, he decided to introduce me to the mysteries of love. He was, however, a frugal man, and decided to escort me himself, to see, in the matter of bargaining, that I would not be taken advantage of . . . Picture me, if you will, as my own dear father . . . *(He calls out to the side)* Antosha! Antosha! Where are you? . . . Don't stand there in the dark shaking like a puppy dog. Come here. We have some adolescence to get over with . . .

(Young Anton appears, nineteen years old, as nervous as a puppy. He frets with his hat in his hand)

BOY I'm not well, Father. I'm sick.

FATHER Sick? Sick? What's wrong with you?

BOY I haven't thought of it yet. Give me a few minutes.

FATHER Fear. That's all it is. Pubescent fear. I was the same way when I was your age.

BOY I never knew you were my age . . . I always thought of you as older.

FATHER How old do you think I was when I was with my first woman?

BOY You were with a woman, Father?

FATHER Certainly, I was with a woman. All men who become fathers have been with a woman at some point in their life.

BOY The same woman?

FATHER *(Yells)* Certainly not the same woman! My God, don't you ever discuss these matters with your young friends?

BOY Oh, yes. All the time. But we get too excited to listen.

FATHER It's a man's obligation to enter a marriage experienced in the ways of love . . . otherwise valuable years are wasted in endless groping.

BOY I don't mind wasting a few years groping, Father.

FATHER It's all in the process of becoming a man, Antosha. First you learned to walk, then you learned to talk—and now it's time to learn this.

BOY Are you sure, Father? I'm really not walking and talking that well.

FATHER *(Irritated)* Antosha, we can't afford to delay any longer. I don't want you becoming an old man waiting to become a young man . . . Now, are you going to walk in there and have your first experience with a woman or do I have to punish you?

BOY Father . . . I don't think we're going to find any women of high moral character around here.

FATHER We're not looking for *high-moraled* women. There are too damn many high-moraled women in the world as it is . . . That's why so many high-moraled men have to come down to places like this . . . Now, let's get on with this business.

BOY Can I hold your hand, Father?

FATHER *Certainly not!* You can't go in there to become a man holding your father's hand . . . Antosha, we don't have all day. Your mother is expecting us home by nine o'clock . . . Now we have exactly an hour and ten minutes for you to mature.

BOY You mean you told mother where we were going?

FATHER Do you think I'm so insensitive? I told her we were going out for a walk just to get some night air.

BOY Won't she become suspicious when she notices that I've come home all grown up?

FATHER It doesn't *show,* Anton. You don't get spots like measles . . . You may possibly have a small smile on your face, that's all . . . Now, come along.

BOY Father, aren't there other ways to become a man? I mean, couldn't I grow a moustache?

FATHER Antosha, tell me the truth, if you'd rather not go through with it, I'll take you home . . .

BOY *(Nods)* Take me home!

FATHER *Wait till I ask the question!* Would you rather not go through with it? I'll take you home . . . ?

BOY Take me home!

FATHER I see! Very well, let's go home . . . You can get in your tub and play with your sailboats until you're ready.

BOY Will you be angry with me?

FATHER No.

BOY Will you be disappointed with me?

FATHER No.

BOY Will you be proud of me?

FATHER No.

BOY All right, I'll do it.

FATHER Good boy, Antosha.

BOY If I like it, can we do it again?

FATHER No! I didn't bring you down here with the intention of leaving you here . . . By God, it's a difficult business being a liberal father.

(The GIRL *enters. She has flaming red hair and a cigarette in her mouth)*

GIRL 'Evening, gentlemen!

BOY Oh, God.

FATHER Steady, boy, steady.

BOY Is she . . . Is she one of the teachers?

FATHER She looks like the principal to me. We're in luck, son. She's a charming-looking girl. I'll go over and attend to your tuition . . .

BOY Father . . . couldn't I take a correspondence course?

FATHER No! Stand there! Don't move! I'll be right back—and don't twiddle with your hat. This is not hat-twiddling business . . . *(He goes over to the* GIRL*)* Good evening, madame . . . A lovely April night, wouldn't you say?

GIRL Is it April already? . . . I don't get out very much.

FATHER No, I can well understand that . . . It's, er . . . it's been a long time since I've been involved in such matters, but I would like to discuss with you a subject of some delicacy—

GIRL Thirty rubles!

FATHER So much for the delicacy . . . Thirty rubles, you say. Well, speaking for myself, I would say thirty rubles was quite fair. But it's not for me. It's for my young, inexperienced son. That's him! The one with the knees buckling.

GIRL It's still thirty rubles, sir. We don't have children's prices down here.

FATHER No, of course not. But thirty rubles does seem a bit high for a boy of nineteen . . . Would you consider fifteen rubles?

GIRL For fifteen rubles I read *Peter Rabbitt.* Sir, a Norwegian ship is due in here tonight and I have to go in and put on my blond wig.

FATHER Wait! There *is* an extenuating circumstance . . . It's the boy's birthday, and I wanted to give him a nice gift . . . What do you say?

GIRL How about an umbrella?

FATHER See here. In my day, thirty years ago, I shared the pleasures of the most delightful girl on this street—Ilka the Milkmaid, she was called—and she cost me a mere ten rubles.

GIRL Well, she's still here. If you want her, she's down to six rubles now.

FATHER Certainly not, good heavens . . .

BOY Father? Oh, Father?

FATHER Yes?

BOY Am I ready yet?

FATHER In a minute. I'm still shopping . . . *(To the* GIRL*)* He's really a lovely boy . . . fragile and sweet. Tells the most delightful stories . . . I'm sure you'll find him most entertaining.

GIRL Haven't you got it the wrong way around, sir?

BOY Father, I'm getting chilly.

FATHER *(To his son)* Well, run around, jump up and down. Be patient. You've waited nineteen years, it's just another few minutes . . . *(To the* GIRL*)* Twenty rubles—not a kopeck more. There's just so much I'm willing to spend on education. Please, it's for my boy.

GIRL *(Looks at him, then smiles)* Settled! You're a good and loving father, sir, and I respect you for it. If I had a father like you, I would never have ended up here on the streets bargaining with fathers like you.

FATHER *(Puzzled)* I'm sure there's a moral in there somewhere, I just don't see it yet . . . Settled, for twenty rubles. *(Gives her the money)* Oh, there's just one other request I have . . . At the conclusion of the evening's festivities, I would appreciate it greatly if you would just say, "Happy Birthday from Poppa."

GIRL *(Nods)* "Happy Birthday from Poppa" . . . Would you like any candles, sir?

FATHER That's not necessary. Just be gentle and kind to him. Gentleness, that's all I ask . . . *(Wipes his eye)* Good heavens, a tear . . . What a thing to cry over.

GIRL I'll wait upstairs. Two flights up, second door on the left. I'll be gentle, sir.

FATHER Thank you. The girls nowadays seem to be so much more understanding.

GIRL May I say, it's men like you who make me proud to serve in my profession.

(She kisses his hand and goes)

FATHER What a wonderful nurse she would have made . . . Antosha, school's in. *(He turns, crosses to the* BOY*)* Settled, my boy. Twenty rubles. You have to know how to bargain with these people. Well, off you go. Two flights up, second door on the left. I'll wait out here. Don't rush.

(The BOY *starts, then stops)*

BOY Father, do I say anything to her?

FATHER Like what?

BOY Like "Hello"?

FATHER "Hello" would be nice . . . "Goodbye" would be good too. Go on, she's waiting.

BOY Are there any "instructions" you want to give me?

FATHER That's what I'm paying *her* good money for. The questions you ask . . . Go on, boy—before I have to pay her overtime.

BOY Yes, Father . . . I'm going, I'm going . . .

(He stops)

FATHER What is it now?

BOY It's funny, but when I come down those stairs and out into the street . . . I won't be your little Antosha any more . . . I'll be Anton the Man. Thank you, Father. Well, goodbye.

(He gets to the door)

FATHER Wait! *(Anton stops)* Wait—Antosha!

BOY What is it, Father?

FATHER I was just thinking . . . Wouldn't you rather have

a nice umbrella? . . . There's plenty of time next year to become a man . . . Plenty of time next year . . .

BOY If you wish, Poppa. Yes, Poppa.

(The FATHER *puts his arm around his son's shoulder, and they turn and walk off into the night . . . Music plays as the stage dims out)*

SCENE FIVE
"The Writer"

The lights come up, and the WRITER *comes downstage carrying his portfolio of writings.*

WRITER I hope that portrait of my father came out with some affection. I loved him very much . . . And yet with him, as with all the other characters I've shared with you tonight, I have a sense of betrayal. When I put down my pen at the end of a day's work, I cannot help but feel that I have robbed my friends of their precious life fluid . . . What makes my conscience torment me even more is that I've had a wonderful time writing today. But before I go . . . What was it we were talking about? Early on, before the story of Cherdyakov? . . . Ahh, yes . . . I was about to say what it was, as a child, I most wanted to do with my life. Well, then—*(He thinks for a moment)* Funny, for the life of me I can't remember . . . But somehow, as I stand here with a feeling of great peace and contentment, in some measure I suspect I must be doing it. Thank you for this visit. If ever you pass this way again, please drop in. Good night . . . Wait! There's an alternative ending . . . If ever you pass this way again, I hope you inherit five million rubles. Good night.

(He turns and moves upstage, as the lights fade)

Curtain

God's Favorite

THE SCENE

The action takes place in the Benjamin mansion on the North Shore of Long Island.

ACT ONE

SCENE ONE Midnight.

SCENE TWO Two weeks later.

ACT TWO

The Holocaust after.

Act One

SCENE I

The scene is the palatial home of wealthy businessman JOE BENJAMIN *on the North Shore of Long Island Sound. The design of the living room is stylized. It is today, and yet it has a feeling of timelessness. Wooden-beamed ceilings seem to stretch up to heaven itself. An enormous French door leads out to a portico which faces the Sound. A large oak door on one side of the room leads to the entrance foyer. An oak door on the other side leads to the dining room. The walls are adorned with paintings worthy of a collection, which indeed one day they will be. Leather-bound volumes of the great works of literature line the shelves.*

Before the curtain rises, we can hear the chiming of a grandfather clock signaling the hour. One . . . two . . . three . . . four . . .

The curtain rises. The room is in darkness. Through the French door, moonlight can be seen reflecting on the snow; it pours an eerie light into the room.

The clock continues. Five . . . six . . . seven . . . eight . . . nine . . . ten . . . eleven . . . twelve. All is silent.

Suddenly, a solitary figure is seen outside on the portico. The light is too dim for us to make out his features. He looks around carefully, blows on his hands, then attempts to open the door. It is locked. He blows on his hands again, looks around once more, and tries the door again, but this time using more pressure. The door opens a few inches—but at that very moment, a piercing burglar alarm goes off.

The figure pulls away from the door in fear. He seems panicked as he starts to run in three different directions, constantly changing his mind. Finally, in desperation, he jumps over the balcony and disappears from sight. An explosion of snow rises up visibly—he must have landed in a snow bank.

The alarm continues its scream. The oak door suddenly

swings open. A man enters. He switches on the lights. He is dressed in a rich silk robe, silk pajamas and monogrammed velvet slippers. He reaches behind the shelf and turns off a switch. The alarm stops.

This is JOE BENJAMIN. *In his late fifties, he gives an impression of great strength of character. He glances around the room quickly, giving a fast look behind the drapes. Then he goes over to the French door and notices it is open.*

Two more people rush in through the oak door in their night clothes. They are BEN BENJAMIN *and* SARAH BENJAMIN, *a pair of twenty-four-year-old twins, or as close as we can approximate. The brother and sister have red hair of the same shade; their I.Q. is 160—between them.*

BEN What is it, Dad? What happened?

JOE I don't know.

SARAH What happened, Dad? What is it?

JOE I said I don't know.

SARAH We heard the alarm go off.

BEN Did you hear the alarm go off, Dad?

JOE Certainly I heard it go off. That's why I'm down here. *(To* SARAH*)* Close your bathrobe.

*(*SARAH *can never keep her robe tied. She closes it)*

SARAH My God, it was really the alarm.

BEN *(Points)* The French door is open. Look!

SARAH It's open, Dad. The French door. Look!

JOE I can see it's open. Stop repeating everything.

(The telephone rings)

BEN It's the phone, Dad.

SARAH Dad, it's the phone.

(It rings again)

JOE I can hear it. Close your bathrobe. Ben, answer the phone.

SARAH Answer the phone, Ben.

JOE I'm going to look outside.

SARAH Suppose someone's out there?

JOE That's why I'm looking. That's the whole point of it. Close your robe. *(The phone rings again)* Answer that.

(JOE goes out to the portico, and BEN picks up the phone)

BEN *(Into the phone)* Hello? . . . Yes?

SARAH Who is it?

BEN The burglar alarm company.

SARAH Daddy, it's the burglar alarm company.

BEN *(Into the phone)* Yes, we just heard it.

SARAH Ben said we just heard it.

JOE *(From out on the portico, yells)* Close your bathrobe!

BEN *(Into the phone)* We found the living-room French door open. My father's checking now.

SARAH What do they think?

BEN *(Into the phone)* What do you think?

JOE *(Coming back into the room)* I think someone tried to break in.

BEN *(Into the phone)* My father thinks someone tried to break in.

JOE I found footprints in the snow.

BEN *(Into the phone)* He found footprints in the snow.

SARAH My God, footprints in the snow.

JOE Close your robe, you want to catch cold? Go to bed. Look at you shivering.

SARAH I'm not cold. I'm scared. My God, someone tried to break in.

JOE Stop using God's name in vain.

SARAH It's not in vain. I'm really scared.

BEN *(Into the phone)* One second, please. *(To* JOE*)* They want to know if they should send somebody.

JOE No one got into the house.

BEN How can you tell?

JOE There's snow outside. There would be footprints on the rug.

SARAH There *are* footprints. *(Points)* Right there!

JOE *Those are mine!* Wasn't I just in the snow?

BEN Suppose he wore galoshes and left them outside?

JOE What kind of a robber wears galoshes? No one got in. Tell them never mind. Everything's all right. I'm going to look around again.

(He goes back out on the portico)

BEN *(Into the phone)* Hello? No one got in . . . Never mind, please. Everything's all right. My father's going to look around again . . . Thank you. We will. *(He hangs up)* Close your bathrobe.

JOE *(Comes back in)* Someone was here. He dropped these outside.

(He holds up a pair of steel-rimmed glasses)

BEN Eyeglasses!

SARAH Look, Daddy, it's a pair of eyeglasses!

JOE *Didn't I just find them?* I can see they're eyeglasses. Well, whoever dropped them won't get far without them. They're a half-inch thick—I can't see two feet through them.

SARAH A half-blind burglar, my God, it gives me the creeps.

(She shivers)

JOE I'm not going to tell you about God's name or your bathrobe again . . . I wouldn't be surprised if he broke both his legs. There are no footprints going down the stairs, so he must have jumped off the balcony.

BEN Jumped off the balcony? Forty feet? He'd break both his legs.

SARAH Oh God, a crippled blind burglar . . .

BEN Why don't we call the police? A crippled blind burglar shouldn't be too hard to find.

JOE First of all, he isn't a burglar because he didn't steal anything. And second of all, I don't want any police around here with your mother in the house. You know how frightened she is.

BEN But whoever it was could still be out there. He could be a dangerous lunatic.

SARAH He could be a rapist! . . . A *sexual* rapist!
(She closes her robe, which always falls open)

BEN *All* rapists are sexual.

JOE *(Looks at her)* He can't see two feet ahead of him, who's he going to find to rape?

SARAH He could feel his way into the house.

BEN Not if he has two broken legs.

SARAH He could *crawl* and feel his way into the house.

JOE *(Yells)* People don't break into houses if they have to crawl and feel around . . . How would they ever get away?

SARAH A girl in my college was attacked by a man with one arm and one leg . . . They still can't figure out how he held her down.

JOE A nineteen-room house with priceless paintings, irreplaceable antiques and a half a million dollars in jewelry, who's going to stop for a rape? He's got other things on his mind.

SARAH What if rape was the thing he had on his mind?

JOE Will you stop talking about rape and close your

bathrobe? Ben, take her upstairs. Go to bed, the both of you.

SARAH Yes, Daddy. Good night, Daddy.

BEN Good night, Dad.

JOE Wait a minute! Did you just hear something? . . . Listen!

(We hear a door screech open, then shut. They all look at each other)

JOE It's in the house.

BEN Someone's in the house!

SARAH Oh God, the rapist!

JOE *(Whispers)* Be quiet! Listen . . . footsteps!

SARAH Coming this way!

BEN Out in the hall!

SARAH Give them what they want, Daddy, don't let them do you-know-what.

JOE Get back, both of you. Near the wall!

(They all move back and pin themselves against the wall)

BEN The burglar alarm is off. We forgot to reset it.

JOE It's too late now.

BEN I could call them. What's the number?

JOE How should I know the number?

BEN Should I call information?

JOE Will you get back against the wall?

SARAH Oh God, I can just feel his hands on me now, his clammy hands rubbing all over me, up and down, up and down—

JOE No one's going to rub you up and down! Stop it! Grab something! *(They each pick up a vase)* The minute I hit him, call the police! Stand back! Here he comes . . . Close your bathrobe! *(They all stand behind the door, and raise the vases over their heads, poised for action—and then the phone rings. They all turn and look at it) Now? Now* the phone rings?

BEN What a time for the phone to ring.

JOE Answer it! Answer it!

(BEN runs over on tiptoe and answers the phone, still speaking in a soft voice)

BEN Hello? . . . Yes? . . . Yes, this is the Benjamin residence—

JOE Who is it?

BEN *(Hand over the receiver, to JOE)* It's a woman. She's asking for Sidney.

JOE Sidney who?

(The vase is still poised over his head)

BEN *(Into the phone)* Sidney who, please? *(He nods. To JOE)* Sidney Lipton.

JOE There's no Sidney Lipton here. She's got the wrong number.

BEN *(Into the phone)* There's no Sidney Lipton here, madam. You've got the wrong number.

SARAH Hang up! Stop talking before the rapist goes away.

BEN *(Into the phone)* Just a minute. *(To JOE)* She says she's *Mrs.* Lipton. Her husband had an appointment here tonight . . . with you. *(JOE shakes his head "No" and shrugs. BEN, back into the phone)* My father doesn't know anything about it . . . Listen, Mrs. Lipton, this is a bad time for us to talk . . . We're expecting someone . . . Yes, I will . . . Thank you.

(He hangs up carefully, then rushes back to his spot against the wall. He doesn't say anything. JOE stares at him)

JOE Yes, you will what?

BEN Tell Sidney that his wife called.

SARAH Here he comes!

(They all stare at the foyer door. But it is the dining room door that opens, slowly, creaking—and a woman appears. It is ROSE BENJAMIN. *In her early fifties, she wears a silk robe, satin slippers, and tons of jewelry—pearls, rings, earrings, bracelets—a walking Harry Winstons. She walks slowly into the room, not noticing anything yet. Then she turns and sees the three poised against the wall, all with their "weapons" raised in the air. She just looks at them)*

ROSE *(Calmly)* What's wrong?

JOE *(Innocently)* Wrong? What could be wrong?

ROSE What?

JOE I said, "What could be wrong?"

ROSE I can't hear you. I have my earplugs in.

JOE Then take them *out!*

ROSE I can't hear you. I have my earplugs in.

JOE *(Yells)* NOTHING'S WRONG!

ROSE David's not home yet. I don't like it when David comes home so late. Tell him I want to speak to him in the morning, Joe. All right?

JOE Yes, Rose. I'll tell him.

ROSE I can't hear you. I have my earplugs in.

JOE I'LL TELL HIM!

ROSE Never mind. You tell him! I'm going to bed. Good night, Joe. Good night, children.

SARAH and BEN Good night, Mother.

ROSE You can at least say good night . . .
(She turns and exits)

JOE *(Relieved)* Ahhh!

SARAH and BEN Ahhh!

JOE I wonder if that was David?

BEN *(Puzzled)* No, Dad. It was Mother.

JOE *(Frowns at him)* Not just now. Before. Maybe he came home late again, drunk as usual, forgot his key and tried to get in through the French door.

BEN That's my guess. That sounds like David.

JOE All right, let's all go to bed. We've had enough for one night. I'll turn the alarm on.

SARAH *(Starting out)* I'll never sleep. I keep picturing some horrid man rubbing his clammy hands all over me, up and down, up and down . . .

JOE No one's going to rub you up and down.

(He turns the lights off and they all leave. The room is empty and dark, except for the moonlight pouring in through the windows. Suddenly a man appears on the portico. He wears a raincoat and a party hat. He wobbles, slightly drunk. He opens the French door and the alarm goes off, screaming through the house. He turns the lights on, then crosses to the other side, removing his raincoat. He wears an expensive tuxedo jacket, silk lace shirt, black tie and, in contrast, filthy, torn blue jeans, with colorful appliqués, and old sneakers. JOE *rushes into the room, but he doesn't see* DAVID. *He dashes to the wall and turns the alarm off. Just as he turns,* DAVID *greets him—and* JOE *screams in terror)*

DAVID Hi, Dad!

JOE Oh! *(Then, relieved)* David—so it was you. Thank God! *(Then he slaps at* DAVID*'s shoulders)* Bum! Drunken bum! Rotten, good-for-nothing drunken bum!

DAVID Oh, good. For a minute I thought I was in the wrong house.

BEN *(Offstage)* Who is it, Dad?

JOE It's David, the bum.

*(*SARAH *and* BEN *enter)*

SARAH David!

BEN It's David.

DAVID Hi, kids. It's David.

JOE You want to scare us all to death? You want to give the three of us a heart attack?

DAVID A *triple* heart attack? I don't think it can be done, Dad.

(He wobbles)

JOE Look at him! Can't even stand up straight. Thank God your mother can't see you, she's got earplugs on.

DAVID How does that affect the eyes, Dad?

JOE Don't you talk back to me . . . I thought it was a burglar. Your brother thought it was a lunatic. Your sister was expecting a rapist.

DAVID Sorry, Sarah, what time were you expecting him?

JOE Go to your room! You hear me? You think you can find your room in your condition?

DAVID Why should my room be in my condition?

JOE Get him out! Get him out before I smack him one!

BEN Cool it, David. Dad is very upset.

(DAVID sits on the end of a fireplace fender)

SARAH Come to bed, David.

JOE A lot of help you'd be if we had a prowler out there now.

DAVID *(He points)* Oh, but we do. I saw something move out there.

(He falls into the fireplace)

JOE What! Someone's out there? You saw him?

SARAH And my bathrobe's open.

JOE *(Looks toward the window)* I knew it! I knew it!

BEN Dad knew it! He knew it!

(DAVID goes over to the bottle of Scotch and pours a drink)

SARAH Dad found his glasses on the porch.

BEN He's probably half blind!

DAVID Lucky dog!

JOE GET AWAY FROM THAT LIQUOR!

DAVID Sorry. Which liquor can I go near?

JOE You hear?

(They glare at each other. Suddenly MORRIS and MADY, two middle-aged black domestics, appear in the room.)

MORRIS Mr. Benjamin.

BEN Dad, it's Mady and Morris!

DAVID Looks like Mady and Morris.

MORRIS Mr. Benjamin, we heard the alarm. Is anything wrong?

JOE No, no, Morris. It was a mistake.

MORRIS Mady thought she saw something run past our window before.

MADY At first I thought it was a dog, but it bumped into a tree. Never saw a dog bump into a tree.

MORRIS Then she heard it call out in the dark.

JOE What'd it say, Mady?

MADY Sounded like "Ohh, my head." Never heard a dog say "Ohh, my head."

JOE No, no. It was probably just the wind.

MADY Never heard the wind say "Ohh, my head" either.

JOE It's nothing. Go back to bed. Don't say anything to Mrs. Benjamin in the morning.

MORRIS Yes, sir. Good night, Mr. Benjamin.

(They start out)

MADY It's gettin' dangerous around here. I don't like livin' in rich neighborhoods.

MORRIS Come on, Mady.

(They go)

DAVID She's right, Dad. Why don't you buy us a nice poor neighborhood so we'd all feel safer?

(He takes another drink. JOE *grabs the glass away from him)*

JOE Give me that. How many times have I told you we only drink in this house on holidays and special occasions?

DAVID If I guess right, can I have a drink?

JOE *I will not tolerate disrespect!*

DAVID I mean no disrespect. I apologize, Dad.

JOE An apology? From you? That's the first one I ever remember.

DAVID Ahh, a special occasion. That means I can have a drink.

(He goes over to the bar)

BEN Come on, David. Let's go to bed.

SARAH Please don't drink any more, David.

JOE *(To* DAVID*)* Why can't you be helpful? There's a professional burglar feeling his way around out there someplace . . . Keep away from this door. I'm going to find out what's going on. *(He opens the French door)* If he attacks me, call the police and try not to wake your mother.

BEN Careful, Dad.

SARAH Be careful, Daddy.

*(*JOE *goes out on the portico; he pulls his robe collar up. We hear the cold wind blow)*

BEN You think it's all right to let him go out there alone?

DAVID In his bathrobe and slippers? How much money could they get off him?

(He gets his usual from the bar)

JOE *(On the portico, calls out in slow, deliberate words . . . like two ships passing in the fog)* Hellooo? . . . Who's out there? *(Silence)* What do you want and where do you come from?

DAVID He expects him to give him his name and address.

(He pours himself one)

JOE *(Calling out again)* What is it you want? . . . If you're cold and want a drink, just say so . . .

DAVID So *that's* how you get one!

JOE *(Yelling out)* Can you see me? I have your glasses in my pocket. If your legs are broken, just crawl up to the house and we'll get you a doctor.

DAVID *(Drinks)* And you can pay us back a little bit each week.

SARAH *(Turns)* Listen! Someone's coming down the stairs.

BEN It's Mother. I hear her jewelry.

SARAH My God, what'll we do? She'll panic.

(The door opens and ROSE *reappears, clutching a huge jewel box to her bosom. There are so many jewels crammed into the box that necklaces, pearls and chains are overflowing it)*

ROSE *(Quickly, nervously)* I heard noises. What were the noises? David, is that you? Yes, it's you. Where were you so late? Do you know you had me so worried? Why is everyone here? Is anything wrong? Where's your father? Why isn't your father here? What's happening? What's going on? What's all this about?

DAVID *(To* BEN*)* You answer the first six, I'll take the rest.

BEN *(To* DAVID*)* She can't hear you. She has earplugs in.

ROSE I can hear you. I don't have my earplugs in. Oh God, I feel weak. My jewel box is so heavy.

JOE *(Still on the terrace, calls out)* We know you're out there! Speak up, damnit, I'm losing patience.

ROSE Who's that? Is that your father? Who's your father talking to?

DAVID You mustn't worry, Mother. It's not another woman.

JOE *(Calling out)* All right, you want to freeze! Freeze! *(He comes back in, and closes the door)* Let 'em freeze!

ROSE Who's out there, Joe?

JOE *(To* BEN*)* Can she hear me? *(*BEN *nods)* No one. No one's out there!

ROSE You're keeping something from me, all of you. I demand to know what it is. I'm the woman of this house. David, Ben, Sarah, I'm your mother. Joe, I'm your wife.

DAVID We all know who you are, Mother.

JOE Rose, please. There's no point in upsetting you.

ROSE *(She sits)* I will not get upset. Why does everyone think I always get upset? I'm perfectly capable of handling a situation as long as I know what it is . . . *Now what is it?*

JOE Someone was trying to break into the house.

(Her head drops as if in a faint—but she never loses her grip on the jewel box) Rose, Rose!

DAVID *(To the others)* You see? Why were you so worried about telling her?

JOE *(Rushes to her, slaps her wrist)* Rose, are you all right?

ROSE *(Screams)* *Agghh! My jewels!*

JOE It's me, Rose. Joe—the one who bought the jewels! It's all right.

ROSE In my house. A burglar in my house.

JOE *(Yells)* Okay, that's enough! *That's enough, everybody!* Do you hear me? One little alarm goes off and everybody goes crazy. There is nothing wrong here.

We're locked in, we're safe, we're well protected, and I don't want to hear any more about it, you understand? I'm your father and that's final.

DAVID We all know who you are, Dad.

JOE *(Points an angry, angry finger)* *You,* I'll talk to later . . . Everybody else, up to bed. I'll turn the lights out.

ROSE *No!* That's what he's waiting for.

JOE Then I'll leave them *on.*

ROSE So he can see better? Are you crazy?

JOE You want me to call the police?

ROSE *Not* the police—they steal more than the crooks.

JOE Then what do you want, Rose? *What do you want?*

ROSE I want to know that we'll be safe in our beds tonight and that some lunatic isn't going to break into the house and cut our throats and steal my jewels, that's what I want.

SARAH And the "other thing." We don't want the "other thing" either, Daddy.

DAVID Why don't we call him in and see if we can negotiate a deal?

JOE Are you finished? All of you? Because I want to say something . . . No one is getting into this house tonight. No one is going to cut our throats, steal our jewels or do the "other thing." I guarantee it . . . but I can't promise it! Because whatever happens, happens. How we live and how we die is in the hands of our maker. We go to sleep and pray we get up in the morning. But if we don't, it's because it's God's will . . . *God's will,* do you understand? *Do you?*

ROSE Yes, Joe.

BEN and SARAH Yes, Daddy.

JOE Then say it!

ROSE, BEN and SARAH We understand! It's God's will!

JOE Thank you! I hope you all feel better . . . Now, let's go to bed.

DAVID And pray it ain't "God's will" tonight!

JOE *(To* DAVID*)* *You* stay! I've postponed that talk we're going to have later to *right now!* Everyone else upstairs.

SARAH Yes, Daddy . . . Good night, Daddy.

(She kisses him and goes out)

BEN Good night, Dad. And don't worry about anything. I just want you to know that you can count on me.

(He goes out)

JOE *(Turns to* DAVID*)* You hear? *That's* a son.

DAVID We all know who he is, Dad.

BEN *(Calls from the hall)* Come, Mother.

ROSE *(To* JOE*)* Don't stay down too long, Joe. Come to bed as soon as you're through yelling at David. *(To* DAVID*)* Good night, darling. Don't aggravate your father too late.

(She leaves. JOE *turns and looks at* DAVID*)*

JOE You want a drink? . . . Go ahead!

DAVID I beg your pardon.

JOE I said, "Have a drink." This is a special occasion . . . You and I are going to communicate with each other for the first time in our lives.

DAVID *(Goes to the bar, picks up a decanter, then puts it down without pouring it)* I can't do it.

JOE Why not?

DAVID It's only fun when you don't like it.

JOE Ohhh, David! David David David David David David David David David David David David David David David David!

DAVID Are you talking to me, Dad?

JOE Yes . . . but *who* are you? Who *are* you, David? Do you know? Because I don't. I don't know who you are. Do *you* know who you are, David?

DAVID Just casually. I've seen me around the house.

JOE *That's* who you are . . . Quick with a flippant answer. Fresh, disrespectful, unambitious, lazy, no interests, no principles, no beliefs, no scruples, a drunkard, a gambler, a playboy, a lover, a bum, a television watcher and a lousy guitar player, that's who you are.

DAVID *(Smiles)* Ah, gee, Dad . . . you remembered!

JOE Last week I tried to make a list of all the things you do that make me proud . . . I didn't even take the top off the fountain pen. In high school, remember the Father and Son Picnic? I went alone. And what makes it so painful to me is that you're the smartest one in the family. You're the smartest one in *anybody's* family. Three college degrees, finished first in your class, and you didn't even show up for your senior year. So why do you throw it all away, David? Why do you drink so much?

DAVID To overcome this terrible condition I have.

JOE *(Concerned)* What condition?

DAVID Soberness! I get it a lot in the mornings. It's terrible—the room stands still, I can see everything clearly, I get single vision. And then I see the most frightening things in this house . . . Money, money, money, money, money, money, money, money . . .

(This breaks DAVID *up)*

JOE Then why do you stay? Why don't you pack your bottles and leave this house?

DAVID I have tried on six separate occasions. But it's such a Goddamn long driveway, I never could make it to the gate . . . Sorry about the God reference.

JOE So you resent all this, is that it? You resent this house, my business, your mother's jewelry, our paintings, the furniture, the swimming pools, is that what you resent?

DAVID Don't forget our own Baskin-Robbins in the playhouse.

JOE Your sister likes ice cream—is that a crime? Is it a crime to be rich? Is it a sin to want only the best for your family?

DAVID I think a man is entitled to whatever he earns in this life. I do, however, think ninety-seven flavors is unnecessary.

JOE This house could go up in smoke tomorrow, I wouldn't blink an eye. I'll tell you something . . . There was a time in my life when the holes in my socks were so big, you could put them on from either end . . . I grew up in a tenement in New York. My mother, my father and eleven kids in one and a half rooms. We had two beds and a cot, you had to take a number off the wall to go to sleep . . . My father was five foot three, weighed a hundred and twenty-seven pounds. He had a bad heart, bad lungs, bad liver and bad kidneys. He was a piano mover. He died at the age of thirty-two from an acute attack of everything . . . My mother had to take a job in a sweatshop working six days a week, fourteen hours a day. At night she washed floors at Madison Square Garden, and on Sundays she sold hot sweet potatoes on the corner of Fourteenth Street and Broadway. What she didn't sell was dinner for the rest of the week. Sweet potatoes every night. On Thanksgiving she'd stuff the sweet potato with a little white potato . . . The clothes we wore were made out of rags she found in the street, or a pair of curtains somebody threw away . . . You know what it is for a young boy growing up in a tough neighborhood in East New York to wear *curtains?* Can you picture that? *Fairies* used to beat me up . . . And through all those freezing winters and hot, hungry summers, through all the years of scrimping and scrubbing, through sicknesses without doctors or medicines—one winter we all had the whooping cough at the same time, eleven kids throwing up simultaneously in one and a half rooms—my mother nursed us on roller skates . . . through all that pain and heartache and suffering, she never complained or cried out against the world, because she knew it was God's will. That was the lesson my mother taught us. "What God has given, God can take away. And for what God has given you, be thankful" . . . When I was fourteen years old I went to work for the Schreiber Corrugated Box Company. A rotten man who made a rotten box. No matter how you packed it, the minute you shipped it, it fell apart. It didn't hold up under any kind of weather—including sunshine. Because Schreiber was interested in a quick profit, not workmanship, not quality. When I bought the business from him in 1942 with six thousand dollars my mother saved, I started to make quality boxes, strong as steel. In the first three months I lost my mother's six thousand dollars. "It's God's will," she kept telling me. And then suddenly business began to pick up. From nowhere, from *everywhere*, people were buying my corrugated boxes. It was like a miracle. The money kept pouring in. I couldn't find banks fast enough to keep it . . . My mother never lived to enjoy my success . . . On the day I made my first million dollars, she died peacefully in her sleep on the BMT subway. Her last words to the conductor were "If God wanted me to live, I would have taken the bus today" . . . All I wanted for my wife and children was not to suffer the way I did as a child, not to be deprived of life's barest necessities. But such riches, such wealth? I never asked for it, I never needed it. But when I ask myself, "Why so much? Why all this?" I hear the voice of my mother say, "It's God's will" . . . I give half of what I have every year to charity, and the next year I make twice as much. Wealth is as much a responsibility as poverty is a burden. I'll accept whatever is given to me and ask for no more or no less . . . Can you understand this,

David? Does anything I've said to you tonight make any sense at all? *(*DAVID *snores)* He's sleeping! Why do you torture me? Why do you twist my heart around like a pretzel? Where is your faith, David? Have I brought you up without faith, or have you just lost it?

DAVID If you want, I'll look in my closet in the morning . . .

JOE I would give away everything I have in this world if I could just hear you say, "Dear God in heaven, I believe in you."

DAVID Listen, I'm willing to discuss it with the man . . . You know his number, call him.

*(*DAVID *gets a whiskey bottle, and heads back to the door)*

JOE Oh, David, David. The son who doesn't believe is the father's greatest anguish. Do you know what it says in the Bible, David?

DAVID Yes, Dad . . . "This book belongs to the Sheraton-Plaza Hotel." Good night, Dad.

(He goes out. JOE *stands there, forlorn and defeated. He sighs a mournful sigh. Then he moves to the switch and turns off the lights. The room is in darkness except for the moonlight shining in through the French door. He looks up and speaks softly and reverently)*

JOE Am I wrong? . . . Is all of this too much for one family? If it is, then why did You give it to me? It's enough already, dear Lord. Don't give me any more . . . Just David. Give me back my David . . . If it be Your Will, dear God, that's all I ask . . . Amen!

(A voice, from somewhere in the room itself, is heard)

VOICE Amen!

*(*JOE *stops in his tracks, then wheels around)*

JOE *(Shocked)* *What?* Who's there? Who said that?

VOICE Don't worry. It's not who you're thinking.

JOE Who is it? I can't see you.

VOICE I can't see you either. I lost my glasses. Are the lights on or off?

JOE You! The one who tried to break in! It's *you*, isn't it?

VOICE Certainly it's me. Are we inside or outside? I can't see a damn thing.

JOE Stay where you are! Don't move. I could have the police here in two minutes.

VOICE You're lucky. In my neighborhood you could wait for them all night . . . Would you please turn the lights on? I get very nervous in the dark.

JOE Don't you try anything funny.

VOICE I'm not here to get laughs.

(Suddenly the lights blaze on. JOE *is standing with his hand on the switch. He wheels around to face the night visitor)*

JOE All right, now who do you— *(But there is no one there)* Where are you? . . . WHERE ARE YOU?

(He turns around quickly . . . Silence. From behind the huge sofa, SIDNEY LIPTON *appears on all fours, crawling and feeling the rug with his hands)*

LIPTON Don't get excited, I'm just looking for my glasses. *(He continues to search. He is not a very impressive-looking person. He wears khaki slacks, a thin raincoat, white sweat socks, Hush Puppies, a tweed cap—a potpourri of cheap clothes)* You think the light helps? I still can't see. Where am I, on the floor?

JOE What do you mean by breaking into my house? Who are you?

LIPTON *(Still feeling around on the floor)* Oh, gorgeous rug. This is all handwoven. Must have cost a fortune. What is it, Persian?

JOE Never mind the rug, I asked you a question. Who are you?

LIPTON *(Still on his knees)* The name is Lipton. Sidney Lipton. By the way, were there any calls for me?

JOE Your wife called.

LIPTON Sylvia?

JOE *What do I know your wife's name?*

LIPTON *(Nods)* Sylvia. She checks on me every minute. Dreadful woman. If she calls again, I'm not here, all right? . . . Where am I, still on the floor?

JOE *(Takes the glasses out of his pocket)* Here. Here's your glasses.

LIPTON You found them? *(Puts out his hand)* Oh, good. Could you put them in my hand, please?

JOE Here.

*(*JOE *puts the glasses into* LIPTON*'s hand)*

LIPTON Is that my hand?

JOE *Certainly* it's your hand.

LIPTON That'll give you an idea how bad my eyes are. *(He puts the glasses on, still on his knees)* Ohh. Ohh, yes, there we are . . . *(Looks up)* Oh, we're inside, aren't we? *(He looks around)* Ohhh! *This—this* is gorgeous! *This* is what I call a gorgeous room. This is one of your better showplaces. What is this, the living room?

JOE Certainly it's the living room . . . What does it look like?

LIPTON Do I know? Was I ever invited before? *(Looks around)* You know what this place reminds me of? Gatsby . . . Did you see *The Great Gatsby?* Wasn't that gorgeous to look at? *Lousy* picture, but beautiful sets—

JOE Is that why you broke in here? To discuss *movies* with me?

LIPTON Certainly not. I'm here on business. *Very* important business.

JOE *What* business?

LIPTON I'll get to it. Be patient. Let me look around. *(Admiringly caresses the carved façade of the fireplace)*

How often does a person like me get inside one of these big-time houses? . . . Do you have something soft to drink? R.C. Cola? A Yoo-hoo?

JOE If you have business with me, you make an appointment like everyone else.

LIPTON *(Looking around)* My business is not the kind of business you think, and I'm not like everyone else. *(Points to an ornate armchair)* I love the chair. I don't fall in love easily, but I am in love with this chair. Just for curiosity, what did you pay? Three thousand? Thirty-four hundred? Am I being pushy?

JOE I don't remember what I paid for chairs. Is that what you are? An antique dealer?

LIPTON Antiques? No. Antiquity, perhaps.

JOE What does that mean?

LIPTON What does *anything* mean?

JOE What do you mean by "What does *anything* mean"?

LIPTON What is meant by meaning? What is the meaning of "meant"? What is real or unreal? What is here, what is there? What the hell are we talking about? I don't know—I'm still dizzy from that fall I took.

JOE I can't make you out. You're not a burglar, that I can tell.

LIPTON A burglar? No. An antique dealer? No. But who am I? What am I? Why am I here? That's the mystery, isn't it? God, I love a good mystery. Did you see *Chinatown?* Jack Nicholson, Faye Dunaway? They cut his nose, he wore a bandaid for two hours. Three-fifty a ticket to see a man with a slit nose, where do they get the nerve? A nice picture, but I can see slit noses for free at Mount Sinai—

JOE If you don't tell me who you are, it's not your *nose* that's going to get slit.

LIPTON Ah, ah, you're losing patience, aren't you? Mustn't lose patience. All in good time. Patience, Joe, patience. *(Looks at a crystal vase)* Lovely crystal. Who picked it out, your wife, Rose?

JOE How do you know my wife, Rose?

LIPTON Did I say I knew her?

JOE But you mentioned her name.

LIPTON To mention her name is not to say I know her. Ergo, to know is to meet . . . Ergo, to be is not necessarily to exist . . . Ergo, to know is to question, to question is to ask . . . Ergo, what is meant by knowing and what is meant by "ergo"? . . . Oh, God, I have such pains in the head. I could use an aspirin, Valium, acupuncture, anything.

JOE You're not getting anything from me until I get some information from *you!*

LIPTON Interesting. You're not as tall as I expected. They led me to believe you were a bigger man—six four, six five. Not that it matters . . . You know how tall Alan Ladd was?

JOE I'M NOT INTERESTED IN ALAN LADD!

LIPTON Two inches shorter than Veronica Lake. They never made a movie where they had a child . . . They couldn't find one small enough. I *love* movie gossip . . .

JOE Who's been talking to you? What do you know about me?

LIPTON I know a lot and I know nothing! Yet to know nothing is to know everything . . . Why do I say things like that? What does that mean? I have cramps in the head. Did you ever get cramps in the head?

JOE A lunatic! A lunatic wandered into my house from the snow. Why do I answer you? Why do I bother talking to you?

LIPTON Curiosity! There is something curious about

me, you've got to admit . . . All right, enough chitchat, enough fiddle-faddle, enough fencing with each other. Let's get down to brass tacks, Joe Benjamin. Let's discuss the reason of the mysterious midnight visit of this most curious and somewhat sinister figure standing in front of you. Why, at this hour, on this night, in this year, in this city, in this house, on this rug, in these shoes, do I, Sidney Leonard Lipton stand before you? WHAT BUSINESS DO WE, STRANGERS TILL NOT FIVE MINUTES AGO, HAVE UNTO EACH OTHER?

JOE Are you selling something? If you're a salesman, I'll kill you with my bare hands!

LIPTON Do I look like a salesman? Do I look like a man who deals in goods and hardware? I am a man of flair, of fancy, a bizarre and unique guide to the world beyond our world, a companion into wild and soaring flights beyond human comprehension.

JOE A travel agent? Is that what you are, a travel agent?

LIPTON *(Yells, angrily)* *You have no imagination!* I am trying to jazz this up. I have a wonderful sense of the theatrical, and you keep pulling my curtain down. What do I have to do to tell you who I am? Think, Joe, think!

JOE I think you're a *nut*, that's what I think, and I want you out! *(He grabs* LIPTON *by the arm)* Out, do you hear me? OUT!

LIPTON Easy, easy. No rough stuff, I'm not a physical person.

JOE Ten seconds and I throw you out that window head-first. One, two—

LIPTON Don't force my hand. I deal a heavy hand—

JOE Three, four—

LIPTON *(Stops; points a long finger)* *STAY! I STAY YOU!* Yea, you would banish He who brings thee the gift of life and the eternal bliss of the joyful soul? . . . Forget that! Forget I said that. That was a slip. A boo-boo. Slipsies! I have a charley horse in the middle of my temple. Does Bengué work on the head?

JOE I'm getting a funny feeling. There's something funny going on here. You're not who you pretend to be at all, are you?

LIPTON Aha! Aha, getting somewhere. Getting warm . . .

JOE This is all an act. A game. Something is up, here . . . Somebody sent you, didn't they?

LIPTON Hot! Getting hot!

JOE Somebody sent you to get something from me!

LIPTON Hotter! Hotter! Boiling hotter!

JOE Somebody important who knows me sent you to get something that I have that has enormous value.

LIPTON Boiling! Roasting, burning, boiling! August fifteenth through the twentieth—scorching.

JOE Something I have that no other man on earth has.

LIPTON *Scalding! Steaming lava!* Two weeks in a sauna bath!

JOE My Bible! My Gutenberg Bible!

LIPTON Cold. Freezing cold. Winter. A room for two in Toronto.

JOE Damn you, what is it?

(He bangs his fist on the table)

LIPTON Hey! Hey hey hey! Calm! Calm, please. Take it easy. Let's not break our blood vessels. Let's behave ourselves. The last thing I want is for you to get sick. I mean, you *are* in good health, aren't you?

JOE *(Knocks wood)* Thank God!

LIPTON *Hot! Boiling hot! Getting hot again!*

JOE What? Good health?

LIPTON Cold.

JOE Knocking on wood?

LIPTON Cold, cold . . .

JOE Thank God?

LIPTON HOT! HOT AS A PISTOL! THE FOURTH OF JULY! AN ALL-TIME RECORD BREAKER!

JOE *(Screams)* What are you saying? You're driving me crazy with these stupid games.

LIPTON Temper, temper. What a nervous disposition. And I was told you were such a patient, wonderful man.

JOE Who told you? Who told you I was a wonderful man?

LIPTON *(Softly; side of his mouth)* You know.

JOE I *don't* know.

LIPTON *(Softly again)* Sure, you do, Joe . . . *He* did.

JOE Who's he?

LIPTON He! Him! Capital "H," small "i" small "m" . . . Do I have to spell it out for you? Oh, I just did, didn't I? Went on and on about you. Crazy about you. I'll tell you the truth, you're His favorite. Out of everyone. I don't mean just this neighborhood, I mean EVERYONE! Yes, you, Joe Benjamin, are considered to be His—that's capital "H" again—His absolute favorite. And that is the honest to God's truth . . . God's truth . . . *(He makes a cross on his chest, then a circle, a square, all sorts of signs—then unbuttons his raincoat, revealing a football jersey with an enormous letter "G" on the front)* Am I getting through to you at all?

JOE I can't understand what you're saying.

LIPTON *Can't* understand or *afraid* to understand?

JOE Afraid? I'm not afraid of anything on the face of this earth except God himself.

LIPTON BINGO! BULL'S-EYE! Ding-a-ling-a-ling-a-ling! Fire, fire, fire! Home run, home run!

(He jumps around in an excited jig)

JOE STOP IT! I beg of you to stop it and tell me who you are, in plain, simple language. I'm a plain, simple man, I can't understand all this fancy hocus-pocus rigamarole. Who are you, please?

(LIPTON stands erect, clasps his fingers together)

LIPTON *(Solemnly)* Very well. Forgive me, my son. I have taken these extraordinary measures, this bizarre form, so that I might present myself to you in some acceptable dimension, for had I told you the truth straight on of my identity, even *I* could not have given you the power to accept or comprehend. Yes, Joe—I am—who you think I am!

JOE *(Sits on the sofa)* Are you trying to tell me that you're—that you're—are you trying to tell me—

LIPTON Say it, Joe. You will only believe if you say the words yourself.

JOE —that you—are you trying to say that you—?

LIPTON Yes, yes . . . I can't answer unless you ask me, Joe.

JOE I can't get the words out. It's so *inconceivable* to me.

LIPTON Conceive it, Joe. Get the words out. *Who,* Joe? Who am I trying to tell you who I am?

JOE *God?* Are you trying to tell me that you're *God?*

LIPTON Who? . . . God? GOD? Is *that* what you thought? That I was going to say I was God? My God, that I never figured on. Nothing personal, but that's really crazy. Why? Do I look like God? Would God wear a filthy Robert Hall raincoat and a pair of leaky Hush Puppies? In the winter? Would God wear glasses? I mean, if anyone's going to have good eyes, it's going to be God. He's the one who gave them out . . . No, Joe, I'm sorry to disappoint you, but I am not God.

(He sits on the sofa)

JOE Then who are you?

LIPTON I'm a friend of God's.

JOE *(His body sags)* I can't take any more of this.

LIPTON Not a *close* friend. We met a few times.

JOE You met God?

LIPTON Twice on business, once on a boat ride.

JOE What business? *What business do you have with God?*

LIPTON My capacity is such that I perform services for Him that deal with vital and important functions in areas related to the contact of individuals whose special interests—

JOE *What business?*

LIPTON *I deliver messages!*

JOE You're a messenger boy?

LIPTON *(Hurt, indignant)* Don't say it like that. I'm not a lousy kid from Western Union, I work for God!

JOE You're a messenger from God?

LIPTON Important documents only; no packages.

JOE I don't believe you.

LIPTON Nobody does. Not even Sylvia. She laughs when I tell her . . . What am I going to do, bring my boss home for dinner?

JOE You're either drunk, a madman or both.

LIPTON Don't start in, please, I have a headache that goes right into my hat. Even my eyeglasses throb. Didn't I tell you you wouldn't believe me? Look,

Mr. Benjamin, I understand you're a wonderful man. Charitable, philanthropic, religious. Am I right?

JOE I serve God as best I can.

LIPTON So if He can have servants, why can't He afford messengers? He's got cleaning people, I've seen them.

JOE All right, if you're who you say you are—

LIPTON I am.

JOE Let me finish!

LIPTON When you finish, I am!

JOE *If you're who you say you are*—a messenger of God—then where do you come from?

LIPTON Oh, you mean like heaven? The Eternal Paradise? Where the angels abide? A place like that?

JOE Yes.

LIPTON Jackson Heights. It's in Queens, just over the Triborough Bridge. Look, I'm not *Here Comes Mr. Jordan.* I'm a nine-to-fiver. This is strictly a job with me. I was sent by an agency, I was interviewed, I had to have a bicycle—it was stolen from me in Central Park. I told them we should work in pairs.

JOE But you said you met God.

LIPTON Not face-to-face. There's always a big light over Him—the glare is murder.

JOE But you've been in His presence.

LIPTON We're *all* in His presence.

JOE But *have you seen Him?* Actually seen him with your own eyes?

LIPTON Without my glasses, I wouldn't recognize my own wife.

JOE *With* your glasses.

LIPTON *With* my glasses? Yes, I'd recognize her.

JOE GOD! GOD! HAVE YOU SEEN GOD?

LIPTON I didn't actually *see* Him. I heard Him.

JOE He spoke to you?

LIPTON He blessed me.

JOE God blessed you?

LIPTON I sneezed and God blessed me—what do you want from me?

JOE This isn't a practical joke, is it? Did David hire you? My son David put you up to this, didn't he? I wouldn't put it past him.

LIPTON I have not had the pleasure of meeting the boy, but personally he sounds like a lot of trouble . . . Can we get on with this, please? I have a migraine starting in my hair.

JOE Get on with *what?* With this *insanity?*

LIPTON *(Loudly)* I cannot deliver God's message until you accept that I am God's messenger! What do I need to prove it to you, *wings?* . . . I should have flapped in here like a Perdue chicken, then you would have believed me, wouldn't you?

JOE Tell me *why?* Then maybe I'll believe you. *Why* would God send a message to me, Joe Benjamin, a plain, simple, ordinary man?

LIPTON *To test your faith, that's why!* . . . Strike that! I didn't say that! You didn't hear it! Erase! Eighty-six on the first sentence! I'm not supposed to tell you that . . . Do you have any uppers? Ask David, I bet he's got pills.

JOE Test my faith? *My* faith? My lifeblood is my faith! Are you saying that God doesn't believe my faith in Him?

LIPTON Oh, no. Not·Him. *He* believes! God's crazy about you . . . It's the other one.

JOE What other one?

LIPTON *(Softly, slyly)* You know . . . the *other* one. From downstairs . . . Mr. Nasty . . . Bad, Bad Leroy Brown . . . Oh, for God's sakes, you have to spell out *everything* for you . . . Satan! Lucifer! The *Devil*, all right? . . . I can't believe this conversation. I feel like I'm on Sesame Street.

JOE *(Smiles)* The *Devil?* The *Devil* questions my faith in God? *(He laughs)* Are you going to tell me now you met the Devil?

LIPTON Who do you think stole my bicycle? . . . Would you like to know what the Devil looks like? Robert Redford, I swear on my mother's grave. Gorgeous. The man is gorgeous. Blond hair, little bend in the nose—

JOE *(Moving toward the phone)* I've wasted enough time with you, I'm calling the police!

LIPTON *(Points a long arm and finger again) Stay! I stay you! I render you powerless and motionless!* (JOE *picks up the phone and dials)* All right, I can't do it, but put down the phone, please. I'll tell you everything. (JOE *looks at him; puts down the receiver)* I'll tell you what I know, take it or leave it . . . God and Satan were sitting around having one of those boring philosophical debates—this was a week ago Tuesday. And Satan was sitting there in this pink suit—gorgeous tan, little mole on his cheek . . . And Satan says there is not one man on the face of the earth, in the entire universe—regardless of race, religion, Polish, whatever—who would not renounce God once the Devil put enough heat on. Can you believe it? Two grown deities talking like this? To which *God* said—this is a quote, they got it on tape—*one* man would never renounce. And that man is . . . *(Makes a bugle sound)* Ta tum ta tum ta tum ta tum ta taaa . . . JOE BENJAMIN! Thrills, right? . . . So they make a bet—I'm only telling you what I heard—and the bet is, the Devil will make your life so miserable, you'll renounce God! So-o-o, that's it. Hell of a story, isn't it?

JOE Renounce God? You think I would renounce God?

LIPTON Tonight, no. When they shut off your steam, who knows?

JOE You think so little of man that he would renounce *God* in the face of adversity?

LIPTON I've seen people with a burning engine on a 747 who would sell out God in a second for a little good news from the pilot . . . So you believe me—good. I can deliver my message and run. *(Takes out a folded, dirty scrap of paper)* You ready?

JOE Let me see that.

LIPTON *(Pulls it away)* I have to read it. It's not official unless I read it . . . *(He takes a pillow from the sofa, throws it on the floor, and indicates that* JOE *should kneel on it.* JOE *looks around hesitantly.* LIPTON *nods that it's all right.* JOE *reluctantly gets on his knees, feeling foolish and embarrassed)* Here we go. "Joseph Marvin Benjamin . . ."

JOE Melvin.

LIPTON What?

JOE Joseph *Melvin* Benjamin.

LIPTON *(Squints at the paper)* Melvin—right. Would you believe God has such a lousy handwriting? . . . "Joseph Melvin Benjamin of 118 Park Place Drive, Oyster Bay, Long Island, zip 11771—"

JOE Come on, come on, get on with it.

LIPTON "Husband of Rose, father of David, Ben and Sarah, son of Arnold and Jeanette—"

JOE Get to the *message* already!

LIPTON "To Joseph Melvin Benjamin, devoted husband and father . . . if you cherish your children and wife, the house that shelters you, the clothes that warm you and the flesh that covers you, if pain, calamity and disaster do not in any manner whatsoever appeal to you, then renounce your God!" That's it! Message delivered. No tip necessary, it's taken care of. Good night, good luck, God bless you . . . but I doubt it!

(He puts the message back in his pocket and starts for the French door)

JOE Wait a minute! Where are you going?

LIPTON If I had a choice, Fort Lauderdale . . . Unfortunately, the bus stop!

(He turns and starts out again)

JOE It doesn't make sense. Why? Why should I, a man who has believed in God all his life, suddenly renounce Him?

LIPTON I take home a hundred-thirty-seven dollars a week. If you want theological advice call Billy Graham. Can I get the number fifteen bus on this corner?

JOE I will *not* renounce God. I will *never* renounce God, do you hear me?

LIPTON Renounce, don't renounce, what do I care? . . . I have to walk out in the freezing snow wearing Supphose.

JOE I am the servant of God, He is my Maker. I fear Him and love Him but come hell or high water, I will never renounce Him!

LIPTON Can I be honest? You can count on the hell and high water. Good luck, Joe. I know you've got what it takes. And no matter what terrible things happen to you, remember that God loves you!

JOE And I love Him!

LIPTON But in case the romance falls apart, here's my number. Renouncements are toll-free calls.

(We hear a fire engine clanging in the distance)

JOE What's that?

LIPTON I don't know.

JOE What's going on out there?

LIPTON *(Looks out the window)* Looks like a fire. Near the water . . . Where's your factory?

JOE Near the water.

LIPTON Ohh . . . Look at that burn. Like a cardboard box . . . What do you make?

JOE Cardboard boxes.

LIPTON Ohh . . . Well, I wouldn't worry unless I got a phone call.

(The phone rings. They both look at it)

JOE It's not my plant. My plant is a hundred percent fireproof.

*(*JOE *picks up the phone)*

JOE Hello? . . . Eddie? . . . What is it? . . . What? . . . *What?*

LIPTON One more "what" and you're in trouble.

JOE *(Into the phone)* WHAT?

LIPTON What is it, a disaster or a calamity?

JOE *(Into the phone)* The *whole plant?*

LIPTON Oh, a catastrophe, wonderful!

JOE Thank you, Eddie . . . I know it wasn't your fault.

(He hangs up)

LIPTON How much did the insurance cover?

JOE *(Dazed)* I didn't have insurance. I didn't believe in insurance . . . GOD was my insurance.

LIPTON Really? Well, that was your mistake. Even God is with John Hancock . . . So long, Joe.

(And he is gone)

Curtain

SCENE 2

The scene is the Benjamin living room, two weeks later, at dinner time. It is dark outside. Some of the furniture has been removed, and some of the paintings. A fruit box replaces a chair. We can hear the bitter cold winter wind howling through the trees. The house seems bleak.

The telephone rings . . . And again. The oak door leading from the dining room opens, and MORRIS *enters. He is wearing his white serving jacket and black tie, but on top of this he has on his heavy winter overcoat, gloves, a muffler and earmuffs. It is obviously freezing in the house. He carries a silver tray from which he has just served food.*

As he crosses to the phone, the family shouts in from the dining room, "Morris, close the door," "It's freezing," etc. A hand from inside slams the dining room door shut. The phone continues to ring. MORRIS *answers it.*

MORRIS Hello. Benjamin residence . . . Who's calling, please? . . . Mr. Benjamin's having a cold dinner with his family just now . . . Yes, sir . . . One moment, sir.

(He puts the receiver down and crosses toward the dining room, blowing on his hands, doing a little dance to keep warm. He opens the door and calls in)
Mr. Benjamin?

JOE Yes?

MORRIS It's a Mr. Lipton.

JOE *(Offstage)* Who?

MORRIS Mr. Sidney Lipton. He wants to know if you'd like it a little colder in the house. Then he giggled.

JOE *(Offstage)* Wait a minute, I'm coming. *(*JOE *comes out of the dining room. He wears a full-length man's fur* *coat, a beaver hat and gloves. He leaves the door open, and they all yell in from the dining room, "Close the door," "It's freezing," etc.)*

JOE Morris, close the door. And sit on my chair—keep it warm.

MORRIS Yes, sir.

(He goes into the dining room and closes the door. JOE *picks up the phone)*

JOE *(Into the phone)* What do you want? . . . I told you last night and the night before and I'll tell you every night you call me, I'm not renouncing anything, you understand? I don't care how cold it gets in here. I'll burn all the furniture before I say yes to you . . . And don't bother calling me any more . . . because they're cutting off my phone tomorrow.

(He bangs up the phone angrily. The dining room door opens again, and ROSE *and* SARAH *come out.* SARAH *wears a ski suit;* ROSE *has on a fur coat, boots and a mink hat)*

ROSE My hands are frozen, Joe. Morris had to cut the meat for me.

SARAH *(Holds her teeth)* My teeth are numb.

*(*BEN *enters wearing a ski suit just like* SARAH*'s)*

BEN Oh, my sinuses. My sinuses, Mother. They're frozen solid.

*(*DAVID *enters wearing a wool jacket and motorcycle helmet)*

DAVID Attention, everybody! I have good news and bad news.

SARAH *(Hopefully)* What's the good news?

DAVID The heat is back on.

BEN What's the bad news?

DAVID I lied.

BEN I hate him! I hate him, Mother!

(The lights dim, then blink up again)

ROSE What's going on? Why is everything suddenly

falling apart? No water, no heat, the electricity is almost gone. What's happening to us?

DAVID *(A big smile)* It's just like living in the city.

(They all chime in with questions—"Yeah, what's going on?," etc.)

JOE Can I have a little decorum? A little decorum, everybody. Please! Mady! Morris! *(*MADY *and* MORRIS *enter, shivering)* Will you all sit down, please? What I have to say to you all now is of grave importance . . . You may have heard it said before, to love God is not to question God. We must accept God as we accept the air and the sky, the earth and the sun.

ROSE Will this take long, Joe? My eyelashes are caking up from the frost.

JOE None of us are very comfortable, Rose. None of us like living under these conditions. We've had it very good for a long time. We're just going to have to learn to live more economically, tighten our belts—

MADY I can't cut the meat thinner unless you want me to shave it.

JOE I understand, Mady . . . There is, however, one thing I haven't had the courage to tell you until tonight . . . My dear children, devoted wife, faithful servants . . . Have any of you stopped to think why, after a lifetime of luxury and prosperity, we're suddenly living in a house that's twelve degrees colder than it is outside? Have you wondered why plumbers, electricians, supermarkets have all turned their backs on us? Why a butcher that I have personally kept in business for fifteen years, by buying the finest beef in the world, sends over meat that three of our cats walked away from? The answer is . . . These things are happening because they are *meant* to happen. The truth is . . . I am being tested! Tested for my courage and strength.

(There is a moment's silence as they all look at him, puzzled)

ROSE Is this for an insurance policy, Joe?

JOE *(Looks heavenward)* How do I explain this? Look . . . I'm fifty-six years old. And in all that time, besides my love for all of you, I've believed in only one thing . . . The Divine Wisdom and Glory of God.

MADY Aaaaa-men! Right on!

JOE Thank you, Mady. Now, God, in His infinite wisdom, has seen fit to give us all the fruits of this earth . . . But now, still in His infinite wisdom, He has seen fit to take it away from us . . . Two weeks ago, I had an experience . . . with a man . . .

ROSE Oh, God! Do you want the children to hear this, Joe?

JOE *(Irritated)* Let me finish! . . . Don't ask me who he was or where he came from. Just accept what I tell you . . . It is my belief, that I have been chosen, for reasons unknown to me, out of all the people on the face of the earth—regardless of race, religion, Polish whatever—to test the faith and courage of man in his love and devotion to God.

(There is a long silence. They all look at each other)

ROSE Is this something that came in the mail, Joe?

JOE It didn't come in the mail.

BEN What do you mean a test, Dad? You have to cut out meats and fish, is that what you mean?

JOE Why doesn't anybody listen to me? Don't you understand? God is asking me to make the supreme personal sacrifice.

ROSE Wait a minute, Joe . . . Does that mean we have to take two of those Jehovah's Witnesses from Ohio in to live with us?

JOE You know what I think? I think *this family* is part of my test. And I'm not so sure I can pass. *(To* DAVID*)* I never thought I would be turning to you for help. You're a bum, but you're smart. Do *you* understand me?

DAVID Yes, Dad. I think so.

JOE Thank you. Will *you* please explain it to them?

DAVID I'm not certain about this, but I think Dad's going into a convent.

(BEN *and* SARAH *giggle,* DAVID *is hysterical)*

JOE *(Glares at him)* You know what I pray for? I pray I had my money back again so I could cut you off without a cent. *(He paces; angrily)* All right, listen to me, everybody. I will try and make this as simple as possible. Two weeks ago a man broke into this house. The one whose glasses we found. His name was Sidney Lipton—a weirdo. A nut, lunatic weirdo. He wore Hush Puppies and talked about Alan Ladd, *Chinatown* with Jack Nicholson and Veronica Lake—

ROSE Veronica Lake wasn't in *Chinatown.*

JOE *(He bites his hat)* Don't analyze it, Rose. Just listen . . . Lipton was not who he pretended to be. He played the fool because he knew I would never accept his real identity until he proved it to me . . . Well, he proved it, all right. Oh, brother, did he prove it.

BEN Are you going to tell us, Dad?

JOE Very well . . . Sidney Lipton, the man who appeared before me, was a messenger—of God!

(A long silence)

ROSE *(To* MADY*) Who* did he say?

JOE For *God! God!* He delivers messages for *God!*

SARAH For *God,* Daddy?

ROSE *Our* God, Joe?

JOE Yes! YES!

ROSE Joe, don't get upset . . . We all know what a strain you're under, getting wiped out and all . . . Think, sweetheart, are you sure he wasn't from UNICEF?

JOE HE-WAS-FROM-GOD! God sent him to talk to me.

ROSE What was it like, Joe? Did you hear organ music? Could you see through him?

JOE He's not what you think. He's a regular person. Like you or me. It's just a job. They hired him. He lives in Jackson Heights. He takes home a hundred and thirty-seven dollars a week. They stole his bicycle. He wants to move to Fort Lauderdale.

ROSE He won't like it there. It's all little condominiums now.

(JOE bangs the floor with his fist in frustration. The family goes into a huddle, then they turn, all smiles)

BEN Dad, you never lied to us in your life. If you saw him, then I believe you. We all do.

JOE Thank you. Thank you, all of you.

DAVID May I ask one question?

MADY Uh-oh.

DAVID Am I to understand that some fruitcake from Queens walks in here and tells you he's a messenger from God?

JOE Important documents only. No packages.

DAVID I see . . . And what was he like. How did he strike you as a person?

JOE He got cramps in his head.

DAVID Figures . . . And how did you know he was a messenger from God? Did he have identification?

JOE Yes.

DAVID What was it?

JOE He had a big "G" on his sweatshirt.

DAVID A big "G"! Are you sure he wasn't from Georgia Tech?

JOE You must believe me. He was God's messenger.

DAVID And what was the message?

JOE The message was . . . I should renounce God.

SARAH Renounce God?

ROSE Joe, that's terrible. Are you sure he had the right address?

JOE There's no mistake. That was the message.

BEN Who asked you this, Dad? Who wants you to renounce God?

JOE God does. God asked me. To prove to the Devil how much I love God.

DAVID Ah, the Devil's in on it too . . . Big "D" on the sweatshirt, Dad?

JOE I didn't see him. The messenger did.

DAVID The messenger saw the Devil? . . . *(Big smile)* And what did he look like?

JOE You'll never believe it.

ROSE Tell us, Joe. We'll believe it.

JOE The good-looking one. From *Butch Cassidy.*

ROSE Paul Newman?

JOE No. The other one.

ROSE Robert Redford? He's such a clean-cut looking boy.

JOE You don't understand anything. He loves me.

ROSE Robert Redford?

JOE No! God loves me.

ROSE We all love you, Joe. But we wouldn't ask you to renounce us. That's why I'm very surprised at God.

JOE Listen to me. He not only loves me, I happen to be His favorite. The messenger told me.

SARAH God's favorite? Oh, Daddy, how wonderful.

BEN *(Very serious)* That's a great honor, Dad. Congratulations.

JOE Can I finish, please? It's God's belief that no matter how much pain and hardship I suffer, I will never renounce Him. So He's putting me to this test. That's why the business burned down, why we have no heat, no water . . . Don't you see how wonderful it is? I've been chosen out of all the people on earth to prove to God Himself how much I love Him.

ROSE Ohhhhhh! Ohhhhhh, I see . . . We all have to suffer because God loves you so much. Oh, Joe, I'm so proud of you. You must be thrilled to death.

BEN Nice going, Dad.

SARAH I can't wait to tell my friends.

MADY Wait'll the girls on the bus hear this.

ALL That's wonderful!, etc.

MADY Mr. Benjamin! Mr. Benjamin!

(They hug each other)

DAVID *(Starts to laugh, then gets hysterical)* I love it! I love it! *(He is beside himself with joy)* A nut with a big "G" on his sweatshirt walks in here and says he's a messenger of God and you all believe it! I love it, I love it, I LOVE IT!

(He crosses to near the French door)

JOE He doesn't believe it. *(To DAVID)* The fire in the factory was *real,* wasn't it? The freezing cold in here is real—and it's just the beginning. The *real* test begins tonight. He just told me on the phone. What we have to face in these next two weeks, don't even try to imagine.

ROSE I can just imagine!

BEN Dad, you know you can count on me.

JOE Thank you, son.

SARAH Me too, Dad.

ROSE *(Goes over to* MADY*)* Just like her twin brother. They were always so close, even as children, weren't they, Mady?

MADY I *still* can't tell them apart.

DAVID Is it my turn to vote? I registered, you know. *(They all turn and look at* DAVID*)*

JOE Yes, David, it's your turn now.

DAVID My personal opinion? We've got a terrific lawsuit on our hands . . . I say we should sue God for property damage.

JOE Don't get smart! You don't know what you're dealing with.

DAVID Are you trying to tell me that God has decided to test man's faith in Him by sending this family a tough cut of pot roast?

JOE Be careful, David, I'm begging you.

DAVID Well, at least let's stand up and fight Him! I mean, the Man's been pushing people around for twenty-five thousand years. I don't think we have to take *any more crap from Him.*

ROSE Oh, my God!

SARAH Wow!

BEN Oh, brother!

MADY If we wasn't in trouble before, we are in trouble *now!*

JOE Don't you talk like that in this house, do you hear me? *I will not have that kind of language in this house!*

DAVID Then how about *outside* the house? *(He quickly opens the French door, goes out on the portico and yells up to the heavens)* Hey, God, You want to test us? Here we are! You want us to show You what we're made of? Show us what *You're* made of! . . . What about it, Big Fella, *show us a little muscle! (He starts to laugh with glee, and at that very moment, an enormous clap of thunder erupts and a bolt of lightning hits the portico, just missing* DAVID *and leaving a ball of smoke. The drapes fall down, and books tumble off their shelves. The women scream and* DAVID *rushes back into the room, ashen white)* Ho-ly *shit!*

(There is another clap of thunder and another bolt of lightning on the portico. The women scream again)

JOE *(To* DAVID*)* *Now* see what you've done!

MORRIS *(To* DAVID*)* Mr. David, I never told you this before, but *you've got a big mouth!*

(Another clap of thunder and another bolt of lightning; more smoke)

JOE In the basement, everybody! Quick, Morris, get everyone down into the basement.

*(*MORRIS *starts to usher everyone out of the room as the thunder and lightning keep coming)*

MORRIS Come on, everyone, follow me!

DAVID Me first! Me first!

(He's the first one out)

ROSE Joe, don't stand there, you'll be killed!

JOE Go on, Rose, go with the children . . . I'll be right down, I promise.

ROSE If you get a chance, get my bracelets.

(And she is gone. They are all gone except JOE. *There is one final clap of thunder and one final bolt of lightning as* JOE *gets on his knees and prays)*

JOE Forgive him, dear God. Forgive my son, David. It's not *his* fault. Let *me* pay for his sins, Lord. Help me to teach him. Help me . . . Help me . . .

(There is another bolt of lightning and a crack of thunder. And suddenly SIDNEY LIPTON *rushes in through the French door, his raincoat smoldering and smoking. He slaps at it, trying to put himself out)*

LIPTON What about helping *me?* Water! Water! Throw water on me, I'm smoking! Hot! Hot! Burning hot! . . . My good raincoat, for Christ's sakes! I needed it dry-cleaned, not toasted!

(He gets a seltzer bottle from the bar and sprays his coat)

JOE What are *you* doing here?

LIPTON You got a crazy son, you know that? I could have been killed! *Never* get God angry when a person is standing under a tree.

JOE I'm sorry. I apologize for David.

LIPTON It's a little late, isn't it? God heard what he said. I'd hate to be driving on the Long Island Expressway with that kid . . . Am I out? Am I still smoldering?

JOE You mustn't pay attention to what David said. He's young, he's angry at the world, at all the injustices he sees . . . He doesn't understand the ways of God.

LIPTON "Crap." He actually said the word "crap" to God. I couldn't believe it. I mean, it's bad enough to fool around with Mother Nature.

(He goes over to the phone and starts to dial. He dials about thirty digits . . .)

JOE Who are you calling?

LIPTON What?

JOE Who are you calling?

LIPTON *(Points heavenward; into the phone)* Hello . . . Is He in? . . . Who's this? . . . Oh, His service . . . No, don't wake Him . . . I'll call back later.

(He hangs up)

JOE If you could just explain to God. He's just a boy. I'll do anything. Give you whatever I have . . .

LIPTON Hey! Hey! What's this—a bribe? Are you offering me a bribe? Are you trying to bribe *me*, a messenger of God?

JOE No! No, of course not!

LIPTON Why not? Too good for you? I'll take anything—cash, clothes, canned goods, sheets, linens—

whatever you got. I took *some* beating on the market this week.

JOE I'm sorry.

LIPTON *You're* sorry? You still got a gorgeous roof over your head. I just got a twelve percent rent increase. And they took out the elevator. Six-floor walk-up and Sylvia just got her report back from the doctors . . . Positive varicose veins. If I don't get her out of New York this winter, they'll have to tie her ankles in knots. SO DON'T TELL ME YOUR TROUBLES WITH YOUR LOUSY SON!

(He sits, and opens up his attaché case)

JOE I'm sorry. Sometimes you get so involved with your own problems, you forget about others.

LIPTON People don't care about people any more. Well, you're finding that out, aren't you? I can't hear myself. *(He rubber-stamps papers)* I think the thunder deviated my septum . . . Well, on with business. *(Takes out papers from his brief case)* If I can just have your signature, I'll be able to get home in time for the *Hollywood Squares. (Hands a pen to* JOE*)* Sign all three copies—write, don't print.

JOE Sign what? *(Looks at the papers)* What is this for?

LIPTON For the ad.

JOE What ad?

LIPTON The ad in *The New York Times.*

JOE What ad? What *New York Times?* What the hell are you talking about?

LIPTON Language, language, please. I can't take any more thunder. I'm sure you and your family have suffered enough too. You don't have to take this any more . . . So we'd like you to take a small ad in the Sunday *Times* saying you've renounced God . . . We pay for it—we get a rate.

JOE Are you mad?

LIPTON At you, no. At your son, a little. Sign here, your full name in triplicate.

JOE Get away! I'm not signing any documents.

LIPTON It's not a document. It's a lousy piece of paper. The Magna Carta was a document. Don't make such a big deal—

JOE Get away! *(He grabs the papers and throws them in the air)* Get away, I said!

LIPTON *(Starts to pick up the scattered papers)* Keep it up! Keep that up and you're going to bring on humidity like you've never seen in your life. You'll have to go to a garage to get your underwear off. *(He has retrieved the papers)* Don't you understand? It's not an official renouncement unless it appears in the Sunday *New York Times* . . . The *Daily News* is acceptable only in the Bronx and Staten Island.

JOE *I am not taking an ad renouncing God!*

LIPTON It's a small ad—tiny little type like "Doggies Lost." Who's even going to see it? The printer and a few nuts who look for renouncements.

JOE Never! Never never never never never never!

LIPTON Joe, you're a businessman. When you go bankrupt, it's not legal unless it's in the paper, right? . . . We'll put it under "Montauk Fishing News"—who the hell reads that?

JOE Didn't you just hear "Never never never never never never"?

LIPTON I heard, I wasn't sure it was definite . . . Here, take the pen.

JOE Get that *poisonous* thing away from me!

LIPTON *(Looks at it)* Poisonous? A Bic Banana? . . . Joe, listen to me. You don't know these people . . . You don't know what discomfort they're capable of. I'm talking about the big-time pain . . . In exactly one minute you're going to start to itch. There is *no* itch which itches like the itch you're going to get, Joe. There is not enough Johnson's baby powder in the world that could help you . . . Sign, Joe!

JOE You think I don't know what hardship is? What bad times are? I grew up in a tenement in New York. My mother, my father and eleven kids in one and a half rooms—*(He suddenly gets an itch on his chest; he scratches himself)*—We had two beds and a cot, you had to take a number off the wall to go to sleep—*(The other side of his chest itches. He scratches it)*—My father was five foot three, weighed a hundred and twenty-seven pounds—*(His back itches. He tries to scratch it)* What the hell is that?

LIPTON Can't get to it, can you? . . . They can put an itch on your back, a *gorilla* couldn't reach it.

JOE Do what you want. Bankrupt me, freeze me, tear out my insides—*(Tries to get at his back again)* Oh, God, that's driving me crazy. *(Turns his back toward* LIPTON*)* Could you just scratch me for a minute? . . . Nobody would know.

LIPTON Certainly. Bend over. I'll scratch while you sign the paper.

JOE *No!* No, I'm not signing anything! Oh! I'd trade my entire hand for one ten-inch finger.

LIPTON Have the bottoms of your feet started to itch yet?

JOE *(Scratching his back)* No. Not yet . . . Now! Now —they just started! *(He flops down on the floor and rips his shoes off, frantically scratching the soles of his feet)* Ohh! Oh, that's worse than the back . . . I'd rather have all my teeth pulled out than have my feet itch.

LIPTON That's scheduled for Thursday . . . Now it starts in-between the fingers.

JOE Oh, it's in-between the fingers now. *(Tries to scratch in-between his fingers, the soles of his feet and his back)* I can't scratch everywhere at once. I need another arm.

LIPTON *(Observing him)* When it starts to itch in your crotch, I'm leaving.

JOE *(Scratching everywhere)* I expected pain but this is

torture . . . Oh, it's in the nostrils now. Now it's up the nose!

(He scratches nose)

LIPTON *(Turns away, shields his eyes)* I'll miss *that* one, if you don't mind! . . . Give in, Joe.

*(*JOE *keeps scratching)*

JOE He's my God. He gave me life and my life meaning. I will not renounce Him. *(Grabs his shoulder in sudden pain)* Oh! Oh, what's that?

LIPTON Neuralgia—with a side order of bursitis . . . Joe, listen to me . . . *Nobody* believes any more. The Church is thinking of closing two days a week . . . Synagogues are selling tickets for the High Holidays at a discount.

JOE *(Grabs other arm)* Ogghhhhhhhhhhh! Oggghhhh! Never, never . . . What is that?

LIPTON Tennis elbow.

JOE Aggghhhhhhh! Get out! Get out and let me suffer alone. Let me bear my pain alone.

LIPTON Who's looking to stay? This is not my idea of *That's Entertainment. (He puts the papers back into his brief case)* Well, Benjy-Boy, what we've got here is a stalemate.

JOE *(Scratching, stomping, writhing—he is being attacked everywhere at once)* Agghhhh! Ogghhhh! It's itching again. Everything and everywhere is itching me. Do something. Help me! Isn't there something you can do?

LIPTON If I could, I would. You think I have no feelings? You think I like to see people suffer? I *hate* this job . . . If only I could get a good Carvel franchise near Miami, I would get out in a minute.

JOE Uggghhhhhhhhhhhh!

LIPTON I'm going. Try not to scream until I'm gone. I'm getting nauseous.

JOE A doctor! Get me a doctor, please . . .

LIPTON Don't ask for doctors. They can't help you and they'll charge you a fortune. Think it over, Joe. If it gets worse . . . you've got my number.

JOE Agggghhhhhhh! That's the worst one. What is that?

LIPTON That, Joe is hemorrhoids. Goodbye!

(He opens the French door and leaps over the balcony railing)

Curtain

Act Two

It is a few days later. The house is gone—burnt to the ground. Parts of the brick walls are still standing, but the roof and wooden-beamed ceilings are no more. Some of the burnt timbers can still be seen on the ground of the "former" living room, where they have crashed during the fire. We can see the sky. It is a cold, bleak, overcast day. Smoke still rises from the smoldering ruins. The furniture has been crushed and burnt. There is very little left worth saving.

Through the portals which once were the entrance from the dining room, and where one charred oak door hangs precariously from a hinge, come MORRIS *and* MADY. *Their clothes are tattered and singed. They enter the room listlessly.* MADY *carries a Gucci shopping bag.* MORRIS *carries a broom and dustpan. They step over debris and twisted furniture.*

MADY *(Looks around at the charred ruins)* Well, I tell you one thing—I ain't cleanin' up *this* mess.

MORRIS *(Morosely)* Well, you got to look on the bright side, Mady . . . At least we only got *one* floor to do now.

MADY Neyer seen a fire spread so fast in all my life. This house got "well done" quicker than a barbecued chicken.

MORRIS It was the wind. Came up outa nowhere blowin' fire every which ways. *(Points off)* Looka that! First time I ever seen a swimming pool burn down.

MADY Now, how come the fire department never answered the alarm? And how come no neighbors bothered comin' over here to help us? And how come when it started to rain, it rained everywhere but right here? I ain't a gamblin' woman, Morris, but somehow I got the feelin' this family has "crapped out"!

MORRIS *(Stops; thinks)* You think it's true, Mady?

MADY What's that?

MORRIS That the Lord is testin' Mr. Benjamin? That it's God who's burned us and froze us and starvin' us just to see if Mr. Benjamin really loves Him the way he say he do?

MADY I hope so. Sure would be a waste if all this misery was nothin' but misery. What time is it?

MORRIS What difference does it make around here? *(Looks at his watch)* Uh-oh. Get ready. It's time for Mr. Benjamin to be gettin' up now. Hold on.

(From the distance we hear a scream—a long, agonizing scream. It is so painful and mournful, it hardly sounds human. It dies slowly. MADY *and* MORRIS *have been looking back in the direction of that horrible sound)*

MADY He sounds a little better today.

MORRIS He ain't gettin' better. He just ain't *screamin'* as good.

ROSE *(Offstage)* Morris? Mady? Are you in the living room?

MORRIS It's Mrs. Benjamin. *(Calls out)* Yes, ma'am, here we are. We're outside in the house.

*(*ROSE *and* SARAH *straggle in through the "portal")*

ROSE Oh, I'm so glad you're both home. I forgot my key.

MORRIS *(Getting up to help her)* Careful, Mrs. Benjamin. Lotta that furniture is still hot.

ROSE Look at my beautiful house . . . my beautiful living room . . . And we just had the windows done.

*(*ROSE *and* SARAH *climb over the rubble)*

SARAH You're tired, Mother. Why don't you sit down and rest?

MORRIS Set yourself here, Mrs. Benjamin. I think it used to be the sofa. *(*ROSE *sits down)* Would you like a carrot to chew on, Mrs. Benjamin?

ROSE No thanks, Morris. I don't want to spoil my dinner.

MADY You won't, 'cause that's it.

ROSE *(Looks around sadly)* You know, Mady, when I was young I always wanted a big house with a little fireplace . . . Now I've got a big fireplace with a little house.

MORRIS If you need to borrow some money, Mrs. Benjamin, we'll be glad to help you out.

ROSE You're both so kind . . . Did I tell you that David is gone?

SARAH He drank a whole bottle of brandy and ran out blind drunk. Ben went out looking for him.

ROSE Don't say anything to Mr. Benjamin. He's got enough on his mind now. If only David were here. He keeps asking for David. "Where is my little David?" he says . . . over and over through his chapped lips.

MORRIS Listen. Someone's comin'.

ROSE Oh, dear. And the place is a mess.

MORRIS It's Mr. Ben.

BEN *(Rushing in)* He's coming! Daddy's coming!

ROSE Everybody, clear all this debris away. He has to be very careful where he steps. Over there. Put it over there.

(They all start to move a large beam to make a path. They move it to the other side of the room)

MADY The Walls of Jericho—that's what we got here is the Walls of Jericho.

(They put it down)

ROSE *(Looks at it)* No, it looks terrible there . . . Never mind.

BEN Here he comes.

ROSE Now, remember, don't touch him. His skin is *very* sensitive. Nobody touch him, please.

(They all turn to the doorway. JOE *stands there, leaning on a stick. He is bent over, half in pain, half because of an aging process that has made him old before his time. Even his hair has grayed. He is in tatters and rags, cloths wrapped around his feet. He is parched, shriveled and weak. His lips are cracked, and when he speaks, it is with great effort and pain)*

JOE Ail . . . Ail in hoo . . .

MORRIS What's that, Mr. Benjamin?

JOE Ail . . . Ail in hoo . . .

ROSE It hurts him to speak. His lips get stuck together. What are you trying to say, dear?

JOE Ail in hoo . . .

ROSE A nail in your shoe?

JOE Ail in hoo . . . hurts!

ROSE Poor Joe.

JOE Daba?

ROSE What, dear?

JOE Daba? . . . Bear daba?

ROSE Where's David? I don't know, dear. David's gone.

JOE Daba gobe?

ROSE Yes. You mustn't worry. He'll be all right . . . You must take care of *yourself* now, Joe.

JOE *(Turns away sorrowfully)* Daba's gobe . . .

MORRIS Well, it's good to see you up and about again, Mr. Benjamin.

MADY Dinner's gonna be ready soon, Mr. Benjamin. We're havin' pot luck tonight.

*(*JOE *seems to be sagging)*

MORRIS You shouldn't be standin' like that, Mr. Benjamin. *(Moves toward him)* Let me help you sit.

JOE *(Panicked, backs away)* Nah! Nah!

ROSE *(Screams)* *Don't touch him!*

MORRIS I won't! I won't touch him!

ROSE You mustn't touch him!

MORRIS I'm not going to touch you, Mr. Benjamin.

JOE Dow tuch . . . Dow tuch . . . Muzzzn tuch . . .

ROSE No one is going to touch you, dear. We know how your skin feels.

JOE Ha! . . . Ski fees ha!

ROSE Skin feels hot. We know, darling.

SARAH *(Sobs)* Oh, Daddy. Poor Daddy!

MADY He needs his strength, that's what he needs . . . You want a nice carrot, Mr. Benjamin?

JOE Ka-hoo!

MADY What?

JOE Ka-hoo!

ROSE He can't chew.

MORRIS You want something to drink?

JOE Ka-swa!

ROSE He can't swallow.

SARAH Isn't there *anything* we can do, Daddy?

JOE Ka-thi!

ROSE He can't think of anything.

JOE *(Looks around)* Gow . . . Evthi gow . . .

ROSE Everything's gone? No, Joe. Not everything. We still have each other. We're still alive and together, Joe.

JOE Evthi gow—in here! *(He indicates his heart by pointing to it. His finger touches his chest and it sets off an agonizing pain)* AaaaaaggggggHHHHHH!!!

ROSE *Don't touch it, Joe,* just point to it.

SARAH *(Turns away)* Poor Daddy.
(She buries herself in BEN*'s arms)*

JOE Away . . . Take away . . .
(He is forming his words a little better by now)

ROSE They're your children, Joe. They love you.

SARAH We're not leaving you, Daddy.

BEN We're sticking, Dad, even if the pain gets worse.

JOE *Worse?* Worse than this? *(He shakes head)* No. There's no worse. This is it!

ROSE That's right, Joe. Things are going to get better, you'll see. David will come home soon and we'll build the house up again and we'll find a nice skin lotion for you. Everything will be all right, Joe. I know it will. We love you, Joe.

JOE And I . . . love you.
*(*ROSE*, filled with love and compassion, rushes to* JOE *and takes him in her arms)*

ROSE Oh, Joe!

JOE AGGGGHHHHHHHHHH!

ROSE *(Backs off)* Oh, I'm sorry, darling!

JOE Dow tuch . . . Dow tuch!

ROSE No. I won't touch you again, Joe. No.

MADY *(Gets on her knees)* Oh, Lord, Help this poor man in his sufferin' . . .

MORRIS *(On his knees)* Amen!

MADY Help this poor man through his pain.

MORRIS Amen!

MADY Help this poor man in his anguish!

MORRIS Amen!

ROSE Joe, isn't that sweet? They're praying for you . . . And it's their day off.

JOE Thank . . . you.

MADY Everybody pray. Everybody down on their knees to God. *(They all start to kneel, including* JOE*) NOT YOU, MR. BENJAMIN!*

*(*JOE *stops)*

ROSE We'll do it, Joe. We'll pray for you.

(He gets up, then nods to them)

JOE Okay.

MADY If you hear us, Lord, give us a sign. Make it known in our hearts, Lord, that you hear us.

MORRIS Make it known.

MADY Make it known in our souls, Lord, that you hear us.

BEN Make it known.

MADY Make it known in our ears, Lord, that you hear us.

JOE *(Loud but not clear)* May it knowwww . . .

MADY Everybody!

ALL Amen, Lord!

JOE Amen, Lord! Oh, I bit my tongue!

(He cries)

ROSE Oh, dear God, his tongue is swelling up. Look at it. He doesn't have enough room in his mouth.

JOE Arrrggghhhhhh!

SARAH *(Sobs)* Oh, Daddy. Poor Daddy.

MORRIS *(On his knees, pounds the floor with his fist)* Poor Mr. Benjamin. Poor Mr. Benjamin. Poor Mr. Benjamin. *(Accidentally hits* JOE*'s foot)* I'm sorry. I'm sorry. I'm sorry.

BEN When's all this gonna be over?

SARAH When, Mother, when?

ROSE *(Defiantly)* When? . . . Now! That's right, I said

"Now!" . . . I've had enough, Joe. We've *all* had enough. I want my David back. I want my house back. I want your tongue to go down . . . Make it stop, Joe. Please make it stop.

JOE *(With difficulty)* There'th nothig I can do . . . I can't thtop it . . .

ROSE *(Screams)* DON'T TELL ME THERE'S NOTHING YOU CAN DO! You *know* what you can do. You can stop it all, Joe, with three little words. You can end our pain, our misery . . . Say it, Joe. Say it, and we can all go to bed and watch some television. Please . . .

(She breaks down sobbing)

JOE Don't . . . Don't ask me, Rose . . .

ROSE I'm not asking, I'm *begging!*

JOE Don't beg me, Rose.

ROSE Then I *demand!* I *demand,* Joe Benjamin, that you give up your precious God. How can you love someone who makes us suffer so much?

JOE David makes me suffer . . . and I love him.

ROSE That's different. He'll grow out of it. But God is millions of years old—He should know better! I believed before, Joe . . . When I was a little girl . . . When I met you . . . When we had the children . . . But not now. Not when I see what He's doing to you. He's not nice, Joe. If you don't renounce Him, Joe . . . then I'm going to renounce *you!*

SARAH Mother!

JOE I can't help myself . . . I love my God . . .

ROSE *(Angrily)* Why couldn't you just have a mistress like other men?

JOE I'm sorry, Rose . . . Forgive me . . .

ROSE Then stay here and suffer—because *I'm* going. I've got five mouths to feed. If there *is* a God, that's what He intended *me* to do . . . I'm going to Welcome Wagon and get some coffee and doughnuts. Come, everybody.

BEN You mean leave Dad here like this?

SARAH We can't leave him alone, Mother. He'll die!

ROSE He won't die. God doesn't want him to die. He wants him to stay here and suffer for a hundred and twenty years. Then they'll *both* be happy. We'll be dead and buried, and your father will be sitting on porcupine needles . . . Have a good time, Joe. Come, children.

BEN All right. We'll go. But as soon as I know the others are all right, I'm coming back. I'm not David. Goodbye, Dad . . . and good luck. *(And without thinking, he grabs* JOE*'s hand to shake it—then realizes his mistake)* That hurts, doesn't it? (JOE *nods quietly)*

BEN Sorry about that.

SARAH Goodbye, Daddy.

JOE Sarah . . . One kiss . . . One goodbye kiss.

SARAH But if I touch you—

JOE A kiss from you could never hurt. *(*SARAH *bends down and kisses his cheek gently)* That's the first time I felt good in three days. Button your coat.

*(*SARAH *bursts into tears and runs to* BEN. *Both leave)*

ROSE Come. It's getting late. With our luck, there'll be a transit strike. Goodbye, Joe.

JOE *(Stopping her)* Rosey!

ROSE You haven't called me Rosey in thirty years.

JOE Take care, Rosey . . . and try and forgive me.

ROSE It was such a nice house. We were all so happy here . . . Why couldn't God have tested a young couple with a small apartment? *(She cries)* I love you, Joe . . . I forgive you.

(And she runs off. Only MADY *and* MORRIS *remain, standing together)*

JOE What are you waiting for? Go.

MORRIS We want to stay with *you*, Mr. Benjamin.

JOE What does a suffering man living all alone in ashes need two in help for? Go with Mrs. Benjamin, Morris. She needs you.

MADY I have a sister who can come in two days a week . . .

JOE Thank you both and God bless you.

MADY Just "Thank you" will be plenty, Mr. Benjamin.

MORRIS May the Lord have mercy on his painful soul.

MADY Hallelujah—and let's get the hell outa here! *(They are gone.* JOE *is alone. He crawls to the sofa in great pain and sits. Then he looks upward)*

JOE Okay, God. What's next? . . . What's next, God? *(Suddenly there is a crack of thunder.* JOE *winces. Then we hear a deep, rich, resonant voice—as if from the heavens)*

VOICE Joe . . .

JOE What?

VOICE Joseph Melvin Benjamin! This—is your God!

JOE *(Leans forward, excited) God?* . . . Is it really you, God?

VOICE Didn't I just say it was? . . . Of all the creatures on this earth you are My favorite, Joe. I love you more than the birds and the butterflies and the crocodiles and the cockroaches . . . especially the cockroaches.

JOE *(Bowing his head)* Oh, thank you, Lord . . .

VOICE Your test is over.

JOE *(With great relief)* Ohhh!

VOICE You have met the challenge of faith and have emerged triumphant . . . I love thee as thou loves thine . . . And thee will be rewarded as thou would wish thine to reward thee . . .

JOE Thank Thee, Thy Lord.

VOICE Raise thyself to be blessed, Joseph. *(*JOE *does)* Knowing now that thy test is over, say the words just for Me . . . As a final tribute of thy love for Me, Joseph, say what thou couldst not say before. Say it, Joseph, say "I renounce God."

JOE *(Puzzled)* What?

VOICE It's all right. The test is over . . . It couldn't hurt, Joe.

JOE What is this? . . . It's a trick. That's what it is! It's a trick, isn't it?

VOICE It is not a trick. God does not trick. God is a busy man. Say it, Joe. Say it before I get upset.

JOE A trick . . . That voice . . . I know that voice . . . It's not God! It's *you,* isn't it?

VOICE It's not me. It's God, I'm telling you. Why would I lie? I'm God, I'm telling you, *I'M GOD! I'M GOD! I'M GOD!*

(And as "God's" voice booms out, the fireplace collapses . . . and standing behind it holding a cordless microphone is SIDNEY LIPTON. *He turns around and looks at* JOE *sheepishly—caught in the act much as the Wizard of Oz was by Dorothy)*

LIPTON *(Smiles and speaks into the microphone)* April Fool!

JOE I knew it! I knew that voice!

LIPTON Tell the truth, did I fool you? Heh? *(Does his "God" voice)* Joseph Benjamin, this is your God. *(Regular voice again)* They hired me once to do that in a temple on Eighty-eighth and Park—I raised over a hundred thousand dollars in donations.

JOE Leave me alone today, please. Besides suffering, I'm not feeling well.

LIPTON *(Looks around)* I don't blame you. Look at this

place . . . If you don't get the screens up, you're going to have one buggy summer.

JOE If I've lost everything else, why can't I lose you too?

LIPTON Can I make a suggestion about the furniture? . . . Try Lemon Pledge. Rub it in for about six years and let it dry.

JOE You're gloating, aren't you? You think you've won. You think you've beaten me. Well, you're wrong. You're wasting your time, Lipton. All I wait for now is my death.

LIPTON Death? You got a long wait. You got fifty, sixty years of healthy suffering in front of you yet. What are you talking about? You're in the prime of pain . . . Oh, by the way, I brought the list with me.

(He takes a sheet of paper out of his pocket)

JOE What list?

LIPTON The previews. The coming attractions. Let me read you what's playing July tenth through August fourteenth . . . *(Reads)* A hernia, gastritis, a double impacted wisdom tooth, a root canal job, the heartbreak of psoriasis, constipation, diarrhea, piles, dysentery, chills, fever, athlete's foot, lumbago, a touch of gonorrhea and a general feeling of loginess . . . All this, mind you, is on the left side of your body.

JOE If I'm alive I'll endure.

LIPTON "I'll endure." I've heard that before. Would you like to know who renounced God today, Joe? If I told you who renounced God today you would be shocked. I couldn't believe it when I heard it.

JOE I don't care.

LIPTON Detroit. The entire city of Detroit renounced . . . including three hundred tourists just passing through.

JOE I am what God made me.

LIPTON And stop talking like you're Moses. You are not Moses. Moses was a big star. You're lucky God even pays attention to you.

JOE I am an infinitesimal speck on the eyelash of the universe . . . but God sees me.

LIPTON With binoculars, maybe. Vain, that's what you are—vain, self-centered and a swellhead. Who do you think you are to take up God's time like this? Do you know something? This will be the first time in nineteen years that he misses the Christmas show at Radio City Music Hall. And for what? Look at you! A mess . . . Walking around in a burnt bathrobe and that *fekokta* stick. You look like a shepherd for the Salvation Army. I didn't want to mention it before— *(He whispers)*—lately you don't smell too good either.

(He puts his scarf to his nose)

JOE It won't work, Sidney. No matter what you say, it won't work.

LIPTON I hate this job. I can't take it any more. I'm having a nervous breakdown . . . Why doesn't God help me? Why should you be the favorite?

JOE I'm sorry, Sidney. Forgive me . . . How can I help you?

LIPTON If you won't renounce God, then—then will —will you—

JOE Will I what, Sidney? Ask me.

LIPTON Will you give me a letter of recommendation? I've been fired!

(He opens his coat—the "G" has been taken off his football jersey)

JOE Oh, Sidney, don't tell me. I'm so sorry.

LIPTON God laid off fourteen hundred people today. Everyone went—messengers, angels, bishops, Hebrew-school teachers . . . I saw two Cardinals trying to get jobs at Chock Full O'Nuts . . . It's because of inflation . . . Do you know what red velvet slippers cost today? . . . I haven't even told Sylvia yet.

JOE She sounds like a good woman. She'll understand.

LIPTON There goes our dream of Florida. You know how far south Sylvia has been in her life? . . . Canal Street . . . not even the downtown side.

JOE Then why did you come here today?

LIPTON *(Shrugs)* I was hoping I could change your mind . . . If I could get this account, they might reconsider.

JOE God loves you, Sidney—he'll provide.

LIPTON He wouldn't even say hello to me in the hallway . . . What am I going to do now? I'm forty-four years old—it's a little late in life to take up pro-football.

JOE We must carry whatever burdens God gives us.

LIPTON Sure. The poor carry their burdens and the rich have them delivered. Where's the justice? . . . Well, I don't care any more . . . What could He do to me now? *(Yells up)* Hey, God! Do You hear me? . . . *I renounce You, God!*

JOE *(Yells)* NO! DON'T DO THAT!

LIPTON *(Yells up again)* I give You up, God! Thanks for nothing. The *Devil* cares more about people. At least *he* entertains them . . . *The Exorcist* grossed over a hundred and thirty million dollars—domestic!

JOE Take it back, Sidney.

LIPTON *(Yells up)* Hey, God, You hear me? May You have the same lousy weather You give *us* every year . . . especially Labor Day weekend.

JOE We all have our own tests to go through, Sidney . . .

LIPTON Why did *you* have to be mine? Even *you*

couldn't take you, believe me. *(Sobs)* What have I done?

JOE Shh . . . Shh . . . It's all right, Sidney.

LIPTON Tell Him I'm sorry, Joe. He knows you, He likes you . . . You, He'll listen to. Tell Him not to forsake me.

JOE Of course I'll tell Him, Sidney. He won't . . . shh . . .

LIPTON *(Wipes his eyes on his sleeve)* Thank you, Joseph. I have to go now . . . I have an interview at two o'clock with United Parcel.

(He stops suddenly; looks around)

JOE Good luck, Sidney.

LIPTON Shh! Listen!

JOE What is it?

LIPTON I hear something. Someone's out there . . .

JOE Where? I can't see.

(He still can't move around freely)

LIPTON *(Points)* There! There, did you see it move?

JOE See what? Where should I look? There's nothing out there but smoke and ashes.

LIPTON And a bush . . . See that one bush over there? It's still burning a little on the bottom . . . There's someone behind there.

JOE Behind the burning bush?

LIPTON *(Stops; looks at* JOE*)* Did you hear what you just said?

JOE What did I say?

LIPTON Behind the burning bush . . . Anything strike you familiar about that phrase?

JOE What are you saying?

LIPTON Nothing.

(He backs away)

JOE What are you implying?

LIPTON Nothing . . . But don't ask me what I'm thinking.

JOE Do you mean—?

LIPTON I doubt it. He never makes house calls. But with you, who knows?

JOE Oh, my God.

LIPTON *(Nods)* It's possible. Your test isn't over yet, Joe . . . Maybe He's going for a big finish . . . This is no place for me. Goodbye, Joe.

JOE *NO!* Stay! Help me!

LIPTON Hold out. Whatever they do to you now, hold out another few minutes . . . Keep saying you love God, and Monday morning you'll be back in the box business, Joe.

JOE I'm not *interested* in the box business any more.

LIPTON Don't turn it down. I could run it for you. I'm available.

(He starts exiting through the fireplace)

JOE Don't leave me now. I need you. Help me, Sidney . . .

LIPTON Goodbye, Joe. Good luck . . . If you think of it, get me an autograph.

(And he is gone. JOE *is alone. He is unable to move with any facility, and whatever movement he does make is still painful. Add to this his immeasurable fear of what may be out there for him . . . We hear a wind come up. It almost sounds like a voice wailing)*

JOE Who's out there? . . . Tell me who's there, please. I'm frightened. Is it—is it who I think it is? . . . Why don't You say something? . . . What more do You want of me? . . . Say *something* to me, PLEASE.

(A clap of thunder is heard. A shaft of light beams a single ray . . . And suddenly someone appears stand-

ing in the ray. It is DAVID. *He looks in* JOE'*s direction, but not directly at him)*

JOE David.

DAVID *(He turns back, waves)* Thanks for the lift.
(A car horn honks; then the sound of it driving away)
What's for dinner? I smell charcoal.

JOE David, David, it's you!
(He reaches out for him)

DAVID We haven't had a cookout in years . . . Ah, a special occasion! Can I have a drink, Dad?

JOE *(Arms extended)* David, help me. Come here, David . . . I've been so worried for you.

DAVID Well, as you can see, I'm fine . . . *(Falls over a beam)* And how is the family? . . . Mother, you seem so quiet tonight.

JOE What are you talking about? Your mother's not here . . . Can't you see they're all gone?

DAVID Really? Mady too? . . . Morris, are you there?

JOE What's wrong with you? Are you drunk again? . . . You're dead drunk, aren't you?

DAVID Not *dead* drunk, Dad. Blind drunk. The only problem is . . . I'm not drunk any more.
(He steps into the room and feels around . . . We realize he is stone blind)

JOE Oh, God . . . Oh, my God! *(He tries to reach out for* DAVID, *then looks up to the sky)* What have You done to my boy? What have You done to my David?

DAVID Who are you talking to? Who came in, Dad?

JOE *(Upward)* God, how could You do such a thing?

DAVID Oh, *Him?* . . . Still on that, are we?

JOE *(Clenches his fists and shakes them at the heavens. His grief, his anger, is enormous)* Is this Your work? . . . Is this Your test of faith and love? . . . You blind my first-born son and still expect me to love you? Punish *me*, not him! Blind *me*, not my son . . . Where is your love? Your compassion? Your justice? . . . I AM ANGRY AT YOU, GOD! REALLY, REALLY ANGRY! . . . And *STILL* I don't renounce you! How do you like *that*, God?

(There is a bolt of lightning and a crack of thunder. DAVID *cries out and holds his eyes, then takes his hands away)*

DAVID *(Lightly)* I think that did it, Pop!

JOE You can see, David? *(*DAVID *nods.* JOE *looks up)* It's over. The test is over! Oh, thank you, God. Thank you! . . . I'm sorry I lost my temper—but after all, I'm only human. You don't know what it's like . . . Try it sometime.

ROSE *(Offstage)* Joe? . . . Joe, are you all right?

JOE In here, Rose! We're in here.

*(*ROSE *appears carrying two huge shopping bags of food)*

ROSE I've come back, Joe. I couldn't leave you . . . Oh, David's home. I was so worried . . . Did you tell him, Joe?

JOE Tell him what?

ROSE That the house burned down? . . . Never mind. *(Hands* DAVID *packages)* Here, David, look for the kitchen. *(He goes out)* I have *food*, Joe. Where is everybody—Mady? Morris? Come on, we're all waiting.

(They all come in)

SARAH Look, Daddy, *food!*

JOE Where did you get it?

ROSE I won it on a TV game show. It started to rain, and we all ducked into this building . . . I didn't know it was a television studio . . . They picked me out of the audience. And today they had a new game where each contestant gets a celebrity helper and both of you have to help each other. And the category I picked was famous Biblical stories, and we got every question right . . . And do you know who the celebrity was who helped me, Joe?

JOE *(Looks slightly upward)* Yes, Rose . . . I think I know.

ROSE Don Rickles . . . He was as sweet as can be.

MADY Oh, it's so good to see you looking well, Mr. Benjamin.

(DAVID reenters)

DAVID Hi.

SARAH David! I'm so glad you're home . . . I think a man followed me on the streets . . . He just kept looking me up and down, up and down.

DAVID No one's going to look you up and down. Button your coat.

JOE You hear? Isn't it wonderful? Mady, Morris . . . Look at David now. *That's* my son.

MADY We all know who he is, Mr. Benjamin.

ROSE Come on everybody, into the kitchen. We're going to have a fat, juicy butterball turkey for dinner.

(They all start to go except DAVID. JOE is the last leaving)

JOE *(Turning back)* Are you coming, David?

DAVID In a minute, Dad . . . I just want to try and clean up around here.

JOE Are you sure you're all right, David?

DAVID I'm fine, Dad . . . Thank God.

JOE *(Nods, smiles)* I'd go through it all again, David, just to hear you say that.

(He goes out. DAVID is alone. He starts to clean up, then turns and looks up to God)

DAVID Okay, God . . . If you got room for one more, count me in . . . I just wanted to thank you for sparing my father's life . . . That's all I wanted to say . . . Amen.

VOICE *(Offstage)* Amen!

DAVID *(Turns)* Who said that?

LIPTON *(Appears)* Don't worry, it's not who you're thinking . . . I wonder if I could talk to you for a minute, young man . . . Guess who's absolutely crazy about you?

Curtain

California Suite

CALIFORNIA SUITE is composed of four playlets whose action takes place in rooms 203 and 204 in the Beverly Hills Hotel.

ACT I

SCENE 1: Visitor from New York
About one in the afternoon on a sunny, warm day in late fall

SCENE 2: Visitor from Philadelphia
Eleven in the morning, mid-December

ACT II

SCENE 1: Visitors from London
About five in the afternoon, early April

SCENE 2: About two o'clock in the morning

SCENE 3: Visitors from Chicago
Four in the afternoon, Sunday July Fourth

Act One

SCENE ONE: *Visitor from New York*

Suite 203–4: a bedroom with an adjoining living room, and a bathroom off the bedroom. The décor is brightly colored and cheerful. Elegant reproductions of Van Gogh and Renoir hang on the walls. There are large color TV sets in both rooms, and a fireplace in the living room.

It is about one in the afternoon on a sunny, warm day in late fall. HANNAH WARREN *is standing at the window, arms folded, a cigarette in one hand, staring pensively out. She is in her early forties, an intelligent and sophisticated woman. She is wearing a tailored woolen suit, too warm for California, just right for New York—where she has just come from. Her packed suitcases are on the bed in the other room, ready for departure. The telephone rings.*

HANNAH *(Into the phone)* Yes? . . . Where are you? . . . Come on up. Room 203. *(She hangs up, takes another drag on her cigarette, then crushes it nervously into the ashtray. She picks up the phone again)* Room service, please. *(She waits tensely. Then, into the phone)* Hello? . . . This is Mrs. Warren in Suite 203 . . . I would like one tea with lemon and one double Scotch on the rocks . . . *(The phone in the bedroom rings)* Yes—203. Thank you. *(She hangs up. The other phone rings again. She goes into the bedroom, sits on the bed and answers the phone)* Yes? . . . Yes, it is . . . Hello? . . . Yes, Bob . . . Well, I was hoping to leave today. I have tickets on the three o'clock flight, but I don't think I'm going to make it . . . It can't be too soon for me . . . This entire city smells like an overripe cantaloupe . . . How is New York? . . . It is? . . . Snow—how wonderful! . . . No, no. The sun is shining, about eighty degrees, on Thanksgiving . . . truly disgusting. *(There is a knock on the living room door. She yells out)* Come in. It's open. *(Back into the phone, a little lower-voiced)* No, nothing's settled yet. But I'm not worried. *(The living room door opens.* WILLIAM WARREN *enters. He is about forty-five, quite attractive, well tanned and trim. He wears brush-denim slacks, an open sport shirt, a cashmere V-neck sweater and tan sneakers. He closes the door and inspects the room as she continues on the phone)* No, he just got here . . . I don't want to bring a lawyer into it yet. We'll see how this goes . . . When have you known me to be intimidated? *(She laughs)* Well, that doesn't count . . . Yes, I remember it in detail . . . You're wasting a perfectly good erotic conversation with my ex-husband in the other room and the operator probably listening . . . Yes, I will . . . As soon as he leaves . . . I do too . . . Bye. *(She hangs up and sits there a moment. She takes a pencil and jots down a note on the pad on the table next to the bed. She is not in any great hurry to greet her visitor. She gets up, gives herself another check in the mirror and goes to the doorway of the living room. He turns and they look at each other)* Sorry. I was on the phone. It's snowing in New York. We're going to have a white Thanksgiving. Don't you love it? *(She sits. He is still standing. He smiles)* Is that wonderful, warm smile for me?

BILLY You still have trouble saying a simple "Hello."

HANNAH Oh, I *am* sorry. You always did get a big thrill out of the "little" things in life . . . Hello, Bill.

BILLY *(With generous warmth)* Hello, Hannah.

HANNAH My God, look at you. You've turned into a young boy again.

BILLY Have I?

HANNAH Haven't you noticed? You look like the sweetest young fourteen-year-old boy. You're not spending your summers at camp, are you?

BILLY Just three weeks in July. How are you?

HANNAH Well, at this moment, nonplussed.

BILLY Still the only one I know who can use "nonplussed" in regular conversation.

HANNAH Don't be ridiculous, darling, I talk that way at breakfast . . . Turn around, let me look at you.

BILLY Shouldn't we kiss or shake hands or something?

HANNAH Let's save it for when you leave . . . I love your California clothes.

BILLY They're Bloomingdale's, in New York.

HANNAH The best place for California clothes. You look so . . . I don't know—what's the word I'm looking for?

BILLY Happy?

HANNAH Casual. It's so hard to tell out here—are you dressed up now, or is that sporty?

BILLY I didn't think a tie was necessary for a reunion.

HANNAH Is that what this is? When I walked in, I thought we were going to play tennis.

BILLY Well, you look fit enough for it.

HANNAH Fit? You think I look fit? What an awful shit you are. I look gorgeous.

BILLY Yes, you do, Hannah. You look lovely.

HANNAH No, no. *You* look lovely. *I* look gorgeous.

BILLY Well, I lost about ten pounds.

HANNAH Listen to what I'm telling you, you're *ravishing.* I love the way you're wearing your hair now. Where do you go, that boy who does Barbra Streisand?

BILLY You like it, you can have my Thursday appointment with him . . . If you're interested, I'm feeling *very* well, thank you.

HANNAH Well, of course you are. Look at that tan. Well, it's the life out here, isn't it? You have an office outdoors somewhere?

BILLY No, just a desk near the window . . . Hey, Hannah, if we're going to banter like this, give me a little time. It's been nine years, I'm rusty.

HANNAH You'll pick it right up again, it's like French. You see, that's what I would miss if I left New York. The bantering.

BILLY San Francisco's only an hour away. We go up there and banter in emergencies.

HANNAH Do you really?

BILLY Would I lie to you?

HANNAH I never liked San Francisco. I was always afraid I'd fall out of bed and roll down one of those hills.

BILLY Not you, Hannah. You roll *up* hills.

HANNAH Oh, good. You're bantering. The flight out wasn't a total loss . . . Aren't you going to sit down, Bill? Or do they call you Billy out here? Yes, they do. Jenny told me. Everybody calls you Billy.

BILLY *(Shrugs)* That's me. Billy.

HANNAH It's adorable. A forty-five-year-old Billy. Standing there in his cute little sneakers and sweater. Please, sit down, Billy, I'm beginning to feel like your math teacher.

BILLY I promised myself driving over here I would be pleasant. I am now being pleasant.

HANNAH You drive everywhere, do you?

BILLY Everywhere.

HANNAH Even to your car?

BILLY Would you mind if I called down for something to drink?

HANNAH It's done.

BILLY I don't drink double Scotches on the rocks any more. I gave up hard liquor.

HANNAH Oh? What would you like?

BILLY A cup of tea with lemon.

HANNAH It's done . . . No hard liquor? At all?

BILLY Not even wine. I'm big on apple juice.

HANNAH Cigarettes?

BILLY Gave them up.

HANNAH Don't you miss the coughing and the hacking in the morning?

BILLY It woke the dogs up. I have dogs now.

HANNAH Isn't divorce wonderful? . . . What about candy? Please don't tell me you've given up Snickers?

BILLY *(Shrugs)* Sorry.

HANNAH That *is* crushing news. You *have* changed, Billy. You've gone clean on me.

BILLY Mind *and* body. That doesn't offend you, does it?

HANNAH May they both live to be a thousand. I don't mean this to seem facetious, but how *do* you take care of yourself?

BILLY I watch my diet, I've cut out meat, and you *do* mean to be facetious. You're dying to make a little fun of me. I don't mind. I have an hour to kill . . . Would you believe I run five miles every morning?

HANNAH After what?

BILLY The newspaper. I have lazy dogs . . . Shall I keep going? I swim twenty laps every night when

I come home from the studio. Eight sets of tennis every weekend. I sleep well. I haven't had a pill in three and a half years. I take vitamins and I eat natural, unprocessed health foods.

HANNAH Ah, aha! Health foods! At last, something in common.

BILLY Don't tell me you've given up P. J. Clarke's chili burgers?

HANNAH No, but I have them on whole wheat now . . . I'm enjoying this conversation. Tell me more about yourself. Jenny tells me you've taken up the banjo.

BILLY The guitar. Classical *and* country.

HANNAH Remarkable. And in New York you couldn't tune in Channel Five . . . More, more!

BILLY I climb.

HANNAH I beg your pardon?

BILLY I climb. I climbed a ten-thousand-foot mountain in the Sierra Nevada last summer.

HANNAH Well, that's no big deal. I climb that three times a week visiting my analyst.

BILLY And no analyst.

HANNAH Yes, I heard that. I'll accept the mountain climbing and, in a stretch, even the guitar. But no analyst? You ask too much, Billy. Why did you quit?

BILLY I went sane.

HANNAH Sane! How exciting. You mean you go out into the world every day all by yourself? *(He smiles, nods)* Don't you ever get depressed?

BILLY Yes.

HANNAH When?

BILLY Now.

HANNAH I'm so glad the sun hasn't dried up your brain completely . . . Tell me more news.

BILLY I moved.

HANNAH Oh, yes. You're not in Hardy Canyon any more.

BILLY Laurel. Laurel Canyon.

HANNAH Laurel, Hardy, what the hell? And where are you now?

BILLY Beverly Hills—a block north of Sunset Boulevard.

HANNAH What style house?

BILLY Very comfortable.

HANNAH Well, I'm sure it is. But what style is it?

BILLY Well, from the outside it looks like a small French farmhouse.

HANNAH A small French farmhouse. Just one block north of Sunset Boulevard. Sounds rugged . . . I passed something coming in from the airport. I thought it was a Moroccan villa—turned out to be a Texaco station.

BILLY We're a colorful community.

HANNAH I love it from the air.

BILLY And how is life over the subway?

HANNAH Fine. I still live in our old apartment. But you would hate it now.

BILLY What did you do to it?

HANNAH Not a thing.

BILLY And I heard you went in for an operation.

HANNAH A hysterectomy. I was out the same day. . . . And I believe you had prostate trouble.

BILLY Small world, isn't it?

HANNAH Well, our past sins have a way of catching up with us . . . What else can I tell you about me?

BILLY Jenny fills me in with everything.

HANNAH Oh, I'm sure.

BILLY I understand you have a new boyfriend.

HANNAH A boyfriend? God forbid. I'm forty-two years old—I have a lover.

BILLY Also a writer.

HANNAH A newspaperman on the Washington *Post.*

BILLY Really? Not one of those two who—

HANNAH No.

BILLY Right.

HANNAH He's fifty-four. He has a heart condition, asthma and leans towards alcoholism. He also has the second-best mind I've met in this country since Adlai Stevenson . . . And what's with you, mate-wise?

BILLY Mate-wise? Mate-wise I am seeing a very nice girl.

HANNAH Are you? And where are you seeing her to?

BILLY *(Annoyed)* Oh, come on, Hannah.

HANNAH What did I say? Have I offended you?

BILLY Can we cut the cute chitchat? I think we've got other things to talk about.

HANNAH I'm sorry. I *have* offended you.

BILLY My God, it's been a long time since I've been involved in smart-ass conversation.

HANNAH I beg *your* pardon, but *you* were the one who said things like "I hear you have a boyfriend" and "I'm seeing a very nice girl." I am *not* the one with the Bobbsey Twin haircut and the Peter Pan phraseology.

BILLY I can see you've really come to hunt bear, haven't you?

HANNAH Hunt bear? Did I actually hear you say "hunt bear"? Is that the kind of nifty conversation you have around those Sierra Nevada campfires?

BILLY Forget the tea. Maybe I *will* have a double Scotch.

HANNAH It's ordered. You're safe either way.

BILLY Can we talk about Jenny?

HANNAH What's your rush? She's only seventeen. She's got her whole life ahead of her. If I'm going to turn my daughter over to you—which I am not—at least I'd like to know what you're like.

BILLY Jenny is *our* daughter! *Ours!*

HANNAH Maybe. We'll see. They've been very slow with the blood test. *(They glare at each other a moment. She suddenly smiles)* So you live in a French farmhouse off Sunset Boulevard. Do you have a pool?

BILLY Christ!

HANNAH Come on, Billy, talk to me. I wrote down seventy-four questions to ask—don't make me look for the list. Do you have a pool? . . . Well, naturally you've got a pool. You've got a tan, so you've got a pool . . . Is it kidney shaped? . . . Liver? . . . Possibly gall bladder?

BILLY Pancreas, actually. The head surgeon at Cedars of Lebanon put it in. You're terrific. You haven't spent fifteen days of your life out here, but you know exactly how we all live, don't you? Too bad you're going back so soon. You're gonna miss the way we spend our holidays. Wouldn't it *thrill* you to see a pink-painted Christmas tree on my lawn . . . or a three-flavored Baskin-Robbins snowman wearing alligator shoes . . . with a loudspeaker on the roof playing Sonny and Cher singing "Silent Night"?

HANNAH When you've seen it once, the thrill is gone.

BILLY Where's that drink?

HANNAH What kind of a car do you have?

BILLY You're really serious, aren't you?

HANNAH I am *dead* serious. If I'm to leave my precious baby with you, I want to know what kind of a car I'm leaving her in.

BILLY A brown Mercedes—450 SEL.

HANNAH You have no class. You never had any class. A red *Pinto* in Beverly Hills would be class . . . Can I throw a few more questions at you?

BILLY Questions? I thought they were spears.

HANNAH What happened to your cute little wife? I don't mean *me,* I mean the cute one *after* me. Divorced her, too, didn't you?

BILLY She was on the road a lot; I like to stay home. The first three years weren't too bad.

HANNAH Oh, that's right, she was a singer, wasn't she? Somebody sent me one of her albums for Christmas, as a gag. They were right . . . I gagged.

BILLY Really? She was number three on the charts, won two Grammys last year. I thought she was good.

HANNAH Pity you didn't take up the guitar sooner,

you could have still been with her . . . And tell me about the one you're seeing now. What does she do?

BILLY She's an actress. Quite good. She was married before. Has a little boy, eleven years old.

HANNAH And is marriage contemplated? . . . Am I being too nosy?

BILLY Not for a *Newsweek* editor . . . Yes. Marriage is contemplated. It is being discussed; it is being considered. Strange as it seems, I like being married.

HANNAH Right. And will there be room for all of you in the little French farmhouse, or will you have to move to an Italian *palazzo* on Wilshire Boulevard?

BILLY What the hell are you so bitter about? You used to be bright and witty. Now you're just snide and sarcastic.

HANNAH It comes with age. When you don't have a fast ball any more, you go to change-ups and sliders.

BILLY Oh, please. Spare me your sports metaphors. You never knew a bunt from a double. The only reason you went to the games is because you thought you looked butch . . . Are you through with your interrogation?

HANNAH I'm still interested in this new girl.

BILLY Her name is Betsy LaSorda. Her father used to be a damned good director. She can catch a trout and she can beat me at tennis. I think she's peachy. What else?

HANNAH Well, I know you've been bouncing around a lot, Billy. Do you really care for her, or do you have someone who gets you a break on marriage licenses?

BILLY God, I can just hear the quips flying when you and the second-best mind since Adlai Stevenson get together. Sitting there freezing under a blanket at the Washington Redskin game playing anagrams with the names of all the Polish players . . . I'll tell you something, Hannah: For one of the brightest women in America, you bore the hell out of me. Your mind clicks off bric-a-bracs so goddamn fast, it never has a chance to let an honest emotion or thought ever get through.

HANNAH And you're so *filled* with honest emotions, you fall in love every time someone sings a ballad. You're worse than a hopeless romantic, you're a *hopeful* one. You're the kind of a man who would end the world's famine problem by having them all eat out . . . preferably at a good Chinese restaurant!

BILLY *(Gets up, starts towards the door, stops)* What do you want to do about Jenny?

HANNAH Who?

BILLY Do you want to discuss this problem sensibly and sincerely, or do you want to challenge me to the *New York Times* crossword puzzle for her?

HANNAH Oh, stop pouting. You may dress like a child, but you don't have to act like one.

BILLY Would you mind terribly if I said "Up yours" and left?

HANNAH What have you done to her, Billy? She's changed. She used to come back to New York after the summers here taller and anxious to see her friends . . . Now she meditates and eats alfalfa.

BILLY She just turned seventeen. Something was bound to happen to her.

HANNAH You have no legal rights to her, of course. You understand that.

BILLY Certainly.

HANNAH Then tell her to come home with me.

BILLY I did. She would like to try it with me for a year. She's not happy in New York, Hannah.

HANNAH *Nobody's* happy in New York. But they're *alive.*

BILLY I can't fight you. If you want to take her, then take her. But I think you'd be making a mistake.

HANNAH She still has another year of high school left.

BILLY Believe it or not, they have good schools here. I can show you some, if you like.

HANNAH Oh, that should be fun. Something like the Universal Studio tour?

BILLY What a snob you are.

HANNAH Thank God there's a few of us left.

BILLY What is there so beautiful about your life that makes it so important to put down everyone else's? Forty square blocks bounded by Lincoln Center on the west and Cinema II on the east is not the center of the goddamn universe. I grant you it's an exciting, vibrant, stimulating, fabulous city, but it is not Mecca . . . It just smells like it.

HANNAH The hell with New York! Or Boston or Washington or Philadelphia. I don't care *where* Jenny lives, but *how.* She's an intelligent girl with a good mind. Let it grow and prosper. But what the hell is she going to learn in a community that has valet parking just to pick up four bagels and the *Hollywood Reporter?*

BILLY I've been to Martha's Vineyard in July, Hannah. Heaven protect me from another intellectual Cape Cod summer . . . The political élite queuing up in old beach sandals to see Bogart pictures, standing there eating ice cream cones and reading the *New Republic.*

HANNAH Neat, wasn't it?

BILLY No. Your political friends never impressed me . . . I remember one hot Sunday afternoon in Hyannisport when our ambassador to some war-torn Middle Eastern country was in a state of despair because he couldn't get the hang of throwing a Frisbee. My God, the absurdity . . . I went to a charity luncheon in East Hampton to raise money for the California grape pickers. There was this teeming mob of women who must have spent a total of twelve thousand dollars on new Gucci pants in order to raise two thousand dollars for the grape pickers . . . Why the hell didn't they just mail them the pants?

HANNAH You were terrific when you used to write like that. . . . I didn't see the last picture you wrote, but they tell me it grossed very well in backward areas.

BILLY Jesus, was I anything like you before?

HANNAH I couldn't hold a candle to you.

BILLY No wonder no one spoke to me here for the first two years.

HANNAH Lucky you.

BILLY Look, I don't want to interrupt your train of venom, but could we get back to Jenny?

HANNAH Jenny. Yes, what a good idea.

BILLY If you respect her as a person, respect her right to make a free choice.

HANNAH You get her for the summers, that's enough. If the judge had seen your life-style, you'd be lucky to get her Labor Day afternoon.

BILLY Funny how we haven't discussed *your* life-style, isn't it?

HANNAH I don't have a life-style. I have a life.

BILLY The hell you do. The only time you're alive is Tuesday mornings when the magazine hits the stands . . . You're a voyeur in newsprint, snooping on everyone else's life-style and editing out the healthy aspects of the human condition because, for a dollar a copy, who the hell wants to read about happiness?

HANNAH Sometimes I actually miss you. You wouldn't consider coming back East and entering into a ménage à trois?

BILLY Would you like to know what Jenny has to say about you?

HANNAH She's told me. She thinks I'm a son-of-a-bitch. She also thinks I'm a *funny* son-of-a-bitch. She loves me but she doesn't like me. She's afraid of me. She's intimidated by me. She respects me but wouldn't want to become like me. We have a normal mother and daughter relationship.

BILLY She told me she feels stifled—that the only time she can really breathe freely is when she's out here.

HANNAH I have a wonderful nose and throat man on East Eighty-fourth Street.

BILLY How the hell can you be so flippant when it comes to your own daughter's well-being?

HANNAH And how the hell can you be so *pompous* not to recognize a very healthy rebellious attitude in an adolescent? If she *didn't* complain, I would probably send her to an expensive shrink. Since she's with *me* ten months of the year, it's only natural *you're* the one she's going to miss . . . I think by and large she and I have managed quite well but it's obvious, like all young girls, she needs a father image. I don't mind. If it's only July and August, it might as well be you.

BILLY This is Thanksgiving and she came out *without* your permission.

HANNAH She never had a very good head for dates.

BILLY What would you do if I just kept her here with me?

HANNAH Don't be ridiculous.

BILLY But what would you do, Hannah?

HANNAH I would find the very best lawyer I could in California . . . and have him beat the shit out of you.

BILLY Would you drag it through the courts if I said I'm keeping her for six months?

HANNAH I will call my friend, the Attorney General of the United States, if she is not on that three o'clock plane.

BILLY *(Sits back and smiles at her)* Why didn't you ever run for office, Hannah? I always thought you'd make a helluva Governor.

HANNAH Because I don't think a democratic system really works. Offer me a monarchy and we'll talk. *(Looks at her watch)* It's one fifteen. Will you call Jenny or shall I?

BILLY No.

HANNAH No what?

BILLY No, *sir!*

HANNAH If you'll tell me how to get to your little French farmhouse, I'll pick her up myself.

BILLY How much time do you spend with her? Do you ever have breakfast with her? How many nights does she eat dinner alone? Do you think she's really happy with that twenty-dollar bill you give her every time you go off to Washington for the weekend? The girl is growing up lonely, Hannah, and if you tell me she's got a cat and a canary, I'll belt you right in the choppers.

HANNAH She has two dogs, a Dominican cook and

twelve different girls who sleep over every time I'm away. Despite her Gothic reports, she is not living the life of Jane Eyre.

BILLY The truth, Hannah . . . You know if we leave it up to Jenny, you don't stand a chance in hell of getting her on that plane. Right?

HANNAH Certainly. Why else would the ninny run away? . . . Who said we don't have problems? She is seventeen years old, and when we go at each other, she needs another shoulder to cry on . . . But I'll be goddamned if I'm giving up a daughter for a cashmere shoulder three thousand miles away.

BILLY My God, you're really afraid . . . This is an event. I think it's the first time I've ever actually seen you nervous.

HANNAH Wrong. I was nervous on our wedding night . . . Unfortunately, it was *after* we had sex.

BILLY Please. No cheap shots. It's not like you. I mean, we may have had a very narrow chance for happiness, but sex was never a stumbling block.

HANNAH Neither was it an architectural marvel . . . Oh, I'm not blaming *you.* Actually you were very skillful in bed. You could ravage me for hours without ever mussing the sheets. But the moment it was over, you would heave a deep sigh and tell me your plans for the future . . . The sex was stimulating but the plans were so freaking boring.

BILLY Boring? And I have made love to women with the television on before, but *never* watching Eric Sevareid.

HANNAH Sometimes we need our private fantasies to help us get to the top of Magic Mountain.

BILLY You know something, Hannah? . . . I don't like you any more.

HANNAH It's okay. I'm not always fond of me either . . . What are we going to do, Billy? I want my daughter back. You're the only one who can help me.

BILLY *(Looks at her)* You're being sincere now, aren't you? . . . What a shame. You do it so seldom, when it finally comes I'm *still* waiting for the zingers.

HANNAH Billy . . . what do you look forward to?

BILLY *(He looks behind him)* Where did *that* non-sequitur come from?

HANNAH You know me. My mind is always on "express." I'd really like to know. You're forty-five years old, you've been married twice, had a child, a half a dozen houses, a promising journalistic career and some questionable but undeniably commercial successes . . . I'd like to know what it is you look forward to.

BILLY *(Pauses)* Saturdays . . . I love Saturdays.

HANNAH For a simple-minded bastard, sometimes you sure are smart . . . You know what I look forward to?

BILLY What?

HANNAH Christ, it's hard for me to say it . . . Are you going to laugh?

BILLY Only if it's not funny. What do you look forward to?

HANNAH I look forward to a granddaughter . . . I think I screwed up the first time.

BILLY *(Good-naturedly)* No one can phrase sentiment like you.

HANNAH Are you going to help me?

BILLY By sending Jenny home? She'd be back in two weeks.

HANNAH Not if I put heavy weights on her feet . . .

Offer me a suggestion, goddamn it, for old times' sake.

BILLY You know my suggestion.

HANNAH I only have one more year with her. In September she'll go to college. In four years she'll come out a revolutionary or a nun . . . or even worse, like you or me.

BILLY A little bit of both wouldn't be so bad.

HANNAH Do you like your mother?

BILLY She's dead.

HANNAH Don't quibble. Did you like her?

BILLY For a neurotic woman, she wasn't too bad.

HANNAH I don't like mine much. Can you imagine being a pain in the ass for seventy-eight years? I felt something was wrong even when I was in the womb. I never felt comfortable. I think I was hanging too low . . . We shouldn't have had Jenny. People like you and me are too selfish . . . I don't want her to grow up hating me and I don't want her growing up here, because I'm liable to hate her . . . Maybe you and I should have stayed together and we could have let *Jenny* go. What do you think?

BILLY I changed my mind. I think I like you again.

HANNAH He's not going to live very long, you know.

BILLY Who isn't?

HANNAH My Washington *Post* friend. He had open heart surgery that was a total waste of time.

BILLY I'm sorry to hear that.

HANNAH Me, too . . . The man could really make me laugh.

BILLY Sounded like it was pretty good.

HANNAH Oh, well, you win some, you lose some.

BILLY *(With admiration)* Talk about resiliency . . .

HANNAH For a smart lady in a man's world, I'm not doing too bad.

BILLY No, you're not . . . Would it comfort you any to meet my actress friend? Just to know that Jenny hasn't fallen into wicked hands?

HANNAH I'm shaky enough right now—I don't have to meet someone with smoother skin than me . . . Thanks a lot.

BILLY For what?

HANNAH You're supposed to say, "She doesn't have smoother skin than you."

BILLY Sorry, she does. It's only in good conversation she comes in second place.

HANNAH The truth . . . Is being in love better now?

BILLY Yes.

HANNAH Why?

BILLY Because it's now.

HANNAH I don't like the way this meeting is going. I think I'm losing ground. Why don't we go to New York and finish it?

BILLY You can have it both ways, you know.

HANNAH What does that mean?

BILLY Take your summer vacation this winter. Come out here, I'll find you a nice place at the beach. This way we can both see Jenny.

HANNAH Two months? Out *here?* . . . I would get constipation of the mind.

BILLY You're afraid.

HANNAH Of what?

BILLY That you might like it. You're afraid you might like *anything*. Happiness is so banal, isn't it?

HANNAH No. Just that statement . . . Let's keep things the way they are, Billy. God only meant us to have nine years together. He knew what He was doing.

BILLY Well, then we haven't settled anything, have we?

HANNAH Well, we've settled that I'm not coming out here for two months. It was worth coming out here just to settle that. That only leaves Jenny to deal with.

BILLY Shall I get her up here? She's downstairs in the car with her bags packed . . . She's willing to abide by any decision we both make.

HANNAH Oh, what a cunning bastard you are. If we say she goes back to New York, she'll think I coerced you. And if we say stay here, she'll think I didn't even put up a fight for her.

BILLY Do you think she has that devious a mind?

HANNAH Certainly. *She's my* daughter . . . I don't suppose *you'd* consider spending two months back East?

BILLY Only if everyone there leaves . . . You want me to make it easy for you, Hannah? I'll throw in my vote. Whatever you say goes. And I'll tell Jenny we *both* made the decision.

HANNAH *(Really perplexed)* Jesus, no wonder there are so many used car salesmen out here. How much time do I have? I was never very good with deadlines.

BILLY As much time as you want.

HANNAH *(Goes over to the window and looks out, trying to see if she can see his car)* Which is your car? They're *all* Mercedes. *(She turns; he is staring at her)* What are you looking at me like that for?

BILLY It's not often I've seen you looking so vulnerable.

HANNAH Well, take a picture of it. You won't see it again . . . Keep her.

BILLY What?

HANNAH I said, keep her—six months, not a year. And *I* pick the school. And whoever I pick, they have to send me three references . . . Christ, what am I doing?

BILLY Stay the weekend, Hannah. Talk it over with Jenny. You don't have to decide because you've got a plane ticket.

HANNAH I'm a fighter, Billy. If I stay the weekend, I not only take Jenny with me, but I'll take your new girlfriend back, too.

BILLY Hannah, don't let me bully you into this. Why can't the three of us talk it out? Let me get Jenny up here.

HANNAH *No,* goddamn it! If I have to give her up to get her back, then let's do it.

BILLY You mean it? You'll let her stay?

HANNAH You think you're in for a picnic? Wait'll you try shopping for clothes with her.

BILLY Can you take a compliment? You're not the Hannah I left nine years ago.

HANNAH And I'm missing the ovaries to prove it . . .

BILLY Well, guess who's nonplussed now?

HANNAH Jesus, you never thought I would say yes, did you? You know, I don't think you're prepared to take on your own daughter. Watching her swim for eight weeks at the beach is not the same as being a parent . . . Don't look now, Billy, but you just lost your sun tan.

BILLY If you think I'm scared, you're damned right.

HANNAH I love it. Oh, God I love it. Wait'll you see how she eats in the winter. You'll be dead broke by Christmas.

BILLY I think you're doing a terrific thing, Hannah.

HANNAH So do I.

BILLY And if for any reason, I feel things aren't working out, I'll send her back to you.

HANNAH The hell you will. You're a Father now, Billy.

BILLY I suppose you want to see her before you leave.

HANNAH Well, you suppose wrong. I've seen her. I'll call her when I get to New York.

BILLY What should I tell her?

HANNAH Tell her I hope she'll be very happy and that I'm selling her record collection.

BILLY *(He starts towards the door)* You know, we couldn't have been too bad together. We produced a hell of a girl.

HANNAH You got that a little wrong . . . I think the two of you produced a hell of a mother.

BILLY Maybe you're right . . . Can we shake hands now? I'm about to leave.

HANNAH Sure. Why not? What more can I lose? *(They shake hands. He holds on to hers)* Serve her plenty of broccoli and lima beans.

BILLY She likes them?

HANNAH *Hates* them. But from now on, what do I care?

BILLY Goodbye, Hannah . . . It was good seeing you again.

HANNAH *(On the point of tears)* I suddenly feel like an artist selling a painting he doesn't want to part with.

BILLY *(Gently)* I'll frame it and keep it in a good light.

HANNAH Do that . . . And take care of Jenny, too. *(*BILLY *looks at her, puts his hands on her shoulders, and kisses her on the cheek. He wants to say something else, then changes his mind, opens the door quickly and leaves. She stands there a moment, then moves back to the window and looks down. Then she goes to the phone and picks up the receiver. Into the phone. About to break down)* Operator . . . Get me room service . . . I never got my goddamn drinks.

(The lights dim)

Blackout

SCENE TWO: *Visitor from Philadelphia*

The morning sunlight is streaming in through the opened drapes in the living room. By contrast, the bedroom is very dark, barely visible. The curtains and shades are drawn. We hear a long, loud, male yawn from the bed.

MARVIN Oh, God . . . *(He rubs his face with both hands)* Ohhhhhhhhhhh. *(He gets up and goes into the bathroom, moving almost zombie-like as he feels the awfulness of his hangover)* MARVIN MICHAELS *is about forty-two. He wears undershorts, T-shirt and* one *black sock. His hair is rumpled. We hear him gargle. He comes out of the bathroom, goes back to the bed, gets in and sits up)* Ugh, never again . . . Never never never . . . *(He sits there trying to breathe, and suddenly, from under the sheets, an arm comes out. A female arm. He recoils, frightened to death)* Oh, God . . . *(He lifts the hand to his face and looks at it. He lifts the cover back, and we see a woman, who, from what we can make out, seems to be attractive. She is wearing the tops of his pajamas)* What are you doing here? I thought you left! *(There is no response from her: she is out like a light)* Hey! *(He nudges her)* Hey, come on, you can't stay here! Hey, wake up! *(He turns, gropes for his watch on the night table, and looks at it) Eleven o'clock! Jesus Christ, it's eleven o'clock! (He jumps out of bed)* Wake up! Come on, get up, it's eleven o'clock, don't you understand? *(He turns back and reaches for the phone)* Crazy! I must be crazy! *(Into the phone)* Operator? . . . What time is it? . . . *(Screams)* Eleven o'clock? . . . Why didn't you call me? . . . I left a wake-up call for eight o'clock . . . I *did!* . . . Mr. Michaels, Room 203, an eight o'clock wake-up call

. . . I *didn't?* . . . I can't understand that . . . Never mind, did I get any calls? . . . Well, take the hold signal off, I'm taking calls. *(He hangs up)* How could I forget to leave a wake-up call? *(He nudges the girl, then starts getting dressed)* Hey, come on. Get up, will ya? You have to get dressed. My wife could walk in any minute. Eleven o'clock—her plane probably got in already. *(He gets his pants and other sock on) Will you get up? We got an emergency here! (He puts his shirt on. The girl hasn't moved)* What's wrong with you? You deaf or something? *(He crosses to the bed. She is breathing but not moving)* Are you all right? *(He nudges her again. She moans but doesn't move. He turns and looks at the floor next to the bed, and picks up a quart-size empty bottle of vodka)* Oh, God, what did you do? An entire bottle of vodka? You drank a whole bottle of vodka with my wife coming in? Are you crazy? *(He nudges her)* Are you all right? Can you hear me? *(She moans)* What? What did you say? . . . I couldn't hear that. *(She moans again. He puts his ear to her mouth)* Sick . . . You feel sick? . . . Six margaritas and a bottle of vodka, I wonder why . . . Listen, you can get dressed and take a cab home and be nice and sick in your own bed all day . . . Doesn't that sound nice? Heh? *(No response)* Oh, God, what am I going to do? . . . Water. You want a little water? *(He rushes to the table, pours a glass of ice water and rushes back to her)* Here, lady. Sip a little cold water. *(He picks her head up and tries to pour some water into her mouth, but her lips won't open and it dribbles down her face)* Drink, sweetheart . . . for my sake . . . Open your lips, you crazy broad! *(To himself)* Don't panic . . . Panic is the quickest way to divorce—mustn't panic! *(He sticks his fingers in the glass and flicks water at her face)* Up, up, up! Here we go! Rise and shine, everybody up! *(He throws more water. She doesn't budge. He shakes her shoulders—she flops about like a ragdoll)* Move! Please God, make her move. I'll never be a bad person again as long as I live. *(She doesn't move; she lies there)* All right, we're gonna get you dressed and down into a cab. Once you're on your feet, you'll be fine . . . I'm really sorry this happened. I don't remember much, but it must have been a wonderful evening, whatever your name is . . . Could you help me a little, honey? Please? . . . You're not gonna help me. All right, Marvin, think. Think, Marvin. *(He slaps his own face to help him think)* I gotta get outta here. *(He picks up phone)* Operator, get me the front desk. *(He looks at the girl,* BUNNY*)* I have two wonderful children who need a father—don't do this to me. *(Into the phone)* Hello? . . . This is an *angry* Mr. Michaels in Suite 203 and 4 . . . Listen, I am very uncomfortable in my room . . . The toilet kept dripping all night. No, I don't want it fixed. I want another room. I could move out immediately . . . I'm expecting my wife in from Philadelphia any minute, and I *know* she's not going to be happy once she sees this room . . . *Who's* here? . . . MY WIFE? MY-WIFE-IS-HERE? . . . You sent my wife up without calling me? . . . How could you do such a thing? What the hell kind of a cheap hotel are you running here? . . . Can't you send someone to stop her? She's not going to like this room! *(There is a knock on the living room door. He slams the phone down and dashes around the bedroom in a frenzy)* Oh, God! *(Whispers to the inert form)* Oh, God! Oh, God! OH, GOD! OH, GOD! OH, GOD! Listen to me . . . I have to go into the other room. When I'm inside, lock the door from in here. Don't open it for anyone, do you understand? . . . For anyone! *(Another knock on the door. He goes into the living room, closing the bedroom door. Then asks softly and innocently)* Who is it?

MILLIE It's me.

MARVIN Millie?

MILLIE Yes.

(He picks up a full ashtray and two champagne glasses and hurls them out the sliding door to the patio. He opens the door)

MARVIN Hello, sweetie.

MILLIE Hello. What took you so long? Why didn't you pick me up at the airport?

MARVIN Why?

MILLIE Yes, why?

MARVIN Why? . . . I've been sick all night. I threw up in the other room. Don't go in there. The doctor just left ten minutes ago. I have acute gastroenteritis . . . It's nothing to worry about.

MILLIE Oh, my God. When did this happen?

MARVIN About two o'clock in the morning.

MILLIE What did you eat?

MARVIN Spaghetti with white clam sauce—and tacos . . . It was a Mexican-Italian restaurant.

MILLIE Spaghetti with tacos?

MARVIN And some tortillas parmegan. Two people got sick at the next table. I thought it was the flu. I never had that kind of food before.

MILLIE Where did you get a doctor?

MARVIN I called my brother. He got me a wonderful stomach man. Greasiest restaurant I ever saw . . . Even the napkins kept slipping off the table.

MILLIE You look terrible. Why don't you get into bed? You'll feel more comfortable.

MARVIN I'm not supposed to lie down. It makes me nauseous . . . I feel a lot better in this room. It's cheerier . . . I need some Compazine spansules.

MILLIE What's that?

MARVIN It stops nausea. Compazine spansules.

MILLIE Did you call the drugstore?

MARVIN They don't carry it. It has codeine in it. The

nearest place that has it is a drugstore on Santa Monica Boulevard. But they don't deliver. I'll have to go over there myself. I'm just nervous about throwing up in the taxi.

MILLIE All right, I'll go. Where's the prescription?

MARVIN What prescription?

MILLIE Didn't the doctor give you a prescription? They're not gonna give you codeine without a prescription.

MARVIN Yes, they will. In California they will . . . Compazine spansules.

(He grabs his stomach)

MILLIE If you don't need a prescription, just send the cab driver. I'm exhausted. I just flew in from Philadelphia.

MARVIN They tell me you can't trust the cab drivers out here. They're notorious for going for medicine and not coming back . . . Oh, God, what I'd give for a good Compazine spansule.

MILLIE What are you going to do about the bar mitzvah?

MARVIN Oh, we're going. I didn't fly all the way from Philadelphia to miss my nephew's bar mitzvah . . . I'm glad you reminded me. Harry called a few minutes ago. He wants us to get over to the temple as soon as possible, so why don't you go down for a cab and I'll finish getting dressed.

MILLIE It's just after eleven. I thought we didn't have to be there until one.

MARVIN That's for the others. Harry wants us to get a seat down front. His kid has a very soft voice and he doesn't want us to miss his speech. So why don't you go down and get the cab and I'll finish getting dressed.

MILLIE And what am I going to wear?

MARVIN What do you mean? Didn't you bring a dress? I told you to bring a dress.

MILLIE They lost it. *(Starts to cry)* They can't find my luggage.

MARVIN Who can't?

MILLIE The airlines. They lost my luggage. My new suitcase with my new dress and my new shoes. I have nothing to wear.

(She sobs)

MARVIN *(Exaggerated anger)* Lost your luggage? Your good luggage that I gave you for Christmas? My God, that gets me insane! In this day and age, to still lose luggage . . .

MILLIE They said they'll call me at the hotel when they find it. I just wanted to come back here, take a hot bath and a nap.

MARVIN There's no time for a nap. I know those airlines. You've got to go down there and make a fuss. Call a cab. We're going back to the airport *right now* and demand satisfaction.

MILLIE I don't want satisfaction. I want my bar mitzvah dress.

MARVIN We'll go shopping in Beverly Hills. This is the best time of day, before they get crowded.

MILLIE This trip is costing us a fortune. Why did you take a suite? It's so expensive.

MARVIN I wanted you to be comfortable. To celebrate —our first trip to California . . . It was a mistake. The bedroom is stifling. It's all those vines outside the window—you can't breathe. I'm going to tell them to close off the bedroom and we'll just keep this room. *This* is cheerful.

MILLIE *(Looks around)* There are no beds in this room.

MARVIN Oh, I didn't know you wanted to stay over. I thought we were going up to San Francisco right after the bar mitzvah.

MILLIE The same day? Then when will I see Los Angeles?

MARVIN There's not much to see. I mean, there aren't that many points of interest.

MILLIE The third largest city in the United States?

MARVIN Only in population. There's plenty of *people* to see, but we don't know any of them.

MILLIE Three thousand miles just to see a bar mitzvah? I've seen them before—they're not worth that much of a trip. Don't you ever do this to me again.

MARVIN *(Guiltily)* Do what? What? Don't do what again?

MILLIE Make us take separate planes—for what? We're so worried that something is going to happen to us and our children will be left alone. So look what happens to us separately. They lose my luggage and you have gastroenteritis. *(She gets up)* I have to go to the bathroom.

MARVIN *(Screeches)* NOW? *(He races around to block the door to the bedroom and bathroom)*

MILLIE I haven't gone in four hours; *now* is a good time.

MARVIN I just told you. I threw up in there. I mean, everywhere—the bathtub, the floor, the mirror. I wouldn't let you go in there.

MILLIE I've seen you get sick before.

MARVIN Not on a holiday. Not on a vacation. I think on a holiday one should try to preserve *some* sense of romanticism . . . At *home,* I wouldn't mind.

MILLIE I can't *wait* till we get home. You're acting very peculiar. Are you sure you don't have a fever or something?

MARVIN It's possible . . . The doctor said I might be getting periods of fever and periods of not knowing how certain inexplicable events may have happened.

MILLIE What inexplicable events?

MARVIN *(Shrugs)* I don't know . . . I mean, in case some trivial thing comes up that I can't explain. The doctor said that's very possible.

MILLIE I don't understand a word you're saying.

MARVIN Exactly my point.

MILLIE I have to go to the bathroom.

MARVIN *Please* . . . Give me the opportunity of making it presentable first. It means a lot to me.

MILLIE We've been married fifteen years, and you've never cleaned up a bathroom for me before.

MARVIN Well, I think it's high time I started. *(He kisses her cheek)* I'll be right out . . . Why don't you thumb through the brochure and find us a nice restaurant for tomorrow? Anything but Mexican-Italian. *(*MILLIE *goes over to the desk and thumbs through the brochure. He goes into the bedroom, locks the door behind him, and rushes to the bed. The girl is still out like a light. He starts to pick her up)* I'm sorry. I don't like doing this, but I'm going to have to leave you out in the hall. *(He drags her towards the door)* You'll be all right, they'll take care of you. They have *wonderful* service here. *(He gets to the door and opens it with one hand, propping her up behind his back. He sticks his head out, sees somebody)* OH! Jesus, you scared me. Hello, how are you?

(He keeps nodding, then pulls the girl away so as not to be seen and closes the door. He starts back for the bed and dumps her on it. Meanwhile in the living

room, MILLIE *is pacing around in her discomfort at needing to use the john. Finally she knocks on the bedroom door)*

MILLIE Marvin? . . . Marvin, the door is locked.

MARVIN I CAN'T HEAR YOU! I'M IN THE BATHROOM.

(He drags the "body" back to the bed and starts to cover it with blankets. He wrestles with her legs to get them to lie flat, and frantically smoothes the bedcovers)

MILLIE Open the door. Why is this door locked?

MARVIN It's not locked. Maybe it's stuck.

(Once the girl is completely covered, he hides her shoes and other female articles under the bed)

MILLIE Well, *open it,* for God's sakes.

MARVIN I'm not through in the bathroom yet.

MILLIE I want to come in the *bed*room! Will you open this door?

MARVIN OPEN THE WHAT?

MILLIE The door, the door.

(This kind of exchange continues until MARVIN *is ready to open the door)*

MARVIN You see? It was open. Don't you know how to work a door?

MILLIE What took you so long? What's the matter, you got a girl in here?

MARVIN *(Playing along with her joke)* That's right. I got a cute redhead in the bed! . . . I cleaned up the bathroom. You can go in there now.

MILLIE It's a nice bedroom. I wish we didn't have to move.

MARVIN I know. Isn't that a shame? *(She closes the bathroom door behind her.* MARVIN *rushes around the room trying to think of how he can dispose of the girl. He looks at the closet, opens it and gets in to see if the body will fit, then he rushes to the bed, hurls the covers off and picks up the helpless girl. He gets her halfway out of bed when he hears the john flush)* I'll never make it.

(He puts the body back into the bed, covers her with sheets and blankets, presses down and flattens her, then arranges himself elaborately on the edge of the bed to conceal the girl, as the bathroom door opens and MILLIE *comes out)*

MILLIE I love the telephone in the john.

MARVIN It's fun, isn't it? Would you like to go back in there and call the kids?

MILLIE Why? I just left the kids and I just used the john . . . How you feeling?

MARVIN Not as good as I would like . . . I was thinking, maybe you could take a shower and I could take a nap for about an hour. We have plenty of time. And maybe by then they'll find your luggage.

MILLIE My God, I hope so. Let's *both* take a nap.

MARVIN *(Stunned)* You mean together?

MILLIE Don't we always?

MARVIN No, no. We *sleep* together. Naps I usually take alone.

MILLIE *(Starts toward the bed)* I never heard you talk so crazy . . . Move over. I'm going to lie down.

MARVIN *(Sits up quickly)* NO! No, please. I—I want you to sit down a minute. I have something to tell you, Millie.

MILLIE You can't tell me lying down?

MARVIN It's the kind of thing you should hear sitting up.

MILLIE *(Shrugs)* You want me to sit up, I'll sit up.

(She sits in the armchair, takes off her shoes)

MARVIN Millie, you mean more to me than you could possibly know . . . but sometimes we transgress. Sometimes we do foolish little things that unwittingly may cause hurt and injury to the other.

MILLIE I don't think you've ever consciously hurt me.

MARVIN Consciously, no. But a careless word here, a thoughtless gesture there . . .

MILLIE Nothing major, Marvin. We've had our disagreements, but nothing major.

MARVIN I'm glad you brought that up, Millie . . . What would you consider major?

MILLIE Major? . . . I don't know . . . I couldn't picture you doing anything "major." A couple of minors maybe, but no major.

MARVIN But if I did . . . If I were not my normal self —temporarily—if illness had caused me to act in some foolish manner, what hurt could I cause you that was major?

MILLIE It's so hard to say . . . I guess if you were cruel to the children, I think that would be major.

MARVIN *(Jumping on it)* I would put that Number One! I think that would be the worst thing a man could do to his wife in a marriage. To be cruel to their children is unpardonable . . . *All else* could be forgiven.

(He looks at the bed)

MILLIE And if I caught you with another woman. That would be major.

MARVIN Let's not get off the children thing so fast! Children are the reflection of the love that two people share . . . Children are the emanations of the spirit of love that—

MILLIE My back is killing me from the plane. I've got to lie down for a few minutes.

(She gets up, going towards the bed)

MARVIN *(He jumps up in front of her)* Let's make love in the living room.

MILLIE What?

MARVIN Let's make love on the living room sofa—like we did on our honeymoon in Florida.

MILLIE That was a love seat.

(She starts for the bedroom)

MARVIN *(Trying to distract her)* How about on the rug? The living room rug. I could order up some champagne. It's been so long since we made love on a rug.

MILLIE That's not a rug. It's carpeting. I don't like to make love on carpeting.

MARVIN Oh, come on. *(He lies flat on the floor)* It's a holiday. We're going to be middle-aged soon.

MILLIE What's the matter with the bed? We've always done very well with a bed.

MARVIN I'm just trying to think of something *different* . . . to break up the monotony of a bed.

(She crosses into the bedroom)

MILLIE *(Hurt)* I didn't think our love-making was so monotonous.

(He follows her)

MARVIN It *isn't!* Our love-making is *wonderful!* It's beds that get repetitious. *(Holds his stomach)* I think I'm getting another attack.

MILLIE *(Angry)* Well, who tells you to eat Mexican-Italian food? You're not the only one who's feeling sick . . . I'm sick, too. *(Starts to cry)* I got my period on the plane . . . The first vacation we've had together in two years and I have to get my goddamn period, so don't tell me how sick you are!

(She suddenly sobs and falls onto the bed, crying into the pillow. She lies right next to the hidden body underneath. He watches in terror)

MARVIN *(Screams)* NO!

MILLIE *(She sits up, then gets off bed and looks at him queerly)* Well, you don't have to be *that* upset. It's not my fault. I didn't time out your lousy nephew's bar mitzvah . . . I'm sorry! I'm sorry, Marvin. I didn't mean to say that. I'm just so cranky and irritable. You know I always get that way when I get my period.

MARVIN I know.

MILLIE *(She sits back on the bed and lies down)* Come here, Marvin. Just lie down with me and hold me. We don't have to make love. Just hold me and tell me you're not upset that I'm so irritable. *(He lies down on the floor near the bed).*

MILLIE *(Looks down at him)* Marvin, why don't you get into the bed?

MARVIN *(He gets up, walks away)* Millie, I can't keep this up any more. I'm going to get a heart attack . . . I've got to tell you something.

MILLIE What, Marvin? What is it, darling?

MARVIN It was never my intention to hurt you, Millie, but it's very possible in the next few minutes you may be terribly, terribly hurt.

MILLIE Is it major or minor?

MARVIN To me it was minor, to you I think it's going to be extremely major.

MILLIE Tell me, Marvin . . . It couldn't be that bad, as long as you're not trying to cover up something.

(BUNNY unconsciously pushes the covers down and reveals herself—but at that moment MILLIE is facing the other way)

MARVIN *(Alarmed, he looks up at the ceiling because he doesn't know where else to look;* MILLIE *looks up also)* There's something I'd like to show you, Millie. But I'm going to ask you to do something for me first . . . Say nothing for ten seconds. Whatever comes to mind, please, for the sake of both of us, say nothing for ten seconds . . . You may turn around now, Millie.

(She turns her head around to the right and sees the body in the bed. She looks at it, and suddenly laughs aloud)

MILLIE One . . . two . . . three . . . I'm praying, Marvin . . . I'm praying the maid came in here to clean, got dizzy from overwork and fainted in your bed . . . I pray to God the maids in this hotel wear pajamas.

MARVIN It's not the maid, Millie.

MILLIE Then I hope it's the doctor . . . Is this your doctor, Marvin? If it's not your doctor, then you're going to need your lawyer.

MARVIN It's not a doctor, Millie . . . It's a woman.

MILLIE That was my *third* guess. You can call American Airlines and tell them to forget my luggage. I won't be needing it . . . Let me ask you a silly question, Marvin. Why doesn't she move?

MARVIN I can explain that.

MILLIE If you tell me you have been carrying on with a helpless paralytic, I won't buy it, Marvin. DON'T PLAY ON MY SYMPATHY!

MARVIN She had six margaritas and a bottle of vodka. She won't wake up till tomorrow . . . Millie, I deny nothing.

MILLIE Interesting, because I accuse you of EVERYTHING! *(She sits on the chair and starts to put on her shoes)* Is it a hooker, Marvin? Is it someone you know or is it a hooker? If it's a hooker, I'm going to divorce you. If it's someone you know, I'm going to kill you.

MARVIN I don't know her. I never met her. She's probably a hooker, I didn't ask.

MILLIE The humiliation . . . The humiliation of lying in bed next to a sleeping hooker and telling you I've got my period!

MARVIN Millie, will you please give me a chance to admit my guilt? I know you're going to take everything else away from me, at least leave me my guilt.

MILLIE You tell that hooker to give you back your pajamas, Marvin, because that's all I'm leaving you with.

(She starts towards the phone. He blocks the way)

MARVIN Is that all you care about? Retribution? What about fifteen years of marriage? Weren't they good years?

MILLIE They were *terrific* . . . but I never bothered looking on the other side of the bed.

(She tries for the phone again)

MARVIN Five minutes . . . If I can't win you back in five minutes, then I'm not worth holding on to.

MILLIE Thank God you *told* me. Can you imagine if I fell asleep and woke up with *her* in my arms?

MARVIN I have sinned. I have transgressed. I have committed adultery.

MILLIE In her condition, it's necrophilia! . . . Get out of my way.

MARVIN She was awake—drunk, but awake. We were both drunk. Do you think I would do something like this *stone sober?*

MILLIE Statements like that are *not* in the direction of winning me back . . . *(Into the phone)* Operator, get me the bell captain, please. *(To* MARVIN*)* And let me tell you something else: Being cruel to the children is Number Two. *This* is Number One!

MARVIN To *you*, Millie . . . I can understand where this is important to you. To me, it was meaningless.

MILLIE That's a shame, Marvin. I always get so upset when you don't have a good time. *(Looks at the lifeless body)* Look how she doesn't move. No *wonder* it wasn't too much fun. Hello, I would like a taxi, please. Mrs. Michaels, Room 203. Thank you. *(Hangs up)* I'll probably get the same cab she came in.

MARVIN Does it help you to know I didn't send for her? I never asked her to come—

MILLIE Really? Who sent her up, room service?

*(*MILLIE *goes into the living room and* MARVIN *follows)*

MARVIN She was a gift! A surprise gift . . . Someone sent her over. I didn't even pay for it.

MILLIE Who did?

MARVIN What's the difference?

MILLIE *Who did?*

MARVIN It's not important.

MILLIE Your brother, Harry! He's the only one you *know* in California. My God, I heard of fancy bar mitzvahs, but this is outrageous. I bet he sent one to *all* the men . . . What do the women get, a bottle of perfume?

MARVIN I'm the only one . . . Harry's four years younger than me. When he was sixteen, I gave him a birthday present—his first woman. He's been wanting to repay me for years . . . He knows in the fifteen years we've been married I never even *looked* at another woman . . . I had dinner at his house, had a few drinks, was feeling pretty good. Harry said to me when I got back to my room he was going to have a present there for me. I never expected anything like this—I thought maybe a basket of fruit . . . Certainly I could have said no, but I didn't. She was in the room, she was attractive, she was a little tight, and she was paid for. And besides, I didn't want to insult Harry. He did it out of love . . . It's not much of an excuse. It will never happen again because not only did I not enjoy it, I don't even remember it . . . That's the story. If you want to leave me, I would understand . . . And when I kill myself, I hope *you* understand.

MILLIE *(Gets up)* I'm in shock . . . I am in total shock. I haven't even reacted to this yet. A tornado of anger will be unleashed when the full weight of lying down next to your husband's hooker really hits me. *(She goes back into the bedroom)* I mean, I'm standing here watching the woman you fornicated, sleeping in the bed *I can't get into!*

MARVIN *(Follows her back in)* Would you like a drink, honey? I could call down for a drink. It'll calm you down.

MILLIE I don't want to be calmed down. I want to remember this moment. Did you bring the camera? I would like to have a picture of our first trip to California . . . Just the three of us.

MARVIN That's okay, Millie. Get it out. The quicker you get it out, the quicker you'll be rid of it.

MILLIE No camera, Marvin? How about calling Harry and getting the official bar mitzvah photographer. The nerve of that man to send you a gift like this. What would you say she cost, Marvin? Fifty? Does she look like a fifty-dollar hooker to you?

MARVIN *(He looks at the girl in the bed)* I don't know. I guess fifty.

MILLIE What a cheap brother you've got. We spent a *hundred and seventy five* on his lousy kid.

MARVIN Millie, I've learned my lesson. I promise it's over and done with.

MILLIE I see. And in the meantime you expect me to go to your nephew's bar mitzvah and say "Congratulations" to the man who *paid* for this woman to fiddle with my husband? You would put me through that humiliation?

MARVIN He doesn't know that you know.

MILLIE I see. Then the joke's on *him.* Only you and *I* know that I know.

MARVIN I'll do whatever you want. Forget the bar mitzvah. If you want to leave on the next plane for Philadelphia, I'll go with you.

MILLIE *(She ponders this a long, long time)* No . . . I will not give you *or* your family that satisfaction . . . I am going to behave with more dignity than you ever dreamed of. I am going to that bar mitzvah with my head held high. I am not going to leave you, Marvin. I am not going to divorce you . . . I am going to forgive you. I am going to forget this ever happened. I am going to understand the reason *why* it happened, and I will never bring it up again as long as we live . . . I am now going into Beverly Hills and spend every cent you've got.

MARVIN Wait, Millie. Let me go with you. I'll get dressed, we'll go shopping, we'll go to the bar mitzvah, and tonight we'll move into another hotel . . . Can we do that, Millie?

MILLIE Yes, Marvin, I would like that. I would like to make a fresh start. I would like to try and rebuild our marriage on trust and faith . . . I don't want something like this ever to happen to us again, Marvin.

MARVIN It won't, Millie, I promise you that. *(He goes over to her)* I'll never do anything to hurt you again as long as I live. You're the most special woman in the world, Millie, and I love you. *(He grabs her)* I love you, Millie—

MILLIE *(Turns away)* Please! Not in front of the hooker.

MARVIN *(Nods)* It'll take me two minutes to shave. I'll be right out. Then we'll go.

MILLIE Should we leave her a note or something?

MARVIN I don't think so. She's probably used to these things . . . You're such a thoughtful woman, Millie. I love you more this minute than I've ever loved you in my life. God, I'm lucky.

(He is about to burst into tears—he runs into the bathroom, closing the door behind him so he can sob in privacy. The phone rings. MILLIE *picks it up)*

MILLIE *(Into the phone)* Hello? . . . Who? . . . Oh, yes. Good. Put them on. *(Calls inside)* Marvin, the kids are calling . . . Hello? . . . Hello, darling. How are you? *(*MILLIE *sits on the bed)* You miss me? Well, I miss you, too . . . *(*MILLIE *lies back on the bed)* Daddy? Daddy's all right. He didn't sleep too well last night . . . On the plane? Oh, some movie with Charles Bronson. *(The hooker's arm flops over* MILLIE. *She looks at it with revulsion)* . . . I do sound funny? . . . Well, to tell you the truth, I *am* a little upset, darling . . . The airline lost my luggage . . . *(The curtain begins to fall)* The new dress I bought for the bar mitzvah, my new shoes, everything . . . I am so upset, darling . . .

(Her tears and the curtain fall)

Act Two

SCENE ONE: *Visitors from London*

The living room is filled with flowers. It is about 5 P.M. *in early April. The shades are open in both rooms, and the light pours through. In the living room sits* SIDNEY NICHOLS *—British, in his early forties. He is in a tuxedo, and is drinking a large gin and tonic. He is reading* Daily Variety. *He glances at his watch, then looks up at the ceiling and drums on the arm of his chair with his fingers.*

DIANA NICHOLS *comes out of the bathroom, fastening her earrings.* DIANA *is English as well. She is wearing a floor-length chiffon gown, obviously very expensive. She looks at herself in the full-length mirror. There is a rather odd bunch of fabric on her left shoulder.*

DIANA Finished, Sidney. I'm dressed. I'm going to have a look. *(She examines herself in the mirror)* Sidney? Disaster! Total disaster . . . The *Titanic* in chiffon! Oh, Christ, what has the dressmaker wrought?

SIDNEY *(Looks at his watch again)* Where the hell is the car?

DIANA There's either not enough chiffon or too much of me . . . I'm listing to the left, Sidney. God, I hope it's the floor. Sidney, come in and look—and try to be gentle.

SIDNEY *(Gets up, crossing toward the bedroom)* It's after five—we should have left ten minutes ago.

(He stops at the doorway and looks in at her)

DIANA Well?

SIDNEY How much was it?

DIANA Nothing. Joe Levine paid for it.

SIDNEY Then I love it.

DIANA You hate it. Damn it, I wish you didn't have such good taste. *(Keeps examining herself in the mirror)* What have they done to me, Sidney? I have a definite hump on my left shoulder. I mean, it's got to be seven hundred dollars if it's a penny, and I look like Richard the Third . . . Do you notice the hump, Sidney?

SIDNEY Isn't that your regular hump?

DIANA Don't joke with me. I'm going on national television.

SIDNEY There are no humps. I see no humps at this particular time.

(He takes a sip of his drink)

DIANA It's all *bulky* on the left side. Don't you see how it bunches up?

SIDNEY Have you taken out all the tissue paper?

DIANA I should have worn something simple . . . My black pants suit. Why the hell didn't I wear my black pants suit?

SIDNEY Because *I'm* wearing it.

DIANA We shouldn't have come. I never know how to dress in this bloody country. It's so easy to dress in England. You just put on warm clothing. Why did we come, Sidney?

SIDNEY Because it's all free, darling.

DIANA Glenda Jackson never comes, and she's nominated every goddamned year. We could have stayed in London and waited for a phone call. Michael Caine could have accepted for me. He would be bright and witty—and no one would have seen my hump.

SIDNEY Use it, sweetheart. People will pity you for your deformity and you're sure to win.

DIANA Maybe if you put your arm on my shoulder . . . *(She places his arm around her)* Keep your arm on my shoulder at all times. If I win, we'll go up together, your arm around me, and they'll think we're still mad for each other after twelve years.

SIDNEY Oh, I thought we were. I keep forgetting.

DIANA *(Looks at him)* How many gin and tonics have you had?

SIDNEY Three gins, one tonic.

DIANA Well, catch up on your tonics. We don't want to be disgusting tonight, do we? *(She fluffs up her hair)* What's wrong with my hair? It looks like I've combed it with a towel.

SIDNEY When you played Elizabeth you looked like a wart hog and you never complained once.

DIANA That's acting, this is living. Living, I want to be beautiful . . . My hair is the strangest color. I asked for a simple rinse and that queen gave me crayons.

SIDNEY Shall I walk with my arm on your head as well?

DIANA That's not funny, Sidney. That's bizarre. You have the most bizarre sense of humor.

SIDNEY Bizarre people often do.

DIANA Oh, Christ, I hate getting dressed like this. Why am I always so much more comfortable as someone else? I would have been perfectly happy going as Hedda Gabbler.

SIDNEY Try Quasimodo.

DIANA Try shutting up. What time is it?

SIDNEY Late. We are definitely late.

DIANA Just check me out. Do I have too much jewelry on?

SIDNEY Jingle it—I can't tell if I don't hear it.

DIANA Will you please be nice to me and pay me one bloody compliment? I've been getting dressed for this horseshit affair since six o'clock this morning.

SIDNEY You look lovely. And if that doesn't do, please accept radiant.

DIANA Why don't we watch it on television? We could stay in bed, have champagne, make love and switch the dial if Faye Dunaway wins.

(The phone rings. He goes toward it)

SIDNEY You can do what you want, love, but I wouldn't miss this circus for the world. *(Picks up the phone)* Hello? . . . Yes, it is . . . Right. We'll be down in two minutes. Thank you.

(He hangs up)

DIANA Why do they have these things so early? No woman can look good at five o'clock in the afternoon, except possibly Tatum O'Neal.

SIDNEY We are being reminded that nominees *must* be there at five thirty for the press.

DIANA The press! I can't *wait* to see how they explain my hump in the newspapers.

SIDNEY Oh, Diana . . .

DIANA What?

SIDNEY I was about to say you're making a mountain out of a molehill, but I didn't think it would amuse you.

DIANA Let me have a cigarette. *(She feels her stomach)*

Oh, Christ, I'm going to be acidic tonight. Be sure and bring a roll of Tums.

SIDNEY And sit there in front of America with a chalky-white mouth? Have a double gin instead; it'll drown all those butterflies.

(He gives her a cigarette, lights it, then goes to make her a drink)

DIANA This whole thing is so bizarre. Eight years with the National Theatre, two Pinter plays, two Becketts, nine Shakespeare, three Shaws, and I finally get nominated for a nauseating little comedy.

SIDNEY That's why they call it Hollywood.

(The phone rings. He hands her the gin. He picks up the phone)

DIANA I'm not here. I don't care if it's the Queen Mother, I'm not here.

SIDNEY Hello? . . . Oh, yes, how are you? . . . Well, she's a bit nervous, I think . . . Do you really think she will? . . . Well, let's hope so . . . And thank you for the flowers, the wine, the suite and everything else you send up by the hour . . . One moment, Joe. *(He puts hand over the phone. To* DIANA*)* Joe Levine. He wants to wish you luck.

DIANA Tell him I'm in the can.

SIDNEY The man paid for this trip, he paid for this suite, and he gave you the best part you've had in five years—I am not going to tell him you are in the can.

DIANA Then I'll tell him. *(She takes the receiver)* Joe, darling, I told Sidney to tell you I was in the can . . . I didn't want to speak to you, that's why . . . Because I feel so responsible . . . I don't want to let you down tonight . . . I know how much the picture means to you, and I want so much to win this for you, Joe . . . There was no picture without you . . . Well, goddamn it, it's true. After four studios turned it down, you deserve some special perserverance award . . . You're a chubby little man and I adore you . . . If I win tonight, darling, it's not going to be an Oscar—it's going to be a Joe Levine . . . You're an angel.

(She hangs up)

SIDNEY That was very sweet.

DIANA Did you like it? That's going to be my speech.

SIDNEY Your acceptance speech?

DIANA All except the part that I was in the can. Naturally we both know I don't have a chance in hell, but you've got to prepare *something.* I can't just stand up there sobbing with a humped back . . . Can I have another drink, darling? And stop worrying. I won't get *pissed* until *after* I lose.

(She takes his drink out of his hand. He starts making himself another one)

SIDNEY You have as good a chance as anyone.

DIANA I don't have the sentiment on my side. You've got to have a sentimental reason for them to vote for you. Any decent actress can give a good performance, but a *dying husband* would have insured everything . . . You wouldn't like to get something fatal for me, would you, angel?

SIDNEY You should have told me sooner. I could have come over on the *Hindenburg.*

DIANA We *are* terrible, Sidney, aren't we? God will punish us.

SIDNEY I think He already has. Drink up.

(He drinks)

DIANA *(Drinks)* Do you know what I might do next year, Sidney?

SIDNEY I pray: anything but Ibsen.

DIANA I might quit. I might get out. Give up acting. I'm not having any more fun. It used to be such fun . . . Do you know what Larry Olivier once said to me?

SIDNEY Can you tell me in the car?

DIANA Larry said, "Acting is the finest and most noble thing you can do with your life, unless, of course, you're lucky enough to be happy." . . . Isn't that incredible, Sid?

SIDNEY It's absolutely awe-inspiring . . . unless of course, you're *un*lucky enough to be married to an actress.

(He starts for the door)

DIANA I'm sorry, Sid. Was that an insensitive thing for me to say? It has nothing to do with us. I've always been unhappy. I think that's why I'm such a damned good actress . . . But that's about *all* I am.

SIDNEY Will you finish your drink? I don't want to miss the sound-editing awards.

DIANA I envy you, Sidney. You have nothing *but* talent. You cook better than I do, you write better than I do, God knows, you *dress* better than I do . . .

SIDNEY Better than *I.* "Do" is superfluous.

DIANA And you speak better than I do. Jesus, I'm glad you came. I would hate to go through this alone tonight.

SIDNEY I don't think they allow nominees to come alone. They give you Burt Reynolds or someone.

DIANA You've never liked any of this, have you? The openings, the parties, any of it.

SIDNEY I *love* the openings. I *adore* the parties. I lead a very gay life. I mean, let's be honest, angel, how many antiques dealers in London get to go to the Academy Awards?

DIANA And I think you hate that dusty little shop. You're never there when I call . . . Where do you spend your afternoons, Sidney?

SIDNEY In London? We don't have afternoons. *(Looks out the window)* I should have waited for you in front of the hotel. I could have gotten a nice tan.

DIANA You shouldn't have given it up, Sidney.

SIDNEY Acting?

DIANA Christ, you were good. You had more promise than any of us.

SIDNEY Really? I can't think what it was I promised.

DIANA You were so gentle on the stage. So unselfish, so giving. You had a sweet, gentle quality.

SIDNEY Yes. I would have made a wonderful Ophelia.

DIANA Well, as a matter of fact, you would.

SIDNEY Pity I couldn't have stayed sixteen forever. What a future I had. Juliet, Roxanne—there were no end to the roles . . .

DIANA You could go back, Sidney. You could if you wanted, you know.

SIDNEY Married to you? Oh, there'd be problems. It would be awful for both of us to be up for the same parts . . . No, no. I'm perfectly happy selling my eighteenth-century door knockers.

DIANA *(A pause)* What do you do with your afternoons, Sidney?

SIDNEY I just told you, darling. I look for knockers . . . Now can we go and get this bloody thing over with?

DIANA First kiss me and wish me luck.

SIDNEY *(Kisses her)* There's your kiss. Now, turn around so I can rub your hump for luck.

DIANA Don't be a shit, Sidney. I'm scared to death.

SIDNEY *(Smiles at her; then warmly and affectionately)* I wish you everything. I wish you luck, I wish you love, I wish you happiness. You're a gifted and remarkable woman. You've put up with me and my shenanigans for twelve harrowing years, and I don't know why. But I'm grateful . . . You've had half a husband and three quarters of a career. You deserve the full amount of everything . . . May the Academy of Arts and Sciences Board of Electees see the beauty, the talent and the courage that I have seen for a quarter of a lifetime . . . I hope you win the bloody Oscar . . . Fifty years from now I'll be able to sell it for a fortune.

(He kisses her again)

DIANA I love you, Sidney.

SIDNEY Then mention me in your speech. Come on.

(He pulls her out as she grabs her purse)

DIANA Ladies and gentlemen of the Academy, I thank you for this award . . . I have a lump in my throat and a hump on my dress.

(They exit, closing the door behind them. Gradually day turns into night, until both rooms are in darkness)

SCENE TWO

It is hours later—about two in the morning. The door opens and SIDNEY *turns on the light. His black tie is undone. He looks a bit under the weather. He leaves the door open and sits in a chair. About ten seconds later,* DIANA *appears. She has had quite a bit to drink and is not in a wonderful mood, to say the least. She stands in the doorway, weaving uncertainly.*

DIANA *(Peering at the number on the door)* What the hell are you doing in here?

SIDNEY *(Looks at her)* It's our room.

DIANA No, it isn't. We're across the hall. Come out of there, you twit.

SIDNEY You're blotto, darling. Go to bed.
(He kicks off his patent leather loafers)

DIANA Give me the key.

SIDNEY I just told you, *this* is our room: 203 and 204.

DIANA *(She turns and looks across the hall)* We are in 201 and 202.

SIDNEY If it makes you happy, go sleep in 201 and 202—you've always made friends easily.

DIANA Ha! *You* should talk! *(She comes in and closes the door)* What time is it?

SIDNEY *(Looks at his watch)* Two thirty-five . . . perhaps *three* thirty-five.

DIANA *(She kicks off her shoes)* Don't give me that "superior than thou" crap.

SIDNEY You *are* stinking, aren't you?

DIANA You've been gloating all evening . . . *(She falls out on the sofa)* all "pardon the expression" evening.

SIDNEY Pardon what expression?

DIANA "Fucking" evening.

SIDNEY Then why didn't you say it?

DIANA Because I'm a lady. A loser and a lady. I'm a great loser and a greater lady.

SIDNEY Who was that girl you threw up on?

DIANA I beg your pardon?

SIDNEY I was asking who that attractive young girl in the Pucci muu-muu that you threw up on *was!*

DIANA How would I know? If I were to start counting all the women in Pucci muu-muus that I throw up on, I would never have time to go shopping.

SIDNEY Well, I think her husband was one of the heads of Universal Pictures. It is my guess that it will snow in Tahiti before you work again at Universal Pictures.

DIANA Unless of course, there's a part that calls for throwing up on Pucci muu-muus . . . In that event, I think it's very likely I'll be considered.

SIDNEY I hate to be clinical about this, but since you had neither lunch nor dinner, nor even a single canapé at the ball, how could you possibly find anything to throw up?

DIANA When you have class, you can do anything.
(She rises and weaves)

SIDNEY You're not going to get "classy" all over me, are you?

DIANA How long do you intend going on like this?

SIDNEY Going on like what?

DIANA Going on here in the wrong suite. I am tired. I would like to take off my hump and go to bed.

SIDNEY I must say it was a dreary affair. Didn't you find it a dreary affair? Aside from losing and throwing up on that girl, it was a completely unmemorable evening.

DIANA Did I tell you I saw what's-her-name in the ladies' room?

SIDNEY Who?

DIANA What's-her-name? The one I saw in the ladies' room.

SIDNEY How would I possibly know?

DIANA Oh, Christ, you know her . . . She was in the ladies' room.

SIDNEY Can you narrow it down a bit more?

DIANA Barbra.

SIDNEY Streisand?

DIANA Was in the ladies' room.

SIDNEY Singing?

DIANA I don't think so. There were no requests.

SIDNEY What was she like?

DIANA Well, in the ladies' room, we're all pretty much the same . . .

SIDNEY I would imagine.

DIANA She thought I should have won.

SIDNEY Did she say that?

DIANA No. I did. But she agreed with me.

SIDNEY Wasn't that sweet of her.

DIANA You never told me what award I missed when I went to the can.

SIDNEY The best documentary short subject.

DIANA *(Furious)* *Damn* it! My favorite category. Who won?

SIDNEY *The Midgets of Leipzig!* . . . a Czech-Polish Production . . . Sigmund Wednetzki, Producer; Directed by Litweil Zumbredowicz and Stefan Vlech.

DIANA *(Looks at him)* I *thought* they would . . . And what was the best picture?

SIDNEY The best picture? You were there when they announced it. It came right after the best actress.

DIANA I was in a deep depression at the time . . . What was the best bloody picture?

SIDNEY You mean what was the best picture of the year or what did they *pick* as the best picture of the year?

DIANA What won the award, you asshole?

SIDNEY I am *not* an asshole. Don't you call me that.

DIANA Sidney, I have just thrown up on some of the best people in Hollywood. This is no time to get sensitive. What was the best picture?

SIDNEY I'm not telling you.

DIANA *(She sits up regally)* I'm not *asking* you, Sidney. I'm threatening you. What was the best picture?

SIDNEY And I said I'm not telling you.

DIANA You're not going to tell me what the best picture was?

SIDNEY I won't even tell you who the nominees were.

DIANA You crud.

SIDNEY Now I'm *definitely* not going to tell you.

DIANA You mean you *were* going to tell me before I called you a crud?

SIDNEY Very possibly.

DIANA I take it back. You are not a crud.

SIDNEY Am I still an asshole?

DIANA Yes.

SIDNEY Then it's back to definitely not telling.

DIANA I'm going to our room. Give me the key.

SIDNEY You behaved abominably tonight.

DIANA I did not.

SIDNEY Abominably.

DIANA *Not!*

SIDNEY A-bom!

DIANA Asshole Crud!

SIDNEY You are behaving better now than you did at the ball . . . That will give you an idea of how badly you behaved tonight.

(He gets up)

DIANA Where are you going, you twit?

SIDNEY I am going to bed. I am going to get some sleep. We have a ten A.M. plane to catch in the morning.

DIANA Ten A.M. *is* the morning. That is redundant. You've been redundant all evening.

SIDNEY When? When? When was I redundant?

DIANA Turning to me and saying "I'm sorry" after they announced that other twit had won *is redundant!*

SIDNEY First you called *me* a twit and now you call *her* a twit. Two twits in one night is redundant.

DIANA Not when the twits are twits. *That* is being specific . . . you A.H.!

SIDNEY Do you think I don't know what you're saying? I can spell.

DIANA Considering that I should have won that effing award tonight, I behaved *beautifully*. I would like a drink, please.

SIDNEY You *drank* everything in California. Try Nevada.

(He crosses to the bedroom, turning out the light in the living room and on in the bedroom)

DIANA Well, *I* had a wonderful time. *(She follows him in)* Did you hear me? I said, *I* had a wonderful time. *(She looks around)* This looks just like *our* room.

SIDNEY *(Sits on the bed, takes off his cuff links and studs)* Have you ever seen a greater assemblage of hypocrites under one roof in all your life?

DIANA Were the hypocrites there? I missed them. Why didn't you point them out to me.

(She crosses and looks in mirror)

SIDNEY Hypocritical hypocrites. They all love you and fawn over you on the way in. And if you come out a loser, it's "Too bad, darling. Give us a call when you're back in town" . . . You should have thrown up on the whole bloody lot of them.

DIANA *(Looking into the mirror)* Sidney?

SIDNEY Yes?

DIANA Was I hit by a bus? I look very much as though I've been hit by a heavy, fast-moving Greyhound bus.

SIDNEY What really infuriated me is how quickly the winners got their cars . . . How could the winners' cars be lined up so quickly outside if they didn't know beforehand who the winners were? Because it's rigged. We come six thousand miles for this bloody affair, and they park *our* car in Vancouver.

DIANA *(Still looking in the mirror)* I've aged, Sidney . . . I'm getting lines in my face . . . I look like a brand new steel-belted radial tire.

SIDNEY That little Polish twerp who won Best Foreign Documentary got *his* car before us—splashed water on my trousers as he drove by . . . They must have snapped fifty photos of us going in. Coming out, a little Mexican boy with a Brownie asked me where Liza Minelli was.

DIANA I'm hungry.

(She heads for the phone)

SIDNEY What are you doing?

DIANA I'm calling room service. I want eggs Benedict.

(She picks up the phone)

SIDNEY *(Taking off his jacket)* You'll just chuck it up again. Please have the decency to find a proper receptacle this time.

DIANA I must drop Barbra a note for agreeing with me . . . *(Into the phone)* Hello? Eggs Benedict, please.

SIDNEY You have to ask for room service first . . . twit.

DIANA Room service, please. *(To* SIDNEY*)* Twit and a half.

SIDNEY Touché.

DIANA *(Into the phone)* No room service? . . . Are you sure? . . . Isn't there anyone there? I just want some eggs Benedict . . . I could come down and make it myself . . . I see . . . Well, it's just not my night, is it?

(She hangs up)

SIDNEY *(Unbuttoning his shirt)* Lost again, did you?

DIANA Bitchy bitchy, darling. *(She reaches back and tries to unzip her dress)* I found the people there singularly unattractive this year. I noticed a general decline in hair transplants and face lifts. Must be the economy, don't you think?

SIDNEY They're not civilized out here, it's as plain as that. Did you notice Jack Nicholson sitting there in tennis shoes? Black patent leather tennis shoes—I've never seen anything like it.

DIANA Really? You must have been the only one there looking at Jack Nicholson's feet . . . By the way, who was that adorable young actor you were chatting with all night? Gorgeous, wasn't he? Where did you find him?

SIDNEY He was at our table. We shared a butter plate. *(He has started to get undressed)*

DIANA How spreadably cozy.

SIDNEY Careful, darling. You're tired and smashed. Let's not get into shallow waters.

DIANA Oh, I *am* sorry. Let's just talk show biz . . . And who did *you* vote for, Sidney?

SIDNEY I don't vote, dear. I am not a member of the motion picture industry. I am an antiques dealer . . . One day when you are an antique, I shall vote for you—that's a promise.

DIANA I mean, who did you vote for privately? In the deep, deep inner twit recesses of your redundant mind, who were you hoping would win?

SIDNEY In what category?

DIANA The strangest thing happened when I lost, Sidney. I actually felt your body relax . . . When Miss Big Boobs ran up there, all teary-eyed and bouncing flesh, I felt all the tension release from every part of you. What could have caused such joy, I wondered to myself. Happy that it was finally over . . . or just happy?

SIDNEY What a nasty streak you have when you drink . . . also when you eat and sit and walk.

DIANA Oh, that's perverse, Sidney. Why are you so perverse tonight? Picky, picky, picky . . . Are you unhappy because you didn't get to wear my dress?

SIDNEY If I had worn your dress, darling, it would have hung properly. Nothing personal.

DIANA There never *is* anything personal with us. Or is that getting too personal?

SIDNEY Diana, I am sincerely sorry you lost tonight. But look at it this way. It's just a little bald, naked statue.

DIANA Just like you'll be one day. *(Still struggling with her zipper)* Would you please get this chiffon tent off me. If you help me, I'll let you sleep in it tonight.

(He unzips her gown)

SIDNEY We are taking a turn for the worse, Diana . . . Let's try and stay as sweet as we were.

DIANA Tell me . . . Did he happen to carve his phone number in the butter patty for you?

SIDNEY Oh, go to hell.

DIANA To hell? What's this? A direct assault? A frontal attack? That's not like you, Sidney. Wit and parry, wit and parry, that's your style.

SIDNEY You make me sick sometimes.

DIANA When, Sidney? *Any*time at your convenience.

SIDNEY When you can't have what you want, you make certain everyone else around you will be equally as miserable.

DIANA I haven't noticed any *equals* around me . . . And I'm not miserable. I'm an artist. I'm creatively unhappy.

SIDNEY It's amazing how you can throw up verbally as well as you can nutritionally.

(He hangs up his shirt in the closet)

DIANA Adam—wasn't that his name? Adam, the first man . . . not very appropriate for you, is it? . . . He did look very Californian, I thought. Sort of a ballsy Doris Day.

SIDNEY Oh, Christ, Diana, come off it. We keep up a front for everyone else, why can't we do it for ourselves?

DIANA You mean lie to each other that we're perfectly well-mated? A closet couple—is that what we are, Sidney?

SIDNEY I have never hidden behind doors, but I *am* discreet.

DIANA Discreet? You did everything but lick his artichoke.

SIDNEY Let's please not have a discretion contest. I have heard about your lunch breaks on the set. The only thing you don't do in your dressing room is dress . . . I'm going to take some Librium. If I'm not up by nine, I've overdosed. *(He crosses into the bathroom. She gets her gown off)*

DIANA I wouldn't like that, Sidney. What would I do without you?

SIDNEY *(From the bathroom)* Everything, darling.

DIANA I'm serious. Don't ever say that to me again. I will not have you dying.

SIDNEY I'll never be far from you. I've left instructions to be cremated and left in a pewter mug near your bed . . . Ash was always a good color for me.

DIANA Why is he coming to England?

SIDNEY Who?

DIANA That boy. He said, "See you in London next week." What is he doing in London?

SIDNEY Acting, of course. He's making a film there . . .

DIANA What film?

SIDNEY I don't follow other people's films. I barely follow yours.

(He comes out of the bathroom in his pajamas)

DIANA *(Furious, throws her dress on the floor)* Goddamn him and goddamn you! *(She kicks the dress across the room)* Goddamn the Oscars, goddamn California, goddamn everything! *(SIDNEY looks at her)*

SIDNEY What is there about this climate that brings out the religion in you?

DIANA *(Abruptly, almost with violence)* Why don't you love me?

SIDNEY What is *that* line from?

DIANA You son-of-a-bitch, answer the question. Why don't you love me?

SIDNEY It didn't sound like a question.

DIANA I am tired of paying for everything and getting nothing back in return.

SIDNEY I thought Joe Levine paid for everything.

DIANA If it wasn't for me you wouldn't have *been* here tonight to meet him in the first place so you could arrange to meet him next week in London . . . Why don't you love me any more, Sidney?

SIDNEY I've never stopped loving you . . . in my way.

DIANA Your way doesn't do me any good. I want you to love me in *my* way.

SIDNEY It's nearly three o'clock in the morning and we're both crocked. I don't think this is a good time to discuss biological discrepancies.

DIANA Faggot!

SIDNEY *(This stops him)* Oh, good. I thought you'd never ask.

(He starts back into the bathroom)

DIANA *(She is sitting. Pleading)* Don't you walk away from me . . . I'm so miserable tonight, Sidney, don't do this to me.

SIDNEY *(Sincere)* I'm sorry. It hasn't been a winning evening, has it?

DIANA Screw the Oscars! Screw the Academy Awards! Screw me, Sidney . . . please.

SIDNEY *(Looks down)* Diana . . .

DIANA I'm sorry. I didn't mean that . . . I don't want to put you off your game.

SIDNEY Funny how some nights go completely downhill.

DIANA Hell of a night to feel sexy . . . You didn't happen to notice anything in my line down at the Polo Lounge?

SIDNEY I didn't take that Librium yet . . .

DIANA Don't force yourself . . . I wouldn't want you to cheat on my account.

SIDNEY I am *always* here for you, Diana.

DIANA My friendly filling station. Why don't you stick to your own kind, Sidney? If it's anything I hate, it's a bisexual homosexual. Or is it the other way around?

SIDNEY It works either way.

(He starts back towards the bathroom)

DIANA *Sidney! (He stops)* Jesus God, Sidney, I love you so much.

SIDNEY I know that . . .

DIANA Why do you stay with me? What do you get from me that could possibly satisfy you?

SIDNEY A wider circle of prospects . . . After a while, relationships with other antiques dealers seem incestuous.

DIANA Sorry I didn't win that award tonight. Your dance card would have been filled for a year.

SIDNEY We haven't done too badly together . . . I'm kinder to you than your average stunt man.

DIANA You didn't answer my question before.

SIDNEY The answer is yes. I love you more than any woman I've ever met.

DIANA Ahh, Christ, I can't get a break.

SIDNEY I do the best I can.

DIANA Thank you.

(She reaches out her hand towards him. He goes to her and holds her hand)

SIDNEY You can't say we don't have fun together.

DIANA Hell, the dinner conversations alone are worth the trouble. *(He puts his arm around her)* It's my fault for being a hopeless romantic. I keep believing all those movies I've made . . . And you do make love so sweetly.

SIDNEY Would it help any if I made some empty promises?

DIANA It never has . . . What's wrong with *me*, Sidney? We've been fighting this for years. Why haven't I ever left you for a hairier person?

SIDNEY Because we like each other . . . And we are each a refuge for our disappointments out there.

DIANA You *do* have a way of putting your finger right on the trouble spot.

(She lies back on the bed. He looks down at her)

SIDNEY Tired?

DIANA Losing Oscars *always* does that to me.

SIDNEY I'll get up first thing and order you eggs Benedict. *(He turns the overhead lights off)*

DIANA You *do* take care of me, Sidney, I'll say that. And good help is so hard to find today.

SIDNEY *(Getting into bed)* You scratch my back, I'll scratch yours.

DIANA It's been an evening of ups and downs, hasn't it?

SIDNEY Mmm.

DIANA Care to continue the motion?

SIDNEY Tacky. You're getting tacky, angel.

DIANA I love you, Sidney. *(*SIDNEY *leans over and kisses her with warmth and tenderness)* Don't close your eyes, Sidney.

SIDNEY I always close my eyes.

DIANA Not tonight . . . Look at *me* tonight . . . Let it be *me* tonight.

(The lights dim)

Blackout

SCENE THREE: *Visitors from Chicago*

It is a Sunday afternoon, about four o'clock—the Fourth of July, as a matter of fact. Both rooms are bright and sunny.

The front door opens, and MORT *and* BETH HOLLENDER *enter. They are in tennis clothes, a bit sweaty.* MORT *carries two tennis rackets and a can of balls—but mostly he carries* BETH. *She has her arm around his shoulder; he has his arm around her waist. She is hobbling on one foot and in enormous pain—she has obviously injured her ankle or foot.*

MORT Easy . . . Easy, now . . .

BETH Slowly . . . Go slowly . . . Please go slowly.

MORT I'm going as slow as I can.

BETH Then go slower . . . Mort, I'm slipping!

MORT I got you.

BETH I'm slipping, I'm telling you! Put down the tennis balls—who needs used tennis balls? I got a broken foot.

MORT *(He drops the balls from his left hand, which was around her waist)* It's not broken. If it was broken, you couldn't step down on it.

BETH I *can't* step down on it. I'm telling you, it feels broken. It's *my* foot, isn't it? Put me down in here.

MORT Which chair would you like?

BETH *(Sarcastic)* The one in my bedroom at home. You want to get it for me?

MORT What are you getting upset for?

BETH Because you ask me such stupid questions. The sofa, all right? *(He heads her for the nearest chair)* Easy . . .

MORT *(Tries to ease her into the chair)* I'm trying . . .

BETH *Put the goddamn rackets down!*

MORT Sorry! I'm sorry.
(He drops the rackets, still holding her in a half standing-half sitting position)

BETH *(She lowers herself into the chair)* Oh, shit . . . Oh shit shit shit shit!

MORT *(Nods sympathetically)* It really hurts, heh?

BETH When have you heard me say shit five times?

MORT Let me try to get a doctor.

BETH First get me some aspirins.

MORT How many do you want?

BETH Forty!
(MORT starts for the bathroom)

MORT The thing that kills me is that they *saw* your shoelaces were untied. That's why they kept lobbing over your head.

BETH Look at that ankle puff up. It's the size of a grapefruit. I'll have to wear your shoes on the plane tomorrow.

MORT *(In the bathroom)* And they just kept lobbing the ball over your head—lob lob lob, the sons-of-bitches.

BETH When I fell, I heard something go snap. I said to myself, "Please God, let it be my brassiere."

MORT *(Comes out with water and aspirins)* That wasn't tennis out there, that was *war!* They only hit it to you when the sun was in your eyes, and they only hit it to me when my shorts were slipping down.

BETH Will you get the doctor?

MORT *(Angry and frustrated)* Who? I don't know any doctors in Los Angeles.

BETH Look in the Yellow Pages under orthopedic.

MORT On Sunday? July Fourth? You expect a doctor to make a house call on Sunday July Fourth?

BETH Mort, it's getting excruciating. If you can't get a doctor, call a druggist . . . I'll take a laundry man, a delivery boy, just get *some*body, please!

MORT *(Thumbs through the phone book with irritation)* Lob lob lob, dirty sons-of-bitches . . . *(He stops at a page, runs his finger down it)* All right, here's the orthopedics . . . Abel, Abernathy, Abromowitz, Barnard, Benson, Berkowitz . . . Pick one.

BETH None of them sound good.

MORT What do you mean, they don't *sound* good? They're just names . . . You want them to come over and audition for you?

BETH Nothing strikes me . . . Keep reading.

MORT Block, Brewster, Brunckhorst . . .

BETH No. I don't want Brunckhorst.

MORT What's wrong with Brunckhorst?

BETH He sounds like a horse doctor. Get me somebody with a soft name.

MORT This is crazy. I'll call the hotel. They must know a doctor.

(He picks up the phone)

BETH Quick, cover the phone, here comes another obscenity!

MORT *(Into the phone)* Can I have the front desk, please?

BETH Oh, *shitty shit!*

MORT . . . No, operator. That was my wife . . . Hello? . . . This is Mr. Hollender in 203 . . . My wife just had an accident on the tennis court. She thinks her foot might be broken. Can you possibly get us a doctor? . . . Would you? . . . Oh, thank you very much. *(He hangs up)* He'll have someone call.

BETH You should have told them what *kind* of a doctor. This Beverly Hills. They'll probably send a psychiatrist.

MORT *(Picks up the phone again)* Room service, please. *(To* BETH*)* He's not gonna get away with this. I'm gonna play him singles someday. I don't know how, but somewhere I'm gonna find a solid steel ball. And on the first serve, I'll break his back, the bastard. *(Into the phone)* Hello? . . . Yes. This is Mr. Hollender in 203 . . . I would like three buckets of ice cubes, please . . . No, no glasses, just the ice cubes.

BETH And a Monte Cristo sandwich.

MORT Are you serious?

BETH I didn't break my stomach, just my foot. I'm hungry. I want a Monte Cristo sandwich.

MORT *(Into the phone)* Hello? . . . Three buckets of ice cubes and a Monte Cristo sandwich. *(He hangs up)* Do you know what the odds must be in Las Vegas for an order like that? *(The phone rings)* Hello? *(Suddenly his tone turns icy)* Yes . . . Yes . . . How *is* she? . . . How do you *think* she is?

BETH Who is it?

MORT *(With his hand over the mouthpiece)* It's them—the "Lobbers" *(Into the phone)* . . . Her foot may be broken, that's how she is . . . It's the size of a coconut . . . What can you do? *(He turns to* BETH*)* They want to know what they can do . . . *(Back into the phone)* I'll tell you what you can do—

BETH Morty, don't—

MORT I want you to go to the pro shop and buy two

cans of Wilson yellow tennis balls, charge them to me, and shove them up your respective asses.

(He slams the receiver down)

BETH *Are you crazy?* Those are our best friends.

MORT *I said I'd pay for the balls, didn't I?*

BETH The four of us never should have taken a vacation together . . . There was trouble from the first day. When he showed up at the airport and said he'd forgotten his credit cards, I knew we were in for it.

MORT I will *never* travel with them again. *Eight* pieces of luggage for two skinny people? What have they got in there?

BETH Where?

MORT In the luggage.

BETH Her make-up. Every new perfume that comes out, she's got it—"Babe," "Charlie," "Harold," "Milton," whatever . . . *(There is a knock on the door)* No wonder I slipped and fell—the court was covered with all her goddamn skin cream and lotion.

(He opens the door. STU *and* GERT FRANKLYN *stand there. She is in a white tennis dress; he is in a yellow warm-up suit. Each carries a racket.* GERT *also has a bottle of skin lotion.* STU *has a can of tennis balls)*

GERT My God, what happened? We thought it was just a sprain. Is it very painful? *(Goes to touch it)* Oh, my poor baby.

BETH Don't do that! I yell shit when you do that!

STU *(Holds up a can of balls; to* MORT*)* Here! This is the can you told me to buy . . . You want me to take the balls out first? *(*MORT *turns away from him in anger. To* MORT*)* Have you called a doctor? *(No response; to* BETH*)* Has he called a doctor?

BETH Yes.

STU Is he a good man?

BETH The hotel is sending somebody.

GERT *(To* MORT*)* Shouldn't she have ice on that leg, Mort? *(He won't answer)* Mort? . . . Should we get some ice?

STU *(To* MORT*)* Gert's talking to you. What the hell's wrong with you?

MORT *(Turns, hands on hips, takes a deep breath)* I'm sorry, Stu. I'm very upset. Beth's foot may be broken—my temper got the best of me. I ordered some ice, okay?

STU I understand.

MORT It's been a rough three weeks. After a while, you start to get on each other's nerves, you know?

STU Sure.

MORT I mean, four people taking a vacation together can get very testy. You can only do it with your best friends . . . And you and Gert are our best friends. Christ, we don't have better friends than you . . . *(*STU *nods)* . . . because if we did—*I would have told you to shove a steel RACKET up your ass!*

GERT Oh, my God!

STU What are you, crazy? What are you blaming *us* for? It wasn't *our* fault.

MORT Lob lob lob wasn't your fault? The woman stood there defenseless with her laces open, and would you hit the ball to me? Oh, no. You hit it over a crippled woman's head.

STU She wasn't crippled until she fell.

BETH *(Closes her eyes in pain)* Could you all please do this in the bedroom. I need this room to yell in . . . *Oh . . . defecation!*

STU *(Starts towards* BETH*)* Can I look at it?

MORT *(To* STU*)* You touch her foot, and they ship you back to Chicago on Air Freight.

STU *(Backs away)* Don't threaten me. I've taken enough crap from you these last few weeks—don't you threaten me.

MORT Ohh, it's coming out now. Now we're all gonna hear about it, right? It started the night *we* got the room with the view in Honolulu, and you got the toilet that kept backing up . . . Only *I* didn't book the rooms, *smart ass—*

STU Watch it, Morty, I don't like being called smart ass.

GERT Stop it, both of you! Somebody go get a cold towel until the ice gets here. *(Neither man moves)* Look at them. Look how they just stand there.

BETH *(To* GERT*)* You smell wonderful. What are you wearing?

GERT It's called "After Tennis." I just bought it . . . I'll get you the towel myself.

(She goes into the bathroom)

STU That woman should be lying flat on her back with her foot up in the air. Let's get her into bed.

MORT I don't need your goddamn advice. Don't start telling me what to do for her. *(To* BETH*)* Come on, honey. Let's get you flat on your back with your foot up in the air.

BETH Let him help you, Morty, you can't do it alone.

*(*STU *rushes over and throws her other arm around his neck)*

STU All right, honey, just put all your weight on us. Here we go. One-two-three . . .

*(*STU *and* MORT *pull in opposite directions)*

BETH Oh, Jesus! Oh, Jesus, that hurts.

STU Don't step down on it.

BETH Not my leg. My *arms.* You're pulling my arms apart.

MORT *(Yells)* Let go of her arm, you shmuck!

STU *(To* MORT*)* It's your fault. You're going the wrong way.

MORT You giving me directions again? Last time you gave me directions, we missed San Francisco.

BETH Can I make a suggestion? Can we talk about all this after the amputation?

MORT *(As they make headway towards the door)* I got you, honey, don't worry. *(Yells out)* Where's the cold towel, for chrissakes?

STU Don't yell at *my* wife while I'm carrying *your* wife.

GERT *(From the bathroom)* Oh, God, no!

STU What?

MORT What is it? What happened?

GERT *(Coming out)* I broke a bottle of perfume. I'm awfully sorry.

(They all bump into the door frame)

BETH My "Bal de Versailles"? My duty-free ninety-dollar "Bal de Versailles"? *(The men get in her way as all three try to get through the connecting door)* Let me through! *I'm* the important one.

MORT Of all the stupid-ass—breaking perfume bottles.

STU It was an accident, for chrissakes! She didn't do it on purpose.

(In his anger he lets BETH *go. She grapples with the wall)*

MORT That's right. So far we got two accidents and

two not-on-purposes. And my wife's got a broken foot and a beautiful-smelling bathroom.

STU We'll *pay* for the perfume. I owe you ninety dollars, all right?

BETH Can we do the accounting from the bed? Just get me on the bed, please.

(They resume carrying her to the bed)

GERT Beth, be careful when you walk in the bathroom. There's broken glass on the floor.

BETH I'm glad you told me. I was going to walk in there a lot today.

*(*GERT *goes back into the bathroom for the cold towel. They are near the bed with* BETH*)*

MORT All right, let's get her down gently.

BETH Yes. Please do it gently.

GERT *(From inside the bathroom)* Dammit to hell! *(She comes out holding her finger in a face towel)* Have you got a Band-Aid? I cut my finger on the glass.

STU *(Concerned)* How did you do that?

GERT Mort, I'm sorry, I know you're busy now. Do you have some Band-Aids and iodine?

MORT In a minute, Gert. Let's take one casualty at a time.

*(*GERT *goes back into the bathroom)*

STU *(At the bed; to* MORT*)* All right, which way are we going to go?

MORT North by northeast. What do you mean, which way are we gonna go?

STU Frontwards or backwards?

BETH Whichever one you do, don't surprise me. Tell me first.

MORT Backwards. Let's put her down backwards.

(MORT and STU turn around with BETH so that they all have their backs to the bed)

STU All right, when I say three, we sit on the bed. Ready, now: One . . . two . . .

BETH Me too?

STU Certainly you too! Who do you think we're doing it for?

MORT *(To STU)* That's right, yell at her. Why don't you *push* her?

STU Can we get this over with? . . . Ready, now: One . . . two . . .

(We suddenly hear a thud from the bathroom and GERT yells out)

GERT OH, SHIT!

(They all freeze)

STU *What? What is it? What happened?*

(GERT comes out of the bathroom staggering, holding the back of her head)

GERT My head . . . I banged my head on the medicine cabinet . . . I think I'm gonna pass out . . . Yes, I am . . .

(And so she does, falling to the floor)

STU Gert! GERT!

BETH First me, then Gert! I was first!

STU One . . . two . . . three! *(The three of them fall backwards onto the bed in their attempt to sit. BETH screams out in pain. Then STU gets up and rushes around to GERT on the floor as MORT attempts to straighten BETH out on the bed)*

STU *(Picking up GERT's head)* She's out like a light! Get me a cold wet towel—hurry!

(GERT moans, opens her eyes)

GERT Ohhhh . . . Stu . . . Did I pass out?

STU Just for a second, hon. Where is it? Where did you hit it?

GERT I had my head down in the sink. I was trying to rush with the towel, and I stood up too quickly . . . I think it's a concussion.

STU *(Turns on* MORT*)* You see what you did! You got her so crazy, the woman's got a concussion.

MORT You're gonna blame *me* because your wife doesn't know how to get up from a sink?

GERT *(Feels the back of her head with her hand, then looks at it)* It's bleeding. My head is bleeding.

STU No, that's your finger. Your finger is bleeding onto your head. *(To* MORT*)* Will you get me a wet towel, for chrissakes!

*(*MORT *rushes into the bathroom)*

BETH *(Lying flat on the bed)* She should have a doctor. Mort, give her our doctor . . . Get her Brunckhorst.

GERT *(Still flat on the floor)* I feel nauseated. I think I'm going to throw up. Help me to the bathroom.

STU I don't think so, honey. I don't think you should be moved.

*(*MORT *comes out of the bathroom with two wet towels. He is limping)*

MORT *(Hands* STU *a towel)* Here! A piece of glass went through my goddamn sneakers—I hope you're satisfied. *(He crosses to* BETH *and puts the wet towel on her ankle)* Does that hurt?

BETH No, because it's on the wrong ankle.

(He changes it to the other ankle. She winces in pain)

GERT Help me up. The floor is cold. I feel chilly.

STU *(To* MORT*)* Give me a hand. Let's put her on the bed.

GERT I bled on the carpet. I got blood on the carpet, Stu.

STU I'm paying for it, don't worry about it. *(*MORT *comes around to* GERT*'s feet)* All right, grab her feet—and don't lift until I tell you.

MORT *(Bending down to get her feet)* Jesus, it's like Guadalcanal in here.

STU All right, one . . . two . . . three, *lift! (They both lift her up and start to carry her towards the bed)* Easy, easy! All right, put her down gently.

(They put her down on the bed, jostling BETH *in the process)*

MORT Goddamnedest vacation I ever took in my life.

STU *(Angrily to* MORT, *taking out his wallet)* All right, let's settle our accounts, I want to get outta here!

MORT Forget it. I don't want your money. Keep your lousy money. *(He limps towards the chair)* I think it went right into the bone.

STU I'm paying for everything, you understand? I want an itemized list: the perfume, the blood on the carpet, the tennis balls I'm shoving up my ass—*everything!* And then I want a receipt for my taxes. *(He takes out a check and starts to write).* What's today's date, bastard?

MORT Hey, hey. Calm down. Take it easy. Let's not get our noses out of joint.

STU You call this a vacation? I had a better vacation when I had my hernia operation . . . I'm sick of your face. I'm sick of your twelve-cent cigars. After three weeks, my clothes smell like they've been in a humidor. I'm sick of your breakfasts. I'm sick of your lightly buttered rye toast and eggs over lightly every goddamned morning. Would it kill you to have a waffle once in a while? One stinkin' little waffle for my sake?

MORT What are you, crazy? We got two invalids in bed and you're talking about waffles?

STU We did everything *you* wanted. *You* made all the decisions. You took *all* the pictures. I didn't get to take *one* picture with my own camera. You picked all the restaurants—nine Japanese restaurants in three weeks. I am nauseated at the sight of watching you eat tempura with your shoes off. I am bored following your wife into every chatska store on the West Coast looking for Mexican bracelets—

MORT Hey, hey, wait a minute. Your wife bought too. What about a pair of African earrings that hang down to her navel?

STU A year I planned for this vacation. You know what I got to show for it? Two purple Hawaiian shirts for *my* kids that *you* picked out. Even *Hawaiians* wouldn't wear them. One entire morning wasted in Honolulu while five Chinese tailors measured you for a thirty-nine-dollar Hong Kong suit that fell apart in the box. I spent half an afternoon on Fisherman's Wharf watching a near-sighted eighty-four-year-old artist sketching a charcoal portrait of you that looks like Charles Laughton. I've had enough! I want to go home! I'm a nervous wreck . . . I need a vacation.

MORT Come on, Buddy, I'll get you a drink. How about a nice Planter's Punch?

STU Please! Don't order another Planter's Punch. I'll go crazy if I have to watch you trying to get the cherry out with your straw. Don't do that to me, Mort.

MORT I won't. I won't play with my cherry again, I promise. Why don't we just shake hands and forget everything?

GERT Shake his hand, Stu. Please
(Leans over on BETH*)*

BETH You're on my leg—

GERT Sorry. I'm sorry.

MORT *(Yells at* GERT*)* Watch what you're doing, you idiot!

STU *(Gets up, slightly crazed)* Take that back! I want an apology. Either you apologize to my wife for calling her an idiot . . . *(Picks up tennis racket)* . . . or I'll take this tennis racket and *backhand you to death!*

MORT *(Backs away)* All right, don't threaten me . . . I got a little bit more meat on me. Never threaten somebody who's got more meat on them.

GERT He's right, Stu. Look how much meat he's got on him.

STU *(Through crazed, gritted teeth)* Apologize! I want a nice apology and I want a smile on your face. You got five seconds . . .

MORT *(Backing away around chairs)* Don't do this, Stu . . . Don't get physical with me. If you attack, I'll counterattack.

STU One . . .

BETH Don't fight! Please don't fight!

STU Two . . .

BETH Someone'll get hurt and fall on me.

STU Three . . .

MORT *(Still backing away)* I'll punch you with my fist, Stu.

STU Four . . .

MORT I'm talking about a closed hard fist, no open hands.

STU Are you going to apologize before I say five?

MORT Say it! Say it! You afraid to say it? I'll say it *for* you. Five! FIVE! I said it, all right? FIVE!

STU I'll say it *myself,* goddamn you! FIVE!

(And STU *lunges out at* MORT, *who is too quick and strong for him.* MORT *grabs* STU *around the head and neck and has him in a hammerlock hold)*

MORT *(Squeezing his neck)* Drop it! Drop the racket!

STU *(A squeaky, airless voice)* Nemmer . . . nemmer . . .

MORT I'll turn you blue! Tell me what shade of blue you like, light or dark?

STU *(Flailing his arms helplessly)* . . . kill you! I'll kill you!

GERT *(Starting to get out of bed)* Leave him alone! Please . . .

BETH *(Grabs her to restrain her)* Let them kill each other, we have to take care of ourselves . . .

(The two women tussle on the bed as MORT *heads towards the living room with* STU*'s head clamped under his arm)*

MORT You want to play? All right, let's play in the bathroom. I'll show you a nice little game in the bathroom called "Kill your friend."

(And the two of them scuffle into the bathroom; now they are both out of view. GERT *and* BETH *stop struggling)*

GERT *(Crying)* He'll kill him! I'll be on the plane with a dead husband, God help me!

BETH I have to go to the john. Get them out of there, I have to go in!

(Suddenly we hear a tremendous crash, the breaking of glass and an awful moan. GERT *whimpers apprehensively . . . The bathroom door opens and* MORT *comes out staggering, holding his groin)*

MORT *(Hoarsely)* He kicked me . . . Oh, God, what a place he kicked me . . .

(He doubles over and sits on the edge of the bed, still holding his groin. STU *comes out with a wet towel over his mouth)*

STU *(Mumbles)* Get a dentist! Look up a dentist, I'm gonna lose some teeth.

BETH Are you two through in there? I have to go in.

GERT *(To* STU*)* Let me see. What did he do to you?

STU It's swelling up. Jesus, my lip is blowing up like a balloon.

BETH Ice is coming. I got enough for all of us.

MORT *(Still holding, still doubled up)* I haven't been kicked there since I played football . . . and then I was wearing protection.

BETH Is anyone going to help me into the bathroom?

GERT I don't believe what's going on here . . . It's like a John Wayne movie.

STU *(Starts to cry)* Jesus . . .

MORT What are *you* crying about? If I could lift my leg, I'd kick you in the same place.

STU *(Stands up, fists poised)* You want more? Come on. Come on, all of youse. I'll take you *all* on!

GERT Are you crazy? Stop it! Stop it! Everybody—JUST *STOP IT!*

*(*GERT *falls back on the chair, and* MORT *falls on top of her.* STU *falls on the bed, right on* BETH*'s bad leg.* BETH *pounds her fist on the bed. There is a long silence . . . a* very *long silence as all four lie there quietly in pain. Then the sobbing subsides, and we just hear them sigh and breathe)*

MORT What was that doctor's name? I think maybe we should all see him.

BETH Did he kick you hard, Mort?

MORT Listen, where he kicked me, even *easy* would hurt.

STU *(On the floor)* I still have a few good teeth left. I'll bite your goddamn leg off unless you apologize to Gert for calling her a moron.

MORT *(On the floor, facing away from him)* I didn't call her a moron. I called her an idiot. *(Suddenly* STU *lets out a war cry and lunges for* MORT*'s leg. He grabs it and bites into his calf.* MORT *screams in pain)* Oh, Jesus! Oh, God, get him off me.

*(*STU *holds on tenaciously)*

GERT *(Screams)* Stu, you'll hurt yourself. He's as hard as a rock.

*(*MORT *starts to pull* STU *off him)*

MORT You crazy bastard!

(He throws STU *to the ground and jumps on top of him, straddling him)*

STU *(Struggling)* Let me go! Let me up, you elephant.

MORT All right, I had enough of you, you skinny little pipsqueak. Don't you ever bite me again. You could give me a blood disease.

STU Gert, hit him! Get a lamp and hit him!

GERT *(She tries to swat* MORT *away with the towel)* Don't sit on him, please! Get off him, you fat water tank . . . Oh, I'm sorry, Beth.

BETH Listen, the truth is the truth.

MORT *(To* STU*)* All right. Now, nobody is leaving this room until we all make up with each other. We came here friends and we're leaving friends. Now, tell me we're friends, you bastard!

(He chokes him)

GERT Make up with him, Stu. It's the only chance we have.

STU I make up . . . I surrender and make up.

MORT Not like that. Like you mean it.

STU I mean it . . . I can't breathe. You're cutting off my air.

BETH *(Lying down flat on the bed—she can't see them)* I don't understand. Why is he cutting off his hair?

MORT And tell me you had a good time on our vacation . . . *Tell me!*

STU I had a good time.

MORT Especially the Japanese restaurants.

STU Especially the goddamned Japanese restaurants. Let me up! My ribs are cracking.

MORT And you want to take another vacation with us next year!

STU Crack my ribs! Crush me! I won't say that!
(The curtain starts to fall)

MORT, BETH and GERT Say it! Say it! Say it!
Curtain

Chapter Two

THE SCENE

The action of *Chapter Two* takes place in Jennifer Malone's upper East Side apartment and George Schneider's lower Central Park West apartment. The play begins on a late February afternoon and continues through to midspring.

Act One

SCENE I

The set consists of two separate apartments on opposite sides of Manhattan—GEORGE SCHNEIDER *lives in one;* JENNIE MALONE, *in the other.*

His apartment, stage left, is located in the mid-seventies on Central Park West. It is one of New York's older buildings, and the ceilings and rooms are higher and larger than the smaller, flatter, uninteresting boxes they build today.

Hers is one of the smaller, flatter, uninteresting boxes they build today. It is in the upper eighties off Third Avenue.

His is decorated in a traditional, comfortable style—large inviting armchairs and sofa, bookcases from floor to ceiling, lots of personal photographs of him and his wife.

Hers is modern, bright, attractive and cheerful. That's because she *is.*

We see the living rooms of both apartments plus the entrance doors. His apartment has a kitchen and an archway that leads into four other rooms. Hers has a small kitchen and single bedroom.

It's about 10:30 P.M. *in his apartment. The door opens and* GEORGE SCHNEIDER *enters. He wears a coat and scarf and carries a large fully packed leather suitcase and an attaché case. He turns on the lights.* GEORGE *is forty-two years old, an attractive, intelligent man who at this moment seems tired and drawn. He puts down his bags, looks around the room, and goes over to a table where his mail has been placed. A large number of letters have piled up. He goes through them, throwing every second and third piece into the wastebasket; the rest he takes with him to a chair, where he sits and starts to look through them.*

LEO SCHNEIDER *appears, carrying* GEORGE*'s other matching suitcase.* LEO *is about forty. He is wearing a suede sheepskin coat, scarf and gloves.*

LEO *(Coming through the door)* George, you're not going to believe this! I found a place to park right in front of the building. First time in four years . . . I think I'll buy an apartment here—I don't want to give up that space. *(Puts the suitcase down)* Christ Almighty, it's four degrees in here. Whooo! Whyn't you rent it out for the winter Olympics, pay your expenses. Where do you turn your heat on? *(GEORGE is reading his mail)* I smell gas. Do you smell gas, George?

GEORGE *(Looks up)* What?

LEO *Gas*, for Chrissakes! *(He runs into the kitchen, to the stove. GEORGE continues to read his mail. LEO comes out)* It was on. Didn't you check it before you left? Thank God I didn't have a cigar on me. One match, we'd *both* be back in Italy. *(Turns on the desk lamp)* Where do you turn the heat on? . . . *George*?

GEORGE What?

LEO Where is the heater?

GEORGE The heater? It's, uh . . .

LEO Take your time. Accuracy is important.

GEORGE I'm sorry . . . The thermostat's on the wall as you come in the bedroom.

LEO *(Looks at him)* Are you all right?

GEORGE No. Am I supposed to be?

LEO You lost weight, didn't you?

GEORGE I don't know. A couple of pounds.

LEO Sure. Who could eat that lousy food in Paris and Rome?

GEORGE Do you smell gas?

LEO What?

GEORGE I smell gas.

LEO I think your nose is having jet lag, George.

(He goes into the bedroom)

GEORGE I was going to stay another week in Rome. Then I said, "No, I have to get back. I'm really anxious to be home." *(He looks around)* I wonder why I thought that.

LEO *(Reentering)* Come on. You walk into Ice Station Zebra with gas leaking in the kitchen and no fresh air in here for four and a half weeks. I mean, this is February and we're standing here breathing January . . . Why don't you make some popcorn, see what's on TV.

(He takes the suitcases into the bedroom. GEORGE *shakes his head)*

GEORGE God!

LEO *(Enters)* You've got to see the bathroom. You left the shower dripping with the little window wide open. There are icicles hanging everywhere. It's beautiful. It looks like the john in *Doctor Zhivago* . . . What are you reading?

GEORGE My mail.

LEO Anything interesting?

GEORGE Not unless you like letters of condolence. I thought I answered my last one when I left . . . Do we have an Aunt Henry?

LEO *(Offstage) Aunt* Henry? We have an *Uncle* Henry. In Kingston, New York.

GEORGE This is signed "Aunt Henry."

LEO *(Offstage)* Uncle Henry's about sixty-three—maybe he's going through a change of life.

GEORGE *(Reading)* " 'Sorry to hear about your loss. With deepest sincerity, Aunt Henry.' "

LEO *(Comes out of the kitchen; holding up the food)* You want to see sour milk? You want to see white bread that's turned into pumpernickel all by itself? You want to see a dish of grapes that have dried into raisins?

GEORGE *(Looking at another letter)* You want to listen to something, Leo?

LEO *(Trying to avoid the past)* George, you just got home. You're tired. Why don't you defrost the bathroom, take a bath?

GEORGE Just one letter: "Dear Mr. Schneider, My name is Mary Ann Patterson. We've never met, but I did know your late wife, Barbara, casually. I work at Sabrina's, where she used to come to have her hair cut. She was so beautiful and one of the warmest people I've ever met. It seems I always used to tell her my troubles, and she always found some terrific thing to say to cheer me up. I will miss her smiling face and the way she used to come bouncing into the shop like a little girl. I feel lucky to have known her. I just wanted to return a little of her good cheer. God bless you and keep you. Mary Ann Patterson." *(He puts down the letter.* LEO *looks at him, knowing not to intrude on this moment)* What the hell did I read *that* for?

LEO It's very nice. It's a sweet letter, George.

GEORGE Barbara knew a whole world of people I never knew . . . She knew that Ricco, the mailman, was a birdwatcher in Central Park, and that Vince, the butcher in Gristede's, painted miniature portraits of cats every weekend in his basement on Staten Island . . . She talked to people all year long that I said hello to on Christmas.

LEO *(Looks at him)* I think you could have used another month in Europe.

GEORGE You mean, I was supposed to come home and forget I had a wife for twelve years? It doesn't work that way, Leo. It was, perhaps, the dumbest trip I ever took in my whole life. London was bankrupt, Italy was on strike, France hated me, Spain was still mourning for Franco . . . Why do Americans go to grief-stricken Europe when they're trying to get over being stricken with grief?

LEO Beats me. I always thought you could have just as rotten a time here in America.

GEORGE What am I going to do about this apartment, Leo?

LEO My advice? Move. Find a new place for yourself.

GEORGE It was very spooky in London . . . I kept walking around the streets looking for Barbara—Harrod's, King's Road, Portobello . . . Sales clerks would say, "See what you want, sir?" and I'd say, "No, she's not here." I know it's crazy, Leo, but I really thought to myself, It's a joke. She's not dead. She's in London waiting for me. She's just playing out this romantic fantasy: The whole world thinks she's gone, but we meet clandestinely in London, move into a flat, disappear from everyone and live out our lives in secret! . . . She would have thought of something like that, you know.

LEO But she didn't. *You* did.

GEORGE In Rome I got sore at her—I mean *really* mad. How dare she do a thing like this to me? I would *never* do a thing like that to her. Never! Like a nut, walking up the Via Veneto one night, cursing my dead wife.

LEO In Italy, they probably didn't pay attention.

GEORGE In Italy, they agree with you. *(He shrugs)* Okay, Leo, my sweet baby brother, I'm back . . . Chapter Two in the life of George Schneider. Where the hell do I begin?

LEO I don't know. You want to go to a dance?

GEORGE You know, you're cute. Does Marilyn think you're cute?

LEO Yeah. It's not enough. I want *all* the women to think so.

GEORGE Everything okay at home?

LEO Couldn't be better.

GEORGE You sure?

LEO Never ask a question like that twice. I gotta go. *(He buttons his coat)* How about poker on Thursday?

GEORGE I'll let you know.

LEO Want me to get tickets for the Knicks game Saturday?

GEORGE We'll talk about it.

LEO How about dinner on Sunday? Monday? Maybe Tuesday will be my good news day? *(Imitates a trombone playing "The Man I Love."* GEORGE *doesn't respond)* Hey! Hey, Georgie . . .

GEORGE I'm okay, Leo. I promise. Just give me a little time, okay?

LEO I don't know what to do for you . . . I feel so goddamn helpless.

GEORGE Well . . . Maybe you can come by tomorrow and show me how to open up tuna fish.

LEO *(Looks at* GEORGE *)* Now *I'm* mad. I think it stinks, too. I'm not going to forgive her for a long time, George. (LEO *goes over and embraces* GEORGE. *Tears well up in* LEO*'s eyes. He pulls away and heads for the door*) I'm coming back next week and the two of us are getting bombed, you understand? I mean, I want you *disgusting*! Then we'll drive up to Kingston and check out this Aunt Henry. If he's got money, he might be a nice catch for you.

(He turns and goes quickly. GEORGE *turns and looks at the apartment, then picks up his attaché case)*

GEORGE *(He takes in a deep breath)* Okay, let's take it one night at a time, folks.

(He heads for the bedroom. The lights come down slowly)

Scene 2

Her apartment. It is mid-February, about four-thirty on a bitter-cold afternoon. The light of a winter's day is fading fast.

The door opens and JENNIE MALONE *enters and switches on the lights. She is an attractive woman, about thirty-two. She wears a camel's-hair coat, leather boots and a woolen hat. She puts down a valise and carries a heavily loaded shoulder bag. She looks around and exhales a deep sigh.*

Right behind her is FAYE MEDWICK, *about thirty-five.* FAYE *dresses a bit more suburban—not chic, but right for the weather. She carries in* JENNIE*'s make-up case.*

FAYE I don't care *how* much traffic there was, no way is it twenty-six dollars from Kennedy Airport to Eighty-fourth Street. *(She closes the door)* It's one thing to pay for his gas, it's another to put his daughter through college. (JENNIE *takes off her coat*) Remember that cabbie last year? Picked up this sweet Mexican family at the airport, drove them into the city and charged them *a hundred and sixty dollars*? He told them in America the cab fare starts from the time you get on the plane. I could kill sometimes . . . It's nice and warm in here. You left the heat on for two weeks?

JENNIE I told the doorman I was coming back today. He probably turned it on this morning.

FAYE Organized. You're so damn organized. I'd give anything to be like you. I'm hungry. We should have stopped off at the grocery.

(She enters the kitchen)

JENNIE I dropped an order off with them before I left. They may have delivered it this morning.

FAYE *(Opens the fridge, looks in)* It's all there! Jesus! You fly two thousand miles to get a divorce and you remember to leave a grocery order?

JENNIE *(Dials the phone)* It's that Catholic upbringing. I majored in Discipline.

FAYE Milk, cheese, butter, eggs, bread . . . Listen, would you like a job in my house? Your own room with color TV?

JENNIE A perfect person. The nuns loved it, but it was murder on a marriage. *(Into the phone)* Four-six-two, please.

FAYE Your plants look nice too. Had them watered, right?

JENNIE Three times a week. *(Into the phone)* Yes?

FAYE You have the nerve to tell that to a woman with a dead lawn and two fallen trees?

JENNIE *(Into the phone)* Thank you. *(Hangs up)* I'm going to change my answering service. I get such boring messages.

FAYE Is there *anything* you forgot?

JENNIE Nothing. I've got everything planned up until five o'clock. Starting at 5:01—help! If it's so warm in here, why am I shivering?

FAYE You just cut off six years of your life. Giggling would be inappropriate.

JENNIE I can still smell the ghost of Gus's cigar. God, what a cheap thing to be haunted by . . . He probably came by to pick up the rest of his clothes.

FAYE Sidney's been complaining the dry cleaner I use does terrible work. I haven't got the nerve to tell him I keep forgetting to send it out.

JENNIE Y'know, I never realized I had so many books I never read . . . Okay, *Catch-22*, we're going to try it one more time.

FAYE You see, I think that's wrong. To tackle heavyweight material is not what you should be doing now. I would read filth.

JENNIE Listen, you're not going to hang around till I've readjusted, are you, Faye?

FAYE Well, you've got to go slowly. I don't want you to get the bends. *(Looking out the window)* Oh, God!

JENNIE What?

FAYE I'm watching the most gorgeous naked person across the street.

JENNIE Man or woman?

FAYE Can't tell. It's a rear view.

JENNIE That's probably Lupe, the Spanish dancer. Beautiful body.

FAYE Fantastic. Women are really terrific. No wonder we drive men crazy . . . some of us . . . Did you ever fantasize making love to a beautiful woman?

JENNIE You're not going to make any advances, are you, Faye? I'm really very tired.

FAYE It's just that sometimes I watch Sidney drooling over those Dallas Cowboy cheerleaders, and I was wondering what I was missing in life . . . Maybe I never should have left Texas.

JENNIE What's wrong this week?

FAYE Sidney and I had dinner with friends last week. A couple married twenty years, the man never stopped fondling his wife for a minute. They both said it was the best time of their lives—that they really never knew how to enjoy each other till now. And I thought to myself, "Shit. Twelve more years to go until the good times."

JENNIE Did you tell that to Sidney?

FAYE *(Putting on her coat)* Not yet. I can't get an appointment with his secretary.

JENNIE I don't understand you. I know more about what's wrong with your married life than Sidney does. Why don't you speak up? What are you afraid of? What do you think would happen to you if you told him what you tell *me* in the privacy of this room?

FAYE That next time you'd be picking *me* up at the airport.

JENNIE Oh, God, that infuriates me. Why are we so intimidated? I wasted five lousy years living with Gus trying to justify the one good year I had with him . . . because I wouldn't take responsibility for my own life. Dumb! You're dumb, Jennie Malone! *All* of us . . . We shouldn't get alimony, we should get the *years* back. Wouldn't it be great if just once the judge said, "I award you six years, three months, two days and custody of your former youthful body and fresh glowing skin"!

FAYE I would be in such terrific shape if you were my mother.

JENNIE Don't give me too much credit. I *talk* a terrific life . . . Now, go on home. I want to crawl into bed and try to remember what my maiden name was.

FAYE Are you sure you'll be all right? All alone?

JENNIE No. But I want to be.

(They embrace)

FAYE You can call me in the middle of the night. Sidney and I aren't doing anything.

(FAYE *leaves.* JENNIE *takes her suitcase into the bedroom*)

SCENE 3

His apartment. It is the next night, about 5 P.M. GEORGE *is obviously having difficulty concentrating at the typewriter. He is wearing slacks, an open-neck shirt, woolen cardigan and slippers. The phone rings as he is typing.*

GEORGE *(Into the phone)* Hello . . . Yes . . . Who's this? . . . Leona Zorn . . . Oh, yes. Yes, I received your note. I was very dismayed to hear that you and Harvey broke up . . . Well, I wouldn't say we were close friends. He's a wonderful chiropracter . . . Dinner on Thursday? Thursday . . . Thursday . . . Ah, nuts, I have something on for Thursday . . . The following Thursday? *(The doorbell rings)* Gee, I think I have something on for that night, too . . . Uh, Mrs. Zorn, will you just hold on? I want to get my doorbell. *(He lays the receiver down; under his breath)* Oh, Jesus!

(He opens the door. LEO *enters)*

LEO Sit down. I have to talk to you.

GEORGE Just a minute, Leo, I'm on the phone. *(Into the phone)* Mrs. Zorn? . . . You said the following Thursday? . . . I think I have something on for that night, but let me check my diary. I'll be right back. *(He puts the receiver down and goes over to* LEO. GEORGE *beckons, gesturing that phone is "open")* Leo, there's a woman on the phone asking me for a date.

LEO Yeah? . . . So?

GEORGE *(Whispers)* Her husband was my chiropracter.

LEO So what?

GEORGE He left her for an ice-skater in Las Vegas.

LEO What does she look like?

GEORGE Like someone you would leave for an ice-skater in Las Vegas.

LEO So what's your problem?

GEORGE *(Annoyed)* What do you mean, what's my problem? I don't want to have dinner with her.

LEO What *do* you want to have?

GEORGE *Nothing!* I want her to hang up. I don't want her to call me. Look, she's probably a very nice woman. I don't want to be cruel to her, but I don't want to have dinner with her.

LEO Would you feel better if *I* took her out? What's her name? I'll talk to her.

(GEORGE *stops him*)

GEORGE Leo! Please! *(Back into the phone)* Mrs. Zorn? . . . I'm sorry to keep you waiting . . . Uh, Mrs. Zorn, I've always found it better to be completely honest . . . and . . . I'm really not all that anxious to go out at this particular time . . . Well, I've tried it a few times and it wasn't all that successful . . . I just don't think I'm psychologically ready . . . Well, I don't think I can give an exact date when I *would* be ready . . . (LEO *does push-ups on the floor*) Well, yes, in a manner of speaking, we *are* in the same boat . . . But we don't necessarily have to paddle together . . . I think we have to go up our own streams.

LEO Jesus!

GEORGE Well, yes, it *is* possible we could meet upriver one day, I don't rule that out.

LEO Is that from *The African Queen*?

(GEORGE *pulls the receiver away so* LEO*'s remark will not be heard*)

GEORGE Leo, please! (Into phone) Yes . . . Yes . . . Well,

you sound charming too . . . Well, if I *do* reconsider, I *will* call . . . Yes. Goodbye. *(He hangs up)* Christ! The guy leaves me with a bad back and *his* wife!

LEO *(Gets up)* There just aren't enough men to go around. I *want* to help out, but Marilyn doesn't understand.

GEORGE Women call me up, Leo. *Women!* They call me up on the *phone.*

LEO What else would they call you up on?

GEORGE But they're so *frank* about it. So open. They just come right out with it. "How do you do. I've been recently widowed myself." Or, "Hi! I'm a divorcee." "I'm legally separated." "I'm *il*legally separated." One woman called, I swear to God, I think her husband was just on vacation.

LEO It's a competitive world, George. The woman who sits waiting by the phone sits waiting by the phone.

GEORGE Do you know I've been invited to three class reunions at schools I never even went to?

LEO Listen, George, next to Christmas, loneliness is the biggest business in America.

GEORGE Do you realize how much courage it must have taken for that woman to call me up just now?

LEO And you think you were the first and only one she's called? She probably has her husband's entire list of clients. If she called you, she's only up to the "Georges."

GEORGE And you don't find that sad?

LEO Certainly I find it sad. That's why they have game shows on TV . . . Now, if you want to feel sorry for yourself and everyone else in the world who's suffered a loss, that's your concern. It is *my* job to brighten up the place. I am God's interior decorator, and he has sent me to paint you two coats of happiness.

GEORGE Leo, don't do this to me again!

LEO This is different. This girl requires a serious discussion. I think I found buried treasure, George. Hear me out.

GEORGE I haven't recovered from *last* week's buried treasure . . . All right, it's my own fault. I should have known in that first phone conversation with her. Three "honeys," two "sugars" and one "babe" was a sure tip-off . . . I'm very busy, Leo. I've written three hundred pages of my new book and I haven't thought of a story yet.

LEO All right, I apologize. I misunderstood. I just thought you wanted someone to have a good time with.

GEORGE Look at me, Leo. I'm a nice, plain, regular person who eats fruit and wears slippers. What makes you think I'm going to like a jazzy blonde who dyes a zigzag streak of dark-blue in her hair? She looked like the cover of a record album.

LEO But a terrific body. You've got to admit that body was put together by someone who's very close to God.

GEORGE I booked a table in one of the finest French restaurants in New York. I put on a nice blue suit, rang her doorbell and this creature from *Star Wars* says hello. You know what kind of a dress she was wearing? Electric! I didn't see where it was plugged in *but this was an electric dress*! I swear to God, we got in and the cab driver got static on his radio. In the restaurant I *prayed* for another blackout.

LEO Did I tell you to take her someplace nice? Putz! You take her to the Rainbow Room, somewhere that only out-of-towners go. But you had a good time, right? Right, George? C'mon, will ya. I went to a lot of trouble. Tell me you had a good time.

GEORGE What do you mean, I had a good time? A thunderstorm came up, and I'm sitting there with a lightning rod. I did not have a good time. She ordered a nine-dollar goose-liver pâté and made a hero sandwich out of it . . . Go home, Leo.

LEO George, I have set that girl up with some very heavy clients from Hollywood, and they've been very nice to me every Christmas.

GEORGE Are you telling me she's a hooker? Are you telling me that outlet from Con Edison is a pro?

LEO Would I do that to you? My brother? Bambi's a terrific girl. A little flashy on the exterior, yes. A little Art Deco around the wardrobe, yes. But no hooker . . . Why? Did she charge you anything?

GEORGE For what? I was wet, I was afraid to touch her.

LEO Bad move on my part, okay? Some like 'em hot, some like 'em milk and cookies. I know better now. But if you're telling me you're ready for a serious woman, George, I met her last night at "21."

GEORGE Close the door on your way out, Leo.

LEO I have a feeling about this, George. Don't deny me my feelings.

GEORGE *(Starting into the bedroom)* Leo, *please*! I have my work. I have my friends. I have the Knicks, the Giants and the Mets. I have jogging and I have watercolors. My life is full. There are no more Barbaras left in the world. If you meet them *once* in your life, God has been more than good to you . . . I *will* go out. I *will* meet people. But I have to find them in my own time, in my own way. I love you for what you're doing . . . but don't do it anymore.

LEO At least let me describe her—a nose, a couple of eyes, one or two ears! *(Following* GEORGE *into the bedroom)* Let me leave her number. You don't have to call her right away. Whenever you feel like it!

(Dimout)

Her apartment. A suitcase is on the sofa; JENNIE *is packing. The phone rings. She answers it.*

JENNIE Hello? . . . Well, what a surprise. How are you, Gus? . . . Fine . . . And how does it feel to be an ex-husband? . . . It's been a long time since I heard your "bachelor" voice. You got your old *pizzazz* back . . . Oh, I found an old pair of your basketball sneakers in the closet, did you want them? . . . Thanks, I can wear them to go shopping . . . *I* sound *down*? . . . Oh, I guess a combination of post-divorce blues and the Mexican water . . . I'm not sure. I've got three more weeks on the soap. I've got an offer to go to Washington and do a year of rep at the Arena Theatre . . . And you? . . . Well, hang in, you always come up with something . . . It was very sweet of you to call, Gus . . . Well, I wish you every happiness, too. This has been the nicest talk we've had in a long time . . . I will . . . *Gus*! . . . I just wanted to say—I'm sorry!

(*On the verge of tears, she hangs up. The doorbell rings; she answers it. It is* FAYE)

FAYE Do you believe in miracles?

JENNIE Do you believe in saying hello?

FAYE Well, two miracles happened last night at "21." The producer of *As the World Turns* saw me at our table, called me today and offered me a part—

JENNIE Congratulations! Oh, Faye, that's fantastic! Well, what's the part?

FAYE Her name is Jarlene Indigo.

JENNIE Jarlene Indigo?

FAYE She's the new cellist with the Boston Symphony.

JENNIE I love it. Will you have to learn to play?

FAYE By Monday.

JENNIE *(Continues her packing)* What's the second miracle?

FAYE Do you remember that fellow Leo Schneider who came over to our table to say hello? Sidney doesn't know, but I used to date Leo when I first got to New York. Anyway, he's got this brother, George. He's recently widowed, about forty-two, forty-three years old I think . . . You're not listening. What are you doing?

JENNIE I am packing. If you don't know this is packing, how will you learn to play a cello?

FAYE Where are you going?

JENNIE Home. To Cleveland. I just have an overwhelming desire to sleep in my old, tiny bed.

FAYE How long will you be gone?

JENNIE A couple of days—maybe a couple of weeks.

FAYE In Cleveland a couple of days are a couple of weeks. Can't you postpone it? Leo was going to try to get George Schneider to call this week.

JENNIE Faye, how many times must I tell you? I don't feel like dating right now.

FAYE Well, that's perfect. Neither does George Schneider. At least you have something in common.

JENNIE I wonder what it is that holds our friendship together.

FAYE He's a writer. A novelist, I think. I met him once a few years ago. Not gorgeous, but sweet-looking. With a very intelligent face.

JENNIE Faye, please stop. I appreciate what you're doing. You and Sidney have been wonderful. I loved the dinner at "21," and the date you fixed me up with was unusual but charming.

FAYE It's all right. I know you didn't like him.

JENNIE It's not that I didn't like him. I couldn't *see* him. The man was six feet eight inches tall. All I could think of at dinner was what if we got married and I had a baby? I'd be giving birth for days.

FAYE If you're going to look for things, you can find fault with everyone.

JENNIE I don't think being uncomfortable with a man who was taller than the waiter *sitting down* is looking to find fault.

FAYE I'm talking about everyone you go out with. You sit there and scrutinize them.

JENNIE I scrutinize?

FAYE Your eyes burn little holes in them. That poor fellow last night kept checking to see if his fly was open.

JENNIE All right. I won't scrutinize if you'll stop arranging my social life for me. I told you it's not important to me—why do you do it?

FAYE I don't do it for you. I do it for me.

JENNIE What?

FAYE I have visions of arranging the perfect romance for you. Someone with a dark tragic background—Jay Gatsby . . . Irving Thalberg . . . Leon Trotsky . . .

JENNIE Jesus, do I have to live out my life with *your* fantasy?

FAYE What the hell, I'm arranging it, I might as well pick who I like . . . I don't understand, Jennie. Are you telling me you're never dating again?

JENNIE *(Putting on her coat)* Yes. YES! I have dated and I have gone to parties and I have had it. If one more man greets me at the door with his silk shirt unbuttoned to his tanned navel, his chest hair neatly combed, and wearing more jewelry around his neck than me, I am turning celibate. . . . I am going to spend the rest of my life doing good work in the theatre. I am going to read all the classics starting with *Agamemnon* . . . I'll work out my sex life the best I can. And don't think I'm not worried. Sometimes I lie in bed thinking, Is it physically possible if you don't have sex for a long, long time, you can go back to being a virgin? Well, I'll find out. But first I'll find out in Cleveland.

(She grabs her suitcase and starts out. The phone rings)

FAYE Oh, my God, maybe that's George Schneider.

JENNIE It's *your* fantasy, *you* answer it.

(She goes. FAYE *runs after her)*

FAYE *(Yells) I'll give you two hundred dollars if you answer that phone!*

(But JENNIE *is gone.* FAYE *closes the door and goes)*

SCENE 5

His apartment. It is two weeks later, about 9 P.M. GEORGE *walks into the living room, carrying a reference book. He looks for something at the desk and around the sofa, then goes to the phone and dials, still looking about him.*

GEORGE *(Into the phone)* Marilyn? . . . George . . . Is Leo there? . . . No, you can just yell into the bathroom . . . Ask him if he remembers where he left the phone number for a Mrs. Jenkins, or Jergins, or something like that. He wrote it down and left it for me somewhere in here last week . . . Jenkins, Jergins . . . *(Looking through some papers)* She's the old woman he told me about who used to work for the Harvard University Library about forty years ago . . . No. It's research for the book . . . Would you? *(Spots a paper under the kitchen phone)* Wait a minute, Marilyn, I'm gonna put you on hold. Just a second. *(Pushes the "hold" button, gets the paper from under the kitchen phone and picks up that receiver)* Marilyn, I found it. It was right under the other phone . . . Yeah . . . Give Tina a kiss for me. Goodbye.

(He hangs up both phones and looks at the paper. He dials again . . . And the phone rings in her empty apartment. Just then we hear the key in the door and JENNIE *enters. She turns on the lights. The phone rings again. She puts down her suitcase and picks up the receiver)*

JENNIE Hello?

GEORGE Hello? Is this, uh . . . I'm sorry. I'm not sure I have your name right . . . This is George Schneider

—Leo Schneider's brother? I believe he told you I would be calling you.

JENNIE George Schneider?

GEORGE The writer.

JENNIE Oh . . . God! Yes . . . George Schneider. It seemed so long ago . . . I'm sorry, you caught me at a bad time. I just got off a plane and walked in the door.

GEORGE Oh, I didn't know. I'm sorry. Can I call you back?

JENNIE Well . . . Yes, I suppose so but, er . . . I'll be very honest with you, Mr. Schneider. I'm going through sort of a transition period right now, and I'm not planning to date for a while.

GEORGE *Date?* Did Leo say I was going to call you for a date?

JENNIE Well, he said you were going to call, so I assumed—

GEORGE No, no. This wasn't a date call. I'm very surprised at Leo, Miss, er . . . Is it Jenkins or Jergins?

JENNIE Is what?

GEORGE Your name.

JENNIE It's Malone. Jennifer Malone.

GEORGE *(Confused, looks at the paper)* Jennifer Malone? . . . No, that's wrong.

JENNIE I could show you my driver's license.

GEORGE That's not the name he gave me . . . *(He looks on the back of the paper)* Oh, geez, it's on the other side. I couldn't read his writing. Serene Jurgens was the one I wanted. She's an elderly woman, about eighty-five years old.

JENNIE Well, you know what you want better than I do.

GEORGE Look, I am so embarrassed. I really was going to call you socially. At another time. I mean, I really was.

JENNIE Well, let's see how it goes with Serene first. Okay? Goodbye.

(She hangs up)

GEORGE *(Looks at the scrap of paper)* God damn you, Leo, get your women straight, will ya?

(JENNIE *takes her suitcase to the bedroom.* GEORGE *thinks a moment about what to do, then looks at the paper and dials again. The phone rings in her bedroom*)

JENNIE *(Answering it)* Hello?

GEORGE It's me. I'm back.

JENNIE You and the old lady didn't hit it off?

GEORGE *Now* I know who you are. The girl Leo met at "21." Jennie Malone.

JENNIE That sounds right to me.

GEORGE Anyway, I'm calling back because I wanted you to know that I got the phone numbers mixed up, and I didn't want you to think I wasn't calling you. I *was*. I mean, I wasn't *then*. I am *now*.

JENNIE For a date?

GEORGE No. Not yet. I thought I'd wait and explain the *last* call before I went ahead with the *next* call.

JENNIE I'm a little slow. Which call are we on now?

GEORGE This is the call back to explain the dumb call. The charming call comes after we hang up from this one.

JENNIE I'm so glad I'm home. If I got this message on my answering service, I'd need a private detective.

GEORGE I'll tell you the absolute truth. I haven't made a call to a nice single girl in fourteen years. I wasn't even good at it then. If I seem inept, please bear with me.

JENNIE You seem ept enough. The point is, Mister . . . er . . .

GEORGE George Schneider. I got it here on the paper.

JENNIE The point is, Mr. Schneider, as I told Faye to tell Leo to tell you, I really have to get my head together right now, and that's what I was going to do for the next few weeks.

GEORGE Oh, I understand that. As a matter of fact, I was doing the same thing. I just didn't want to leave you with the image of some retarded romantic walking around town with your number and a handful of dimes.

JENNIE Knowing that, I will sleep better . . . It was very nice talking to you, George. Goodbye.

(She hangs up. He hangs up. She turns and goes into the kitchen. He thinks a moment, then looks at the paper and dials again. The phone rings in her apartment. She comes out of the kitchen, a little annoyed, and answers it) Hello?

GEORGE This is the charming call.

JENNIE I think I have a problem on my hands.

GEORGE You don't. I promise. This is definitely our last conversation.

JENNIE Then why did you call back?

GEORGE I couldn't resist saying, "This is the charming call" . . . Seriously, I'm sorry if I intruded on your privacy. I know very much how you feel. And I liked the sound of your voice, and I also wanted to say, "I hope you get your head together in good health." This is now the end of the charming call. Goodbye.

(He hangs up. Caught off-guard, she looks at the

phone, then hangs up. His call stops her halfway to her kitchen)

JENNIE *(Returns to the phone)* Hello? *(A laugh bubbles out of her)*

GEORGE I was just trying to place your voice. California girl, right? U.C.L.A.?

JENNIE Born in Cleveland and I went to Bennington in Vermont.

GEORGE How about that? I was *so* close.

JENNIE That's where I've just come from.

GEORGE Bennington?

JENNIE Cleveland. I was visiting family.

GEORGE Aha.

JENNIE Aha what?

GEORGE Just aha. Acknowledgment. Comprehension. I understand.

JENNIE Oh. Well, aha to you, too.

GEORGE Leo told me what you did but I didn't pay any attention.

JENNIE Why not?

GEORGE His previous social arrangements for me all ended like the *Andrea Doria*.

JENNIE And yet here you are calling me.

GEORGE Only by mistake.

JENNIE No, no. The first call was a mistake, and the second one was a call back explaining the mistake. The charming call was yours.

GEORGE That's true. You have a very good mind, Jennie Malone. Now you see why you got the charming call.

JENNIE You're a writer, that's for sure. I took English Lit. This is what they call "repartee," isn't it?

GEORGE No. This is what they call "amusing telephone conversation under duress" . . . So what is it you do?

JENNIE I'm an actress. *(He doesn't respond)* No "aha"?

GEORGE Leo didn't tell me you were an actress.

JENNIE I'm sorry. Wrong career?

GEORGE No. No. Actresses can be, uh, very nice.

JENNIE Well, that's an overstatement but I appreciate your open-mindedness.

GEORGE Wait a minute, I'm now extricating my mouth from my foot . . . There, that's better. So you're an actress and I'm a writer. I'm also a widower.

JENNIE Yes. Faye told me.

GEORGE Faye?

JENNIE Faye Medwick. She's the one pushing from my side.

GEORGE Leo is getting up a brochure on me. We'll send you one when they come in . . . I understand you're recently divorced?

JENNIE Yes . . . How deeply do you intend going into this?

GEORGE Sorry. Occupational hazard. I pry incessantly.

JENNIE That's okay. I scrutinize.

GEORGE Well, prying is second cousin to scrutiny.

JENNIE Wouldn't you know it? It turns out we're related.

GEORGE I don't know if you've noticed but we also talk in the same rhythm.

JENNIE Hmmm.

GEORGE Hmmm? What is "hmmm"?

JENNIE It's second cousin to aha! . . . You're a very interesting telephone person, Mr. Schneider. However, I have literally just walked in the door, and I haven't eaten since breakfast. It was really nice talking to you. Goodbye. *(She hangs up, waits right there expectantly. He hurriedly dials. Her phone rings; she picks it up)* As you were saying?

GEORGE Listen, uh, can I be practical for a second?

JENNIE For a second? Yes.

GEORGE They're not going to let up, you know.

JENNIE Who?

GEORGE The Pushers. Leo and Faye. They will persist and push and prod and leave telephone numbers under books until eventually we have that inevitable date.

JENNIE Nothing is inevitable. Dates are man-made.

GEORGE Whatever . . . The point is, I assume you have an active career. I'm a very busy man who needs quiet and few distractions. So let me propose, in the interest of moving on with our lives, that we get this meeting over with just as soon as possible.

JENNIE Surely you jest.

GEORGE I'm not asking for a date. Blind dates are the nation's third leading cause of skin rash.

JENNIE Then what are you suggesting?

GEORGE Just hear me out. What if we were to meet for just five minutes? We could say hello, look each other over, part company and tell Leo and Faye that they have fulfilled their noble mission in life.

JENNIE That's very funny.

GEORGE And yet I hear no laughter.

JENNIE Because it's not *funny* funny. It's stupid funny.

GEORGE You think it's smart to suffer an entire evening rather than a quick five-minute "hello and goodbye"?

JENNIE Because it's demeaning. It's like shopping. And I don't like being shopped.

GEORGE Do you prefer window-shopping? I could stand across the street, look up and wave.

JENNIE Am I talking to a serious person?

GEORGE My friends tell me I have a certain charm. It's like gold, though. You have to pan for it.

JENNIE And what if during these five minutes we took a liking to each other?

GEORGE Then we take a shot at six minutes.

JENNIE *But* if you take a fancy to me and I don't to you—or, God forbid, vice versa—what then?

GEORGE It's a new system. We don't have all the bugs out yet.

JENNIE I can't believe this conversation.

GEORGE Look, if five minutes is too exhausting, we could have two-and-a-half-minute halves with an intermission.

JENNIE Why am I intrigued by this? . . . When would you like this momentous occasion to take place?

GEORGE How about right now?

JENNIE Right now? That's crazy.

GEORGE You mean, not possible?

JENNIE Oh, it's possible. It's just crazy.

GEORGE Why not? I'm having trouble working anyway. And next week could be too late. Mrs. Jurgens and I could be a hot item.

JENNIE But I just got off a plane. I look terrible.

GEORGE So do I, and I got off one two months ago. And besides, fixing yourself up is illegal. That's a date. This is just a quick look for Leo and Faye.

JENNIE For Leo and Faye, huh? . . . Oh, what the hell, let's give it a shot.

GEORGE Hey, terrific! Where would you like to meet?

JENNIE How does Paris strike you?

GEORGE Outside is no good. Then it gets down to who says goodbye and who leaves first. Very messy . . . How about your place?

JENNIE That's out of the question.

GEORGE Why?

JENNIE I don't *know* why . . . 386 East Eighty-fourth Street, apartment 12F.

GEORGE Got it.

JENNIE Write it down. You have a bad history with numbers.

GEORGE I'll be there in eight minutes.

JENNIE And you don't think this is a bizarre thing to do?

GEORGE It is the weirdest thing I've ever come up with. But we may be blazing the trail for millions of others.

JENNIE And neither of us will be disappointed if we're disappointed, right?

GEORGE Please. Let's not build down our hopes too much. See you. Goodbye.

JENNIE Goodbye.

(He hangs up. She hangs up)

GEORGE Smart! Smart move, George!

JENNIE Dumb! You're a dumb lady, Jennie Malone!
(They head in opposite directions)

Her apartment. Twenty minutes later. The phone rings. JENNIE *comes out of the bedroom. She has taken off her blouse and is buttoning a new one. She goes to the phone quickly.*

JENNIE *(Into the phone)* Hello? . . . Faye, I can't talk to you now . . . He's on his way over . . . George Schneider . . . Yes, *your* George Schneider . . . It's not a date. It's a look! He looks at me and I look at him and then you don't bother us anymore . . . Faye, I can't talk to you now. I'll call you back when he leaves in five minutes . . . Because that's all it takes. *(The doorbell rings)* Dammit, he's here . . . I hate you. Goodbye.

(She hangs up, tucks her blouse into her skirt, looks in the mirror, does a last-minute brush job, then goes to the door. She takes in a deep breath, and then opens it. GEORGE *stands there, arm extended, leaning against the doorframe. They look at each other . . . Finally he smiles and nods his head)*

GEORGE Yeah! Okayyyyyy!

JENNIE Is that a review?

GEORGE No. Just a response . . . Hello.

JENNIE *(Smiles)* Hello.

(They are both suddenly very embarrassed and don't quite know what to say or how to handle this situation)

GEORGE *(Good-naturedly)* This was a dumb idea, wasn't it?

JENNIE Extremely.

GEORGE *(Nods in agreement)* I think I've put undue pressure on these next five minutes.

JENNIE You could cut it with a knife.

GEORGE I think if I came in, it would lessen the tension.

JENNIE Oh, I'm sorry. Please, yes.
(He steps in. She closes the door behind her)

GEORGE *(Looks around the room and nods)* Aha!

JENNIE Does that mean you comprehend my apartment?

GEORGE No. It means I like it. "Aha" can be used in many situations, this being one of them.

JENNIE Can I get you anything to drink?

GEORGE No, thanks. I don't drink.

JENNIE Oh, neither do I.
(There is an awkward pause)

GEORGE Although I'd love a glass of white wine.

JENNIE So would I. *(She goes to the kitchen)* Please, sit down.

GEORGE Thank you. *(But he doesn't. He wanders around the room looking at things. She brings in an opened bottle of white wine in an ice bucket set on a tray with two glasses. He spots a framed photograph of a football player in action)* Is it all right if I pry?

JENNIE Sure.

GEORGE You can scrutinize later. *(He examines the picture)* Oh, are you a football fan?

JENNIE That's my ex-husband. He was a wide receiver for the New York Giants.

GEORGE No kidding! What's his name?

JENNIE Gus Hendricks.

GEORGE *(Looks at picture again)* Gus Hendricks? . . . Funny, I can't remember him. How wide a receiver was he?

JENNIE He was cut the beginning of his second year. Bad hands, I think they call it. Couldn't hold on to the football.

GEORGE Well, some coaches are very demanding. What does he do now?

JENNIE Well, he was in mutual funds, he was in the saloon business, he was in broadcasting, he was in sports promotion—

GEORGE Very ambitious.

JENNIE He did all those in three months. He has some problems to work out.

(She pours the two glasses of wine)

GEORGE Who doesn't?

JENNIE True enough.

(She hands him a glass)

GEORGE Thank you.

JENNIE Here's to working out problems.

(They both drink. He looks at her)

GEORGE Leo was right. You're very attractive.

JENNIE Thank you.

GEORGE I'm curious. You don't have to answer this . . . How was *I* described?

JENNIE "Not gorgeous, but an intelligent face."

GEORGE *(Smiles)* That's true. I have. You can ask my face anything. (JENNIE *sits.* GEORGE *is still standing*) No matter how old or experienced you are, the process never seems to get any easier, does it?

JENNIE What process?

GEORGE Mating.

JENNIE *Mating?* My God, is *that* what we're doing?

GEORGE *(Sits next to her on the sofa)* Haven't you noticed? First thing I did as I passed you, I inhaled. Got a little whiff of your fragrance. In our particular species, the sense of smell is a determining factor in sexual attraction.

JENNIE This is just a guess. Do you write for *Field and Stream*?

GEORGE *(Laughs)* Please, give me a break, will you? I haven't done this in fourteen years. If you're patient, I get interesting with a little kindness.

JENNIE You're not uninteresting now.

GEORGE I'll tell you the truth. You're not the first girl Leo's introduced me to. There were three others . . . All ranked with such disasters as the *Hindenburg* and Pearl Harbor.

JENNIE *Now* I see. That's when the Five-Minute Plan was born.

GEORGE Necessity is the Mother of Calamity.

JENNIE Tell me about them.

GEORGE Oh, they defy description.

JENNIE Please. Defy it.

GEORGE All right. Let's see. First there was Bambi. Her name tells you everything.

JENNIE I got the picture.

GEORGE Then there was Vilma. A dynamite girl.

JENNIE Really?

GEORGE Spent three years in a Turkish prison for carrying dynamite . . . Need I go on?

JENNIE No, I think I've had enough.

GEORGE Since then I've decided to take everything

Leo says with a grain of panic . . . And now I feel rather foolish because I was very flippant with you on the phone, and now I find myself with an attractive, intelligent and what appears to be a very nice girl.

JENNIE You won't get a fight from me on that.

GEORGE With an appealing sense of adventure.

JENNIE You think so?

GEORGE It's your five minutes, too.

JENNIE I was wondering why I said yes. I think it's because I really enjoyed talking to you on the phone. You're very bright, and I found I had to keep on my toes to keep up with you.

GEORGE Oh. And is that unusual?

JENNIE I haven't been off my heels in years . . . What kind of books do you write?

GEORGE Ah, we're moving into heavy territory. What kind of books do I write? For a living, I write spy novels. For posterity, I write good novels. I make a good living, but my posterity had a bad year.

JENNIE Name some books.

GEORGE From column A or column B?

JENNIE Both.

GEORGE Well, the spy novels I write under the name of Kenneth Blakely Hyphen Hill.

JENNIE Hyphen Hill?

GEORGE You don't say the hyphen. You just put it in.

JENNIE Oh, God, yes. Of course. I've seen it. Drugstores, airports . . .

GEORGE Unfortunately, not libraries.

JENNIE Who picked the name?

GEORGE My wife. You see, my publisher said spy novels sell better when they sound like they were written in England. We spent our honeymoon in London, and we stayed at the Blakely Hotel, and it was on a hill and the hall porter's name was Kenneth . . . If we had money in those days, my name might have been Kenneth Savoy Grill.

JENNIE And from column B?

GEORGE I only had two published. They were a modest failure. That means "Bring us more but not too soon."

JENNIE I'd like to read them someday.

GEORGE I'll send you a couple of cartons of them. *(They both sip their wine. He looks around, then back at her)* I'm forty-two years old.

JENNIE Today?

GEORGE No. In general.

JENNIE Oh. Is that statement of some historic importance?

GEORGE No. I just wanted you to know, because you look to be about twenty-four and right now I feel like a rather inept seventeen, and I didn't want you to think I was too young for you.

JENNIE I'm thirty-two.

(They look at each other. It's the first time their gaze really holds)

GEORGE Well. That was very nice wasn't it? I mean, looking at each other like that.

JENNIE I wasn't scrutinizing.

GEORGE That's okay, I wasn't prying.

JENNIE My hunch is that you're a very interesting man, George.

GEORGE Well, my advice is—play your hunches.

JENNIE Can I get you some more wine?

GEORGE No thanks. I think I'd better be going.

JENNIE *Oh?* . . . Okay.
(They rise)

GEORGE Not that I wouldn't like to stay.

JENNIE Not that you're not welcome, but I understand.

GEORGE I think we've hit it off very well, if you've noticed.

JENNIE I've noticed.

GEORGE Therefore, I would like to make a regulation date. Seven to twelve, your basic normal hours.

JENNIE Aha! With grown-up clothes and make-up?

GEORGE Bath, shower—everything.

JENNIE Sounds good. Let's make it.

GEORGE You mean now?

JENNIE Would you rather go home and do it on the phone?

GEORGE No, no. Dangerous. I could get the wrong number and wind up with Mrs. Jurgens . . . Let's see, what is this?

JENNIE Tuesday.

GEORGE How about Wednesday?

JENNIE Wednesday works out well.

GEORGE You could play hard to get and make it Thursday.

JENNIE No. Let's stick with Wednesday and I'll keep you waiting half an hour.

GEORGE *(At the door)* Fair enough. This was nice. I'm very glad we met, Jennie.

JENNIE So am I, George.

GEORGE I can't believe you're from the same man who gave us Bambi and Vilma.

(He goes. She closes the door, smiles and heads for her bedroom. The lights fade)

Her apartment. It is a week later, about 6:30 P.M. FAYE *is staring out the window through binoculars, a cigarette in her hand. She is looking a little glum.*

FAYE She's putting on weight.

JENNIE *(Offstage)* Who?

FAYE Lupe, across the street. Sagging a little, too. Another six pounds, she'll start pulling down her shades.

JENNIE *(Offstage)* You sound terrible. Is anything wrong?

FAYE We're not going away for Easter. Sidney's ear infection still hasn't cleared up. He's lost his sense of balance. He keeps rolling away from me in bed. It's a very sad state of affairs when things are worse at home than they are on the soap . . . They tell me you're coming back to work on Monday.

JENNIE *(Offstage)* Maybe. We'll see.

FAYE You haven't given me a straight answer in a week. What's all the mystery about? . . . Can I come in now? Jennie? I'm alone enough at nights.

JENNIE *(Offstage)* Give me ten more seconds.

FAYE Four nights in one week, he's got to be someone special. Who is he, Jennie? Have I met him? Oh, God, I hate it when I'm left out of things! (JENNIE *comes out, shows off her new backless dress*) It's gorgeous. I love everything but the price tag.

(They remove it)

JENNIE Oh, damn, I'm a basket case. I haven't worried about looking good for someone in such a long time.

FAYE What is going on, my angel?

JENNIE I don't know. I've been on a six-day high and I've had nothing stronger than a Diet Pepsi.

FAYE My God, it's George Schneider, isn't it? (JENNIE *nods*) Why didn't you tell me?

JENNIE I was afraid to.

FAYE Why?

JENNIE Because after six days I think I'm nuts about him, and I was afraid if I told anyone they'd have me put in the Home for the Over-Emotional. Come on, I'm going to be late.

FAYE *(Going into the corridor)* Well, tell me about him. What's he like?

JENNIE Well, he's everything you've always wanted...

(She closes the door, and they are gone)

His apartment, later that night.

JENNIE *(Outside his door)* Don't worry, I paid for the cab. *(She opens the door)* Where are the lights, George?

GEORGE *(In the corridor)* I don't want you to look at me.

JENNIE George, where are the lights?
(She finds them, turns them on)

GEORGE *(Entering, puts his hand to his eyes)* Oh, God, that hurts.

JENNIE Do you want to lie down, George?

GEORGE I'm so embarrassed. Just let me sit a few minutes. I'll be all right.

JENNIE Just keep taking deep breaths.

GEORGE *(Dizzy, sitting on the sofa)* That's the closest I've ever come to passing out.

JENNIE Loosen your collar. I'll take your shoes off.
(She kneels, starts to untie his laces as he loosens his tie and wipes his brow)

GEORGE First I thought it was the wine. Then I thought it was the fish. Then I figured it was the bill.

JENNIE You don't know where they get the fish from anymore. *(She has his shoes off, massages his feet)* You read about tankers breaking up every day, oil spilling all over. For all we know, we just ate a gallon of Texaco.

GEORGE Ohh. Ohh. Careful.

JENNIE What?

GEORGE I have very sensitive feet.

JENNIE I'm sorry.

GEORGE That's the weakest part of my system. Even baby powder hurts.

JENNIE You're perspiring all over. Let me get you a cold towel.

(She gets up, looks around, goes to the kitchen)

GEORGE You mean my feet were sweaty? Oh, God! Is it over between us, Jennie?

JENNIE *(Coming back in with a wet cloth)* Oh, shut up. I've rubbed sweaty feet before.

GEORGE You have? You've really been around, haven't you? . . . I don't want you to think this is a regular thing, passing out on dates. I mean, I played varsity football at Hofstra.

JENNIE I faint all the time. It's the only thing that relaxes me.

(She puts the cloth on his forehead)

GEORGE Jesus! You paid for the taxi. How humiliating! I don't want to live anymore.

JENNIE You're not taking in enough air.

(She starts to unbuckle his belt and the top button of his pants)

GEORGE Hey! What are you doing?

JENNIE Oh, stop. I'm just unbuttoning your pants.

GEORGE Please! No premarital unbuckling! I'm all right, Jennie, really.

JENNIE *(She kneels down beside him)* You look about twelve years old right now.

GEORGE Seventeen last week, twelve this week—I'll be back in the womb by the end of the month. *(She kisses the back of his hand, then caresses it with her cheek. He touches her hair with his other hand)* You are the sweetest girl.

JENNIE *(Looks up at his face, smiles)* Thank you.

(He leans over and kisses her gently on the mouth)

GEORGE I can't believe it's just a week. I feel like we're into our fourth year or something.

JENNIE Have you felt that, too? As though it's not a new relationship at all. I feel like we're picking up in the middle somewhere . . . of something that started a long, long time ago.

GEORGE That's exactly how it was when I walked in your door that night last week. I didn't say to myself, "Oh, how pretty. How interesting. I wonder what she's like." I said, "Of course. It's Jennie. I know her. I never met her but I know her. How terrific to find her again."

JENNIE It's nice bumping into you again for the first time, George. *(They smile and kiss again. She looks up at him. He seems to have a pained expression on his face)* What is it? . . . Is it the pain again? *(He shakes his head "no," then turns away to hide the tears. He takes out a handkerchief to wipe his eyes)* George! Oh, George, sweetheart, what? Tell me.

(She cradles his head in her arms as he tries to fight back his emotions)

GEORGE I don't know, Jennie.

JENNIE It's all right . . . Whatever you're feeling, it's all right.

GEORGE I keep trying to push Barbara out of my mind . . . I can't do it. I've tried, Jennie.

JENNIE I know.

GEORGE I don't really want to. I'm so afraid of losing her forever.

JENNIE I understand and it's all right.

GEORGE I know I'll never stop loving Barbara, but I feel so good about you . . . and I can't get the two things together in my mind.

JENNIE It all happened so fast, George. You expect so much of yourself so soon.

GEORGE On the way over in the cab tonight, I'm yelling at the cab driver, "Can't you get there faster?" . . . And then some nights I wake up saying, "I'm never going to see Barbara again and I hope to God it's just a dream."

JENNIE I love you, George . . . I want you to know that.

GEORGE Give me a little time, Jennie. Stay next to me. Be with me. Just give me the time to tell you how happy you make me feel.

JENNIE I'm not going anywhere, George. You can't lose me. I know a good thing when I see it.

GEORGE *(Managing a smile)* Jeez! I thought I had food poisoning and it's just a mild case of ecstasy.

JENNIE *(Embraces him)* I just want you to be happy. I want you to have room for all your feelings. I'll share whatever you want to share with me. I'm very strong, George. I can work a sixteen-hour day on a baloney sandwich and a milk shake. I have enough for both of us. Use it, George. Please. Use me . . .

GEORGE *(Wipes his eyes, puts the hanky down)* Really? Would you knit me a camel's-hair overcoat?

JENNIE With or without humps? *(Touches his hand)* Why did it scare you so, George? We were sitting there touching hands, and you suddenly broke into a cold sweat.

GEORGE Because it's not supposed to happen twice in your life.

JENNIE Who said so?

GEORGE Don't ask intelligent questions. You're talking to a man who just swooned into his butter plate. *(He rises)* Come on. I'll show you the house that Kenneth Blakely-Hill built.

JENNIE And don't forget to give me those books tonight.

GEORGE They're four ninety-five each, but we can talk business later. *(Puts his arm around her waist)* Now, then . . . This is the living room. That's the hallway that leads to the bedroom. And this is the rug that lies on the floor that covers the wood of the house that Kenneth Hyphen built.

JENNIE I want to see everything.

GEORGE Shall we start with the bedroom?

JENNIE Okay.

GEORGE If we start with the bedroom, we may *end* with the bedroom.

JENNIE Endings are just beginnings backwards.

GEORGE It's going to be one of those fortune cookie romances, huh? Okay, my dear . . . *(They head toward the bedroom)* Trust me.

JENNIE I do.

GEORGE Sure. I pass out at fish. What have *you* got to be afraid of?

(They enter the bedroom as the lights fade)

SCENE 9

His apartment. It is three days later, mid-afternoon. LEO *paces in* GEORGE*'s living room, takes some Valium from his attaché case and swallows one with club soda.*

LEO George, will you let somebody else in New York use the phone?

GEORGE *(Enters from the bedroom, wearing a sweater over an open-necked shirt)* I'm sorry, Leo. It was an important call. I had to take it.

LEO Are you all right?

GEORGE I'm wonderful! I'm terrific! I haven't felt this good in such a long time . . . Listen, Leo, I'm glad you dropped by.

LEO You look tired. You don't have good color in your face.

GEORGE I'll have a painter come in Tuesday, he'll show me some swatches. Leo, will you stop worrying about me? I want to talk to you.

LEO I called you one o'clock in the morning last night, you weren't in.

GEORGE I'm glad I wasn't. Why did you call me at one o'clock in the morning?

LEO I couldn't sleep. I wanted to talk to you.

GEORGE *(Impatient)* *Leo*! I am *fine*! Everything is *wonderful*!

LEO I wanted to talk about *me* . . . I'm in trouble, George.

GEORGE What?

LEO *(Nods)* Marilyn wants to leave me.

GEORGE *(Looks at him)* Oh, come on.

LEO What is that, a joke? My wife wants to leave me.

GEORGE Why?

LEO She's got a list. Ask her, she'll show it to you . . . She doesn't like my lifestyle, she doesn't like the hours I keep, my business, my friends, my indifference, my attitude, my coldness—and our marriage. Otherwise we're in good shape. Christ! I said to her, "Marilyn, show me a press agent who comes home at six o'clock and I'll show you a man who can't get Jimmy Carter's name in the newspapers." I'm in the theater. Life begins at eight o'clock. The world isn't just matinees.

GEORGE She's not going to leave you, Leo. This has been going on for years.

LEO I took on two extra shows this season. The money was good, we needed it. I can't tell what the future is. I've got to make it *now*! I've got two kids. I could be dead tomorrow.

GEORGE *(Nods)* That's possible. I guess she just wants to enjoy you while you're still alive.

LEO *(Referring to* GEORGE*'s wife)* I'm sorry, George.

GEORGE Oh, come on, Leo. I know how you feel. You'll work it out. You always have.

LEO Not this time . . . She's leaving me the morning after *Pinocchio*.

GEORGE *Pinocchio*? What's that?

LEO Tina is doing *Pinocchio* at school. Marilyn doesn't want to upset her until it's over. The kid isn't even playing the lead. She's a herring that gets swallowed by the whale.

GEORGE When is the show?

LEO The show is Thursday night. The only chance I have to keep her is if the play runs four years! I don't know what the hell I'm holding on to, anyway. I swear to God, I'll never get married again. You spend half your married life fighting to get back the feeling you had just before you got married.

GEORGE Come on, Leo. You've got a good marriage— I *know.*

LEO Really? I'll invite you to sleep in our bedroom one night, you can listen. I'll tell you, George. The trouble with marriage is that it's relentless. Every morning when you wake up, it's still there. If I could just get a leave of absence every once in a while. A two-week leave of absence. I used to get them all the time in the Army, and I always came back . . . I don't know. I think it was different for you and Barbara. I'll tell you the truth, I always thought the two of you were a little crazy. But that's what made it work for you. You had a real bond of lunacy between you . . . Marilyn has no craziness. No fantasies. No uncharted territories to explore. I'm sitting there with maps for places in my mind I've never been, and she won't even pack an overnight bag. In eleven years she never once let me make love to her with the lights on. I said to her, "Marilyn, come on, trust me, I won't tell anybody." So we stop growing, stop changing. And we stagnate . . . in our comfortable little house in the country . . . Oh, well, another thirty, thirty-five years and it'll be over, right? *(He sits back)* All right, I've told someone. I feel better . . . Now, what the hell is it you feel so wonderful about?

GEORGE *(Smiles)* You're an interesting man, Leo. Someday I'll have to get to know you . . . In the meantime there's this girl I've met—

LEO You've gone out with her? You like her?

GEORGE I like her, Leo. She's extraordinary.

LEO *(Pleased)* Isn't that wonderful! You see, I knew you'd like her. I only spoke to her for ten minutes, but I saw she had a vitality, a sparkle about her—I knew she would interest you.

GEORGE She more than interests me, Leo. I'm crazy about her.

LEO Listen, I don't blame you. If I wasn't married, I'd have beaten you to the punch. Isn't that terrific! Terrific! Well, I knew once you left yourself open, you'd start to meet some women you can relate to—

GEORGE I'm in love with her, Leo—I mean, crazy in love with her.

LEO Well, we'll see. The point is, you enjoy being with her and that's very important for you at this time.

GEORGE Leo, you don't hear what I'm saying . . . I'm going to marry her.

LEO Look, it's possible. *I* hope so. She seems very sweet. Very bright. Faye tells me there isn't a person who ever met her who doesn't like her. She could be wonderful for you. When things calm down, when you get to be your old self again, I would *love* to see it happen.

GEORGE We're getting married on Monday.

(LEO *looks at him*)

LEO Monday's a terrific day to get married. You miss the weekend traffic. Seriously, George, I'm glad you like the girl.

GEORGE We took the blood test. I got the license. It's Monday morning, ten o'clock, Judge Ira Markowitz's chambers. I'd like you and Marilyn to be there.

LEO To be where?

GEORGE *(Annoyed)* Come on, Leo, you heard me. Jennie and I are getting married on Monday morning.

LEO Wait a minute, wait a minute, back up! Play that again. What are you telling me? You mean on Monday morning you're marrying a girl I met for twelve seconds in a restaurant?

GEORGE I'm marrying Jennie! *Jennie Malone!*

LEO Oh, good. You know both names. So you must have had a chance to talk to her.

GEORGE I've lived with her twenty hours a day for the last two weeks, and I know everything I want to know about her.

LEO Two weeks? You've known her two weeks? I eat eggs that are *boiled* for two weeks—what the hell is *two* weeks?

GEORGE Wait a minute. What happened to "how interesting she is"? What happened to her vitality, her sparkle?

LEO Can't you wait to see if she's still sparkling in six months?

GEORGE Six days, six months—what the hell difference does it make? I only knew Barbara eight weeks, and the marriage lasted twelve years.

LEO George, you're vulnerable now. You're in no shape to make a decision like this.

GEORGE Wait a minute. You know me, Leo. I'm not self-destructive. I wouldn't do something to hurt me *and* Jennie just to satisfy a whim. I love her. I want to be with her. I want to make this commitment.

LEO It's my fault, George. I never should have introduced you to Bambi. After Bambi you were ready for anything.

GEORGE Leo, it was the same thing when I met Barbara. I could have married her after the third date. I knew then she was the most special girl in the world. Well, it's twelve years later and Barbara is gone. And suddenly, miraculously, this incredible person comes into my life—a sensitive, intelligent, warm, absolutely terrific human being. I don't know. Maybe it *is* crazy. You always said I was. But I'm miserable every minute I'm away from her, and she feels the same way. I think marrying her is a Class-A idea, Leo.

LEO Okay, okay. But what is she—Cinderella? She's leaving at twelve o'clock? Wait! You'd wait six weeks for a dentist appointment, and that's with *pain* in your mouth.

GEORGE Have dinner with us tonight. You and Marilyn.

LEO I really don't think a couple breaking up is the best company for a couple starting out.

GEORGE Call Marilyn. Tell her. Maybe being around us will give you both a chance to work things out.

LEO *(Annoyed)* Why can't you accept the fact that Marilyn and I are separating?

GEORGE Why can't you accept the fact that Jennie and I are getting married?

LEO Because my separation makes sense. Your getting married is crazy!

GEORGE Have it your own way. But I would still like you both to be there on Monday.

LEO George, you've always been a lot smarter than me in a lot of ways. You have the talent and the discipline I've always admired. I'm very proud of you. But once in a while I've steered you straight, and I don't think you've ever regretted it . . . Wait a couple of months. Let her move in here with you. Is she against that? She's not a Mormon or anything, is she?

GEORGE What's the point of delaying what's inevitable? She'll wait if I ask her.

LEO Ask her.

GEORGE She'll move in if I ask her.

LEO Ask her. Please, George, ask her.

GEORGE Monday morning, Criminal Courts building. I'm wearing a blue suit.

LEO Wait a month. Wait a month for *me*.

GEORGE I'm not marrying *you*!

LEO Wait a month for me, and I'll wait a month for you. I'll try to work things out with Marilyn. I'll keep us together somehow, for a month, if you and Jennie will do the same for me.

GEORGE Leo, we're not trading baseball cards now. This is my life, that's your marriage. Save it for you and Marilyn, not for me.

LEO George, I realize I'm not the best marriage counselor you could go to—the toll-taker in the Lincoln Tunnel is more qualified than me—all I'm saying is take the time to catch your breath. Sleep on it. Take twelve Valiums and wake up in a month.

GEORGE We're wasting a lot of time, you know that, Leo? This conversation used up my entire engagement period.

LEO Would you mind if I talked to her?

GEORGE Jennie?

LEO Yes. Would you mind if I met with her, alone, and told her how I feel about all this?

GEORGE Yes, I certainly would. She doesn't need an interview to get into this family.

LEO Are you afraid she might agree with me?

GEORGE Leo, I was always bigger than you . . . and

you always beat up the kids who picked on me. What Pop didn't do for me, you did. I was the only kid on the block who had to buy *two* Father's Day presents . . . All right. Look, you want to protect me? Go ahead. You want to talk to Jennie, talk to her. But I promise you—a half-hour with her and you'll come back wondering why I'm waiting so long.

LEO Thank you. I'll call Jennie tonight.

GEORGE Would you like me to talk with Marilyn? I could wrap up the four of us in one night.

LEO Listen, I could be wrong. I've been wrong before.

GEORGE When?

LEO I can't remember when, but I must have been . . . *(Goes to the door)* I don't know what the hell I'm doing in publicity. I was born to be a Jewish mother.

(He leaves. GEORGE *thinks a moment, then goes to the phone and dials. In* JENNIE*'s apartment the phone rings. She's been reading* Catch-22)

JENNIE *(Answering the phone)* Hello?

GEORGE I love you. Do you love me?

JENNIE Of course I do . . . Who is this?

GEORGE You're going to get a call from my brother. He thinks we're crazy.

JENNIE Of course we are. What else is new?

GEORGE Jennie, I've been thinking . . . Let's call it off. Let's wait a month. Maybe a couple of months.

JENNIE All right . . . Whatever you say.

GEORGE And I'd like you to move in here with me. Until we decide what to do.

JENNIE I'll move in whenever you want.

GEORGE I'm crazy about you.

JENNIE I feel the same way.

GEORGE Then forget what I said. It's still on for Monday morning.

JENNIE I'll be there with my little bouquet!

(They hang up. JENNIE *looks thoughtful.* GEORGE*'s gaze is drawn to a framed photo of Barbara)*

Curtain

Act Two

SCENE I

His apartment. It's the next afternoon. GEORGE *is stretched out on his sofa, the phone to his ear. He is in the midst of a difficult conversation.*

GEORGE Of course I am . . . Yes . . . An incredible girl . . . Mom, why would I marry her if I wasn't? . . . Her father sells insurance in Cleveland . . . Yes, he also lives there, that's why he works there. *(He holds the receiver aside and emits a deep sigh of exasperation. Then he puts the phone back to his ear)* . . . I just told you. Monday morning. In a judge's office . . . How can it be, Mom? How can it be a big wedding in a judge's office? . . . You'll meet her when you come up from Florida. *(Another deep sigh. The doorbell rings)* Hold it a second, Mom, the doorbell's ringing . . . No. *Mine!*

(He shakes his head, puts down the phone, opens the door. JENNIE *stands there, beaming)*

JENNIE I'm so crazy about you, it's ridiculous. *(She throws her arms around him and kisses him)* You're the most perfect man who ever lived on the face of the earth.

GEORGE Jeez, if I hear that one more time today . . . What are you doing here?

JENNIE I just had a physical, a facial and a dental. I don't want to get returned because of an imperfection. And I bought you a present.

(She takes a package from her purse and hands it to him)

GEORGE What is it?

JENNIE Open it. *(He does. It is two books bound in fine leather)* Two from column B. I bought them at Doubleday's. They had to order them from the publisher.

GEORGE *(Overwhelmed)* You had them bound? In leather?

JENNIE Guaranteed to last as long as Dickens and Twain.

GEORGE I'm speechless. I'm so thrilled, I don't know what to say . . . I mean, the leather binding is beautiful—but to think I sold two more books! *(He hugs her)* Hey! I left my mother on the phone.

JENNIE In Florida? I want to speak to her.

GEORGE Mom? . . . The next voice you are about to hear is that of Jennie Malone, a girl who brings dignity and respect to the often maligned phrase, "future daughter-in-law"!

JENNIE *(Into the phone)* Mrs. Schneider? . . . Hello . . . I'm very happy to meet you . . . Oh, how nice . . . Well, I am too . . . I hope you know you have a very special and wonderful son.

GEORGE She knows, she knows.

JENNIE No . . . No, it's not going to be a big wedding. It's going to be in a judge's office.

GEORGE *(Into the phone extension)* She drinks, Mom . . . And she's a jockey at Belmont.

(He hangs up)

JENNIE All right, I will . . . Yes . . . As soon as we get back from Barbados . . . God bless you, too.

(JENNIE, *suddenly taken with tears, hands the phone to* GEORGE)

GEORGE *(Into the phone)* Mom, I'll be right with you.

Hang on. Watch Merv Griffin. (He lays the phone down and embraces JENNIE) She can drive you completely nuts and then say something that just wipes you out.

JENNIE Listen, I'll let you work. Don't be late tonight. I'm making spaghetti with fresh basil sauce.

GEORGE Wait a minute. I bought you a present too. *(He goes to a drawer, opens it and takes out a ring box)* I was going to wait until after dinner, but I think I'm going to be eating a long time.

(He hands it to her. She is excited, knowing full well what it probably is)

JENNIE *(Beside herself)* Oh, George, George, what have you done?

GEORGE It's a car.

JENNIE *(Taking out a small diamond ring)* Oh, George...

GEORGE It's no big deal. It's just a wholesale engagement ring.

JENNIE But we'll only be engaged for two more days.

GEORGE Well, what I paid, that's all it's going to last.

JENNIE This is too much emotion for me in one day. Come a half-hour late—I need more time to cry. *(And she rushes to the door, stops and goes back to the phone)* Hello, Mom, he gave me a ring.

(She runs out, and into her own apartment)

GEORGE *(Into the phone)* Mom? . . . No, she left . . . Thank you . . . Of course she knows about Barbara . . . Well, in *my* day we discuss things, Mom . . . What else am I doing? You mean besides getting married? . . . Well, I bought a new sports jacket . . . Gray . . . You can never have too much gray, Mom . . .

(Dimout)

SCENE 2

Her apartment. The doorbell rings. JENNIE *goes over to it. The lights come up on his apartment.* GEORGE, *having finished his long conversation with his mother, dials the phone, sitting up.* JENNIE *opens the door.* FAYE *stands there, her hair in curlers, covered with a scarf.*

JENNIE I thought you were taping two shows today.

FAYE We're on a lunch break. If I asked you for an enormous favor, would you say yes and not ask any questions?

JENNIE Yes.

FAYE How long are you keeping this apartment? *(The phone rings)*

JENNIE My lease is up in two months. Why?

FAYE Would you let me have the key? (JENNIE *looks at her. The phone rings again. She picks it up. It is* GEORGE)

JENNIE Hello?

GEORGE My mother said no. I'm awfully sorry.

JENNIE I am too.

GEORGE I think we could have made a go of it, but this is too great an obstacle.

JENNIE Don't worry about it. I have other things to do.

GEORGE She found someone else for me. But good news: You're invited to the reception.

JENNIE So we can still see each other.

GEORGE Certainly. We can chat over an hors d'oeuvre . . . I'm going to take a bath now. I know you like to follow my schedule.

JENNIE I read it. It was in the *Times*.

GEORGE Then there's no point in talking. Goodbye.

JENNIE 'Bye! (*They both hang up. He turns and heads for his bathroom as the lights go down on his apartment.* JENNIE *turns to* FAYE) Why do you want the key?

FAYE You promised no questions.

JENNIE That's before I knew the favor.

FAYE Please.

(JENNIE *sees that* FAYE *is serious. She crosses to her dresser, takes out a spare key, goes to* FAYE *and hands it to her*)

JENNIE I don't want to know, Faye, but if it's something stupid, please don't do it.

FAYE Then take the key back, because I don't know a smart way to have an affair.

JENNIE Ohhh, Christ! What have you done?

FAYE Everything but consummation. That's why I need the key.

JENNIE When did all this happen?

FAYE All what? So far it's only ten percent cocktail talk . . . But I'm leaning toward "happening."

JENNIE I don't want to know who it is.

FAYE It's a secret I'll keep to my grave.

JENNIE Why won't you tell me?

FAYE Because it's not important who it is. It's only important that I want to do it. Don't you understand, Jennie? If I don't have something like an affair, I'll scream.

JENNIE Then scream!

FAYE Well, I thought I'd try this first.

JENNIE Listen, maybe you're right. You're a grown lady, you know what you're doing.

FAYE The hell I do.

JENNIE Then why are you doing it?

FAYE You tell me. Why are you getting married to a man you've known two and a half weeks who was married to a woman he idolized for twelve years? Because yesterday was lousy and it seems right today. I'll worry about tomorrow the day after.

JENNIE "The Wit and Wisdom of Women in Trouble." Someday we'll collaborate on it . . . Is there anything I can do to help?

FAYE Just leave me a map of all quick exits from the apartment . . . I've got to get back to making America cry. *(Holding up the key)* Listen, I may never use this, but you're the best friend I ever had.

JENNIE When is this—*thing* going to take place?

FAYE Oh, not for a few days. I have to be hypnotized first.

(She exits. The phone rings; JENNIE *answers it)*

JENNIE Hello? . . . Hello, my angel . . . I thought you were taking a bath . . . Oh, you are! . . . No, I do *not* want to hear you blow bubbles . . . I do not want to hear your rubber duck. You're down to three years old, George, and sinking fast. *(The doorbell rings)* Oh, I think that's Leo . . . I'll see you for dinner . . . Well, I'm having spaghetti and you're having baby food. 'Bye!

(She hangs up and opens the door)

LEO Hello, Jennie.

JENNIE Leo—come on in. *(He enters)* I really enjoyed dinner the other night. Marilyn is a very sweet girl.

LEO Thank you. We'll have to have you out to the house when you two get settled.

JENNIE I'd love it . . . Would you like some coffee and stale cookies? I'm trying to clean out the kitchen.

LEO A few minutes. That's all I'm staying. I just wanted to state my case and leave.

JENNIE Oh? That sounds serious . . . All right. Please sit.

LEO *(Decides to stand)* This is none of my business, you know. I have no right coming up here.

JENNIE I think loving your brother is very much your business.

LEO I'm glad you feel that way. Because I do. The reason I wanted to talk to you, Jennie—and if I'm out of line here, tell me . . . the reason I came up here today . . . The foundation for my thoughts . . . The . . . the structure for my desire to . . . to delineate the . . . What the hell am I saying? The structure to delineate—what is that?

JENNIE You think George and I are going too fast.

LEO Exactly. Thank you! Christ! I thought that sentence would take me right into middle age.

JENNIE Two weeks *is* very fast.

LEO In some circles it's greased lightning . . . Be that as it may—and I hasten to add that I have never used expressions like "Be that as it may" or "I hasten to add"—but I'm having trouble. This is delicate territory, and I'm dealing with someone I care very much about.

JENNIE Leo, I told George I'd wait as long as he wanted. Two weeks, two months—I don't care how long. He said, "No. It's got to be Monday, the twenty-third. It's all arranged" . . . What is it you're afraid will happen, Leo?

LEO *(Takes a news clipping from his wallet)* I don't know . . . I'm not sure. Listen, I once did some work for an insurance company and they published these statistics—it was in every national magazine . . . *(Reads)* "The greatest loss that can happen to a man or woman, in terms of traumatic impact to the survivor, is the death of a spouse. The loss of a parent, a child, a job, a house—any catastrophe—is not deemed as devastating as the death of a husband or wife." In time, thank God and the laws of nature, most people work through it. But it needs the time . . . And I wouldn't want you and George to be hurt because that time was denied to him—to both of you.

JENNIE I see . . . Have you and George talked about this?

LEO I can't always read George's mind. He keeps so much bottled up. Maybe he spills it all out when he's alone—at the typewriter. I don't know.

JENNIE Can I ask you a question?

LEO What?

JENNIE What was it like when Barbara died?

LEO Ohhh . . . I don't think you want to go through that, Jennie.

JENNIE No, I don't . . . But you just made it clear how important it is that I do. Tell me, Leo.

LEO *(Thinks, takes his time)* All right . . . They were very close. I mean, as close as any couple I've ever seen. After ten years, they still held hands in a restaurant. I'm married eleven years and I don't pass the salt to my wife . . . When George first found out how ill Barbara was, he just refused to accept it. He knew it was serious, but there was no way she was not going to beat it. He just couldn't conceive of it. And Barbara never let on to a soul that anything was ever wrong. Her best friend, at the funeral, said to George, "I just didn't know" . . . She was beautiful, Jennie, in every way. And then in the last few months you could see she was beginning to slip. George would go out to dinner or a party and leave early, trying not to let on that anything was wrong —and especially not letting on to themselves . . . And then one morning George called me from the hospital, and he said very quietly and simply, "She's gone, Leo." And it surprised me because I thought when it was finally over, George would go to pieces. I mean, I expected a full crackup, and it worried me that he was so held together . . . I saw him as often as I could, called him all the time, and then suddenly I didn't hear from him for about five days. He didn't answer the phone. I called the building. They said they didn't see him go in or go out, and I got plenty scared. I went up there—they let me in with the passkey—and I found him in the bedroom sitting in front of the television set, with the picture on and no sound. He was in filthy pajamas, drenched in perspiration. There was a container of milk on the floor next to him that had gone sour. He must have dropped eight or nine pounds. And I said to him, "Hey, George, why don't you answer your phone? Are you okay?" And he said, "Fine. I'm fine, Leo." Then he reached over and touched my hand, and for the first time in a year and a half, the real tears started to flow. He cried for hours—through that whole night. I still couldn't get him to eat, so the next morning I got our doctor to come over, and he checked him into Mount Sinai. He was there for ten days. And he was in terrible shape. His greatest fear was that I was going to commit him someplace. When he came out, he stayed with me about a week. I couldn't even get him to take a walk. He had this panic, this fear he'd never make it back into the house. I finally got him to walk down to the corner, and he never let go of my arm for a second. We started across the street and he stopped and said, "No, it's too far. Take me back, Leo." A few weeks later he went into therapy. A really good doctor. He was there about a month, and then suddenly he decided he wasn't going back. He wouldn't explain why. I called the doctor and he explained to me that George was making a very determined effort not to get better. Because getting better meant he was ready to let go of Barbara, and there was no way he was going to let that happen. And then one day, bang, he took off for Europe. But not new places. Only the ones he'd visited with Barbara before. When he came back he looked better, seemed more cheerful. So in my usual dumb, impulsive way, I figured he would want what I would want if I were in his place—companionship. Well, companionship to him and me, I found out, were two different things. But he has good instincts. He knows what's right for him. And God knows what I offered wasn't right . . . until the night I saw you sitting there with Faye and I said, "Oh yeah, that's for George." I swear to you, Jennie, you are the best thing that could happen to that man. I was just hoping it would happen a little later . . . I'm sorry. No matter how I say all this, it doesn't seem to come out right. But you wanted to hear it. I just felt I had an obligation to say it. I hope you understand that, Jennie.

JENNIE I'm trying hard to.

LEO In other words, I think the smart thing to do is wait . . . to get one thing over with before you start something new. Is it unfair of me to say that?

JENNIE Maybe it was your timing that was wrong. It was the most detailed, descriptive, harrowing story any woman who's just about to get married ever heard.

LEO I'm sorry. The bluntness comes from twenty-one years in the newspaper business.

JENNIE Jesus God, what a thing to hear. I know you're concerned about your brother—maybe you should have given a little consideration to your future sister-in-law.

LEO Jennie, please . . .

JENNIE Forgive me. I'm sorry. But just let me get angry a second, because I think I deserve it.

LEO I came here to talk, I didn't come here to fight.

JENNIE No, maybe you're right, Leo. Maybe George really hasn't dealt with Barbara's death yet. And maybe I haven't asked enough questions. I can only deal with one thing at a time. Let me experience my happiness before I start dealing with the tragedies . . . Even if there were no Barbara to deal with, this is scary enough. And I'm goddamned petrified!

LEO Well, you shouldn't be.

JENNIE What do you mean, I shouldn't be? The thing I was most frightened to hear, you just sat there and told me.

LEO That he loved her?

JENNIE Yes!

LEO That he was miserable when she died?

JENNIE Yes! Yes! Of course I know it, but I don't want to hear it. Not now. Not today. My God, I'm moving into the woman's house Monday afternoon.

LEO That's my point.

JENNIE I'll wait as long as he wants. But it was his choice. He picked the date. And if that's not the sign of a man who wants to get healthy quickly, I don't know what is . . . Who picked me out as the stable one, Leo? I've just come from five years of analysis and a busted marriage. I couldn't believe how *lucky* I was when George came into my life . . . that he was going to make everything all right. And look at me —I'm so damned nervous everything might fall apart. It all feels like it's hanging by a string, and this sharp pair of scissors is coming towards me— snapping away.

LEO Jennie, I swear to you, the only reason I brought it up at all is because I feel so responsible. I'm the one who made this match.

JENNIE Well, let me put your mind at rest. There are powers even higher than matchmakers. I promise you, Leo, even if what we're doing is not right, I'll *make* it right.

LEO *(After a pause)* Okay, I'll buy that. *(Shakes her hand, smiles)* I'll see you Monday, kid.

(He starts out)

JENNIE Leo, do me a favor. Don't tell George what we talked about. Give us time to get to that ourselves.

LEO I'm not even talking to George. I can't understand why he waited this long.

(He opens door and leaves. She heads for the bedroom)

SCENE 3

His apartment. Monday morning, about 9 A.M. GEORGE, *dressed in a neat blue suit, is looking in the mirror at the tissue covering a shaving cut on his jaw. He glances at his watch; he is very nervous. He goes over to the phone and dials.*

GEORGE *(He listens for a minute, then speaks distinctly into the phone)* Doctor Ornstein . . . It's George Schneider again . . . I don't think I can wait any longer for you to get out of your session . . . I know this is a weird message to be leaving on a recording . . . I realize I should have called you sooner, but frankly I was nervous about it . . . I'm getting married in about forty-five minutes and . . . She's a wonderful girl and I know I'm doing the right thing . . . I'll be at 273–4681, extension 1174, Judge Markowitz's chambers, in case you have to tell me something of the utmost importance, uh . . . Goodbye. *(He hangs up and wipes his brow with a hanky, realizes he's wearing slippers, runs toward the bedroom. The doorbell rings. He yells out)* It's open!

(The door opens and LEO *comes in wearing a dark-blue suit and a white carnation in his lapel)*

LEO I've been waiting downstairs fifteen minutes. I watered my carnation three times. Are we getting married today or not?

GEORGE *(Returning, shoes in hand)* I cut myself shaving. I can't stop bleeding. Was there any royalty in our family?

LEO Yeah. King Irving from White Plains. Come on.

The cab is going to cost you more than the honeymoon.

GEORGE I slept twelve minutes—and I woke up *twice* during the twelve minutes.

LEO Let's go, George. The judge has a lot of murderers to convict today.

GEORGE *(Looks at him)* Who is she, Leo? I'm marrying a girl, I don't know who she is.

LEO Don't start with me! Don't give me trouble, George! You drove me and all your friends half-crazy and now suddenly you want information?

GEORGE I can't breathe. What a day I pick not to be able to breathe. What should I do, Leo?

LEO I'll buy you a balloon, you can suck on it! George, I've got to know. Are you calling this off? Because if you are, I can still catch a workout at the gym.

GEORGE *(Yells, annoyed)* Will you have a little goddamn compassion! I can't even get my ex-analyst on the phone. A lot *they* care. Fifty dollars an hour and all they do is protect you from doing neurotic things in *their* office. *(Gets a boxed carnation from the refrigerator)* Listen, if you're too busy, run along. Take the cab. I don't want you at my wedding anyway. You're going to stand there and make funny faces. You do it all the time.

LEO I did it at *my* wedding, never at yours. *(Sees* GEORGE *fumbling hopelessly with the cellophane wrapping of the carnation)* What are you doing? What is that, a forest fire? Hold it, hold it, *hold it!*

(He pins the carnation on GEORGE*'s lapel)*

GEORGE You never told me what you and Jennie talked about.

LEO She wasn't home.

GEORGE She told me I'm very lucky to have such a concerned brother.

LEO And she told me *I'm* the one she really wants. She's just marrying you to make me jealous. Let's go, George. *(Starts to push* GEORGE *to the door)* If you're late, this judge fines you.

(LEO *ushers* GEORGE *almost all the way out. He balks at the door*)

GEORGE You were right, Leo. It's all too soon. I should have waited until eleven, eleven-thirty. Ten o'clock is too soon.

LEO Will you *come on*?

GEORGE I didn't even have breakfast!

LEO I'll buy you an Egg McMuffin at McDonalds!

(LEO *hustles* GEORGE *out*)

SCENE 4

Her apartment. FAYE *comes out of the bedroom in a sexy black negligee, wearing dark glasses, nervously smoking a cigarette, brushing her hair. She takes perfume from her bag, sprays it all over. Music plays on the radio. She goes to the door, looks out furtively.*

His apartment. A key opens the door. LEO *rushes to the phone, dials a number, takes the phone with him as he searches through desk drawers in a slight panic. The phone rings in* JENNIE*'s apartment.* FAYE *is startled, looks at it. It rings again as* LEO *mutters, "Answer it, come on!" Finally she turns off the music and answers the phone.*

FAYE Yes?

LEO Faye?

FAYE What number did you want, please?

LEO It's all right, Faye. It's me, Leo.

FAYE Leo who?

LEO Faye, I haven't got time to play espionage! I can't meet you now. I've got to rush back out to the airport. George forgot the airline tickets and his traveler's checks, the limousine had a flat on the Long Island Expressway, and Jennie's got the heaves . . . Can we do it tomorrow?

FAYE No. Tomorrow's no good. Sidney and I are going to the marriage counselor.

LEO What time do you get through?

FAYE I'm going *there* so I don't have to come *here!*

LEO Cool it, cool it! Let's not get untracked before the train gets started—

FAYE Leo, please. Let's forget it. I can't go through with it.

LEO Why?

FAYE I was seen by two little girls in the elevator.

LEO Faye, please stop treating this like it's the Watergate break-in. You think we're the only ones doing this? What do you think they have lunch hours for? . . . I've got to run. There are two people about to leave for their honeymoon who aren't talking to each other. I'll call you later.

FAYE No, Leo—

LEO I'm hungry for you . . . hot, steaming, roasting, burning hungry with desire. *(Kissing and hissing sounds)* 'Bye. *(Hangs up, looks at his watch)* Oh, shit!

(He rushes out of the apartment. FAYE *hangs up and sits there glumly)*

FAYE This is definitely my last affair.

(She goes into the bedroom. Dimout)

SCENE 5

His apartment. It is a week later, about 8 P.M. *We hear the sound of thunder, then of rain. The door opens.* GEORGE *enters, carrying straw bags and suitcases. He looks rather bedraggled.* JENNIE *follows him in, carrying suitcases and her shoulder bag, along with a large straw hat and bongo drums —bought in the tropics, no doubt. She drops them with a thud, then goes over to the sofa and falls into it, exhausted, her legs outstretched.*

GEORGE *picks up his mail, which was tied with a rubber band and left inside his door. He closes the door, and stands there going through the letters meticulously. Both are silent and there is some degree of tension between them.*

JENNIE *(Looks up at the ceiling, mournfully)* That was fun! Three days of rain and two days of diarrhea. We should have taken out honeymoon insurance.

GEORGE *(Without looking up)* Don't forget to put your watch back an hour.

JENNIE I don't want the hour. Let 'em keep it! . . . Any mail for me?

(He opens and reads a letter)

GEORGE *(Looks at her)* You've only been *living* here thirty-eight seconds.

JENNIE Are you going to read your mail *now*?

GEORGE It's from my publisher. He wants some revisions.

JENNIE Again? You "revised" in Barbados . . . Is there anything soft to drink?

GEORGE *(Testy)* I think there's some beer. I could strain it if you like.

JENNIE No, thanks. We have all the "strain" we can handle. *(She crosses to the fridge)* I read somewhere you can tell everything about a person by looking inside his refrigerator. *(She opens it)* Oh, God! Is this the man I married? Cold and empty, with a little yogurt?

GEORGE I'll call the grocer in the morning and have him fill up my personality.

JENNIE *(Takes out a half-empty bottle of Coke with no cap on it)* You want to share a half a bottle of opened Coke? None of that annoying fizz to worry about.

(She takes a swig)

GEORGE *(Looks at her, not amused)* How many glasses of wine did you have on the plane?

JENNIE Two.

GEORGE How many?

JENNIE Four.

GEORGE You had seven.

JENNIE I had six.

GEORGE And two at the airport. That's *eight*.

JENNIE All right, it was eight. But it wasn't seven. Don't accuse me of having seven.

GEORGE *(Gets up)* You're tight, Jennie.

(He picks up the suitcases and coats)

JENNIE Ohhh, is that what's been bothering you all day, George? That I drank too much? I can't help it: I don't like flying. I asked you to hold my hand, but you wouldn't do it. So I drank some wine instead.

GEORGE *(Starts for the bedroom with the bags)* I *did* hold your hand. And while I was holding it, you drank my wine.

(He goes into the bedroom)

JENNIE All right, George. Get it all out. You're angry because I ate your macadamia nuts, too, aren't you? And your package of Trident chewing gum. And I read the *Time* magazine you bought *before* you. You're sore because I knew what happened to "People in the News" ahead of you.

(She glances through the mail)

GEORGE Don't mix up my mail, please.

JENNIE *(Puts it back)* *Pardonnez-moi*. I'll "revise" it later. *(He takes off his jacket. She tries to be more cheerful)* It's a little glum in here . . . We need plants. Lots of plants, from the floor to the ceiling. And sunshine. How do we get some sunshine in here?

GEORGE I think our best bet is to wait for the morning.

(He picks up her bags)

JENNIE Oh, God! Humor! At last, humor!

GEORGE Look, it's been a lousy day. And because of the time difference, we get an extra hour of lousy. Why don't we just write it off and go to bed.

JENNIE I'm hungry.

GEORGE *(Starts to unpack some tropical souvenirs)* You just had dinner on the plane.

JENNIE Airplane food is not dinner. It's survival. Come on, let's get a chili-burger.

GEORGE I don't want one.

JENNIE Don't be ridiculous. *Everybody* wants a chili-burger. Come on, George, a big, greasy, nongovernment-inspected burger dripping with illegal Mexican chili.

(She gooses him with the Coke bottle)

GEORGE *(Pulls away angrily)* *Cut it out, dammit!*

JENNIE *(Startled by his sudden hostility)* I'm sorry.

GEORGE How many times do I have to tell you? I don't want a goddamn chili hamburger!

JENNIE Chili-*burger*. The ham is silent, like Hyphen Hill.

GEORGE Oh, very good. Give the girl two gallons of wine and the repartee really gets quick.

JENNIE Well, never as quick as you, George. Ah'm jes a dumb ole country girl from Cleveland.

GEORGE I noticed. Sitting on the plane with pen poised over the *New York Times* crossword puzzle for three and a half hours without ink ever *once* touching paper.

JENNIE I'm sorry, George. Am I not "literary" enough for you? How's this? "Up your syntax!"

GEORGE Swell. I'll try it tonight. I've been looking for a thrill.

(He goes into the kitchen. She sits, angry now, trying to figure out how to handle all this. GEORGE *comes back in with a glass of water)*

JENNIE I've tried everything, including my funniest faces, to get a smile out of you since eight o'clock this morning.

GEORGE Why don't you try an hour of quiet?

(He pops a Tylenol)

JENNIE I tried it in Barbados and it turned into twenty-four hours of gloom.

GEORGE Listen, I'm walking a very fine line tonight. There are a lot of things I would like to say that would just get us both in trouble. I don't want to deal with it now. Let's just go to bed and hope that two extra-strength Tylenol can do all they claim to do. Okay?

(He starts to cross back into the bedroom)

JENNIE I'd just as soon hear what you had to say.

GEORGE I don't think you would.

JENNIE Why don't you be in charge of saying it and I'll be responsible for not wanting to hear it.

(He looks at her, nods, then looks around and decides to sit opposite her. She looks at him. He stares at the floor)

GEORGE As honeymoons go, I don't think you got much of a break.

JENNIE Really? I'm sorry if you felt that way. *I* had an intermittently wonderful time.

GEORGE Well, I don't know what you experienced in the past. I'm not a honeymoon expert, but personally I found me unbearably moody.

JENNIE Two days in seven isn't much of a complaint —which I never did. And I think we ought to limit this conversation to present honeymoons.

GEORGE Why?

JENNIE Because that's where we're living.

GEORGE You can't get to the present without going through the past.

JENNIE Jesus, George, is that what you did in Barbados? Compare honeymoons?

GEORGE *(Stares at her)* Why don't you ever ask me questions, Jennie? Why do you treat our lives as though there never was a day that happened before we met?

JENNIE I'm not overly curious, George. If there are things you want to tell me, then tell me . . . but *Christ*, does it have to be our first night in this house?

GEORGE Jesus, I was wondering when that perfectly calm exterior was going to crack. Thank God for a little antagonism.

JENNIE Antagonism, hell. That's pure fear. We haven't even started this conversation yet and I'm scared to death.

GEORGE Why?

JENNIE I have terrific animal instincts. I know when my life is about to be threatened.

GEORGE Aren't you even curious to know who the hell we are? I mean, I think you've got some goddamn romantic image of this man with a tragic past right out of *Jane Eyre*.

JENNIE You're the one with the writer's imagination, not me.

GEORGE All right, I'll start. Who is Gus? I would appreciate some biographical information on the man you spent a few important years of your life on. I mean, he's got to be more than a comic figure in a football jersey who pops up in a conversation every time we need a laugh.

JENNIE I never thought of him as comic.

GEORGE Really? Well, anyone who's described as pulling the wine cork out of the bottle with his teeth didn't seem like heavyweight material to me.

JENNIE I wish to hell I knew what you're trying to get at.

GEORGE Oh, come on, Jennie. Tell me *some*thing—anything . . . What was your honeymoon like? Would you say your sex life was A) good; B) bad; or C) good and bad. Pick one!

JENNIE Why are you doing this to me? I don't understand. Do you expect me to stand there and give a detailed description of what it was like in bed with him? Is that what you want to hear?

GEORGE Okay, Jennie, forget it.

JENNIE If you want the truth, I don't think I ever knew the first damn thing about sex, because what happened to you and me in Barbados was something I never dreamed was possible. I hope you felt the same way, George. You never gave me any cause to doubt it . . . I'm sorry. This is very painful for me to talk about . . . But I'll try, George, I'll try anything that's going to make us move closer to each other.

GEORGE I said forget it.

JENNIE *(Yells)* No, *goddammit!* You're not going to open me up and walk away from it. I went through one marriage ignorant as hell. At least let me learn from *this* one. What else? *Ask me!*

GEORGE You're doing fine on your own.

JENNIE Please, George. I'm not going to blow five years of analysis in one night because you haven't got the nerve to finish what you've started. I've always had problems with confrontations. If my father just looked at me with a curve in his eyebrow I fell apart. But I swear to God, I'm going to get through this one. *(He tries to leave the room; she blocks his way)* No other questions? *(He doesn't answer)* Then can I ask you a few?

GEORGE Why not?

JENNIE Tell me about Barbara.

GEORGE *(Looks at her)* She was terrific.

JENNIE Oh, I know she was pretty. I see enough pictures of her around here. Tell me about your honeymoon. You went to Europe, didn't you?

GEORGE Paris, London and Rome. And if you want a romantic description, it was a knockout.

JENNIE I got the adjectives, George, what about the details? Big room? small room? view of the park?

overlooking the Seine? fourposter bed? What was the wallpaper like?

GEORGE Stop it, Jennie!

JENNIE Why? What's wrong? Would you rather make out a list? What's safe to talk about and what's hands-off?

GEORGE *(A deep breath)* Jesus, I don't have the strength for this kind of thing anymore.

JENNIE You were doing fine two minutes ago.

GEORGE *(Looks at his hands)* Sweating like crazy . . . I'm sorry, Jennie, I don't think I'm up to this tonight.

JENNIE Why, George? Why is it so painful? What are you feeling now? Do you think that I'm expecting you to behave a certain way?

GEORGE No. *I* expect it. I expect a full commitment from myself . . . I did it twelve years ago . . . But I can't do it now.

JENNIE I'm in no hurry. What you're giving now is enough for me. I know the rest will come.

GEORGE *How* do you know? How the hell did you become so wise and smart? Stop being so goddamn understanding, will you? It bores the crap out of me.

JENNIE Then what *do* you want? Bitterness? Anger? Fury? You want me to stand toe to toe with you like Barbara did? Well, I'm not Barbara. And I'll be damned if I'm going to re-create *her* life, just to make *my* life work with you. This is *our* life now, George, and the sooner we start accepting that, the sooner we can get on with this marriage.

GEORGE No, you're not Barbara. That's clear enough.

JENNIE *(Devastated)* Oh, Jesus, George. If you want to hurt me, you don't have to work that hard.

GEORGE Sorry, but you give me so much room to be cruel, I don't know when to stop.

JENNIE I never realized that was a *fault* until now.

GEORGE I guess it's one of the minor little adjustments you have to make. But I have no worry—you'll make them.

JENNIE And you resent me for that?

GEORGE I resent you for *everything*!

JENNIE *(Perplexed)* *Why*, George? *Why?*

GEORGE Because I don't feel like making you happy tonight! I don't feel like having a wonderful time. I don't think I *wanted* a "terrifically wonderful" honeymoon! You want happiness, Jennie, find yourself another football player, will ya? I resent everything you want out of marriage that I've already had. And for making me reach so deep inside to give it to you again. I resent being at L or M and having to go back to A! And most of all, I resent not being able to say in front of you . . . that I miss Barbara so much.

(He covers his eyes, crying silently. JENNIE *has been cut so deeply, she can hardly react. She just sits there, fighting back her tears)* Oh, Christ, Jennie, I'm sorry . . . I think I need a little outside assistance.

JENNIE *(Nods)* What do you want to do?

GEORGE *(Shrugs)* I don't know . . . I don't want to make any promises I can't keep.

JENNIE Whatever you want.

GEORGE We got, as they say in the trade, problems, kid.

(He goes to her, embraces her head, then goes into the bedroom, leaving her stunned and alone. Dimout)

SCENE 6

Her apartment. It is two days later, about three o'clock on a sunny afternoon. The living room is empty.

FAYE *comes in from the bedroom, wearing a sheet—and apparently nothing else. Her hair is disheveled. She is distraught.*

LEO SCHNEIDER *comes out of the bedroom, zipping up his pants. He is nude from the waist up.*

LEO I'm sorry.

FAYE Forget it.

LEO Don't be like that.

FAYE What *should* I be like?

LEO It was an important phone call. I *had* to take it.

FAYE It's not taking it that bothered me. It's *when* you took it I felt was badly timed.

LEO Half my year's gross income depended on that call. He's my biggest client. Come on back . . . Faye? What do you say? They won't call again.

FAYE You mean you actually left this number? I changed taxis three times and walked with a limp into the building and you gave out this number?

LEO It's just a number. It could be a luncheonette. He doesn't know. Faye, that phone call meant thirty thousand dollars to me.

FAYE Jesus—I'm worried I'm going to be emotionally scarred for life, and you're getting rich.

LEO You're so tense, Faye. You've been tense since I walked in the door. I knew when I came in and we shook hands, things weren't going to be relaxed.

FAYE I'm no good at this, Leo. I'm nervous and I'm clumsy.

LEO Don't be silly. You've been wonderful.

FAYE I'm sorry about your shoes.

LEO It's just a little red wine. They're practically dry.

FAYE Your socks too?

LEO Don't worry about it . . . Hey, Faye—Faysie! Have I offended you in some way? Have I been inconsiderate? Insensitive?

FAYE Aside from adultery, you've been a perfect gentleman. I don't know . . . I just didn't think it would be so complicated. So noisy.

LEO Noisy? What noise?

FAYE My heart. It's pounding like a cannon. They must hear it all over the building.

LEO I'll turn on the radio, they'll think it's the rhythm section . . . Hey! Would you like to dance?

FAYE Are you serious?

LEO Absolutely! You think it's corny? Well, I happen to be a very corny guy. Come on. Come dance with me.

FAYE With red wine in your shoes? You'll squeak.

LEO *(Pulling* FAYE *to her feet)* C'mon.
(Singing)
Flamingo . . .
Like a flame in the sky . . .
Flying over the island . . .
(Taking her cigarette) Gimme that.
(Singing)
To my lover nearby . . .

(Sings a scat phrase, starts dancing with FAYE*)*
Hey, Flamingo . . .
In your tropical hue . . .

FAYE You're crazy, Leo.

LEO
Words of passion and romance . . .

FAYE You're embarrassing me.

LEO
And my love for you . . .
(Sings a scat phrase)
One dip. Just give me one old-fashioned dip.
(He dips her)

FAYE Let me up, Leo. I'm in no mood to be dipped!
(She slips a little and they slide to the floor)

LEO Jesus, you're pretty.

FAYE I'm not.

LEO Don't tell me you're not. I'm telling you you're pretty.

FAYE All right, I'm pretty. I don't want to argue.

LEO You're pretty and you're sweet and you've got the softest face.

FAYE You've done this a lot, haven't you, Leo?

LEO You get some particular thrill in dousing me with ice water?

FAYE You're so good at it. I admire your professionalism. It's all so well-crafted. Like a really well-built cabinet.

LEO Where do you find a parallel between my love-making and woodwork?

FAYE I may be new at this, Leo, but I'm not naïve. You've had affairs with married women before, haven't you?

LEO No . . .

FAYE Leo . . .

LEO There was one woman, but she was waiting for her divorce to come through.

FAYE A lot?

LEO Maybe one other.

FAYE You've done it a lot.

LEO A few times, I swear.

FAYE A lot.

LEO Yes, a lot. But they were never important to me. *Today* is important to me. *(Trying to caress her, he struggles with the sheet)* What is this tent you're wearing?

FAYE *(She gets up, moves away)* Please, Leo. A lot of meaningless affairs does not raise my appreciation of what we're doing.

LEO It's not just the phone call that's bothering you. It's something else. You know what the problem is? You don't have a good enough reason to be here.

FAYE That's a funny thing to say to a woman who shopped in twelve stores for the right underwear.

LEO Well, then, maybe we rushed it. *I* rushed it, okay? Maybe this isn't the right time for you, Faye.

FAYE What do *you* know about it? A couple of lousy affairs and you're suddenly Margaret Mead? Listen, when Jennie began having trouble with Gus, she decided to see an analyst. And I asked her, "When was the day you finally realized you needed one?" And she said, "It was the day I found myself in his office." Well, I'm *here* in your office . . . and I need something in my life. I already tried Transcendental Meditation, health foods and jogging. And I am now serenely, tranquilly and more robustly unhappy than I have ever been before . . . So don't tell me this isn't the right time, Sidney!

LEO Leo.

FAYE *Leo!* Oh, shit!

LEO Oh, Faye, sweet Faye . . . You are so much more interesting-looking than you were twelve years ago. You've got so damn much character in your face.

FAYE Why does that not overjoy me? Why is life going by so fast, Leo? First I was pretty. Now I'm interesting-looking with character! Soon I'll be handsome followed by stately and finally, worst of all, remarkable for her age.

LEO Gloomy! You're taking a gloomy perspective, Faye. Gloom is the enemy of a good time.

FAYE You were right before, Leo. I don't have a good enough reason to be here. Because what I want, I can't have. I want what Jennie has: the excitement of being in love again. I'm so much smarter now, I could handle everything so much better. I am so jealous of her I could scream. I did for her what I wish I could have done for myself. And in return I got her apartment to do exactly what I swore, when I was young and pretty, I would never end up doing when I became interesting-looking with character.

LEO I think you're a very confused person, Faye.

FAYE I've noticed that . . . I think you'd better leave first, Leo. I have to stay for a while and practice my limp.

LEO I was crazy about you, Faysie . . . Never stopped thinking about you all through the years. I used to skim through the trades to see if you were working or not—

FAYE Why didn't you ever try to get in touch with me?

LEO I heard you were happily married.

FAYE I heard you were, too.

LEO Go trust people.

FAYE I never told you this, but my mother didn't like you.

LEO I never met her.

FAYE I know, but I used to tell her about you. She said, "I know his type. He's the kind that needs lots of women.' I could call her and say, "You were right, Mom"—but how do I explain how I found out?

LEO I wonder what would have happened if we had married each other?

FAYE Well, I would hope a hell of a lot more than happened today . . . What's your opinion?

LEO I think we'd have turned out swell.

FAYE You don't really believe that, do you?

LEO No.

FAYE Then why did you say it?

LEO I thought it would make you happy.

FAYE You're awful.

LEO Why? Because I want to please you? Are we better off deluding ourselves that ours would have been one of the great love affairs of midtown Manhattan? I know what it is and *you* know what it is —why do we have to call it something we both know it isn't?

FAYE Because a woman *needs* delusion.

LEO *(Putting on the rest of his clothes)* Not me. I need something new. It's why I like show business. There's another opening every three weeks. I can't be monogamous, Faye. What can I do, take shots for it? But in our system I'm put down as a social criminal. I can't be faithful to my wife, and I hate the guilt that comes with playing around. So I compromise. I have lots of unpleasurable affairs. And what makes it worse—I really do care for Marilyn. I can't stop, and I don't expect her to understand. So we end up hurting each other. I don't like it, Faye. I don't like crawling into bed at two o'clock in the morning and feeling the back of a cold, angry woman. And I don't like you coming up here under any false pretenses. I would love to make love to you, but that's the end of the sentence. I don't want a fine romance. I don't want to dance on the ceiling or have my heart stand still when "she" walks in the door. Because I really don't want to hurt anyone anymore. All I want is a little dispassionate passion . . . Let George and Jennie handle all the romance for the East Coast. The man is half-crazed right now, and he's welcome to it . . . I'll tell you what I *do* want, Faye. I want a woman who looks exactly like you and feels like you and thinks exactly like me.

FAYE Boy, did I ever come to the wrong store to shop.

LEO So what have we got here? We got one romantic unhappy woman, one indifferent frustrated man and one available and unused bedroom . . . is what we got here.

FAYE It's too bad. You finally got me in the mood, and your honesty got me right out of it.

LEO Anyway, I like you too much. Making love to people you like is very dangerous.

FAYE Good. Save it for your enemies.

LEO *(Looks at his watch)* Well, I can still get some work done. Can I drop you downtown?

FAYE You mean, leave together? Suppose someone sees us?

LEO Listen, they could have seen us in bed and never suspected anything. Come on, get dressed.

FAYE Leo, as a lover, you make a terrific friend. Would you mind giving me one warm, passionate and very sincere kiss? I'll be goddamned if I'm going home empty-handed.

LEO *(Steps toward her)* Hold on to your sheet, kid, kissing is my main thing.

(He gently puts his arms around her and gives her a soft, warm kiss on the lips. She pulls back, looks at him, and then suddenly feeling very safe, she leans forward again and they kiss deeply and passionately. His hands start to roam over her back. He gently puts her down on the sofa and begins to kiss her neck and her face as . . . the door opens and JENNIE *walks in. She sees them and freezes)*

JENNIE Oh, God! I *am* sorry!

(They both jump up. LEO *backs away)*

FAYE Oh, Jesus!

LEO Oh, Christ!

JENNIE I should have called. I didn't think—

LEO It's all right. It's okay. No harm done. We're all adults. It's a grown-up world. These things happen. We have to be mature—

FAYE Oh, shut up, Leo.

JENNIE I just came by to pick up the rest of my summer clothes. I can do it later. I'm so sorry.

(She backs up toward the door)

FAYE Don't think, Jennie. Don't think until I talk to you tonight. Promise me you won't think.

JENNIE I won't. I promise . . . Goodbye, Leo. Say hello to Maril—! Goodbye, Leo!

(She turns and goes out, closing the door)

FAYE This is one of those situations in life that a lot of people find humor in—I don't!

(She goes into the bedroom)

LEO That's a first for me. That has never happened before. Never caught by a sister-in-law. *Never!*

(He leaves, slamming the front door)

SCENE 7

His apartment, about an hour later. GEORGE *comes out of the bedroom, wearing a sports jacket and carrying a raincoat and fully packed suitcase and attaché case. He puts a note on the desk and starts for the door.*

JENNIE *enters, looking a little glum, sees* GEORGE *and his luggage.*

GEORGE Hi.

JENNIE Hi.

GEORGE You had some messages. *(Takes the piece of notepaper from the desk)* I was going to leave this for you. I don't know if you can read my writing . . . Jill James at CBS called and said you start shooting again on Monday. They'll send the pages over tonight. Also, Helen Franklyn called and said you have a reading for the new Tom Stoppard play Monday at ten. And Faye called a few minutes ago, said it was urgent she talk to you and can you have lunch with her on Tuesday, Wednesday, Thursday and Friday . . . And that was it.

JENNIE *(Stunned; doesn't respond immediately)* I'm sorry, I wasn't listening . . . I couldn't take my eyes off your suitcase.

GEORGE I tried to explain everything in a letter. I left it on the bed.

JENNIE Good. I was worried that I wasn't getting any mail . . . Where are you going?

GEORGE Los Angeles. Someone at Paramount is interested in *The Duchess of Limehouse* as a film.

JENNIE When did all this come up?

GEORGE Two weeks ago.

JENNIE Why didn't you tell me?

GEORGE I had no reason to go two weeks ago.

JENNIE Leave it to you to make a point clear. How long will you be gone?

GEORGE I don't know.

JENNIE Where will you stay?

GEORGE I don't know.

JENNIE Just going to circle the airport for a few days?

GEORGE You never lose your equilibrium, do you?

JENNIE You think not? I'd hate to see an X-ray of my stomach right now.

GEORGE I don't think being apart for a while is going to do us any damage.

JENNIE Probably no worse than being together the past few days.

GEORGE But if it's really important to get in touch with me, Leo will know where I am.

JENNIE And I'll know where Leo is.

GEORGE *(Goes to the door, turns back uncomfortably)* I don't think I have anything else to say. How about you?

JENNIE *(Shrugs)* I have no statement to make at this time.

GEORGE I'm glad a lot of work is coming your way. I know it's important to you. It's what you want.

JENNIE I'm glad you know what I want, George . . . If you told me five years ago, I could have saved a lot of doctor money.

GEORGE I was busy five years ago.

JENNIE You don't have to remind me. Interesting how this all worked out. You pack up and go and leave *me* with all your memories.

GEORGE I'm sorry, but you can't get a five-room apartment in the overhead rack.

JENNIE Is there anything you want me to take care of while you're gone?

GEORGE You seem to be taking care of it fine right now.

JENNIE Oh, I tripped over the wire and set off the trap, didn't I? . . . Everything I say can be so cleverly twisted around by you that you always end up the victim and I'm the perpetrator. God forbid I'm not as fast with a thought or a phrase as you, and you pounce on it like a fat cat.

GEORGE Fat cats are very slow on the pounce because they're fat, but I got your point.

JENNIE *(Very angry)* Oh, go on, get the hell out of here, will you! If you're going to leave, leave! Go! Your Mystery Plane is waiting to take you, shrouded in secrecy, to your Phantom Hotel on the intriguing West Coast. Even your life is turning into a goddamn spy novel—

GEORGE *(Puts down the valise)* I've got a few minutes. I don't want to miss what promises to be our most stimulating conversation since I thought you were an eighty-five-year-old woman on the phone.

JENNIE Isn't it amazing the minute I get angry and abusive, it's one of the few times I can really hold your attention . . . What can I say that will really hurt you, George? I want to send you off happy.

(She swarms over him, punching him. He throws her onto the sofa)

GEORGE Just going is reward enough.

(He starts out. She runs ahead of him and grabs the suitcase to fling it out. He throws her to the floor)

JENNIE You know what you want better than me, George . . . I don't know what you expect to find out there, except a larger audience for your two shows a day of suffering . . . I know I'm not as smart as you. Maybe I can't analyze and theorize and speculate on why we behave as we do and react as we do and suffer guilt and love and hate. You read all those books, not me . . . But there's one thing I *do* know. I know how I *feel*. I know I can stand here watching you try to destroy everything I've ever wanted in my life, wanting to smash your face with my fists because you won't even make the slightest effort to opt for happiness—and still know that I love you. That's always so clear to me. It's the one place I get all my strength from . . . You mean so much to me that I am willing to take all your abuse and insults and insensitivity—because that's what you need to do to prove I'm not going to leave you. I can't promise I'm not going to die, George, that's asking too much. But if you want to test me, go ahead and test me. You want to leave, leave! But *I'm* not the one who's going to walk away. I don't know if I can take it forever, but I can take it for tonight and I can take it next week. Next month I may be a little shaky . . . But I'll tell you something, George. No matter what you say about me, I feel so good about myself —better than I felt when I ran from Cleveland and was frightened to death of New York. Better than I felt when Gus was coming home at two o'clock in the morning just to change his clothes. Better than I felt when I thought there was no one in the world out there for me, and better than I felt the night before we got married and I thought that I wasn't good enough for you . . . Well, I am! I'm wonderful! I'm nuts about me! And if you're stupid enough to throw someone sensational like me aside, then you don't deserve as good as you've got! I am sick and tired of running from places and people and relationships . . . And don't tell me what I want because *I'll* tell you what I want. I want a home and I want a family—and I want a career, too. And I want a dog and I want a cat and I want three goldfish. I want *everything*! There's no harm in wanting it, George, because there's not a chance in hell we're going to get it all, anyway. But if you don't *want* it, you've got even less chance than that . . . Everyone's out there looking for easy answers. And if you don't find it at home, hop into another bed and maybe you'll come up lucky. *Maybe!* You'd be just as surprised as me at some of the "maybe's" I've seen out there lately. Well, none of that for me, George . . . You want me, then fight for me, because I'm fighting like hell for you. I think we're both worth it. I will admit, however, that I *do* have one fault. One glaring, major, monumental fault . . . Sometimes I don't know when to stop talking. For that I'm sorry, George, and I apologize. I am now through!

(She sits back on the sofa, exhausted)

GEORGE *(Looks at her for a long time, then says warmly)* I'll tell you one thing—I'm glad you're on *my* side.

JENNIE *(Looks over at him)* Do you mean it, George?

GEORGE I didn't hear half of what you said because I was so mesmerized by your conviction. I'm not a doctor, Jennie, but I can tell you right now, you're one of the healthiest people I ever met in my life.

JENNIE *(Smiles)* Funny, I don't look it.

GEORGE I am crazy about you. I want you to know that.

JENNIE I know that.

GEORGE No. You don't know that I'm absolutely crazy nuts for you.

JENNIE Oh. No, I didn't know that. You're right.

GEORGE I want to walk over now and take you in my arms and say, "Okay, we're finished with the bad part. Now, what's for dinner?" But I'm stuck, Jennie . . . I'm just stuck someplace in my mind and it's driving me crazy. Something is keeping me here, glued to this spot like a big, dumb, overstuffed chair.

JENNIE I could rearrange the furniture.

GEORGE Don't make it so easy for me. I'm fighting to hold on to self-pity, and just my luck I run into the most understanding girl in the world.

JENNIE I'm not so understanding.

GEORGE Yes, you are. You just said so yourself. And I swear to God, Jennie, I can't find a thing I would want to change about you . . . So let me go to Los Angeles. Let me try to get unstuck . . . I'll be at the Chateau Marmont Hotel. I'll be in my room unsticking like crazy.

JENNIE Couldn't I go with you? I wouldn't bother you. I would just watch.

GEORGE Then the people next door would want to watch, and pretty soon we'd have a crowd. *(He picks up his suitcase)* Take care of yourself.

JENNIE George! *(He stops, looks at her)* Would you mind very much if I slept in my apartment while you're gone? I feel funny about staying in this place alone.

GEORGE *(Nods)* I understand . . .

JENNIE If you don't call me, can I call you?

GEORGE *(A pause)* You know, we may have one of the most beautiful marriages that was ever in trouble.

(He goes out. She goes to the door, watches him go, then comes in and closes the door. Dimout)

SCENE 8

Her apartment. The next day. The doorbell rings. FAYE *opens the door. It is* LEO.

LEO Oh? Hello! Do I look as surprised as you?

FAYE What are you doing here?

LEO I just dropped by.

FAYE To see me?

LEO No.

FAYE Thank God. I was afraid it was one of those habits you can't break.

LEO Is Jennie home?

FAYE She's in the shower. She moved back last night . . . So much for our matchmaking business.

LEO Actually I came back hoping to find my wallet. I think I dropped it in the bedroom yesterday during the mass exodus.

FAYE Jennie found it. She woke up in the middle of the night with a credit card lump under her head. *(She gives him a small Manila envelope, held with a rubber band. He looks at it)*

LEO She didn't have to put my name on it. It's humiliating enough. Did she say anything about us?

FAYE That's not her style . . . I was prepared to tell her I'd been drugged. You don't mind, do you?

LEO Look, why don't we just write off yesterday? Even my horoscope said, "Stay outdoors."

FAYE I'm in the process of forgetting about it. I'm seeing Jennie's old doctor on Monday.

LEO That's terrific. I'm glad you're doing something constructive about your problems.

FAYE And what about you, Leo? What are you doing?

LEO *(Shrugs)* Nothing! I have no intention of changing. So why should I pay some doctor to make me feel guilty about it?

FAYE And what about you and Marilyn? Are you going to separate?

LEO Yes. But not this year. We have too many dinner dates . . . *(He stands)* Well, I'll see you around, kid.

FAYE Every place but here.

LEO Keep your options open. It makes life more interesting.

FAYE Why is it the more you say things I don't like, the more attractive you get?

LEO That's what's going to cost you fifty bucks an hour to find out . . . We never did finish that warm, passionate, friendly kiss.

FAYE You know what? I think I'm just crazy enough to do it.

(They kiss. JENNIE *walks in from the bedroom in a bathrobe, drying her hair with a towel)*

JENNIE Faye, was that the phone I heard befo—? *(She stops, seeing them. They break apart)* Jesus, is that the same kiss from yesterday?

LEO My regiment was just called up and I'm trying to say goodbye to everybody . . . Maybe next week the three of us can meet in a restaurant, because I'd like to explain this whole silly business. We'll all wear hoods, of course.

JENNIE Leo . . . Have you heard from George?

LEO No . . . but give him a couple of days, Jen. He'll figure it out. *(Kisses her, starts out, stops)* Jesus, life was so simple when we were kids. No matter how much trouble you got into outside, when you got home you always got a cupcake.

(He leaves)

FAYE (*Looks sheepishly at* JENNIE) I feel so foolish. Do you hate me?

JENNIE *(Smiles)* I could never hate you.

FAYE Well, I have another confession to make to you . . . Leo was never the one I wanted to have an affair with.

JENNIE Who was?

FAYE A certain ex-wide receiver from the New York Giants.

JENNIE *Gus?*

FAYE I lusted for that man in more places than my heart.

JENNIE Then why did you pick Leo?

FAYE Because I was intimate with him before I met Sidney . . . I just wanted to practice with someone I already knew.

JENNIE You have a peculiar bookkeeping system.

FAYE Anyway, Sidney and I are going to an adult motel in New Jersey this weekend. From now on, I'm only cheating with the immediate family . . . I've got to go. Are you sure you'll be all right? I mean, staying here all alone?

JENNIE Wait a minute. Am I having a déjà vu or have we played this scene before?

FAYE The dialogue *does* seem awfully familiar. I remember saying, "Shit. Twelve more years to go until the good times" and then falling in love with the girl across the street.

JENNIE Oh, God. Our life is on a loop. Does this mean I have to go out with the giant from Chicago again?

FAYE I'd better go before Leo comes in with a bottle of red wine. *(She crosses to the door, opens it, then turns back)* There's a lesson to be learned from all this . . . I wonder what the hell it is.

(She leaves. Fadeout)

SCENE 9

His apartment. The door opens. GEORGE *enters and turns on the lights. He looks a little travel-weary.*

GEORGE *(Putting down his suitcase)* Jennie? Jennie? *(He looks around, then goes into the bedroom. It's apparent no one is home. He comes back into the living room. In her apartment,* JENNIE *goes to the refrigerator, takes out an apple, then goes to the sofa and sits.* GEORGE *picks up the phone, and starts to dial just as* JENNIE *picks up the receiver. She dials 213-555-1212. He finishes dialing and gets a busy signal. He hangs up, takes a manuscript from his attaché case)*

JENNIE *(Into the phone)* Los Angeles . . . I'd like the number of the Chateau Marmont Hotel . . . Yes, I think it *is* West Hollywood . . . *(She waits. He paces)* 656–1010 Thank you. *(She disconnects with her finger, then starts to dial just as he goes back to the phone, picks it up and starts to dial. She gets halfway through the number when she suddenly hangs up)* Patience, Jennie! Don't pressure him. *(She sits back just as he completes his dial. Her phone rings. She jumps and clutches her bosom)* Oh, God, I'm so smart! *(She reaches over and picks up the phone)* Hello?

GEORGE Serene?

JENNIE Who?

GEORGE Is this Serene Jurgens? . . . It's George Schneider, Leo's brother . . . I just arrived on the Coast, darling. At last, I'm free.

JENNIE *(Near tears)* Tell me you're joking, George. Right now I wouldn't know humor if it hit me with a truck.

GEORGE Oh. Well, then you'd better pull off the highway . . . How are you? What have you been doing?

JENNIE Watching the telephone. Nothing good on until now . . . How's the weather there?

GEORGE *(Looks around)* Oh, about eighty-four degrees. A little humid.

JENNIE Same here . . . How are you, George?

GEORGE Dumb. Dummy Dumbo.

JENNIE Why?

GEORGE Well, when Barbara and I had a fight, I'd walk around the block and come back twenty minutes later feeling terrific . . . At the airport I said to myself, "Of course. That's what I should do." And that's what I did.

JENNIE I can't believe it. You mean, you just walked around the block?

GEORGE Yes.

JENNIE What's so dumb about that?

GEORGE I was in the Los Angeles airport when I thought of it.

JENNIE Well, where are you? Here or there?

GEORGE Wait, I'll look. *(He looks around)* Looks like here.

JENNIE You're back! You're in New York!

GEORGE I never even checked into the Chateau Marmont . . . I got unstuck in the TWA lounge.

JENNIE Oh, George . . .

GEORGE I sat there drinking my complimentary Fresca, and I suddenly remembered a question Dr. Ornstein told me to ask myself whenever I felt trouble coming on. The question is "What is it you're most afraid would happen *if*?"

JENNIE I'm listening.

GEORGE So I said to myself, "George, what is it you're most afraid would happen—*if* you went back to New York . . . to Jennie . . . and started your life all over again?" And the answer was so simple . . . I would be happy! I have stared happiness in the face, Jennie—and I embrace it.

JENNIE *(Tearfully)* Oh, George. You got any left to embrace me?

GEORGE From here? No. You need one of those long-armed fellas for that.

JENNIE Well, what are we waiting for? Your place or mine?

GEORGE Neither. I think we have to find a new one called "Ours."

JENNIE Thank you, George. I was hoping we would.

GEORGE Thus, feeling every bit as good about me as you do about you, I finished the last chapter of the new book on the plane. *(He takes up the manuscript. The last few pages are handwritten)* I've got it with me. You want to hear it?

JENNIE The last chapter?

GEORGE No. The whole book.

JENNIE Of course. I'll be right over.

GEORGE No, I'll read it to you. I don't want to lose my momentum. *(He opens the manuscript folder, settles back; so does she. He reads)* You ready? . . . *Falling Into Place*, by George Schneider. Dedication: "To Jennie . . . A nice girl to spend the rest of your life with

. . ." *(He turns the page)* Chapter One . . . "Walter Maslanski looked in the mirror and saw what he feared most . . . Walter Maslanski . . ." *(The curtain begins to fall)* "Not that Walter's features were awesome by any means . . . He had the sort of powder-puff eyes that could be stared down in an abbreviated battle by a one-eyed senior-citizen canary . . ."

Curtain

ABOUT THE AUTHOR

Since 1960, a Broadway season without a Neil Simon comedy or musical has been a rare one. His first play was *Come Blow Your Horn,* followed by the musical *Little Me.* During the 1966–67 season, *Barefoot in the Park, The Odd Couple, Sweet Charity* and *The Star-Spangled Girl* were all running simultaneously; in the 1970–71 season, Broadway theatergoers had their choice of *Plaza Suite, Last of the Red Hot Lovers* and *Promises, Promises.* Next came *The Gingerbread Lady, The Prisoner of Second Avenue, The Sunshine Boys, The Good Doctor, God's Favorite, California Suite, Chapter Two* and the new musical hit, *They're Playing Our Song.*

Mr. Simon began his writing career in television, writing *The Sgt. Bilko Show* and Sid Caesar's *Your Show of Shows.* He has also written for the screen: the adaptions of *Barefoot in the Park, The Odd Couple, Plaza Suite, The Prisoner of Second Avenue, The Sunshine Boys* and most recently, *California Suite.* Other original screenplays he has written include *The Out-of-Towners, The Heartbreak Kid, Murder by Death, The Goodbye Girl* and *The Cheap Detective. Chapter Two* is now in production.

The author lives in California and New York with his actress wife, Marsha Mason. He has two daughters, Ellen and Nancy.